HIDDEN ®

San Francisco & Northern California

HIDDEN®

San Francisco & Northern California

Ray Riegert

ELEVENTH EDITION

Ulysses Press®

BERKELEY, CALIFORNIA

Published by:
ULYSSES PRESS
P.O. Box 3440
Berkeley, CA 94703
www.ulyssespress.com

ISSN 1097-1572
ISBN 1-56975-402-0

Printed in Canada by Transcontinental Printing

30 29 28 27

MANAGING EDITOR: Claire Chun
PROJECT DIRECTOR: Kate Allen
COPY EDITOR: Lily Chou
EDITORIAL ASSOCIATES: Laura Brancella, Kaori Takee
TYPESETTING: Lisa Kester, James Meetze
CARTOGRAPHY: Pease Press
COVER DESIGN: Leslie Henriques, Sarah Levin
INDEXER: Sayre Van Young
COVER PHOTOGRAPHY: Getty Images
   (fog shrouding the Golden Gate Bridge)
ILLUSTRATOR: Glenn Kim
CONTRIBUTING WRITER: Marty Olmstead

Distributed in the United States, Great Britain, and Europe by Publishers Group West and in Canada by Raincoast Books

To Leslie,

for the wonderful years behind us and the many ahead

Acknowledgments

As soon as I finish revising a book, everyone who worked on it applies for an unlisted phone number. The zany pace and fatal deadlines cost me colleagues, friends, even relatives. A few stalwart souls, however, stick it out, and to them I feel a tremendous sense of gratitude.

Foremost is my wife Leslie, who contributed to every aspect of the project. She served as researcher, designer, writer, editor, proofreader, and in countless other roles, working impossible hours under incredible pressure. She gave inspiration to the author and life to the book.

Claire Chun also added her many abilities, helping to research, copy edit, and typeset the material. I have to give special thank yous to Kate Allen, the project director for this edition, and Lily Chou, the copy editor. Sayre Van Young once again lent her ample talents as indexer. Lisa Kester, James Meetze, Laura Brancella, and Kaori Takee also assisted with the revision of the current edition.

Ulysses Press would like to thank the following readers who took the time to write in with suggestions that were incorporated into this new edition of *Hidden San Francisco & Northern California*:

Belinda Cole of Charleston, SC; Linda and Annie Lee of San Francisco, CA; David Polaner via e-mail; Allison Rost of Fremont, CA; Meera Sankaran of Cupertino, CA; Doug Smith via e-mail; Vivien Wong of Alameda, CA; Leda Young of San Francisco, CA.

What's Hidden?

At different points throughout this book, you'll find special listings marked with a hidden symbol:

◀ HIDDEN

This means that you have come upon a place off the beaten tourist track, a spot that will carry you a step closer to the local people and natural environment of San Francisco and Northern California.

The goal of this guide is to lead you beyond the realm of everyday tourist facilities. While we include traditional sightseeing listings and popular attractions, we also offer alternative sights and adventure activities. Instead of filling this guide with reviews of standard hotels and chain restaurants, we concentrate on one-of-a-kind places and locally owned establishments.

Our authors seek out locales that are popular with residents but usually overlooked by visitors. Some are more hidden than others (and are marked accordingly), but all the listings in this book are intended to help you discover the true nature of San Francisco and Northern California and put you on the path of adventure.

Write to us!

If in your travels you discover a spot that captures the spirit of San Francisco and Northern California, or if you live in the region and have a favorite place to share, or if you just feel like expressing your views, write to us and we'll pass your note along to the author.

We can't guarantee that the author will add your personal find to the next edition, but if the writer does use the suggestion, we'll acknowledge you in the credits and send you a free copy of the new edition.

ULYSSES PRESS
P.O. Box 3440
Berkeley, CA 94703
E-mail: readermail@ulyssespress.com

Contents

Maps

OUTDOOR ADVENTURE SYMBOLS

The following symbols accompany national, state, and regional park listings, as well as beach descriptions throughout the text.

▲	Camping			Surfing
	Hiking			Waterskiing
	Biking			Windsurfing
	Horseback Riding			Canoeing or Kayaking
	Downhill Skiing			Boating
	Cross-country Skiing			Boat Ramps
	Swimming			Fishing
	Snorkeling or Scuba Diving			

ONE

California Dreaming

Travelers today possess an awareness and imagination lacking in their outlandish predecessors. Vacations were once escapes from routine. People charted two weeks a year as an island-in-time where they changed from wool suits to bathing suits. In desperate attempts to forget office hours and car payments, they gravitated to overcrowded tourist areas where life proved as frenzied as back home.

Now travel is becoming a personal art form. A destination no longer serves simply as a place to relax: it's also a point of encounter, where experience runs feverish and reality unravels. To many, this new wave in travel customs is labeled "adventure travel" and involves trekking glaciers or dusting granite walls in a hang glider; to others, it connotes nothing more daring than a restful spell at a hidden country inn. Actually, it's a state of mind, a willingness not only to accept but seek out the uncommon and unique.

This book is written for those taking up the challenge of this freewheeling style. It's intended not for tourists but travelers—people who are equally at ease on a mountain trail or a city boulevard. As a guide, it leads you through San Francisco, then combs the Bay Area and beyond in search of adventure.

Many traditional tourist spots are described, but I have tried to take you a step further. In San Francisco, for instance, you'll visit ever-popular Chinatown, but after walking the crowded blocks of Grant Avenue, the tour leads down an alleyway to a fortune cookie factory. I've listed well-known restaurants and also uncovered the tradition of dim sum dining. In North Beach, the walking tour carries you from Broadway's neon strip to a silent street lined with wooden sidewalks and flowering gardens. At Fisherman's Wharf, you skirt the tacky tourist section and wander the barnacle-caked waterfront, where fishermen still ply an ancient trade.

Then head for The Neighborhoods, far from the Gray Line crowds, to discover the soul of the city. Union Street is a strange mix of historic Victorian homes and swinging singles bars; Russian Hill contains pocket parks and hills so steep that steps replace sidewalks; the Haight, once scene of the Summer of Love, has become thoroughly gentrified; the South of Market District, once called SOMA Multimedia Gulch, stood as the epicenter of SF's dot-com boom; the rapidly changing Mission District is a fascinating neighborhood with its colorful murals and authentic mariachi bands. San Francisco's gay neighborhoods, particularly Castro and Polk streets, are fully described.

You can explore Golden Gate Park, the West Coast answer to New York's Central Park. Farther afield lies the Golden Gate National Recreation Area with its joggers and hang gliders; the Presidio, a spacious forest in the midst of a major city; and Land's End, where San Francisco marks its finale in a wild tangle of fractured cliffs and untracked coastline.

For the Bay Area, there are descriptions of Sausalito's unique houseboat community and the secluded country towns of Port Costa and Benicia. In Berkeley, you will learn how the '60s revolution surrendered to a revolution in the kitchen. During the '70s and '80s "California cuisine" seized the time and created some of the nation's finest restaurants. There are bayside parks galore, plus a look at the hills and dales of Silicon Valley, a boomtown kind of place that has seen property values rocket sky-high.

The tourism industry has a knack for transforming everyday life into a spectacle and making tourists feel like visitors to a huge, outdoor human zoo. The result is a kind of Heisenberg-uncertainty-principle-of-tourism whereby the mere presence of outsiders changes the human landscape forever. Local residents become actors, historic places are transformed into theme parks, and visitors see something that more nearly reflects themselves than the indigenous culture.

Like Heisenberg's dilemma, the phenomenon is unavoidable. But given the sensitivity and circumspection contemporary travelers are demonstrating, it is possible to gaze into America's cultural kaleidoscope without greatly disturbing the glass pieces.

In the following pages, I've provided a quiet and intimate approach to Northern California, taking you beyond the surface and into the heart of the place. Visiting the Wine Country, for instance, the book explores the burgeoning winegrowing regions of Sonoma and Napa valleys, stopping at tiny wineries where quality is a matter of family pride. Then it rolls west through the Russian River resort area, a getaway destination for gay men and lesbians. Families also vacation here because of the numerous outdoor opportunities.

Along the magnificent California coast, you'll range from Big Sur to Oregon, stopping at quaint bed-and-breakfast inns and tiny restaurants. The book describes picnics amid the redwoods, hiking trails high above the Pacific, nude beaches, and twisting country roads.

Then it heads for California's golden hills, the Sierra Nevada. Climbing through the Gold Country, where the ghosts of '49ers still wander falsefront towns, it leads to Lake Tahoe and Yosemite. Traditional tourist places are examined in detail, but the important moment is when the tour leaves the beaten track to include hideaway hotels, cozy nightspots, and remote campgrounds.

While this fresh style of travel appeals to people ranging in age from sprout to senior citizen, it has been taking shape for only a few decades. The transformation began in the '60s. The Peace Corps demonstrated we could swim freely in

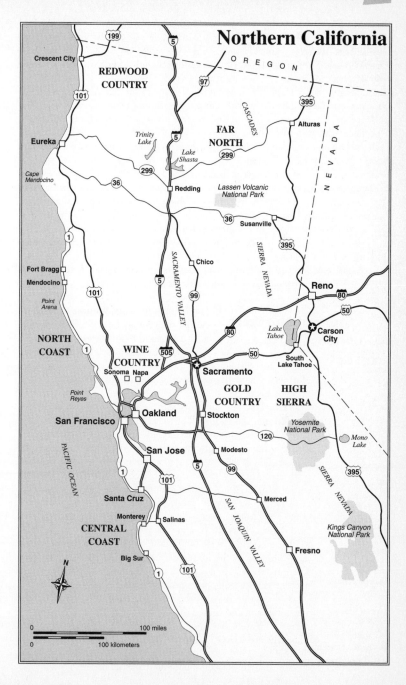

Northern California

OREGON

Crescent City

REDWOOD COUNTRY

199

5

101

97

395

CASCADES

FAR NORTH

Alturas

Eureka

Trinity Lake

5

299

Lake Shasta

Redding

299

36

Cape Mendocino

36

Lassen Volcanic National Park

NEVADA

Susanville

36

SIERRA NEVADA

395

1

Fort Bragg

Mendocino

101

Point Arena

Chico

5

99

Reno

80

50

NORTH COAST

1

SACRAMENTO VALLEY

Lake Tahoe

80

Carson City

WINE COUNTRY

505

50

South Lake Tahoe

Sonoma Napa

Sacramento

Point Reyes

GOLD COUNTRY

HIGH SIERRA

San Francisco

Oakland

Stockton

Yosemite National Park

Mono Lake

PACIFIC OCEAN

1

San Jose

Modesto

120

101

5

99

SIERRA NEVADA

395

Santa Cruz

Monterey

Salinas

Merced

CENTRAL COAST

SAN JOAQUIN VALLEY

Kings Canyon National Park

Big Sur

1

101

Fresno

N

| 0 | | 100 miles |
| 0 | | 100 kilometers |

foreign seas; Vietnam taught us not to thrash about in the water. Then the pre-occupation with self in the '70s, narcissistic though it was, opened us to unmapped experiences. We have changed from a society perceived as "ugly Americans" to a people in search of unique cultures and history. Better informed, more sensitive and adventurous, we travel for education as much as enjoyment. Rather than proclaiming answers, we ask questions. Cyberspace, with the Bay Area as its epicenter, overlays the region with a whole new dimension of existence, and the kaleidoscope of cultures, philosophies, and dreams invites us to reach out and touch the ephemeral spirit of place.

More than anywhere in the country, Northern California is a place for creative travelers. It's a multicultural extravaganza as well as a region of exceptional natural beauty. Continents have drifted into San Francisco Bay in ways geologists will never explain. Asia overlaps the entire state, Mexico is shifting north, and tides are carrying the rest of the world closer. Chinese are moving into Italian neighborhoods, French vintners have invaded the Wine Country, and Scandinavians are discovering the snows of the High Sierra.

Northern California is a destination best suited to a particular pattern of exploration, one requiring an open spirit and unquenchable curiosity. It's a place where experience and adventure form a pattern of overlapping layers that the new traveler, like an archaeologist, will personally uncover.

▼▼▼▼▼▼▼▼▼▼▼▼▼▼▼▼

The Story of Northern California

GEOLOGY

For billions of years, natural forces have carved the geology of California, creating a land as grand as it is beautiful. Bounded to the west by the cold waters of the Pacific and on the east by sharp mountain ranges and dense forests, Northern California has developed a diverse landscape rich in geologic history.

As a whole, the interior of Northern California can be divided into four natural regions. The first is the Sierra Nevada, the largest single mountain range in the United States. It's a solitary block of earth, tilted and uplifted, 430 miles long and 80 miles wide. A mere child in the long count of geologic history, it rose from the earth's surface a few million years back and did not reach its present form until 750,000 years ago. During the Pleistocene epoch, glaciers spread across the land, grinding and cutting at the mountains. They carved river valleys and deep canyons, and sculpted bald domes, fluted cliffs, and stone towers.

The glaciers left a landscape dominated by ragged peaks where lakes number in the hundreds and canyons plunge 5000 feet. There are cliffs sheer as glass that compete with the sky for dominance. It is, as an early pioneer described it, a "land of fire and ice."

Millions of years ago, the Klamath region separated from the Sierra Nevada and drifted 60 miles to the northwest. Composed of rocky uplands extending as high as 7000 feet in elevation, the Klamaths are deeply etched by the Smith, Klamath, and Trinity rivers. Heavy precipitation and fog have created dense coniferous forests that now dominate the landscape.

To the east of the Klamaths is the third natural region, which encompasses the southern extension of the volcanic Cascade Range and includes Mount Shasta and Lassen Peak. Mt. Shasta, rising over 14,000 feet, is lord of the land, a white-domed figure brooding above a forested realm. Lassen Peak, its infernal cousin, is an active volcano that last erupted in 1921. Composed of andesite volcanic rock and dated at several million years of age, the Cascade Range developed as a result of the process of subduction.

The fourth natural region consists of the Coast Ranges, which extend up the San Francisco peninsula, through Northern California to Oregon. Built of shale, sandstone, and other sedimentary rocks, the Coast Ranges are a product of pressure from the Pacific Plate beneath the western border of North America. These peaks include the Santa Cruz Mountains, which rise to the west and south of San Francisco Bay; on the other side of the Bay are the East Bay Hills and the Diablo Range; to the north looms Mt. Tamalpais. At the mouth of the Bay is the Golden Gate, a rocky conduit through which California's major drainage system empties into the Pacific.

The California coast is lined with softly rolling hills and bounded by a pacific sea. The shoreline is actually a head-on collision between the edge of the ocean and the rim of North America. Two tectonic plates, those rafts of land that float upon the earth's core, meet in California. Here the North American Plate and the Pacific Plate push against each other in a kind of international arm wrestle. Between them, and under colossal pressure from both sides, lies the San Andreas Fault. Villain of the 1906 San Francisco earthquake, it also brought the Loma Prieta quake in 1989 that measured 7.1 on the Richter scale.

Things were not always as they are. About 150 million years ago, the California coast rested where the Sierra Nevada mountains reside today. Then the North American Plate shifted west, riding roughshod over the Pacific Plate, compressing and folding the earth upward to create the Coast Ranges, and moving the continent 100 miles westward.

Today the northern section of the San Andreas Fault runs up the San Francisco peninsula, heading briefly out to sea just south of San Francisco, then cutting north through Stinson Beach, Bo-

A FLOODED CANYON

According to geologists, San Francisco Bay is a drowned river valley. Glaciers melting 10,000 years ago created it by raising sea levels and causing the ocean to flood a canyon carved earlier by the Sacramento and San Joaquin rivers.

dega Bay, and Point Arena, before heading seaward again near
Shelter Cove. Meanwhile the Pacific Plate, carrying Los Angeles,
is shifting north along the North American Plate, which holds
San Francisco, at a pace that should position the rival cities next to
each other in about ten million years. Anyone planning to hitch
a ride north should pack extra sandwiches and prepare for a long
wait at the side of the road.

FLORA   From dark redwood forests to sunny alpine meadows to a coastline colored by wildflowers, California's habitats are heaven to
natural history lovers. Radical climatic differences within the
state are largely responsible for creating this unique diversity.

Heavy precipitation and cold temperatures in the Sierra Nevada create the perfect environment for dense coniferous forests
of Ponderosa pine, white fir, and red fir. Higher
up, the sugar pines and Sierra redwoods tower over
manzanita, deer brush, and Sierra gooseberry. Also
included in this high-altitude habitat is California's
own giant sequoia, which is the pride of Sequoia and
Kings Canyon national parks.

More than 30 percent
of the plant species
in California are
endemic.

In the riparian woodlands of the Sierra Nevada, smaller
trees and larger shrubs including willows, cottonwoods,
white alders, and dogwoods thrive. Often bounded by lodgepole forests, Sierra meadows are home to an array of springtime
wildflowers—phloxes, paintbrushes, lupines, elephants head, and
the brilliant scarlet gilia.

In the Far North region of the Klamath mountains, abundant
rainfall and moderate temperatures combine to create a dense forest similar to that of the Alaskan coast. Species include Alaskan
cedar, Douglas fir, and silver fir. At higher elevations, wind-eroded
foxtail pine, a close relative of the ancient bristlecone pine of Southern California, survive. The lower slopes along the coast are host
to Pacific madrone, tan oak, and California laurel, while different
species of shrubby willow trees are found from Humboldt County
to Del Norte County.

East of the Klamaths, the volcanic soils of the Cascades support a unique conifer known as the Baker cypress, which flourishes despite the area's cold weather conditions. In the lowlands,
rainfall and fog have created forests dotted with ponderosa and
Jeffrey pine.

From the rim of the sea to the peaks of surrounding mountains, the coastline is covered with a complex variety of plant life.
Several plant communities flourish along the shore, each clinging
to a particular niche in the environment. Blessed with a cooler,
more moderate climate near the ocean, they are continually misted
by sea spray and must contend with more salt in their veins.

On the beaches and along the dunes are the herbs, vines, and low shrubs of the coastal strand community. Among their numbers are beach primrose, sand verbena, beach morning-glory, and sea figs, those tenacious succulents that run along the ground sprouting magenta flowers and literally carpeting the coast. Characterized by leathery leaves that retain large quantities of water, they are the plant world's answer to the camel.

Around the mud flats and river mouths grow rushes, pickleweed, tules, cord grass, and other members of the salt marsh community. Low, shrubby plants growing in clumps, these hearty fellows are inundated by tides and able to withstand tremendous concentrations of salt.

Coastal sage scrub inhabits a broad swath from above the waterline to about the 3000-foot elevation. White and black sage, wild buckwheat, and California sagebrush belong to this community of short, tough plants.

Along the northern coastal ranges, cold ocean waters create heavy fog, an essential nutrient for the eerily beautiful coastal redwoods. The fabled Monterey cypress inhabits a picturesque region along the Monterey coast, the only place in the world it is found. Closed-cone pines including the Monterey, Bishop, and knobcone skirt the shoreline. Shrubs in the northern coastal ranges include brown dogwood, Western rose-bay, and bunchberry. Scattered along the rolling hills of the coastal interior are the dignified, gnarled oak trees while the coastal woodlands are also sown with drought-tolerant species of dry grasses and assorted wildflowers including the California poppy, the state flower.

FAUNA

From the black bears of Yosemite Valley to the black-tailed deer of the East Bay hills, Northern California is home to a variety of wildlife. This is true despite the environmental stress of humans on the state's wilderness areas, which has caused the extinction of many species. The California grizzly bear, for instance, is no longer found in the Sierra Nevada; and because of the damming of rivers and streams, salmon spawning has become a rare phenomenon. Conservation efforts have increased in the past few years, and many species are now under governmental protection. For example, attempts to preserve the habitat of the bighorn sheep have been so intense that a marked increase in their population occurred for several years. Debates continually rage over the status of mountain lions and coyotes, both of which are coming into increased contact with humans as open land has given way to residential developments.

The rich habitat of the High Sierra is home to a variety of species including ground squirrels, yellow-bellied marmots, pikas, gophers, jackrabbits, hares, snakes, lizards, golden trout, salamanders, bighorn sheep, and great gray owls. In the lower fields of the

Sierra riparian woodlands, multicolored butterflies and a diverse selection of birds such as starlings, sparrows, blackbirds, American dipper, and the belter kingfisher make their homes. Lower yet, the cavities in oak trees provide shelter for gray squirrels, owls, woodpeckers, and bluebirds.

The moist forests of the Klamath region are a fertile backdrop for a wide array of wildlife. There are approximately 15 colorful species of salamanders in these northern forests, including the cave-dwelling Shasta salamander and the water-loving Olympic salamander. Colorful hummingbirds, bald eagles, pileated woodpeckers, elusive spotted owls, and the marbled murrelet dart around the forests. Other critters include chipmunks, porcupines, raccoons, weasels, river otters, and Roosevelt elk.

Six species of seals and sea lions inhabit the coast, together with sea otters, those playful creatures that delight visitors and bedevil fishermen.

In the northern Coast Ranges, the insects can be as interesting as reptiles and amphibians. The monarch butterfly migrates between Canada and Central Mexico, stopping off in Pacific Grove every year. The Western pond turtle is found along the coast, while alligator lizards inhabit the coastal interior. The scrub jay helps create oak forests by storing hundreds of acorns underground. Another acorn-loving species is the acorn woodpecker, which stores its provisions in the cavities of oak trees.

Somehow the mud flats of San Francisco Bay are the last place you may think to go sightseeing, particularly at high tide, after the flood has stirred the ooze. But it is at such times that birders gather to view flocks of as many as 60,000 birds.

The California shore is one of the richest bird habitats anywhere in North America. Over 500 species are found across the state, many along the coast and its offshore islands. There are near-shore birds like loons, grebes, cormorants, and scoters, that inhabit the shallow waters of bays and beaches. Others birds are situated offshore; these include shearwaters, which feed several miles off the coast; and pelagic or open-ocean species like albatross and Arctic terns, which fly miles from land and live for up to 20 or 30 years.

Joining the shore birds along California's beaches are ducks, geese, and other waterfowl. Both waterfowl and near-shore birds flee the scene each year, flying north in spring to Canada and Alaska or south during autumn to Mexico and Central America, following the Pacific flyway, that great migratory route spanning the western United States.

The peregrine falcon nests on rock ledges and is capable of diving at 200 miles an hour to prey on ducks, coots, and terns. Among the most beautiful birds are the egrets and herons. Tall, slender, elegant birds, they live from January until July in Bolinas and other coastal towns. Together with sea gulls, sandpipers, and pelicans, they tend to turn travelers into birdwatchers and make inconvenient times, like the edge of dawn, and unusual places, like swamps, among the most intriguing possibilities Northern California has to offer.

California's marine mammals inspire great myth and magic. Foremost are the ocean-going animals like whales, dolphins, and porpoises, members of that unique Cetacean order that left the land 30 million years ago for the alien world of the sea.

While dolphins and porpoises range far offshore, the region's most common whale is a regular coastal visitor. Migrating 12,000 miles every year between the Bering Sea and Baja Peninsula, the California gray whale cruises the shoreline each winter. Measuring 50 feet and weighing 40 tons, these distinguished animals can live to 50 years of age and communicate with sophisticated signaling systems.

Northern California stretches over 400 miles from Big Sur to Oregon and almost 200 miles from east to west. Within that broad expanse lies the Pacific coastline, a broad interior valley, the lofty Sierra Nevada, and a weather pattern that varies as dramatically as the terrain.

When to Go

SEASONS

Generally, there are three different climatic zones. San Francisco and the rest of the Pacific shore enjoy mild temperatures year-round, since the coastal fog creates a natural form of air conditioning and insulation. The mercury rarely drops below 40° or rises above 70°, with September and October being the hottest months, and December and January the coolest.

Spring and particularly autumn are the ideal times to visit. During the winter, the rainy season brings overcast days and frequent showers. Summer is San Francisco's peak tourist season, when large crowds can present problems. It's also a period of frequent fog; especially in the morning and evening, fog banks from offshore blanket the city and head inland through the Golden Gate.

The seasons vary much more in the interior valleys, creating a second climatic zone. In the Wine Country, Delta, and Gold Country, summer temperatures often top 90°. There's less humidity, winters are cooler, and the higher elevations receive occasional snowfall. Like the coast, this piedmont region experiences most of its rain during winter months.

The Sierra Nevada and Cascade Ranges experience Northern California's most dramatic weather. During summer, the days are warm, the nights cool. Spring and autumn bring crisp temperatures and colorful foliage changes (which the coastline, with its unvarying seasons, rarely undergoes). Then in winter, the thermometer plummets and snow falls so heavily as to make these mountain chains spectacular ski areas.

CALENDAR OF EVENTS

JANUARY   **San Francisco**   During late January or early February, the **Chinese New Year** features an extravagant parade with colorful dragons, dancers, marching bands, and fireworks.

FEBRUARY   **San Francisco**   The **Pacific Orchid Exposition** celebrates its floral namesake at the Fort Mason Center.
North Coast   The **World Famous Crab Races and Crab Feed** takes place in Crescent City; if you forgot to bring your own, you can rent a racing crab. Who said California lacks culture?
Far North   During the winter months, Mount Shasta Ski & Snowboarding Park sponsors a series of **Demo Days** during which you can test-drive all the latest ski and snowboarding equipment.
Central Coast   The AT&T **National Pebble Beach Pro-Am Golf Championship** swings into action early in the month.

MARCH   **San Francisco**   Bands, politicians, and assorted revelers parade through the city on the Sunday closest to March 17, marking **St. Patrick's Day**.
Wine Country   The blooming of wild mustard marks the start of the **Napa Valley Mustard Festival**, which runs February through March and includes cooking demonstrations, art exhibits, and (of course) chowder- and winetasting.
North Coast   Mendocino and Fort Bragg celebrate a **Whale Festival** with whale-watching cruises, art shows, and winetasting.
High Sierra   The **SnowFestival** along Lake Tahoe's North Shore is a celebration with fireworks, ski races and dancing.

APRIL   **San Francisco**   Japantown's **Cherry Blossom Festival** features parades, tea ceremonies, theatrical performances, and martial arts displays. **Opening Day on the Bay** launches the yachting season with a blessing of the fleet and a parade of decorated boats. The **San Francisco International Film Festival** offers a wide selection of cinematic events.
Wine Country   The entire town of Sebastopol turns out for an **Apple Blossom Festival**, staging exhibits, parades, and pageants.
North Coast   The two-day wildlife festival at Lower Lake, **Heron Days**, features boat rides to heron rookeries on Clear Lake, nature walks, slide shows, and fun for the kids.
Central Coast   Monterey presents its **Annual Wine Festival**, with winetasting, gourmet food, and cooking demonstrations.

MAY   **San Francisco**   Over 70,000 hearty souls (soles?) run the **Bay to Breakers Foot Race**, many covering the 7.5-mile course in costumes. San Francisco celebrates **Cinco de Mayo** in the Mission with arts, crafts, food, and a festive parade.

Gold Country   Up in Angels Camp, the **Calaveras County Fair and Jumping Frog Jubilee**, immortalized by Mark Twain, includes not only frog-jumping contests, but a wine show, and county fair as well.

San Francisco   The **San Francisco Lesbian, Gay, Bisexual, Transgender Pride Parade**, with its colorful floats and imaginative costumes, marches down Market Street to the Civic Center. June launches the performances of the two-month-long **Stern Grove Festival**, which showcases international music and dance, vocal ensembles, opera, and jazz.

JUNE

Bay Area   Artists throughout the East Bay display their work two weekends every June during the **Pro Arts Open Studios**.

Gold Country   A parade helps kick off a series of rodeo competitions at Sonora's **Mother Lode Round Up**.

San Francisco   Here at Fisherman's Wharf and throughout Northern California, firework displays commemorate the **Fourth of July**.

JULY

Bay Area   The **Jewish Film Festival**, in existence for more than two decades, celebrates new independent films from around the world, focusing on Jewish history, culture, and identity.

Central Coast   Gilroy celebrates its favorite crop with a **Garlic Festival** featuring the cuisine of local gourmet chefs. The **California Rodeo** in Salinas ranges from horse races to trick riders to clown acts. Browse the wares of local artists, accompanied by live jazz, at Santa Cruz's outdoor **Art on the Wharf**.

Gold Country   Plymouth's **Amador County Fair** includes demonstrations of antique farming, mining, and lumbering equipment.

San Francisco   Celebrate the Bay Area's diverse Asian community at the annual **Nihonmachi Street Fair**. Local artisans display their wares, and there's live music and authentic Asian cuisine as well as an area for kids to make traditional Asian crafts. **Comedy Celebration Day** is a free "comedy concert" in Golden Gate Park featuring stand-ups from around the world. The **San Francisco Chronicle Marathon** begins at the Ferry Plaza, then winds for 26.2 miles past many of the city's sights before heading back to the Ferry Building.

AUGUST

Central Coast   Pebble Beach sponsors the **Blackhawk Collection Exposition of Classic Cars**, a classic auto show featuring pre- and postwar cars. Salinas celebrates its four-day **Steinbeck Festival** with walking tours, lectures, films, and plays.

Gold Country   Sample the fare of a number of local restaurants and wineries at the **Nimbus Winery Wine and Food Festival** in Rancho Cordova. Grass Valley hosts the **Nevada County Fair**, with entertainment, food, music, livestock, living-history displays, and gold panning.

SEPTEMBER **San Francisco**   This month for music is marked by the opening of the **San Francisco Opera** and the **San Francisco Symphony**, as well as the annual **Blues Festival** and **Opera in the Park**. The **San Francisco Blues Festival** at Fort Mason is known not only for being the oldest of its kind in America, but also for attracting some of the best musicians in the world. The end of the month and Leather Pride Week brings a San Francisco tradition: the **Folsom Street Fair**. The event is peopled with San Francisco's kinkiest citizens (it's the biggest leather event in the world), but tolerant adults of all kinds also join in the fun.

Bay Area   The **Santa Clara Art and Wine Festival**, one of the nation's largest sidewalk art displays, features food, entertainment, and local and regional artists at Central Park. Sausalito also celebrates the arts and Memorial Day weekend with the **Sausalito Art Festival**. More than 20,000 works are displayed, accompanied by live entertainment and gourmet delights.

Central Coast   It's also the magic month for the internationally renowned **Monterey Jazz Festival**.

Gold Country   The **Gold Country Fair** in Auburn features a harvest festival, livestock auction, plenty of food, and country music. The capital city of Sacramento hosts the **California State Fair**, which features concerts, exhibits, and competitions galore.

OCTOBER **San Francisco**   **Columbus Day** is marked by a parade, bocce ball tournament, and the annual blessing of the fishing fleet. The **San Francisco Jazz Festival** kicks off in late October to present two weeks' worth of concerts, dance, performances, and tributes to the masters. The **Castro Street Fair** features food, art, and loads of quirky San Francisco culture.

Central Coast   The **Art and Pumpkin Festival** in Half Moon Bay features food booths, crafts exhibits, and pie-eating contests.

Gold Country   The festivities at Murphy's **Old Rush Street Faire** include grape stomping, a team costume contest, a waiters' race, and belly dancers.

NOVEMBER **San Francisco**   Cowboys do their celebrating at the **Grand National Rodeo, Horse & Stock Show**.

North Coast   Mendocino hosts a **Thanksgiving Art Fair** with over 40 crafts booths and refreshments.

DECEMBER **San Francisco**   The **Great Dickens Christmas Fair**, which goes from Thanksgiving to Christmas, and the **Tree Lighting at Union Square** commemorate the holiday season. There are also **Christmas Parades** in towns throughout Northern California. The San

Francisco Ballet (the world's oldest ballet company and one of the best) mounts its annual production of Tchaikovsky's classic **Nutcracker**.

Bay Area   Locals head to Oakland's Jack London Square to view the annual **Lighted Yacht Parade**.

Several agencies provide free information to travelers. The **California Office of Tourism** will help guide you to areas throughout the state. ~ 801 K Street, Suite 1600, Sacramento, CA 95812; 916-322-2881, 800-862-2543; www.gocalif.com.

Before You Go

VISITORS CENTERS

For information on the North Coast counties between San Francisco and Oregon, contact the **Redwood Empire Association**. ~ c/o The California Welcome Center, Pier 39, Suite Q-5, San Francisco, CA 94133; 415-956-3491; www.redwoodempire.com.

The **San Francisco Visitors Information Center** is another excellent resource. ~ Hallidie Plaza, Lower Level, Powell and Market streets; 900 Market Street, San Francisco, CA 94102; 415-391-2000; www.sfvisitor.org.

Also consult local chambers of commerce and information centers, which are mentioned in the various area chapters.

PACKING

There are two important guidelines when deciding what to take on a trip. The first is as true for San Francisco and Northern California as anywhere in the world—pack light. Dress styles here are relatively informal and laundromats or dry cleaners are frequent. The airlines allow two suitcases and a carry-on bag; try to take one suitcase and perhaps a small accessory case.

The second rule is to prepare for cool weather, even if the closest you'll come to the mountains is the top of Nob Hill. "The coldest winter I ever spent," Mark Twain remarked, "was a summer in San Francisco." While the city's climate is temperate, temperatures sometimes descend below 50°. Even that might not seem chilly until the fog rolls in and the ocean breeze picks up. A warm sweater and jacket are absolute necessities. Pack shorts for the summer or autumn. You'll encounter similar weather conditions in all coastal areas of Northern California, where the Pacific Ocean moderates the climate. If you plan to tour inland, though, it's a different story. The Wine Country, the Delta, and the Gold Country can be very hot during the summer, and you'll want the lightest, coolest clothing possible.

Yosemite and other parts of the Sierras have deep snow and subfreezing temperatures for most of the winter, so a parka, hat, gloves, and warm boots are in order. The best plan, whenever you're planning a trip around the interior of California, is to dress in layers and be prepared for anything.

LODGING   Overnight accommodations in Northern California are as varied as the region itself. They range from highrise hotels and neon motels to hostels and bed-and-breakfast inns. One guideline to follow with all is to reserve well in advance. This is an extremely popular area, particularly in summer, and facilities fill up quickly.

Throughout the book, hotel facilities are organized geographically. Check through the various regional sections of each chapter and you're bound to find something to fit your budget and personal taste.

The neon motels offer bland facilities at low prices and are excellent if you're economizing or don't plan to spend much time in the room. Larger hotels often lack intimacy, but provide such conveniences as restaurants and shops in the lobby. My personal preference is for historic hotels, those slightly faded classics that offer charm and tradition at moderate cost. Bed-and-breakfast inns present an opportunity to stay in a home-like setting. Like hostels, they are an excellent way to meet fellow travelers; unlike hostels, Northern California's country inns are quite expensive.

> Even in early fall and late spring, campers in the Sierras will discover that the thermometer quickly plunges below freezing as the sun goes down.

To help you decide on a place to stay, I've described the accommodations not only by area but also according to price (prices listed are for the high season; rates may decrease in low season). *Budget* hotels are generally less than $60 per night for two people; the rooms are clean and comfortable, but lack luxury. The *moderately* priced hotels run $60 to $120, and provide larger rooms, plusher furniture, and more attractive surroundings. At *deluxe*-priced accommodations you can expect to spend between $120 and $175 for a homey bed and breakfast or a double in a hotel or resort. You'll check into a spacious, well-appointed room with all modern facilities; downstairs the lobby will be a fashionable affair, and you'll usually see a restaurant, lounge, and a cluster of shops. If you want to spend your time (and money) in the city's very finest hotels, try an *ultra-deluxe* facility, which will include all the amenities and a price above $175.

Contact **California Association of Bed & Breakfast Inns** to give you a hand in finding a cozy place to stay. ~ 2715 Porter Street, Soquel; 831-462-9191, fax 831-462-0402; www.cabbi.com.

DINING   It seems as if Northern California has more restaurants than people. Particularly in San Francisco, they line the streets; vendor stands and lunch wagons line the curbs as well. To establish a pattern for this parade of dining places, I've described not only the cuisine but also the ambience and general price structure of each establishment. Restaurants listed offer lunch and dinner unless otherwise noted.

Within a particular chapter, the restaurants are categorized geographically, with each restaurant entry describing the establishment as budget, moderate, deluxe, or ultra-deluxe in price. Dinner entrées at *budget* restaurants usually cost $9 or less. The ambience is informal café-style and the crowd is often a local one. *Moderately* priced restaurants range between $9 and $18 at dinner and offer pleasant surroundings, a more varied menu, and a slower pace. *Deluxe* establishments tab their entrées above $18, featuring sophisticated cuisines, plush decor, and more personalized service. *Ultra-deluxe* dining rooms, where $25 will only get you started, are gourmet gathering places where the cooking (hopefully) is a fine art form and service is a way of life.

Breakfast and lunch menus vary less in price from restaurant to restaurant. Even deluxe-priced kitchens usually offer light breakfasts and lunch sandwiches that place them within a few dollars of their budget-minded competitors. These early meals can be a good time to test expensive restaurants.

TRAVELING WITH CHILDREN

Visiting Northern California with kids can be a real adventure, and if properly planned, a truly enjoyable one. To ensure that your trip will feature the joy, rather than the strain, of parenthood, remember a few important guidelines.

Children under age 5 or under 40 pounds must be in approved child restraints while riding in cars/vans. The back seat is safest.

Use a travel agent to help with arrangements; they can reserve spacious bulkhead seats. Also plan to bring everything you need on board—diapers, food, toys, and extra clothes for kids and parents alike. If the trip to Northern California involves a long journey, plan to relax and do very little during the first few days.

Always allow extra time for getting places. Book reservations well in advance and make sure the hotel has the extra crib, cot, or bed you require. It's smart to ask for a room at the end of the hall to cut down on noise. Also keep in mind that many bed-and-breakfast inns do not allow children.

Most towns have stores that carry diapers, food, and other essentials; in cities and larger towns, 7-11 stores are often open all night (check the Yellow Pages for addresses). In San Francisco, **Cala Foods** has several large groceries, including locations at 6333 Geary Boulevard, 4041 Geary Boulevard, 4201 18th Street, and South Van Ness and Mission streets, which are open 24 hours a day.

Hotels often provide access to babysitters or you can check the Yellow Pages for state licensed and bonded babysitting agencies.

A first-aid kit is always a good idea. Also, check with your pediatrician for special medicines and dosages for colds and diarrhea. Finding activities to interest children in Northern California could not be easier. Especially helpful in deciding on the day's outing are *Places to Go with Children in Northern Califor-*

nia (Chronicle Books) and the "Datebook" or "pink section" of the Sunday *San Francisco Chronicle*.

WOMEN TRAVELING ALONE

It is sad commentary on life in the United States, but women traveling alone must take precautions. It's entirely unwise to hitch-hike and probably best to avoid inexpensive accommodations on the outskirts of town; the money saved does not outweigh the risk. Bed and breakfasts, youth hostels, college dorms, and YWCAs are generally your safest bet for lodging.

If you are hassled or threatened in some way, never be afraid to scream for assistance. It's a good idea to carry change for a phone call and to know the number to call in case of emergency.

Northern California boasts nearly 900 women's organizations, including rape crisis centers, health organizations, battered women's shelters, National Organization of Women (NOW) chapters, business networking clubs, artists' and writers' groups, and one-of-a-kind organizations ranging from Women as Allies in the Santa Cruz area to the Women's Mountain Bike & Tea Society (WOM-BATS) in Fairfax.

Emergency services, including rape crisis and battered women's hotlines, can be found in local phone books or by calling directory assistance. A good place to start when seeking information about other resources is the local women's center, often affiliated with a university. Among them are **University of California–Berkeley Gender and Equity Resource Center**, 202 Cesar Chavez Student Center, Berkeley, 510-642-4786; **University of California–Santa Cruz Women's Center**, Cardiff House, University of California, Santa Cruz, 831-459-2072; **University of California–San Francisco Center for Gender Equity**, 100 Medical Center Way, San Francisco, 415-476-5222; **Stanford Women's Community Center**, 433 Santa Teresa Street, Stanford, 650-723-0545; **Women Escaping a Violent Environment** (WEAVE), Sacramento, 916-920-2952; **Women's Center House 55**, Humboldt State University, Arcata, 707-826-4216; and **Women's Resources and Research Center**, North Hall, University of California, Davis; 530-752-3372.

GAY & LESBIAN TRAVELERS

Without doubt, San Francisco is one of the premier gay and lesbian vacation spots in the country. The Castro Street and Polk Street neighborhoods, as well as the South of Market district, are all major gay areas. Each offers gay-owned and gay-friendly lodging, restaurants, and nightspots. (See the "Gay Neighborhoods" and "South of Market" sections in Chapter Two, and "Gay and lesbian travelers" in the index.) One of the largest of its kind, the **San Francisco Lesbian, Gay, Bisexual, and Transgender Community Center** (LGBT) offers a plethora of services from health and legal referrals to lodging and activity suggestions. ~ 1800 Market Street; 415-865-5555, fax 415-865-5501; www.sfcen

ter.org. The **Billy DeFrank LGBT Community Center** in San Jose, has lots of information online. ~ www.defrank.org.

San Francisco AIDS Foundation Hotline is the area's best resource for counseling and referrals. ~ 415-863-2437, 800-367-2437 (within California); www.sfaf.org. The AIDS **Nightline** staffs operators from 5 p.m. to 5 a.m. ~ 415-434-2437, 800-628-9240.

The **Community United Against Violence Support Line** is available 24 hours a day to assist gay, lesbian, bisexual, and transgender people who have been physically assaulted. ~ 415-333-4357; www.xq.com/cuav.

Despite its name, the **Women's Building** is a community center with a non-profit auditorium for rent, and bulletin boards loaded with information and job listings for gays, lesbians, and bisexuals. ~ 3543 18th Street, San Francisco; 415-431-1180, fax 415-861-8969. Medical attention for lesbian and transgender women can be had at the **Lyon-Martin Women's Health Services**. ~ 1748 Market Street, Suite 201, San Francisco; 415-565-7667. **The Pacific Center for Human Growth** offers low-cost counseling, peer-support groups, job listings, and housing bulletins, as well as an information referral line for anything that is pertinent to the gay-lesbian-bisexual-transgender community. ~ 2712 Telegraph Avenue, Berkeley; 510-548-8283; www.pacific center.org, e-mail info@pacificcenter.org.

> In many ways, the entire city of San Francisco is a gay-friendly enclave. Gays and lesbians constitute a powerful voting block in local politics, and several currently serve on the Board of Supervisors.

For weekly updates on the gay community, pick up a *Bay Area Reporter*, which focuses on local news and arts and entertainment. ~ 415-861-5019. *SF Frontiers* is biweekly, publishing feature and news articles of interest to the gay community. ~ www.frontiers newsmagazine.com. The monthly *San Francisco Bay Times* deals with gay issues and doubles as a resource guide as well. ~ 415-626-0260.

The Russian River area, an hour north of the city, is another key gay and lesbian resort area. (See the "Russian River" section in Chapter Four, and "Gay and lesbian travelers" in the index.) **Gay/Lesbian Information Referral Line** is a traveler-friendly phone line that provides information and referrals about lodging, dining, and nightlife in the area, along with just about any other information you might need. ~ 707-526-0442. The local gay and lesbian newspaper is *We the People*, which comes out once a month and is available throughout the Wine Country and the Russian River region. The free bimonthly *Mom . . . Guess What!* serves Sacramento and Northern California with political scoops, travel tips, restaurant reviews, and more. ~ 916-441-6397; www.mgwnews.com.

Northern California is an ideal spot for older vacationers. The mild climate makes traveling in the off-season possible, helping to **SENIOR TRAVELERS** cut down on expenses. Many museums, theaters, restaurants, and hotels offer discounts to seniors (requiring a driver's license, Medicare card, or other age-identifying card). Be sure to ask your travel agent when booking reservations.

The **American Association of Retired Persons,** or AARP, offers members travel discounts and provides escorted tours. ~ 601 E Street NW, Washington, DC 20049; 800-424-3410; www.aarp.org.

For those 55 or over, **Elderhostel** offers educational programs in California. ~ 11 Avenue de Lafayette, Boston, MA 02111; 877-426-8056; www.elderhostel.org.

The California redwood, the state tree, is the tallest living thing in the world.

Be extra careful about health matters. Bring any medications you use, along with the prescriptions. Consider carrying a medical record with you—including your current medical status, and medical history, as well as your doctor's name, phone number, and address. Also be sure to confirm that your insurance covers you away from home.

DISABLED TRAVELERS

California stands at the forefront of social reform for persons with disabilities. During the past decade, the state has responded to the needs of the blind, wheelchair-bound, and others with a series of progressive legislative measures.

The **Department of Motor Vehicles** provides special parking permits for the disabled. Many local bus lines and other public transit facilities are wheelchair accessible. ~ 1377 Fell Street, San Francisco; 415-557-1179; www.dmv.ca.gov.

There are also agencies in Northern California assisting travelers with disabilities. For tips and information about the San Francisco Bay Area, contact the **Center for Independent Living,** a self-help group that has led the way in reforming access laws in California. ~ 2539 Telegraph Avenue, Berkeley; 510-841-4776, fax 510-841-6168; www.cilberkeley.org.

There are many organizations offering general information. Among these are:

The **Society for Accessible Travel & Hospitality.** ~ 347 5th Avenue #610, New York, NY 10016; 212-447-7284; www.sath.org.

The **MossRehab ResourceNet.** ~ MossRehab Hospital, 1200 West Tabor Road, Philadelphia, PA 19141; 215-456-9600; www.mossresourcenet.org.

Flying Wheels Travel operates as a full-service travel agency for the disabled. ~ 143 West Bridge Street, Owatonna, MN 55060; 800-535-6790; www.flyingwheelstravel.com.

Travelin' Talk, a network of people and organizations, also provides assistance. ~ P.O. Box 1796, Wheat Ridge, CO 80034; 303-232-2979; www.travelintalk.net. Its sister organization,

Access-Able Travel Service has worldwide information online. ~ 303-232-2979; www.access-able.com.

Or consult the comprehensive guidebook, *Access to the World —A Travel Guide for the Handicapped,* by Louise Weiss (Holt, Rinehart & Winston). Though out-of-print, it can be found through second-hand book dealers.

Be sure to check in advance when making reservations. Many hotels and motels feature facilities for those in wheelchairs.

Passports and Visas   Most foreign visitors are required to obtain a passport and tourist visa to enter the United States. Contact your nearest United States Embassy or Consulate well in advance to obtain a visa and to check on any other entry requirements.

FOREIGN TRAVELERS

Customs Requirements   Foreign travelers are allowed to bring in the following: 200 cigarettes (1 carton), 50 cigars, or 2 kilograms (4.4 pounds) of smoking tobacco; one liter of alcohol for personal use only (you must be 21 years of age to bring in alcohol); and US$100 worth of duty-free gifts that can include an additional 100 cigars. You may bring in any amount of currency, but must fill out a form if you bring in over US$10,000. Carry any prescription drugs in clearly marked containers. You may have to produce a written prescription or doctor's statement for the customs officers. Meat or meat products, seeds, plants, fruits, and narcotics are not allowed to be brought into the United States. Contact the **United States Customs Service** for further information. ~ 1300 Pennsylvania Avenue NW, Washington, DC 20229; 202-927-1700; www.customs.treas.gov.

Driving   If you plan to rent a car, an international driver's license should be obtained prior to arrival. Some rental car companies require both a foreign license and an international driver's license, along with a major credit card and require that the lessee be at least 25 years of age. Seat belts are mandatory for the driver and all passengers. Children under the age of 5 or 40 pounds should be in the back seat in approved child-safety restraints.

Currency   American money is based on the dollar. Bills in the United States come in six common denominations: $1, $5, $10, $20, $50, and $100. Every dollar is divided into 100 cents. Coins are the penny (1 cent), nickel (5 cents), dime (10 cents), quarter (25 cents), half-dollar (50 cents), and dollar (100 cents). You may not use foreign currency to purchase goods and services in the United States. Consider buying traveler's checks in dollar amounts. You may also use credit cards affiliated with an American company such as Interbank, Barclay Card, VISA, and American Express.

Electricity and Electronics   Electric outlets use currents of 110 volts, 60 cycles. For appliances made for other electrical systems, you need a transformer or other adapter. Travelers who use lap-

Text continued on page 22.

Old Gold Mountain

The tiny village of Yerba Buena, pop. 400, slumbered on the edge of the bay, waiting for the whaling ships that occasionally dropped anchor there for supplies. Once the northernmost Spanish colonial capital in the Americas, it had begun to decline when the old Franciscan mission on the other side of the hill shut down. By 1846, when the region became United States territory, most Californians had moved south into Mexico. Meanwhile, a few Anglo adventurers had begun to arrive; by 1848, about 1000 of them had homesteaded in Northern California.

When local newspaper publisher Sam Brannan announced in the town plaza that gold had been discovered 150 miles inland, all hell broke loose. Within a year, the population of the village—newly renamed San Francisco after the old mission nearby—grew from 400 to 24,000, and another 60,000 pioneers had taken up residence in the gold country of the Sierra. In ten more years San Francisco's population would reach 57,000, and by 1870 it would be 150,000, while the total population of Northern California would exceed 500,000.

Many newcomers were Southerners who brought black slaves with them; but California was admitted to the Union as a free state, and in 1851 a woman named Biddy Mason won a Supreme Court decision that any slave owner who remained in the state for three years lost his property rights to his slaves, thus instantly freeing about 1000 African Americans in California. The presence of an established black community made California seem a land of opportunity for many newly freed slaves who migrated west after the Civil War.

At the same time, famine was sweeping China, and American brokers brought thousands of refugees to the United States to work in mines and build railroads. Japanese immigrants also came to California, but most dispersed in rural areas to become farmers. Prejudice ran high, and as the numbers grew, Anglo Californians prevailed on the federal government to pass laws prohibiting Asian immigration—with a few exceptions. After the Philippines became United States territory in the Spanish-American War, Filipinos could move to the U.S., and many did.

Before World War II, there were no restrictions on Mexicans entering the United States. Many Mexican citizens came to California seasonally to work in the fast-growing agricultural industry, and many stayed between seasons. During the war, fears that Mexicans would fill the jobs vacated by American soldiers prompted the federal government to tighten the border and deport many people of Mexican descent. But those who could prove they had been born in the U.S. or had been naturalized were allowed to stay and form the nucleus of a Mexican American population that has been growing ever since.

Also during World War II, Japanese Americans in California were taken from their homes and put in internment camps around the western U.S. While some returned after the war, California's Japanese population has never regained its pre-war level. Laws against Asian immigration stayed in effect until 1965. After they were lifted, the Asian population grew rapidly. Thousands of Cambodian, Vietnamese, and Laotian refugees settled in San Francisco. With the Silicon Valley high-tech boom, a new wave of highly educated immigrants from many parts of Asia arrived to meet the seemingly limitless demand for engineers and technicians.

As civil wars ravaged Central America during the 1980s, many Guatemalan, Salvadoran, and Nicaraguan people chose to live in California with its long-established Spanish-speaking community. In San Francisco, Central Americans now comprise the majority of the Latino population.

According to recent official population estimates, 66 percent of Northern Californians are of European descent; 12 percent are African American; 16 percent are Asian American; and 6 percent are "other." Latinos (who may fall into any of the above categories) account for 14 percent of Northern California's population.

In San Francisco, 49 percent are of European descent; 7 percent are African American; 31 percent are Asian; and 13 percent are "other." Within the Asian population, 63 percent are Chinese; 16 percent are Filipino; 5 percent are Japanese; 4 percent are Vietnamese; and the remaining 12 percent include Koreans, East Indians, Cambodians, Hmong, Laotians, and Thais. Of all San Franciscans, 14 percent are Latino, including 44 percent Mexican Americans, 50 percent Central Americans, 3 percent Puerto Ricans, and 1 percent Cubans.

Statistics alone, however, cannot tell the whole story of Northern California's kaleidoscope. Consider, for instance, the rich Italian heritage that infuses the Wine Country, as well as the Irish character of many communities in the Gold Country. Above all, there's San Francisco's reputation for tolerance, which has consistently attracted people whose lifestyles lie outside the American mainstream. Beatniks, gay men and lesbians, hippies, and cyberspace pioneers have all helped shape the character of one of the most unique and culturally vibrant cities anywhere.

top computers for telecommunication should be aware that modem configurations for U.S. telephone systems may be different from their European counterparts. Similarly, the U.S. format for video-tapes is different from that in Europe; National Park Service vis-itors centers and other stores that sell souvenir videos often have them available in European format on request.

Weights and Measurements   The United States uses the English system of weights and measures. American units and their met-ric equivalents are as follows: 1 inch = 2.5 centimeters; 1 foot (12 inches) = 0.3 meter; 1 yard (3 feet) = 0.9 meter; 1 mile (5280 feet) = 1.6 kilometers; 1 ounce = 28 grams; 1 pound (16 ounces) = 0.45 kilogram; 1 quart (liquid) = 0.9 liter.

Outdoor Adventures

The state oversees close to 300 camping facil-ities. Amenities at each campground vary; for more information on state-run campgrounds

CAMPING   call or write the **California Department of Parks and Recreation** for a free **California Escapes** guide packet. ~ P.O. Box 942896, Sacramento, CA 94296; 916-653-6995, 800-777-0369. Reser-vations for campgrounds may be made by calling 800-444-7275.

For general information on federal campgrounds, contact the **National Park Service**. ~ Pacific West Region, 1111 Jackson Street, Suite 700, Oakland, CA 94607; 510-817-1300. To reserve specific campsites call 800-436-7275.

For maps and information contact the **U.S. Forest Service**. ~ 1323 Club Drive, Vallejo, CA 94592; 707-562-8737; www.r5.fs.fed.us. Campsites must be booked through **National Recreation Reservation Center**. ~ 877-444-6777. A fee is charged at these facilities and the length of stay varies from park to park. It's best to reserve in advance, though many parks keep some sites open to be filled daily on a first-come, first-serve basis.

In addition to state and national campgrounds, Northern California offers numerous municipal, county, and private facili-ties. See the "Beaches & Parks" sections in each chapter for the locations of these campgrounds.

PERMITS   **Wilderness Permits**   For camping and hiking in the wilderness and primitive areas of national forests, a wilderness permit is re-quired. Permits are free and are issued for a specific period of time, which varies according to the wilderness area. You can obtain permits from ranger stations and regional information centers, as described in the "Beaches & Parks" sections in each chapter. Information, but not permits, is available through the **U.S. Forest Service**. ~ 1323 Club Drive, Vallejo, CA 94592; 707-562-8737; www.r5.fs.fed.us.

Fishing Licenses   For information on the fishing season and state license fees, contact the **Department of Fish and Game**. ~ 3211 S Street, Sacramento, CA 95816; 916-445-0411; www.dfg.ca.gov.

TWO

San Francisco

It is a city poised at the end of the continent, civilization's last fling before the land plunges into the Pacific. Perhaps this is why visitors demand something memorable from San Francisco. People expect the city to resonate along a personal wavelength, speak to them, fulfill some ineffable desire at the center of the soul.

There is a terrible beauty at the edge of America: the dream begins here, or ends. The Golden Gate Bridge, that arching portal to infinite horizons, is also a suicide gangplank for hundreds of ill-starred dreamers. Throughout American history, those who crossed the country in search of destiny ultimately found it here or turned back to the continent and their own past.

Yet San Francisco is only a city, a steel-and-glass metropolis mounted on a series of hills. With a population of about 780,000, it covers 47 square miles at the tip of a peninsula bounded by the Pacific Ocean and San Francisco Bay. A gateway to Asia, San Francisco supports a multicultural population with large and growing concentrations of Chinese, Latinos, African Americans, Italians, Filipinos, Japanese, and Southeast Asians. In the last few years, though San Francisco's population remained virtually the same, an estimated 64,000 U.S. citizens moved out of the city, while about the same number of recent immigrants moved in.

The myth of San Francisco originates not only from its geography, but its history as well. If, as early Christians believed, the world was created in 4004 B.C., then the history of San Francisco began on January 28, 1848. That day a hired hand named James Marshall discovered gold in California. Year One is 1849, a time etched in the psyche of an entire nation. The people swept along by the mania of that momentous time have been known forever since as "'49ers." They crossed the Rockies in covered wagons, trekked the jungles of Panama, and challenged the treacherous seas around Cape Horn, all because of a shiny yellow metal.

Gold in California was the quintessence of the American Dream. For anyone with courage and ambition, it represented a chance to blaze trails, expand a young nation, and become rich in the flash of a fortuitous find.

God granted Divine Right to Britain, creating a kingdom that ruled the oceans. To America, God gave Manifest Destiny, a hunger for territory which drove an entire nation west like a fever through the body. Gold was the currency of Manifest Destiny, a myth that lured 100,000 people across an implacable land, and created a civilization on the fringes of a continent.

San Francisco became the capital of that civilization. The peaceful hamlet was transmogrified into a hellbent city, a place to make the Wild West look tame. Its population exploded from 900 to 25,000 in two years; by 1890 it numbered 300,000.

During the Gold Rush, a Barbary Coast ghetto grew along the Bay. Over 500 businesses sold liquor; gambling, drugs, and prostitution were rampant; gangs roamed the boomtown and iron-fisted vigilance committees enforced law and order. Sailors were shanghaied and failed prospectors committed suicide at the rate of 1000 per year.

By 1850, about 500 ships, whose crews had deserted for the gold fields, lay abandoned in San Francisco Bay. Some were used as stores, hotels, even lunatic asylums; others became landfill. Speculators wildly divided the city into tiny plots.

Amid all the chaos, San Francisco grew into an international city. Ambitious Americans, displaced Mexicans, indentured Chinese, itinerant Australians, and Chilean immigrants crowded its muddy streets. The populace soon boasted over a dozen newspapers, published in a variety of languages. Because of its multicultural population, and in spite of periodic racial problems, San Francisco developed a strong liberal tradition, an openness to the unusual and unexpected, which prevails today.

Long before Americans discovered gold in the Sierra Nevada foothills, Spaniards spoke of a mythical land filled with gems and precious metal. A 16th-century Spanish novel described it as an island called California, inhabited by beautiful amazons. San Francisco lay near the northern tip of the colony that the Spanish eventually named after that fabled land.

In 1769 an expedition led by Gaspar de Portolá, intent on expanding Spanish control in California, marched up the San Francisco peninsula and discovered the Golden Gate. Then in 1776, while the American Revolution raged on the East Coast, Captain Juan Bautista de Anza established a mission and presidio near San Francisco Bay.

Of course, the Costanoan Indians had been occupying the area for thousands of years, moving among the hills, marshes, forests, and meadows. They hunted deer, elk, and grizzly bears, ground acorns to make meal, dug roots, and caught shellfish off the coast. After the conquistadors arrived, the Costanoans built churches. In ever-imperious fashion, the Spanish "civilized" the American Indians, forcibly removing them from ancestral homes, crowding the Indians into dingy quarters, and teaching them the glories of Christianity.

Using slave labor and fortifying a chain of 21 missions, the Spanish eventually colonized the coast from San Diego to San Francisco to Sonoma. When Mexico gained independence from Spain in 1821, this colonial prize became Mexican territory. At the same time, San Francisco and environs began attracting American whalers, Russian seal hunters, French adventurers, and British entrepreneurs.

Finally, in 1846, American settlers, with assistance from the United States government, fomented the Bear Flag Revolt. Seizing California from Mexico, they created an independent republic that soon became part of the United States. Just two years before gold would be found in Spain's mythic land of amazons, the stars and stripes flew over San Francisco.

The Gold Rush not only lured prospectors to the pulsing young city: many of America's finest writers were soon mining literary material. Mark Twain, fresh from the gold fields, took in the scene during the 1860s, as did local colorist Bret Harte. Ambrose Bierce excoriated everyone and everything in his column for William Randolph Hearst's *Examiner*. In 1879, Henry George published a book in San Francisco called *Progress and Poverty*, which propounded a revolutionary system of taxation. Robert Louis Stevenson explored the Bay Area a few years later, and Jack London used it as a setting for his adventure tales.

The funeral of "Emperor Norton," a Gold Rush–era character, drew 10,000 mourners.

With characters like Joshua Abraham Norton roaming the streets, San Francisco was a natural place for storytellers. A riches-to-rags victim, Norton made and lost a fortune within a few years of the Gold Rush, then, unhinged by the ordeal, declared himself the emperor of the United States. Rather than committing the crackbrain, San Francisco welcomed him and made "Emperor Norton" a municipal mascot.

Even a society willing to accept eccentrics can sometimes turn upon itself, bitterly excluding part of its populace. There is a dark side of the dream that blackens the fate of some and casts a shadow upon all. During the 1860s, Chinese immigrants were brought in to build the transcontinental railroad. When they completed it in 1869, San Francisco was linked with the rest of the United States and railroad owners like the Big Four (Mark Hopkins, Leland Stanford, Collis Huntington, and Charles Crocker) were fabulously wealthy. Chinese labor helped stimulate the boom that made San Francisco a city of cable cars and stately Victorians by the end of the century. Regardless, the Chinese were victims of vitriolic racism. "Yellow Peril" hysteria was rampant in San Francisco during the 1880s, and led to beatings, murder, and a ban on Asian immigration to the United States.

Social upheaval gave way to devastating convulsions of the earth on April 18, 1906. Dream turned to nightmare at 5:12 that morning as a horrendous earthquake, 8.3 on the Richter scale, rocked and buckled the land. Actually, the infamous San Francisco earthquake owed its destructive ferocity more to the subsequent fires than the seismic disturbance. One of the few people killed by the earthquake itself was the city's fire chief. Gas mains across the city broke and water pipes lay shattered. Within hours, 50 separate fires ignited, merged, and by nightfall created firestorms that tore across the city. Three-quarters of San Francisco's houses were destroyed in the three-day holocaust, 452 people died, and 250,000 were left homeless.

The city whose municipal symbol is a phoenix rising from the ashes quickly rebuilt. City Hall and the Civic Center became part of a resurrected San Francisco. The Golden Gate and Bay bridges were completed in the 1930s, and during

Text continued on page 28.

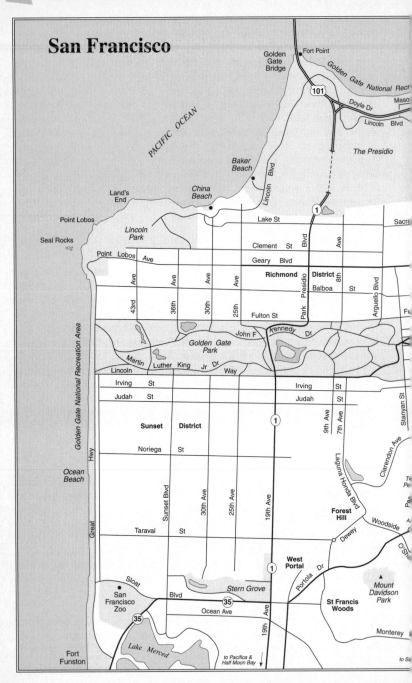

San Francisco

PACIFIC OCEAN

Golden Gate Bridge

Fort Point

Golden Gate National Recr

101

Doyle Dr

Maso

Lincoln Blvd

The Presidio

Baker Beach

Lincoln Blvd

Land's End

China Beach

Point Lobos

Lake St

Sacra

Lincoln Park

Clement St

Blvd

Ave

Seal Rocks

Point Lobos Ave

Geary Blvd

Richmond **District** 8th

Presidio

Arguello Blvd

Ave

Ave

Ave

Ave

43rd

36th

30th

25th

Balboa St

Fulton St

Fu

Park

John F Kennedy Dr

Golden Gate Park

Martin Luther King Jr Dr Way

Lincoln

Golden Gate National Recreation Area

Irving St

Irving St

Judah St

Judah St

Stanyan St

Sunset **District**

9th Ave

7th Ave

Noriega St

1

Laguna Honda Blvd

Clarendon Ave

Ocean Beach

Hwy

Sunset Blvd

30th Ave

25th Ave

19th Ave

Forest Hill

Woodside

Tw

Pe

Pa

Taraval St

Dewey

O St

Great

1

West Portal Dr

Portola Dr

▲ Mount Davidson Park

Sloat

San Francisco Zoo

Stern Grove

35

Blvd

35

Ocean Ave

19th Ave

St Francis Woods

Monterey

Fort Funston

Lake Merced

to Pacifica & Half Moon Bay

to Se

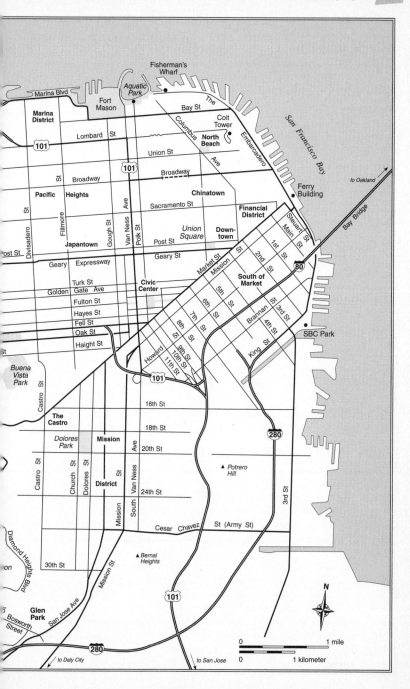

World War II the port became a major embarkation point for men and materiel. A city of international importance, San Francisco was the site for the signing of the United Nations charter in June 1945.

It entered the post–World War II era at the vanguard of American society. San Francisco's hallmark is cultural innovation. This city at the continent's edge boasts a society at the edge of thought. During the 1950s it became the Beat capital of the world. The Beats blew cool jazz, intoned free form poems, and extolled the virtues of nothingness.

Allen Ginsberg, Jack Kerouac, Gary Snyder, and other Beat poets began haunting places like Caffe Trieste and the Co-Existence Bagel Shop in the 1950s.

Lawrence Ferlinghetti opened City Lights Bookstore in 1953. Two years later Ginsberg publicly read a poem called "Howl" that redefined the American dream and outraged the Eisenhower society. In 1957, Jack Kerouac, ricocheting between San Francisco and the East Coast like some kind of human missile, defined the generation in On the Road. Later he would pen his finest book, The Dharma Bums, using Northern California settings and characters.

Not even Kerouac was prepared for San Francisco's next wave of cultural immigrants. This mecca for the misplaced became a mystical gathering place for myriads of hippies. The Haight-Ashbury neighborhood was the staging area for a movement intent on revolutionizing American consciousness.

Ken Kesey and his Merry Pranksters created the Trips Festival in 1966, combining dynamic light shows and massive doses of LSD in a grand effort to entertain while enlightening. The Jefferson Airplane, Big Brother and the Holding Company, and the Grateful Dead blew minds with an electric sound called acid rock. Then, in January 1967, about 20,000 people gathered in Golden Gate Park for a "Human Be-In." Ginsberg chanted, the Hells Angels blasted through on Harleys, and Tim Leary advised the assembled to "Turn on, tune in, and drop out." It was a happening of colossal proportions, leading to the fabled "Summer of Love" when hippies from around the world set out to make San Francisco the center of cosmic consciousness.

By the 1970s San Francisco was becoming home to a vital and creative minority, gay men and women. The city's gay population had increased steadily for decades; then, suddenly, San Francisco's open society and freewheeling lifestyle brought an amazing influx of gays. In 1977, Supervisor Harvey Milk became the nation's first outfront gay to be elected to a major municipal post. That same year the city passed a landmark gay rights ordinance. With an advancing population that today numbers perhaps 200,000, gays became a powerful social and political force.

Then the dark face of the dream appeared once again. More than 900 members of the People's Temple, one of the countless sects headquartered in San Francisco, committed mass suicide at their outpost in Guyana. Shortly afterwards, on November 27, 1978, in an unrelated incident, Supervisor Dan White assassinated fellow supervisor Harvey Milk and San Francisco Mayor George Moscone.

The dual murder stunned the world and outraged the gay community. When White received a relatively mild sentence the next year, a night of rioting swept the Civic Center, with damages totaling $300,000. And then, within a few years, the AIDS epidemic swept the gay community.

Throughout the 1980s, '90s, and into the 21st century, San Francisco has retained a gay supervisor whose constituency remains an integral part of the city's life. A multi-cultural society from its early days, San Francisco remains a city at the edge, open to experiment and experience. The national media still portray the region as a kind of open ward, home to flakes and weirdos. They point to events like the mayoral election in which a character named Jello Biafra, then a singer for a punk band called the Dead Kennedys, polled over three percent of the vote.

The city does sometimes seem to contain as many cults as people, but it also boasts more than its share of artists and activists. The national ecology movement, which began in this area with the pioneering work of John Muir, also flourishes here. This is headquarters for dozens of concerned organizations.

There are some problems: during the last few decades, San Francisco's skyline has been Manhattanized, crowded with clusters of dark skyscrapers. The AIDS epidemic has taken a terrible toll, particularly among the area's gay population. And the city has allowed its port to decline. Most cargo ships travel across the Bay to Oakland, while San Francisco's once great waterfront is being converted into gourmet restaurants and chic shopping malls. It is a city in love with itself, trading the mundane business of shipping for the glamorous, profitable tourist industry.

In October 1989, television viewers across America who had tuned in for the third game of the World Series between the San Francisco Giants and neighboring Oakland Athletics in Candlestick Park witnessed a 7.1-level earthquake that rocked the stadium and rolled through Northern California, leaving 67 dead and causing more than $10 billion in damage. As with previous disasters, however, San Francisco quickly rose from the rubble to achieve a new level of prosperity. The rebuilding process provided ideal investment opportunities for the new money flooding the Bay Area thanks to booming high-tech companies in nearby Silicon Valley. Condemned warehouses were bulldozed to make way for luxury condominium and office complexes. Artsy, affordably run-down districts were transformed almost overnight into yuppie enclaves of richly renovated Victorian mansions, their former carriage houses converted to garage space for Lexuses and BMWs. Ultimately, Candlestick Park itself was abandoned by the Giants in favor of a new, state-of-the-art ballpark in another part of the city. But by the turn of the 20th century, the dot-com crash hit hard, knelling a death blow for much of SF's computer industry. Technology continues to be an important sector, though it has lost its explosive and vibrant nature.

Perhaps Rudyard Kipling was right. He once called the place "a mad city—inhabited for the most part by perfectly insane people." William Saroyan saw it as "a city that invites the heart to come to life . . . an experiment in living." The two thoughts do not contradict: San Francisco is madly beautiful, a marvelous and zany place. Its contribution to the world is its lifestyle.

The people who gravitate here become models—some exemplary, others tragic—for their entire generation. Every decade San Francisco moves further out along the edge, maintaining a tradition for the avant-garde and iconoclastic that dates back to the Gold Rush days. The city is a jigsaw puzzle that will never be

Text continued on page 32.

Three-day Weekend

San Francisco

DAY 1 • Starting at the **San Francisco Visitor Information Center**, find your way to some of the city's most unique areas—**Chinatown**, **North Beach** and **Fisherman's Wharf**. You can see all these and more along the **Barbary Coast Trail** (page 44), or, if urban hiking isn't your idea of a good time, you can reach all three areas on the Powell-Mason **cable car**.

• In these areas of the city, you're never far from a great place for lunch. Try a dim sum restaurant in Chinatown, an Italian café in North Beach, or a sidewalk seafood cocktail stand on Fisherman's Wharf.

• Evening is the time to discover why San Francisco enjoys a reputation for the best restaurants and live theater on the West Coast. Out-of-towners—to find out about upcoming stage productions ahead of time and get phone numbers for reservations, check www.sfweekly.com or the "pink section" at www.sfgate.com/chronicle.

DAY 2 • Pack a picnic lunch and head for **Golden Gate Park** (page 118). With three world-class museums plus a thousand acres of formal gardens, meadows, lakes, forests, and spectacular vistas, it's easy to while away a whole day here. Weather permitting, the best way to tour the park is on a bicycle; rentals are available at shops near the east end of the park.

• Dine out at another tempting restaurant this evening. Afterwards, there are limitless possibilities for evening entertainment. Feeling adventuresome? For a look at another element that makes San Francisco unique, check out the gay and lesbian nightclub scene. Straight people are welcome in most places.

DAY 3 • This could be the perfect day for a spending spree. You might start at Union Square, surrounded by department stores and art galleries, and then move on to more esoteric districts like North Beach, Japantown, and the Haight, or to such exclusive—and expensive—shopping enclaves as Union Street and Upper Fillmore.

- If shop-'til-you-drop isn't your idea of fun, consider a boat trip from Fisherman's Wharf. It could be a harbor tour, a visit to Alcatraz, or an excursion to Angel Island.

- Round out your San Francisco culinary experience with a climactic splurge at one of the city's top restaurants, such as **Boulevard** (page 61), the **Empress of China** (page 68), or **La Folie** (page 93).

- Leave your heart in San Francisco and come back soon.

IF YOU ONLY HAVE ONE DAY

If you have only one day free for San Francisco sightseeing, hit the highlights using the Day 1 itinerary above.

completed. Its residents, and those who come to love the place, are parts from that puzzle, pieces that never quite fit, but rather stand out, unique edges exposed, from all the rest.

Downtown

Visit any city in the world and the sightseeing tour will begin in a vital but nebulous area called "Downtown." San Francisco is no different. Here, Downtown is spelled Union Square (Geary and Stockton streets), a tree-dotted plot in the heart of the city's hotel and shopping district. Lofty buildings bordering the area house major department stores while the network of surrounding streets features many of the city's poshest shops and plushest hotels.

SIGHTS

Union Square's most intriguing role is as San Francisco's free-form entertainment center. On any day you may see a brass band high-stepping through, a school choir singing the world's praises, or a gathering of motley but talented musicians or mimes passing the hat for bus fare home.

Cable cars from the nearby turnaround station at Powell and Market streets clang past en route to Nob Hill and Fisherman's Wharf. So pull up a patch of lawn and watch the world work through its paces, or just browse the Square's hedgerows and flower gardens.

While you're here, you'd be wise to stop by the **San Francisco Visitors Information Center** for some handy brochures. ~ Hallidie Plaza, Lower Level, Powell and Market streets; 415-391-2000; www.sfvisitor.org.

At street level you'll see the **Flood Building**, which overlooks the Powell Street BART station and houses The Gap. This was the only downtown building besides the U.S. Mint to survive the 1906 earthquake intact.

Then you can head off toward the city's high voltage Financial District. Appropriately enough, the route to this pinstriped realm leads down **Maiden Lane**, headiest of the city's high-heeled shopping areas. Back in Barbary Coast days, when San Francisco was a dirty word, this two-block-long alley-way was wall-to-wall with bawdy houses. But today it's been transformed from redlight district to ultra-chic mall. Of particular interest among the galleries and boutiques lining this pedestrian-only thoroughfare is the building at **140 Maiden Lane**. Designed by Frank Lloyd Wright in 1948, its circular interior stairway and other unique elements foreshadow the motifs he later used for the famous Guggenheim Museum.

LODGING

BUDGET LODGING The cheapest accommodations in town are found in the city's Tenderloin district. Situated between Union Square and the Civic Center, this area is an easy walk from restaurants and points of cultural interest. The Tenderloin is a sometimes

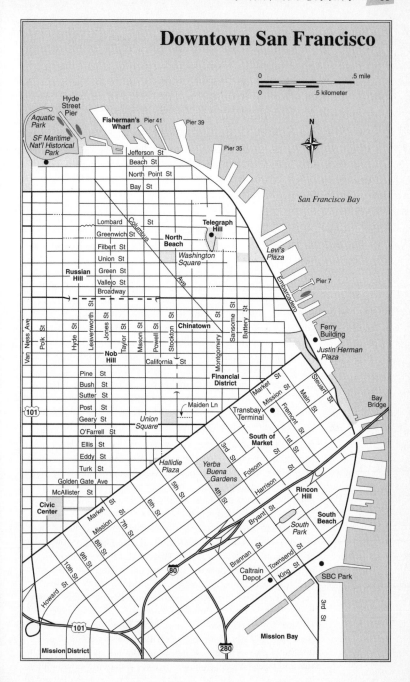

Downtown San Francisco

dangerous, sleazy neighborhood filled with interesting if menacing characters, the kind of place you stay because of the low rents rather than the inherent charm. Still, if the spirit is willing, the purse will certainly be appreciative. Just don't flaunt the purse—or camera, for that matter.

Hostelling International—Downtown is *the* place if you are looking for budget accommodations in the heart of the city. There are 32 private rooms as well as shared rooms with two to six bunks per room; a kitchen is available for guests to use. Internet access is also available. ~ 312 Mason Street; 415-788-5604, fax 415-788-3023; www.norcalhostels.org, e-mail sfdowntown@norcalhostels.org.

> Union Square is a scene—where the rich and powerful come to view the merely talented, where panhandlers sometimes seem as plentiful as pigeons.

For native funk at rock bottom rates consider the **Adelaide Inn**. Billed as "San Francisco's unique European pensione," it is an 18-room, family-operated establishment. There is a small lobby plus a coffee room and kitchen for the guests. The room prices, with continental breakfast included, are friendly to the pocketbook. Rooms are small, tidy, and plainly furnished; each is equipped with a sink and television; bathrooms are shared. Most important, the inn is located in a prime downtown location, not in the Tenderloin. ~ 5 Isadora Duncan Place; 415-441-2261, fax 415-359-1940.

Also away from the Tenderloin, the **Grant Hotel** is basic and clean. The furniture in the guest rooms doesn't exactly match, and the color scheme is not especially coordinated, but the price is right, and a friendly, helpful staff makes this 76-room hotel a pleasant place to stay. Every room has a color TV; continental breakfast is included. ~ 753 Bush Street; 415-421-7540, 800-522-0979, fax 415-989-7719; www.granthotel.citysearch.com.

MODERATE LODGING   In my opinion the best hotel buys in San Francisco are the middle-range accommodations. These usually offer good location, comfortable surroundings, and reasonable service at a cost that does not leave your pocketbook empty. Happily, the city possesses a substantial number of these facilities, the best of which are listed below.

Close to Union Square is the **Ansonia Abby Hotel**, situated in a turn-of-the-20th-century building. Although the lobby looks plush, the 123 guest rooms are basic and tidy; some have shared baths but all have phones, TVs, refrigerators and free wireless internet. Guests here are mostly international, many of them students. Complimentary breakfast and dinner are served buffet-style in the dining room (no dinner on Sunday). ~ 711 Post Street; 415-673-2670, 800-221-6470, fax 415-673-9217; www.ansoniahotel.com, e-mail ansonia@sbcglobal.net. MODERATE.

Somehow the **Commodore Hotel** does not quite live up to its baronial name. The place does feature a spacious lobby with bas-relief work along the walls, and there is a coffee shop and a hip cocktail lounge (the Red Room) attached. But the rooms are undistinguished. Decorated with neo-deco furnishings, they include wall-to-wall carpeting, televisions, shower-tub combos, and the usual creature comforts. Rooms vary in price, depending on "newness" and location. Recommended as a backup hotel, the Commodore is a fair buy, but does not match other hotels in its class. ~ 825 Sutter Street; 415-923-6800, 800-338-6848, fax 415-923-6804; www.thecommodorehotel.com, e-mail commo dorehotel@jdvhospitality.com.

The **Sheehan Hotel** was once the YWCA, which means it offers facilities not usually found in a moderately priced hotel, like a swimming pool and exercise rooms. But it's definitely not the Y anymore. The rooms have been nicely decorated with prints on the walls and antique-looking lamps, and the bathrooms are large. Guests can enjoy a complimentary continental breakfast in the lobby tearoom. ~ 620 Sutter Street; 415-775-6500, 800-848-1529, fax 415-775-3271; www.sheehanhotel.com, e-mail sheeho tel@aol.com.

The brilliant polished wood facade of the **Savoy Hotel** provides only a hint of its luxurious interior. The lobby is the first word in elegance with black and white marble floors, brass fixtures, and dark woods. The rooms at this lavish but affordable hotel second the invitation of the lobby. Sporting a French-country motif, they blend floral prints with attractive wood furniture. An afternoon wine-and-cheese reception is included. Add a tile bath-shower, goosedown featherbeds, plus color television, and you have one very noteworthy hotel. ~ 580 Geary Street; 415-441-2700, 800-227-4223, fax 415-441-0124; www.thesavoyhotel. com, e-mail savoysf@usa.com.

The **Touchstone Hotel** sits smack-dab in the center of the theater district, but even more important, it is located over David's Delicatessen, one of the best delis in town. The lobby is nearly nonexistent, but the rooms are attractively done in modern deco style, with warm woods and red bedspreads. This hotel is immaculately clean, and anyone would be hard-pressed to find a speck of dust anywhere. The rate includes a complimentary breakfast and discount coupons for the deli. This place is a true original. ~ 480 Geary Street; 415-771-1600, 800-524-1888, fax 415-931-5442; www.thetouchstone.com, e-mail reservations@thetouchstone.com.

The upscale **Nob Hill Hotel** boasts rooms and suites decorated in Victorian style, appointed with antiques and marble bathrooms. In addition, suites are equipped with wet bars and hot tubs. There's a complimentary wine tasting every evening. Continental breakfast included. ~ 835 Hyde Street; 415-885-2987, 877-662-4455, fax 415-921-1648; www.nobhillhotel.com, e-mail nobhill@nob hillhotel.com.

DELUXE LODGING If your wallet is willing, the city's deluxe-priced hotels are waiting. Among them are several that I suggest you consider.

European elegance at reasonable cost: that's what the **Hotel Beresford** has offered its clientele for years. You'll sense a touch of class immediately upon entering the richly decorated lobby. There's a historical flair about the place, highpointed by the adjoining White Horse Tavern and Restaurant, with its Olde England ambience. Upstairs the individually wall-papered rooms are outstanding—wooden headboards, comfortable furnishings, small refrigerators, and a marble-top vanity in the bathroom. Complimentary continental buffet. All this, just two blocks from Union Square. If you can beat it, let me know how. ~ 635 Sutter Street; 415-673-9900, 800-533-6533, fax 415-474-1317; www.beresford.com, e-mail info@beresford.com.

The **Beresford Arms** is a sister hotel to the Beresford in more than name. Featuring a similar antique lobby, the Beresford Arms has gracefully decorated its public area with a crystal chandelier, leather-tooled tables, stuffed armchairs, and an old grandfather clock. Casting that same European aura, rooms often feature mahogany dressers and headboards as well as the expected amenities like wall-to-wall carpeting, tile tubs, and spacious closets and VCRs with movie rentals at the desk. All at the same prices as the Beresford. The Arms has suites with whirlpools, kitchenettes, and wet bars. ~ 701 Post Street; 415-673-2600, 800-533-6533, fax 415-929-1535; www.beresford.com, e-mail info@beresford.com.

The **Carlton Hotel** features a rich lobby with marble floors, brass wall sconces, and a fireplace. The rooms have been decorated subtly and with great care and are reasonably priced. Complimentary wine is served from 6 to 7 p.m. in the lobby. Shuttle services take guests to and from downtown shopping and restaurants. Though located about five blocks from Union Square, the Carlton is highly recommended. ~ 1075 Sutter Street; 415-673-0242, 800-922-7586, fax 415-673-4904; www.carltonhotel.com, e-mail carlton@carltonhotel.com.

Clarion Hotel Bedford is another European-style hotel. The lobby here is a fresh, bright place hung with crystal and dotted about with potted plants. Upstairs the private rooms are brilliantly coordinated and possess an air of artistry with their gallery prints, floral drapes, and white furniture. ~ 761 Post Street; 415-673-6040, 800-794-6011, fax 415-563-6739; www.hotelbedford.com, e-mail reservations@hotelbedford.com.

Another upscale establishment is the **Hotel Union Square**. Built early in the 20th century to accommodate visitors to the Panama–Pacific International Exposition, this 131-plus room hotel has been exquisitely decorated. Mystery writer Dashiell Hammett and playwright Lillian Hellman, who reportedly once frequented the place, might recognize it even today. The lobby still possesses a contemporary ambience with its mosaic murals. The old speakeasy is reputed to have included a secret "chute entrance" from Ellis Street. Walls upstairs have been sandblasted to expose original brick and the rooms are decorated in rich colors with cherrywood furniture. ~ 114 Powell Street; 415-397-3000, 800-553-1900, fax 415-885-3268; www.hotelunionsquare.com, e-mail reservations@personalityhotels.com.

Or if you prefer an English theme, try the **King George Hotel**. The lobby at this tasteful establishment is done in a lovely cream with a traditional English coutryside motif. A marble staircase ascends to the "Windsor Tea Room." Convenient in both price and location, featuring comfortable, spiffy rooms, the King George is a noteworthy competitor in its class. ~ 334 Mason Street; 415-781-5050, 800-288-6005, fax 415-835-5991; www.kinggeorge.com, e-mail kgeorge@kinggeorge.com.

Elegance *and* style? That would be the **White Swan Inn**. A six-story, English-style building with curved bay windows, the White Swan was originally built in 1908 as a small hotel. Today it is a fashionable bed and breakfast with a living room, library, solarium, and small courtyard. The decorative theme, reflected in the garden, wallpapers, and art prints, is English. Each room contains a fireplace, television, telephone with voicemail, wet bar, coffeemaker, and private bath. Like the public rooms, they are all beautifully appointed. ~ 845 Bush Street; 415-775-1755, 800-999-9570, fax 415-775-5717; www.whiteswansf.com, e-mail whiteswan@jdvhospitality.com.

ULTRA-DELUXE LODGING   In lower Pacific Heights, a mile or two from the Downtown district, stands **The Majestic**. As a hotel this five-story structure dates from 1902 when The Majestic opened as one of the city's first grand hotels. It underwent several incarnations before finally being reincarnated as The Majestic. The current 58-room establishment features a bar and attractive lobby.

NOTHING STAID IN THIS HOTEL

From the wild and crazy lobby with its dervish chairs to the sapphire theater curtains in all 140 rooms, the **Hotel Triton** is a place with a sense of humor. If you are seeking a hotel with a fantasy mural, furniture that appears to undulate, iridescent throw pillows, starburst light fixtures, and room service from several trendy restaurants, look no further. Several of its suites were designed by celebrities (think Carlos Santana and Jerry Garcia). An added plus is its proximity to Chinatown. ~ 342 Grant Avenue; 415-394-0500, 800-433-6611, fax 415-394-0555; www.hoteltriton.com. ULTRA-DELUXE.

Some rooms are strikingly appointed with canopied beds, European antiques, and marble bathrooms. Rates start in the deluxe range. ~ 1500 Sutter Street; 415-441-1100, 800-869-8966, fax 415-673-7331; www.thehotelmajestic.com, e-mail info@thehotel majestic.com.

The **Hotel Rex** is one of those quirky kinds of places that sets itself apart from more ordinary hostelries. The lobby looks like a library, where you long to spend the evening curled up in front of the fireplace, with a glass of sherry and an antique book chosen from the hundreds on shelves around the room. The rooms have a modern edge with a Provençal color-scheme and artwork from local artisans on the walls. ~ 562 Sutter Street; 415-433-4434, 800-433-4434, fax 415-433-3695; www.jdvhospitality.com, e-mail info@jdvhospitality.com.

Among the latest in Joie de Vivre's chic boutique hotel line, **The Maxwell** is a deco lair, stylish and sumptuous, its 153 guest rooms done in jewel-toned velvets and brocades, walls of garnet and gold, soft carpets and long, flowing draperies. One of the twin penthouses has a black-tiled kitchen with a black toaster and refrigerator, and a fabulous rooftop deck set with candles. All the rooms come with conveniences like two phones and writing desks. Downstairs is Max's on Union Square, which provides room service. Outside, The Maxwell looks like a great yellow and maroon theater, and no wonder: It's right in the heart of the theater district. ~ 386 Geary Street; 415-986-2000, 888-734-6299, fax 415-397-2447; www.maxwellhotel.com, e-mail ammax @jdvhospitality.com.

A small boutique hotel in the heart of SF's theater district, **Hotel Monaco** offers luxury accommodations with a funky edge.

AUTHOR FAVORITE

When a travel writer is reduced to writing about a hotel's hallways, the establishment is either problematic or exceptional. Corridors at **The Inn at Union Square** are fashionably done along their entire length with mirrors and brass wall sconces, and most rooms leading off the halls are equipped with a brass lion-head door knocker. All that brass is a polisher's nightmare, but adds immeasurably to the charm of this pocket hotel. The entire inn numbers only 30 rooms, so intimacy is a primary consideration here. There is a small lobby with a fireplace on each floor where wine and evening hors d'oeuvres are served. Rooms are plush and cozy with quilted bedspreads, wooden headboards, and antique Georgian furnishings. In sum, a marvelous establishment, one of the city's finest small hotels. ~ 440 Post Street; 415-397-3510, 800-288-4346, fax 415-989-0529; www.unionsquare.com, e-mail inn@unionsquare.com. ULTRA-DELUXE.

Vibrant colors meet eclectic furniture in guest rooms that feature pillowtop beds, down pillows, and whirlpools (in most suites). Pop uptown for some morning shopping with their free chauffeur service, then come back for an evening wine-and-cheese reception with tarot readings and neck massages. This hotel is so pet-friendly, they even sponsor a "Guppy Love" program, matching guests up with overnight goldfish companions. ~ 501 Geary Street; 415-292-0100, 866-622-5284, fax 425-292-0111; www. monaco-sf.com. ULTRA-DELUXE.

A sparkling, well-run hotel in one of the best shopping blocks in town is always worth checking out—or checking into. The 114-room **Cartwright Hotel** offers eight floors of accommodations individually decorated in personally selected antiques. The attention to detail shows in touches such as plump reading pillows. There's a daily wine hour in the evenings. ~ 524 Sutter Street; 415-421-2865, 800-919-9779, fax 415-398-6345; www. cartwrighthotel.com, e-mail reservations@cartwrighthotel.com.

Once inside the 21-story **Pan Pacific San Francisco**, some guests simply cannot believe there are 329 rooms and suites here; the ambience is more like that of an intimate small hotel. Guest rooms have fine furnishings, custom cabinetry, and distinctive arched windows. Despite their size, they feel cozy, almost too much so. Oversized marble baths and attentive valet service are extra indulgences at this ultra-deluxe-priced hotel one block west of Union Square. ~ 500 Post Street; 415-771-8600, 800-533-6465, fax 415-398-0267; www.panpacific.com.

Home to Wolfgang Puck's Postrio eatery, the **Prescott Hotel** is more famous for its restaurant than its rooms. It shouldn't be, for the accommodations are equally as outstanding, from the Early California living room warmed by a big stone hearth to 164 rooms and suites beautifully arranged with Empire and neoclassical furnishings. Cherry armoires, silk wallpapers, and nightstands inlaid with black granite are embellished by rich tones of purple and gold and hunter green. There's complimentary coffee and tea in the mornings, and wine in the afternoons. And if you don't feel like going out for dinner, you can always order room service from Postrio. ~ 545 Post Street; 415-563-0303, 800-283-7322, fax 415-563-6831; www.prescotthotel. com, e-mail diane.wes ley@prescotthotel.com.

Accommodations at the 25-story **Hotel Nikko** exude *shibui*, a Japanese word that expresses elegant simplicity. Smooth-edged contemporary furnishings and natural colors. Rates include access to business services and fitness facilities, including a glass-enclosed rooftop swimming pool. ~ 222 Mason Street; 415-394-1111, 800-645-5687, fax 415-394-1106; www.hotelnikko sf.com, e-mail reservations@hotelnikkosf.com.

The ultra-posh **Four Seasons Hotel** features over 250 modern units. Suites have an office area separated from the living space by French doors, and even the more moderate rooms have marble bathrooms complete with deep-soaking tubs. If your pampering needs exceed the comforts of your guest room, the resident spa will step in and offer massage, aromatherapy, and a tempting array of peels and wraps. There's a pool and an elegant dining room. ~ 757 Market Street; 415-633-3000, 800-819-5053, fax 415-633-3009; www.fourseasons.com. ULTRA-DELUXE.

It's a one-class-fits-all establishment. Of course, at the 17-story **Campton Place Hotel**, the class is definitely first: 110 luxurious rooms and suites are outfitted with sinfully comfortable beds, armoires, writing desks, limited edition art, and European baths. Innumerable services are available around the clock. Located half a block from Union Square, this is the place to stay when you can afford to pay ultra-deluxe prices. ~ 340 Stockton Street; 415-781-5555, 800-235-4300, fax 415-955-5536; www.campton place.com, e-mail reserve@campton.com.

DINING   Whether they are hungry or not, Dashiell Hammett fans always track down **John's Grill**. It's the restaurant that detective Sam Spade popped into during a tense scene in *The Maltese Falcon*. Today the wood-paneled walls, adorned with memorabilia and old photos, still breathe of bygone eras. Waiters dress formally, the bartender gossips about local politicians, and the customers sink onto bar stools. The menu features broiler and seafood dishes as well as a nostalgic platter of chops, baked potato, and sliced tomato (what Spade wolfed down on that fateful day). Live jazz nightly. No lunch on Sunday. ~ 63 Ellis Street; 415-986-3274, fax 415-982-2583; www.johnsgrill.com. MODERATE TO DELUXE.

Sushi Man is a matchbox sushi bar with matchless style. If that's not evident from the plastic sushi displays in the window, then step inside. The tiny wooden bar is decorated with serene silk screens and fresh flowers. Owner Ryo Yoshioka has earned a deserved reputation for his sushi creations. There's *sake* (smoked salmon) and *mirugai* (clam), as well as sashimi. Dinner only. ~ 731 Bush Street; 415-981-1313, fax 415-668-3214. MODERATE.

Maiden Lane used to be a perfect spot for slumming; today it's a fashionable shopping district. But there's one place along the high-priced strip that brings back the easy days. **Bistro 69** is an unassuming deli serving an array of sandwiches, salads, homemade pastas, and mouth-watering pastries. Dine alfresco at one of the tables out front or pull up a chair inside this brick-walled establishment. At lunch there will likely be a line extending out the door. Also open for breakfast. ~ 69 Maiden Lane; 415-398-3557, fax 415-981-3735. BUDGET.

What do you get when you cross an American restaurant with a French fad? A pastrami croissant. At **Franciscan Croissants** you will get many other strange combinations, like smoked turkey, ham, and cheese, or prosciutto croissants. Things are more sub-dued at breakfast, when they feature apple and berry croissants. These are not your ordinary pastries, but colossal croissants served fresh and steaming. *Pourquoi pas?* ~ 301 Sutter Street; 415-398-8276. BUDGET.

It is the rare restaurateur who can please both Los Angeles and San Francisco, but that's exactly what Wolfgang Puck has done in bringing his talents north to **Postrio**. Puck's innovative food pairings, such as grilled quail with spinach and soft ravioli and roasted king salmon with toasted almond lavender sauce, com-pete for attention with a stunning dining room and impressive art collection. Reserve far in advance. ~ 545 Post Street; 415-776-7825, fax 415-776-6702; www.postrio.com, e-mail mail@postrio.com. ULTRA-DELUXE.

The atmosphere is classy and the food fancy at **Scala's Bistro**. Gilt mirrors adorn the walls and deep mahogany booths evoke the charm of an upscale, modern Parisian bistro. Choose from any of their lavish regional Italian or French country dishes: seared salmon filet with buttermilk mashed potatoes or a duck confit with risotto. There's even a cheese list with scrumptious choices to peruse and sample. ~ 432 Powell Street; 415-395-8555, fax 415-395-8549; www.scalasbistro.com. DELUXE TO ULTRA-DELUXE.

After dining at **Tempura House**, you'll understand why the Financial District crowd goes out of its way to eat there. What's delivered to your table looks exactly like the plastic meals dis-played in the front window, and everything's delicious. Tempura is the specialty of the house, but the grilled fish, sukiyaki, and

DEEP-SEA DINING

In addition to being a dining extravaganza, **Farallon** is a total immersion experience. Step into this uniquely designed restaurant and it's like plunging beneath the waves; every aspect of the decor reflects an aquatic motif. Light fixtures resembling jellyfish hang suspended two stories overhead, handrails look like tendriling kelp, and bar stools stand on octopus tentacles. The Gothic arches in the dining room (called, naturally, the "Pool Room") sport mermaid mosaics and sea urchin light fixtures. After easing into a booth, you can order from a menu laden with seafood dishes. The menu, which changes every few weeks, might feature Atlantic black bass, poached sea scallops, parchment roasted monkfish, or, for those who don't get the point—grilled filet of beef. No lunch on Sunday and Monday. ~ 450 Post Street; 415-956-6969; www.farallonrestaurant. com, e-mail pdr@farallonrestaurant.com. ULTRA-DELUXE.

sushi also rate highly. ~ 529 Powell Street; 415-393-9911, fax 415-393-9523. MODERATE.

Cortez is like a skewed Mondrian painting brought to life. Oversized mobiles fashioned from hanging globe lamps, illuminated panels, and occasional primary color splashes provide edgy contrast to the earthy, Mediterranean-inspired menu. These small plates are best shared with friends. Favorites include the Moroccan date and mint–crusted lamb and shoestring fries with *harissa* and *zaatar*-spiced mayonnaise. The desserts are sinful. ~ 550 Geary Street; 415-292-6360, fax 415-673-7080; www.cortezrestaurant.com, e-mail info@cortezrestaurant.com. DELUXE.

Indonesia Restaurant has developed a loyal following among the many San Franciscans who have lived or traveled in Indonesia. And for good reason. The complex and diverse flavors in this tiny, crowded hole-in-the-wall establishment tantalize the taste buds. Such favorite dishes as *gado-gado*, *soto ayam*, beef curry, *mie goreng*, *rendang*, and *sate* are included on the menu, as well as many others. ~ 678 Post Street; 415-474-4026, fax 415-858-8095. BUDGET.

Stuck for a place to dine? There are more than 3000 restaurants in this city of 780,000.

San Francisco offers several European-style gourmet restaurants. Most are located in major hotels and feature exquisite surroundings as well as fine cuisine. Others are dotted about town in small, intimate locales. The tab at these exclusive addresses is in the ultra-deluxe range. Two of the very best are listed below. Remember, they usually serve dinner only, require guests to be well-dressed, and recommend advance reservations.

HIDDEN ▶

Campton Place Restaurant transforms fresh all-American ingredients into haute cuisine, all in a creamy room where the candlelight dances on the white tableclothes and gold accents. Breakfast is worth a special trip for items like French toast with pear butter and vanilla ice cream. At lunch and dinner, seafood shares the menu with entrées such as braised ragout of beef oxtail with truffles and poached pheasant with savoy cabbage and vegetable mousseline. ~ 340 Stockton Street in the Campton Place Hotel; 415-781-5555, fax 415-955-5536; www.camptonplace.com, e-mail reserve@campton.com. ULTRA-DELUXE.

Another small and romantic dining room, **Masa's** is one of my favorite San Francisco restaurants. Elite yet understated, the decor is a mix of dark woods, softly colored upholstered chairs, and floral arrangements. Changing daily, the contemporary French menu might include filet mignon with foie gras mousse and black truffles, roasted squab with wild rice risotto, or sautéed medallions of fallow deer with caramelized apples and zinfandel sauce. Dinner only. Reservations highly recommended.

Closed Sunday and Monday. ~ 648 Bush Street; 415-989-7154, fax 415-989-3141; e-mail masas@creative.net. ULTRA-DELUXE.

Craving authentic Italian pizza, but don't want to trek out to North Beach? Hit up **Uncle Vito's**. It's casual, homestyle Italy with what some San Franciscans claim are the best pies around. Everyone has a favorite, and pasta dishes are available, too. ~ 700 Bush Street; 415-392-5808. BUDGET.

Union Square quite simply is *the* center for shopping in San Francisco. First of all, this grass-and-hedgerow park (located between Post and Geary, Stockton and Powell streets) is surrounded by department stores. **Macy's** is along one border. ~ 170 O'Farrell Street; 415-397-3333. **Saks Fifth Avenue** guards another. ~ 384 Post Street; 415-986-4300. **Neiman-Marcus**, the Texas-bred emporium, claims one corner. ~ 150 Stockton Street; 415-362-3900. Once the haven of European specialty boutiques, Union Square is becoming a hot address among sport-shoes shops, entertainment-company merchandising centers, and mass-appeal clothing stores.

SHOPPING

Of course, that's just on the square. Beyond the plaza are scads of stores, including those along **Maiden Lane**. One notable Maiden Lane shop is **Xanadu Gallery Folk Art International**, offering icons, folk sculptures, baskets, pottery, and other crafts from Africa, Oceania, Latin America, and Asia, as well as antique jewelry from India and gem-quality Baltic amber from Poland and Denmark. Closed Sunday. ~ FLW building, 140 Maiden Lane; 415-392-9999; www.folkartintl.com, e-mail info@folkart intl.com.

Along Stockton, one of the streets radiating out from the square, you'll find a number of prestigious shops.

Then if you follow Post, another bordering street, there's **Crocker Galleria**, a glass-domed promenade lined with fashionable shops. A center for well-heeled business crowds, the mall showcases designer fashions and elegant gifts. ~ 50 Post Street; 415-956-2846; www.shopatgalleria.com.

Farther along, you'll find **Gump's**, which features fine jewelry, objets d'art, and imported decorations for the home. If you get bored looking through the antiques, china pieces, and oriental art, you can always adjourn to the Crystal Room. ~ 135 Post Street; 415-982-1616, fax 415-984-9361; www.gumps.com.

Nestled on the sixth floor of a building at Grant and Post, **Hats on Post** features two rooms filled with elegant and expensive women's headwear. ~ 210 Post Street, Suite 606; 415-392-3737.

For a vicarious "rich and famous" experience, take a stroll through **Giorgio Armani** at Union Square. This boutique is one of only eleven American stores carrying the designer's premier

Text continued on page 46.

The Barbary Coast Trail

This thoroughly urban "trail" blazed along San Francisco's sidewalks introduces you to some of the city's best-known districts on an easy four-mile trek. Because of stoplights and storefronts, city hiking takes longer than country hiking, so allow four to five hours for the whole route. The Barbary Coast Trail is marked by well-worn circular bronze plaques embedded in the sidewalks, each with one arrow pointing where you're coming from and another pointing the way you want to go.

DOWNTOWN   If you're driving, the nearest lots are between Harrison and Market on 5th Street. Start at the intersection of Powell and Market—location of the cable car turnaround, the Powell Street BART station, and the **San Francisco Visitors Information Center** (page 32). Walk three blocks north on Powell Street to **Union Square** (page 32). Stroll through the square to cross the intersection at the corner of Post and Stockton streets. Half a block south, facing the square, is the entrance to **Maiden Lane** (page 32). Walk a block east through this narrow alley lined with cafés and boutiques to Grant Avenue and turn north (left). Proceed three blocks on Grant to the Chinatown gate.

CHINATOWN   Stroll three blocks along Chinatown's tourist-tacky **Grant Avenue** (page 64), past **St. Mary's Square** and **Old St. Mary's Church**, California's oldest cathedral. Turn west (left), go half a block, and turn north (right) onto **Waverly Place** (page 66) and plunge into the real heart of Chinatown. You can't get lost—directly east is the Transamerica Building, the city's tallest, visible from every streetcorner; you can pick up the Barbary Coast Trail again in front of it. Wander down Waverly, past ornate tong buildings and Taoist temples. Walk two blocks to Washington Street, turn west (left) and go half a block, turning north (right) into **Ross Alley** (page 66), home of the **Golden Gate Fortune Cookie Factory**. At the north end of the alley, turn east (right) down Jackson Street for a block. Turn south (right) on Grant to the corner of Washington and the landmark **Bank of Canton** with its elaborate facade and triple pagoda roof. Go one block south on Washington, crossing Lum Place, to historic **Portsmouth Square** (page 64), the city's original town plaza. Strolling across the square to Clay Street, turn east (left) half a block to Kearny Street, south (right) one block to Commercial Street, and east (left) on Commercial. There you'll find the **Chinese Historical Society of America** (page 63) and the **Pacific Heritage Museum** (page 54). Turn left onto Montgomery Street.

TAKE A BREAK IN THE WOODS   Officially, the Barbary Coast Trail takes you along Montgomery Street past the west side of the **Transamerica Building** (page 54) but why not detour to **Redwood Park**, one of the city's shadiest and most peaceful spots, on the building's east side? Back on Montgomery, walk north to Jackson Street and turn east (right).

IMAGINE THE BARBARY COAST   San Francisco's oldest historic district, **Jackson Square** (page 55) occupies the site of the old Barbary Coast. During the gold rush, stage star Sarah Bernhardt called it "the most fascinatingly wicked place on earth." Leveled by the 1906 earthquake, the Barbary Coast tried to re-establish its houses of ill repute but ultimately became infested by lawyers—notably tort king Melvin Belli, whose worn red-brick former office building still dominates the block. At Jackson Street, turn east (right) and walk one block, passing across the street from the the the ornate **Hotaling Buildings** (445–473 Jackson). The trail turns north (left) on Balance Street and goes a short distance to Gold Street, site of the first assay office during the Gold Rush. Turning east (right) on Gold, go to Sansome Street, turn north (left) and walk one block to Pacific Avenue. Turn west (left) and walk two blocks to Columbus Avenue. The copper-sheathed seven-story flatiron building at **916 Kearny**, where Pacific, Columbus, and Kearny meet, is the headquarters for filmmaker Francis Ford Coppola's **Zoetrope Studios**.

NORTH BEACH   Walk northwest (right) up Columbus Street, passing such historic Beat hangouts as **City Lights Bookstore** (page 71) and **Vesuvio Café** (page 72) before crossing **Broadway** with its strip clubs and porn houses. Three more blocks up Columbus, through a mixed Italian and Chinese neighborhood, brings you to **Washington Square** (page 73). Rest in the park, then proceed one block east on Union Street, turn north (left) on Grant, and go two blocks north. Here, if you're feeling athletic, you can climb the steps to the 495-foot summit of **Telegraph Hill** and ride the elevator up **Coit Tower** (page 72) for a great view of the city. The designated route skips the hill and continues three more blocks up Grant, past hidden **Jack Early Park**, to Francisco Street; turn east (right) into the cul-de-sac, then north (left) down a flight of stairs to Kearny Street. Continue two more blocks north to the Embarcadero.

THE WATERFRONT   You don't need the Barbary Coast Trail markers to find your way west along the waterfront. Just turn left from Kearny onto the Embarcadero, passing **Pier 39** (page 79), and follow the throngs of sightseers, street vendors, and silver-painted mimes down **Fisherman's Wharf** to **Aquatic Park** (page 81).

CABLE CARS   The **Powell-Hyde Cable Car** turnaround is at Hyde and Beach streets, between **The Cannery** and **Ghirardelli Square** (page 82). Anticipate a half-hour wait in line—possibly much more on weekends and in summer. The cable car climbs steeply up and down **Russian Hill** and **Nob Hill** before reaching Powell and Market streets, where this tour began. If you wish to stop at the **Cable Car Museum** (page 66) or other sights along the way, you can get off and on the cable car on the same ticket.

Black Label line. Formalwear and sportswear are elegantly displayed under the tutelage of attentive salespeople, who discreetly disclose the cost of the apparel. Closed Sunday. ~ 278 Post Street; 415-434-2500, fax 415-434-2546; www.giorgioarmani.com.

The streets all around host a further array of stores. You'll encounter jewelers, dress designers, boutiques, furniture stores, tailor shops, and more. So take a gander—there's everything out there from the unexpected to the bizarre.

Braunstein/Quay Gallery is an outstanding place to view the work of local artists. As the catalog claims, owner Ruth Braunstein "embodies the brash, irreverent, and irrepressible energy of the San Francisco art world." This contemporary gallery also exhibits works from other parts of the world. Closed Sunday and Monday except by appointment. ~ 430 Clementina Street; 415-278-9850; e-mail bgg@serious.com.

The "On Broadway" theater scene in San Francisco is on Geary Street, near Union Square; while the "Off Broadway," or avant-garde drama, is scattered around the city.

San Francisco's answer to Boston's famous Filene's Basement discount apparel chain is **Loehmann's**, a clothing store with alarmingly low-priced designer clothes. ~ 222 Sutter Street; 415-982-3215; www.loehmanns.com.

Just steps from Union Square, you'll find **Borders Books & Music**, with four floors of books, CDs, national and international newspapers and periodicals, and chairs for serious reading. Stop by the Cafe Espresso for a cup of coffee, an Italian soda, or a snack. ~ 400 Post Street; 415-399-1633, fax 415-399-1898; www.borders.com.

If you've ever struggled to find that perfect pair of jeans, look no further: **Levi's** will make 'em fit. They'll also make them sequined, beaded, rhinestoned—whatever design you have in mind. Be forewarned, though: you'll pay for your custom-made denim. Prices can hit four digits for a heavily accessorized pair. ~ 300 Post Street; 415-501-0100, fax 415-501-0110.

Harold's International Newstand is a shop specializing in "hometown newspapers." There are dailies from all over the world. For homesick travelers, or those just interested in a little local news, it's a godsend. ~ 454 Geary Street; 415-441-2665.

A nine-story vertical mall, the **San Francisco Shopping Centre** sports six stacked spiral escalators that ascend through an oval-shaped, marble-and-granite atrium toward the retractable skylight. The mall includes nearly 65 upscale shops selling everything from men's and women's sportswear to jewelry and unique gifts. The center is all crowned by a five-floor **Nordstrom**, the high-quality fashion department store. ~ 5th and Market streets; 415-495-5656, fax 415-512-6770; www.sanfranciscocentre.com.

NIGHTLIFE   Since its rowdy Gold Rush days, San Francisco has been renowned as a wide-open town, hard-drinking and easygoing. Today there are over 2000 places around the city to order a drink, including saloons, restaurants, cabarets, boats, private clubs, and even a couple of hospitals. There's a bar for every mood and each occasion.

When looking for nightlife, it is advisable to consult the *SF Bay Guardian*, the *SF Weekly*, or the "Datebook" (commonly called the "pink section") in the Sunday *San Francisco Chronicle* for current shows and performers. However you decide to spend the evening, you'll find plenty of possibilities in this city by the Bay.

San Francisco's answer to a Scottish pub is **Edinburgh Castle**, a cavernous bar complete with dart board. There are chandeliers hanging from the ceiling, heavy wooden furniture, and convivial crowd—Scotland incarnate. ~ 950 Geary Street; 415-885-4074.

The **Warfield Theatre**, owned by the late rock impresario Bill Graham's company, brings in top groups from around the country. Bill Graham Presents produces other shows regularly throughout the Bay Area. ~ 982 Market Street; 415-775-7722.

The **Plush Room** in the York Hotel caters to an upscale clientele and draws big-name cabaret acts. It's a lovely setting. Cover. ~ 940 Sutter Street; 415-885-2800; www.plushroom.com.

A favored relaxing place for the rich is the **Redwood Room** in the Clift Hotel. With art-deco lamps, marble tables, and burnished redwood paneling, it is nothing less than sumptuous. Men will feel more comfortable wearing coats and ties, women dresses. ~ Geary and Taylor streets; 415-775-4700, fax 415-776-9238.

Calling itself a "shrine to the blues" is no exaggeration. Located about a block from Union Square, **Biscuits & Blues** represents all that's right about the American South. With Southern cuisine and live music in an elegant basement nightclub, it's the perfect place to relax, appreciate the wail of a harmonica, and have a drink after taking in a play in the theater district. ~ 401 Mason Street; 415-292-2583; www.biscuitsandblues.com, e-mail sfwine@sbc.net.

You wouldn't expect to find a vibrant nightclub in a restored Victorian ballroom, but **Ruby Skye** mixes lavish surroundings with a club atmosphere. If you're not into the bump-and-grind scene, stop in for drinks before 10 p.m. and enjoy the interior architecture. Open Thursday through Sunday. Cover. ~ 420 Mason Street; 415-693-0777; www.rubyskye.com.

Built in 1910, the Beaux Arts–style **Geary Theater** reopened in 1996 after extensive repair and renovation, and now features a sky lobby. This state historic landmark is home of the **American Conservatory Theater**, or ACT, the biggest show in town. It's also one of the nation's largest resident companies. The season runs from September to July, and the repertory is traditional, ranging from Shakespeare to French comedy to 20th-century drama. Closed Monday. ~ Geary Theater, 415 Geary Street; 415-749-2228, fax 415-439-2322; www.act-sf.org.

The **Curran Theatre** brings Broadway musicals to town. ~ 445 Geary Street; 415-551-2000; www.bestofbroadway-sf.com. **Golden Gate Theatre** attracts major shows and national companies. Built in 1922, the theater is a grand affair with marble floors and rococo ceilings. ~ 1 Taylor Street, at the corner of 6th and Market streets; 415-551-2000. Among the city's other playhouses is the **Marines Memorial Theatre**. ~ 609 Sutter Street; 415-771-6900; www.marinesmemorialtheatre.com. Close to the Civic Center is the **Orpheum Theatre**. ~ 1192 Market Street; 415-551-2000.

Civic Center

On the other side of the Downtown district, to the southwest, rises the Civic Center, the architectural pride of the city. The prettiest pathway through this municipal meeting ground begins in United Nations Plaza at Fulton and Market streets.

SIGHTS

Every Wednesday and Sunday this promenade is home to the **Heart of the City Farmers' Market**, an open-air produce fair that draws farmers from all over Northern California.

To experience one of the country's most modern information centers, saunter on over to the main branch of the **San Francisco Public Library** in its $104.5 million headquarters that opened in 1996. Exemplifying the fact that libraries are not just about books anymore (in fact, critics charge that the architectural splendor and special features have resulted in a lack of shelf space), the main branch's facilities include 400 electronic workstations with free connection to the internet. Among the library's 11 special-interest research centers are the San Francisco History Center, the Gay and Lesbian Center, and the Art and Music Center. ~ 100 Larkin Street; 415-557-4400, fax 415-557-4205; www.sfpl.lib.ca.us, e-mail info@sfpl.lib.ca.us.

With its bird-whitened statues and gray-columned buildings, the **Civic Center** is the domain of powerbrokers and political leaders; ironically, its grassy plots and park benches also make it the haunt of the city's homeless. Guided tours of the Civic Center begin at the San Francisco Public Library. ~ Tour information, 415-557-4266; www.sfcityguides.org.

As you pass the reflecting pool and formal gardens of **Joseph L. Alioto Performing Art Piazza**, an area often used for outdoor events and named in honor of one of San Francisco's most beloved mayors, you'll see **City Hall**, recently reopened after a three-year, $300 million renovation during which it was lifted from its foundation and set on 600 steel-and-rubber base insulators designed to make it earthquake-proof. Its gold-leafed dome is 307 feet tall—the fifth-tallest domed building in the world, 20 feet taller than the U.S. Capitol. It also surpasses other government centers in technology, with interactive touch screens that let supervisors vote, call staff, and retrieve documents during meetings. Free guided tours of City Hall are offered daily. ~ 1 Dr. Carlton B. Goodlett Place. ~ 415-554-6023; www.ci.sf.ca.us/cityhall.

Since you're in earthquake country, why not stop by **The Museum of the City of San Francisco**. Historic photographs, paintings, and relics tell the tale of that fateful day in 1906 and shed new light on California's greatest natural disaster. Rotating exhibits feature local artifacts such as the Goddess of Liberty statue from the old city hall. Closed Sunday. ~ City Hall South Light Court, Grove Street and Van Ness Avenue; 415-928-0289, fax 415-731-0204; www.sfmuseum.org.

Across from City Hall and housed in a historic 1917 Beaux Arts building, the **Asian Art Museum** features major pieces from China, Tibet, Japan, Korea, Iran, Syria, and throughout the continent. This institution is the largest museum in the country devoted exclusively to Asian art. Some of the 14,000-plus pieces date back 6000 years. Admission. ~ 200 Larkin Street; 415-581-3500, fax 415-581-4700; www.asianart.org.

Centerstage of the Civic Center is the **War Memorial Opera House**, home of one of the world's finest opera companies as well as the San Francisco Ballet Company. Considered by such performers as Placido Domingo to be one of the world's finest opera houses and called "the most attractive and practical building of its kind in the U.S." by *Time Magazine*, the grandiose building's interior features lofty romanesque columns, a gold-leafed proscenium and a five-story-high ceiling. Although conceived in 1918 as a tribute to the nation's World War I veterans, the opera house was

Civic Center

not completed until 1932. Perhaps its finest moment came in 1945, when the opera house and adjacent Veterans Auditorium (now Herbst Theatre) hosted the signing of the United Nations Charter and the first official sessions of the U.N. ~ 301 Van Ness Avenue at Grove Street.

To the left, that ultramodern glass-and-granite building is the **Louise M. Davies Symphony Hall**, home of the San Francisco Symphony. Through the semicircle of green-tinted glass, you can peer into one of the city's most glamorous buildings. Or if you'd prefer to be on the inside gazing out, tours of the hall and its cultural cousins next door are given Monday from 10 a.m. to 2 p.m. Admission. ~ Van Ness Avenue and Grove Street; information, 415-552-8338.

One of the best places in town to appreciate the city's rich cultural tradition is the **San Francisco Performing Arts Library and Museum**. The collection covers San Francisco's musical and theatrical heritage with photos, programs, books, and audio and visual recordings. Recent exhibitions include a Kronos Quartet retrospective and a centennial celebration of Broadway composer Richard Rogers. Library open Wednesday through Saturday; galleries open Tuesday through Saturday. Researchers should call the librarian in advance. ~ Veterans Building, 401 Van Ness Avenue; 415-255-4800, fax 415-255-1913; www.sfpalm.org, e-mail info @sfpalm.org.

LODGING   For fans of the opera (or the symphony or the ballet), the **Inn at the Opera** is heaven on earth. Located virtually within earshot of the major performing-arts houses, it plays the ham with concierge services (especially helpful for last-minute tickets) and little touches (such as sheet-music drawer liners) in the 30 rooms and 18 suites. Rooms have tasteful furnishings with mini-fridges. ~ 333 Fulton Street; 415-863-8400, 800-325-2708, fax 415-861-0821. ULTRA-DELUXE.

A two-story motor court flanking a pool courtyard, spacious rooms and suites with a '50s bungalow theme, an aquatically inspired restaurant and lounge . . . can this be the heart of San **HIDDEN ▶**   Francisco? It is, and it's the **Phoenix Hotel**, just a long block from Civic Center. Concierge services and the patronage of music-business mavens may make the Phoenix the hippest inn in town. There's a chic restaurant on-site. ~ 601 Eddy Street; 415-776-1380, 800-248-9466, fax 415-885-3109; www.thephoenixhotel. com, e-mail mwilliams@jdvhospality.com. MODERATE TO ULTRA-DELUXE.

Located on the border between the city's stately Civic Center and unwashed Tenderloin district, **San Francisco Central YMCA** has singles and doubles with shared baths. In traditional Y-style, the rooms are as clean as they are sterile; they are scantily furnished and tend to be cramped. But for these prices—which include a continental breakfast and free use of the sunroof, pool, sauna, steam room, weight room, laundry, aerobics area, and basketball and racquetball courts—who's complaining? ~ 220 Golden Gate Avenue; 415-885-0460, fax 415-885-5439; www.central ymcasf.org, e-mail yhotel@ymca.org. BUDGET.

Located right on the edge of the Civic Center, the **Hotel Renoir** is one of the more economical spots to rest. The lobby is lined with Renoir prints and decorated in gold and soft peach colors. There's a Brazilian restaurant, a lounge and a friendly ambience about the place. The only detraction is its location on busy Market Street and proximity to the city's Tenderloin district. Rooms are reasonably well furnished. The accommodations I saw featured wall-to-wall carpeting, color televisions, steam heat, plush furniture, and tile bathrooms with shower-tub combinations. ~ 45 McAllister Street; 415-626-5200, 800-576-3388, fax 415-626-0916; www.renoirhotel.com, e-mail reservations@renoirhotel.com. DELUXE TO ULTRA-DELUXE.

DINING

Find a little bit of the South in San Francisco at **Powell's Place**. Opened in 1927 by gospel singer Emmitt Powell, this is the real deal. Mouth-watering fried chicken, yummy mashed potatoes and dee-lish sweet potato pie come served with a side of soul and a home-style atmosphere. This certainly ain't your mama's kitchen—it's better. ~ 511 Hayes Street; 415-863-1404. BUDGET TO MODERATE.

This area spotlights several outstanding dining rooms. One of the best in my opinion is **Hayes Street Grill**, situated within strolling distance of the opera and symphony. Specializing in fresh fish dishes, they also serve grilled porkchops, dry-aged steak, and chicken breast. Excellent food. No lunch on the weekend. ~ 320 Hayes Street; 415-863-5545, fax 415-863-1873; www.hayesstreetgrill.com. DELUXE.

CLASSROOM CUISINE

With two restaurants and a deli, the **California Culinary Academy** offers everything from a half pint of delicious potato salad to a global buffet. Here students under faculty supervision hone their talents. Located in a skylit neoclassic hall, the Carême Room serves three-course lunches and dinners as well as buffets. The budget take-out fare at The Culinary Shoppe includes pastries, salads, and desserts. Closed Sundays. ~ 625 Polk Street; 415-771-3500, fax 415-775-5129; www.baychef.com. BUDGET TO DELUXE.

Few, if any, places in the Hayes Valley gourmet ghetto are more popular than **Caffe Delle Stelle**. Cans of tomatoes stacked in pyramids grace the windows, and wreaths of dried red peppers adorn the walls of this quirky, cute Tuscan trattoria. Conversation buzzes, but it's not too loud to enjoy an intimate discussion of your own. The cuisine is Italian country cooking, and meals begin with fresh bread and a bowl of *pansanela*, a dip made from olive oil, bread, tomato juice, and spices. Entrées include a selection of pastas, baked chicken, roasted salmon fillet, and daily specials like ravioli barbarossa stuffed with arugula, ricotta, and walnuts in a basil sauce. ~ 395 Hayes Street; 415-252-1110, fax 415-863-5224. MODERATE.

The two blocks of Polk Street within the Civic Center were renamed Dr. Carlton B. Goodlett Jr. Place in honor of the San Francisco civil rights leader who died in 1997.

HIDDEN ►   **Vicolo Pizzeria** may be a bit hard to find, but the reward is gourmet pizza different from any you may have tasted before. The restaurant's decor, with high ceilings and tall windows, acts as a reminder that the building was formerly an auto mechanic's shop. Served primarily by the slice, Vicolo's pizza is characterized by its distinctive cornmeal crust. Sausage, four cheese, and two vegetarian varieties are the standards, with other choices changing regularly. Usually no lunch on weekends. ~ 201 Ivy Street; 415-863-2382, fax 415-863-7202. MODERATE TO DELUXE.

Max's Opera Café serves a variety of fare that ranges from smoked barbecued ribs to California cuisine, but the standouts are the thick pastrami, corned beef, and turkey breast sandwiches accompanied by tangy coleslaw and potato salad. A lively bar area features occasional impromptu entertainment by the staff, some of whom are budding tenors and sopranos. ~ 601 Van Ness Avenue; 415-771-7301, fax 415-474-9780; www.maxsworld.com. MODERATE.

A café setting that features brass fixtures, pastel walls, bentwood furniture, and Asian artwork make **Thepin** an inviting Thai establishment. The fare, ranging from red curry duck to marinated prawns and chicken breast, is also a winner. Specialties include sliced chicken and shrimp with spinach in peanut sauce, marinated filet of salmon in curry sauce, and sliced green papaya salad with tomatoes and chili pepper. No lunch on the weekend. ~ 298 Gough Street; 415-863-9335, fax 415-863-9276. BUDGET TO MODERATE.

SHOPPING   Hayes Valley lies directly west of the Civic Center and has as its focus the block bounded by Hayes, Franklin, Grove, and Gough streets. Of particular importance here is the **Vorpal Gallery**. One of the city's finest galleries, it features works by Jesse Allen, Kathleen Dunn, and other contemporary artists. There are also paintings and prints by such 20th-century masters as Pablo Picasso and M.

C. Escher, as well as by Yozo Hamaguchi, the master of mezzo-tint. Closed Sunday and Monday. ~ 393 Grove Street; 415-397-9200, fax 415-864-8335; www.vorpalgallery.com, e-mail vorpal @concentric.net.

F. Dorian specializes in crafts from all over the world including ethnic and contemporary items. Although their selection varies, you may be lucky enough to find antique Filipino furniture, Indian oil lamps, Indonesian diary boxes, and exotic jewelry. ~ 370 Hayes Street; 415-861-3191; e-mail fdorian@earthlink.net.

Just a few blocks away lies **Opera Plaza** (at Van Ness and Golden Gate avenues), an atrium mall with shops, restaurants, a good bookstore, and a movie theater collected around a courtyard and fountain. It's a pretty place to sit and enjoy the day.

NIGHTLIFE

San Francisco is rich culturally in its opera, symphony, and ballet, located in the Civic Center area. Since tickets to major theatrical and other cultural events are expensive, consider buying day-of-performance tickets from TIX **Bay Area** in Union Square, on Powell Street between Geary and Post. Open from 11 a.m. until just before showtime, they sell tickets at half-price on the day of the show (cash only) and full price for future events. Closed Monday. ~ 415-433-7827; www.theatrebayarea.org, e-mail tix@ theatrebayarea.org.

San Francisco takes nothing quite so seriously as its opera. The **San Francisco Opera** is world class in stature and invites operatic greats from around the world to perform. As a result, tickets can be very difficult to obtain. The international season begins in mid-September and runs through June. The box office is closed on weekends. ~ 301 Van Ness Avenue; 415-864-3330, fax 415-626-1729; www.sfopera.com.

The **San Francisco Symphony** stands nearly as tall on the world stage. The season extends from September through July. Michael Tilson Thomas conducts, and guest soloists have included Jessie Norman and Itzhak Perlman. Closed Sunday. ~ Davies Hall, Van Ness Avenue and Grove Street; 415-864-6000, fax 415-554-0108; www.sfsymphony.org.

The **San Francisco Ballet**, performing since 1933, is the nation's oldest professional ballet, and one of the finest. Featuring *The Nutcracker* during December, the company's official season runs at the Opera House from February until May. In addition to original works, they perform classic ballets. The box office is closed late May to September, and weekends. ~ 301 Van Ness Avenue; 415-865-2000, fax 415-865-0740; www.sfballet.org, e-mail sfbmktg@sfballet.org.

Over at the **Great American Music Hall**, a vintage 1907 building has been splendidly converted to a nightclub featuring a variety of entertainers. Included in the lineup are international acts such as Jimmy Cliff, Bonnie Raitt, and Shawn Colvin. ~ 859 O'Farrell Street; 415-885-0750, fax 415-885-5075; www.music hallsf.com, e-mail pr@gamh.com.

▼▼▼▼▼▼▼▼▼▼▼▼
Financial District

Beyond the Downtown district, as Maiden Lane debouches into a complex of streets, you'll come upon the "Wall Street of the West," Montgomery Street, locus of the Financial District. The center of Pacific commerce and trade, this is the roosting place for San Francisco's skyscrapers. Here you'll encounter windswept canyons of glass and steel inhabited by exotic birds dressed in three-piece suits or tailor-trim skirts.

SIGHTS

Behind the granite and marble along Montgomery are more banks than one could imagine. **A. P. Giannini Plaza**, a combination mall and office building, memorializes the brilliant Italian banker who developed an upstart savings company into one of the world's largest financial institutions, the Bank of America. ~ Montgomery Street, between Pine and California streets.

Another bank on Montgomery hosts the **Wells Fargo History Museum**. In addition to glistening gold specimens and postal artifacts, there are photos recapturing the raffish days of the Old West. Central to the entire exhibit is an 18-passenger stagecoach reconditioned to sparkle like this year's model. (Remember, this pocket museum is open during banker's hours only.) Closed Saturday and Sunday. ~ 420 Montgomery; 415-396-2619, fax 415-391-8644; www.wellsfargohistory.com.

Or consider the Bank of Canton of California (now part of United Commercial Bank), which has reconstructed a 19th-century federal mint and incorporated it into the **Pacific Heritage Museum**. The rest of the facility features rotating exhibitions on the art and culture of the Pacific Basin. Closed Sunday and Monday. ~ 608 Commercial Street; 415-399-1124, fax 415-989-0103; www.ibankunited.com.

The history-minded will also keep a sharp eye for the bronze markers spotted here and there along this fabled street. Montgomery has always been a center for San Francisco financial adventures. One plaque near 505 Montgomery commemorates the **Hudson's Bay Company headquarters**. It seems that in 1841 the British-owned company set up shop here, sending shivers through the American traders who were beginning to consider California their own preserve. On the side of the California National Bank at Montgomery and Clay streets rests a marker noting the spot where the first Pony Express rider arrived in 1860 after the dangerously harrowing relay from St. Joseph, Missouri.

That bizarrely shaped edifice between Clay and Washington streets is none other than the 48-story **Transamerica Building**.

Designed like a pyramid that's been put through a wringer, it stands 853 feet tall and is the most striking feature along San Francisco's skyline. Although not open to the public, it's still a marvel to gaze upward at. Situated on the east side of the building is a half-acre pocket park—a significant attraction in itself. It features metal sculptures, a fountain, and a child's-eye view of the stone needle rising straight above. ~ 415-983-4100, fax 415-983-4309; www. thepyramidcenter.com.

The 700 block of Montgomery contains a cluster of buildings dating back to 1850. They are part of the **Jackson Square** area, a misnomered enclave extending from Washington to Pacific streets and from Columbus Avenue to Sansome Street. There is no "square" here, but you will find an official historic district sprinkled with brickface buildings and interior courtyards. During the

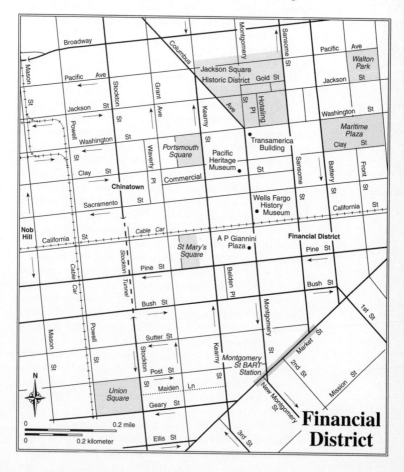

1850s, this represented the black heart of the Barbary Coast. Prospectors on the make and convicts on the lam haunted its gambling dens and flophouses. The local denizens' penchant for kidnapping drunken sailors gave rise to the word "shanghaied."

As with Downtown's Maiden Lane, a mixture of time and irony has transformed the area. Fashionable galleries and other upscale emporia have replaced the brothels and dives. Though prices here are as staggering as the neighboring skyscrapers, you might want to browse the shops, which include some of the city's finest antique stores.

DINING

Sam's Grill, established in 1867, is a classic San Francisco businessperson's restaurant. With a new menu printed every day, it features fresh fish, shellfish from surrounding waters, charcoal-broiled steaks and chops, plus seafood casseroles. The menu is the same at lunch or dinner, and you can order a martini anytime from 11 a.m. on. There are diner car booths, waitstaff in bow ties and tuxedos, a friendly bar, and white walls adorned with hunting scenes. Closed Saturday and Sunday. ~ 374 Bush Street; 415-421-0594, fax 415-421-2632; www.samsgrill.com, e-mail smsgrill@sbc.net. MODERATE TO DELUXE.

No, you're not at a Paris metro station, even though the designer of **Cafe Bastille** would like to make you think so. This popular bistro boasts a basement dining room, with floors done in multicolored marble, walls painted with steel girders, and a giant Bastille Metro sign. You can also dine on the ground floor, by the bar, or at umbrella-covered tables in the front alleyway. The daily menu is written on a blackboard and includes crêpes, sandwiches, quiche, and such entrées as roasted chicken breast. Closed Sunday ~ 22 Belden Place; 415-986-5673, fax 415-986-1013; www.cafebastille.com, e-mail oliva@cafebastille.com. MODERATE.

Tadich Grill means wood-paneled walls, tile floor, and art-deco light fixtures. It also means a counter running the length of the grill, white linen–covered tables, and wooden booths. The history of the place is so rich it consumes the first page of the menu. It all began during that gilded year, 1849, and has continued as a businessperson's restaurant in the heart of the Financial District. A new menu is printed daily, though on any given day, lunch and dinner remain the same. The specialty is seafood (sole, salmon, snapper, swordfish, shrimp, and scallops), but charcoal-broiled steak, chops, and chicken are also available. Proud in tradition and cuisine, this San Francisco institution remains top-flight all the way. Closed Sunday. ~ 240 California Street; 415-391-2373. MODERATE.

HIDDEN ►

There are only about 25 tables, but **Sai's Restaurant** packs in the Financial District lunch crowds, who wait in line to enjoy Vietnamese food at this popular family-run establishment. The decor is simple, with a few paintings on the wall, but the food has a devoted following. Favorite dishes include lemongrass chicken, eggplant with garlic sauce, Sai's special chow mein, and coconut curries. ~ 505 Washington Street; 415-362-3689. BUDGET.

London Wine Bar is a rare vintage indeed. Established in 1974, it is "America's first wine bar." Fittingly, there is an impressive and fashionable list of California, boutique, and imported wines; over 50 are sold by the glass. To quench the appetite, they serve lunch and evening hors d'oeuvres like salmon, pâtés, cheeses, and quesadillas. A fashionable treat. Closed Saturday and Sunday. ~ 415 Sansome Street; 415-788-4811, fax 415-788-4808; www.londonwinebar.com, e-mail garylwb@worldnet.att.net. MODERATE.

Dim sum is the Chinese tradition of selecting dishes from trays that are continuously wheeled about the dining room at brunchtime. You'll discover designer dim sum at a restaurant that has elevated the tea house idea to a culinary art. While tea houses are usually like cafeterias, **Yank Sing** provides a serene setting with white linen, fresh flowers, and cane-back chairs. Simple but suave, the restaurant offers dim sum delights like stuffed snow crab claws, seafood-stuffed green peppers, Peking duck by the slice, and rabbit-shaped shrimp dumplings. Open only for lunch, it is an important dining innovation. ~ 101 Spear Street; 415-957-9300; www.yanksing.com, e-mail yanksing@yanksing.com. MODERATE TO DELUXE.

The land east of the Transamerica Building was San Francisco's harbor until 1855, when it was filled in. Abandoned by sailors turned gold miners, at least ten ships still lie buried beneath the streets of the Financial District.

Though just a little hole in the wall, **Yo Yo's** long lines prove there's more to a restaurant than just location. Businessfolk love to pop in and grab some sobe noodle soup, teriyaki chicken or sushi. After all, Yo Yo's is mainly take-out with little seating and a fast turn-around. So just take your fare down to the waterfront for some great views and delicious grub. Lunch only. ~ 318 Pacific Avenue; 415-296-8273. BUDGET.

Chic, moderne, and popular is the best way to describe **MacArthur Park**. Particularly favored by the pin-stripe crowd, this brick-wall dining room serves dishes specially prepared in an oakwood smoker and a mesquite grill. There are baby back ribs, dry-aged steak, and fresh fish. The decor is casual but self-conscious: blackwood and Matisse prints and padded park benches, track lights and a skylight, as well as a marble bar with mirrors and wine racks. No lunch on the weekend. ~ 607 Front Street; 415-398-5700, fax 415-296-7827; www.spectrumfoods.com, e-mail kgitter@aol.com. MODERATE TO DELUXE.

A favorite bar in this world of finance is the **Carnelian Room** atop the Bank of America. Perched on the 52nd floor, this luxurious

NIGHTLIFE

lounge has the best views of all, sweeping from little old San Francisco Bay out across the boundless deep. Reservations required. Dress code. ~ 555 California Street; 415-433-7500; www.carnelian room.com, e-mail carnelianroomsf@hotmail.com.

The comedy scene has been ripping through San Francisco since the early days of Lenny Bruce and Mort Sahl. Today the city has more stand-up comedians than cab drivers. **The Punch Line** books a wide variety of acts from around the country. Closed Monday. ~ 444 Battery Street; 415-397-7573.

▼▼▼▼▼▼▼▼▼▼▼

Embarcadero

Below the Financial District, where the city's skyscrapers meet the Bay, is the Embarcadero. This waterfront promenade has become increasingly appealing since the 1989 earthquake, which resulted in the dismantling of a freeway that once ran along the bayfront. Today the vistas are unobstructed and the strip is wide open for wandering.

Back in Gold Rush days, before the pernicious advent of landfill, the entire area sat beneath fathoms of water and went by the name of Yerba Buena Cove. Matter of fact, the hundreds of tall-masted ships abandoned here by crews deserting for the gold fields eventually became part of the landfill.

Nature is rarely a match for the shovel. The Bay was pressed back from around Montgomery Street to its present perimeter. As you head down from the Financial District, walk softly; the world may be four billion years old, but the earth you're treading has been around little more than a century.

SIGHTS

Fittingly enough, the first place encountered is **Embarcadero Center**, a skein of five skyscrapers rising sharp and slender along Sacramento Street to the foot of Market Street. This $645 million complex, oft tagged "Rockefeller Center West," features a three-tiered pedestrian mall that links the buildings together in a labyrinth of shops, restaurants, fountains, and gardens.

That blocky complex of cement pipes from which water pours in every direction is not an erector set run amok. It's **Vaillancourt Fountain**, situated smack in the Hyatt's front yard. The surrounding patchwork of grass and pavement is **Justin Herman Plaza**, a perfect place for a promenade or picnic. Craft vendors with engraved brass belt buckles, silver jewelry, and beanbag chairs have made the plaza their storefront and skaters have made it their playground. It's also the starting point for the monthly roving bicycle protest known as Critical Mass.

Just across the road, where Market Street encounters the Embarcadero, rises San Francisco's answer to the Statue of Liberty. Or what was the city's answer at the turn of the 20th century, when the clock tower of the **Ferry Building** was as well-known a landmark as the Golden Gate Bridge is today. Back then there were no bridges, and 100,000 ferryboat commuters a day poured through the portals of the world's second-busiest passenger terminal. Built in 1896, the old landmark has made a comeback with a complete renovation. Now the building houses a plethora of shops and restaurants. Tours of the building are available through City Guides (415-557-4266; www.sfcityguides.org) on Saturday, Sunday, and Tuesday at 12 p.m.

You might want to walk the ramp that leads up to the **World Trade Center**, on Embarcadero at the foot of Market Street. It's lined with Covarrubias' murals that were preserved from the 1939 Golden Gate International Exposition. They look like those maps in your old sixth grade social studies book: one vividly depicts "the people of the Pacific" with aborigines sprouting up from the Australian land mass and seraped Indians guarding the South American coast. Another pictorial geography lesson features the Pacific economy with salmon swimming off the North American shore and rice bowls growing in China.

One positive result of the horrendous 1989 Loma Prieta earthquake was the demolition of the Embarcadero Freeway, a longtime eyesore that ran like a concrete scar through the waterfront area. Now that the freeway is gone, there is a lighter and brighter look to the area, with palm trees planted along the Embarcadero and more expansive views of the Bay Bridge and Treasure Island. In 1996, the city named the pedestrian promenade that parallels the boulevard **Herb Caen Way**, in honor of San Francisco's famous gossip columnist who died in 1997. At the same time, a new neighborhood is fast growing up around and to the south of lower Market Street with apartments, restaurants, nightspots, and a Saturday-morning farmers' market. A popular gathering spot for locals, especially at noontime, is the **Rincon Center**, which fea-

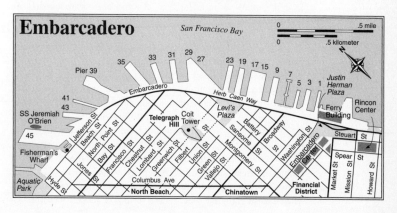

tures a cluster of eateries offering everything from Korean noodles to Indian curries. The eateries surround a central indoor courtyard dining area and spectacular, rainfall-like fountain. ~ 101 Spear Street; 415-777-4100.

The Rincon Annex is a restored 1930s post office with magnificent WPA murals glorifying science and technology.

Stretching from either side of the Ferry Building are the rows of **shipping piers** that once made San Francisco a fabulous harbor. Today much of the commerce has sailed across the Bay to the Port of Oakland. To recapture San Francisco's maritime era, head north on Embarcadero from the Ferry Building along the odd-numbered piers. The city looms to your left and the Bay heaves and glistens before you. This is a world of seaweed and fog horns where proverbial old salts still ply their trade. Blunt-nosed tugboats tie up next to rusting relics from Guadalcanal. There are modern jet ferries, displaying the latest aeronautical curves and appearing ready at any moment to depart from the water for open sky. The old, big-girthed ferries have been stripped of barnacles, painted nursery colors, and leased out as office space; they are floating condominiums.

Along this parade of piers you'll see cavernous concrete wharves astir with forklifts and dockhands. Locomotives shunt with a clatter, trucks jockey for an inside post, and container cranes sweep the air. Other piers have fallen into desuetude, rust-caked wharves propped on water-rotted pilings. The only common denominators in this odd arithmetic progression of piers are the seagulls and pelicans whitening the pylons.

Across from Pier 23, **Levi's Plaza** features a grassy park ideal for picnicking; just beyond Pier 35 there's a waterfront park with a wonderful vantage for spying on the ships that sail the Bay. ~ 1155 Battery Street.

The Embarcadero continues along the waterfront all the way to Fisherman's Wharf. Joggers, skaters, and skateboarders all favor this long smooth stretch of Herb Caen Way.

LODGING   The lobby of the **Hyatt Regency**, on the corner of Market and California streets, features a towering atrium that rises 170 feet— a triangular affair lined with a succession of interior balconies that ascend to a skylighted roof. Along one side, plants cascade in a 20-story hanging garden, while another wall is designed in a zigzag shape that gives the sensation of being inside a pyramid. Fountains and flowering plants are all about, glass capsule elevators scale the walls, and sun flecks splash in through the roof. The 805 large, fashionable guest rooms, accented with tall green plants and fresh-cut flowers, come with business-oriented amenities such as two telephones, voice mail and computer hookups, as well as such luxury touches as hair dryers, plush robes and optional turndown service. Most rooms have exterior balconies, and many have bay views. ~ 5 Embarcadero Center; 415-788-1234, fax 415-398-2567; www.hyatt.com, e-mail sales@sforspo.hyatt.com. ULTRA-DELUXE.

Just one block from the Embarcadero and convenient to the Financial District, the **Hotel Griffon** offers 62 attractive rooms and suites appointed with modern art, window seats, oversized mirrors, and, in a few cases, bay views. A cozy lobby features a reading nook and fireplace, and there's an adjacent fitness center. A continental breakfast is included. ~ 155 Steuart Street; 415-495-2100, 800-321-2201, fax 415-495-3522; www.hotelgriffon.com, e-mail reservations@hotelgriffon.com. ULTRA-DELUXE.

On the same block is **Harbor Court Hotel**, where some of the 131 rooms and suites also offer marine views. Guest accommodations are small but attractively appointed with nautical prints, big mirrors, canopied beds, and brass sconces. The lobby is large and comfortable, and ideal for leisurely afternoons. Complimentary wine is served daily between 5 and 6 p.m. You can also relax at the health club and indoor pool adjacent to the hotel. ~ 165 Steuart Street; 415-882-1300, 800-346-0555, fax 415-777-5457; www.harborcourthotel.com, e-mail sales@harborcourthotel.com. DELUXE TO ULTRA-DELUXE.

DINING

Consistently ranked among the city's top restaurants, **Boulevard** is the brainchild of famed San Francisco chef Nancy Oakes and interior designer Pat Kuleto. Art-deco decor unifies three distinct seating areas—a casual central section around an open kitchen where you can watch the chefs at work, a front bar, and a more formal back dining area. The food is as chic as the decor, and the menu changes regularly. Representative entrées have included glazed quail, vanilla-cured pork loin and grilled ahi tuna in ginger salsa. There's also an exceptional list of hard-to-find California wines. No lunch on weekends. ~ 1 Mission Street; 415-543-6084; www.boulevardrestaurant.com, e-mail blvd@sirius.com. ULTRA-DELUXE.

San Francisco's modern version of camp is **Fog City Diner**. It is the most upscale diner you've ever seen. Check out the exterior with its art-deco curves, neon lights, and checkerboard tile. Then step into a wood-and-brass paneled restaurant that has the feel of a club car on the Orient Express. Featuring California cuisine, the menu changes frequently, though on a given day it will be the same for both lunch and dinner. Everything is à la carte, including the Fog City T-shirts. What can I tell you except to book a reservation in advance. ~ 1300 Battery Street; 415-982-2000, fax 415-982-3711; www.fogcitydiner.com, e-mail fogcitydiner@aol.com. MODERATE TO DELUXE.

One of San Francisco's finest and most authentic Hong Kong–style restaurants is not located in Chinatown, but is tucked into a corner of the Embarcadero Center. **Harbor Village** serves exquisite Cantonese dishes such as crisp, juicy roast chicken, steamed catfish, and shark's fin soup in an elegant setting of Chinese antiques and teak furnishings. At lunchtime, its dim sum selections are among the best in the city. ~ 4 Embarcadero Center; 415-781-8833; www.harborvillage.net, e-mail hvrsfo@aol.com. DELUXE.

HIDDEN ►

Head on down to **Pier 23 Cafe**, a little shack between Fisherman's Wharf and downtown, for unique waterfront dining. The place is funky but nice, with white tablecloths and linen napkins on the tables. Dine inside or on the huge back patio overlooking the bay. This restaurant specializes in seafood and offers several fish specials daily. The deep-fried calamari appetizer and the oven-roasted crab with garlic, parsley, and butter dipping sauce are two of the most popular items on the menu. ~ Pier 23; 415-362-5125; www.pier23cafe.com, e-mail pier23cafe@aol.com. MODERATE.

SHOPPING

Shoppers along the Embarcadero head for the **Embarcadero Center**, located on Sacramento Street near the foot of Market Street. It's a vaulting glass-and-concrete "town" inhabited by stores and restaurants. This multifaceted mall consists of the lower three levels of five consecutive skyscrapers. You pass from one building to the next along corridors that open onto a galaxy of shops. Verily, what Disneyland is for kids, Embarcadero Center is to shoppers. The place has positively everything. There are bookstores, bakeries, jewelry stores, gift bazaars, newsstands, and camera shops. There's even a "general store," plus dozens of restaurants, cocktail lounges, and espresso bars, a luggage shop, a store devoted entirely to nature, and on and on and on in labyrinthine fashion.

NIGHTLIFE

The Holding Company is crowded with young professionals on the make. Closed Saturday and Sunday. ~ 2 Embarcadero Center; 415-986-0797.

Over at the Hyatt Regency, there's a revolving rooftop bar, **The Equinox**. A glass-encased elevator whisks you to this aerie, where you can pull up a window seat and watch the world spin. ~ 5 Embarcadero Center; 415-788-1234.

Pier 23 is a funky roadhouse that happens to sit next to the San Francisco waterfront. The sounds emanating from this saloon are live jazz, reggae, salsa, and blues. Highly recommended to those searching for the simple rhythms of life. There's music nightly; Wednesday evening features a salsa class. Cover. ~ Embarcadero and Pier 23; 415-362-5125, fax 415-362-8138; www.pier23cafe.com.

It's the largest Chinatown outside Asia, a spot that older Chinese know as *dai fao*, Big City. San Francisco's China-town also ranks as the city's most densely populated neighborhood. Home to 40,000 of the city's 150,000 Chinese, this enclave has been an Asian stronghold since the 1850s. Originally a ghetto where Chinese people were segregated from San Francisco society, the neighborhood today opens its arms to burgeoning numbers of immigrants from a host of Asian nations.

▼▼▼▼▼▼▼▼▼▼
Chinatown

On the surface, this pulsing, noisy, chaotically colorful 70-square-block stretch projects the aura of a tourist's dream—gold and crimson pagodas, stores brimming with exquisite silks and multicolored dragons, more restaurants per square foot than could be imagined, roast ducks strung up in shop windows next door to Buddhist temples and fortune cookie factories.

But Chinatown is far more than a tourist mecca. This crowded neighborhood is peopled with families, powerful political groups, small merchants, poor working immigrants and rising entrepreneurs molding a more prosperous future. Although the "city within a city" that Chinatown once symbolized now encompasses only a quarter of San Francisco's Chinese people, it's still a center of Chinese history, culture, arts, and traditions that have lived for thousands of years.

In appropriately dramatic fashion, you enter Chinatown through an arching gateway bedecked with dragons. Stone lions guard either side of this portal at Grant Avenue and Bush Street.

It was during the Gold Rush that "Celestials" sporting queues and exotic costumes arrived en masse in California. Often forced into indentured servitude, they worked the gold fields and later helped build the transcontinental railroad. During the 1870s and 1880s these proud people, who had arrived in San Francisco with visions of the "Great City on the Golden Hill," became vic-

◆◆

CHINATOWN—A DIFFERENT PERSPECTIVE

Just off the notorious Columbus/Broadway intersection lies a museum that will open wide your perspective on Chinatown's history. The **Chinese Historical Society of America** graphically presents the history of San Francisco's Chinese population. In the museum is a magnificent collection of photos and artifacts re-creating the Chinese experience from the days of pig-tailed "coolies" to the recent advent of ethnic consciousness.

Wide in scope, the museum is a treasure house with a helpful and congenial staff. Closed Monday; call ahead for hours. Admission. ~ 965 Clay Street; 415-391-1188, fax 415-391-1150; www.chsa.org, e-mail info@chsa.org.

tims of the "yellow peril" mentality sweeping the nation. They were beaten and lynched, their homes torched. Racist whites, eyeing the prime real estate upon which the Chinatown ghetto had grown, tried to run the entire population out of town.

It took an earthquake to uproot them. The calamity of 1906 devastated Chinatown, leaving countless dead and homeless. When the smoke and rubble were cleared, a new Chinatown arose; gone were the opium dens and houses of prostitution for which the old ghetto was notorious; in their stead grew a neighborhood that became modern-day Chinatown.

SIGHTS   To stroll the eight-block length of Chinatown's **Grant Avenue** is to walk along San Francisco's oldest street. Today it's an ultramodern thoroughfare lined with Chinese arts-and-crafts shops, restaurants, and Asian markets. It's also one of the most crowded streets you'll ever squeeze your way through. Immortalized in a song from the musical *Flower Drum Song*, Grant Avenue, San Francisco, California, U.S.A., is a commotion, clatter, a clash of cultures. At any moment, a rickety truck may pull up beside you, heave open its doors, and reveal its contents—a cargo of chinaware, fresh produce, or perhaps flattened pig carcasses. Elderly Chinese men lean along doorways smoking fat cigars, and Chinatown's younger generation sets off down the street clad in sleek leather jackets.

At the corner of California Street, where cable cars clang across Grant Avenue, rises the lovely brick structure of **Old St. Mary's Church**. Dating to 1854, this splendid cathedral was originally built of stone quarried in China. Just across the way in **St. Mary's Square**, there's a statue of the father of the Chinese Republic, Dr. Sun Yat Sen, crafted by San Francisco's foremost sculptor, Beniamino Bufano. You might take a hint from the crowds of businesspeople from the nearby financial center who bring their picnic lunches to this tree-shaded plaza.

Next you'll encounter **Mam Kue School**. With an iron fence, mullioned doors, and pagoda-like facade, it's an architectural beauty ironically backdropped by a glass-and-concrete skyscraper. ~ 755 Sacramento Street.

As you walk along Grant Avenue, with its swirling roof lines and flashing signs, peek down **Commercial Street**. This curious brick-paved street permits a glimpse into "hidden" Chinatown. Lined with everything from a noodle company to a ginseng shop, this tightly packed street also holds the **Mow Lee Company**, Chinatown's second-oldest establishment. ~ 774 Commercial Street.

After you've immersed yourself in Chinese history, head down to **Portsmouth Square** (Kearny and Washington streets) for a lesson in the history of all San Francisco. Formerly the city's central plaza, it was here in 1846 that Yankees first raised the Stars and

Stripes. Two years later, the California gold discovery was announced to the world from this square. At one corner of the park you'll find the bronze statue of a galleon celebrating the ocean-going Robert Louis Stevenson. Today this gracious park is a gathering place for old Chinese men playing chess and practicing tai chi. From the center of the plaza, a sky bridge arches directly into the **Chinese Culture Center**, with its displays of Chinese art. Located on the third floor of the Holiday Inn Hotel, it's closed Sunday and Monday. ~ 750 Kearny Street; 415-986-1822, fax 415-986-2825; www.c-c-c.org, e-mail info@c-c-c.org.

Now that you've experienced the traditional tour, you might want to explore the hidden heart of Chinatown. First take a stroll along **Stockton Street**, which runs parallel to, and one block above, Grant Avenue. It is here, not along touristy Grant Avenue, that the Chinese shop.

The street vibrates with the crazy commotion of Chinatown. Open stalls tumbling with vegetables cover the sidewalk, and crates of fresh fish are stacked along the curb. Through this maze of merchandise, shoppers press past one another. In store windows hang Peking ducks, and on the counters are displayed pigs'

Chinatown

Map of Chinatown showing streets including Broadway, Pacific Ave, Jackson St, Washington St, Clay St, Sacramento St, California St, Pine St, Bush St, and cross streets Taylor St, Mason St, Powell St, Stockton St, Grant Ave, Kearny St, Columbus Ave. Landmarks shown include Cable Car Museum, Golden Gate Fortune Cookie Factory, Tian Hou Temple, Portsmouth Square, Merchant St, Chinese Historical Society of America, Mow Lee Company, Commercial St, Mam Kue School, Nob Hill, Grace Cathedral, Huntington Park, Cushman, Old St Mary's Church, St Mary's Square, Quincy St, Joice St, Stockton Tunnel, Ross Alley, Spofford Ln, Hang Ah St, Pagoda St, Waverly Pl, Lum Pl, Financial District.

heads and snapping turtles. Rare herbs, healing teas, and chrysanthemum crystals crowd the shelves.

The local community's artwork is displayed in a fantastic **mural** that covers a half-block between Pacific and Jackson streets.

To further explore the interior life of Chinatown, turn down Sacramento Street from Stockton Street, then take a quick left into Hang Ah Street. This is the first in a series of alleyways leading for three blocks from Sacramento Street to Jackson Street. When you get to the end of each block, simply jog over to the next alley.

HIDDEN ▶

A universe unto themselves, these **alleyways of Chinatown** are where the secret business of the community goes on, as it has for over a century. Each door is a barrier beyond which you can hear the rattle of mah-jongg tiles and the sounds of women bent to their tasks in laundries and sewing factories.

Along Hang Ah Street, timeworn buildings are draped with fire escapes and colored with the images of fading signs. As you cross Clay Street, at the end of Hang Ah Street, be sure to press your nose against the glass at **Grand Century Enterprise**. Here the ginseng and other precious roots sell for hundreds of dollars a pound. ~ 858 Clay Street; 415-392-4060, fax 415-392-4063.

Rudyard Kipling, Jack London, and Robert Louis Stevenson once wandered the grounds of Portsmouth Square.

The next alley, **Spofford Lane**, is a corridor of painted doorways and brick facades humming with the strains of Chinese melodies. It ends at Washington Street where you can zigzag over to **Ross Alley**. This is the home of the **Golden Gate Fortune Cookie Factory**. At this small family establishment you can watch your fortune being made. ~ 56 Ross Alley; 415-781-3956.

The last segment in this intriguing tour will take you back to **Waverly Place**, a two-block stretch leading from Washington Street to Sacramento Street. Readers of Dashiell Hammett's mystery story, *Dead Yellow Women*, will recall this spot. It's an enchanting thoroughfare, more alley than street. At first glance, the wrought-iron balconies draped along either side of Waverly evoke images of New Orleans. But not even the French Quarter can boast the beauty contained in those Chinese cornices and pagoda swirl roof lines.

Prize jewel in this architectural crown is **Tian Hou Temple**. Here Buddhists and Taoists worship in a tiny temple overhung with fiery red lanterns. There are statues portraying battlefields and country landscapes; incense smolders from several altars. From the pictures along the wall, Buddha smiles out upon the believers. They in turn gaze down from the balcony onto Chinatown's most magical street. ~ 125 Waverly Place.

Just uphill from Chinatown stands the **Cable Car Museum**, a brick goliath which houses the city's cable cars. The museum here provides a great opportunity to see how these wood-and-steel masterpieces operate. The system's powerhouse, repair, and storage facilities are here, as are the 14-foot diameter sheaves which neatly wind the cable into figure-eight patterns. The museum also has on display three antique cable cars from the original cable car company. ~ 1201 Mason Street; 415-474-1887, fax 415-929-7546; www.cablecarmuseum.com.

Though you'll notice doors and stairways throughout Chinatown advertising hotel accommodations, these are usually residential buildings serving the local Chinese community. Look for the permanent "no vacancy" signs that accompany many of the hotel insignia and you'll realize that these facilities are Asian boarding houses, closed to the general public. There are, however, two hotels and a YMCA providing adequate accommodations for budget travelers. Any of them will give you a chance to fully experience this amazing neighborhood.

LODGING

If you're after a real budget find, the **Chinatown** YMCA has rooms with shared bath facilities. The rooms are devoid of decoration and furnished in spartan fashion with bed, dresser, and table. If your room depresses you (we've received complaints and critiques at times), you can escape to the pool, gym, or weight room, all free of charge to guests. Men only. ~ 855 Sacramento Street; 415-576-9622, fax 415-782-2260; www.ymcasf.org/chinatown. BUDGET.

On the edge of Chinatown, less than a block from North Beach, the **Obrero Hotel** provides clean, but very basic, hotel accommodations on the second and third floors of a building squeezed between a row of shops. Each room has been furnished a bit differently, but all have a large double bed and a sink, and some sport brass beds. Bathrooms are shared. All rooms are nonsmoking and soundproofed. ~ 1208 Stockton Street; phone/fax 415-989-3960; e-mail h1208@aol.com. BUDGET TO MODERATE.

Immediately up from the Grant Avenue gateway to Chinatown you'll encounter **Grant Plaza Hotel**. Staff and management here are quite hospitable and the security guard and buzzer system makes this a safe hotel for women. The place features a small, tastefully decorated lobby and a selection of remodeled rooms. They feature plush carpeting, telephones, color televisions, and private baths. The hotel's location right on Grant Avenue has the advantage of being at the very heart of the district and the disadvantage of being noisy. ~ 465 Grant Avenue; 415-434-3883, 800-472-6899, fax 415-434-3886; www.grantplaza.com, e-mail info@grantplaza.com. BUDGET TO MODERATE.

Chinatown is one of the best places in the city to find exceptional food at rock-bottom prices. Look for it at the kind of plain-looking places where most of the diners appear to be from the neighbor-

DINING

hood and children roam around as freely as if they were at home. A good example is **Hon's Wun Tun House,** where spotless formica, shared tables and counter seating set the stage for noodle dishes and soups as tasty as they are affordable. Closed Sunday. ~ 648 Kearny Street; 415-433-3966, fax 415-433-1506. BUDGET.

Among budget restaurants, **Sam Wo** is a San Francisco classic. Dining in this jook house is a rare adventure. The entrance is also the kitchen, and the kitchen is just a corridor filled with pots, stovepipes, cooks, and steamy smells. Sam Wo's menu is extensive and the food is quite good for the price. ~ 813 Washington Street; 415-982-0596. BUDGET.

HIDDEN ►

Concealed along one of Chinatown's back alleyways, the **Pot Sticker** has the feel of a local secret, part social club, part take-out place serving neighborhood families, and so exotic that it seems a world apart from the more touristy restaurants of Grant Street. Specializing in its namesake—meat-filled dumplings that are first steamed and then fried—the Pot Sticker also offers a full menu of Mandarin-style dishes. ~ 150 Waverly Place; 415-397-9985, fax 415-397-3829. MODERATE.

For luxurious dining in the heart of Chinatown, no place matches the **Empress of China.** Set on the top floor of the China Trade Center, with nothing between you and heaven, it is a culinary temple. Dining rooms are adorned with carved antiques and the maitre'd dons a tuxedo. Lunch at this roof garden restaurant begins with appetizers like Shanghai dumplings and barbecued quail, then graduates to lichee chicken and Manchurian beef. Dinner is the true extravagance. The menu includes a royal variety of chicken, duck, lamb, shellfish, pork, and beef dishes. There are also unique selections like hundred blossom lamb, prepared with sweet and sour ginger; lobster *see jup* in black bean sauce; and phoenix dragon, a medley of shrimp, chicken, and onions sautéed in wine. ~ 838 Grant Avenue; 415-434-1345, fax 415-986-1187; www.empressofchinasf.com. DELUXE TO ULTRA-DELUXE.

Of course, the ultimate Chinatown experience is to dine dim sum style. Rather than choosing from a menu, you select dishes

AUTHOR FAVORITE

My favorite dim sum restaurant is tucked away in an alley above Grant Avenue. Personalized but unpretentious, more cozy than cavernous, **Hang Ah Tea House** is a rare find. Enter the dining room with its Chinese wood carvings and fiberglass tables. Serving a full Mandarin cuisine as well as dim sum portions, it warrants an exploratory mission into the alleys of Chinatown. Open late for dessert. ~ 1 Hang Ah Street; 415-982-5686. BUDGET.

from trundle carts laden with steaming delicacies. A never-ending convoy of waitresses wheels past your table, offering plates piled with won tons, pork tidbits, and Chinese meatballs. It's up to you to create a meal (traditionally breakfast or lunch) from this succession of finger-size morsels.

Many dim sum establishments are cavernous restaurants, sparsely decorated like cafeterias. But each has a particular personality and generates warmth from the crowds passing through. Do not be fooled by the neon facades, for an Asian adventure waits within these dining palaces. You should be careful about prices, however: most dim sum courses cost only $2 or $3, but it's easy to lose count as you devour dish after dish. Figure that the restaurants noted below will be moderate in price, unless you become a dim sum addict.

The brightly lit yellow sign outside **Gold Mountain Restaurant** attracts its share of tourists and passersby. Nonetheless, this clean and modern dining room serves trusty claypot specialties, traditional seafood and noodles, and dim sum at lunch. Try the three treasures in black bean sauce, a colorful dish with red bell peppers, eggplant and stuffed tofu. ~ 644 Broadway near Powell Street; 415-296-7733, 415-296-7782. BUDGET TO MODERATE.

Overlooking Portsmouth Square on the second story of a nondescript building, the **Oriental Pearl** serves sophisticated, gourmet dim sum, a step above the usual Chinatown teahouse. Here dim sum is ordered from a menu, allowing diners to concentrate on conversation and cuisine, rather than being distracted by the contents of passing carts. Such treats as shrimp and scallop dumplings, pork buns, and chicken meatballs emerge hot and fresh from the kitchen. White tablecloths, mahogany chairs, and classical Chinese music make this a quiet oasis from the busy streets of Chinatown below. ~ 760–778 Clay Street; 415-433-1817, fax 415-433-4541; www.orientalpearlrestaurant.com. BUDGET TO MODERATE.

Shopping in Chinatown brings you into immediate contact with both the common and the unique. If you can slip past the souvenir shops, many of which specialize in American-made "Chinese products," you'll eventually discover the real thing—Chinese arts and crafts as well as Asian antiques.

SHOPPING

Grant Avenue is the neighborhood's shopping center, but local Chinese favor **Stockton Street**. My advice is to browse both streets as well as the side streets between. Some of the city's best bargains are right here in Chinatown.

After this soft-spoken introduction, continue on to that buzzing, clanging commercial strip called **Grant Avenue**. Sensory overload and crazed consumerism are facts of life along this neon thoroughfare. But don't be discouraged by the painted face: beneath that garish exterior Grant Avenue reveals its own particular culture.

The soul of the place resides somewhere between the Hong Kong souvenirs and the antique tapestries. While there is a lot of gimcrackery sold here, many specialty shops provide a sense of the richness of Chinese arts and crafts. Slip into one of the district's silk stores to admire the kimonos, or drop by a tea shop and sample one of the hundreds of varieties of teas.

First stop along Grant Avenue is a mandatory one: **Canton Bazaar**. This three-story emporium is a browser's warehouse. Six-foot-high wooden statues and laughing Buddhas surround the entrance, drawing in the canny and unwary alike. From the ceramic pieces to the silver jewelry, the shelves are laden with exceptionally tasteful goods. The bottom floor is filled with furniture and decor items while the top floor is devoted to clothing and textiles. Among the antiques are Buddhist religious paintings, raw-silk wallhangings, and intricately carved statues. ~ 616 Grant Avenue; 415-362-5750; e-mail cantonbazaar@aol.com.

As you continue down Grant Avenue, several specialty shops are worth noting. The **Chinatown Kite Shop** is hung with a variety of kites, including dragonfly and box kites. ~ 717 Grant Avenue; 415-391-8217; www.chinatownkite.com.

The **Wok Shop** sells every kind of wok imaginable—carbon steel, cast iron, stainless steel, electric—as well as all the accessories to cook up a tantalizing stir-fry, succulent roasted chicken, or savory *shiu mai*. There are also bamboo steamers, cleavers, claypots, and books. ~ 718 Grant Street; 415-989-3797, fax 415-982-2299; www.wokshop.com.

Nearby the **Far East Flea Market** you'll find everything from clothing to birdcages. Also available at this Asian emporium are fans and decorative boxes from mainland China. ~ 729 Grant Avenue; 415-989-8588.

At the New China Trade Center there's a store, **Chong Imports**, which seems to offer every item found anywhere else on Grant Avenue. The prices at this multitiered wonderland are as alluring as the merchandise. ~ 838 Grant Avenue; 415-982-1434.

NIGHTLIFE **Li Po,** a dimly lit Chinatown bar, is complete with incense, lanterns, and carved statuary, plus an incongruous jukebox featuring Caucasian favorites. The potions they mix here are powerful and exotic; the place has an air of intimacy. ~ 916 Grant Avenue; 415-982-0072, fax 415-982-1903.

▼ ▼ ▼ ▼ ▼ ▼ ▼ ▼ ▼ ▼ ▼

North Beach

It's a region of contrasts, a neighborhood in transition. North Beach combines the sex scene of neon-lit Broadway with the brooding intellect and Beat heritage of Grant Avenue and Columbus Street. Traditionally an Italian stronghold, North Beach still retains its fabulous pasta palaces and bocce ball courts, but it's giving way to a growing influx of Chinese residents.

Introductions to places should be made gradually, so the visitor comes slowly but certainly to know and love the area. In touring North Beach, that is no longer possible, because the logical spot to begin a tour is the corner of Broadway and Montgomery streets, at night when the neon arabesque of Broadway is in full glare.

SIGHTS

Broadway, you see, has long been San Francisco's answer to Times Square, a tawdry avenue that traffics in sex. While the neighborhood is steadily changing, it still features strip joints, peekaramas, and X, Y, Z-rated theaters—a modern-day Barbary Coast.

After you've dispensed with North Beach's sex scene, your love affair with the neighborhood can begin. Start at **City Lights Bookstore**. Established in 1953 by poet Lawrence Ferlinghetti, City Lights is the old hangout of the Beat poets. Back in the heady days of the '50s, a host of "angelheaded hipsters"—Allen Ginsberg, Jack Kerouac, Gary Snyder, and Neal Cassady among them—haunted its book-lined rooms and creaking staircase. Today the

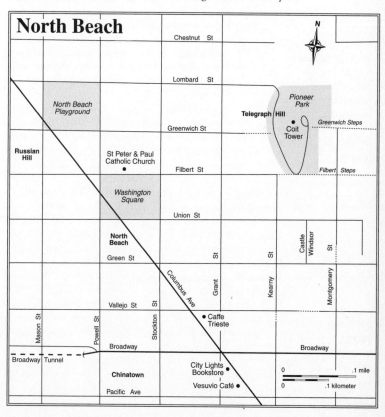

North Beach

place remains a vital cultural scene and gathering point. It's a people's bookstore where you're invited to browse, carouse, or even plop into a chair and read awhile. You might also check out the paintings and old photos, or perhaps the window display in this official national landmark. Forty years after the Beats, the inventory here still represents a who's who in avant-garde literature. ~ 261 Columbus Avenue; 415-362-8193, fax 415-362-4921; www.citylights.com, e-mail staff@citylights.com.

Vesuvio Café next door was another hallowed Bohemian retreat. ~ 255 Columbus Avenue; 415-362-3370; www.vesuvio. com. Then head up nearby Grant Avenue to the **Caffe Trieste**, at the corner of Vallejo Street. With its water-spotted photos and funky espresso bar, the place has changed little since the days when bearded bards discussed cool jazz and Eisenhower politics. ~ 601 Vallejo Street; 415-392-6739, fax 415-982-3045; www. caffetrieste.com.

You're on "upper Grant," heart of the old Beat stomping grounds and still a major artery in the city's Italian enclave. Chinatown is at your back now, several blocks behind, but you'll see from the Chinese script adorning many shops that the Asian neighborhood is sprawling into the Italian. Still remaining, however, are the cafés and delicatessens that have lent this area its Mediterranean flair since the Italians moved in during the late 19th-century.

Some of the nation's most outstanding WPA murals decorate Coit Tower's interior. Done as frescoes by New Deal artists, they sensitively depict the lives of California laborers.

Beyond Filbert Street, as Grant Avenue continues along the side of Telegraph Hill, the shops give way to Italian residences and Victorian houses. When you arrive at Lombard Street, look to your left and you'll see the sinuous reason why Lombard is labeled "The Crookedest Street in the World." Then turn right as Lombard carries you up to the breeze-battered vistas of Telegraph Hill.

Named for the semaphore station located on its height during the 1850s, **Telegraph Hill** was a Bohemian haunt during the 1920s and 1930s. Money moved the artists out; today, this hillside real estate is among the most desirable, and most expensive, in the city.

Poking through the top of Telegraph Hill is the 180-foot-high **Coit Tower** (admission for elevator to observation platform). Built in 1934, this fluted structure was named for Lillie Hitchcock Coit, a bizarre character who chased fire engines and became a fire company mascot during the 1850s. Lillie's love for firemen gave rise to stories that the phallic tower was modeled after a fire hose nozzle. Architectural critics scoff at the notion.

Upstaging these marvelous artworks is the view from the summit. All San Francisco spreads before you. That sinewy structure to the right is the **Bay Bridge**, which stretches for eight and one quarter miles, the world's longest steel bridge. It is interrupted in its arching course by **Yerba Buena Island** and **Treasure Island**, the latter a manmade extension created for the 1939 Golden Gate International Exposition. The Bay Bridge's gilded companion to the left is the **Golden Gate Bridge**. Between them lies San Francisco Bay. Tugs and freighters slide past in search of mooring. Fog horns groan. From this aerie the distant sloops and ketches look like children's toys blown astray in a pond puffed with wind.

The island moored directly offshore is **Alcatraz**, named for the pelicans that still inhabit it, but known for the notorious prisoners who have long since departed its rocky terrain. Looming behind America's own Devil's Island is **Angel Island**. That high point on the horizon, between the Golden Gate and Angel Island, is **Mt. Tamalpais**, crown jewel in Marin County's tiara. Across the water, where the Bay Bridge meets terra firma, are the East Bay cities of **Berkeley** and **Oakland**. Behind you, past the highrise cityscape, the hills and streets of San Francisco sweep out toward the sea.

Now that all San Francisco has been spread before you like a tableau, it's time to descend into the hidden crannies of the city. Unlike Coit Tower, there will be no elevator to assist on the way down, but then again there won't be any tourists either.

After exiting Coit Tower, turn right, cross the street, and make your way down the brick-lined staircase. In the middle of San Francisco, with wharves and factories far below, you have just entered a countrified environment. Ferns and ivy riot on either side of the **Greenwich Steps**, while vines and conifers climb overhead.   ◄ *HIDDEN*

At the bottom of the steps, turn right, walk a short distance   ◄ *HIDDEN*
along Montgomery Street, then head left down the **Filbert Steps**. Festooned with flowers and sprinkled with baby tears, the steps carry you into a fantasy realm inhabited by stray cats and framed with clapboard houses. Among the older homes are several that date to the 1870s; if you follow the Napier Lane Boardwalk that extends from the steps, there are falsefront buildings from which sailors reportedly once were shanghaied.

Retracing your tracks back up the steps, then descending the other side of Filbert Street, you'll arrive at **Washington Square**, between Filbert and Stockton streets in the heart of North Beach. Nestled between Russian and Telegraph hills, this is the gathering place for San Francisco's "Little Italy." In the square, old Italian men and women seek out wooden benches where they can watch the "young people" carrying on. From the surrounding delis and cafés you might put together a picnic lunch, plant yourself on the lawn, and catch this daily parade. But if you come early in the morning, you will see evidence of the slow transition North Beach is undergoing: 50 or more Chinese and Westerners practice tai chi in the square.

St. Peter & Paul Catholic Church anchors one side of the square. Its twin steeples dominate the North Beach skyline. The façade is unforgettable, an ornate affair upon which eagles rest in the company of angels. The interior is a wilderness of vaulting arches hung with lamps and decorated in gilt bas-relief. Tourists proclaim its beauty. For my taste, the place is overdone; it drips with architectural jewelry. Everything is decoration, an artistic happening; there is no tranquility, no silent spot for the eye to rest. ~ Filbert Street, between Powell and Stockton streets; 415-421-0809, fax 415-421-0217; www.stspeterpaul.san-francisco.ca.us, e-mail gibbons@stspeterpaul.sanfrancisco.ca.us.

LODGING
As a nighttime visit to North Beach will clearly indicate, this neighborhood was not made for sleeping. The "love acts" and encounter parlors along Broadway draw rude, boisterous crowds until the wee hours.

But if noise and neon have a soporific effect upon you, or if you have some bizarre and arcane need to know what sleeping on the old Barbary Coast was like, check out **Europa Hotel**. The price is certainly right, and you get a clean, carpeted room and shared bath. ~ 310 Columbus Avenue; 415-391-5779, fax 415-391-0499. BUDGET.

HIDDEN ▶
Or better yet, retreat a little farther from Broadway to the **Hotel Bohème** and take a step back into North Beach history. This European pensione–style hotel has been decorated to reflect the Beat-generation era, complete with a black-and-white photo retrospective. Poet Allen Ginsberg even stayed here. Rooms feature antique wardrobes, tile bathrooms, and black iron beds. Ask for one of the rooms in the back, which are quieter than those along busy Columbus Avenue. ~ 444 Columbus Avenue; 415-433-9111, fax 415-362-6292; www.hotelboheme.com, e-mail mail@hotelboheme.com. DELUXE.

DINING
Dining at **Helmand** is like visiting the home of an upper-class Afghani family. Lush handmade Afghan carpets, beautiful chandeliers, and paintings add a touch of elegance, and the food is first-rate. You can feast on grilled rack of lamb, roasted chicken, and many vegetarian dishes. *Aushak*, Afghan ravioli stuffed with leeks and topped with ground beef marinated in yogurt, can be habit-forming. A true find among the sleazy strip joints of Broadway. Dinner only. ~ 430 Broadway; 415-362-0641, fax 415-362-0862. MODERATE.

Some of the best pizza in town is served at **Tommaso's Neapolitan Restaurant,** where the chefs bake in an oak-fired oven.

The creations they prepare have resulted in this tiny restaurant being written up in national magazines. As soon as you walk in you'll realize it's the food, not the surroundings, that draws the attention. Entering the place is like stepping down into a grotto. The walls are lined with booths and covered by murals; it's dark, steamy, and filled with inviting smells. Filmmaker Francis Ford Coppola drops by occasionally, as should every pizza and pasta lover. Dinner only. Closed Monday. ~ 1042 Kearny Street; 415-398-9696, fax 415-989-9415. MODERATE.

At least once during a North Beach visit, you should dine at a family-style Italian restaurant. Dotted all around the neighborhood, these establishments have a local flavor unmatched by the area's chic new restaurants. A good choice is **Capp's Corner**, a local landmark adorned with celebrity photos, more celebrity photos, and a few photos of celebrities. The prix-fixe dinner includes soup, salad and an entrée. Among the dishes are osso buco, linguini with steamed mussels and clams, and lamb shanks. ~ 1600 Powell Street; 415-989-2589, fax 415-989-2590. MODERATE.

If there is any place in San Francisco that elevates dining to the level of high adventure, it is **Caffe Sport**. First, the place introduces itself a block before you arrive; if you're not buried beneath the waves of garlic it wafts along Green Street, you'll be visually assaulted by the garish orange facade. Once inside, you'll discover a baroque nightmare; the place is chockablock with bric-a-brac—faded photos, tacky candelabra and antiques circa 1972. Besides that, it's hot, steamy, unbelievably crowded, and the waiters are rude. What more can I say, except that you'll either love or hate the place. Lunch only offered Friday and Saturday. Closed Sunday and Monday. ~ 574 Green Street; 415-981-1251; www.caffe sport.citysearch.com. MODERATE TO DELUXE.

It's hard to imagine that Washington Square was a tent city back in 1906. The great earthquake and fire totally devastated North Beach, and the park became a refuge for hundreds of homeless.

A big blue neon moosehead marks the entrance to **Moose's** located on Washington Square. When Ed Moose opened his namesake restaurant, San Francisco's politicians and powerbrokers promptly declared the long bar in the front of the restaurant their "second office." Here, it's said, more deals are made than in any conference room in the city. The main dining area is bright, modern-looking, and spacious, with a view of the adjoining open kitchen. The menu runs the gamut from the trademark Mooseburger (actually made from quality ground beef, but mooselike in its hugeness) to haute cuisine such as mahimahi colorfully presented with purple potatoes, green garlic, and blood orange. No lunch Sunday through Wednesday. ~ 1652 Stockton Street; 415-989-7800; www.mooses.com, e-mail sarah@mooses.com. MODERATE TO ULTRA-DELUXE.

Dessert in North Beach means Italian ice cream, and few places make it better than **Gelato Classico**. Creamy and thick, Italian ice cream is made without air, so it's denser and more delicious than other ice cream. At Gelato they also use fresh fruit and other natural ingredients to guarantee great taste. If you try it in summer, you can have fresh strawberry, blackberry, burgundy cherry, or raspberry. During the rest of the year, they serve a host of flavors ranging from coppa mista and banana to good old chocolate and vanilla (made, of course, from vanilla beans). *Viva Italia!* ~ 576 Union Street; 415-391-6667.

Okay, not everybody likes garlic, but those who don't probably have no business dining in predominantly Italian North Beach anyway. On the other hand, those who *really* like garlic will love **The Stinking Rose**. Everything, from scrambled eggs to cocktails, is laced with garlic. Though mainly California-Italian, the menu runs the gamut from 40-clove garlic chicken to garlic-roasted Dungeness crab. Garish inside and out, the decor is conducive to fun-loving rowdiness, and the waitpeople take their jobs anything but seriously. An added bonus is that you can get your garlic fix until midnight, daily. ~ 325 Columbus Avenue; 415-781-7673; www.thestinkingrose.com. MODERATE TO DELUXE.

The heart of North Beach beats in its cafés. Gathering places for local Italians, the neighborhood's coffee houses are also literary scenes. Step into any of the numerous cafés dotting the district and you're liable to hear an elderly Italian singing opera or see an aspiring writer with notebook in one hand and espresso cup in the other.

The best North Beach breakfasts are the continental-style meals served in these cafés. But any time of day or night, you can order a croissant and cappuccino, lean back, and take in the human scenery. Foremost among these people-watching posts is **Caffe Trieste**, the old Beatnik rendezvous. ~ 601 Vallejo Street; 415-392-6739, fax 415-982-3045; www.caffetrieste.com. Another prime location is **Caffe Puccini**, with heavenly homemade *tiramisu*. ~ 411 Columbus Avenue; 415-989-7033. Right on Washington Square is the popular **Mario's Bohemian Cigar Store Cafe**. ~ 566 Columbus Avenue; 415-362-0536, fax 415-362-0112.

The *New Yorker* once called **Hunan Restaurant** "the best Chinese restaurant in the world." Those are pretty big words, hard to substantiate this side of Beijing. But it's certainly one of the best San Francisco has to offer. Understand now, we're talking cuisine, not ambience. The atmosphere at Hunan is characterized by noise and crowds; there is a bar and a contemporary-style dining room adorned with color photographs. But the food will transport you to another land entirely. It's hot, spicy, and delicious. From the dining room you can watch masterful chefs working the woks, preparing pungent sauces, and serving up bean curds with meat sauce, Hunan scallops, and a host of other delectables. A culinary experience well worth the price. ~ 924 Sansome Street; 415-956-7727. MODERATE.

Shopping in North Beach is a grand escapade. As you browse the storefronts here, do like the Sicilians and keep an eye out for Italian treasures such as the hand-painted ceramics and colorful wallhangings still brightening many a home in old Italia.

SHOPPING

Biordi Art Imports provides the Italian answer to gourmet living. Specializing in Italian ceramics, the place is loaded. There are hand-painted pitchers from Florence and De Simone folk art from Palermo, noodle makers and hand-painted dinnerware, wall mirrors framed in ceramic fruit, hand-painted umbrella stands and other high-kitsch items. Walking through this singular shop is like browsing an Italian crafts fair. Closed Sunday. ~ 412 Columbus Avenue; 415-392-8096; www.biordi.com, e-mail info@biordi.com.

No North Beach shopping spree would be complete without a visit to **A. Cavalli & Company**. Operating since 1880, this family business caters to all sorts of local needs. They offer an assortment of Italian cookbooks as well as records and tapes ranging from Pavarotti to Italian new wave. Cavalli's also stocks Italian travel posters, Puccini opera prints, Italian movies on cassette, and magazines from Rome. Closed Sunday. ~ 1441 Stockton Street; 415-421-4219; e-mail jvac@sbcglobal.net.

A longtime East Bay tradition, **Black Oak Books** has opened several sister stores, one of which is in North Beach (across from City Lights, incidentally—the more books the better, I say). In addition to its excellent literary collection, Black Oak also sponsors author readings. ~ 540 Broadway; 415-986-3872.

North Beach, the old Beatnik quarter, is the area for slumming. It's door-to-door with local bars and nightclubs, not to mention the few topless and bottomless joints that still remain along Broadway.

NIGHTLIFE

AUTHOR FAVORITE

A diverse crowd packs the tables and barstools at **Vesuvio Café**, a major North Beach scene, rich in soul and history. The place hasn't changed much since the Beat poets haunted it during the days of Eisenhower, Kerouac, Corso, Ginsberg, and the crew spent their nights here and their days next door at City Lights Bookstore. ~ 255 Columbus Avenue; 415-362-3370, fax 415-362-1613; www.vesuvio.com.

Spec's **Museum Café** is a bohemian haunt. There's nary a bald spot on the walls of this literary hangout; they're covered with all manner of mementos from bumperstickers to a "walrus' penis bone." A great place to get metaphysical. ~ 12 Saroyan Place; 415-421-4112.

To step uptown, just walk down the hill to the **San Francisco Brewing Company**. Built the year after the 1906 earthquake, it's a mahogany-paneled beauty with glass lamps and punkah wallah fans. Legend tells that Jack Dempsey once worked here as a bouncer. It's also the first pub in San Francisco to brew its own beer on the premises. ~ 155 Columbus Avenue; 415-434-3344; www.sfbrewing.com, e-mail greatbeer@sfbrewing.com.

Club Fugazi features an outlandish musical revue, *Beach Blanket Babylon*, which has been running since 1973 (although the script is frequently updated). The scores and choreography are good, but the costumes are great. The hats—elaborate, multi-layered confections—make Carmen Miranda's adornments look like Easter bonnets. Cover. ~ 678 Green Street (Beach Blanket Babylon Boulevard); 415-421-4222; www.beachblanketbabylon. com, e-mail bbb@beachblanketbabylon.com.

Bimbo's 365 Club, a snazzy North Beach institution since 1951, showcases an eclectic mix of live music from jazz and rock to French pop. Call for a list of events. Cover. ~ 1025 Columbus Avenue; 415-474-0365; www.bimbos365club.com.

Fisherman's Wharf

▼ ▼ ▼ ▼ ▼ ▼ ▼ ▼ ▼ ▼ ▼ ▼ ▼

Places have a way of becoming parodies of themselves—particularly if they possess a personal resonance and beauty or have some unique feature to lend the landscape. People, it seems, have an unquenchable need to change them.

Such is the fate of Fisherman's Wharf. Back in the 19th century, a proud fishing fleet berthed in these waters and the shoreline was a quiltwork of brick factories, metal canning sheds, and woodframe warehouses. Genoese fishermen with rope-muscled arms set out in triangular-sailed *feluccas* that were a joke to the west wind. They had captured the waterfront from the Chinese and would be supplanted in turn by Sicilians. They caught sand dabs, sea bass, rock cod, bay shrimp, king salmon, and Dungeness crab. Salt caked their hands, wind and sun gullied their faces.

Today the woodplanked waterfront named for their occupation is hardly a place for fishermen. It has become "Tourist's Wharf," a bizarre assemblage of shopping malls and penny arcades that make Disneyland look like the real world. The old waterfront is an amusement park with a wax gallery, a Ripley's museum, and numerous trinket shops. The architecture subscribes to that modern school which makes everything look like what it's not—there's pseudo-Mission, ready-made antique Victorian, and simulated falsefront.

But salt still stirs the air here and fog fingers through the Bay. There are sights to visit along "the Wharf." It's a matter of recapturing the past while avoiding the plastic-coated present. To do that you need to follow a basic law of the sea—hug the shoreline.

On the corner of Embarcadero and Beach Street, **Pier 39** itself is an elaborately laid-out shopping mall catering primarily to tourists who spill over from neighboring Fisherman's Wharf. In addition to a plethora of waterfront shops and restaurants, Pier 39 features jugglers, yo-yo champs, and other entertainers who delight the crowd with their sleight of hand.

SIGHTS

The central attraction at Pier 39 is the colony of **sea lions** that has taken up residence on the nearby docks. Numbering 400 at times, these thousand-pound pinnipeds are a cross between sea slugs and sumo wrestlers. They began arriving in 1989, taking over a marina, causing a ruckus, and creating the greatest stench this side of a sardine factory. But when Pier 39 attracted over 10 million people the next year, placing it behind Orlando's Walt Disney World and Anaheim's Disneyland as the most popular tourist spot in the country, the local merchants decided to welcome the smelly squatters as permanent residents. On weekends, you can join docents from the Marine Mammal Center for free educational talks about the sea lion's habitat. Meet at the K Dock at Pier 39's west marina. ~ 415-289-7325, fax 415-289-7333; www.tmmc. org, e-mail com@tmmc.org.

For an up-close look at other residents of the San Francisco Bay, including sharks and fish, go to **Aquarium of the Bay**. Journey along moving walkways through a 300-foot-long transparent tunnel into two giant two-story tanks. These tanks contain rays, sal-

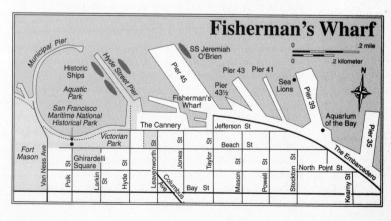

mon, crabs, jellyfish, eels, and more than 150 examples of the six shark species found in surrounding waters. Touch live seastars and other shoreline creatures in the Touch the Bay area. Admission. ~ Pier 39; 415-623-5300, 888-732-3483, fax 415-623-5324; www.aquariumofthebay.com, e-mail info@aquariumofthebay.com.

Among Pier 39's attractions is the shuttle boat to **Forbes Island**, a 50-foot-long fantasyland complete with live palm trees, a sand beach, a waterfall, and a 40-foot-tall lighthouse with an observation deck. Given the theme-park ambience of Fisherman's Wharf, it should come as no surprise that the "island" is actually a self-propelled 700-ton motor vessel in disguise. Admission. ~ Pier 39; 415-951-4900; www.forbesislands.com.

Pier 45 is a working wharf, bleached with bird dung and frequented by fishing boats. From here it's a short jog to the docks on Jefferson Street, located between Jones and Taylor streets. The remnants of San Francisco's fishing fleet lies gunnel to gunnel here. The *Nicky-D*, *Ocean Star*, *Daydream*, *Phu Quy*, *Hai Tai Loc*, and an admiralty of others cast off every morning around 4 a.m. to return in late afternoon. With their brightly painted hulls, Christmas tree rigging, and roughhewn crews, they carry the odor and clamor of the sea.

At the intersection of Taylor Street and the Embarcadero is the **Musée Mécanique**, a collection of vintage mechanical amusements dating to a simpler time. You can put in your change and see them still do their thing. ~ Pier 45; 415-346-2000; www.musee mecanique.com.

Docked at Pier 45 at the Embarcadero is the **S.S. Jeremiah O'Brien**, one of two 2751 World War II Liberty Ships to remain in original condition (the other is docked in Boston). A beamy hulk, the *Jeremiah O'Brien* numbers among its combat ribbons the D-Day invasion of Normandy. Visitors may walk the decks of the old tub, explore the sailors' quarters, and descend into the depths of the engine room. Call ahead for tour information. Admission. ~ 415-544-0100, fax 415-544-9890.

HIDDEN ►   **Fish Alley** is a nostalgic nook. Just duck into the narrow corridor next to Castagnola's Restaurant on Jefferson Street and walk out towards Scoma's Restaurant. Those corrugated metal sheds lining the docks are fish-packing operations. The fleet deposits its daily catch here to be processed for delivery to restaurants and markets. This is an area of piers and pilings, hooks and hawsers, flotsam and fish scales, where you pay a price to recapture the past: as you work farther into this network of docks, approaching nearer and nearer the old salty truths, you'll also be overwhelmed by the putrefying stench of the sea.

For a breather, it's not far to the Hyde Street Pier, where history is less offensive to the nose. Here you'll find the **San Fran-**

cisco **Maritime National Historical Park**. Docked along the length of this wharf are historic ships. You can board the *Eureka*, an 1890 paddlewheeler that ferried commuters between San Francisco and Sausalito for almost 30 years. Recently the largest floating wooden structure on earth, it served as police headquarters for the crime-fighting crew on TV's now-defunct "Nash Bridges." To walk this pier is to stride back to San Francisco's waterfront at the turn of the 20th century. The *Eppleton Hall* is an old paddlewheeler and the *Alma* a "scow schooner" with a flat bottom and square beam. A three-masted merchant ship built in Scotland in 1886, the *Balclutha* measures 301 feet. This steel-hulled craft sailed around Cape Horn 17 times in her youth. She loaded rice in Rangoon, guano in Callao, and wool in New Zealand. Today the old ship's cargo boasts exhibits and a hold full of memories. Stop by the Small Boat Shop and watch volunteers work on restoration projects or try your hand at knot-tying and block-and-tackle work. A visitors center (415-447-5000) is located across from the Hyde Street Pier. Admission. ~ 415-561-7100, fax 415-561-6660; www.nps.gov/safr.

> On a given day there might be jugglers, clowns, or other entertainers performing free at Pier 39.

The nearby **San Francisco Maritime Museum,** in case you mistook it for a ferryboat run aground, is actually an art-deco building designed to resemble the bridge of a passenger liner complete with wildly colorful murals along the first floor. Onboard there's a weird collection of body parts from old ships plus models, scrimshaw displays, and a magnificent photo collection. But perhaps the neatest exhibit is "Sparks, Waves and Wizards." Using a live feed from the U.S. Coast Guard, visitors can use a telescope to spot a vessel entering the Golden Gate, find the ship on a computer screen, and with a click of a button pull up all sorts of information, from vessel speed to cargo contents. ~ Beach and Polk streets; 415-561-7100, fax 415-556-6293; www.nps.gov/safr.

All these nautical showpieces are anchored in **Aquatic Park,** which sports a lovely lawn that rolls down to one of the Bay's few sandy beaches. A mélange of sounds and spectacles, the park has a bocce ball court where you'll encounter old Italian men exchanging stories and curiously eyeing the tourists. There are street vendors galore. If that's not enough, you can watch the Powell and Hyde Street cable cars being turned around for their steep climb back up Nob Hill. Or catch an eye-boggling glimpse of San Francisco Bay. Alcatraz lies anchored offshore, backdropped by one of the prettiest panoramas in this part of the world.

Of course no tour of Fisherman's Wharf is complete without a stop at **The Cannery,** a shopping center with 30 specialty shops. ~ Jefferson and Leavenworth streets; 415-771-3112.

If you're sightseeing with young children, don't miss the **Basic Brown Bear Factory**, located in the Cannery building. Despite the plain-sounding name, the factory makes more than 30 different furry characters and 40 outfits for them. The guided tour includes a history of teddy bears and a demonstration of how they are designed and manufactured. Then the staff helps kids stuff their own bears on the big, noisy stuffing machine, give them "bear baths" to remove excess fuzz, and select personalized outfits and accessories. Daily tours run hourly. Admission. ~ 2801 Leavenworth Street; 800-554-1910; www.basicbrownbear.com, e-mail info@basicbrownbear.com.

Be sure to stop at **Ghirardelli Square**, former site of the chocolate factory, which has been converted into an open-air shopping courtyard. ~ 900 North Point Street; 415-775-5500; www.ghira dellisq.com. For more information, see "Shopping" below.

LODGING   Fisherman's Wharf contains more hotels than fishermen. Most facilities here are overpriced and undernourished. I'm only going to mention a few, since I think you'll do much better financially and experience San Francisco more fully in a downtown or neighborhood hotel.

The first is **The Wharf Inn**, which underwent a major renovation in 2002. With a fresh coat of paint inside and out, new beds and furniture, this four-story affair has 51 moderate-size rooms. Unlike its nearby competitors, free onsite parking is included. The place is clean and bright, offering the same type of facility you could have downtown at a lesser cost. In an area of pricey hotels, The Wharf Inn has some of the best rates around. ~ 2601 Mason Street; 415-673-7411, 800-548-9918, fax 415-776-2181; www.wharfinn.com, e-mail mlaplante@wharfinn.com. DELUXE TO ULTRA-DELUXE.

Lodging in the **Sheraton Fisherman's Wharf**, a sprawling 529-room facility, feature spacious rooms tastefully furnished in Sheraton fashion, plus room service and nightly turndown service. The hotel has other alluring features like a brick-paved entranceway, liveried doormen, swimming pool, and an attractive gift shop. ~ 2500 Mason Street; 415-362-5500, 800-325-3535, fax 415-956-5275; www.sheratonatthewharf.com, e-mail sheraton@meristar. com. ULTRA-DELUXE.

The **Hyatt at Fisherman's Wharf** is a 313-room luxury retreat that is faced in antique brick and illuminated through skylights. It comes complete with a pool, a spa, and a fitness center. ~ 555 North Point Street; 415-563-1234, 800-233-1234, fax 415-749-6122; www.hyatt.com ULTRA-DELUXE.

Smaller in scale than the Hyatt, the 221-room **Tuscan Inn Best Western** is richly decorated and more intimate. This Italian-style boutique hotel features a garden court and an Italianate

Cruising the Bay

Ground zero (water zero?) for the Blue and Gold Fleet—which sponsors Bay cruises, Alcatraz tours, and ferry service to Angel Island, Sausalito, and Tiburon—is Pier 41 near Fisherman's Wharf. ~ 415-773-1188, fax 415-705-5429; www.blueandgoldfleet.com.

The trip to **Alcatraz** is highlighted with a National Park Service tour of the infamous prison. Originally a fort and later a military prison, Alcatraz gained renown as "The Rock" when it became a maximum security prison in 1934. Al Capone, "Machine Gun" Kelly, and Robert "Birdman of Alcatraz" Stroud were among its notorious inmates. On the tour, you'll enter the bowels of the prison, walk the dank corridors, and experience the cage-like cells in which America's most desperate criminals were kept. Be sure to tune in to the audio cassette tour of former guards and prisoners remembering their time at The Rock.

The prison closed in 1963; then in 1969 a group of American Indians occupied the island for almost two years, claiming it as Indian territory. Today Alcatraz is part of the Golden Gate National Recreation Area.

A cruise to **Angel Island State Park** is a different adventure entirely. Unlike "The Rock," this star-shaped island is covered with forest and rolling hills. During previous incarnations it has served as a military installation, quarantine station, immigration center, and prisoner of war camp. Today, the largest true island in San Francisco Bay is a lacework of hiking and biking trails and flowering meadows. For an overview stop by the Visitors Center at Ayala Cove. Here you'll find a diorama and map of the island, historical exhibits, a self-starting 20-minute video that reviews the history of the island and the light fixture from an old lighthouse. You can trek five miles around the island or climb to the top for 360° views of the Bay Area.

Deer graze throughout the area and there are picnic areas galore. It's a perfect spot for a day in the sun. Along the way you can visit the small Immigration Station Museum, which is dedicated to the history of the island's early immigration station. Touching photographs document the story of this "West Coast Ellis Island." Except for the visitors center, which is open year-round, the buildings on Angel Island are open weekends only April through October. A tram operates on weekends in the summer. (The day-use fee is included in the ferry price; however, there is a $5 day-use fee if you bring your own boat.) ~ 415-435-5390; www.angelisland.org.

lobby complete with fireplace. ~ 425 North Point Street; 415-561-1100, 800-648-4626, fax 415-561-1100; www.tuscaninn.com, e-mail sales@tuscaninn.com. ULTRA-DELUXE.

If you're looking for a place with a little more history, try the **Argonaut Hotel**. Housed in the old Haslet warehouse and built in 1907 to store canned goods, this four-story building takes its nautical theme to the limit: a steamer-like front desk, wooden plank floors, and yellow and deep blue hues dominate the decor. It can be a bit much, but certainly adds to the experience. Most rooms feature great views of the bay; the Maritime National Historical Park visitors center is located adjacent to the lobby. Evening wine reception included. ~ 495 Jefferson Street; 800-790-1415, fax 415-563-2800; www.argonauthotel.com. DELUXE TO ULTRA-DELUXE.

DINING   Dining at Fisherman's Wharf usually means spending money at Fisherman's Wharf. The neighborhood's restaurants are over-priced and over-touristed. If you look hard enough, however, it's possible to find a good meal at a fair price in a fashionable res-taurant. Of course, the easiest way to dine is right on the street, at one of the **seafood cocktail stands** along Jefferson Street. An old wharf tradition, these curbside vendors began years ago feed-ing bay fishermen. Today they provide visitors an opportunity to sample local catches like crab, shrimp, and calamari. ~ BUDGET.

A San Francisco favorite, sourdough bread, can be tasted at **Boudin Bakery**. A pungent French bread particularly popular in seafood restaurants, sourdough is the staff of life in these parts. Boudin Bakery, founded in 1849, has had plenty of time to fit its recipe perfectly to the local palate. ~ 156 Jefferson Street; 415-928-1849, fax 415-922-2575. BUDGET.

STARRING GARY DANKO

Dinner at **Gary Danko**, one of San Francisco's top-rated restaurants, is an extravaganza. The eponymous owner, who once built stage sets, envisions each evening as a "performance" featuring a "multi-act meal." The restaurant setting is certainly dramatic enough—with contemporary paintings on taupe walls and a decor that combines oak panels, plantation-style shutters and pin-spot lights to create an intimate but active atmosphere. The seasonal cuisine focuses on freshness and includes signature dishes like lamb loin and roast lobster. They also boast an exceptional wine cellar, special tea service, and a cheese service for which they are renowned. It's a special place for special occasions. Highly recommended. Dinner only. ~ 800 North Point Street; 415-749-2060, fax 415-775-1805; www.gary danko.com, e-mail info@garydanko.com. ULTRA-DELUXE.

Situated between the Wharf and North Beach, **Café Francisco** enjoys the best of both worlds—it's strolling distance from the water and possesses a bohemian flair. A great place for light and inexpensive meals, this trendy café serves salads and sandwiches for lunch. Breakfast at the espresso bar ranges from a continental repast to bacon and eggs. Decorated with changing exhibits by local artists, it attracts a local crowd. ~ 2161 Powell Street; 415-397-2602; www.cafefrancisco.com. BUDGET.

The **Eagle Café** is another old-timer. It's so much a part of San Francisco that plans to tear the place down years ago occasioned a public outcry. Instead of flattening the old woodframe building, they lifted it—lock, stock, and memories—and moved it to the second floor of the Pier 39 shopping mall. Today it looks like an ostrich at a beauty pageant, a plain all-American café surrounded by glittering tourist shops. The walls are covered with faded black-and-white photos, Eagle baseball caps, and other memorabilia. Actually, the bar is more popular than the restaurant. Who wants to eat when they can drink to old San Francisco? The bar is open all day and into the night. ~ Pier 39; 415-433-3689, fax 415-434-9253. BUDGET TO MODERATE.

Would you believe a hidden restaurant in tourist-mobbed Fisherman's Wharf? **Scoma's** is the place. Seafood is the password ◄ HIDDEN to this chummy restaurant. There's *cioppino alla pescatore*, a Sicilian-style broth; *calamone alla anna*, squid prepared "in a totally different manner"; or just plain old sole, snapper, shrimp, or scallops. There's lobster tail, too, and Dungeness crab. ~ Pier 47 near the foot of Jones Street; 415-771-4383, fax 415-775-2601; www.scomas.com. DELUXE TO ULTRA-DELUXE.

For the sights, sounds, and seafood of the San Francisco waterfront, Scoma's is the catch of the day. For spicy food from the subcontinent, everyone's choice is **Gaylord India Restaurant**. From its third floor corner roost in Ghirardelli Square, this fashionable dining emporium enjoys a startling view of San Francisco Bay. It also hosts an extensive menu that varies from tandoori chicken and spiced lamb to meatless entrées such as eggplant baked in a clay oven, creamed lentils, or spiced cauliflower and potatoes. Gaylord creates a warm ambience into which it introduces a deliciously tangy cuisine. ~ 900 North Point Street; 415-771-8822; www.gaylords.com, e-mail gaylords@best.com. MODERATE.

Crisp, clean, and classy is the way to describe **McCormick & Kuleto's**, a popular seafood restaurant in Ghirardelli Square. Natural woods predominate, white tablecloths adorn the tables, and faux tortoiseshell lamps hang from the high ceilings, but the focus of attention is the incredible view of the bay from the floor-to-ceiling windows. The extensive menu changes daily depending on what fish is available and includes such specialties as crab cakes, seafood pastas, seared ahi, alder-smoked salmon, and mesquite-grilled bass fillet. There's also a very lengthy wine list. ~ 900 North Point Street; 415-929-1730, fax 415-567-2919; www.mccormickandkuletos.com. DELUXE TO ULTRA-DELUXE.

Albona Ristorante Istriano is a high-heeled hole-in-the-wall, a small but fashionable restaurant serving Venetian and Central European dishes. The interior is a mélange of beveled mirrors, white linen tablecloths, burgundy banquettes, and fresh flowers. The menu, not to be upstaged, includes sauerkraut braised with prosciutto, pan-fried gnocchi, and exotic entrées like braised rabbit with juniper berries and *brodetto alla Veneziana* (fish stew or soup). Valet parking is complimentary. Dinner only. Closed Sunday and Monday. ~ 545 Francisco Street; 415-441-1040, fax 415-441-5107. MODERATE.

SHOPPING   Fisherman's Wharf is a shopper's paradise . . . if you know what you're doing. If not, it's a fool's paradise. This heavily touristed district houses a mazelike collection of shops, malls, arcades, and galleries. Most of them specialize in high-priced junk. How someone can arrive in the world's most splendid city and carry away some trashy trinket to commemorate their visit is beyond me. But they do. Since you're certainly not the type searching out an "I Got Crabs at Fisherman's Wharf" T-shirt, the best course is to go where the natives shop.

Though its wooden boardwalks and clapboard buildings look promising, **Pier 39** proves hardly the place for bargains or antiques. It's a haven for tourists and features gift stores that range from cutesy card shops to places selling ceramic unicorns. There are restaurants and stores galore, plus an amusement arcade. Kids often enjoy the carnival atmosphere here. ~ Embarcadero and Beach Street; 415-981-7437.

My main objection is to the ticky-tacky shops. Every year, however, millions of tourists disagree with me. They flock to this two-tiered mall, popping in and out of the more than 110 shops and enjoying the ersatz early-20th-century atmosphere.

AUTHOR FAVORITE

Before I buy anything in the City, I go to **Cost Plus World Market** and see if it's there. If so, it's cheaper; if not, maybe I don't really need it. You'll find ceramics, wallhangings, and a host of other items. There are temple rubbings from Thailand, Indian mirrorcloths, scenic San Francisco posters, household furnishings, clothes, gourmet foods, wine, etc. Everything under the sun, at prices to brighten your day. ~ 2552 Taylor Street; 415-928-6200, fax 415-921-2657; www.costplusworldmarket.com.

One noteworthy exception to Pier 39's tourist-oriented selection of shops is **The National Park Store**, the only bookshop I know that comes with a view of sea lions basking in the sun. It offers a complete selection of travel, hiking, and wildlife books and also sells educational toys, American Indian arts and crafts, and other gifts. ~ Pier 39; 415-433-7221.

For locally crafted goods, be sure to watch for the **street vendor stalls**. Located along Beach Street between Hyde and Larkin, and on side streets throughout the area, they offer hand-fashioned wares with homemade price tags. You'll find jewelry, leather belts, statuary, framed photos of the bay city, tie-dye shirts, kites, and anything else the local imagination can conjure.

A popular spot among San Franciscans is the old brick canning factory on Jefferson and Leavenworth streets. Thanks to innovative architects, **The Cannery** has been transformed into a tri-level marketplace dotted with interesting shops. The central plaza, with its olive trees and potted flowers, contains picnic tables, several cafés, and snack kiosks, and features free daily entertainment. Among the dozens of shops are many selling handcrafted originals. ~ 415-771-3112; www.thecannery.com, e-mail info@thecannery.com.

The chocoholics who don't know will be delighted to discover that the home of Ghirardelli chocolate, **Ghirardelli Square**, has been converted into yet another shopping complex. This early-20th-century factory is another example of old industrial architecture being turned to contemporary uses. Around the factory's antique chocolate-making machines is a myriad of shops varying from designer outlets to sundry stores. There are also import stores, boutiques, and so on. ~ 900 North Point Street; 415-775-5500; www.ghirardellisq.com, e-mail laura-ba@sbc.net.

So there you have the secret of shopping Fisherman's Wharf: simply ignore everything else and beeline between the street vendors, Cost Plus, The Cannery, and that brick-red chocolate factory.

The **Eagle Café** appears like some strange bird that has landed in **NIGHTLIFE** the wrong roost. All around lies touristville, polished and preening, while the Eagle remains old and crusty, filled with waterfront characters. Old photos and baseball caps adorn the walls, and in the air hang age-old memories. ~ Pier 39; 415-433-3689, fax 415-434-9253.

Don't know any local people, but still like to party? Head for **Lou's Pier 47**, have a meal, and dance the afternoon and night away. For eats, there are sandwiches, burgers, pastas, and fried, grilled, or sautéed fish and seafood. The bands that play each week in the glass-enclosed nightclub upstairs range from rhythm-and-blues and Motown to light rock. The music begins around 4 p.m. daily. Cover. ~ 300 Jefferson Street; 415-771-5687, fax 415-771-7060; www.louspier47.com.

Buena Vista Café, situated near Fisherman's Wharf, is popular with local folks and tourists alike. There's a fine old bar and friendly atmosphere, and the place claims to have introduced America to the Irish coffee. ~ 2765 Hyde Street; 415-474-5044, fax 415-474-2207.

▼▼▼▼▼▼▼▼▼▼

Russian Hill

Among the city's better-kept secrets is a tumbling residential area called Russian Hill. According to legend, the neighborhood's vaulting slopes were once the site of a cemetery for Russian seal hunters. The Russians have long since departed, leaving the district to local folks and a few canny travelers.

SIGHTS

There's a single block amid Russian Hill's checkerboard streets that stands out in the public imagination. Located along **Lombard Street** between Hyde and Leavenworth, it has earned for Lombard the sobriquet of "The Crookedest Street in the World." Whether

◆◆◆◆◆◆◆◆◆◆◆◆◆◆◆◆◆◆◆◆

Where Filbert Street plummets from Hyde to Leavenworth is the steepest street in the city.

this block represents the planet's most serpentine road remains to be measured; it is certainly the street most congested with shutter-snapping visitors.

Visitors come from around the world to stand astride Lombard's crest and take in the postcard views that stretch in several directions. The western window opens onto the Presidio's wooded expanse; to the north are moored the old ships of Hyde Street Pier and just offshore, Alcatraz Island; eastward rises Telegraph Hill, crowned by Coit Tower and backdropped by Yerba Buena Island. **George Sterling Park**, named for the poet who in turn named San Francisco the "cool grey city of love," stands in the southwest corner of Lombard and Hyde. Its wooded walkways and sunny tennis courts are a cool counterpoint to the surrounding cityscape.

They're also a prelude to the trip down Lombard Street. This dizzying descent happens to be along a beautifully landscaped street. The brick-paved road winds around hedgerows and banks of hydrangea bushes; at the corners, where zig gives way to zag, trees have been planted. You'll have to see for yourself: it's one of those places so cluttered with tourists you never want to admit visiting, but so beautiful you don't want to miss it.

Afterward you'll be ready for even more ethereal realms. Heaven always seems to evoke images of pearl-encrusted gates and shimmering white boulevards. One hopes the saintly place possesses a few country paths as well. If so, they'll undoubtedly be modeled on **Macondray Lane**. To those who wish a preview of eternal life, Macondray waits off Jones between Green and Union streets. For a solitary block, its cobblestone path leads

HIDDEN ►

through a garden, then opens onto a wooden staircase overlooking the Bay. You enter a tunnel of greenery, walled on one side with shingle houses and on the other with an ivy-embowered hillside. It's a realm of flower pots and fluttering birds, one of San Francisco's secret and magical walks.

Lombard Street represents only one of Russian Hill's two crests. Tourists jam the first, while literary historians know the second. To join the cognoscenti, travel up **Vallejo Street** to the 1000 block. Together with Russian Hill Place and Florence Street, nearby cul-de-sacs, this enclave was a gathering place for 19th-century writers. Ambrose Bierce, Frank Norris, and a sheaf of other California authors were part of the area's famous salon. The beauty they sought can be found among the Mediterranean-style haciendas lining **Russian Hill Place**, and the Pueblo Revival houses that have taken over **Florence Street**.

In 1893, Willis Polk, the master architect for whom Polk Street is named, designed and occupied the gingerbread brown-shingle house at **1013–1019 Vallejo Street**. A few things have been added to the Bay view that Polk enjoyed. Today it sweeps from Fisherman's Wharf to Coit Tower to San Francisco's skyscrapers. Nor did Polk have the steps that lead down Vallejo Street's eastern flank one block to **Ina Coolbrith Park** at Vallejo and Taylor streets. This steep swath of green was named for the Oakland librarian who helped a young fellow named Jack London find his way around the literary world.

People go to Union Street for two reasons—shopping and singles bars. Sightseeing is an afterthought. The fact of the matter, however, is that many of the district's trendy shops are housed in magnificent Victorians. So sightseeing can become a case of shopping in architectural wonders.

Union Street

Foremost is the **Octagon House**, built in 1861. This eight-sided heirloom is capped with a turret. The National Society of Colonial Dames of America, which runs the old place, opens it to the public on the second and fourth Thursdays and second Sunday of each month (except January) from noon until 3 p.m. ~ 2645 Gough Street; 415-441-7512.

SIGHTS

The park next door, with its easy slope and tall timber, is a lone remnant from the days when Union Street was "Cow Hollow." Thirty dairies once operated from this grassy dale. What is today the sidewalk of Union Street was then the shoreline of "Washerwoman's Lagoon," a small lake where housewives gathered on laundry day.

The structure at 1980 Union Street gained a mark on the map when an eccentric father built this Siamese twin of a house for his two daughters. It seems they were newlyweds needing dowries, who soon found themselves cozily ensconced in these **Twin Wedding Houses**.

Actually, a grander example of the Victorian-in-a-mirror can be seen in the imposing pair of houses across the street at **1923–1929 Union Street**.

Vendanta House is another structural curiosity. No, it wasn't levitated here from Moscow. It was built on the spot to celebrate the Hindu religion. At the risk of trying to portray the indescribable, it's a sprawling three-story house, maroon and gray, capped with several towers. One tower sports battlements, another a bulbous dome, and yet another a cluster of cupolas. ~ 2963 Webster Street.

Don't neglect the brick courtyard of **St. Mary's Church**. Graced with a garden and wood-shingled church, St. Mary's also has a fountain. A very special fountain. It's actually a spring where early dairy farmers watered their herds back in Cow Hollow days. ~ Union and Steiner streets.

The **Casebolt House** is the last link in this chain of architectural jewels. With two magnificent palm trees guarding the entranceway and a flanking retinue of willows, it presents an imposing sight. Dating from 1865, it was built in an Italianate style; today the ornate white edifice, set on a rise above the street, is as grand as it was back in California's younger days. ~ 2727 Pierce Street.

LODGING   Amid elegant shops and Victorian homes are some of San Francisco's stateliest bed-and-breakfast inns.

Union Street Inn is an excellent choice. The emphasis at this six-room hostelry is on personalized service. Guests are often served full breakfast in the garden, an urban oasis of fruit trees and flowering plants. The rooms are quite cozy, grandly decorated, and imaginatively furnished. The Golden Gate Room features burgundy decor. Cherrywood armchairs cluster around an

---

A SUNNY STAY

An affordable and hip hotel in the Marina? Yes, Virginia, it does exist. Formerly a '50s-style motor lodge, **Hotel Del Sol** uses vibrant colors to re-create the feel of a California beach house. Lounge around the courtyard pool, browse the pillow-lending library (yes, pillow-lending), or borrow the hotel's stash of kites and beach balls to entertain the kids. Fifty-seven guest rooms, ten one-bedroom suites (three with kitchenettes), and one family suite complete with bunk beds and board games are available. Continental breakfast included. ~ 3100 Webster Street; 415-921-5520, 877-433-5765, fax 415-931-4137. DELUXE.

oriental rug and the bed is covered with a quilted spread and topped by a canopy. The "carriage house," a cottage snugly set in the garden, and two other rooms feature private jacuzzis. ~ 2229 Union Street; 415-346-0424, fax 415-922-8046; www. unionstreetinn.com, e-mail innkeeper@unionstreetinn.com. ULTRA-DELUXE.

"Ours is an attempt to return to the original B&B concept popularized in Britain: a modest room at a practical price." At **Edward II Inn** the proprietors have fully realized their motto. Taking the old Hotel Edward, which provided accommodations for the nearby Panama–Pacific International Exposition of 1915, they transformed it into the 32-room (7 of which are suites) Edward II. In the process they provided an opportunity for guests to enjoy bed-and-breakfast luxury at a lower cost. The room I saw was English in decor and included such features as quilted bedspread and a dresser with beveled mirror; the bathroom was tiled and trimmed in wood. Guests enjoy a complimentary continental breakfast and evening sherry. While I highly recommend this facility, I also advise that you ask for a room in back, away from noisy Lombard Street. ~ 3155 Scott Street; 415-922-3000, 800-473-2846, fax 415-931-5784; www.edwardii.com, e-mail reservations@edwardii.com. MODERATE TO ULTRA-DELUXE.

Among the many motels lining busy Lombard Street, only the **Marina Motel** seems to possess character; others are part of the mondo condo world. The Marina is located near a noisy thoroughfare, but most guest rooms are set back off the street. This 38-unit motel resembles a white adobe structure with the clean and tidy rooms surrounding a flower-filled courtyard. About half have kitchens, while all have fridges. Dogs are welcome in certain rooms. ~ 2576 Lombard Street; 415-921-9406, 800-346-6118, fax 415-921-0364; www.marinamotel.com, e-mail marinamotel@value.net. MODERATE.

DINING

Romantic candlelight and hanging Chianti bottles create an inviting ambience at **Luisa's**. The cuisine is Italian with the accent on dishes such as linguine with calamari and osso buco. There are numerous pasta dishes; Luisa also offers homemade gnocchi and bread. Dinner only. Closed Monday. ~ 1851 Union Street; 415-563-4043. MODERATE TO DELUXE.

◀ **HIDDEN**

Joji's House of Teriyaki is a hole in the high-priced wall of Union Street that happens to serve outstanding Japanese and American dishes. In addition to the eponymous teriyaki plates, there's sashimi, pot stickers, and a vegetarian dish. There are also burgers, sandwiches, and salads. For breakfast the ingenious owner serves up "Egg McJoji" on an English muffin with ham and melted cheese, plus numerous omelettes and other egg dishes. A good bet any time of day. ~ 1919 Union Street; 415-563-7808. BUDGET.

Hankering for good food and the feel of an Upper East Side bar? Try **Perry's on Union**. Their menu runs the gamut from grilled ahi tuna sandwiches to meatloaf and chicken fajitas, with more traditional American fare dominating the selection. Wednesday and Saturday nights mean "Lobster Madness" (one and a quarter pounds of fresh Maine catch for a reasonable price) and crowds, so make reservations. You might also enjoy their weekend brunch, especially if you secure a coveted spot outside. ~ 1944 Union Street; 415-922-9022, fax 415-922-0843; www.perrys usa.com, e-mail perry@perrysusa.com. DELUXE.

With its brass rails and mirrored walls, **Prego** is high-tech to the max. The Milanesque interior features a brick oven in which many of the Italian dishes are prepared. There's grilled chicken, veal chops, and fresh fish. The pasta is homemade and the pizza is garnished with everything from prosciutto and artichokes to grilled zucchini and eggplant. Very *chic* and highly recommended. ~ 2000 Union Street; 415-563-3305, fax 415-563-1561. MODERATE TO ULTRA-DELUXE.

The history of the **Balboa Café** is almost as rich as its brass, oak, and stained-glass interior. In operation since 1914, it specializes in California cuisine. The menu varies from lunch to dinner, and includes fresh fish, pork chops, and New York steak. There are appetizers like potato cakes with smoked salmon and calamari *fritti*. A splendid restaurant. ~ 3199 Fillmore Street; 415-921-3944, fax 415-921-3957. DELUXE.

For an intimate pub setting, check out the **Brazen Head**. Its low ceiling, deep woodwork, and burgundy carpeting make it a warm getaway from any lingering SF fog. Meat is the standard fare here, and those who like solid Continental dishes will get their fill. There's an extensive wine list and full bar. Dinner only. ~ 3166 Buchanan Street; 415-921-7600. MODERATE TO DELUXE.

HIDDEN ► Over on Chestnut Street, a few blocks from the chic Union Street corridor, you'll find **Judy's Café**. As the local crowds flowing in here every day attest, it's an excellent dining choice. Judy's is small, intimate, and decorated with signed artwork. There's side-

ALL-AMERICAN

The all-American eatery hereabouts is **Mel's Drive In**, a classic '50s-style joint with push-button jukeboxes and posters of vintage cars. I don't have to tell you we're talking burgers, hot dogs, and chili here. For something more substantial, how about meat loaf or a "ground round plate." And don't forget a side of "lumpy mashed potatoes" or "wet fries" (with gravy). ~ 2165 Lombard Street; 415-921-3039, fax 415-921-3521; www.melsdrive-inn.com. BUDGET TO MODERATE.

walk dining where you can enjoy a lunch menu that features sandwiches and omelette specials. Judy's also offers breakfast and Sunday brunch. No dinner. ~ 2268 Chestnut Street; 415-922-4588, fax 415-922-0149. BUDGET TO MODERATE.

For inexpensive Asian food, try **Yukol Place Thai Cuisine**. The dinner menu includes fried mussels with chile, ginger chicken, and sautéed pork. It's a comfortable restaurant. Dinner only. Closed Sunday. ~ 2380 Lombard Street; 415-922-1599. MODERATE.

Ristorante Parma is a tiny place with mirrored walls and leatherette banquettes, it serves popular southern European dishes nightly. Offerings range from eggplant scallopine, stuffed veal, and saltimbocca to prawns in garlic and lemon-butter sauce or baked petrale. Closed Sunday. ~ 3314 Steiner Street; 415-567-0500, fax 415-567-0457. MODERATE.

Fashionable, French, intimate, and imaginative—**La Folie** combines all the ingredients required of a small San Francisco restaurant. Those heavy French sauces of yore have been replaced with natural sauces and vegetable purées. The menu includes specialties like roti of quail and squab stuffed with wild mushrooms and wrapped in crispy potato strings, and broiled salmon with horseradish and celery-root crust cooked in wine sauce and served with baby vegetables. Dinner only. Closed Sunday. ~ 2316 Polk Street; 415-776-5577, fax 415-776-3431; www.lafolie.com, e-mail la folie@juno.com. ULTRA-DELUXE.

No doubt about it, Union Street is a budget-busting boulevard. Rich in designer fashions and rare imports, this Victorian street sports some of the finest merchandise and heftiest price tags in town. But as the saying goes, it doesn't cost to look.

SHOPPING

Maxamillian is one of those chi chi stores that's more about ultramodern interior design than clothing. A beautiful open room is dotted here and there with racks of beige, tailored women's clothes that make you feel too loud and colorful. They also sell upper-end uniforms. The jewelry is pretty but make sure you speak in muted tones while you look at it. Open afternoons and evenings. Closed Tuesday. ~ 1650 Union Street; 415-922-6668.

Model railroad engineers will find enough new and old model trains, including Marklin, Lionel, and LGB brands, to engineer for the rest of their lives at **Chan's Trains & Hobbies**. A mecca for Bay Area hobbyists, model trains chug on tracks overhead and in the front display window. You'll have to drag your kids out of this place—and maybe yourself, as well. ~ 2450 Van Ness Avenue; 415-885-2899, fax 415-885-6584.

◀ HIDDEN

Kozo sells sheets of exquisite Japanese handmade paper, beautiful fountain pens, blank books, and handmade photo albums, all excellent examples of one of Japan's many art forms. ~ 1969-A Union Street; 415-351-2114; www.kozoarts.com.

One place where you can look, or more properly gaze, is **Enchanted Crystal**. Aglitter with art glass pieces by about 70 artists, this glass palace is also known for its world-class collection of quartz pieces. The window displays—extravagant, wildly imaginative affairs in rock and glass—are magical. As a matter of fact, in addition to its ordinary clientele, this shop caters to metaphysical covens and others knowledgeable in the mesmerizing powers of crystal. ~ 1895 Union Street; 415-885-1335, fax 415-885-0619.

Collectors come from all over the country to purchase the Alaskan and Canadian Inuit art sold at **Images of the North**. This gallery represents artists from across the Artic and sells museum-quality stone sculptures of people, wildlife, and mythological beings carved from soapstone, serpentine, and musk-ox horn, as well as walrus ivory jewelry. The gallery also features prints, masks, jewelry and photography. Even if you can't afford to buy, it's a great place to look. ~ 2036 Union Street; 415-673-1273; www.imagesnorth.com, e-mail mail@imagesnorth.com.

For rare pieces and exquisite decorative items, consider **Silkroute**. Even if you have no intention of buying, this intriguing locale is worth a browse through. You're bound to find carpets from India, ceremonial masks from Africa, and handicrafts from Afghanistan. For history buffs and fans of the Beats, Silkroute is home to The Six Gallery, where Allen Ginsberg first read "Howl." Beat fans are welcome to hang out and share a cup of Afghani tea. ~ 3119 Fillmore Street; 415-563-4936, fax 415-563-3324.

NIGHTLIFE   **Tongue & Groove** is a warm and friendly San Francisco bar and nightclub. Live bands bring the crowds to the dancefloor Thursday through Saturday with rock, hip-hop, and funk. There are several couches for lounging. Cover. ~ 2513 Van Ness Avenue; 415-928-0404; www.tongueandgroovesf.com.

For an archetypal San Francisco fern bar, head to **The Royal Oak**. With its plush Victorian parlor couches, it's a cozy spot for a nightcap. Be sure to open the drawers of any end table; you'll find them full of napkins scrawled with poetry. ~ 2201 Polk Street; 415-928-2303.

To take a rest from the crowds, drop into **Perry's**, where you can actually get a seat at the bar on the weekends. It's a friendly spot and reminiscent of San Francisco in decades past. ~ 1944 Union Street; 415-922-9022, fax 415-922-0843.

If you're in the mood for another kind of action, check out the scene at **Balboa Café**. It's a meat market for the young and upwardly mobile. ~ 3199 Fillmore Street; 415-921-3944.

Perhaps the most famous of all the knolls casting their loving shadows on San Francisco is a prominent promi-nence called Nob Hill. It is a monument to San Fran-cisco's crusty rich—those old powerbrokers who trace their her-itage back to the Big Four. It seems that in the 19th century, Misters Crocker, Huntington, Hopkins, and Stanford—the tycoons who built the transcontinental railroad—chose Nob Hill as the place to honor themselves. They all built estates on top of the 338-foot rise, each more ostentatious than the other. It became, as Robert Louis Stevenson described it, "the Hill of palaces." Until 1906, that is: the fire that followed the great earthquake burned Nob Hill's mansions to the ground.

Nob Hill

All that remains from the robber baron age is the **Pacific Union Club**, a blocky brownstone built in 1855 for a silver king named James Flood. ~ 1000 California Street.

SIGHTS

The **Fairmont Hotel** across the street is a partial survivor. Built just prior to 1906, the shell of this grand building endured; the interior was refurbished in time for the hotel to open on the first anniversary of the earthquake. Today the hotel lobby, with its marble columns and gilt bas-relief, evokes memories of the Big Four. ~ 950 Mason Street.

Once the domain of San Francisco's wealthiest families, Nob Hill now is home to the city's finest hotels. Strung like pearls along California Street, a doorman's whistle from the Fairmont, are three luxurious hotels. Fittingly, the **Stanford Court Hotel, Mark Hopkins Inter-Continental Hotel**, and the **Huntington Hotel**

BRUNCH 'TIL YOU BURST

Reserve a Sunday for brunch at **The Terrace**, located within the Ritz-Carlton, possibly the best in Northern California. A jazz quartet sets the mood for this feast, and dining in the outside courtyard is an option when the sun's out. The gourmet spread includes traditional brunch fare such as eggs Benedict and crêpes, plus a stomach-expanding banquet featuring several varieties of caviar, an assortment of sushi, exotic salads, fresh-from-the-sea shrimp, and oysters on the half shell. And if that isn't enough, you'll definitely want to save room for the to-die-for desserts. Top it off with a glass of cham-pagne, mimosa, or fresh-squeezed orange juice and you won't have to eat for a week. It's worth the splurge for the ultra-deluxe price. Reser-vations advised. ~ 600 Stockton Street; 415-773-6198, 800-241-3333, fax 415-291-0288, www.ritzcarlton.com. ULTRA-DELUXE.

were built upon the ruins of Big Four mansions. That tree-dotted resting place across the street, *naturalement*, is **Huntington Park**.

The nearby **Grace Cathedral** marks San Francisco's attempt at Gothic architecture. Consecrated in 1964 and constructed of concrete, it's not exactly Notre Dame. But this mammoth, vaulting church does have its charm. Foremost are the doors atop the cathedral steps; they represent Lorenzo Ghiberti's "Doors of Paradise," cast in bronze from the artist's original work in Florence. The church interior is graced with a series of wall murals and tiers of stained-glass windows picture such latter-day luminaries as labor leader John L. Lewis, social worker Jane Addams, and astronaut John Glenn. In addition to these architectural adornments, the cathedral is filled with objects as dear as they are sacred—a 15th-century carved oak altar piece, a 13th-century Spanish crucifix, a 16th-century Belgian tapestry, and an organ boasting 7000 pipes. ~ 1051 Taylor Street.

Cathedral, hotels, the park—all are perched in a gilded nest known sarcastically among local folks as "Snob Hill." When you're ready to come down from these heady heights, you might want to decompress slowly by touring some of the area's small townhouses.

You needn't be a millionaire to live along Sacramento Street; you just need lots of money. Take the sprightly **townhouse** at 1172 Sacramento, for instance. With its mansard roof and cast-iron filigree, it could probably be had for a relative pittance. The **1200 block of Sacramento** boasts a string of lovely townhouses, including two structures adorned with wrought-iron tracery. At 1298 Sacramento Street, **Chambord Apartments** is a singular Beaux Arts–style building featuring curved balconies and elaborate exterior ornamentation.

Actually it's only the three square blocks at the very top of Nob Hill that possess the pretension of wealth. The neighborhood below, where the hill slopes westward, is rather folksy. One *HIDDEN* ► enclave is downright rural. That, of course, is **Priest Street**, which rises from Washington Street between Jones and Leavenworth. Priest is not really a street but a staircase, an ivy-banked country lane in the heart of San Francisco. It requires a bit of imagination to fully experience the place. For one thing you have to always gaze to the right, where slender townhouses are bordered with hedges.

On the left side someone has built an astonishingly hideous apartment house. To add irony to insult, they've barricaded the beast behind a chain-link fence topped with a menacing roll of barbed wire. Follow the trail at the end of the road and emerge on an overgrown hill that looks out upon the city. If you continue on this semicircular course, you'll come out on **Reed Street**. Like its counterpart, this "street" is a narrow walkway planted with gardens and tucked between clapboard houses. Perhaps we should call Priest and Reed streets "the Tiny Two," the common

Nob Hill, Pacific Heights, and Japantown

Stockton St
Broadway
Chinatown
Powell St
Stockton Tunnel
Union Square
Powell St
Sacramento St
Fairmont Hotel
Pacific California
Pine St
Bush St
Sutter St
Post St
Geary St
Mason St
Cable Car
Mason St
Huntington Park
Pacific Union Club
Taylor St
Jackson St
Washington St
Clay St
Grace Cathedral
Cable Car
Jones St
Nob Hill
Broadway
Tunnel
Priest St
Reed St
Leavenworth St
Hyde St
Cable Car
Hyde St
Larkin St
Vallejo St
Broadway
Pacific Ave
Jackson St
Washington St
Clay St
Sacramento St
Polk St
California St
Pine St
Bush St
Sutter St
Post St
Geary St
O'Farrell St
Van Ness Ave
Franklin St
Haas-Lilienthal House
Grenlee Terrace
Golden Gate Church
Gough St
Royal Swedish Consulate
Octavia St
old Soto Zen Mission
Geary Expwy
Whittier Mansion
Spreckels Mansion
Lafayette Park
Laguna St
Pacific Heights
Broadway
Pacific Ave
Jackson St
Washington St
Clay St
Sacramento St
Buchanan St
Japantown
Peace Plaza
Japan Center
Mall
Hamlin School
Bourn Mansion
Pacific Heights
Webster St
Pine St
Bush St
Sutter St
Post St
Japan Center
Fillmore St

N
0.4 mile
0.4 kilometer
0
0

folk's answer to Nob Hill's "Big Four." You can take any of the city's three cable car lines to Nob Hill's **Powell–California Street stop**, the only spot in San Francisco where they all intersect.

LODGING

There's an emphasis on style and service at **The Stanford Court**. Its hallmark is the *porte cochère*, illuminated through a leaded-glass dome. The 393 guest rooms combine antiques and modern pieces to create a singular effect. Indulge in a personal morning wake-up call, where tea or coffee is brought to your room. There are two restaurants, a fitness room, several shops and a piano lounge, plus an excellent staff. Of the several well-known hotels that adorn Nob Hill, this is my favorite. Five stars. ~ 905 California Street; 415-989-3500, 800-227-4736, fax 415-391-0513; www.renaissancehotels.com, e-mail sales@stanfordcourt.net. ULTRA-DELUXE.

Of major Nob Hill hotels, **The Huntington** is no doubt the least known, and it seems to like it that way. Constructed in the 1920s as an apartment house, the building was the first steel-and-brick highrise west of the Mississippi. An aura of understated elegance pervades the hotel and its 140 guest rooms and suites, most of which are individually decorated. The Big 4 restaurant, named after the four great railroad magnates—Stanford, Hopkins, Crocker, and Huntington—is a mini-museum of San Francisco and Western memorabilia and also serves exceptional meals in a comfortable, clublike atmosphere. ~ 1075 California Street; 415-474-5400, 800-227-4683, fax 415-474-6227; www.huntingtonhotel. com, e-mail reservations@huntingtonhotel.com. ULTRA-DELUXE.

NIGHTLIFE

If San Francisco tourists were given an association test and asked the first thing that came to mind when a "bar with a view" was mentioned, about 101 out of every 100 would list **The Top of the Mark**. With good reason: from its roosting place in Nob Hill's Mark Hopkins Hotel, this venerable lounge provides extraordinary vistas of the bay and beyond. There's also live music nightly. Dress code. No cover on Tuesday and Wednesday. ~ California and Mason streets; 415-392-3434; e-mail sanfrancisco @interconti.com.

The view ain't shabby at the Huntington Hotel's **Big 4**, either. The intimate, softly lit, wood-paneled bar has comfortable chairs encircling round tables, and live piano music is performed nightly. ~ 1075 California Street; 415-771-1140, fax 415 474-6227.

Japantown

Center of culture for San Francisco's burgeoning Japanese population is Japantown, a self-contained area bounded by Geary, Post, Laguna, and Fillmore streets. This town-within-a-city consists of two sections: the old part, where residential housing is located, and a newer commercial area.

Japan Center, designed by architect Minoru Yamasaki, is a five-acre monstrosity. Built in 1968, it exemplifies the freeway architecture of the era. There are, nonetheless, fascinating shops and outstanding restaurants located in this Asian mall.

SIGHTS

You'll also encounter special features here and there. Like the **Peace Pagoda,** a five-tiered structure designed by world-renowned architect Yoshiro Taniguchi as an expression of friendship and goodwill between the people of Japan and America.

During the April Cherry Blossom Festival, August Street Fair, Autumn Bon Dances, and the Aki Matsuri festival in September, Japantown turns out in splendid costumes for musical celebrations. All year round you can enjoy **Nihonmachi Mall** (on Buchanan Street) with its cobblestone pathway and lovely Ruth Asawa origami fountains. There are also park benches featuring bas-reliefs done by local children. Pass through the *torii* gate here, then head up to 1881 Bush Street, and you'll encounter the time-battered **Soto Zen Mission,** a center for the city's ardent *go* players.

Japantown has two excellent hotels that provide a "chance to experience the tranquilities of the East and the amenities of the West."

LODGING

One of the most reasonable accommodations in the area, the **Best Western Miyako Inn** has 125 rooms. The lobby is simple but comfortable, featuring plump armchairs. There is also a restaurant on the premises. ~ 1800 Sutter Street; 415-921-4000, 800-528-1234, fax 415-563-1278; www.bestwestern.com/miyakoinn, e-mail miyakoin@ix.netcom.com. MODERATE TO DELUXE.

Its sibling, and foremost among the city's Asian-style hotels is the **Radisson Miyako Hotel.** Architecturally the building lacks appeal. The interior is another matter. Pass through the sliding glass doors and you'll enter an oriental milieu. The private rooms

◆◆

AAHHH!!

For the ultimate in relaxation after a full day of sightseeing, visit **Kabuki Springs & Spa,** where the main attraction is a series of hot and cold traditional Japanese communal baths. The baths are open to women only on Sunday, Wednesday, and Friday, and men only on Monday, Thursday, and Saturday, bathing suits optional. Tuesday is coed, suits required. In addition, a wide range of spa services are available, including shiatsu and Swedish massage, seaweed wraps, acupuncture, Ayurvedic rebalancing, and Javanese lulur body treatments. None of this is inexpensive, of course, but you'll leave feeling like a million bucks. ~ 1750 Geary Boulevard; 415-922-6000, fax 415-922-6005; www.kabukisprings.com.

are adorned with Japanese prints; behind the colorful shoji screens are balconies overlooking a garden. Be sure to ask for a sunken Japanese tub. Some of the special rooms are entirely Japanese in furnishing and decoration with tatami mats, futons, and built-in saunas. The Miyako represents one of the city's most exotic hotels. ~ 1625 Post Street; 415-922-3200, 800-333-3333, fax 415-921-0417; www.miyakohotel.com, e-mail info@miyako hotel.com. ULTRA-DELUXE.

DINING

The Japan Center building houses several Japanese dining establishments, including a *shokuji dokoro*, or traditional bistro, called **Koji Osakaya**. Here the atmosphere is mannered and reserved. Japanese tradition at its finest. ~ 1737 Post Street; 415-922-2728. MODERATE.

Tired of humdrum sushi bars? Bored with sea urchin platters? Then **Isobune** is the place for you. Here those raw fish finger foods scud past you on wooden boats along a miniature canal. No joke—we're talking sushi on a stream. You simply sit at the counter and pluck off your favorite cargo as the boat goes by. There are numerous sushi selections, as well as soup and sashimi. ~ 1737 Post Street; 415-563-1030, fax 415-563-3337. MODERATE.

Recommended by local residents and gourmets alike, **Sanppo Restaurant** serves excellent food at fair prices. In addition to outstanding sushi, they offer lemon steak, garlic chicken, *chanko nabe* (a fish, chicken, and vegetable dish), tempura, and *donburi* dishes. The interior is unsophisticated café-style, but the cuisine is worthy of a plush establishment. Three stars over Japantown. ~ 1702 Post Street; 415-346-3486. MODERATE.

SHOPPING

In this Asian neighborhood, most shopping is done in Japan Center, a modern mall. As you'll discover, most of the listings below are located in this commercial complex.

Shige Nishiguchi Kimono & Antiques specializes in antique kimonos, those gorgeous heavy silk garments but have new kimonos as well. They also have dolls dressed in kimono miniatures. ~ 1730 Geary Boulevard; 415-346-5567.

Similarly, **Asakichi** features antique furniture as well as Asian arts and crafts. Take special note of those heavy wood antique chests called *tansu*. Cluttered but fascinating, this shop also carries porcelain dinnerware, sake cups, tea ceremony utensils and antique fabrics. ~ 1730 Geary Boulevard #150; 415-921-2147, fax 415-928-1987.

Also worthy of notice is **Kinokuniya Stationery and Gift**, which stocks Japanese postcards, calendars, and writing supplies. ~ 1581 Webster Street; 415-567-8901.

One of Japan Center's most captivating stores is **Mashiko Folkcraft**, a museum-cum-shop displaying Japanese folk art. Among the exhibits, you might find an 18th-century tobacco set or a hand-painted papier-mâché pillow. The prices often match the age of these precious objects, but there are affordable items—like ceramic dishes and porcelain chopstick rests. ~ 1581 Webster Street; 415-346-0748.

Pacific Heights

San Francisco's most prestigious neighborhood resides on a hill looking down upon the Bay. In addition to Rolls-Royces and Mercedes Benzes, Pacific Heights contains some of the city's most outstanding architecture. Stroll the wide streets and you will encounter straitlaced Tudor homes, Baroque confections, and elaborate Victorians.

SIGHTS

Best place to begin touring this palatial ridgetop is the corner of Franklin and California streets. That twin-turreted structure on the corner is a **Queen Anne–style Victorian**, built for a 19th-century figure who made his fortune in gold and lumber. Its poorer neighbors up the hill are **Italianate-style Victorians**, characterized by slanting edge bay windows; both date to the 1870s.

Head north on Franklin Street to 1735 Franklin, a brick **Georgian-style house** built at the turn of the 20th century for a family of coffee barons. The **Golden Gate Church** is a Baroque Revival structure built in 1900 for the Crockers, one of California's most powerful families. ~ 1901 Franklin Street.

The **Haas-Lilienthal House**, perhaps the grandest of all San Francisco's Victorians, is a Queen Anne gingerbread fantasy adorned with gables and bas-relief figures. Today it's a house museum, operated by San Francisco Architectural Heritage, open to the public Wednesday, Saturday and Sunday afternoons on docent-led tours only. Admission. ~ 2007 Franklin Street; 415-441-3004; www.sfheritage.com, e-mail info@sfheritage.org.

Turn left on Jackson and continue uphill to **Grenlee Terrace**. With its white stucco facade and red tile roof, this sophisticated apartment house follows a Mission Revival motif and dates from 1913. ~ 1925 Jackson Street. The stately brick building across the street houses the **Royal Swedish Consulate**. ~ 1950 Jackson Street. Also nearby is the **Whittier Mansion**, a red sandstone structure built in 1896. ~ 2090 Jackson Street.

Turn right on Laguna, go downhill, then left on Broadway. That stern three-story edifice with lions on either side of the entranceway is the **Hamlin School**. Designed as a Baroque Revival mansion, it was constructed in 1901. ~ 2120 Broadway. James

> Despite the bold tower, ornate design, and sheer size of the place, the Haas-Lilienthal House cost less than $20,000 to build. Of course, that was back in 1886.

Flood, the man who commissioned the building, also built the white marble **Renaissance-style palazzo** at 2222 Broadway.

Go back a half-block and turn uphill on Webster Street. The **Bourn Mansion** is a Georgian townhouse that was built in 1896 by William Bourn, one of California's wealthiest businessmen. ~ 2550 Webster Street.

Take a left on Washington Street and continue to **Lafayette Park** between Washington and Laguna streets, a beautiful tree-dotted park with a rolling lawn. Across the street at 2080 Washington Street rises the **Spreckels Mansion**, an ornate edifice with a white limestone surface that is beginning to fall to the forces of San Francisco's wind and weather. There are literally hundreds more houses to visit in this neighborhood. If this thumbnail tour has merely whetted your architectural appetite, you can continue alone, strolling these heights, searching out vestiges of San Francisco's baronial history.

LODGING

For fashionable living, consider **Hotel Drisco**. This 48-room hotel survived the 1906 earthquake and fire and went on to serve four generations of guests. Located in the city's poshest area, the Drisco has undergone a complete renovation. Both the small standard rooms and the roomier suites combine modern and antique furnishings and offer oversized baths. And the place still retains some of its old charms—like the downstairs dining room, the dark wood lobby, the nightly wine reception, and the complimentary buffet breakfast. ~ 2901 Pacific Avenue; 415-346-2880, 800-634-7277, fax 415-567-5537; www.hoteldrisco.com, e-mail resinfo@hoteldrisco.com. ULTRA-DELUXE.

Chain establishments sometimes get a bad rap, but the **Laurel Inn** is a boutique hotel that's truly lovely. The art-deco interior hides super-modern comforts. Eighteen of the forty-nine colorful guest rooms have kitchenettes; many have pretty views of the neighborhood. Continental breakfast is included, as is a lending library of CDs and videos. ~ 444 Presidio Avenue; 415-567-8467, 800-552-8735, fax 415-928-1866; www.laurelinn.com, e-mail khegre@jdvhospitality.com. DELUXE.

DINING

While Pacific Heights is primarily residential there are a few options. You'll also find dining rooms in the "Upper Fillmore" area and along Sacramento Street. Both of these gentrified districts feature a host of gourmet restaurants. The best way to uncover them is by exploring the area.

Upper Fillmore reaches from Bush Street to Jackson Street, wedged between a proletarian neighborhood and posh Pacific Heights. The accent is on the latter locale, however, and the street is lined with good dining places. Most are restaurants characterized by canvas awnings, hand-lettered signs, brass rails, and ever-changing menus.

At **Little Joe's** the food is outstanding and it's prepared before your eyes by some of the city's great showmen. Working a row of oversized frying pans, these jugglers rarely touch a spatula. Rather, with a snap of the wrist, they flip sizzling veal, steak, or calamari skyward, then nonchalantly catch it on the way down. This restaurant also serves delicious fish, roast chicken, and sausage dishes, each accompanied by pasta and sautéed vegetables. Very crowded, especially on weekends. ~ 2550 Van Ness Avenue; 415-433-4343. MODERATE.

My personal favorite is the **Élite Café**, a spiffy establishment with overhead fans and private oak-paneled booths. Open for dinner and Sunday brunch, the Élite specializes in Cajun-Creole cuisine. Appetizers include gumbo and Gulf oysters; the main courses vary daily and may feature blackened fish, filet mignon with Cajun butter, housemade sausage and jambalaya, or broiled sea bass with pecan rice. ~ 2049 Fillmore Street; 415-346-8668, fax 415-346-9324. DELUXE TO ULTRA-DELUXE.

La Méditerranée, or La Med, as regulars like to call it, is an excellent Mediterranean restaurant squeezed into small digs. The lighting is low and seating cozy, but the hummus and tabbouleh are to die for. Customers rave about the Mezze (there's also a veggie version), which lets couples sample almost everything on the menu. Try the Middle Eastern plate or opt for a phyllo-dough creation. ~ 2210 Fillmore Street; 415-921-2956; www.lamediter ranee.net. MODERATE.

Away from the hustle and bustle of Fillmore Street lies **Osteria**, a charming neighborhood eatery. With a soft cream-colored interior and murals of vineyards on the walls, rural Tuscany comes to life. Fresh pastas (wonderful capellini and homemade gnocchi) and tasty salads keep a consistent clientele coming back for more. Friendly service and great food make this little place a true find. Dinner only. Closed Monday. ~ 3277 Sacramento Street; 415-771-5030. MODERATE.

SHOPPING

Upper Fillmore and Sacramento Street are convenient shopping districts close to Pacific Heights. "Upper" Fillmore is a doubleentendre referring to class as well as altitude. Stretching from Sutter Street

RETRO-CHIC REVIVED

The clothing at **Betsey Johnson** may look used, but the pricetags will tell you otherwise. The ultimate in retro designer fashion, Betsey's will make you wish you hadn't thrown out those old clothes in the back of your closet. You could sell them and make a fortune. ~ 2031 Fillmore Street; 415-567-2726; www.betseyjohnson.com.

to Jackson Street in Pacific Heights, it's a gently sloping boulevard lined with designer shops. Along this seven-block row are galleries, gourmet food outlets, boutiques, and bath accessory stores. *Très chic.*

Speaking of *chic*, consider **Seconds To Go**, which has used clothing for guys and gals. ~ 2252 Fillmore Street; 415-563-7806.

Francophiles will adore **Nest**, with its funky collection of handbags, jewelry, and French-inspired houseware. ~ 2300 Fillmore Street; 415-292-6199.

One of the streets crossing this upper Fillmore promenade is Sacramento. Follow it several blocks west and you'll discover another fast-growing shoppers' strip. The stores here are not as concentrated, but scattered between Broderick and Lyon streets are a number of boutiques and trendy shops.

A real neighborhood shopping area, **Sacramento Street** combines galleries, boutiques, and antique stores with shops serving the immediate needs of local folks. You can combine your shopping with a tour of this vintage area, which contains a number of impressive Victorian homes.

NIGHTLIFE   Located just below Pacific Heights in the Fillmore District, the **Fillmore** showcases national rock, folk, blues, and country acts, this Victorian-style venue continues the legacy started by promoter Bill Graham in 1966, when bands such as the Jefferson Airplane and the Grateful Dead rang in a new era. Stained-glass chandeliers highlight the huge dancefloor and balcony seats. ~ 1805 Geary Boulevard; 415-346-6000; www.thefillmore.com, e-mail fillmore@sfx.com.

▼ ▼ ▼ ▼ ▼ ▼ ▼ ▼ ▼ ▼ ▼ ▼ ▼ ▼
Golden Gate National Recreation Area

One of San Francisco's most spectacular regions belongs to us all. The Golden Gate National Recreation Area, a 74,000-acre metropolitan park, draws about 20 million visitors annually. A place of natural beauty and historic importance, this magnificent park stretches north from San Francisco throughout much of the Bay Area. In the city itself, the Golden Gate National Recreation Area forms a narrow band around the waterfront. It follows the shoreline of the Bay from Aquatic Park to Fort Mason to the Golden Gate Bridge. On the ocean side it encompasses Land's End, an exotic and untouched preserve, as well as the city's finest beaches.

SIGHTS   The most serene way to begin exploring the Golden Gate National Recreation Area is via the **Golden Gate Promenade**. This three-and-a-half-mile walk will carry you across a swath of heaven that extends from Aquatic Park to the shadows of the Golden Gate Bridge.

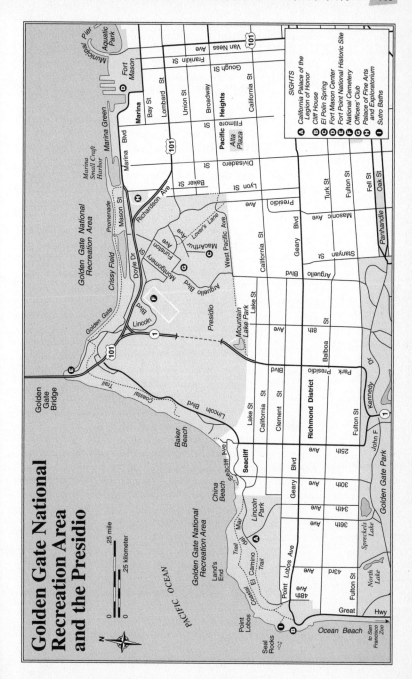

Golden Gate National Recreation Area and the Presidio

PACIFIC OCEAN

SIGHTS
- **A** California Palace of the Legion of Honor
- **B** Cliff House
- **C** El Polin Spring
- **D** Fort Mason Center
- **E** Fort Point National Historic Site
- **F** National Cemetery
- **G** Officers' Club
- **H** Palace of Fine Arts and Exploratorium
- **I** Sutro Baths

0 25 mile
0 25 kilometer

Aquatic Park
Municipal Pier
Fort Mason
Marina Green
Marina Small Craft Harbor
Promenade
Crissy Field
Golden Gate National Recreation Area
Golden Gate Bridge
Baker Beach
China Beach
Seacliff
Lincoln Park
Golden Gate National Recreation Area
Land's End
Point Lobos
Seal Rocks
Ocean Beach
to San Francisco Zoo

Van Ness Ave
Franklin St
Gough St
California St
Broadway
Union St
Lombard St
Bay St
Marina
Pacific Heights
Alta Plaza
Fillmore St
Divisadero St
Baker St
Lyon St
Richardson Ave
Mason St
Doyle Dr
Lincoln Blvd
Montgomery St
Funston Ave
MacArthur Ave
Lover's Lane
West Pacific Ave
Arguello Blvd
Lincoln Blvd
Coastal Trail
Presidio
Golden Gate National Recreation Area
Presidio Ave
Geary Blvd
Turk St
Fulton St
Fell St
Oak St
Panhandle
Masonic Ave
Stanyan St
California St
Lake St
Mountain Lake Park
8th Ave
Balboa
Park Presidio Blvd
Richmond District
California St
Clement St
Fulton St
25th Ave
30th Ave
34th Ave
36th Ave
43rd Ave
48th Ave
Point Lobos Ave
Geary Blvd
Seacliff Ave
El Camino Del Mar
Coastal Trail
Golden Gate Park
Spreckels Lake
North Lake
John F. Kennedy Dr
Fulton St
Great Hwy

Just start in the park and make the short jaunt to the **Municipal Pier**. This hook-shaped cement walkway curls several hundred yards into the Bay. As you follow its curving length, a 360-degree view unfolds—from the Golden Gate to the Bay Bridge, from Mt. Tamalpais to Alcatraz to downtown San Francisco. The pier harbors fisherfolk and seagulls, crabnetters and joggers; few tourists seem to make it out here.

From the pier it's uphill and downstairs to **Fort Mason Center**, a complex of old wharves and tile-roof warehouses that was once a major military embarkation point. Fort Mason today is the cultural heart of avant-garde San Francisco. This National Historic Landmark houses theaters, museums, and a gourmet vegetarian restaurant, and hosts thousands of programs and events. ~ Marina Boulevard and Buchanan Street; 415-441-3400, fax 415-441-3405; www.fortmason.org, e-mail contact@fortmason.org.

Nearly all the arts and crafts are represented—several theater groups are home here; there is an on-going series of workshops in dance, creative writing, painting, weaving, printing, sculpture, music, and so on. A number of environmental organizations also have offices in the center. As one brochure describes, "You can see a play, stroll through a museum or gallery, learn how to make poetry films, study yoga, attend a computer seminar, or find out about the rich maritime lore of San Francisco."

At the **San Francisco Craft and Folk Art Museum** exhibitions range from Cook Island quilts to San Simeon architect Julia Morgan's craftware. You'll also want to visit the gift shop where they sell native and tribal goods, as well as a wide variety of jewelry and contemporary craft. Closed Monday. Admission. ~ Building A; 415-775-0991, fax 415-775-1861; www.mocfa.org, e-mail admin@sfcraftandfolk.org.

Museo ItaloAmericano presents samplings of Italian artistry. The museum is dedicated to displaying the works of Italian and Italian-American artists and culture. The permanent collection features the work of several artists, some of whom have made San Francisco their home for years. Docent-led group tours available by appointment. Closed Monday and Tuesday. Admission. ~ Building C; 415-673-2200, fax 415-673-2292; www.museoitaloamericano.org, e-mail museo@firstworld.net.

Now that you're fully versed in the arts, continue on the shoreline to the **Marina**, along Marina Boulevard. (The remainder of the tour can be completed by car, though walking is definitely the aesthete's and athlete's way.) Some of this sailor-city's spiffiest yachts are docked along the esplanade.

Nearby **Marina Green**, a stretch of park paralleling the Bay, is a landlubber's haven. Bicyclers, joggers, jugglers, sunbathers, and a world of others inhabit it. The park's most interesting denizens are the kitefliers who fill the blue with a rainbow of soaring colors.

Continue on past a line-up of luxury toys—boats with names like *Haiku*, *Sea Lover*, *Valhalla*, and *Windfall*. When you arrive at the far end of that small green rectangle of park, you'll have to pay special attention to your navigator; you're on Marina Boulevard at the corner of Yacht Road; if going by car, proceed directly ahead through the U.S. Army gate and follow Mason Street, Crissy Field Avenue, and Lincoln Boulevard, paralleling the water, to Fort Point; if on foot, turn right onto Yacht Road, then left at the waterfront, and follow the shoreline toward the Golden Gate Bridge.

Before doing either, you have an alluring detour in store. Turn left at Yacht Road, cross Marina Boulevard, and proceed to that magnificent Beaux-Arts monument looming before you. It's the **Palace of Fine Arts**, a domed edifice built of arches and shadows. Adorned with molded urns and bas-relief figures, it represents the only surviving structure from the 1915 Panama–Pacific International Exposition. Happily, it borders on a sun-shivered pond. The pond in its turn is peopled by mallards and swans, as well as pintails and canvasbacks from out of town. Together, the pool, the pillars, and surrounding park make this one of the city's loveliest spots for sitting and sunning.

But enough for detours; we were embarked on a long march to the bridge. If you cheated and drove, you're already at Fort Point, and we'll catch up with you later; otherwise you're on foot, with the Bay at your side and the Golden Gate dead ahead. This is a land where freighters talk to foghorns, and sloops scud along soundlessly. The waterfront is a sandy beach, a rockpile in seeming upheaval, then beach again, sand dunes, and occasional shade trees. That wooded grove rising to your left is the Presidio; those bald-domed hills across the Bay to the right are the Marin Headlands, and the sharp-rising buildings poking at your back are part of the San Francisco skyline. You'll pass a Coast Guard Station and a fishing pier before arriving at the red brick fort that snuggles in the arch of the Golden Gate Bridge.

> At Fort Point, if you follow the spiral granite staircase to the roof, you'll stand directly beneath the Golden Gate Bridge and command a sentinel's view out into the Pacific.

Modeled on Fort Sumter and completed around the time Confederate forces opened fire on that hapless garrison, **Fort Point National Historic Site** represents the only brick fort west of the Mississippi. With its collection of cannons and Civil War–era exhibits, it's of interest to history buffs. Open Friday through Sunday. Call for hours and information on guided tours and special programs. ~ End of Marine Drive; 415-556-1693, fax 415-561-4390; www.nps.gov/fopo.

From Fort Point, a footpath leads up to the observation area astride the **Golden Gate Bridge**; if driving, take Lincoln Boulevard to the vista point. By whichever route, you'll arrive at "The Bridge at the End of the Continent." Aesthetically, it is considered one of the world's most beautiful spans, a medley of splayed cable and steel struts. Statistically, it represents one of the longest suspension bridges anywhere—6450 feet of suspended concrete and steel, with twin towers the height of 65-story buildings and cables that support 200 million pounds. It is San Francisco's emblem, an engineering wonder that has come to symbolize an entire metropolis.

If you're game, you can walk across, venturing along a dizzying sidewalk out to one of the most magnificent views you'll ever experience. The Bay from this height is a toy model built to scale; beyond the bridge, San Francisco and Marin, slender arms of land, open onto the boundless Pacific.

The Golden Gate Promenade ends at the bridge, but Lincoln Boulevard continues along the cliffs that mark the ocean side of San Francisco. There are **vista points** overlooking the Pacific and affording startling views back toward the bridge. After about a mile you'll reach **Baker Beach**, a wide corridor of white sand. Ideal for picnicking and sunbathing, this lovely beach is a favorite among San Franciscans. ~ Off Lincoln Boulevard on Gibson Road. Adventurers can follow this strand, and the other smaller beaches with which it connects, on a fascinating walk back almost all the way to the Golden Gate Bridge. With the sea unfolding on one side and rocky crags rising along the other, it's definitely worth

HIDDEN ► a little sand in the shoes. As a final reward, there's a **nude beach** on the northern end, just outside the bridge.

Lincoln Boulevard transforms into El Camino del Mar, which winds through Sea Cliff, one of San Francisco's most affluent res-

IT'S HANDS-ON TIME HERE

If education is on your mind, note that the Palace of Fine Arts houses the **Exploratorium**. A great place to bring children, this "hands-on" museum, with imaginative exhibits demonstrating the principles of optics, sound, animal behavior, etc., was once deemed "the best science museum in the world" by *Scientific American*. It's an intriguing place with constantly changing temporary exhibits and permanent displays that include a "distorted room" lacking right angles and an illusionary mirror into which you seemingly pass. Also check out the Tactile Dome (reservations required; separate admission), a pitch-black crawl-space of textural adventures. Closed Monday from September through May, except on holidays. Admission. ~ Marina Boulevard and Lyon Street; 415-561-0360, fax 415-561-0370; www.exploratorium.edu.

idential neighborhoods. This exclusive area has something to offer the visitor in addition to its scenic residences—namely **China Beach** (formerly known as James Phelan Beach). More secluded than Baker, this pocket beach is backdropped by a rocky bluff atop which stand the luxurious plate-window homes of Sea Cliff. Named for the Chinese fishermen who camped here in the 19th century, the beach has a dilapidated beach house and restroom facilities. (To get there, turn right on 25th Avenue, left on Sea Cliff Avenue, then follow until it dead ends.)

Continuing on El Camino del Mar as it sweeps above the ocean, you'll come upon San Francisco's prettiest museum. With its colonnaded courtyard and arching entranceway, the **California Palace of the Legion of Honor** is modeled after a gallery in Paris. In fact, a mini pyramid mirroring the one at the Louvre sits in the courtyard, letting light into the gallery below. Appropriately, it specializes in European art and culture. The exhibits trace European aesthetic achievements from ancient Greek and Roman art to the religious art of the Middle Ages to Renaissance painting, the Baroque and Rococo periods, and the Impressionists of the 19th and 20th centuries. Closed Monday. Admission. ~ Lincoln Park, 34th Avenue and Clement Street; 415-750-3600, fax 415-750-3656; www.legionofhonor.org, e-mail guestbook@famsf.org.

After you've drunk in the splendid view of city and Bay from the museum grounds, head downhill on 34th Avenue past the golf course, turn right on Geary Boulevard, which becomes Point Lobos Avenue, then turn right on to El Camino del Mar and follow it to the end. (Yes, this is the same street you were on earlier; no, I'm not leading you in circles. It seems that years ago landslides collapsed the midriff of this highway, leaving among the survivors two dead-end streets known forever by the same name.)

This is **Land's End**, a thumb-like appendage of real estate that ◄ HIDDEN
San Francisco seems to have stolen from the sea. It is the nearest you will ever approach to experiencing San Francisco as the Costanoan Indians knew it. Hike the trails that honeycomb the hillsides hereabout and you'll enter a wild, tumbling region where winds twist cypress trees into the contours of the earth. The rocks offshore are inhabited by slithering sea creatures. The air is loud with the unceasing lash of wave against shoreline. Land's End is San Francisco's grand finale—a line of cliffs poised at the sea's edge and threatening imminently to slide into eternity.

From the parking lot located at the end of El Camino del Mar, walk down the steps that begin at the U.S.S. *San Francisco* Memorial Flagpole, and head east on the trail to the water. That dirty blonde swath of sand is a popular **nude beach,** perfectly sit- ◄ HIDDEN
uated here in San Francisco's most natural region.

(Note: While hiking the footpaths in the region, **beware!** Land's End is plagued by landslides and foolish hikers. Remain on the trails. Exercise caution and this exotic area will reward you with eye-boggling views of Marin's wind-chiseled coast.)

Continuing down Point Lobos Avenue, at the corner where the road turns to parallel the Pacific Ocean, rest the ruins of the **Sutro Baths**. From the configuration of the stones, it's a simple trick to envision the foundation of Adolf Sutro's folly; more difficult for the mind's eye is to picture the multitiered confection that the San Francisco philanthropist built upon it in 1896. Sprawling across three oceanfront acres, Sutro's baths could have washed the entire city. There were actually six baths total, Olympian in size, as well as three restaurants and 500 dressing rooms—all contained beneath a stained-glass dome.

Towering above them was the **Cliff House**, a Gothic castle that survived the earthquake only to be consumed by fire the next year. Following several reincarnations, the Cliff House is a rather bland structure housing several restaurants and tourist shops. It is currently undergoing a major renovation. Only one dining room and the gift shop remain open during construction. The main floor is scheduled for completion in summer 2004; the rest of the site will re-open later that year. However, from this crow's nest you can gaze out over a sweeping expanse of ocean. ~ 1090 Point Lobos Avenue.

A controversy once surrounded the **Camera Obscura** (415-750-0415), the camera-shaped kiosk near the Cliff House. The National Park Service, which leases the land on which this venerable old-time tourist attraction stands, wanted to tear the building down and move the camera's inner workings to a visitors center. Public outcry resulted in the addition of the Camera Obscura to the National Register of Historic Places, which will protect it permanently. So rest assured that you'll be able to stand inside this dark chamber and watch as a rotating lens and mirror, based on a 16th-century design by Leonardo da Vinci, projects a panoramic view that takes in the Cliff House, the Sutro Baths and the

AUTHOR FAVORITE

Located on Skyline Boulevard at the far end of Ocean Beach, **Fort Funston** is the prettiest stretch to stroll. The fort itself is little more than a sequence of rusting gun emplacements, but there is an environmental education center and a half-mile nature trail here that winds along cliffs overlooking the sea. It's a windblown region of dune grass and leathery succulent plants, with views that span San Francisco and alight on the shore of Marin. Hang gliders dust the cliffs of Fort Funston, adding another dramatic element to this spectacle of sun and wind.

Golden Gate Bridge, and **Seal Rocks,** which lie just offshore. (The seals for which the rocks were named have all moved to Pier 39 at Fisherman's Wharf, but other sea lions take up residence on the rocks during the spring months.) Admission. Note: During Cliff House renovations, the Camera Obscura will remain closed.

Below the Cliff House, extending to the very end of vision, is the Great Highway. The salt-and-pepper beach beside it is **Ocean Beach,** a slender ribbon of sand that decorates three miles of San Francisco's western perimeter. Remember, this is San Francisco— land of fog, mist, and west winds—beachwear here more often consists of sweaters than swimsuits. The water, sweeping down from the Arctic, is too cold for mere mortals; only surfers and polar bear swimmers brave it. Nevertheless, to walk this strand is to trek the border of eternity. American Indians called San Francisco's ocean the "sundown sea." If you'll take the time some late afternoon, you'll see that the fiery orb still settles nightly just offshore.

At the intersection of Skyline and Lake Merced boulevards lies **Lake Merced,** a U-shaped reservoir that has the unusual distinction of once having been salt water. Bounded by the Harding Park golf links and hiking trails, it provides a pretty spot to picnic. If you decide to pass up the hang gliding at Fort Funston, you might rent a rowboat or canoe at the clubhouse here and try a less nerve-jangling sport. The lake is stocked with catfish and trout.

Heading back along the Great Highway, you'll encounter the **San Francisco Zoo.** Countless changes have taken place over the past few years as part of an ambitious rebuilding progam. The long-time main entrance on Sloat Boulevard has moved to the Great Highway and a new Entry Village now greets visitors. Guests can stroll up Zoo Street and visit the Lemur Forest, while Puente al Sur ("bridge to the south") brings together such South American species as the giant anteater, tapir, and capybara. There's a children's zoo, home to the Meerkat and Prairie Dog exhibits, as well as an extensive facility for classes and educational programs. Other unique exhibits include Gorilla World, one of the world's largest gorilla habitats; Koala Crossing, one of the few zoo habitats of this teddybearlike marsupial; and the Primate Discovery Center, a home for rare and endangered apes, monkeys, and lemurs. The daily (except Monday) big-cat feeding at the Lion House is especially popular. More than most zoos, this one goes out of its way to prove it's not just for kids. Besides a full calendar of events for children and families, the zoo sponsors adults-only mating season parties, including a popular Valentine's Day Sex Tour. Admission. ~ 47th Avenue and Sloat Boulevard; 415-753-7080; www.sfzoo.org, e-mail webmaster@sfzoo.org.

LODGING

Say the word "hostel" and the first pictures to come to mind are spartan accommodations and shabby surroundings. At **Hostelling International–San Francisco–Fisherman's Wharf** that simply is not the case. Set in Fort Mason, an old military base that is now part of a magnificent national park, the hostel overlooks San Francisco Bay. In addition to eye-boggling views, the facility is within walking distance of the Marina district and Fisherman's Wharf. The hostel itself is contained in a Civil War–era infirmary and features a living room, kitchen, and laundry, as well as a café that offers stunning views of the bay. The rooms, carpeted and quite clean, are dorm-style with 8 to 12 bunk beds in each. Rates also include a continental breakfast. No smoking or alcohol-imbibing; strict noise curfew at midnight. Free walking tours, music, and movies are offered. Reservations recommended. ~ Fort Mason, Building 240, Bay and Franklin streets; 415-771-7277, fax 415-771-1468; www.norcalhostels.org, e-mail sfhostel@norcalhostels.org. BUDGET.

If you're seeking a hotel near the ocean, removed from the hubbub of downtown San Francisco, consider **Seal Rock Inn**. Perched on a bluff overlooking the Pacific, it's located just outside the Golden Gate National Recreation Area, a stone-skip away from Ocean Beach and Golden Gate Park. The 27 guest rooms are spacious, easily sleeping four people. Furnishings and decor are unimaginative but quite comfortable; the rooms are carpeted wall-to-wall and equipped with televisions and phones. Also, a godsend in this region of frequent fog, some rooms have fireplaces. These are a little extra, as are rooms featuring minikitchenettes and panoramic ocean views. ~ 545 Point Lobos Avenue; 415-752-8000, 888-732-5762, fax 415-752-6034; www.sealrockinn.com, e-mail reservations@sealrockinn.com. MODERATE TO DELUXE.

San Francisco's first motel is a 24-room art-deco beauty. Built in 1936, the same year as the Golden Gate Bridge, the **Ocean Park Motel** combines modern furnishings, cedar paneling, and floral wallpapers. In addition to attractive rooms with refrigerators (some with kitchens) and large family suites, it offers guests an outdoor hot tub, garden courtyard, and small playground. Dogs are welcome. ~ 2690 46th Avenue; 415-566-7020, fax 415-665-8959; www.oceanparkmotel.com, e-mail ocnprk36@aol.com. MODERATE.

DINING

One of San Francisco's most popular vegetarian restaurants is incongruously situated in an old waterfront warehouse. With pipes exposed and a metal superstructure supporting the roof, **Greens at Fort Mason** possesses the aura of an upscale airplane hangar. But this eatery, run by the Zen Center, has been deftly furnished with burlwood tables, and there's a view of the Golden Gate out of the warehouse windows. The lunch menu includes vegetable brochettes fired over mesquite charcoal, pita bread stuffed with hummus, grilled tofu, soups, and daily specials. Dinner menu is à la carte Monday through Friday, pre-set on Saturday. The menu changes daily: a typical multicourse repast would be fougasse with red onions; spinach linguine with artichokes, shiitake mushrooms, pinenuts, rosemary, and parmesan; Tunisian salad; eggplant soup; Gruyère tart; lettuce salad; tea; and dessert. Reservations recommended for lunch and dinner. No lunch on Monday, no dinner on Sunday. ~ Fort Mason Center, Building A; 415-771-6222, fax 415-771-3472; www.greensrestaurant.com. MODERATE TO DELUXE.

In a city famed for its amazing array of ethnic restaurants, there's only one place where you can try Tibetan cuisine. (Some say it might be the only place in the United States.) Nope, you won't find yak burgers at **Lhasa Moon**. In fact, at first glance the menu looks like fairly standard Asian fare—curries, noodles, steamed dumplings, and beef, poultry, and vegetarian stews. But the minute you wrap your taste buds around any item served here, you'll know you're not in Kansas any more. The difference is in the seasoning, a kaleidoscope of distinctive and exotic flavors developed over centuries of isolation. The warm, friendly staff, mainly Tibetan refugees, and the authentic decorative touches make a meal here a memorable experience. Dinner nightly except Monday; lunch Thursday and Friday only. ~ 2420 Lombard Street; 415-674-9898. MODERATE.

◄ HIDDEN

Try as you might to escape the trodden paths, some places in the world are simply inevitable. Such a one is the Cliff House, a historic structure at the edge of the sea that is positively inundated with tourists. Since there's little else out on the city's ocean side, you may find yourself at the only dining area left open during construction. **Upstairs at the Cliff House** offers a great view in a café-cum-formal setting. The breakfast and lunch menu boasts

CLIFFSIDE DELIGHT

For a tad less expensive meal than at the nearby Cliff House, head uphill a few steps to **Louis'**, a cliffside café that's been family-owned since 1937. The dinners, served with soup or salad, include New York steak, prawns, scallops, and hamburger steak. Breakfast and lunch are similar all-American affairs. Add a postcard view of the Sutro Baths and Seal Rocks and you have one hell of a bargain. Limited dinner hours during winter. ~ 902 Point Lobos Avenue; 415-387-6330. MODERATE.

Text continued on page 116.

Clement Street Restaurants

For any city in the country, there's a rule of thumb to good eating: to dine where the locals dine, go where the locals live. In San Francisco that means Clement Street. Paralleling Golden Gate Park and the Presidio and set midway between the two, this friendly street is the center of a multicultural neighborhood. Irish, Russians, Chinese, Japanese, Jews, and others have called the district home for varying periods of time.

The result is a marvelous mix of ethnic restaurants. Stroll Clement Street, from 1st to 12th Avenue or 19th to 26th Avenue, and encounter Italian, Danish, Thai, and Indonesian restaurants. There are Irish bars, French patisseries, bistros, health food stores, open-air vegetable stands, and numerous Asian dining places. The only difficulty you'll encounter is deciding on a particular place (and maybe finding parking). I have a few suggestions, but if they don't fit your fancy, you'll doubtless find a dozen places that do.

I heartily recommend **Mai's**. The dining room is small and informal with a simple decor. Serene and personable, Mai's prepares a host of tempting entrées, among them coconut chicken, lemongrass barbecued beef, Vietnamese pork shish kebab, as well as several vegetarian dishes. ~ 316 Clement Street; 415-221-3046. BUDGET.

With over 300 dishes from all over China to choose from, **Yet Wah** has something for everyone. The main dining room is rather large and franchise-esque, sporting the same look as other popular Chinese restaurants. But that doesn't detract from the food, which remains tasty and well-prepared. Weekend dim sum is especially popular, with carts whizzing by and chatter filling the room. ~ 240 Clement Street; 415-387-8040; www.yetwah.com. MODERATE.

Proving a perennial favorite among San Franciscans, **Fountain Court** offers a slew of Shanghai specialties. The lights are a bit bright, but wicker-back chairs and large potted plants help calm the starkness. This is the place for seafood: eel, catfish, fresh crab, or even sea cucumber. Then again, almost all of their dishes are divine. Dim sum is also available, but you'll be ordering from a menu, not the carts. Lunch only on weekends. ~ 354 Clement Street; 415-668-1100. MODERATE TO DELUXE.

For north Indian cooking, it's hard to beat the **India Clay Oven**, where house specialties include chicken *tikka* and other tandoori oven–cooked entrées. Bright decor suggestive of an Indian village sets the tone in this low-key family restaurant. ~ 2435 Clement Street; 415-751-0544. BUDGET TO MODERATE.

The **King of Thai Noodle House** is a genuine hole in the wall: a narrow, fluorescent-lit eatery with a few tables in the back where young locals hang out late into the night. The food, like the atmosphere, more closely approximates what you'd actually find in Thailand than what you'd expect of a Thai restaurant in the U.S.—an assortment of spicy soups and noodle bowls ranging from vegetarian to meat and seafood. ~ 639 Clement Street; 415-752-5198. BUDGET.

Haig's Delicacies, a long-established specialty food shop, is where many chefs from San Francisco's finest restaurants go for unusual and hard-to-find ingredients from around the world, such as Indian chutneys, Turkish olive oil, Israeli soup mixes, and Lebanese hot red-pepper sauce. There are a few tables where old-timers linger over cups of Turkish coffee and diners can eat on the premises (but why not pick up the makings for a classy picnic and head up to Golden Gate Park?). The hummus and tabbouleh come highly recommended. Closed Sunday. ~ 642 Clement Street; 415-752-6283. BUDGET TO MODERATE.

Chandeliers in a hamburger joint? **Bill's Place** ain't just any hamburger joint! Many San Franciscans insist it's a hamburger palace, the best in the city. There's the '49er burger with bacon and avocado; the Giants burger; the Letterman burger; the Red Skelton burger (garnished like a clown); and so on. If you want to be gauche, you can order a sandwich or hot dog instead. And if you'd rather forego the counter or table service out front, there's an open-air patio in back. Bill's is *the* place for fast food with a flair. ~ 2315 Clement Street; 415-221-5262, fax 707-836-9104. BUDGET.

End your meal on a sweet note with a shake, malt, or sundae from the **Toy Boat Dessert Cafe**. Though mainly an ice cream parlor, you'll also find espresso drinks, pies, cakes, and cookies. If you're young at heart, you probably won't be able to resist the mind-boggling display of old and new collectible toys. Their price tags, however, are another matter. ~ 401 Clement Street and 5th Avenue; phone/fax 415-751-7505. BUDGET.

One block south of and parallel to Clement Street, Geary Boulevard is a broad street with storefronts that harken back to an earlier decade. It, too, boasts an array of ethnic eateries, old-fashioned ice cream parlors, and friendly watering holes.

If you're a fan of baked goods, prepare to spend some time in the **Moscow & Tbilisi Bakery Store**. Sure, you'll have to get in line to purchase the freshly baked black, rye, and white breads, but that's not why you'll take so long—it's the process of deciding which desserts and pastries *not* to buy! To make things more difficult, the piroghis, filled with meat, cheese, or potatoes, are delectable. ~ 5540 Geary Boulevard; 415-668-6959, fax 415-752-5721. BUDGET.

omelettes as well as soups and sandwiches. At dinner the wait-staff changes into nicer clothes, the linen goes on the tables and the café becomes a formal dining room. There are pasta dishes, several seafood selections, and a few chicken, steak, or lamb entrées. ~ 1090 Point Lobos Avenue; 415-386-3330; www.cliff house.com, e-mail info@cliffhouse.com. MODERATE TO DELUXE.

Seafood lovers start lining up early at the popular **Pacific Café** in the outer Richmond District where the wait for a table is soothed by a complimentary glass of wine and convivial talk. Then it's time to sink into a high-backed wooden booth and ponder the daily specials, which always include a wide assortment of grilled fresh fish and frequently ahi tuna garnished with wasabe butter, crab cakes, and garlic-infused steamed mussels. Dinner only. ~ 7000 Geary Boulevard; 415-387-7091. DELUXE.

Leave your shoes at the door and step into Southeast Asian elegance. **Khan Toke** offers all the culinary and aesthetic delights of fine dining without the hefty price. Sunken-floor seating, intricate wood carvings, and gold inlay transform the interior into an exotic locale. Try the fried tofu appetizer with peanut sauce, green curry chicken, or any of their other Thai delights. Ask for a spot in the back and get your own secluded table. Reservations suggested. ~ 5937 Geary Boulevard; 415-668-6654. MODERATE.

Out in San Francisco's southwest corner, in Harding Park on the shores of Lake Merced, you'll discover a spiffy dining room, **The Boathouse Sports Bar and Restaurant**. With pretty views, it offers a lunch and dinner menu of steak, seafood, sandwiches, and salad. They take their sports themes seriously. Corridor walls are lined with photos of local athletes and every corner (as in all four) has a television to keep you posted on the latest scores. If you're out here to begin with, it's probably to go golfing, boating, hiking, or hang gliding, so the athletic ambience shouldn't bother you. Saturday and Sunday brunch. ~ 1 Harding Park Road; 415-681-2727, fax 415-681-3067. MODERATE.

NIGHTLIFE The **Magic Theatre** has premiered several plays by Pulitzer Prize–winning dramatist Sam Shepard, who was playwright-in-residence here for several years. Plays by new playwrights are performed nearly year-round. ~ Fort Mason Center, Building D; 415-441-8822, fax 415-771-5505; www.magictheatre.org.

▼▼▼▼▼▼▼▼▼▼▼

The Presidio

What was previously the oldest active military base in the country is now part of the country's largest urban national park. The Presidio is also a National Historic Landmark. It was established by the Spanish in 1776 and taken over by the United States in 1846. Civil War troops trained here, and the Sixth Army established the base as its headquarters. Even when it was a military base, the Presidio had the feel of a country retreat. Hiking trails snake through the 1400 acres of undulating hills sprinkled with acacia, madrone, pine, and redwood trees, and there are expansive bay views. Although still under development, there are plans for new hiking trails, museums, education centers, and conference facilities.

SIGHTS

The best way to explore the Presidio is by stopping first at the **Visitor Center**. The folks here are very knowledgeable; they'll provide you with a map and information about free public programs. The center is temporarily located at the **Officers' Club**, a tile-roof, Spanish-style structure. It includes part of the original 1776 Presidio, one of the first buildings ever constructed in San Francisco. ~ Building 50, Moraga Avenue; 415-561-4323, fax 415-561-4310; www.nps.gov/prsf.

The **National Cemetery**, with rows of tombstones on a grassy knoll overlooking the Golden Gate Bridge, is San Francisco's salute to the nation's war dead. ~ Lincoln Boulevard.

The remainder of our Presidio tour is of a more natural bent. There's **El Polin Spring**, where, as the brass plaque proclaims, ◄ HIDDEN "the early Spanish garrison attained its water supply." History has rarely been made in a more beautiful spot. The spring is set in a lovely park surrounded by hills upon which eucalyptus trees battle with conifers for strategic ground. Hiking trails lead down and outward from this enchanted glade. ~ Located at the end of MacArthur Avenue.

Mountain Lake Park, stationed along the Presidio's southern flank, is another idyllic locale. With grassy meadows and wooded walkways, it's a great place to picnic or stroll. The lake itself, a favorite watering hole among ducks visiting from out of town, is skirted with tule reeds and overhung with willows. There's also a playground here. ~ Lake Street between 8th and Funston avenues.

The base's prettiest walk is actually in civilian territory along the **Presidio Wall** bordering Lyon Street. Starting at the Lombard Street Gate, where two cannons guard the fort's eastern entrance,

THE LAST STAND

The battle lines are drawn at **Lover's Lane**. March, or even stroll, along this narrow pathway, and review these armies of nature. On one side, standing sentinel straight, out-thrust arms shading the lane, are the eucalyptus. Mustered along the other front, clad in darker uniforms, seeming to retreat before the wind, are the conifer trees. Forgetting for a moment these silly games soldiers play, look around. You are standing in an awesome and spectacular spot, one of the last forests in San Francisco. ~ In the southeast corner of the Presidio.

walk uphill along Lyon Street. That wall of urbanity to the left is the city's chic Union Street district, breeding place for fern bars and antique stores. To the right, beyond the Presidio's stone enclosure, are the tumbling hills and towering trees of the old garrison.

After several blocks, Lyon ceases to be a street and becomes a staircase. The most arduous and rewarding part of the trek begins; you can follow this stairway to heaven, which happens to be Broadway, two heart-pounding blocks above you. Ascend and the city falls away—the Palace of Fine Arts, Alcatraz, the Marina, all become landing points for your vision. Closer to hand are the houses of San Francisco's posh Pacific Heights district, stately structures looming several stories and sprawling across the landscape. When you reach the stone steps at the top of Broadway, they will still rise above, potent and pretentious, hard contrast to the Presidio's leafy acres.

DINING   Creative California cuisine may be everywhere you look in San Francisco, but rarely will you find it served in such a restfully sylvan setting as at the **Presidio Café**, located in the clubhouse of the Presidio Golf Course. The indoor dining area features an exposed-beam cathedral ceiling, a massive stone fireplace, and picture windows looking out on the golf course, while the heated outdoor area is sandwiched between the links and the forest. Developed by veteran chef Thomas Doyle, the menu features specialty sandwiches, appetizers, and daily fresh fish specials. Prices are reasonable, and there's ample free parking. Hours, designed to accommodate golfers, are 6:30 a.m. to 6 p.m. (Hours vary slightly on weekends.) ~ 300 Finley Road (at the Arguello gate); 415-561-4661 ext. 203; www.presidiogolf.com. MODERATE.

▼▼▼▼▼▼▼▼▼▼▼▼▼
Golden Gate Park   It is the Central Park of the West. Or perhaps we should say that Central Park is New York's answer to Golden Gate Park. It extends from the Haight-Ashbury neighborhood, across nearly half the width of the city, all the way to the ocean. With its folded hills and sloping meadows, its lakes and museums, Golden Gate is everyone's favorite park.

Once an undeveloped region of sand dunes, the park today encompasses over 1000 acres of gardens, lawns, and forests. The transformation from wasteland to wonderland came about during the late-19th and early-20th centuries through the efforts of a mastermind named John McLaren. A gardener by trade, this Scotsman could rightly be called an architect of the earth. Within his lifetime he oversaw the creation of the world's largest human-made park.

What he wrought was a place that has something to suit everyone: there are tennis courts; lawn bowling greens; hiking trails; byways for bicyclists, rollerskaters, skateboarders, even uni-

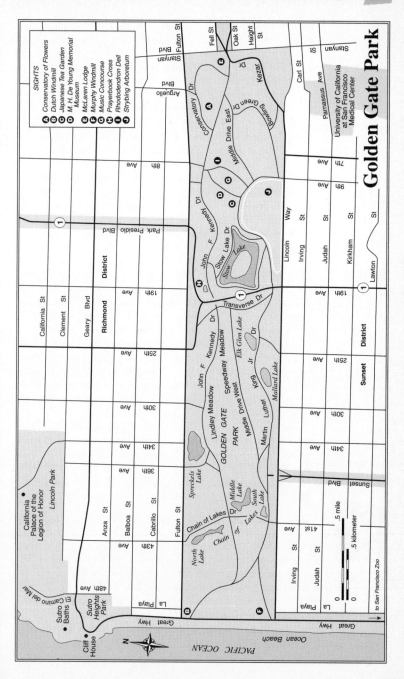

SIGHTS

Ⓐ Conservatory of Flowers
Ⓑ Dutch Windmill
Ⓒ Japanese Tea Garden
Ⓓ M. H. De Young Memorial Museum
Ⓔ McLaren Lodge
Ⓕ Murphy Windmill
Ⓖ Music Concourse
Ⓗ Prayerbook Cross
Ⓘ Rhododendron Dell
Ⓙ Strybing Arboretum

Golden Gate Park

cyclists; a nine-hole golf course; an archery field; flycasting pools; playgrounds; fields for soccer and football; riding stables; even checker pavilions. Facilities for renting bikes and skates are located just outside the park along Haight and Stanyan streets.

Or, if you'd prefer not to lift a finger, you can always pull up a shade tree and watch the parade. The best day to visit Golden Gate Park is Sunday when many of the roads in the eastern end of the park are closed to cars but open to skaters, jugglers, cyclists, troubadours, mimes, skateboarders, impromptu theater groups, sun worshippers, and anyone else who feels inspired.

Touring the park should be done on another day, when you can drive freely through the grounds. There are two roads spanning the length of the park. Each begins near Stanyan Street on the east side of Golden Gate Park and runs about four miles westward to the Pacific. The best way to see this area is to travel out along John F. Kennedy Drive and back by Martin Luther King, Jr. Drive, detouring down the side roads that lead into the heart of the park.

SIGHTS

The first stop along John F. Kennedy Drive lies immediately after the entrance. That red-tile building is **McLaren Lodge**, park headquarters and home base for maps, brochures, pamphlets, and information. ~ Stanyan and Fell streets; 415-831-2700, fax 415-221-8034; www.parks.sfgov.org, e-mail elizabeth_goldstein@ci.sf.ca.us.

The glass palace nearby is the **Conservatory of Flowers**. Built in 1878 and Victorian in style, it houses a plant kingdom ruled by stately palm trees and peopled with tropical flowers, pendent ferns, and courtly orchids. The Conservatory makes for a stunning photo op. Closed Monday. Admission. ~ John F. Kennedy Drive; 415-466-7001; www.conservatoryofflowers.org.

Just down the street is **Rhododendron Dell**. A lacework of trails threads through this 20-acre garden; if you're visiting in early spring, when the rose-hued bushes are blooming, the dell is a concert of colors.

Just beyond this garden beats the cultural heart of Golden Gate Park. Located around a tree-studded concourse are the De Young

AUTHOR FAVORITE

If you're like me, you won't be in Golden Gate Park more than an hour or two before museum fatigue sets in and dinosaur vertebrae start looking like rock formations. It's time for the **Japanese Tea Garden**. Here you can rest your heavy eyes on carp-filled ponds and hand-wrought gateways. There are arch footbridges, cherry trees, bonsai gardens, and, of course, a tea house where Japanese women serve jasmine tea and cookies. Admission.

Museum, Academy of Sciences, and Japanese Tea Garden. The **M. H. De Young Memorial Museum** houses an impressive collection. Exhibits trace the course of American art from colonial times to the mid-20th century, including an important collection of colonial-era art donated by the Rockefellers. The Art of the Americas gallery features ancient art from Central and South America as well as North American art of the past 400 years. There's also an intriguing display of works from Africa and Oceania. The De Young has one of the largest collections in the nation. Closed for renovations until 2005. Admission. ~ 415-750-3600, fax 415-750-7386; www.thinker.org, e-mail guestbook@famsf.org.

All these cultural gathering places cluster around a **Music Concourse.**

You can get back on John F. Kennedy Drive and resume your self-guided tour by continuing to **Stow Lake.** This is a donut-shaped body of water with an island as the hole in the middle. From the island's crest you can gaze across San Francisco from Bay to ocean. Or, if an uphill is not in your day's itinerary, there's a footpath around the island perimeter that passes an ornate Chinese pagoda. There are also rowboats, pedalboats, and electric motorboats for rent, and a small snack bar.

Next along John F. Kennedy Drive you'll pass **Rainbow Falls.** That monument at the top, from which this cascade appears to spill, is **Prayerbook Cross,** modeled after an old Celtic cross.

This is followed close on by a chain of meadows, a kind of rolling green counterpoint to the chain of lakes that lie ahead. **Speedway Meadow** and **Lindley Meadow** offer barbecue pits and picnic tables; both are fabulous areas for sunbathing.

Spreckels Lake is home to ducks, seagulls, and model sailboats. Nearby is the **Buffalo Paddock,** where American bison still roam, though within the confines of a barbed wire fence.

Immediately beyond is the **Chain of Lakes,** a string of three reservoirs stretching the width of the park, perpendicular to John F. Kennedy Drive. Framed by eucalyptus trees, they offer hiking paths around each shoreline. As you circumnavigate these baby lakes, you will notice they are freckled with miniature islands. Each lake possesses a singular personality: North Lake is remarkable for its hip-deep swamp cypress; Middle Lake features an island tufted with willows; and South Lake, tiniest of the triplets, sprouts bamboo along its shore.

If these ponds be babies, the great mother of them all rests nearby. Where the road meets the Pacific you'll come upon the **Dutch Windmill,** a regal structure built in 1903. With its wooden struts and scale-like shingles, it stares into the face of the sea's inevitable west winds. The Dutchman's cousin, **Murphy Windmill,** an orphan with broken arms, lives several hundred yards down the coast.

From here at continent's edge, it's a four-mile trip back through the park along Martin Luther King, Jr. Drive. After picking it up at Murphy Windmill, you'll find that this softly curving road passes lakes and forests, meadows and playgrounds. More importantly, it borders **Strybing Arboretum**, a place specially made for garden lovers. Strybing is a world within itself, a 55-acre flower quilt stitched together by pathways. Over 7000 species peacefully co-exist here—dwarf conifers and sprawling magnolias, as well as plants from Asia, the Andes, Australia, and America. There is a "redwood trail" devoted to native California plants, a "garden of fragrance" redolent of flowers, and a Japanese strolling garden. It's a kind of park within a park, a glorious finale for your visit to this park within a city. ~ 415-661-1316, fax 415-661-7427; www.strybing.org.

▼▼▼▼▼▼▼▼▼▼▼

The Haight

Places that are part of the cultural mythology have usually gained their prominence centuries before. For the Haight that is simply not the case. This neighborhood of quiet streets and Victorian houses blazed across the public consciousness within the past few decades, leaving a vapor trail that may never vanish.

For an entire generation, 1967 was the "Summer of Love," a heady season when psychedelic drugs were food for thought and acid rock was king. On January 14, 1967, about 20,000 enlightened folks streamed through the Haight on the way to a "Human Be-In—A Gathering of the Tribes," where they tuned in to a succession of speakers, singers, and seers. By that summer, San Francisco had become a mecca for young people seeking religious truth and righteous dope. A new breed thronged to the Haight—clad in motley and carrying bells, feathers, beads, and cymbals. For one brief period it was a kind of dreamland, a creation of the collective imagination. Like all dreams, it was ephemeral, momentarily transmogrified into reality by Vietnam and an increasingly repressive society.

SIGHTS

While many of us will carry the memory of those days to the grave, the Haight has lost many of its countercultural trappings. As it was before the first hippie floated along its streets, the Haight is an upper-middle-class neighborhood resplendent with tree-lined avenues and backyard gardens. With its multihued Victorian houses, it is continually undergoing a process of gentrification. Old buildings are remodeled and chic shops move. As a result, shoppers will find that Haight Street is a hip, bustling boulevard.

Tucked between two of San Francisco's prettiest parks—Golden Gate and Buena Vista—the Haight sports some of the city's loveliest Victorians. There are Queen Anne styles marked by solitary turrets and boldly painted facades. On **Ashbury Heights,** the hillside overlooking Haight Street, are houses drawn from a gingerbread cakeboard. In the entire neighborhood there are over a thousand Victorians.

Today the Haight is still an area in transition. The district has been partially gentrified but still retains vestiges of its bohemian past. On **Haight Street,** between Masonic and Stanyan streets, the sidewalks are door-to-door with mod shops, trendy bars, used clothing stores, art galleries, and funky restaurants.

Before strolling this refurbished street, be sure to explore **Buena Vista Park.** Dense with conifers and eucalyptus trees, the park's angling hills offer splendid views of San Francisco from ocean to bay. Buena Vista possesses the beauty of Golden Gate Park but lacks the crowds. ~ Haight and Lyon streets.

Just off Haight Street are several spots vital to the history of the '60s counterculture. For a vibrant retrospective on psychedelic art, wander past the **mural** that decorates an entire outside wall at 1807 Page Street. Painted in striking colors, it pictures a visionary eye radiating down upon a multiracial band of musicians. Along one side, green hills roll to infinity, while from the other extends the open sea. In the busy but vital style of the era, it is packed with an endless series of images.

To add a ghoulish element to your otherwise pleasant tour, check out the nondescript house at **636 Cole Street.** It served during the "Summer of Love" as home to a man named Charles Manson.

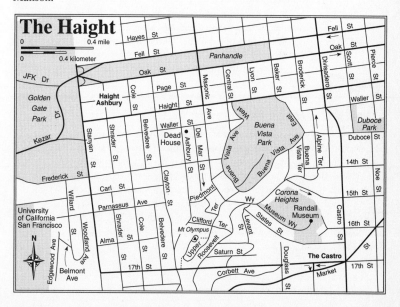

Or, if you like visiting these places-that-are-still-spoken-of-around-town-even-though-they-are-no-longer-what-they-are-known-for, you'll be interested in the pretty Victorian at 710 Ashbury Street. Back in the halcyon days of live music and electric drugs it was the **Dead House**, home to San Francisco's foremost acid rock ensemble, the Grateful Dead.

A rewarding way to discover the Haight is by wandering on your own through the neighborhood, seeking out old Victorians and soaking up local ambience. You might also head to **Corona Heights** for a city view known only to San Franciscans. This six-block uphill walk from Haight Street carries one past some pretty Victorians (take Masonic Street to the end, then continue one-half block after it turns into Roosevelt Avenue). At the top is a rocky, wind-haunted outcropping that commands a sweep of the city from Russian Hill to the Financial District to the southern stretches of the Bay. Backdropped by Twin Peaks, Corona Heights is a lesser promontory, but one that you'll often have to yourself.

HIDDEN ▶

Near the southern edge of Corona Heights Park is the **Randall Museum**, the spot to aim for if you have kids in tow. Interactive exhibits focus on the culture of San Francisco, from science to art. Free audience-participation animal sessions are held every Saturday at noon. A model-railroad exhibit is also open Saturday. There's a playground adjacent to the museum. Closed Sunday and Monday. ~ 199 Museum Way; 415-554-9600, fax 415-554-9609; www.randallmuseum.org, e-mail info@randall museum.org.

Beauty appears not only in open spaces, but in narrow corridors as well. After descending Corona Heights, you might also consider **Edgewood Avenue**. The climb begins on Farnsworth Lane (off Parnassus Avenue, above the University of California Medical Center). Farnsworth is a country lane banked with ivy and trim

HIDDEN ▶

hedges that someone accidentally placed in the city. It opens on to Edgewood Avenue, a brick-paved street that local resident Else Reisner considers one of San Francisco's prettiest walks. If you ever plan to live in San Francisco, you might as well settle here; you'll never find a more congenial place. The houses on either side are faced with brown shingle or brick; they end at the edge of a forest amid trees heavy with vines. If you're game, a hiking path leads into this primeval wood.

LODGING One of San Francisco's most reasonable B&B hotels can be found right along Haight Street, center of the fabled Summer of Love. **The Red Victorian Inn** evokes a sense of that era. Owner Sami Sunchild promotes an individualistic atmosphere in her 18-room hotel. Each chamber is decorated according to a different theme. The Peacock Suite and the Rainbow Room reflect the style of the 1960s. All rooms are nicely appointed with handsome wood tables and chairs and lacy curtains. The public areas display the owner's artwork as well as historic photos of Golden Gate Park and San Francisco. A continental breakfast is served. ~ 1665 Haight Street; 415-864-1978, fax 415-863-3293; www.redvic. com, e-mail redvic@sbcglobal.net. MODERATE TO ULTRA-DELUXE.

If the wackiness of Haight Street proves too much, retreat to **Inn 1890**. A stately Victorian built in, you guessed it, 1890 boasts rooms with brass or iron queen-sized beds, down comforters, and kitchenettes. A full kitchen and dining room is available around the clock and guests enjoy nearby health club facilities (slight fee). Continental breakfast included. ~ 1890 Page Street; 415-386-0486, 888-466-1980, fax 415-386-3626; www.inn1890.com, e-mail inn1890@pacbell.net. MODERATE TO DELUXE.

DINING Stepping into **Kan Zaman** is like entering into a dream of Arabian Nights. The lighting is dim, and the walls are covered with desert murals done in relaxing earth tones. Lounge on the big, comfortable cushions set on the floor around low tables and choose from couscous, falafel, grape leaves, and so on. After dinner you may want to indulge in one of the large hookah pipes filled with your choice of apricot, honey, strawberry or apple tobacco. No lunch on weekdays. ~ 1793 Haight Street; 415-751-9656. BUDGET TO MODERATE.

Amid Santería altars and glittering shrines hanging on the black brick walls, **Cha Cha Cha** conjures up a bewitching mix of Latin and Caribbean flavors that can range from Jamaican jerk chicken over white rice to Cajun shrimp in a spicy cream sauce. Fortunately, most menu choices are tapas plates allowing diners to sample a variety of tastes. ~ 1801 Haight Street; 415-386-7670, fax 415-386-0417; chachacha.citysearch.com. MODERATE.

Text continued on page 128.

Unique Bookstores

San Francisco has a long tradition of supporting unusual, often quirky bookstores, large and small. Yes, these days you'll find bookselling behemoths Borders, Barnes & Noble, and B. Dalton downtown, but serious readers still head for personality-packed independent shops.

At the **Rand McNally Map & Travel Store**, there's everything the wanderer could conceivably desire: guidebooks, maps, globes, language tapes, and geography games for kids. ~ 595 Market Street; 415-777-3131; www.randmcnally.com.

For used books and magazines, try **McDonald's Bookshop** in the Tenderloin. This musty warren of crowded aisles could keep you browsing for hours. It boasts more than a million books and a vast array of magazines that dates back to the 1920s, including a complete selection of *Life*, which began publication in 1936. There are also hundreds of old photos and a collection of James Dean pictures and books. Call for hours; scheduled to open in spring 2004. ~ 48 Turk Street; 415-673-2235; e-mail mcdonaldsbookshop@prodigy.net.

Near the Civic Center, the excellent **A Clean Well-Lighted Place for Books** carries a broad range of literature, cooking, music, and travel books. ~ 601 Van Ness Avenue; 415-441-6670; www.bookstore.com.

For Chinatown books and periodicals, be sure to peek into **New China Bookstore**. Opened by Mr. Jimmy Lee in 1970, the shop has an exciting collection of books for adults and children alike. ~ 642 Pacific Avenue; phone/fax 415-956-0752.

San Francisco's most famous independent bookshop, **City Lights Bookstore** in North Beach stocks both the traditional and the avant-garde. Within the hallowed confines of this oddly shaped store is a treasure trove of magazines on arts and politics, plus books on everything from nirvana to the here and now. Once a roosting place for Beat writers like Allen Ginsberg, Jack Kerouac, and Neal Cassady, it still remains a vital gathering point for local artists. The book selection is unique, featuring many contemporary poetry and prose volumes that are unavailable elsewhere. More importantly, City Lights is a place where you're welcome to pull up a chair and immerse yourself in conversation or classic literature *and* they're open daily until midnight. ~ 261 Columbus Avenue; 415-362-8193, fax 415-362-4921; www.citylights.com, e-mail staff@citylights.com.

In Pacific Heights, **Browser Books** is noteworthy. Its stock focuses on literature, psychology, religion, and philosophy. ~ 2195 Fillmore Street; 415-567-8027.

Japantown's **Kinokuniya Bookstore** is a warehouse of a store, chocka-block with volumes on Japanese language and culture. Among the works in both English and Japanese are books on history, travel, and cooking. ~ Japan Center, 1581 Webster Street; 415-567-7625; www.kinokuniya.com.

Located in the heart of the Castro, **A Different Light** carries the most popular titles for and about the lesbian, gay, bisexual, and transgender community. ~ 489 Castro Street; 415-431-0891; www.adlbooks.com.

The Mission District offers perhaps the richest and most eclectic mix of used and special-interest bookstores in the city. The **Book Building** at 2141 Mission Street offers worthwhile places to browse. Go to **Bolerium Books** for writing on American labor and radical history, gay and lesbian history, African-American history, Spanish Civil War, and other ethnic social movements. They also specialize in psychoceramics (the satudy of crackpots, of course). Closed Sunday. ~ 415-863-6353; www.bolerium.com, e-mail wackos@bolerium.com. **Meyer Boswell Books** has books on the history of law. Closed weekends. ~ 415-255-6400; www.meyerbos.com. **Mark Post Booksellers** specializes in books on American, European, and military history, Scotland, and all liturature. Open by appointment only. ~ 2555 Ocean Avenue, Suite #101; 415-583-2363; www.markpostbooks.com.

Of all the used bookstores in the Mission, none is more pleasant to browse than **The Abandoned Planet Bookstore**. Neatly arranged books, dark woods, and a red carpet create a used-book lovers' heaven. There are easy chairs for serious readers and resident cats to pet. In the back room is a poetry mural painted by the late beat poet Jack Micheline. ~ 518 Valencia Street; 415-861-4695. Specializing in books on contemporary culture, feminism, sexuality, and politics, **Modern Times Books** also has a multicultural, international selection of children's books and books in Spanish. ~ 888 Valencia Street; 415-282-9246; www.moderntimesbookstore.com. For dramatic-arts aficionados, **Limelight Bookstore** has an impressive selection of books on film, theater, and performing arts. Plop into one of their comfy chairs and thumb through a new play. ~ 1803 Market Street; 415-864-2265. **Get Lost Travel Books** carries an extensive selection of guidebooks, travel literature, and maps. ~ 1825 Market Street; 415-437-0529; www.getlostbooks.com.

The Haight is crammed with countless burrito joints, but **Sweet Heat** goes beyond your standard Mexican fare. The dishes are fresh and healthy, and many of their wraps come with grilled fish in infinite intriguing preparations. It's a bright and cheery place where the mango and peach margaritas are always flowing. ~ 1725 Haight Street; 415-387-8845. BUDGET.

SHOPPING   In addition to an imaginative name, **Off The Wall** has an appealing collection of contemporary poster art and a large line of new rock art. There are assorted eclectic artworks, particularly by ethnic artists. ~ 1669 Haight Street; 415-863-8170.

At **Planet Weaver's Treasure Store** you'll find native peoples' crafts and clothing, masks, drums, books, cards, music, body products, and hundreds of other items from every corner of the globe. ~ 1573 Haight Street; 415-864-4415, fax 415-575-1196; www.planetweavers.com.

Dress to fit your fantasy at **Piedmont Boutique**. Join the drag queens and strippers who frequent the store for fancy custom-made gowns, boas, baubles, and bangles. You can buy a great outfit for a costume party or something to help you blend into the Haight Street fashion scene. There aren't too many stores like this one. ~ 1452 Haight Street; 415-864-8075; www.piedmontsf. com, e-mail glitz@piedmontsf.com.

Though the hippies of the Haight may have gone off to graze in greener pastures, their spirit infuses **Pipe Dreams**, an anachronistic '60s survivor that still has a good selection of pipes, rolling papers, nostalgic posters, roach clips, and water pipes, as well as a small selection of shirts, books, and incense burners. ~ 1376 Haight Street; 415-431-3553, fax 415-431-5689.

Gargoyle Beads sells thousands of beads in hundreds of varieties. Just take an ice cube tray and fill it with seed, crystal, ceramic, or whatever other types of beads grab your fancy. Purchase a spool of thread and you'll be ready to create necklaces, earrings, and hanging curtains. ~ 1310 Haight Street; 415-552-4274.

Distractions offers underground electronic CDs, smoking paraphernalia, and popular items of the hippie era such as bells, incense, jewelry, and reggae and urban clothing. In the back, a spe-

---

STOCKING UP

The **Ashbury Market** is a great neighborhood market for picnic stuff to bring to Golden Gate Park. You'll find fresh-baked breads, California wines, a wide array of deli items and tempting gourmet specialties. ~ 205 Frederick Street; 415-566-3134.

cial section specializes in waterpipes and used records and CDs. ~ 1552 Haight Street; 415-252-8751.

Located a block north of Haight Street, **San Francisco Stained Glass** has stained-glass supplies and creates custom windows. Closed Sunday. ~ 345 Divisadero Street; 415-626-3592; www. sfgw.com.

NIGHTLIFE

The Lower Haight is home to many bars and clubs, and on weekends they seem to have a revolving door as people cruise from one to the other and back again. **Mad Dog in the Fog** resembles a British pub and attracts quite a crowd with its dart boards and extensive beer selection (20 on tap plus about 20 bottled). There are deejay-spun tunes on Friday night, live music on Saturday night, and a pub quiz on Monday, Tuesday, and Thursday. On weekend mornings, they show live English soccer via satellite, if you're so inclined. ~ 530 Haight Street; 415-626-7279; www. maddog.citysearch.com.

A bit more pretentious than Mad Dog is **Noc Noc**, marked by old televisions in the storefront windows. It's quiet enough here to actually have a conversation with your drink. ~ 557 Haight Street; 415-861-5811.

For a game of pool or serious dancing go to **Nickie's Haight Street BBQ**. There's a different deejay or band Monday through Saturday, playing everything from hip-hop to Latin and jazz. Closed Sunday. Cover. ~ 460 Haight Street; 415-621-6508.

Gay Neighborhoods

San Francisco's gay neighborhoods center around Castro Street, Polk Street, and in the South of Market area. The city's lesbian community focuses along Valencia Street in the Mission District. With a population that today numbers perhaps 200,000, the community has become a powerful social and political force. In 1977, Supervisor Harvey Milk became the nation's first openly gay man elected to a major municipal post. Since then, despite the AIDS epidemic, San Francisco has retained gay supervisors and the gay community has remained an integral part of the city's life.

LODGING

Throughout the Castro and Polk districts are numerous hotels catering primarily to gay travelers. Others in these areas serve a wide-ranging clientele, including many gay guests.

There are several hotels located in the center of the action. The first is the **Inn on Castro**, an eight-room bed and breakfast housed in an old Victorian. A class establishment all the way, the inn adds subtle touches like fresh flowers. Each room is decorated in a different fashion, and the house atmosphere is comfortable and personal. The rooms all have private baths. Because of its popularity, the hotel recommends reservations. ~ 321 Castro Street;

phone/fax 415-861-0321; www.innoncastro.com, e-mail info@inn oncastro.com. MODERATE TO DELUXE.

Several blocks from Castro Street is **The Willows Bed and Breakfast Inn**, a beautiful 12-room facility that attracts both gay and straight guests. Each room has been furnished with antique wooden pieces and adorned with French art prints (while all have a contemporary mini-fridge). The trademark of this cozy hostelry, however, is the willow-branch furniture designed expressly for the Inn. It's personal touches like this that make it a special place. Shared bath. ~ 710 14th Street; 415-431-4770, fax 415-431-5295; www.willowssf.com, e-mail vacation@willowssf.com. MODERATE TO DELUXE.

Castro Suites is a beautiful pair of comfortable and colorfully decorated apartments a couple of blocks from the heart of the Castro. The kitchens include a dishwasher, laundry facilities, and a microwave. (The upstairs kitchen is painted an appropriate bright purple.) If you give them some warning, they'll have the kitchen fully stocked for you. ~ 927 14th Street; 415-437-1783, fax 415-437-1784; www.castrosuites.com, e-mail jmrsrc@castrosuites.com. DELUXE.

Nancy's Bed is a friendly, private lesbian home offering sleeping accommodations to women travelers, and small children are welcome. Located in a quiet residential neighborhood near Twin Peaks, the house is full of female energy and decorated with women's art. There are two bedrooms (one overlooks a green garden), and a sliding glass door leads from one bedroom to a deck in the back. The bathroom is shared. There's an old cat on the premises. It's also close to public transit. ~ 415-239-5692; www.nancysbed.com, e-mail nancysbed@aol.com. BUDGET.

Although not just for gay and lesbian travelers, the nonsmoking **Dolores Park Inn** sits in a garden behind a wrought-iron fence in the heart of the Castro. This bed and breakfast, built in 1874, is filled with antiques, and one room has a four-poster Victorian bed. The ultra-deluxe suite, which sleeps up to four, features a 20-foot sundeck, a kitchen, a marble bath, and other luxuries. There are also a formal dining room and a double parlor, both with fireplaces. A full breakfast is served, as is afternoon coffee, wine, and tea. Two-night minimum required; reservations recommended. ~ 3641 17th Street; phone/fax 415-621-0482; www. doloresparkinn.net. DELUXE TO ULTRA-DELUXE.

The **Inn San Francisco** resides in a 19th-century world. Set in a grand four-story Victorian, this splendid mansion has been furnished entirely with period pieces. There are gilded mirrors and beveled glass in the parlors, wall sconces and marble sinks in many rooms, as well as other antique flourishes. The rooftop sundeck provides a great view of the city, and an English garden in the back has a gazebo and hot tub. Room prices in this elegant establishment all include a full buffet breakfast; the moderate prices are for shared bath; some moderate and deluxe rooms have private facilities; ultra-deluxe rooms come with hot tubs or jacuzzis. The clientele is both gay and straight. ~ 943 South Van Ness Avenue; 415-641-0188, 800-359-0913, fax 415-641-1701; www.innsf.com, e-mail innkeeper@innsf.com. MODERATE TO ULTRA-DELUXE.

Midway between Castro Street and the Haight-Ashbury neighborhood is the **Metro Hotel**. Appealing to a mixed clientele, there are 23 rooms, a small lobby, an adjoining café downstairs, and an English garden. The guests rooms are carpeted wall-to-wall, furnished with oak pieces, and decorated with wallhangings. Each has a private bath (shower only) and color television with cable. Set in a white Victorian building, it is clean and comfortable. While the location is not ideal, it is close enough to key neighborhoods to make the hotel worth the cost of admission. ~ 319 Divisadero Street; 415-861-5364, fax 415-863-1970; www. metrohotelsf.com, e-mail metrohotelsf@sbcglobal.net. BUDGET TO MODERATE.

The **Alamo Square Inn** offers not one but three Victorian mansions, a Queen Anne, a Georgian, and a Tudor Revival, both predating the 1906 earthquake by a decade. The bed-and-breakfast hostelry, which welcomes both gays and straights, is just a ten-minute walk from Castro Street and offers a choice of nine individually decorated rooms, a self-contained apartment and three suites, including one with a sunken jacuzzi and private deck. ~ 719 Scott Street; 415-922-2055, fax 415-931-1304; www.alamoinn.com, e-mail wcorn@alamoinn.com. MODERATE TO ULTRA-DELUXE.

VISIT A PAINTED LADY

Those in search of the quintessential "Painted Lady" Victorian will not want to miss **Chateau Tivoli**, a dazzling three-story 1892 mansion resplendent with gold leaf, stained-glass windows, and elaborate woodwork. Many of the rooms and suites are named for famous painted ladies of San Francisco, including actress Lola Montez and flapper Aimee Crocker. Accommodations include five rooms, three suites, and one efficiency, most with private marble bathrooms and some with canopy beds, fireplaces, and private decks. The clientele is both straight and gay. Wine and cheese are served in the afternoon, and champagne brunch on Sunday is included in the rates. Non-smoking. ~ 1057 Steiner Street; 415-776-5462, 800-228-1647, fax 415-776-0505; www.chateautivoli.com, e-mail mail@chateautivoli.com. MODERATE TO ULTRA-DELUXE.

DINING

Over in the Castro Street neighborhood, **Caffe Luna Piena** is a good choice. You can dine indoors or outside on a tree-studded patio. They feature a breakfast menu that includes poached eggs, omelettes, and eggs Benedict. Lunch consists of hamburgers, sandwiches, salads, and pasta. The restaurant serves dinner as well. No dinner on Monday. ~ 558 Castro Street; 415-621-2566. MODERATE.

Anchor Oyster Bar is a hole-in-the-wall café that happens to serve delicious shellfish. There are oysters on the half shell, steamed clams and mussels, seafood cocktails, and various daily specials. Recommended for lunch or dinner. No lunch on Sunday. ~ 579 Castro Street; 415-431-3990. MODERATE TO DELUXE.

To appease your sugar cravings, stop in at **Sweet Inspiration**. Though the café doesn't sport a particularly Castro-esque vibe, it has the most delectable cakes and pastries around. The slices are so huge, you'll have to share. Try the cheesecake, tiramisu, or fresh fruit tart. ~ 2239 Market Street; 415-621-8664. BUDGET.

Exceptionally popular with the locals, **Cafe Flore** has a partially enclosed outside patio and sidewalk, where diners can watch life in the Castro go by. Inside, the floor is tiled, the atmosphere casual and relaxed. You order at the window from a blackboard menu listing soups, pastas, sandwiches, and burgers. There's also an espresso bar. ~ 2298 Market Street; 415-621-8579, fax 415-252-0464. BUDGET TO MODERATE.

After a long night of clubbing or an attack of the midnight munchies, hit up **Sparky's Diner**. Open 24 hours, they serve traditional American fare—burgers, fries, and omelettes—to a less-than-typical clientele. The restaurant gets packed in the wee hours of the morning, offering a loud and vibrant environment while the rest of the city sleeps. ~ 242 Church Street; 415-626-8666. BUDGET.

If a hamburger craving hits, try **Barney's Gourmet Hamburgers**. The service is sometimes spotty but you'll be thrilled with the food: huge, juicy burgers with a variety of add-ons (cheese, avocado, grilled onions). Alternate options include ground-turkey burgers, portobello-mushroom burgers, falafel, eggplant sand-

EATS 'ROUND THE CLOCK

A good place after a late movie at the Castro Theater is **Orphan Andy's**, one of the few San Francisco restaurants open 24 hours. Decorated with a colorful 1950s diner theme with a counter and leatherette booths, Orphan Andy's serves good burgers, sandwiches, omelettes, and other classic coffee-shop fare. ~ 3991 17th Street; 415-864-9795. BUDGET.

wiches, and the ol' garden-burger standby. And the seasoned curly fries are among the best I've ever had. ~ 4138 24th Street; 415-282-7770, fax 415-282-1920. BUDGET.

For a bite between bar hopping or a quick snack, try **Tom Peasant Pies**. This shop has a few stools and a counter, but the business is mostly carry-out. There's a good selection of sweet and savory pies that include clam and tomato, spicy eggplant, leek and red peppers, mushroom and zucchini, chocolate raspberry, and blueberry pear. ~ 4108 24th Street; 415-642-1316. BUDGET.

Open for breakfast and lunch, catering to a mixed clientele, and particularly popular with women, is **Just For You**. This diner just outside the Potrero Hill district has counter service and tables and is decorated with artwork by local artists. The cuisine is a mix of American and Cajun, with cornmeal pancakes and grits for breakfast, hamburgers and crabcake sandwiches at lunch. ~ 732 22nd Street; 415-647-3033; www.justforyoucafe.com. BUDGET.

Dollar for dollar, the best dining spot along Polk Street is **Swan Oyster Depot**. It's a short-order place serving fresh prawns, crabs, lobster, shrimp, and oysters, all displayed in trays out front. The place consists simply of a counter lined with stools and is always packed. The depot opens at 8 a.m. and closes at 5:30 p.m. Closed Sunday. ~ 1517 Polk Street; 415-673-1101. MODERATE.

Running a close second is **The Grubstake**, a brightly painted café adorned with a skylight and exotic murals. The menu consists of hamburgers, sandwiches, salads, omelettes, and a number of Portuguese dishes. At night they serve pork chops, steaks, and a daily fish special. Better yet, it stays open until 4 a.m. Lunch is only served on the weekend. ~ 1525 Pine Street; 415-673-8268; e-mail fao@jps.net. BUDGET TO MODERATE.

There are about a thousand restaurants in San Francisco named Hunan, and the second most popular name seems to be Cordon Bleu. The place claiming to be the original **Cordon Bleu Vietnamese Restaurant** is a simple café-style establishment serving a wide array of Southeast Asian dishes. There are imperial rolls, shish kabobs and five-spice roast chicken. No lunch on Sunday. Closed Monday. ~ 1574 California Street; 415-673-5637. BUDGET.   ◄ HIDDEN

SHOPPING   The Castro Street shopping district stretches along Castro from 19th Street to Market Street, then continues for several blocks on "Upper Market"; there are also several interesting stores along 18th Street. The entire area is surprisingly compact, but features a variety of shops. Together with Polk Street, it represents the major gay shopping area in San Francisco.

For African trade beads, turquoise and silver jewelry, as well as other bodily adornments, try **The Bead Store**. It's a tiny one-room shop positively crammed with attractive items. ~ 417 Castro Street; 415-861-7332.

Speaking of generic names, how about **Brand X Antiques?** They feature an assortment of antiques and decorative artworks that are perfect as gifts and souvenirs. Estate jewelry is another very popular part of their line. Silver cigarette cases, glass figurines, Chinese Buddhas, rare porcelain, and objets d'art are often among the extraordinary pieces in this fascinating shop. ~ 570 Castro Street; 415-626-8908.

Along "Upper Market," look into **Image Leather** for black leather. ~ 2199 Market Street; 415-621-7551.

Polk Street is wall to wall with designer fashion shops, boutiques, and all manner of clothing outlets. The central gay area stretches from Post Street to Washington Street, but savvy shoppers will continue on to Union Street, since several intriguing stores lie on the outskirts of the neighborhood.

At the **Tibet Shop** are *sili* bangles, painted lanterns, Buddha figurines, prayer beads, and monastic incense. This wonderful little shop also has vests, skirts, dresses, shirts, and jackets made in Nepal and Bhutan. ~ 4100 19th Street; 415-982-0326; www.tibetshopsf.com.

There are enough plates, saucers, pitchers, bowls, and cups at **Naomi's American Art Pottery Dinnerware** to furnish an entire neighborhood of dining rooms, whether in the homes of hip young professionals or traditional grandparents. Closed Sunday and Monday. ~ 1817 Polk Street; 415-775-1207.

Dozens of fragrances in a variety of classic and floral bouquets line the shelves at **Denis Dumont Parfumerie**. There are perfumes, colognes, soaps, lotions, and perfume spray bottles from France. The perfumer-in-residence can even create a custom scent just for you, if you can afford it. Just schedule an appointment, and three weeks later you'll have a one-of-a-kind perfume. ~ 1741 Polk Street; phone/fax 415-441-0341.

SHOPPING FOR A GOOD CAUSE

Shopping at **Under One Roof** is like giving to a good cause. This store is underwritten by individuals and corporations, so 100 percent of the profits are donated to dozens of AIDS service organizations. It sells a wide selection of items, including candles, soaps, lotions, candy, T-shirts, jewelry, and gay and lesbian books. Most of the personnel are volunteers. ~ 549 Castro Street; 415-503-2300, 800-525-2125, fax 415-503-2301; www.underoneroof.org, e-mail info@underoneroof.org.

Good Vibrations, a sex toy, book, and video emporium designed in the late 1970s especially for women, has become a Bay Area institution. The store sells erotic literature, self-help sex books, feminist erotica, videos and sex education films, and an unbeatable array of vibrators and electric massagers. A highlight of the store is an antique vibrator museum with some rather unusual items like a cranked version that looks like a rolling pin. ~ 603 Valencia Street; 415-522-5460; www.goodvibes.com, e-mail good vibe@well.com.

At **X21** the good stuff is strewn throughout a 9000-square-foot, two-story space. There's a huge assortment of mid-20th-century design fixtures, vintage office furniture, paintings, sculpture, industrial design, glass, and ceramics. ~ 890 Valencia Street; 415-647-4211; www.x21modern.com.

One example of San Francisco's wide-open tradition is the presence of almost 200 gay bars in the city. There's everything here from rock clubs to piano bars to stylish cabarets. Some are strictly gay, others mix their customers, and some have become so popular that straights have begun to take them over from gays.

NIGHTLIFE

There are a dozen or so bars in the Castro Street area, many open from early morning until the wee hours. Among the nicest is **Twin Peaks Tavern** with its overhead fans and large windows overlooking the street. ~ 401 Castro Street; 415-864-9470.

Nearby, you'll find **The Stud**, everybody's favorite gay bar. Everybody in this case includes aging hippies, multihued punks, curious straights, and even a gay or two, all packed elbow to armpit into this pulsing club. Cover on most nights. ~ 399 9th Street; 415-863-6623; www.studsf.com.

The scene is different down the street at the **The Eagle Tavern**, a Levis and leather bar with occasional live music. Cover on Thursday. ~ 398 12th Street; 415-626-0880; www.sfeagle.com.

San Francisco's lesbian bars are located not only around Valencia Street, but in other parts of the city as well. Catering to a mixed gay and lesbian crowd, **The Café** is a mirrored club with pool tables, pinball machines, three full bars and outdoor patios. Occasional cover. There's deejay music nightly in the lounge. ~ 2369 Market Street; 415-861-3846; www.cafesf.com.

A Bernal Heights bar, **The Wild Side West** operates out of a purple Victorian house. The bar is open to all, but is mainly frequented by women. The red walls and ceiling are adorned with photos and paintings, as well as masks, vintage clothing, and shoes. Guests can play video games and enjoy music from the jukebox. ~ 424 Cortland Street; 415-647-3099.

Closer to the Castro you'll find the **Lexington Club**, a mellow nightspot especially popular with lesbians. There's a pool table, a jukebox, and, perhaps most significantly, two women's restrooms. ~ 3464 19th Street; 415-863-2052; www.lexingtonclub.com.

For women who are ready to relax, there's **Osento Bath House**, a quiet and comfortable Japanese-style bath for women. There are also massage and sauna facilities and a sun deck for lounging and picnicking. Open from 1 p.m. to 1 a.m. Fee. ~ 955 Valencia Street; 415-282-6333; www.osento.com.

Cafe du Nord is *the* hip hangout for gays and straights alike. Built in 1907, the historic building's past life as a speakeasy is still visible in its bordello-red interior and dim lighting. Sidle up to the 40-foot mahogany bar or hunker down in a separate room where there's live entertainment most nights. ~ 2170 Market Street; 415-861-5016; www.cafedunord.com, e-mail hey@cafedunord.com.

Nicest of all the Polk Street neighborhood bars is **Kimo's**. With mirrors and potted palms all around, it's a comfortable atmosphere. Cover for occasional live music. ~ 1351 Polk Street; 415-885-4535.

The **N'Touch** has a disco dancefloor plus video monitors. There's always a lively Asian crowd here. With flashing lights and ample sound, it's a good spot for dancing and carousing and watching the go-go boys. Most nights have shows or other entertainment. Cover on weekends. ~ 1548 Polk Street; 415-441-8413; www.ntouchsf.com, e-mail stewart@creative.net.

A small club in Pacific Heights, the **Lion Pub** has been around for years and is a pleasant place for a drink. Clientele is a welcoming mix of gay and straight. ~ 2062 Divisadero Street; 415-567-6565.

Plays with gay, bisexual, transgender, and lesbian themes are the focus of **Theatre Rhinoceros**, an acclaimed company that presents performances at two theaters, Rhino's Mainstage and Rhino's Studio. ~ 2926 16th Street; 415-861-5079; www.the rhino.org.

San Francisco's answer to off-off-Broadway is **The Marsh Theater**, a small, informal theater billed as a "breeding ground for new performances," which offers plays and spoken-word entertainment frequently, but not exclusively, on women's topics.

NOE VALLEY

Noe Valley, a district near the Mission, features an opportunity to shop far from the tourist areas. All along 24th Street between Church and Castro streets, small stores line either side of the road. There are bookstores, galleries, handicrafts shops, open-air fruit stalls, and numerous other locally owned establishments. There's a distinctive neighborhood feeling here, which makes shoppers seem more like friends than consumers.

Monday nights are reserved for performers trying out new work.
~ 1062 Valencia Street; 415-826-5750; www.themarsh.org, e-mail
gotmarsh@yahoo.com.

Mission District

Depending on your personal taste or maybe just your mood, you'll come away from the Mission District thinking it either a poem or a ghetto. In truth, it's both. "The Mission," San Francisco's own Spanish barrio, is the vibrant home of the city's Mexican, Colombian, Guatemalan, Nicaraguan, and Salvadoran population. It's a neighborhood where brilliant murals vie with graffiti-scrawled walls, and where children compete with old folks for a seat on the bus or park bench.

The Mission District is a scene not just of transition but of social turmoil. In the early 1990s, zoning regulations opened the neighborhood to "live/work lofts," which originally meant artists' studios, and "bohos" (short for bohemians) moved in. Then city planners created NEMIZ—the Northeast Mission Industrial Zone—to encourage development of biotechnology industries. But while an influx of capital from pre-Communist Hong Kong poured in to finance new construction, the biotech boom passed San Francisco by. As a result, all that development money went into luxurious, very expensive live/work loft projects to accommodate the overflow of dot-com firms from the South of Market district, creating population densities that are now approaching ten times what city planners anticipated—with no increase in parking spaces. Skyrocketing rents and property taxes are rapidly forcing long-time Latino residents, bohemian artists, and the vibrant lesbian subculture out of the Mission.

Today, the Mission is a controversy-ridden patchwork quilt of a neighborhood, where young multimillionaires pedal down the bike lanes of Valencia Street, one of the fastest-gentrifying streets in the city, passing within a block or two of makeshift car repair shops and hole-in-the-wall *taquerías* that could as easily be in Guatemala City, and equally close to chic boutiques, restaurants, and galleries; where hilly, quiet, beautiful Dolores Street rolls down past the park of the same name, shared by picnicking families and one of the city's largest concentrations of drug dealers; where the same magical murals that brighten the exteriors of dozens of buildings are also displayed with pride on dozens of websites. Here you'll find the oldest building in San Francisco and some of the newest. In fact, wandering the streets of the Mission, you'll probably find whatever you want, along with a few things you never imagined.

The *corazón* of the Mission is 24th Street with its outdoor markets and indoor murals. Start your tour at 24th and York streets, about six blocks east of Mission Street.

SIGHTS

St. Francis Candies, right on the corner, is a classic. With its cozy booths, old-fashioned fountain, and pink ceiling, the place seems suspended in time since 1955. Actually this after-school ice cream parlor dates from 1918.

Those **murals** in the park across the street are a striking example of *la raza* (the Latino people). The artists who worked those walls might be part of the ever-changing exhibits at **Galería de la Raza.** Innovative and provocative, the gallery is as liable to feature a show on the revolutionary movement in El Salvador as a photographic display or artistic exhibit. Hours vary—call for details. Closed Sunday through Tuesday. ~ 2857 24th Street; 415-826-8009, fax 415-826-6235; www.galeriadelaraza.org, e-mail info@galeriadelaraza.org.

Another **mural** on the side of 2884 24th Street depicts scenes that also correspond with this theme, and the painting on the facade of **China Books** is modeled after the style of Chinese peasant paintings. Closed on weekends. ~ 2929 24th Street; 415-282-2994; www.chinabooks.com, e-mail info@chinabooks.com.

Even the alleyways hereabouts are home to art—check out the colorful **children's mural** decorating the Mission Neighborhood Family Center. ~ On the corner of 24th Street and Balmy Avenue.

There's more street art just past South Van Ness Avenue—a **wall mural** depicting multihued parrots and thrashing fish. Then, space-age counterpoint to this folk art, is the **mural** at 24th and Mission streets, illustrating San Francisco's modernistic BART subways.

If 24th Street is the heart of the barrio, **Mission Street** is its nerve center, a neon ganglia delivering electric charges throughout the community. By day it's a collection of shoe stores, hair salons, and pawn shops. At night, particularly on weekends, the area is transformed into a cruising strip. Although the gaudy, outrageous low-riders have been pushed out of the Mission in recent years, there are still plenty of macho cars competing with spit-shine sleek vans with multicolored designs.

Surprisingly, just one block from this area is **Valencia Street,** center of the city's lesbian community. Along this nondescript thoroughfare are bars, boutiques, bookstores, and cafés serving the vibrant artists' community. The **Women's Building** is an important gathering place here. Closed on weekends. ~ 3543 18th Street; 415-431-1180, fax 415-861-8969; www.womensbuilding.org, e-mail info@womensbuilding.org.

Unless you've sidetracked down Mission or Valencia, you're still on the corner of 24th and Mission, staring at that futuristic mural. Cross Mission and continue along 24th Street uphill several

HIDDEN ►

blocks to **Quane Street.** Walk the three-block length of this alleyway and you'll be convinced the city fathers and mothers meant to name it Quaint Street. It's not much—just picket fences, shade trees, and clapboard houses—but rarely has so little spoken so eloquently.

The Mission

Jackson Playground

Basic Brown Teddy Bear Factory

Mariposa St
18th St
19th St
20th St
Rhode Island St

Carolina St
De Haro St

Potrero Hill
Southern Heights Ave

16th St
17th St

Kansas St

Vermont St

San Bruno Ave

San Bruno Ave

McKinley Square

22nd

23rd

Vermont St

Cesar Chavez Ave exit

Utah St

101

San Francisco General Hospital

24th St

Potrero Ave

Potrero Ave

Franklin Square

Mariposa St

18th St
19th St
20th St
21st St
22nd St

Hampshire St

York St

Galería de la Raza

Bryant St

23rd St

St Francis Candies

Florida St

Alabama St

China Books

Harrison St

Harrison St

Treat Ave

Treat Ave

Folsom St

24th St

16th St
17th St
18th St
19th St
20th St

Shotwell St

S Van Ness Ave

Book Building

Capp St

Mission St

16th Street Mission BART Station

24th Street Mission BART Station

Valencia St

16th St
17th St

Lapidge St

Women's Building

Guerrero St

18th St
19th St
20th St
21st St
22nd St
23rd St

Murphy House

Dolores St

Mission Dolores

Chula Ln

Dolores Park

Liberty St

Church St

0.5 miles

0.5 kilometers

N

When this woodframe corridor debouches into 21st Street, turn left, then take a quick right onto Dolores Street. Head down for one block and take a right onto Liberty Street for a view of some magnificent old Victorians. That Italianate-style home at 159 Liberty is the old **Murphy House**. Built in 1878, the place gained notoriety in 1896 when the famous suffragette Susan B. Anthony visited. Five other majestic Victorians, including a turreted Queen Anne–style structure, sit just beyond this fine old home.

Back on **Dolores Street**, you can continue downhill along one of San Francisco's prettiest boulevards. Bordered on either side by bay window homes, Dolores Street's proudest feature is the grassy median planted with stately palm trees. Better still, this marvelous promenade opens onto **Dolores Park**, between Dolores and 20th streets, a rectangle of rolling hills dotted with magnolia and pepper trees. You can follow the sinuous walkways down to the tennis courts or head for the high ground and a luxurious view of the city. Remember, this is the Mission District, the city's sunniest sector, and there's no better place than Dolores Park for hanging out, people watching, and sunbathing.

Farther downhill, at Dolores and 16th streets, stands the historic building that gave the neighborhood its name. Crown jewel of the city, **Mission San Francisco de Asís**, or Mission Dolores, completed in 1791, was one of the 21 Spanish missions established along the California coast by Franciscans. Here you can wander back to the last great days of the Spanish empire: the tabernacle came from the Philippines, the main altar along with several side altars were imported from Mexico, the ceiling design was created by Costanoan Indians— all unfortunate subjects of 18th-century Spain. There's a mini-museum behind the chapel and a massive 20th-century basilica next door, but the most intriguing feature on the mission grounds is the cemetery. Studded with yew trees and tombstones, it is the last resting place of several famous (and infamous) San Francisco figures. Captain Louis Antonio Arguello, California's first Mexican governor, is interred here. So are Charles Cora and James Casey, a notorious pair who died at the hands of San Francisco's Vigilance Committee. Admission. ~ 415-621-8203, fax 415-621-2294; www.missiondolores.citysearch.com, e-mail mdolores@earthlink.net.

The thick adobe walls—and perhaps a few prayers— helped Mission San Francisco de Asís (Mission Dolores) survive the 1906 earthquake and fire; today it is the city's oldest building.

LODGING   A short six blocks away from the Mission District, **Noe's Nest** could be your home away from home. Perhaps a more lavish domicile, with a hot tub, steam room, fireplace, and gorgeous views of the city. The six cozy rooms at this bed and breakfast feature private baths. Children are welcome. Reservations recommended. (The innkeepers go to sleep after 9 p.m.) ~ 3973 23rd Street; 415-

821-0751, 888-663-6378, fax 415-821-0723; www.noesnest.com, e-mail noesnest@aol.com. DELUXE TO ULTRA-DELUXE.

DINING

The pastel-colored walls, paintings, and statuary add to the charm of **Bangkok 16**. Thai specialties served at your candlelit table include duck in a spicy lemon sauce, calamari salad, yellow curry, pad Thai noodles, lamb on a skewer served with a peanut sauce, and filet of snapper in a spicy tamarind sauce. Try the fried bananas for dessert. Dinner only. ~ 3214 16th Street; 415-431-5838. BUDGET TO MODERATE.

In Brittany, Ti-Couz means The Old House, and worn hardwood floors, blue-and-white-painted walls, and wooden china cabinets give **Ti-Couz Creperie & Seafood Bar** that homey feeling. The seafood bar (available at dinner only) features oysters, shrimp, and fresh whole crab. But it's the savory crêpes that draw the crowds. Made from buckwheat flour in the style of Brittany, the crêpes are cooked to order one at a time, filled with cheese, sausage, or smoked salmon, and garnished with crème fraîche. Flavored butters, ice cream, white chocolate, and fruit are folded into the sweet crêpes. Delicious. ~ 3108 16th Street; 415-252-7373, fax 415-252-7712; www.ticouz16.com. BUDGET.

It looks and smells like south of the border in **La Cumbre**. By the size of the crowd here, those rumors about the best burritos must be true. For a price comfortable to any budget, you can order pork, tongue, chicken, or steak burritos, as well as tacos and other Mexican finger foods. They also feature vegetarian dishes at this simple but special *taquería*. ~ 515 Valencia Street; 415-863-8205. BUDGET.

If you're craving something less traditional, head across the street to **Mariachi's**, where you'll find tacos and burritos with a decidedly Californian twist. Bright and festive decorations match the equally zesty menu. Try the snapper soft tacos with tangy mango salsa. Vegan dishes available. ~ 508 Valencia Street; 415-621-4358. BUDGET.

It's Christmas every day at **La Rondalla**. Where else will you encounter gold tinsel decor in the middle of July? Not to mention multihued foil snowflakes and a religious scene illuminated with, you guessed it, Christmas lights. The menu is nearly as unique: those pots on the stove are liable to contain *albóndigas* (meatball soup) or even *birria de chivo* (barbecued goat meat). For the less daring, there are enchiladas, rellenos, *y mucho más*. Closed Monday. ~ 901 Valencia Street; 415-647-7474. BUDGET TO MODERATE.

Esperpento shines among the city's many tapas places, distinguished by its colorful atmosphere. Fans, ceramic plates, shawls, and pictures of bullfights adorn the walls, and the tables are painted with flowers and giant suns. You can linger over plates of paella and tapas of fried fish, garlic shrimp, pork kebab, and salads, while enjoying lively conversation and good Spanish wine. ~ 3295 22nd Street; 415-282-8867. MODERATE.

Food and films go hand in hand at **Foreign Cinema**, a favorite evening destination for locals. The California-Mediterranean menu might include lavender-scented pork chop and King salmon with green olive tapenade. The menu changes daily and there's a full oyster bar. But it's the atmosphere here that's most distinctive. The high, stark, concrete walls create a warehouse-like feel that's at odds with the elegant dining and conciliatory service. In the large courtyard outside, films (mainly foreign and art flicks) are projected onto a 25-foot wall. If you plan to focus on the movie, eat outdoors: there are heat lamps and private speakers at each table. Weekend brunch available. Closed Monday. ~ 2534 Mission Street; 415-648-7600; www.foreigncinema.com, e-mail bruce@foreigncinema.com. MODERATE TO ULTRA-DELUXE.

At **Butterfly Mission Lounge**, your meal is combined with live deejay music. The excellent food is North Vietnamese–inspired (think tumeric-grilled red snapper or sweet potato and shrimp tempura) and served until midnight. The decor is cool and modern, studded with skylights, glass, and an indoor *koi* pond, designed with clear sightlines of the stage. Dinner only. Closed Sunday and Monday. ~ 1710 Mission Street; 415-864-5575; www.butterflysf.com, e-mail butterflymission@hotmail.com. BUDGET TO MODERATE.

SHOPPING This Latin American neighborhood once favored shoe stores and groceries over boutiques and galleries. Today, however, those old-timey stores are being joined by some screamingly modern places.

Arik Surplus stocks American Army surplus clothing. They also have outdoor wear, boots, camping equipment, and rain gear. ~ 2650 Mission Street; 415-285-4770.

Sometimes a person needs to find that perfect mounted beetle, exotic plant, or rare Japanese gardening tool. If this should occur on your San Francisco travels, stop by **Paxton Gate**, where

AUTHOR FAVORITE

Rainbow Grocery Cooperative has always been a perfect expression of the spirit of the Bay Area for me. It's a one-of-a-kind food emporium offering a wide array of organic, vegetarian, and health food items, as well as specialty cookbooks, aromatherapy candles, massage, and other household necessities. More importantly, the grocery has been worker-owned and -operated since 1976. ~ 1745 Folsom Street; 415-863-0620, fax 415-863-8955; www.rainbow.coop.

all your butterfly needs will be met. ~ 824 Valencia Street; 415-824-1872; www.paxtongate.com.

The Mission is known for its secondhand shops, but few beat **Community Thrift Store**. When people donate items to this massive emporium of previously owned furniture, books, posters, records, dishes, and clothes, they designate their favorite charity, which receives the proceeds. Because of the store's policy, it receives better-than-average donations. ~ 623 Valencia Street; 415-861-4910, fax 415-861-7483.

Roccapulco Supper Club, at the edge of the Outer Mission, features live music on Friday and Saturday. Thursday there's hip-hop and rock—in Spanish. For beginners, there are salsa lessons on Wednesday. The ballroom is as big as a warehouse, with enough tables and dance space to fit a Latin American army. It's hot. Closed Sunday through Tuesday. Cover. ~ 3140 Mission Street; 415-648-6611; www.roccapulco.com, e-mail roccapulco@aol.com.

NIGHTLIFE

Valencia street between 15th and 20th streets teem with trendy watering holes.

The **Elbo Room** is lively and the people are having a blast. There are a few pool tables, and live music upstairs ranges from jazz to rockabilly. Upstairs cover. ~ 647 Valencia Street; 415-552-7788; www.elbo.com.

Are loud, smoky nightspots passé? Find out for yourself at the trendy new alternative: **2202 Oxygen Bar**. The oxygen is combined with various scents such as lavender ("for the severely uptight") and patchouli ("for mental bliss"). Paying for what you can get free may seem frivolous, but it's a surprisingly pleasant feeling to sit and breathe herb-infused air for awhile. When you get the bill, remember to take a deep breath. Closed Monday. ~ 795 Valencia Street; 415-255-2102; www.2202bar.com, e-mail oxygensf@yahoo.com.

This area is also home to many outstanding dance companies. Featuring modern and experimental dance, they include the **Margaret Jenkins Dance Company**. ~ 3973-A 25th Street; 415-826-8399; www.mjdc.org. Also based in the Mission is ODC/San Francisco. ~ 3153 17th Street; 415-863-9834; www.odcdance.org.

South of Market

In the 1970s, South of Market, popularly known as SOMA, had the reputation as one of the most unattractive and unsafe neighborhoods in the city. Filled with residential hotels, vacant warehouses, and seedy bars, it was long ignored by many of the city's residents. This neglect presented an opportunity for those who wanted to be isolated, and SOMA became a hub for the gay-bathhouse crowd and the gay-leather crowd.

During the '80s SOMA metamorphosed again. Gay bathhouses were closed in a sweeping move by government officials and replaced by trendy nightclubs; gay-leather bars with names like "The Arena" converted into popular dance clubs with names like the "DNA Lounge."

The underutilized warehouses then brought in a different countercultural crowd—artists. Modeling themselves after the residents of New York City's SOHO (South of Houston) district, Bay Area artists converted SOMA warehouses into combination live/work spaces featuring art galleries, music studios, and performance spaces. Many of San Francisco's most creative people still live and display (or perform) in small galleries and theaters throughout SOMA.

Ephemeral as ever, SOMA next burst into another transitional phase, flaunting its formerly low-profile cyber-art industry with the promotional flair of a P. T. Barnum. Centering on Yerba Buena Gardens as the town square of the area, developers quickly packed the blocks between Market Street and Moscone Convention Center with family-oriented entertainment attractions, many of them showcasing interactive media.

Meanwhile, decrepit old hotels and office buildings in the surrounding neighborhood were replaced by upscale live/work complexes as builders petitioned City Hall for exemptions from San Francisco's strict anti-growth regulations, claiming that more condominiums and office suites in SOMA were needed to keep high-tech companies from moving elsewhere. Today, the artist and gay communities are being squeezed out of SOMA block by block. And oddly enough, all this urban redevelopment is meeting with less public protest than the traffic and noise associated with the big, glitzy nightclubs that are replacing the local leather bars of old.

Still, there are many restaurants and cafés that offer a true SOMA twist to their atmosphere and menu. Don't be surprised if your café table has a computer hooked up to the internet, or the restaurant you're dining at has decor created during the slow hours before lunch.

SIGHTS Named for George Moscone, the San Francisco mayor who was assassinated in 1978, **Moscone Convention Center** is a mammoth convention center that extends across 11 acres. With restaurants, hotels, apartments, and stores encircling it like satellites, the center is the dominant feature in San Francisco's fastest-changing district. ~ Howard Street between 3rd and 4th streets.

An important addition to the area is **Yerba Buena Gardens**, a project that was 30 years in the making but has proven to be worth the wait by providing a forum for the visual and performing arts as well as some much-needed green space.

One component of the ten-acre complex located on top of the underground Moscone Convention Center is the **Yerba Buena Center for the Arts** with two buildings, one designed by the acclaimed Japanese architect Fumihiko Maki. It includes three galleries devoted to visual arts and high-tech installations, as well as a screening room for video and film. A large multipurpose room called "The Forum" hosts special events. In addition, a 755-seat theater offers a diverse lineup of music, dance, and performance art. Closed Monday. Admission.

Softening the contemporary hard edges of Yerba Buena is a five-and-a-half-acre esplanade of gardens and outdoor public art. A focal point of Yerba Buena Gardens is the **Martin Luther King Jr. Memorial**, a graceful waterfall spilling over Sierra granite. Behind the waterfall are a series of 12 thick glass panels etched with quotations drawn from speeches Dr. King made in San Francisco. Each quote is paired with a translation into a different language, including Chinese, Spanish, Hebrew, and Swahili, and representing the origins of the city's major ethnic groups. ~ 415-978-2787, fax 415-978-9635; www.yerbabuenaarts.org, e-mail comments@yerbabuenaarts.org.

The **San Francisco Museum of Modern Art** is one of the top-ten most-visited museums in the United States. The building, designed by Swiss architect Mario Botta, is a Modernist work of art in itself, distinguished by a tower finished in alternating bands of black and white stone. Inside are three large galleries and more than 20 smaller ones, totaling 50,000 square feet. The

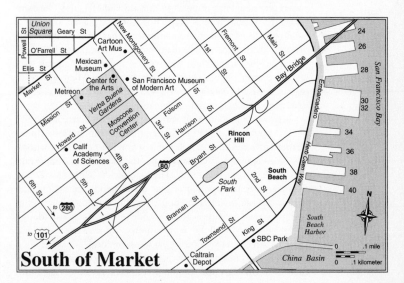

South of Market

second floor displays selections from the museum's permanent collection. The third-floor gallery features photographs and works on paper. The top two gallery floors accommodate special exhibitions and large-scale art from the museum's collection. Closed Wednesday. Admission. ~ 151 3rd Street; 415-357-4000, fax 415-357-4037; www.sfmoma.org.

A peculiar blend of theme park and shopping mall, the **Metreon** combines San Francisco's largest motion picture complex (15 screens plus an IMAX theater), nine restaurants, play areas based on children's books, a futuristic video arcade, and nine retail stores, plus plenty of high-tech advertising. The self-styled "entertainment center" looks like a giant concrete cube from the outside and stands four stories tall to accommodate the 50-by-100-foot IMAX screen. Almost everything here is associated with Sony's entertainment and technology empire and supported by sponsorships from other huge corporations, and many of the management team members are veterans of Disney, so don't be surprised if you feel like you've stepped into the world's largest advertisement for corporate America. If you're traveling with kids, the Metreon is a must-see—sort of. Among the multimedia "tie-ins" is the 175-seat Action Theatre featuring anime movies and live performances, and **Where the Wild Things Are**, a live-action adventure based on Maurice Sendak's book. Another Sendak children's book is the basis for the family-friendly **Night Kitchen** restaurant. You gotta be a teen to fully appreciate **Portal 1**, an arcade designed by French comic artist Moebius (*Heavy Metal*) that features expensive video games played against opposing teams instead of against the computer. A standout here is **HyperBowl**, where players use actual bowling balls in interactive environments that simulate the streets of San Francisco, the surface of an alien planet, or the rocking deck of an ancient sailing ship. Meanwhile, mom and dad can play with the latest high-tech toys at the Sony and Microsoft retail outlets. ~ 4th and Mission streets; 415-3537-3400, 800-638-7366; www.metreon.com, e-mail information@metreon.com.

Just over a second-floor walkway from the Metreon, on top of the Moscone Convention Center, the **Rooftop at Yerba Buena Gardens** presents another collection of family-oriented attractions, this time created not by megacorporations but by the San Francisco Redevelopment Agency. The high-tech draw here is **Zeum**, an art-and-technology center that offers hands-on, behind-the-scenes experiences in animation, video production, digital photography, web page design, 3-D modeling, and stage set design and production. Call for winter hours. Admission. ~ 4th and Howard streets; 415-777-2800; www.zeum.org.

In striking contrast to the futuristic Zeum is the antique **1906 Charles Looff Carousel**, originally the centerpiece of San Francisco's former Playland-at-the-Beach amusement park. The large, beautifully restored carousel has all-white horses that gleam like new. Admission. ~ 4th and Howard streets; 415-541-0312.

In addition, the rooftop complex includes the **Yerba Buena Ice Skating Center** (admission), an Olympic-size ice rink with huge windows overlooking the San Francisco skyline to create the feel of skating outdoors, and the adjoining 12-lane **Yerba Buena Bowling Center.** ~ 750 Folsom Street; 415-777-3727; www.scsf.org/rink.html.

Also located in the Yerba Buena neighborhood, the **Cartoon Art Museum** features rotating exhibits of cartoon art in all its various incarnations: newspaper strips, political cartoons, comic books, and animation are amply represented. Highlights include a children's gallery and a bookstore. One of only two museums of its kind in the United States, this rare treat should not be missed. Closed Monday. Admission. ~ 655 Mission Street; 415-227-8666, fax 415-243-8666; www.cartoonart.org, e-mail funnies@sirius.com.

◀ *HIDDEN*

For a look at the rich arts and cultures of our neighbors to the south, visit the **Mexican Museum.** There are rotating exhibits of pre-Columbian art, Mexican Colonial art, and Chicano contemporary art and art of the Americas. Exhibits in the galleries change every several months. Undergoing move, check website. ~ 718 Mission Street; 415-202-9700; www.mexicanmuseum.org, e-mail emma louise@mexicanmuseum.org.

Called the "Smithsonian of the West," Golden Gate Park's **California Academy of Sciences** has been relocated to SOMA until 2008. Here you will find an array of African animals grouped in jungle settings and a "roundabout" aquarium in which you stand at the center of a circular glass tank while creatures of the deep swim around you. However, it's still a tremendous place for kids. This natural history museum also features numerous "hands-on" exhibits. Admission. ~ 875 Howard Street; 415-750-7145, fax 415-750-7346; www.calacademy.org, e-mail info@calacademy.org.

If your attention wanders during a game at SBC Park, don't blame your team: it may be the food. In addition to basic hot dogs, there's Caribbean food, fruit smoothies, microbrews, and sushi. You *are* in San Francisco, after all.

Tucked into an area bordered by Bryant, Brannan, 2nd, and 3rd streets is **South Park,** an oval-shaped park ringed by cafés and artists' studios. The surrounding neighborhood is an industrial district that includes multimedia companies operating out of lofts in converted warehouses.

To see a startling example of the force with which the 1906 earthquake warped and buckled San Francisco buildings, drive down the alleyway between 5th and 6th streets just south of Mission Street to **479 and 483 Tehama Street**. These old warehouses look like the earth collapsed beneath them at the same time a giant hand shoved them backwards.

Opened at the beginning of the 2000 baseball season as Pacific Bell Park, the recently rechristened SBC **Park** is situated on the south side of the South of Market warehouse district, along the China Basin waterfront and readily accessible from the Embarcadero or Route 280. Baseball's San Francisco Giants left 3Com Park (known as Candlestick Park until a Silicon Valley conglomerate bought the naming rights) in favor of this more cost-efficient facility, which has just over one-half the seating capacity. The $319 million ballpark features classic architecture inspired by Wrigley Field and Fenway Park, together with state-of-the-art lighting and electronics and an innovative seating alignment that provides the best possible views of the field from most seats. Speaking of views, fans also find themselves surrounded by a panorama of the San Francisco skyline, the Bay, and the distant East Bay Hills. Just outside the stadium, a wharfside promenade near center field lets passersby view ball games knothole-style. Tours, offered hourly from 10:30 a.m. to 12:30 p.m. daily except game days, include looks at the press box and the dugout. ~ King Street between 2nd and 3rd streets; 415-972-2400.

LODGING

As soon as you spot the Twister painting on the lobby wall—complete with life-sized mannequin assuming the position—you know you've entered the land of the terminally hip. The **W Hotel** provides trendy types upscale accommodations done in sleek Euro-Asian style. Rooms are spacious enough to launch a start-up inside. ~ 181 3rd Street; 415-777-5300, 877-946-8357, fax 415-817-7823; www.whotels.com. ULTRA-DELUXE.

DINING

It's not every day you can enjoy a dry martini while seated at a curved pink leatherette bar right out of the '50s and then be treated to a postmodern nouvelle American dinner, but that's the case at **Julie's Supper Club**. Despite the loud music, insist on a table in the front room to enjoy the passing array of trendy SOMA club-goers. Stick with the imaginative salads for starters, followed by outstanding chicken, lamb, or fish dishes. Dinner only. Closed Sunday and Monday. ~ 1123 Folsom Street; 415-861-4084, fax 415-861-8078; www.juliessupperclub.com. MODERATE TO ULTRA-DELUXE.

A hotspot not far from the Yerba Buena Gardens complex is **Restaurant Lulu**, a noisy warehouse-sized restaurant that draws in crowds at lunch and dinner for superb meats and chicken prepared on a brick rotisserie. Also noteworthy are the shellfish selections such as iron skillet–roasted mussels and Dungeness crab with garlic. The wine bar offers over 70 wines by the glass. Reservations recommended. ~ 816 Folsom Street; 415-495-5775, fax 415-495-7810; www.restaurantlulu.com. MODERATE TO ULTRA-DELUXE.

South Park Café is a sunny and cheery dining spot facing, as its name suggests, South Park. With only a long zinc bar and a few tables, it is a popular gourmet dining spot known for its imaginative salads and daily meat and fish specials. Dinner only. Closed Sunday. ~ 108 South Park; 415-495-7275, fax 415-495-7295; www.southparkcafe.com. MODERATE TO DELUXE.

Or try **Max's Diner**, the millennial version of a classic old diner. The music is vintage, the menu is meat and potatoes, and the bar is jammed with nostalgic people. ~ 311 3rd Street; 415-546-6297, fax 415-546-9231; www.maxsworld.com. MODERATE.

Trained in New Orleans and Paris, Loretta Keller, chef and founder of **Bizou**, is perhaps single-handedly responsible for the consumption of beef cheeks in San Francisco. Her menu is so good she managed to convince her trusting customers to try the Parisian delicacy and is now serving 100 pounds a week of the dish. If you're not ready for that, try the tomato-braised veal shank or the grilled scallops with fried artichokes. The service here is excellent. No lunch on Saturday. Closed Sunday. ~ 598 4th Street; 415-543-2222, fax 415-543-2999. DELUXE.

If you're looking to nosh on a bagel, burgers, sandwich, or salad while your duds spin around in the suds, drop by **Brain Wash**. This innovative address combines a café with a laundromat. Check out their cheap ($2.99) breakfasts Monday through Friday. ~ 1122 Folsom Street; 415-861-3663; www.brainwash.com, e-mail getlost@brainwash.com. BUDGET.

A kind of faux Pompeiian eatery, **Café Rustico** offers excellent pizza, panini, calzone, sandwiches, and salads. Homemade

❖❖❖

FEAST ALL YOUR SENSES

There's another side to San Francisco beyond the bridge-dotted skyline and bustling capitalism; past the elaborate Victorians and winding streets; behind the inline skaters and Sunday strollers. It's a world of camp and fashion, where the drinks are mixed, the music is intoxicating, the clothing is sleek, and the men are women. Welcome to **AsiaSF**. Make no mistake, the food is good: lots of grilled seafood, chicken satay, "baby got back" ribs and other Asian-influenced entrées. But no one comes for the food. They come for the "gender illusionists"—men you'd swear on your partner were women—performing cabaret numbers on a red runway when they're not filling water glasses. After dinner, work off the calories in the state-of-the-art danceclub downstairs. ~ 201 9th Street; 415-255-2742; www.asiasf.com. DELUXE.

soups, quiche, vegetarian lasagna, and tasty tarts are also served in the dining area or at sidewalk tables. Convenient to the South of Market discount outlets, this is the place to refuel on the bargain trail. ~ 300 DeHaro Street; 415-252-0180, fax 415-252-1533. BUDGET.

SHOPPING The highly regarded auction house **Bonhams & Butterfields** has regular sales that are open to the public. You must register on-line before you can bid. ~ 220 San Bruno Avenue; 415-861-7500; www.butterfields.com.

Also located South of Market is the **Flower Mart**, where dozens of florists offer excellent prices. ~ 6th and Brannan streets.

Walking or driving around will net additional possibilities, from furniture stores to gallery shops and artist studios.

NIGHTLIFE SOMA is the epicenter of San Francisco's nightclub scene, and "something for everybody" seems to be the motto. For some live acoustic sounds from local bands or deejay-spun jazz, check out **Brain Wash**. There's always something happening at this hip café that also doubles as a . . . laundromat! Wednesday is "spoken word" night, Thursday is comedy night, and Friday and Saturday feature live bands. ~ 1122 Folsom Street; 415-861-3663; www.brainwash.com, e-mail getlost@brainwash.com.

There is only one thing in the world better than a rocking nightclub: three rocking nightclubs. That's what you get over at 3rd and Harrison streets. **The X** features alternative music on Friday night; on Saturday **City Nights** jumps to the sound of Top-40 hip-hop, R&B, and house at the same location; and on Thursday, it's gay and lesbian night at **Club Faith**. Cover. ~ 715 Harrison Street; 415-546-7938; www.sfclubs.com, e-mail sharonsfclubs@aol.com.

Not sure what you're in the mood for tonight? Then head to **Ten 15**, a SOMA club with three floors and five separate dance environments, each featuring a different sound from house to trance to techno. The club is open after-hours, often going on until 7 a.m. Open Friday and Saturday. The first Thursday of the month caters to an art crowd and the first Sunday to a gay clientele.

THREE BABES AND A BUS

If you find SF's nightlife options overwhelming, **3 Babes and a Bus** allows you a 45-minute taste of different scenes, from '70s disco and Top-40 to salsa and R&B. For a flat fee, this nightclub-touring company takes care of the driving and cover charges while ensuring priority entry to a number of clubs on this four-hour tour. Reservations recommended. ~ 800-414-0158; www.threebabes.com, e-mail info@threebabes.com.

Cover. ~ 1015 Folsom Street; 415-431-1200; www.1015.com, e-mail 1015@1015.com.

Hip, black-clad twenty-somethings with funky haircuts and dancing feet converge on the two dancefloors at the **Cat Club**. Deejays spin '80s hits, Brit pop, indie rock, and hip-hop most nights; on Tuesday, bands crank out rock and metal. Cover. ~ 1190 Folsom Street; 415-431-3332; www.catclubsf.com.

The DNA **Lounge** has lasted much longer than most trendy clubs. The scene is high-decibel with a mixed crowd clearly born to dance. And dance they do, all over this two-story club. There's also occasional live music. Cover. ~ 375 11th Street; 415-626-1409; www.dnalounge.com, e-mail info@dnalounge.com.

A self-proclaimed "white trash bistro," **Butter** serves up a host of snacks and drinks—all to the sound of a funky house beat provided by deejays. Just follow the 30-something model-chic hipsters in always-fashionable black. Closed Sunday through Tuesday. ~ 354 11th Street; 415-863-5964; www.smoothasbutter.com.

Some of the classic Bay Area rock and blues performers appear at **Slim's**, possibly because entertainer Boz Scaggs is an owner. But there is also a hefty line-up of alternative rock bands, so the crowd could be grey- or green-haired at this all-ages club. Usually a cover. ~ 333 11th Street; 415-522-0333, fax 415-255-0427; www.slims-sf.com.

The **Paradise Lounge** offers three dancefloors and four full bars, so grab a drink and get your groove on. Feeling adventurous? Climb into a go-go cage for maximum dance exposure. Open Friday and Saturday only. Cover. ~ 308 11th Street; 415-621-1912; www.paradiselounge.com.

An important member of the city's group of small theaters is the **Asian American Theater Company**, which represents the city's burgeoning Asian community. ~ 690 5th Street, Suite 211; 415-543-5738; www.asianamericantheater.org.

With over 40 tables, **The Great Entertainer** is one of the largest poolhalls on the West Coast. Located in a former warehouse, this vast establishment also offers snooker tables, shuffleboard, ping pong, darts, video games, and a full bar. ~ 975 Bryant Street; 415-861-8833; www.tge.com, e-mail jim@tge.com.

San Francisco's "Backyard"

There is an area of San Francisco, stretching across the southern sector of the metropolis that I call the city's "Backyard." Dotted throughout this sprawling residential region are a number of inviting places. Most are unknown to tourists; some remain hidden even to native San Franciscans. To find them you'll require a feel for adventure, a touch of patience, and a good road map. Plus a special desire to uncover secret locales.

SIGHTS

HIDDEN ▶

Everyone knows about the 1906 quake, just as everyone has heard of Lombard, San Francisco's "crookedest street." Few are aware of **Vermont Street**, even though it might just be crookeder than the crookedest. That's because it's located out on Potrero Hill, a clapboard neighborhood that has been gentrified by artists, craftspeople, and imaginative others. From a public park at Vermont and 20th streets, there's a back-door view of San Francisco's skyline; in the opposite direction loom Twin Peaks, Mt. Davidson, and a ridgeline of lesser hills. From this coign of vantage, Vermont snakes down to 22nd Street in a mesmerizing series of zigs and zags.

For another splendid view, head to **Bernal Heights**. This working-class neighborhood is similar to Potrero Hill, though economically more upscale and geographically a bit upslope. Bernal Heights Boulevard encircles a shale-strewn hill from the top of which the entire Bay Area spreads before you. Just park on the street and climb a short distance uphill. To the north stands the Golden Gate and beyond it the fog-curled mountains of Marin. Then as the eye moves clockwise, the San Francisco skyline appears in the foreground. The Bay, long and narrow here, draws a line along the eastern perimeter as it ebbs and flows from San Jose. Complete this 360° sweep and your eye will hike the ridgeline that protects San Francisco from the rolling fogs of the Pacific Ocean.

Of course, the view of views is from **Twin Peaks** on Twin Peaks Boulevard. Atop these bald knobs the eye traces a circle around the entire Bay. The Golden Gate Bridge becomes a mere corridor

SF'S WEST COAST   Head out to San Francisco's west coast to visit two different kid-pleasers: the **Exploratorium** (page 108) and the **San Francisco Zoo** (page 111).

METREON   One of the most child-friendly restaurants in town is **Portal 1** (page 146) in the Metreon. Although some moms report that their media-savvy kids are unimpressed with other Metreon attractions, two places not to miss are the adjacent **Zeum** and the **1906 Charles Looff Carousel** on the Rooftop at Yerba Buena Gardens (page 146).

TOYS   Take the warm-and-fuzzy industrial tour at the **Basic Brown Bear Factory** (page 82).

THE HAIGHT   Fool your kids into learning while they have a blast at the **Randall Museum** (page 124), where the interactive fun may change their minds about museum outings.

that opens onto a mountain range called Marin. The Bay is a pond inhabited by sailboats. The cityscape lies before you, and buildings appear as out of the wrong end of a telescope. Jostled and teeming, civilization stretches to the west, only to pile up at the Pacific's edge. It is a view for travelers who can wander back in the mind to the days before humankind when wind and water were all the land could see.

After leaving the metropolis in the dust, spur your mount toward **Glen Canyon Park**. With its meandering stream, dense underbrush, and twisted geologic formations, there's something about this steep canyon that evokes the Old West. Granted, the sunglinted windows of civilization surround the hillsides, but deep in the heart of this draw are hiking trails that are escapes from urbanity. Like all treasures, Glen Canyon is hard to find and requires a map. Most visitors to the park come along Portola Drive to O'Shaughnessy Boulevard, then down to Elk Street. Turning left onto Elk, there's a ballfield and tennis courts, followed immediately by a road. Turn onto the road as it parallels the courts; it becomes a dirt road that forks into several hiking trails.

Another wooded retreat rests nearby atop **Mt. Davidson**. A trail from the corner of Myra Way and Sherwood Court climbs sharply to the 938-foot summit of San Francisco's highest peak. The concrete cross at the top measures another 103 feet; for more than 60 years the Council of Churches has celebrated its Easter sunrise services here. If today doesn't happen to be Easter, you can still peer through the eucalyptus forest out over the Pacific.

Stern Grove is known for its free summer concerts in the park. Aficionados of jazz and classical music flock every Sunday to this natural amphitheater. The San Francisco Opera and Ballet companies always put on one performance each during the summer here. Regardless of the day or season, the grove offers visitors grassy meadows, shady spots, and a tiny lake encircled by eucalyptus trees and freckled with ducks. It's a beautiful stroll from the gingerbread house (once an infamous gambling den) to the lake, even when there's nary a symphonic sound to be heard. ~ Corner of 19th Avenue and Sloat Boulevard; 415-252-6252.

DINING

Out in the Sunset district, a tiny storefront restaurant that serves some of the most flavorful and authentic Mexican dishes north of Veracruz is **Casa Aguila**. Mini tamales are good for starters. As for the entrées, seafood paella and pork steaks marinated in citrus juices and fresh herbs are standouts, as are chicken *mole* and chile rellenos with pork, dried fruits, marinated vegetables, and walnuts. A reservation is a good idea; otherwise, be prepared to wait while munching on the free tamales. Closed Monday. ~ 1240 Noriega Street; 415-661-5593. BUDGET TO MODERATE.

SHOPPING

Near Potrero Hill, **Petco's Pet World** is much more than a pet shop. It's more like a zoo. Petco's has all kinds of exotic birds, reptiles, and snakes, as well as more run-of-the-mill pets such as hamsters and goldfish. Bring Fluffy home a new jeweled collar or buy yourself some animal motif jewelry. ~ 85 Bryant Street; 415-863-1840, fax 415-861-7570.

NIGHTLIFE

At **Trad'r Sam** you sit in booths named Guam, Samoa, and various Hawaiian islands and slowly sip such tropical concoctions as Tahitian deep purples, mai tais, and banana cows. Soak in the 1940s Polynesian atmosphere. This bar is a classic. ~ 6150 Geary Boulevard; 415-221-0773.

For more information on Stern Grove's free June-through-August concerts, visit www.sterngrove.org. You can also check newspapers or call 415-252-6252.

Perhaps the closest thing to an authentic Dublin pub in San Francisco is **The Plough and the Stars** with its burnished wood paneling and framed political cartoons hanging on the walls. A stage in the back presents rousing Irish folk bands on most nights. Cover on Friday and Saturday. ~ 116 Clement Street; 415-751-1122, fax 415-831-1538.

The **Last Day Saloon** is a neighborhood watering hole that features jazz, rock, reggae, and hip-hop groups. It's attractively decorated, yet informal and friendly. No live music Sunday and Monday. Cover. ~ 406 Clement Street; 415-387-6343; www.lastdaysaloon.com.

Theater of Yugen Noh Space (415-621-7978) and **A Traveling Jewish Theatre** (415-399-1809; www.atjt.com) are among the companies in permanent residence in the Project Artaud complex. ~ 450 Florida Street; 415-621-7797.

If you hanker to spend a day deep-sea fishing for rock cod, bass, salmon, and other gamefish, check out **Wacky Jacky**, which takes you out on her 50-foot *Delta*, often heading out to the Farallon Islands in search of salmon. ~ Fisherman's Wharf, Berth 1; 415-586-9800. Bring a lunch and dress warmly.

Outdoor Adventures

SPORT-FISHING

Some of the world's most challenging sailing can be found on San Francisco Bay. Spend an afternoon cruising the Bay on a motorized yacht with **Pacific Marine Yachts**, which has three yachts ranging from 75 to 150 feet. They offer a two-hour brunch excursion around the Bay on Sunday. ~ Pier 39; 415-788-9100, 800-292-2487; www.signaturesf.com, e-mail sales@signaturesf.com.

From the deck of the **Oceanic Society**'s 63-foot vessel you'll observe elephant seals and sea lions, dolphins, puffins, porpoises, and humpback, blue, and gray whales also frequent the waters. Day-cruises to the Farallon Islands are offered June through November; whale-watching tours go from December until mid-May. Reservations required. ~ Fort Mason Center, Building E; 415-474-3385, 800-326-7491, fax 415-474-3395; www.oceanic society.org.

SAILING & NATURE CRUISES

If you like to soar the skies, try hang gliding. There are sites at Fort Funston (Skyline Boulevard at the far end of Ocean Beach) and Westlake (just south of Fort Funston). For lessons in paragliding, contact **Merlin Flight School**. Flights offer views of the coastline. ~ 415-456-3670; www.merlinflightschool.com, e-mail wally@merlinflightschool.com. If you're not ready to test those wings, you'll find it's fun just to watch.

HANG GLIDING

When weekends roll around, several hundred folks are apt to don inline skates and rollerskates and careen along the sidewalks and streets of Golden Gate Park. John F. Kennedy Drive, on the east side of the park, is closed to cars on Sundays and holidays. It's great exercise, and a lot of fun to boot. Rentals are available outside of the park at **Skates on Haight**. Closed Sunday in winter. ~ 1818 Haight Street; 415-752-8376; www.skates.com, e-mail le ecole@skates.com. Try their 1219 Polk Street location, too. You can also rent on the park's north side from **Golden Gate Park Skates and Bikes**. ~ 3038 Fulton Street at 6th Avenue; 415-668-1117.

SKATING

In a city of steep hills, where walking provides more than enough exercise, jogging is nevertheless a favorite pastime. There are actually places to run where the terrain is fairly level and the scenery

JOGGING

spectacular. Most popular are the Golden Gate Bridge, the Presidio Highlands, Glen Canyon Park Trail, Ocean Beach, Golden Gate Park, and Angel Island.

Parcourses, combining aerobic exercises with short jogs, are located at Justin Herman Park (the foot of Market Street near the Ferry Building; half course only), Marina Green (along Marina Boulevard near the foot of Fillmore Street), Mountain Lake Park (Lake Street between 8th and Funston avenues), and the Polo Field in Golden Gate Park.

SWIMMING   Although the air temperature remains moderate all year, the ocean and bay around San Francisco stay cold. If you're ready to brave the Arctic current, join the hearty swimmers who make the plunge regularly at Aquatic Park. Many of these brave souls belong to either the **Dolphin Club** or the **South End Rowing Club**. Both clubs are open to the public (on alternating weekdays, call for open dates) and provide saunas and showers for a small fee (bring your own towel and swimgear). ~ Dolphin Club: 502 Jefferson Street; 415-441-9329. South End Rowing Club: 500 Jefferson Street; 415-776-7372.

SURFING   West of Golden Gate Park there are several spots along San Francisco's wide, sandy **Ocean Beach**; however, the conditions vary seasonally and, because of strong rip currents, this is not a place for beginners. **Fort Point**, located on the bay side of the Golden Gate Bridge's south tower, is another surf break in the city. Fast-flowing currents moving out the Gate make this another spot for experts only.

GOLF   For the earthbound, golf can be a heavenly sport in San Francisco. Several courses are worth checking out. With two separate tee boxes, the **Glen Eagles International Golf Club** features a nine-hole course that's hilly and narrow. This public course rents power carts, and has a small pro shop. ~ 2100 Sunnydale Avenue; 415-587-2425. **Golden Gate Park Golf Course** is a short but tricky nine-hole course close to the ocean. They rent pull carts and clubs at this public course. ~ 47th Avenue and Fulton Street; 415-751-8987. **Harding Park Golf Course** is considered to be one of the finest public courses in the country. There is an 18-hole course and a 9-hole course. Power carts are available for rent, as well as golf clubs. ~ Harding Park Road and Skyline Boulevard; 415-661-1865. The 18-hole **Presidio Golf Course**, the only golf course in a U.S. national park, was originally built in 1895 for Army officers to use and doubled as a drill field for troop reviews. Opened to civilians in 1995, it has quickly gained a reputation as one of the finest public courses in Northern California. Cart and club rentals are available. ~ Presidio; 415-561-4664; www.presidio golf.com, e-mail presidiogc@palmergolf.com.

With more than 150 free public courts, San Francisco could easily be called The City of Nets. **Golden Gate Park** has 21 courts. There *is* a fee to play, however. ~ John F. Kennedy and Middle drives. In the Marina try the four lighted courts at the **George Moscone Playground**. ~ Chestnut and Buchanan streets. A popular spot in the Mission is **Mission Dolores Park**, with six lighted courts. ~ 18th and Dolores streets. On Nob Hill the three courts at the **Alice Marble Memorial Playground** are recommended. ~ Greenwich and Hyde streets. In Chinatown try the one lighted court at the **Chinese Playground**. ~ Sacramento Street and Waverly Plaza. Over in North Beach the **North Beach Playground** has three lighted courts. ~ Lombard and Mason streets. For more information on all city courts call the San Francisco Parks and Recreation Department. ~ 415-753-7032, fax 415-753-7105.

TENNIS

San Francisco is not a city designed for cyclers. Some of the hills are almost too steep to walk and downtown traffic can be gruelling. There are places, however, that are easy to ride and beautiful as well. **Golden Gate Park**, the **Golden Gate Promenade**, and **Lake Merced** all have excellent bike routes.

BIKING

Among the city's most dramatic rides is the bicyclists' sidewalk on the **Golden Gate Bridge**. Or, if you're less adventurous, the **Sunset Bikeway** begins at Lake Merced Boulevard, then carries through a residential area and past views of the ocean to the Polo Field in Golden Gate Park.

Bike Rentals   Near Fisherman's Wharf is **Blazing Saddles Bike Rentals**, with mountain bikes, hybrids, and tandems. ~ 1095 Columbus Avenue; 415-202-8888; www.blazingsaddles.com. Located nearby, **Bike and Roll** provides a complimentary windbreaker for summers in San Francisco. ~ 734 Lombard Street; 415-771-8735, 888-544-2453; www.bicyclerental.com. Near the southeast corner of Golden Gate Park is **Avenue Cyclery**, which

STOP TRAFFIC

If you find yourself on a bike on the last Friday of the month, head over to Justin Herman Plaza at 5:30 p.m. and join **Critical Mass** for a huge group ride. This slow-paced, moderate bike expedition lasts about two hours; the route varies each time, but expect to bring traffic to a halt as you maneuver through thoroughfares and up inclines with hundreds of other two-wheelers.

rents mountain bikes, tandems, hybrids, and kids' bicycles. ~ 756 Stanyan Street; 415-387-3155. The **Angel Island Company** rents 21-speed mountain bikes, tandems, junior bikes, and child trailers to explore that state park's paved paths. ~ Angel Island; 415-897-0715.

▼▼▼▼▼▼▼▼▼▼▼▼
Transportation

CAR

The major highways leading into San Francisco are **Route 1**, the picturesque coastal road, **Route 101**, California's coastal north–south thoroughfare, and **Route 80**, the transcontinental highway that originates on the East Coast.

AIR

San Francisco International Airport, better known as SFO, sits 15 miles south of downtown San Francisco off Routes 101 and 280. A major destination from all points of the globe, the airport is always bustling.

Most domestic airlines fly into SFO, including Alaska Airlines, American Airlines, Continental Airlines, Delta Air Lines, Hawaiian Airlines, Northwest, and United Airlines.

International carriers are also prominent here: Aeroflot, Air Canada, British Airways, China Airlines, Canadian Air, Japan Airlines, Lufthansa, Mexicana, Philippine Airlines, Singapore Airlines, and TACA International Airlines have regular flights into San Francisco's airport.

The **SFO Ground Transportation Information Service** is a free service that will help you plan your way to and from the airport via buses, shuttles, taxis, limousines, and more. ~ There's an information booth in the baggage claim area of each SFO terminal.

BART (650-992-2278) now runs from the airport to all its destinations. Or, to travel from the airport to downtown San Francisco, call SFO **Airporter,** which runs frequently. ~ 650-624-0500. **Supershuttle** provides door-to-door service. ~ 415-558-8500; www.supershuttle.com. Or catch a **San Mateo County Transit,** or **SamTrans,** bus (800-660-4287, fax 650-817-1717) to the Transbay Terminal (425 Mission Street). Taxi and limo service are also available, or try **Lorrie's Airport Service.** ~ 415-334-9000; www.lorries-shuttles.com.

BUS

Greyhound Bus Lines (800-231-2222) services San Francisco from around the country. Buses arrive and depart from the Transbay Terminal. ~ 425 Mission Street; 415-495-1569; www.greyhound.com.

TRAIN

For those who prefer to travel by rail, **Amtrak** has train service via the "Coast Starlight," "California Zephyr," and "San Joaquin." These trains arrive at and depart from the Emeryville train station, with connecting bus service to San Francisco's Ferry Building, where Market Street meets the Embarcadero. ~ 5885 Landregan Street, Emeryville; 800-872-7245; www.amtrak.com.

The easiest way to explore San Francisco is by foot or public transit. Driving in San Francisco can be a nightmare. Parking spaces are rare, parking lots expensive. Then there are the hills, which require you to navigate along dizzying inclines while dodging cable cars, trollies, pedestrians, and double-parked vehicles. The streets of San Francisco make Mr. Toad's wild ride look tame.

CAR RENTALS

If you do decide to rent a car, most major rental agencies have franchises right at the airport. These include **Avis Rent A Car** (800-331-1212), **Budget Rent A Car** (800-527-0700), **Dollar Rent A Car** (800-800-4000), **Hertz Rent A Car** (800-654-3131), and **National** (800-227-7368).

PUBLIC TRANSIT

San Francisco is a city where public transit works. To get anywhere in the city, call **San Francisco Muni** and an operator will direct you to the appropriate mode of public transportation. ~ 415-673-6864; www.sfmuni.com.

Over 90 bus lines travel around, about, and through the city. Trolley buses, street cars, light-rail subways, and cable cars also crisscross San Francisco. Most lines operate daily (with a modified schedule on weekends and holidays). Free transfers allow a 90-minute stopover or connection to two more lines. Exact fares are required. For complete information on the Muni system, purchase a copy of the "Muni Street and Transit Map" from the Visitor Information Center (900 Market Street; 415-391-2000), the Information Desk at City Hall, or local bookstores and corner groceries.

Unlike San Francisco's classic cable cars, the **Bay Area Rapid Transit System,** or BART, operates streamlined cars that zip beneath the city's streets. This space-age system travels from Downtown to the Mission District, Glen Park, and SFO. It also runs under the San Francisco Bay to the cities of Oakland, Berkeley,

◆◆

SLOW AND STEADY WINS THE RACE

An alternative to Greyhound is the **Green Tortoise**, a New Age company with a fleet of funky buses. Each is equipped with sleeping platforms that allow travelers to rest as they cross the country. The buses stop at interesting sightseeing points en route. The Green Tortoise, an endangered species from the '60s, travels to and from the East Coast, Grand Canyon, Alaska, Baja Mexico, and elsewhere. It provides a mode of transportation as well as an experience in group living. ~ 494 Broadway; 415-956-7500; www.greentortoise.com, e-mail tortoise@greentortoise.com.

and other parts of the East Bay. Trains run every 8 to 20 minutes depending on the time of day. BART opens at 4 a.m. (6 a.m. on Saturday and 8 a.m. on Sunday) and closes at midnight every night. ~ 650-992-2278; www.bart.gov.

Many surrounding communities feature transportation services to and from San Francisco. To the north, **Golden Gate Transit** provides both bus and ferryboat service. ~ 415-923-2000; www.goldengatetransit.org. South of San Francisco, **San Mateo County Transit**, or **SamTrans**, offers bus service as far south as Palo Alto. ~ 800-660-4287; www.samtrans.com. In addition, **Caltrain** provides daily commuter service from San Jose to San Francisco with stops along the way. ~ Fourth and Townsend streets; 800-660-4287; www.caltrain.com. Across the Bay, **Alameda–Contra Costa Transit**, or **AC Transit**, carries passengers from Oakland, Berkeley, and other East Bay cities to the Transbay Terminal in San Francisco. ~ 510-839-2882; www.actransit.org. For more information on ferry services, see the "Transportation" section in Chapter Three.

CABLE CARS

Cable cars, those clanging symbols of San Francisco, are *the* way to see this city of perpendicular hills. This venerable system covers a ten-mile section of downtown San Francisco.

The cable car was invented in 1873 by Andrew Hallidie and works via an underground cable that travels continuously at a speed of nine and a half miles per hour. Three of the system's original twelve lines still operate year-round. The Powell–Mason and Powell–Hyde cars travel from the Downtown district to Fisherman's Wharf; the California Street line runs east to west and passes through Chinatown and Nob Hill.

TAXIS

Cabs are plentiful, but flagging them down is a trick—it's best to call by phone. The main companies are **DeSoto Cab Company** (415-970-1300), **Luxor Cabs** (415-282-4141), **Veteran's Taxi Cab Company** (415-552-1300), and **Yellow Cab** (415-626-2345).

CLANG, CLANG, CLANG GOES THE CABLE CAR

Built partially of wood and furnished with old-style running boards, cable cars are slow and stylish. Edging up the city's steep heights, then descending toboggan-run hills to the Bay, these open-air vehicles provide many of San Francisco's finest views. Half the joy of riding, however, comes from watching the operators of these antique machines. Each has developed a personal style of gripping, braking, and bell-ringing. In addition to the breathtaking ride, they will often treat you to a clanging street symphony.

San Francisco is a city made for walkers. Appropriately, it offers a number of walking tours that explore various neighborhoods and historical spots.

WALKING TOURS

Chinese Heritage Walks, conducted by the Chinese Culture Center, reveal the true Chinatown. They also offer a **Culinary Walk** that visits markets and herb shops, then stops for lunch in a dim sum restaurant. Call ahead for tour times. Reservations required. Fee. ~ Holiday Inn (third floor), corner of Kearny and Washington streets; 415-986-1822; www.c-c-c.org, e-mail info@c-c-c.org.

Wok Wiz Walking Tours, led by cookbook author Shirley Fong-Torres and staff, features local markets, herbal pharmacies, temples, and other attractions. A dim sum lunch is optional. This daily two-and-a-half-hour walk is a tasty way to get acquainted with Chinatown's historical and culinary world. Fee. ~ 654 Commercial Street; 415-981-8989; www.wokwiz.com, e-mail wokwiz@aol.com.

The **Dashiell Hammett Walking Tour** is a three-mile search for the old haunts of the mystery writer and his fictional sleuth, Sam Spade. Hammett lived in the bay city from 1921 to 1930, and used it as the setting for numerous short stories and novels, including *The Maltese Falcon*. Following the tracks of Sam Spade, the tour combs the city from the Tenderloin to Nob Hill. The tour is given every Sunday in May and September and begins at noon at the northwest corner of the San Francisco Public Library at 100 Larkin and Fulton streets. Fee. ~ P.O. Box 8755, Emeryville, CA 94662; 510-287-9540; www.donherron.com/tour.html, e-mail dashdude@donherron.com.

Folks at the Mexican Museum lead a tour of the **San Francisco City Club**, an early-20th-century building that once housed the San Francisco Stock Exchange and features a fresco by Diego Rivera. First Wednesday of every month at 3 p.m. Fee. ~ 155 Sansome Street; 415-285-0495, fax 415-441-7683. Tours are also given by **Precita Eyes Mural Arts Center**. Fee. ~ 2981 24th Street; 415-285-2287.

City Guides, a volunteer organization sponsored by the Friends of the San Francisco Public Library, offers free tours of various locations throughout the city. They include separate tours of the Ferry Building, Pacific Heights Victorians, North Beach, Nob Hill, Coit Tower, and other points of interest. For information, call 415-557-4266; www.sfcityguides.org, e-mail tours@sfcityguides.org.

For a look at some of San Francisco's tourist-free zones and their array of Victorian homes, consider a two-and-a-half-hour **Victorian Home Walk**. Hosted by Jay Gifford, the tour's pace and tone are set by the group of two or more. Tours depart daily from Union Square. Fee. ~ 415-252-9485; www.victorianwalk.com, e-mail jay@victorianwalk.com.

Experience San Francisco's gay community by **Cruisin' the Castro** with host Trevor Hailey. Approximately four hours long, this entertaining walking tour includes a visit to the 1922 vintage Castro Theater, Pink Triangle Memorial Park (the first of its kind to commemorate gays who died in WWII's concentration camps), and a lunch stop. Reservations required. No tours January through May; no tours Sunday and Monday. Fee. ~ 415-550-8110; www.webcastro.com/castrotour, e-mail trvrhailey@aol.com.

Discover the sights and tastes of the Mission and Noe Valley with **J Walks**. Tours last three hours and include a substantial amount of snacking at shops and cafés. Guides Jean Feilmoser and Joyce Ferman provide a delightful look at the pretty Victorians, funky shops, and vibrant murals that dominate the neighborhood. Reservations required. No tours December through April. Fee. ~ 415-806-0049; www.jwalks.com, e-mail tours@jwalks.com.

THREE

Bay Area

Geologists demythologize even the most romantic places. San Francisco Bay, they state, is a drowned river valley. Glaciers melting 10,000 years ago created it by raising sea levels and causing the ocean to flood a canyon that earlier had been carved by the Sacramento and San Joaquin rivers.

Mountains surround the entire area. The Santa Cruz Mountains rise to the west and south; on the other side are the East Bay Hills and Diablo Range; to the north looms Mt. Tamalpais. At the mouth of the Bay is the Golden Gate, a rocky conduit through which California's major drainage system empties into the Pacific.

Then the geographers take over, explaining that San Francisco Bay covers 900 square miles. It extends 50 miles south from the Golden Gate to San Jose, and ranges east for 30 miles through San Pablo and Suisun bays to the Delta.

Along the west side of the Bay sits the Peninsula. Containing wealthy suburban towns, it reaches to Palo Alto, home of Stanford University. Santa Clara Valley, better known as Silicon Valley, capital of the computer industry, sprawls along the South Bay. San Jose, with a population greater than San Francisco, dominates the area. The East Bay, directly across the water from San Francisco, features Oakland, one of the world's largest container shipping ports, and the dynamic campus town of Berkeley. To the north lies Marin County, a posh enclave highlighted by the town of Sausalito, with its aura of the Mediterranean. (Western Marin, along the Pacific, is covered in Chapter Five.)

That last word is important to meteorologists, who use it to describe the Bay Area climate. With an average temperature of 57°, it resembles sections of southern Europe. Summers are warm and dry and the warm winters bring plentiful rainfall. Though snow is extremely rare, annual precipitation varies from 20 inches in the warm South Bay to 33 inches in cooler Marin. Fog is a fact of life, particularly around the Golden Gate.

Historians perceive the area differently. They begin with the Ohlone Indians, part of the Costanoan language group, who occupied the region perhaps as early as 7000 B.C. In Marin, the Coast Miwok held sway. By the 18th century, on the eve of the white man's appearance, the Indian population numbered about 9000.

The Spanish arrived in 1769. Gaspar de Portolá explored the length of the Peninsula, and was probably the first European to see San Francisco Bay. By 1777, his countrymen founded San Jose, building Mission Santa Clara de Asís and establishing a pueblo with 66 residents. They pressed on to Marin in 1817, creating Mission San Rafael Archangel in the town of San Rafael.

By then the Spanish were already in decline, and San Rafael represents the next-to-last of their 21 California missions. The Bay was becoming a major shipping point for merchants from several countries. Traders bartered sugar, spices, and other goods for cattle hides, better known as "California banknotes."

After the Americans took over California in 1846, the fruit farming industry blossomed in the South Bay and lumbering dominated elsewhere. Timber was stripped from surrounding mountains and shipped through the Golden Gate. Then the Gold Rush brought further prosperity to towns along the Bay and made the Delta a vital corridor for goods shipped upriver to Sacramento and the Gold Country. After Chinese and other workers built a labyrinthine system of levees later in the century, the Delta became the nation's richest agricultural area.

Communities in the East Bay and Marin bloomed after the 1906 earthquake as thousands of refugees sought new homes. When the Golden Gate and Bay bridges opened during the 1930s, another trans-Bay migration occurred.

By the 1950s, the South Bay was moving to center stage. The electronics boom sounded and computer manufacturing replaced fruit farming. Between 1940 and 1998, the population of Santa Clara County increased exponentially from about 300,000 to almost 1,700,000. Today, a staggering percentage of the nation's high-tech components originate from this Silicon Valley region. A victim of its own success, Santa Clara County began losing population in 1999 as high rents and real estate prices forced many Silicon Valley workers to live in other counties and commute an average of 150 miles a day. By the beginning of the 21st century, however, the high-tech industry and the astronomical housing prices were in retreat. Now the area remains in limbo, buoyed by past successes, but decidedly stagnant.

History in the 1960s was written in red and black. Berkeley became a rallying point, first for the Free Speech Movement in 1964, and later for the anti–Vietnam War mobilization. Its provocative populace set the pace for a nationwide movement that helped force the United States out of Southeast Asia. In 1967, Huey Newton and Bobby Seale founded the Black Panther Party in Oakland. The East Bay was a staging ground for revolution with demonstrations and riots continuing into the early 1970s.

Later in that decade, as the "Me Generation" matured, sybaritic Marin became known for its hot tubs and peacock feather massages. Berkeley politics mellowed and moved from the radical fringes to the liberal center. Oakland expanded its port at the expense of San Francisco's shrinking waterfront, and San Jose overtook San Francisco as the state's third largest city. Meanwhile, the entire Bay Area (including San Francisco) grew to more than six million population.

Rather than visualizing the Bay Area as geologists and historians, it's time to look at the region through the eyes of the traveler. To ease the visitor's entry, this

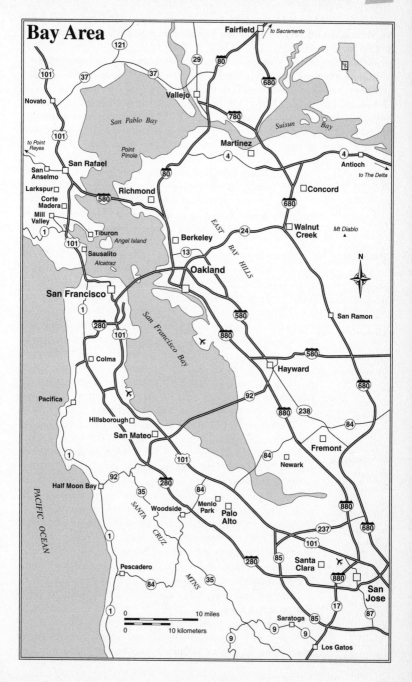

Bay Area

to Sacramento

Fairfield

Vallejo

Novato

San Pablo Bay

Point Pinole

to Point Reyes

San Rafael

San Anselmo

Larkspur

Corte Madera

Mill Valley

Tiburon

Angel Island

Sausalito

Alcatraz

San Francisco

Colma

Pacifica

Hillsborough

San Mateo

Half Moon Bay

PACIFIC OCEAN

SANTA CRUZ MTNS

Pescadero

Woodside

Menlo Park

Palo Alto

Martinez

Antioch

to The Delta

Concord

Walnut Creek

Mt Diablo

N

San Ramon

Suisun Bay

EAST BAY HILLS

Oakland

Berkeley

San Francisco Bay

Hayward

Fremont

Newark

Santa Clara

San Jose

Saratoga

Los Gatos

0   10 miles

0   10 kilometers

121

37

37

29

80

680

780

4

4

680

24

13

580

580

880

92

880

238

84

880

680

101

280

101

1

1

1

92

35

280

84

280

85

101

237

880

680

17

87

85

9

9

9

chapter is divided into five sections. Proceeding counterclockwise from San Francisco, they are the Peninsula, South Bay, East Bay, and Marin, followed by a northeastern tangent out into the Delta.

Within this lazy loop reside two of the nation's finest universities—Stanford, with its 8100-acre campus, and Berkeley. There is also the Santa Clara Valley, where the box-shaped architecture of the high-tech industry gives way to fruit orchards and rolling hills. Marin, one of the nation's richest counties, features picturesque towns and opulent estates. The Delta is a dreamy maze of waterways linked by drawbridges. Together these diverse sections form a circle and salient, along which lie some of the prettiest land west of the Atlantic.

▼ ▼ ▼ ▼ ▼ ▼ ▼ ▼ ▼
The Peninsula

The Peninsula of which San Francisco is the tip extends south and encompasses some of the Bay Area's wealthiest bedroom communities. Here you will find Hillsborough, Atherton, and Palo Alto, a series of high-toned towns adorned with wooded realms and prestigious homes.

SIGHTS

The best way to explore an area is to scout it out first. So the initial stop in a Peninsula tour should be **San Bruno Mountain**, a bald-domed rise from which to survey the entire region. With its steep flanks and wooded ravines, this park overlooks all the Bay Area. To get there, take Bayshore Boulevard to Guadalupe Canyon Parkway, which goes through the park to the summit. You'll have to share the heights with radio antennas, but there are nearby hiking trails to escape civilization. ~ Summit Road, Brisbane.

Peer south and the world spreads before you, with the Pacific to the west, San Francisco Bay to the east, and the Santa Cruz Mountains running down the Peninsula like a spine. (The ocean side of the Peninsula is covered in Chapter Six.)

To explore the Bay side of the Peninsula, you can choose between three highways. Route 101, closest to the Bay, is a major freeway that streams past San Francisco International Airport, then beelines south. It is quick, painless (except during commute hours), and downright ugly. Route 82, or El Camino Real, named for the old royal road, is a commercial highway lined with shopping areas. Passing through the heart of most peninsula towns, it involves a lot of stop-and-go traffic and is largely uninteresting. The third option is Route 280, farther inland. To call a parkway pretty takes gall and imagination, but this high-speed freeway does possess beautiful stretches. It has been nicely landscaped and skirts the eastern fringe of the Santa Cruz Mountains.

All these highways will pass some of the Bay Area's most exclusive towns. Like Marin County to the north, the Peninsula is a suburban enclave filled with wealthy bedroom communities. In the towns of Hillsborough, Belmont, and Atherton, along winding roads above the Bay, are outlandish mansions and secluded estates.

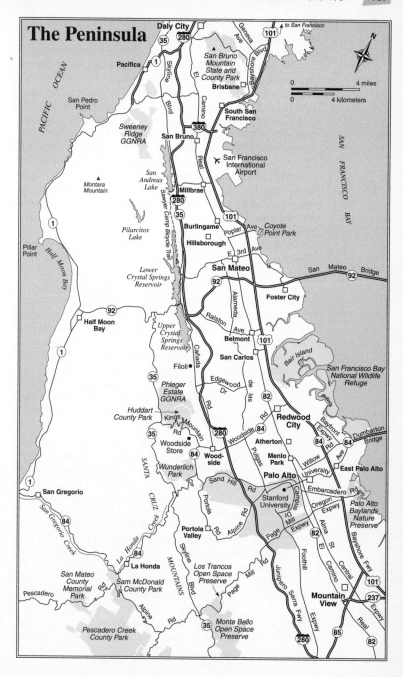

The Peninsula

to San Francisco

PACIFIC OCEAN

Daly City

35 280

Geneva Ave

Bayshore Blvd

101

Pacifica

1

Skyline Blvd

San Bruno Mountain State and County Park

Brisbane

N

0   4 miles
0   4 kilometers

San Pedro Point

Sweeney Ridge GGNRA

Camino Real

South San Francisco

San Bruno

380

SAN FRANCISCO BAY

Montara Mountain

San Andreas Lake

San Francisco International Airport

Sawyer Camp Bicycle Trail

280

Millbrae

35

Pilarcitos Lake

101

Burlingame

Poplar Ave

Coyote Point Park

Pillar Point

Half Moon Bay

Hillsborough

E 3rd Ave

Lower Crystal Springs Reservoir

San Mateo

92

San Mateo Bridge

92

Alameda

Foster City

Ralston Ave

92

Half Moon Bay

Upper Crystal Springs Reservoir

Belmont

101

Bair Island

de las

Cañada Rd

San Carlos

San Francisco Bay National Wildlife Refuge

Filoli

Edgewood Dr

1

35

Phleger Estate GGNRA

Huddart County Park

Kings

Mountain

Rd

82

Redwood City

Bayfront Expwy

Dumbarton Bridge

35

Woodside Store

84

280

Woodside

84

Woodside

Pulgas

84

Rd

84

Atherton

SANTA

Wunderlich Park

Menlo Park

Willow

East Palo Alto

1

San Gregorio

Sand Hill Rd

Palo Alto

University

84

CRUZ

Portola

Rd

Stanford University

Campus

Embarcadero Rd

Palo Alto Baylands Nature Preserve

San Gregorio Creek

La Honda Creek

Portola Valley

Alpine Rd

Oregon Expwy

82

Alma St

El Camino

Bayshore Fwy

84

MOUNTAINS

Skyline Blvd

Page Mill Rd

Junipero Serra Fwy

Foothill Expwy

Central Expwy

101

La Honda

Los Trancos Open Space Preserve

Mountain View

237

Pescadero

San Mateo County Memorial Park

Sam McDonald County Park

Rd

85

82

Alpine Rd

35

Monte Bello Open Space Preserve

280

El Camino Real

Pescadero Creek County Park

The town of **Woodside** is a rural version of these elite communities. Situated near Route 280 along the Santa Cruz Mountains, its fabulous homes are tucked away in forested heights.

The most splendid of all is **Filoli**, a sumptuous 43-room mansion designed in 1915 by Willis Polk. Built for William Bourn II, whose wealth derived partially from the Empire Mine in Grass Valley, the house features a gilded ballroom. The floors are inlaid with exquisite designs, murals decorate the ballroom, and the marble work is impeccable. The gardens surrounding the house, equally beautiful, once required the maintenance of 18 gardeners. Today visitors may take a self-guided tour with a brochure; docent-led tours available by reservation. A café on the grounds serves light lunches. Gates close at 2:30 p.m. Closed Sunday and Monday, and late October to mid-February. Admission. ~ Canada Road, Woodside; 650-364-8300, fax 650-366-7836; www.filoli. org, e-mail filolifriend@earthlink.net.

Also of interest is the old **Woodside Store**, a bare wood structure that dates back to 1854. A general store in the days when this region was a lumbering center, the establishment is now a three-room museum containing old tools and other artifacts. Closed Monday, Wednesday, and Friday. ~ 3300 Tripp Road (at King's Mountain Road), Woodside; 650-851-7615.

If you decide to follow Route 280 and visit Woodside, consider getting off the freeway in Hillsborough and taking the small side roads that parallel the main road. Skyline Boulevard (Route 35), Ralston Avenue, and Canada Road link together to form an alternate north–south route between Hillsborough and Woodside. Passing through the **San Francisco State Fish and Game Refuge**, they provide splendid views of Crystal Springs Reservoir and the Santa Cruz Mountains.

STANFORD UNIVERSITY   Regardless of the highway you take, you will ultimately arrive in **Palo Alto**, home to one of America's prettiest college campuses. Named for a "tall tree" that served as an early landmark, this wealthy community is still noted for its beautiful arbors. The centerpiece of the town is Stanford University, an immense campus created by railroad baron Leland Stanford during the 1880s. ~ For information on walking tours, call **Stanford Visitor Information** at 650-723-2560, fax 650-725-6232; www.visitorinformation.stanford.edu, e-mail visinfo@sher lock.stanford.edu.

The arcade of trees lining the entrance along Palm Drive will provide an idea of Palo Alto's arboreal heritage and of Stanford's magnificent landscaping. You'll also pass the **Iris and B. Gerald Cantor Center for Visual Arts**. Among the pieces in this diverse collection are an Egyptian mummy, California landscape oil paintings, a 19th-century Yurok canoe carved from a redwood log, and the golden spike that marked completion of the transcontinental railroad. Ongoing exhibits highlight art and artifacts from around the world. One of the main attractions is the outdoor Rodin sculpture garden, accessible 24 hours a day. Closed Monday and Tuesday. ~ Museum Way and Lomita Drive, Palo Alto; 650-723-4177, fax 650-725-0464; www.stanford.edu/dept/ccva.

The center of campus, the **Quadrangle**, lies at the end of Palm Drive. Built of sandstone and capped with red tile, it's an elegant Spanish-style courtyard. The architecture throughout the university is Romanesque, and the Quad's colonnaded walkways evoke the image of a cloister.

Fittingly, the **Memorial Church** anchors the far edge of the plaza. That tile mosaic facade portraying the Sermon on the Mount was fashioned in Venice, Italy. Inside, the cathedral is a vaulting structure illuminated through stained glass and adorned with stone filigree. Behind the altar, past the candelabra and solitary cross, hangs "The Last Supper," re-created from the Sistine Chapel original with special permission from the Pope.

A major stop along the Pacific Flyway, the marshlands of the City of Palo Alto Baylands Nature Preserve are visited by over one million birds each year.

Just east of the Quad rises **Hoover Tower**, a 285-foot landmark from the top of which you can survey the campus and beyond. Home to the Hoover Institution, a conservative think tank, the tower also houses the memorabilia of one of Stanford's most famous graduate, President Herbert Hoover. Closed during finals and other relevant academic occasions. Admission. ~ 650-723-2053, fax 650-725-6232; www.stanford.edu/home/visitors, e-mail visinfo@sherlock.stanford.edu.

Ingenuity is the password to the **Museum of American Heritage**. Truly an original, this little showplace traces the history of mechanical and electrical invention with displays of cameras, calculators, cash registers, and kitchenware. There is a 1890s-era "stocking knitter," as well as electric trains, antique bicycles, and a player piano. Closed Monday through Thursday. ~ 351 Homer Avenue, Palo Alto; 650-321-1004, fax 650-473-6950; www.moah.org, e-mail mail@moah.org.

In addition to these historic and academic heights, Palo Alto possesses mucky lowlands along the shores of San Francisco Bay. Though the contrast between the two is startling, both are well worth exploring. **City of Palo Alto Baylands Nature Preserve** is a land of pickleweed and cord grass, home to the endangered clapper rail and salt marsh harvest mouse. It takes a special person to appreciate the beauty of a salt marsh. For those who don't mind black mud and pungent smells, this preserve offers unique opportunities. There's a small interpretive center here, as well as a boardwalk that leads through the marsh to the edge of the Bay. Closed Monday. ~ Located on the east end of Embarcadero Road, Palo Alto; 650-329-2506, fax 650-443-5239; e-mail deborah_bartens@city.palo-alto.ca.us.

◀ HIDDEN

Most important, the preserve is a birdwatcher's paradise—on a single day, there were once 10,000 western sandpipers in residence. You may see a great egret, four-foot tall great blue heron, northern harrier, canvasback duck, or a burrowing owl.

Also on Embarcadero Road near Baylands is 40-acre **Byxbee Park**. Created on an old landfill site, this waterfront spot features environmental art displays and plenty of room for peacefully contemplating the universe. Mysteriously arranged poles scattered across the moguled landscape make this an intriguing place (as do the wind waves, oyster shell pathways, and industrial flair).

To get in tune for a visit to these mudflats, you can follow a route from Stanford that leads along one of Palo Alto's tree-shaded streets. Most people take University Avenue, the main drag. Instead take Hamilton Avenue, one block to the south, then turn right on Greer Road, and pick up Embarcadero Road to the Bay. Along this **arboreal route** are trees exotic in name and appearance—Irish yews, sugarplums, bottle-brushes, bunya-bunyas, Australian brush cherries, and monkey puzzle trees.

LODGING   At the **Best Western Grosvenor Hotel** you're just ten minutes from the San Francisco Airport (which is really the only reason to check in to the hotel in the first place). This nine-story facility offers 207 rooms and suites; the suites feature queen-size beds and comfortable sofas. If you like watching planes take off, this is the place for you. Fortunately the rooms are all soundproofed. There's a pool and 24-hour airport shuttle, and an extensive business center on the ground floor. ~ 380 South Airport Boulevard, South San Francisco; 650-873-3200, 800-722-7141, fax 650-589-3495; www.grosvenorsfo.com. DELUXE.

Just half a mile from the Stanford campus, the European-style **Stanford Park Hotel** offers 163 rooms and eight suites. English yew wood furniture adds to the charm of rooms decorated with landscape paintings. Many offer courtyard views. You can work out in the exercise room and pool. This is a place that manages to retain Old World hospitality. ~ 100 El Camino Real, Menlo Park; 650-322-1234, 800-368-2468, fax 650-322-0975; www.stanfordparkhotel.com. ULTRA-DELUXE.

Located on the main drag, the **Townhouse Inn** is a convenient place to stay in Palo Alto. The digs are comfortable and spacious, done up in typical motel decor. Some rooms have kitchenettes; laundry facilities are on site. A continental breakfast is included in the rates. ~ 4164 El Camino Real, Palo Alto; 650-493-4492, 800-458-8696, fax 650-493-3418; www.townhouseinn.com, e-mail hosts@townhouseinn.com. MODERATE.

The **Victorian on Lytton** is a gorgeous bed and breakfast, a startling counterpoint to the high-tech surroundings of Palo Alto. Built in 1895 and restored almost a hundred years later, most of the guest rooms are decorated with Victorian antiques, including canopy or four-poster beds in each of the ten rooms. Be sure to stroll the English garden before you leave. A continental breakfast, served in your room, is included. ~ 555 Lytton Avenue, Palo Alto; 650-322-8555, fax 650-322-7141; www.victorianonlytton.com, e-mail innkeeper@victorianonlytton.com. ULTRA-DELUXE.

There's no need to fly across the Pacific for authentic dim sum. Just head to the **Hong Kong Flower Lounge**, where servers wheel around carts laden with savory delicacies such as shrimp dumplings, steamed pork buns, stuffed bell peppers, and shark-fin dumplings. In addition to this lunchtime favorite, diners can order traditional Cantonese dishes from the menu. ~ 51 Millbrae Avenue, Millbrae; 650-692-6666; e-mail hkflower@sprynet.com. MODERATE TO ULTRA-DELUXE.

DINING

Located at the only busy intersection for miles around is **Alice's Restaurant**. It sports little more than a counter, a few tables and chairs, and a 12-table outdoor eating area facing Route 35. Alice's is open for breakfast, lunch, and dinner (in the summer), primarily serving egg dishes, sandwiches, and a variety of vegetarian dishes. ~ Skyline Boulevard and La Honda Road, Wood side; 650-851-0303. BUDGET TO MODERATE.

Tresidder Memorial Union on the Stanford University campus has several restaurants. The **Corner Pocket** (650-723-0374) serves student-made pizza, smoothies, ice cream, and "fro-yo." **The Treehouse** (650-723-4500) serves Mexican food. At **Bon Appetit** next door (650-723-4324), you can order breakfast pastries, or sandwiches and salads at lunch and dinnertime. Each place will be crowded with students. Since the eateries are located

AUTHOR FAVORITE

To dine in style while visiting Stanford, I recommend **MacArthur Park**. Located between campus and downtown, it rests in a 1918 building designed by noted Bay Area architect Julia Morgan. Originally serving as a World War I hospitality house, the structure now contains a lovely restaurant specializing in food prepared in an oakwood smoker or mesquite grill. There's roasted chicken breast, famous barbecued baby back ribs, petite filet medallions, shrimp, sizzling whole catfish, as well as other fresh fish. Vegetarian dishes are also available. The menu is similar at dinner and lunch; they also serve Sunday brunch. Private rooms for up to 100 people are also available. ~ 27 University Avenue, Palo Alto; 650-321-9990, fax 650-328-4066. MODERATE TO ULTRA-DELUXE.

near the central quadrangle, they're convenient when touring the campus. ~ 520 Lagunita Drive, Palo Alto. BUDGET.

Singapore cuisine meets dot-com trendiness at **Straits Cafe**. Entrées reflect a pan-Asian romance—Indian-flavored noodles listed next to tuna sashimi, for instance. The setting is equally exotic with teak, orchids, and a lavish patio. Appetizers are plentiful and highly recommended, especially the grilled scallops, Poh Pia (a spring roll creation), and Dungeness crab cakes with mango salsa. No lunch on weekends. ~ 3295 El Camino Real, Palo Alto; 415-650-7168; www.straitsrestaurants.com. DELUXE.

When the yuppified streets of Palo Alto prove too much, find solace in old-fashioned and unpretentious diner fare at the **Peninsula Fountain & Grill**. Known as the Peninsula Creamery to regulars, this joint has been turning out burgers and fries since the 1920s. Breakfast is served all day, the jukebox spits out oldies nonstop, and there's a tantalizing display case full of deliciously sinful desserts. Forgoing a milkshake is criminal. ~ 180 El Camino Real, Palo Alto; 650-327-3141. BUDGET.

St. Michael's Alley is an intimate bistro—a good place to go for quiet conversation and a taste of hearty California cuisine. Seasonal entrées may include artichoke and cheese ravioli, pork medallions, Idaho trout, and potato gnocchi. Closed Sunday night and Monday. ~ 806 Emerson Street, Palo Alto; 650-326-2530, fax 650-326-1436; www.stmikes.com. MODERATE TO DELUXE.

HIDDEN ► Way up in the hills above Palo Alto, there's a roadhouse called the **Alpine Inn** that dates back to the 1850s. It's a simple, homey place serving locally famous hamburgers, sandwiches, and other basic fare. The spot is very popular with local folks. You can dine indoors beneath trophy heads or outside at a picnic table. ~ 3950 Alpine Road, Portola Valley; 650-854-4004. BUDGET.

SHOPPING   For detailed maps and cartographic information, it's hard to top the **United States Geological Survey Earth Science Information Center**. In addition to excellent USGS topographic maps, this facility sells thematic maps and various literary works. Closed weekends. ~ 345 Middlefield Road, Menlo Park; 650-329-4390, fax 650-329-5130.

If you've got kids in tow, the Saturday-morning children's storytime at Kepler's Books is a great alternative to TV cartoons.

One of the Peninsula's best bookstores, **Kepler's Books** is a "literary living room" where residents of the Stanford University area come to meet friends, argue politics, and share gossip. The huge, eclectic stock of books is hand-picked to appeal to an extremely well-educated, affluent clientele, and the staff stays knowledgeable by meeting daily to compare notes on the latest books they have read. Kepler's hosts monthly fiction discussions and writers' workshops as well as author appearances. ~ 1010 El Camino Real, Menlo Park; 650-324-4321; www.keplers.com, e-mail contactus@keplers.com.

If you can't find it at Kepler's, that elusive volume will doubtless be in one of downtown Palo Alto's many bookstores. This campus town has practically as many booksellers as restaurants. To browse shops in downtown Palo Alto, plan to stroll University Avenue from Alma Street to Webster Street, then return along Hamilton Avenue. Like the side streets between, these thoroughfares are door-to-door with boutiques, galleries, and knickknack shops. An exceptional example is the **Gallery House**, which contains striking works of contemporary art and pottery by local artists. Closed Sunday and Monday. ~ 320 California Avenue, Palo Alto; 650-326-1668.

University Avenue boasts countless galleries, shops, and restaurants, making it a neat place to do some browsing. **Meadowlark Gallery**, which represents over 400 American artists, sells a multitude of hand-crafted objects like ceramics, jewelry, furniture, and woodwork. ~ 516 University Avenue; 650-330-1490. If you're ready to plunk down some serious moolah, visit **Gleim Jewelers** and drool over their dazzling collections of "old-time" jewelry. ~ 322 University Avenue; 650-323-1331.

NIGHTLIFE

Night owls flying south from San Francisco will find plenty of diversions along the Peninsula. **Molloy's**, a few miles from the City, is a century-old bar crowded with memories and memorabilia. ~ 1655 Old Mission Road, Colma; 650-755-9545.

◄ HIDDEN

In an unlikely spot near the San Francisco International Airport, **Caribbean Gardens** bills itself as an international dance club and is undoubtedly one of the peninsula's hottest places to dance to salsa, merengue, reggae, African, house, and soca music. Closed Monday through Wednesday. Cover. ~ 1306 Bayshore Avenue, Burlingame; 650-344-1797.

With a warm atmosphere and 16 microbrewed beers on tap, the **Empire Grill & Tap Room** is a choice spot for a candlelit evening drink. Out back, the spacious patio is complemented by lush greenery and a fountain. ~ 651 Emerson Street, Palo Alto; 650-321-3030.

Popular with folks 18 to 21, **The Edge** offers modern deejay rock, dancing, and special events. Cover. ~ 260 California Avenue, Palo Alto; 650-289-0222.

Check the "Intermission" section of the *Stanford Daily* and other university publications for information about programs on the Stanford campus. You can also call 650-723-0336 for a tape-recorded calendar of events.

BEACHES & PARKS

SAN BRUNO MOUNTAIN STATE AND COUNTY PARK 🚶 🚲
This 2000-acre facility seems to be perennially under construction. After bitter debates between conservationists and developers, the park was finally established in the late 1970s. Today, it is one

of San Francisco's last wild places, harboring 14 endangered plant species and three endangered butterflies. A spectacular time to visit is during the wildflower season from February through May. Scenically, it provides one of the Bay Area's most spectacular views, a 360° panorama from atop 1314-foot San Bruno Mountain. This hillside park is also a fine place to picnic. There are 12 miles of hiking trails, picnic areas, and toilets. Day-use fee, $5 (weekends only). ~ In Brisbane a few miles south of San Francisco. From 101 South, take the Sierra Point exit to Lagoon Road. Follow through to Bayshore Boulevard and go right. Follow to Guadalupe Canyon Parkway and go left; 650-992-6770, fax 650-992-1682.

COYOTE POINT PARK A multiuse facility, this bayshore park contains everything from a museum to a firing range, with stops in between for a marina and two playgrounds. There's a pebble beach for sunbathers, a nearby golf course, a salt marsh ideal for wildlife viewing, and the Coyote Point Museum (admission), which houses rotating exhibits of local wildlife. Because of the proximity to San Francisco Airport, jets pass overhead continually, but there are excellent views of the Bay, and the park is extremely popular with local residents. Facilities include restrooms, picnic areas, and a museum (admission); showers in summer. Day-use fee, $5. ~ Located in San Mateo; from Route 101 south take the Poplar Avenue exit to Coyote Point Drive; 650-573-2592, fax 650-573-3727; www.coyotepointmuseum.org.

HUDDART COUNTY PARK Situated on the Bay side of the Santa Cruz Mountains, this densely forested park provides a touch of the wild within whistling distance of San Francisco. Rising to 2000 feet, it features redwood and mixed evergreen forests. Twenty-five miles of hiking trails crisscross the landscape, and the park is a habitat for blacktail deer, raccoons, coyotes, and an occasional bobcat or gray fox. There are picnic areas (some with shelters and electricity), restrooms, playground, and archery range. Day-use fee, $5. ~ Located in Woodside; take Woodside Road off Route 280, then go three and a half miles west to 1100 Kings Mountain Road; 650-851-0326, 650-851-1210, fax 650-851-9558; e-mail hud@netwiz.net.

WUNDERLICH PARK Also set along the eastern slopes of the Santa Cruz Mountains, this facility is largely undeveloped. It does have a private stable, however, and is very popular with equestrians. Hikers also favor the 25 miles of trails that wind along mountain streams, across rolling meadows, and through redwood groves. The only facilities here are portable toilets. ~ Route 84 in Woodside, two miles west of the town center; 650-851-1210, fax 650-851-9558; e-mail hud@netwiz.net.

MIDPENINSULA REGIONAL OPEN SPACE DISTRICT 🚶 🚲 🐎

The contiguous preserves of Los Trancos and Monte Bello cover 3000 acres of rolling countryside. They're located in the hills above Palo Alto and provide sweeping views from San Francisco to Mount Diablo. The terrain varies from grassland to mixed evergreen forest to canyons shaded with oak trees. Most visitors are drawn here by the San Andreas Fault, which bisects Los Trancos and can be explored along one of the area's many hiking trails. From these heights, it's possible to visually follow the fault past San Francisco. The only facilities are toilets at Monte Bello. ~ From Route 280 in Palo Alto, take Page Mill Road seven miles southwest. The entrances to both preserves are along the roadside; 650-691-1200, fax 650-691-0485; www.openspace.org, e-mail info@openspace.org.

▲ Campers can spend the night at the very primitive Black Mountain Backpack Camp, which is a one-and-a-half-mile hike from Page Mill Road. A permit is required for overnight camping.

▼▼▼▼▼▼▼▼▼▼▼▼
The South Bay

Located about 50 miles south of San Francisco, the San Jose area is a sprawling collection of cities and towns laid out like Los Angeles. It's one of California's wealthiest sections, home to the state's vaunted high-tech industry. Scattered around this Santa Clara Valley region are several points of interest.

SIGHTS

Today, **San Jose** is best known as the super-rich "capital" of Silicon Valley, epicenter of the microelectronics industry in America. Among the city's custom home developments, shopping malls, and congested thoroughfares, though, visitors can discover some unique and eccentric reminders of an earlier, simpler time.

For sightseeing information, your best resource is the **Visitor Information and Business Center**. Located in San Jose Convention Center, it can provide details and directions for the entire area. ~ 150 West San Carlos Street, San Jose; 408-977-0900, fax 408-295-3937; www.sanjose.org. For information on San Jose and the Santa Clara Valley in general, contact the **San Jose Silicon**

◆◆◆

CHEAP AND EASY

The **San Jose Convention & Visitors Bureau**'s unique, free concierge service will make hotel and restaurant reservations for you and arrange theater, sports, and special events tickets, all at discounted prices. ~ 888-726-5673, fax 408-295-3937; www.sanjose.org, e-mail concierge@ sanjose.org.

Valley Chamber of Commerce. Closed Saturday and Sunday. ~ 310 South 1st Street, San Jose; 408-291-5250, fax 408-286-5019; www.sjchamber.com, e-mail info@sjchamber.com.

Downtown, a billion-dollar renovation brought a metamorphosis to this formerly rundown area. Center stage stands the 425,000-square-foot **San Jose Convention Center.** Critical raves met this unique soft peach–colored structure—with its enormous vaulted entranceway highlighted by a porcelain-tile mural, its multilevel glass-enclosed arcade and concourse, and its black-and-white marble terrazzo promenade—upon its completion in 1989. ~ West San Carlos Street between Almaden Boulevard and Market Street, San Jose; 408-277-3900, fax 408-277-3535; www.sjcc.com.

High-class hotels, restaurants, shops, and financial centers dot the area, where people zip along via a modern light-rail system. Landscaping has not been forgotten amid all this glass and concrete. The city planted 600 sycamore trees to shade the downtown transit mall, and there's **Plaza Park,** a green oasis with palms and acres of grass along Market Street across from the convention center.

The nearby **Children's Discovery Museum** presents an amazing collection of interactive exhibits. Kids can climb on real fire trucks and ambulances, operate traffic lights along simulated roadways, make their own cornhusk doll, or build a bridge. Your kids can also explore a hands-on art studio and an interactive bubble exhibit. Closed Monday except in July and August. Admission. ~ 180 Woz Way, San Jose; 408-298-5437, fax 408-298-6826; www.cdm.org.

For older kids and adults there's the **Tech Museum of Innovation.** Here you'll discover a collection of interactive exhibits in which you can drive a space rover through a Martian landscape, compare genetic profiles with other visitors, or take a virtual bobsled ride, complete with auditing and visual feedback. The museum's 87-foot Hackworth IMAX Dome Theater, which wraps the audience in images ten times larger than the largest conventional movie screens. Closed all non-holiday Mondays. Admission. ~ 201 South Market Street, San Jose; 408-294-8324, fax 408-279-7167; www.thetech.org.

The **San Jose Museum of Art,** housed in a century-old Romanesque-style building, is complemented by a wing featuring a barrel-vaulted ceiling and two outdoor sculpture courts. Focusing on 20th- and 21st-century art, the collection includes such contemporary artists as Robert Arneson, Richard Diebenkorn, Rupert Garcia, Raymond Saunders, and Deborah Oeopallo. The museum features changing exhibitions of contemporary art, as well as a number of special programs. Closed Monday. ~ 110 South Market Street, San Jose; 408-294-2787, fax 408-294-2977; www.sjmusart.org, e-mail info@sjmusart.org.

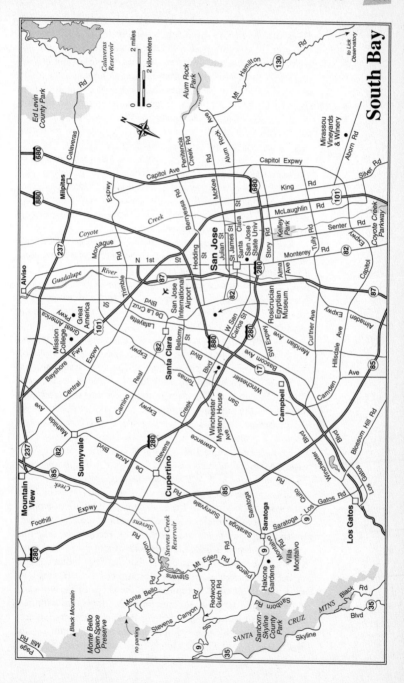

South Bay

Two restored historic houses in San Pedro Square, the Fallon House and Peralta Adobe, form a living-history museum designed to honor the city's roots. The **Peralta Adobe**, San Jose's only surviving adobe structure, illustrates California pueblo life in both the 1790s and 1840s. The **Fallon House**, an Italianate Victorian mansion built by an early mayor, shows how a prosperous family lived in the 1850s. Open Saturday and Sunday by appointment. Closed Monday. Admission. ~ 175 West St. John Street, San Jose; 408-993-8182, fax 408-993-8184; www.historysanjose. org, e-mail education@historysanjose.org.

Located near the Museum of Art, the **San Jose Museum of Quilts and Textiles** is another recommended stop. Quilts and other textiles from around the world are featured in changing exhibits. Closed Monday. Admission. ~ 110 Paseo de San Antonio, San Jose; 408-971-0323, fax 408-971-7226; www.sjquiltmuseum.org, e-mail info@sjquiltmuseum.org.

Kelley Park contains more than 150 wooded acres with picnic areas and recreation facilities. There's a petting zoo (admission) for children that also contains rides and puppet shows. Next to this playland sits the Japanese Friendship Garden, a serene setting with *koi* pond, footbridges, and a teahouse. ~ Story and Senter roads, San Jose; 408-277-5254, fax 408-297-0779; www.ci.san-jose.ca. us/cae/parks.

Of Kelley Park's several attractions, the highlight is the **History San Jose**, an outdoor museum featuring several antique buildings in a plaza setting. Inside the old Pacific Hotel, you'll find displays tracing San Jose's history from the Indians through the trappers, miners, and farmers. The nearby soda fountain, still operating, is definitely the highpoint of any visit. Not far from here rise the old firehouse, a clapboard livery stable complete with rickety wagons, a printing office, a Gothic-style house from the 1870s, a Chinese temple, and a 1927 gas station with gravity-feed pumps. Closed Monday. Admission. ~ 1650 Senter Road, San Jose; 408-287-2290, fax 408-287-2291; www.historysanjose.org.

Certainly San Jose's most unique and exotic site is the **Rosicrucian Egyptian Museum**. The landscaping and buildings throughout the elaborate complex effectively re-create ancient Egypt. There are sphinxes, and temples decorated with hieroglyphs. The museum entranceway is lined on either side by stone statues of rams, reproducing an ancient avenue in Thebes. Inside are mummies dating back 3000 years, alabaster urns, bronze pieces portraying lion-headed goddesses, incense burners in the shape of falcon heads, statues of the Nile gods, and mummy shrouds painted with holy insignia. Also featuring Babylonian, Persian, and Assyrian artifacts, it's a place to make you ponder the texture of life and the structure of infinity. Closed Monday. Admission. ~ Park and Naglee avenues, San Jose; 408-947-3600, fax 408-947-3638; www.egyptianmuseum.org.

If the Rosicrucian Museum represents humankind's search for universal meaning, the **Winchester Mystery House** is a study in the meaningless lives of the idle rich. Numbering 160 rooms and covering four acres, this Victorian monstrosity is still unfinished. It was built by Sarah Winchester, heiress to the Winchester rifle fortune, who kept adding on rooms for 38 years. She believed that the ghosts of everyone killed by Winchester rifles were out to get her and hoped to lose them within the maze of the house. Unfortunately for her, the floor plans weren't revenge-proof—she died in 1922. Her legacy is an architectural riddle complete with stairways leading nowhere and closets that open onto walls. The interior design is very beautiful, however, and there are ghost stories galore surrounding the house and its unbalanced owner. Admission. ~ 525 South Winchester Boulevard, San Jose; 408-247-2101, fax 408-247-2090; www.winchestermysteryhouse.com.

Nearly destroyed by fire on the eve of its completion in 2002, **Santana Row** rose from the ashes to become a thriving San Jose addition. Its wide tree-lined sidewalks, homey storefronts, and old-town streetlamps hide the chic and upscale shops that dominate the setting. People come here to spend, spend, spend, whether it be on dinner, deluxe accommodations, or a new Gucci tote. ~ 355 Santana Row; 408-552-4600; www.santanarow.com.

For hair-raising excitement, there's **Great America**. This 100-acre theme park features movies, theatrical revues, concerts, video galleries, a flight simulator, and white-knuckle rides with menacing names such as Invertigo, Demon, Vortex, Xtreme Skyflyer, and

AUTHOR FAVORITE

I found my visit to the **Intel Museum** a humbling experience; mastering my e-mail is nothing compared to the feats of technology being performed today. This is one of the few places visitors can learn firsthand about the technology industry that drives Silicon Valley. Exhibits trace the history of microchip development and explain the functions of different types of chips. A live video feed displays microchips being produced in Intel's contamination-free factory environment. Interactive exhibits let visitors try the latest educational and entertainment software and explore the Internet. A futuristic "Intelligent Home" exhibit shows what it may be like to live in a computer-controlled house. Closed Sunday. ~ 2200 Mission College Boulevard, Santa Clara; 408-765-0503, fax 408-765-1217; www.intel.com/go/museum.

Drop Zone, the world's tallest freefall ride. The newest addition is Nickelodeon Central, which features kid-themed rides like Sponge-Bob's Boatmobile or the Rugrats Runaway Reptar Rollercoaster. Closed in winter. Admission. ~ Great America Parkway, Santa Clara; 408-988-1776, fax 408-986-5855; www.pgathrills.com.

The South Bay's other features are farther afield, and far more placid. **Los Gatos**, a wealthy and luxurious town in the foothills of the Santa Cruz Mountains, provides peaceful country lanes and Carpenter Gothic–style homes. **Saratoga** also contains sumptuous hillside homes.

None, however, match the grandeur of **Villa Montalvo**. This Mediterranean-style mansion and surrounding estate was home to James Phelan, a three-term mayor of San Francisco and former U.S. Senator. Today his 19-room house serves as a cultural center featuring artistic exhibits and events; the luxurious grounds have been converted to an arboretum laced with nature trails. There are gardens, rare plants, creeks, and forests of maple and oak. Call for hours and events. ~ 15400 Montalvo Road, Saratoga; 408-961-5800, fax 408-961-5850; www.villamontalvo.org, e-mail general@villamontalvo.org.

Hakone Gardens, smaller and more modest, is a lovely Japanese-style retreat with wisteria arbors, dwarf pines, and a wooden footbridge. Irises and rushes border the *koi* pond and a waterfall spills across the landscape. A perfect place to meditate, or simply soak up the sun, this enchanting garden also contains a house built without nails that serves as a cultural exchange center. On summer weekends docent-led tours of the grounds are available by reservation. On the first Thursday afternoon of each month, a tea ceremony is performed. Admission. ~ 21000 Big Basin Way, Saratoga; 408-741-4994, fax 408-741-4993; www.hakone.com.

The Santa Clara Valley supports numerous wineries, some offering tours and winetasting. **La Rochelle Vineyards & Winery** is a sixth-generation family concern producing generic and varietal wines as well as champagne. While the grapes here don't match those of Napa Valley, the winery is well worth a visit, and the tasting is complimentary. ~ 3000 Aborn Road, San Jose; 408-

DONUT PILGRIMAGE

The joking claims of **Lou's Living Donut Museum** to have fueled the technological revolution may not be far off. Maple-glazed, honey whole wheat, pumpkin, and jelly-filled—whatever your poison, Lou's got the freshest. You can watch them create in their open kitchen; tours are also available. Closed Sunday. ~ 387 Delmas Street, San Jose; 408-295-5887, fax 408-295-8053; e-mail lousdonuts@yahoo.com.

274-4000, 888-775-1936, fax 408-270-5716; www.lrwine.com, e-mail email@lrwine.com.

The 45-minute drive to the **Lick Observatory**, atop 4209-foot Mount Hamilton, will carry you even farther from the smoggy center of San Jose. One of the world's largest telescopes, a giant eye 120 inches in diameter, it stares heavenward from this lofty perch. In operation since 1888, the observatory sponsors guided tours and a visitors center. ~ Mount Hamilton Road, San Jose; 408-274-5061; www.ucolick.org.

Mount Hamilton Road (Route 130) winds over 20 miles past rolling ranch lands, oak groves, and flowering fields en route to the summit. With the white-domed observatory above you and the entire South Bay spread below, there are views no telescope can hope to match.

An art-deco gem restored to its 1931 grandeur is the **Hotel De Anza**, a 100-room boutique hotel that is a fine component of the impressive urban facelift that took place in downtown San Jose. Rooms are light and airy, decorated with the blond woods and geometric prints reflective of the 1930s. ~ 233 West Santa Clara Street, San Jose; 408-286-1000, 800-843-3700, fax 408-286-0500; www.hoteldeanza.com. DELUXE TO ULTRA-DELUXE.

LODGING

Of Northern California's many hostels, **Sanborn Park Hostel** is among the prettiest. It sits in a striking 1908 building fashioned from redwood logs in the midst of a county park. Dense forest surrounds the place and nearby hiking trails lead up into the Santa Cruz Mountains. There are several bunk rooms, as well as a laundry, kitchen, and living room with stone fireplace. Nightly curfew. ~ 15808 Sanborn Road, Saratoga; 408-741-9555; www.sanbornparkhostel.org. BUDGET.

Where do the rich and famous stay and play when not in Hollywood? **The Cypress Hotel**. Built at the height of the dot-com boom, this nine-story extravaganza caters to the lavish lifestyles of the region's nouveau riche. Don't let the hotel's suburban surroundings fool you: inside are plush comforters, richly decorated rooms, and all the trappings of a Mediterranean villa with splashes of animal print and deep velvet fabrics. Due to the local economic downturn, guests can get rock-bottom prices on top-quality rooms. Ask about special packages. ~ 10050 South Deanza Boulevard, Cupertino; 408-253-8900, 800-499-1408, fax 408-342-4841; www.thecypresshotel.com. ULTRA-DELUXE.

In downtown San Jose, home of business professionals and urban developers, there's an invitingly informal place called **Eulipia Restaurant and Bar**. With its local crowd and light, airy, bistro-like atmosphere, the place is a prime choice when you're in the mood for casual dining. Serving lunch and dinner, they offer an

DINING

array of fresh fish, chicken, and pasta dishes. Closed Monday. ~ 374 South 1st Street, San Jose; 408-280-6161; www.eulipia.com, e-mail eulipia@eulipia.com. DELUXE TO ULTRA-DELUXE.

For that special occasion there's **Paolo's Restaurant**, a lavishly decorated dining room with a sophisticated Italian cuisine. The seasonal menu has more than a dozen pasta dishes as well as such entrées as roast duck, braised veal, and seared ahi tuna. No lunch on Saturday. Closed Sunday. ~ 333 West San Carlos Street, San Jose; 408-294-2558; www.paolosrestaurant.com, e-mail cucinasj@aol.com. MODERATE TO ULTRA-DELUXE.

Part of a whole new infusion of sophisticated bistro-style restaurants in downtown San Jose is **Bella Mia**, which packs in the upwardly mobile at lunch and dinner for flatbread pizzas, pastas, and succulent meat entrées such as spit-roasted duck with raspberry vinegar sauce and grilled pork chops with sour cherries and orange brandy sauce. No lunch on weekends. ~ 58 South 1st Street, San Jose; 408-280-1993, fax 408-280-6087; www.bella mia.com, e-mail bellamia@bellamia.com. MODERATE.

Bella Saratoga, in the heart of Saratoga village, offers a similar menu in the more laidback setting of a yellow Victorian house with sunny patio. ~ 14503 Big Basin Way, Saratoga; 408-741-5115, fax 408-868-9774; www.bellasaratoga.com. MODERATE TO DELUXE.

You'll have to travel many leagues to find a seafood restaurant as good as **Steamer's Grillhouse**. Serving fresh fish, shrimp, and crab, they also offer calamari plus a host of seafood pasta dishes. Attractively paneled in hardwood, the establishment features an oyster bar, dining area, and fashionable saloon. Quite popular with young professionals, this gourmet spot is usually very crowded. ~ 31 University Avenue, Los Gatos; 408-395-2722, fax 408-354-4203; www.steamers-restaurant.com. MODERATE TO ULTRA-DELUXE.

INDIAN SPICE AND ALL THINGS NICE

Santana Row is chock full of good restaurants, but **Amber India** deserves special consideration. Yes, there are standards like *baingan bharta* and *palak paneer*, but their best dishes are seasonal ones that combine classic regional spices with Western favorites. Try the *bhara jung khumb*, a portobello mushroom stuffed with spiced *paneer* and topped with artichokes and wild mushroom sauce. With words from the Bhagavad Gita painted above your head, modern Indian artwork on the walls, and a delicious dinner on your plate, outings at Amber are always scrumptious and soothing. ~ 377 Santana Row, San Jose; 408-238-5400. MODERATE TO DELUXE.

Much of San Jose's downtown district is continuing to be refur- **SHOPPING** bished. Already refurbished, amid the stately palms and 1920s houses of the Willow Glen neighborhood is **Lincoln Avenue**, a street lined with craft and antiques shops, cafés, and gourmet delis.

For gifts at reasonable prices, step over from the Japan Center to **Nichi Bei Bussan**. Here is a huge collection of Asian wares ranging from standard kimonos and martial arts supplies to Japanese cultural books and rice paper wallets; they specialize in Japanese textiles. There are also a few special treasures, such as Noren wall-hangings and Japanese shoes. Closed Sunday. ~ 140 East Jackson Street, San Jose; 408-294-8048; www.nbstore.com, e-mail nichi beibu@aol.com.

Valley Fair remains the mall to end all malls, with department store stalwarts Macy's and Nordstrom, and a dizzying array of some 200 shops, including the flagship Banana Republic. ~ 2855 Stevens Creek Boulevard, San Jose; 408-248-4451. The buying frenzy continues across the street at **Santana Row** and its high-end stores like Burberry, Cole Haan, and Escada. ~ 355 Santana Row, San Jose; 408-551-4600; www.santanarow.com.

For hours of interesting shopping and some of the best bargains in the South Bay, head for the **San Jose Flea Market**. It has over 2000 vendors selling everything from bicycles to books and 35 food stalls for a quick order of chow mein or a plate of nachos. You could get lost here. Closed Monday and Tuesday. ~ 1590 Berryessa Road, San Jose; 408-453-1110, fax 408-437-9011; www.sjfm.com.

Some of the area's better shops have moved to the suburbs, where they cater to Silicon Valley's affluent young executives. Two towns are particularly noteworthy.

Saratoga features an upscale shopping strip in the center of town along **Saratoga Avenue**. There are antique stores and galleries galore, as well as malls with an assortment of shops.

Los Gatos is quite simply a window browser's dream. Along **Santa Cruz Avenue** are block on block of posh establishments. There are stores specializing in antique interiors, teddy bears, magic tricks, and travel accessories. You'll find high-fashion boutiques, gourmet food outlets, novelty shops, custom clothiers, and antique garment stores. ~ From Saratoga–Los Gatos Road to Main Street. **Old Town**, a misnomered mall, is another prime shopping enclave. Attractively landscaped with flowering gardens, it features a string of stores in a hacienda-style building. ~ 50 Universal Avenue, Los Gatos.

The focus for San Jose high culture is the **Center for the Performing Arts**, located in the downtown district. The **American Musical Theatre of San Jose**, which puts on wonderful productions of **NIGHTLIFE**

Broadway musicals, performs here. ~ 1717 Technology Drive; 408-453-7100, 888-455-7469; www.amtsj.org. Also consider the **San Jose Repertory Company**. ~ San Jose Repertory Theatre, 101 Paseo de San Antonio; 408-367-7255; www.sjrep.com.

Head on over to **Agenda** in SOFA, South of First Street Area, San Jose's SOHO/SOMA/hip and trendy district. This three-level establishment is a dinner club serving California regional cuisine on the ground floor, a lounge with deejay music nightly upstairs, and a speakeasy in the basement. On the patio there's live jazz. Restaurant closed Sunday and Monday; speakeasy only open Friday and Saturday. ~ 399 South 1st Street, San Jose; 408-287-3991; www.agendalounge.com.

Scores of bars and restaurants make Santana Row great for late-night drinks. With its mesh metal curtains, red lights, and swank crowds, the Hotel Valencia's **V Bar** is one of the poshest. ~ 355 Santana Row, San Jose; 408-551-0010.

For some laughs, hit up **Rooster T. Feathers Comedy Club**, where top-bill comedians make their South Bay debuts Thursday through Sunday. Reservations recommended. Cover. ~ 157 El Camino Real, Sunnyvale; 408-732-7781.

Mountain Charley's Saloon is a down-home drinking hole with a magnificent old wooden bar that must weigh four tons. The live sounds here include rock of the '80s and '90s; most of the bands hail from the Bay Area. Wednesday is karaoke night. Closed Sunday through Tuesday. Cover. ~ 15 North Santa Cruz Avenue, Los Gatos; 408-395-8880.

BEACHES & PARKS

SANBORN-SKYLINE COUNTY PARK 🚶 🐎 ⛺ Rising from the foothills of the Santa Cruz Mountains to 3000 feet, this outstanding area is covered with Douglas fir and second-growth redwoods. It covers about 3600 acres, spreading across several ecological zones. Along the 20 miles of hiking trails, there are extraordinary views of the Santa Clara Valley; the trails also connect with a network leading all the way to the Pacific. Facilities include restrooms, picnic areas, a science museum, and a hostel. Dogs and bikes are not allowed on the trails. Day-use fee, $4. ~ Off Route 9 about three miles west of Saratoga, the park is at 16055 Sanorn Road; 408-867-9959, fax 408-867-1859; www.parkhere.org.

▲ There are 33 walk-in sites (closed in winter) at $8 per night; 15 RV sites with full hookups at $25 per night; reservations required. Information, 408-358-3751.

▼▼▼▼▼▼▼▼▼▼

The East Bay

Point your compass east from San Francisco, cross the Bay Bridge, and lo and behold, you have arrived in the East Bay. Framed by wooded hills and looking out on the Golden Gate, Oakland and Berkeley are the two key towns in this suburban enclave.

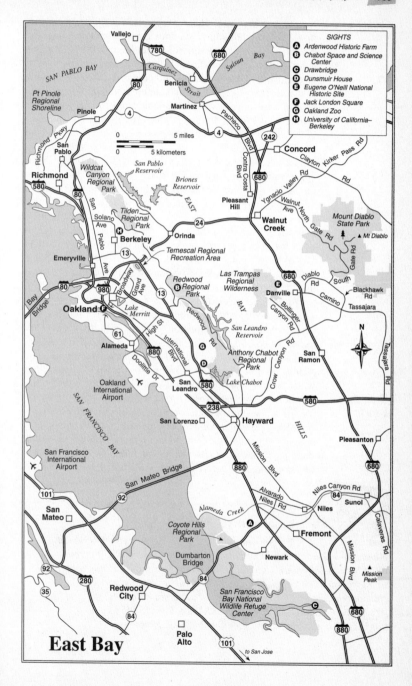

SIGHTS
Ⓐ Ardenwood Historic Farm
Ⓑ Chabot Space and Science Center
Ⓒ Drawbridge
Ⓓ Dunsmuir House
Ⓔ Eugene O'Neill National Historic Site
Ⓕ Jack London Square
Ⓖ Oakland Zoo
Ⓗ University of California–Berkeley

East Bay

SIGHTS   In past decades, **Oakland** had a reputation as the Bay Area's bad neighborhood, notwithstanding the gracious hillside homes that line the city's higher elevations. Since the mid-1990s, however, urban renewal and an influx of high-tech money have done much to transform Oakland into a multi-ethnic enclave as welcoming as it is diverse. To tour Oakland, a city of 400,000 people, pick up the maps and brochures available from the **Oakland Convention and Visitors Bureau**. ~ 463 11th Street, Oakland; 510-839-9000, fax 510-839-5924; www.oaklandcvb.com, e-mail oakcvb@inreach.com.

Secluded among the trees of the Oakland hills is the **Chabot Space and Science Center**. The space theme is reflected in the modern-looking concrete and steel architecture of the facility. In addition to interactive science exhibits there is a dome theater where wide-format science films are shown, and a planetarium that offers a variety of shows. The three powerful telescopes are open for public viewing on weekends when the skies darken. Closed Monday and Tuesday. Admission. ~ 10000 Skyline Boulevard, Oakland; 510-336-7300; www.chabotspace.org, e-mail info@chabotspace.org.

Also in the hills is the **Oakland Zoo**, which displays a wide array of native and exotic animals, and is known for its efforts in elephant breeding. Admission. ~ 9777 Golf Links Road, Oakland; 510-632-9525, fax 510-635-5719; www.oaklandzoo.org.

The prettiest place in all Oakland is **Lake Merritt**, an unassuming body of water that happens to be the world's biggest saltwater tidal lake located within a city. Now that you've digested another meaningless statistic, you can work it off by joining the legions of joggers and bicyclists who continually circle the lake's three-mile perimeter. Or you can practice lawn bowling, stroll the park's botanical gardens, or rent a sailboat, rowboat, paddle boat, kayak, or canoe. Romantics can hire a gondola (510-663-6603; www.gondolaservizio.com). ~ Sailboat House: 568 Belle-

AUTHOR FAVORITE

One of the grandest mansions in the Bay Area, the **Dunsmuir House and Gardens** sits in a hidden valley in the Oakland hills. The 37-room mansion, carriage house, and formal gardens make this baronial spot a favorite retreat of mine and practically everyone who has visited. The grounds are closed to the public seasonally; call ahead for details. Admission. ~ 2960 Peralta Oaks Court, Oakland; 510-615-5555, fax 510-562-8294; www.dunsmuir.org, e-mail dhgi@dunsmuir.org.

vue Avenue, Oakland; 510-238-2196, fax 510-238-7199; www.
oaklandnet.com/parks.

For kids, there are duck feeding areas and a **Children's Fairy-
land** complete with rides and puppet shows. Closed Monday and
Tuesday in the spring and fall; closed Monday through Thursday
in winter. Admission. ~ Grand Avenue at Bellevue Avenue, Oakland; 510-238-6876, fax 510-452-2261; www.fairyland.org.

Also part of this lakeside complex is the **Camron-Stanford
House,** an 1876 Victorian home decorated with art and furniture
from that historic era. Open Sunday and Wednesday afternoon
and by appointment. Admission. ~ 1418 Lakeside Drive, Oakland;
510-444-1876, fax 510-874-7803; e-mail pelican@cshouse.org.

For complete information about Lake Merritt, stop by the
Office of Parks and Recreation. ~ 1520 Lakeside Drive, Oakland;
510-238-7275, fax 510-238-2224; www.oaklandnet.com.

Located just a few blocks from Lake Merritt sits the **Oakland
Museum of California,** a beautifully landscaped, triple-tiered facility. With its terraced gardens, courtyards, and lily ponds, the place
has won international acclaim. The theme here is California—its
history, art, and environment. Historical exhibits trace the area's
development from early Indian settlements to the present day,
artistic works present California artists from the Gold Rush era
forward, and the natural science exhibits carry visitors along a
simulated exploration route from the Pacific to the Sierra Nevada peaks. Closed Monday and Tuesday. Admission. ~ 1000 Oak
Street, Oakland; 510-238-2200, 888-625-6873, fax 510-238-
4901; www.museumca.org, e-mail webmaster@museumca.org.

Chinatown in Oakland is a miniature neighborhood compared   ◀ HIDDEN
to San Francisco's crowded enclave, but it's still an intriguing area
to stroll. Most of the markets and restaurants lie along 8th and
9th streets between Harrison and Franklin streets. Early morning
is the time to visit. That's when you'll see live catfish being delivered to local restaurants and shopkeepers shelving daikon roots,
Napa cabbage, and other Chinese-style vegetables.

Another area of increasing interest is **Preservation Park** on
9th Street between Broadway and Washington. All around this
cluster of old Victorian houses, downtown blocks are being refurbished and developed. Hotels, restaurants, shops, and offices
are moving to this formerly rundown section of town and promise to turn it into one of Oakland's premier commercial districts.

Jack London Square is everyone's favorite Oakland sightseeing spot. Today it harbors retail shops, overpriced restaurants,
and heavily touristed bars, but the place packs a lot of history.
Located on the Alameda estuary and overlooking one of the world's
busiest ports, it marks the city's early days. Richard Henry Dana
visited the area in 1835 while gathering material for *Two Years
Before the Mast*; by 1852 the waterfront boasted a couple of

rickety wharves from which the hamlet's oak timber was shipped to San Francisco. ~ At the foot of Broadway, Oakland.

Jack London, who grew up in Oakland, was in turn a sailor and oyster pirate along this hard-bitten waterfront. You can stroll the boardwalks, conjuring visions of the fabled adventure writer, then visit the **Jack London Cabin**. It's a classic log cabin, little more than a dozen feet across, where London lived in 1897 during the Klondike gold rush. Back then it rested along the north fork of Henderson Creek up in the Yukon. Today it sits next to **Heinold's First and Last Chance**, a funky woodframe saloon that London haunted as a young man. They still serve spirits, so you can engage in a little historical research while toasting the writer who made Oakland infamous. ~ 56 Jack London Square, Oakland; 510-839-6761.

At the edge of Jack London Square, in the shadows of the port's loading cranes, is Franklin D. Roosevelt's 165-foot yacht, the **USS Potomac**. A step back to another era, the beautifully refurbished vessel allows you to see where FDR liked to escape to and relax during the Depression years. Open for dockside tours and cruises around the bay on selected days. Admission. ~ 540 Water Street, Oakland; 510-627-1502, fax 510-839-4729; www.usspotomac.org, e-mail usspotomac@aol.com.

The recovery ship for the *Apollo 11* and *12* astronauts, and a significant player in World War II, the **USS Hornet** has a long history of American service. Recently refurbished by a group of dedicated volunteers, the decommissioned aircraft carrier is now a museum at Alameda Point. Cavernous hangar bays, claustrophobic hallways, and a wide-open flight deck create an unusual contrast of environments well worth experiencing. Closed Tuesday. Admission. ~ Pier 3, Alameda Point, Alameda; 510-521-8448, fax 510-521-8327; www.uss-hornet.org, e-mail info@uss-hornet.org.

From Oakland, **Telegraph Avenue** beelines to the University of California campus in the college town of **Berkeley**. During the tumultuous '60s and early '70s, "Telegraph" was the battleground for a wave of riots. Demonstrators protesting the Vietnam War spilled out from the campus to confront phalanxes of police and National Guardsmen. Protesters trashed the Bank of America's plate-glass windows so many times the bank finally replaced them with brick. Police brutality ran rampant.

The **mural** at the corner of Telegraph Avenue and Haste Street brilliantly depicts this chaotic era. Tracing the history of the Berkeley movement in overlapping images, it portrays the Free Speech Movement, anti-war protests, flower children, and the battle for People's Park.

In May 1969, a patch of Berkeley ground became a symbol for an entire generation. **People's Park**, a vacant lot owned by the University, was expropriated early in 1969 by radicals and converted to a public facility. The University responded by fencing the area, demonstrators promptly tore down the enclosure, and several days of vicious rioting followed. National Guardsmen and police occupied the town, killing one bystander and blinding another. Today the park remains a public area planted with flowers and occupied by street people as well as neighborhood folks looking for a game of frisbee or basketball. ~ Bowditch Street between Haste Street and Dwight Way, Berkeley.

UNIVERSITY OF CALIFORNIA–BERKELEY One of the nation's finest schools, the University of California–Berkeley (UCB) is home to over 30,000 students. Founded in 1868, it covers over 1200 acres and is easy to tour with a map available at University Hall. Guided tours are given Monday through Saturday at 10 a.m. and Sunday at 1 p.m. ~ 101 University Hall, 2200 University Avenue, Berkeley; 510-642-4636; www.berkeley.edu, e-mail visitor_info @pa.urel.berkeley.edu.

From here you can stroll across **Sproul Plaza**, site of countless rallies and demonstrations during the Vietnam era. Sproul Hall, the administration building, was the scene of a massive sit-in during the 1964 Free Speech Movement. Led by Mario Savio, over 700 people were dragged from the building, the largest mass arrest in California history.

Centerpiece of the campus is **Sather Tower**, a 307-foot spire modeled after St. Mark's campanile in Venice. A 61-bell carillon tolls from this lofty perch, and an elevator (admission) carries visitors to an observation perch from which there are extraordinary views. Just west of the campanile sits **South Hall**, the oldest and prettiest building on campus, and **Bancroft Library**, which houses the world's finest Western Americana collection.

Among its many features, the University also offers several important museums. The **Phoebe Hearst Museum of Anthropology**, boasting a half-million specimens, has fine collections of American Indian artifacts and archaeological and ethnographic materials from Europe, Asia, Egypt, South America, and the Pacific Islands. Call to find out what is currently on display, as all exhibits are temporary. Closed Monday and Tuesday. Admission.

THE WAY IT WAS
Just a minute from the freeway and blissfully behind the times, 205-acre **Ardenwood Historic Farm** is a charming farmstead preserving the region's agrarian tradition. Tour the Queen Anne home, watch a blacksmith at work, enjoy craft and cooking displays, visit the cornfield, and see living history demonstrations. Closed Monday. Admission. ~ 34600 Ardenwood Boulevard, Fremont; 510-796-0663, fax 510-796-0231; www.ebparks.org, e-mail ardn@ebparks.org.

~ Kroeber Hall, UC Berkeley; 510-643-7648, 510-642-3682; www.
hearstmuseum.berkeley.edu, e-mail pahma@uclink4.berkeley.edu.

The **Berkeley Art Museum**, with its skylights and spiraling
ramps, features a permanent collection of Western and Asian artworks. There are oils by old masters and contemporary artists
alike, as well as a sculpture garden on the grounds. Closed Monday and Tuesday. Admission. ~ 2626 Bancroft Way, Berkeley; 510-
642-0808, fax 510-642-4889; www.bampfa.berkeley.edu.

HIDDEN ►

Not far from the University, the **Judah L. Magnes Museum** is
an important center for Jewish history and art. Occupying a
stately 1908 three-story house, its collections include ceremonial
pieces from around the world, works by contemporary and traditional artists, and a wealth of rare books, oral histories, and
original documents. Closed Friday and Saturday. ~ 2911 Russell
Street, Berkeley; 510-549-6950, fax 510-849-3673; www.magnes.
org, e-mail magnes40@magnes.org.

En route to the next museum, located in the hills above the
Berkeley campus, visit the **Botanical Garden**. One of the finest in
the state, it contains over 12,000 species
arranged geographically. There are environments planted with African, South American, Mexican–Central American, Asian,
Mediterranean, New World Desert, Australian, and Californian species, as well as Western
and Chinese medicinal herb gardens, a Japanese
pool, and a palm garden. Closed first Tuesday of
the month. Admission. ~ 200 Centennial Drive,
Berkeley; 510-642-3343; www.mipberkeley.edu/
garden, e-mail garden@uclink4.berkeley.edu.

The area around the UC campus,
particularly on Telegraph and
Durant avenues, is crowded with
an array of cheap eats: pizza,
salads, ramen, falafel, sushi,
curry. On weekends vendor
stands line Bancroft Way,
peddling an eclectic selection of handicrafts.

Continue uphill to the **Lawrence Hall of Science**,
an oddly shaped structure that looks more like a Southwestern
rock formation than a building. Intended for the eight-to-eighty
set, this marvelous place is a hands-on museum with labs where
you perform experiments and play computer games. Kids can
handle animals in the biology lab, and the planetarium features a
series of stellar shows on weekends. Admission. ~ Centennial
Drive, Berkeley; 510-642-5132; www.lhs.berkeley.edu, e-mail
lhsinfo@uclink.berkeley.edu.

For a tour of the **Berkeley hills**, follow Centennial Drive up
to Grizzly Peak Boulevard and continue north; Euclid Avenue
will lead you back down to central Berkeley. All through these
magnificent hills are splendid houses of brick and brown shingle;
others re-create Spanish styles with red tile roofs and whitewashed
facades. The views spread across the Bay to San Francisco and
out beyond the Golden Gate.

Off Grizzly Peak Boulevard and stretching across the hills of
Berkeley and Oakland, 2000-acre **Tilden Regional Park** is a pop-

ular recreation spot, especially on sunny weekends. See "Beaches & Parks" below for more information.

To experience some of the East Bay's lesser-known locales, head south on Route 880 to the **San Francisco Bay National Wildlife Refuge**. Within this broad, flat expanse of marsh and pickleweed you'll find 30 miles of trails and 250 bird species. Visitors center closed Monday. ~ Near the junction of Route 84 and Thornton Avenue, on Marshland Road, Newark; 510-792-0222, fax 510-792-5828; desfbay.fws.gov. ◄ *HIDDEN*

Heading east on Route 84 will bring you to the town of **Niles**. Actually part of Fremont, this falsefront community played an important role in the history of Hollywood (it has its own "Hollywood" sign constructed on a neighboring hillside—only this one proclaims "Niles"). More than 450 one-reel films were shot here after Essanay Studios made it their West Coast headquarters around 1910. Charlie Chaplin's classic *The Tramp* was filmed in town. You can still see a few of the silent stars' cottages on 2nd Street between F and G streets. It's still a great neighborhood if you like to poke around its countless antique shops. If you head east into Niles Canyon on Route 84 you'll pass the rolling hills where Bronco Billy filmed his fabled Westerns. ◄ *HIDDEN*

While you're in the canyon, you can board a vintage train on the **Niles Canyon Railway**. The trip, which runs on the first and third Sunday of the month October through March, and every Sunday April to October, lasts about an hour. Admission. ~ Along Route 84, Sunol; 925-862-9063; www.ncry.org, e-mail pla_ncry @ncry.com.

Over the East Bay hills in Danville rests the **Eugene O'Neill National Historic Site**. In 1937, America's only Nobel Prize–winning playwright Eugene O'Neill built and resided in a beautiful home overlooking Mt. Diablo while writing some of his greatest dramas—*The Iceman Cometh*, *A Moon for the Misbegotten*, and *Long Day's Journey into Night*. Decorated in the fashion of the era, Tao House and its grounds are open to the public. Access is by reservation only; arrangements can be made through the National Park Service. Tours are run twice a day, Wednesday through Sunday, at no charge. Closed Monday and Tuesday. ~ 925-838-0249, fax 925-838-9471; www.nps.gov/euon.

Pay homage to Henry Ford's invention at the **Blackhawk Museum**, which has a collection of classic cars dating back to the 1890s—among them Clark Gable's 1935 Duesenberg convertible. The museum houses traveling exhibits from the Smithsonian. Closed Monday and Tuesday. Admission. ~ 3700 Blackhawk Plaza Circle, Danville; 925-736-2277, fax 925-736-4818; www.black hawkmuseum.org, e-mail museum@blackhawkmuseum.org.

Just a short jaunt from BART, the **Oakland Marriott City Center** sits at the heart of downtown. It's standard large-chain fare with **LODGING** close to 500 rooms stacked into 21 stories, but you can expect the top-quality services and amenities that come with a big hotel. The location is close to Chinatown and perfect for easy access to the Bay Area's countless treasures. ~ 1001 Broadway, Oakland; 510-451-4000, fax 510-835-3466; www.marriott.com. DELUXE TO ULTRA-DELUXE.

For help in booking rooms at Berkeley B&Bs, contact **Bed & Breakfast Accommodations in Berkeley**. ~ 2235 Carleton Street, Berkeley; 510-548-7556.

One of the coziest spots in the Bay Area is the **Rose Garden Inn**, a 1905 Tudor-style house converted to an inn. The public areas in this homey establishment include several ornately designed sitting rooms as well as a spacious yard and deck. There are 11 guest rooms in the main house plus 29 more in four adjacent buildings. Many are creatively appointed with hand-carved headboards, antique wardrobes, quilts, and plump armchairs, but the primary antiques at the inn are the houses themselves. The price includes a full buffet breakfast. The Rose Garden Inn provides the best of both worlds: a country inn in the city. ~ 2740 Telegraph Avenue, Berkeley; 510-549-2145, 800-992-9005, fax 510-549-1085; www. rosegardeninn.com, e-mail info@rosegardeninn.com. MODERATE TO ULTRA-DELUXE.

When looking for a convenient location, it's hard to top the **Hotel Durant**. This 144-room facility sits just one block from the Berkeley campus and includes a restaurant and pub. The rooms are creatively decorated with photographs from Berkeley's early days, contain hardwood furniture, and feature all the creature comforts from cable television to shower-tub combinations. ~ 2600 Durant Avenue, Berkeley; 510-845-8981, 800-238-7268, fax 510-486-8336; www.hoteldurant.com, e-mail durant@sfo.com. ULTRA-DELUXE.

HIDDEN ►   Set amidst a tree-lined section of Durant Avenue is the Gothic-style **Berkeley City Club**. Built in 1929, this historic landmark functions as both a private social club and a bed and breakfast. The rooms, which feature private baths, are small and spartan,

AUTHOR FAVORITE

The most intriguing place I can think of to spend the night is on one of the yachts of the **Dockside Boat & Bed** fleet. The 15 moored sailboats and power yachts ranging up to 60 feet in length are fully equipped for the night. They are available in both Oakland and San Francisco. Continental breakfast is included. ~ 57 Clay Street, Oakland; 510-444-5858, 800-436-2574, fax 510-444-0420; www.boatandbed.com, e-mail boatandbed@ aol.com. DELUXE TO ULTRA-DELUXE.

recalling women's residences of the 1920s. Among the amenities here are a grand indoor swimming pool, a fitness center, and a hair salon. It's located just a block from the UC Berkeley campus. Tours of this Julia Morgan–designed building are held the fourth Sunday of every month except December. ~ 2315 Durant Avenue, Berkeley; 510-848-7800, fax 510-848-5900; www.berkeley cityclub.com, e-mail berkeleycityclub@aol.com. DELUXE TO ULTRA-DELUXE.

Right across the street from the Berkeley campus is the **Bancroft Hotel**, a 22-room boutique hotel listed on the National Register of Historic Places. A prime example of the Arts and Crafts architecture that once flourished in Berkeley, the 1928 building was designed by Walter T. Steilberg, one of Julia Morgan's associates, as a private clubhouse for the College Women's Club. Many rooms feature balconies and the rooftop has panoramic views of San Francisco Bay. Continental breakfast included. ~ 2680 Bancroft Way, Berkeley; 510-549-1000, 800-549-1002, fax 510-549-1070; www.bancrofthotel.com, e-mail reservations@bancrofthotel.com. DELUXE.

DINING

Oakland's Chinatown has no shortage of eateries to fit all budgets. Most, of course, are Chinese, but you'll also find Vietnamese gems. Here, there's a restaurant that can compete dish for dish with many of San Francisco's popular Chinese restaurants. **Hunan Restaurant** serves Mandarin-style cuisine with special flair. Among the dozens of dishes are smoked tea duck, Szechuan prawns, Peking spareribs, squid, braised fish, and ginger crab. This family restaurant is highly recommended. ~ 396 11th Street, Oakland; 510-444-0212, fax 510-444-0219. MODERATE.

Jack London Square, a high-rent area situated along the Oakland waterfront, specializes in expensive restaurants. **Il Pescatore**, however, is a reasonably priced place with a view of the marina and estuary. The decorative motif is nautical and the menu follows the theme, specializing in seafood entrées like scampi, calamari, and salmon. There are also numerous Italian-style dishes, including veal scallopine, chicken cacciatore, and eggplant parmigiana. ~ 57 Jack London Square, Oakland; 510-465-2188, fax 510-465-0238. MODERATE TO DELUXE.

Exquisite Japanese meals, ranging from teriyaki and tempura to yakitori and sushi, are served at **Yoshi's at Jack London Square**. The exceptional Shokado Bento, a two-tiered box meal, includes a wide variety of seasonal specialties and is a compact version of *kaiseki* cuisine, Japan's most elegant culinary tradition. Yoshi's also presents hot jazz sounds in the adjoining club. ~ 510 Embarcadero West, Oakland; 510-238-9200, fax 510-238-4551; www.yoshis.com. MODERATE TO DELUXE.

Off the main drag lies **Le Cheval**, a large bright dining room with a delicious Vietnamese menu. There isn't a lot for decoration, aside from the giant bronze horse in the foyer (hence its name), but it's a convivial place with well-prepared dishes. Some good choices: the bird's nest, a bowl of crispy noodles filled with vegetables; marinated grilled meat; seafood claypots. It's a popular place, so reservations are recommended. No lunch on Sunday. ~ 1007 Clay Street, Oakland; 510-763-8495. BUDGET TO MODERATE.

Old-town Oakland with its red-brick facades has catered to the new trend in social life, the microbrewery. Down on Washington Street, a block away from the Convention Center, the **Pacific Coast Brewing Company** boasts award-winning microbrew and an elbow-polished hardwood bar where executives battle for the bartender's attention after 5. At lunch, expect hearty blue-collar fare like bangers and mash or meat pies. The service is notoriously slow, but beer gourmets don't mind. ~ 906 Washington Street, Oakland; 510-836-2739, fax 510-836-1987; www.pacific coastbrewing.com, e-mail info@pacificcoastbrewing.com. BUDGET TO MODERATE.

HIDDEN ▶ **L. J. Quinn's Lighthouse** claims to be Oakland's best-kept secret, and it may very well be. Hidden away across from Coast Guard Island along the Oakland/Alameda estuary, the building where Quinn's is located dates to 1903, once served as the Oakland harbor entrance lighthouse, and was moved to its present site in 1965. The main dining room is decorated in a nautical motif and has views of the marina below and downtown Oakland in the distance. An upstairs deck proves a wonderful place to dine on a sunny day. Specialties of the house include salmon Wellington, blackened prawns, and seafood pastas. ~ 1951 Embarcadero Cove, Oakland; 510-536-2050, fax 510-532-4156;

AUTHOR FAVORITE

When I first dined at **Lalime's**, I felt as though I had stumbled into a secret retreat. Set in the midst of a pretty residential neighborhood, the restaurant looks like an ordinary home from the outside. But I've never been in a private residence that serves grilled juniper-berry cured pork chop on buttermilk mashed potatoes with apple chutney. The service is excellent, as is the Mediterranean-inspired food, and the intimate dining is ideal for a quiet evening out. Dinner only. ~ 1329 Gilman Street, Berkeley; 510-527-9838, fax 510-559-7025; www.lalimes.com, e-mail chef@lalimes.com. DELUXE.

www.quinnslighthouse.com, e-mail bonoae@aol.com. BUDGET
TO DELUXE.

T. J.'s Gingerbread House is the place to enjoy "Louisiana
Fancyfine" gourmet Creole dishes while a gallery of rag dolls
adorning the shelves of a Victorian dining room looks on. This
enchanted cottage serves up hunks of "sassy" cornbread, heaping
bowls of jambalaya and such specialties as whiskey-stuffed lobster
and smoked prime rib. There is also a dining annex that looks like
a greenhouse and a retail shop selling handicrafts and the restaurant's baked goods. Open for breakfast, lunch, and two dinner
seatings; reservations are required. ~ 741 5th Street, Oakland;
510-444-7373, fax 510-444-2204. DELUXE TO ULTRA-DELUXE.

College Avenue, running directly from Broadway in Oakland
to the Berkeley campus, boasts a bevy of cafés, bistros, trattorias,
diners, and restaurants in all price ranges. One is **Zachary's
Chicago Pizza**, blessing the East Bay with Chicago-style *stuffed*
pies. Dough, then cheese and toppings, then more dough, then
sauce. The result is so good that both locations of the restaurant
are constantly packed. The mood is usually jovial, however, as locals know the wait is well worth it. ~ Two locations: 5801 College
Avenue, Oakland, 510-655-6385; 1853 Solano Avenue, Berkeley,
510-525-5950. MODERATE.

In the Elmwood district of College Avenue lies **Shen Hua**. A
favorite among East Bay folk, this is, simply put, a fantastic
Chinese restaurant. The dining room is light and airy with full-
length sliding glass windows, high ceilings and an open kitchen,
while the food is exquisite. Along with a host of delightful meat,
poultry, and seafood dishes, you'll also find veggie selections like
braised green beans and Szechuan eggplant. If you're looking for
great Chinese food on this side of the bay, you've found it.
Reservations recommended. ~ 2914 College Avenue, Berkeley;
510-883-1777. MODERATE.

Located in Berkeley's gourmet ghetto, **Café de la Paz** serves
tasty Latin American, vegetarian, and seafood specialties. Ecuador,
Venezuela, Brazil, and Argentina are among the countries represented on the menu. Mouth-watering tapas include *platanos
fritos* (ripe fried plantains with ancho-chile *crema*). For the main
course, try *vatapá de mariscos* (seasonal seafood simmered in a
peanut-ginger-habanero-chile sauce). They also have a full bar
and serve Latin-tinged weekend brunch. ~ 1600 Shattuck Avenue, Berkeley; 510-843-0662; www.cafedelapaz.net, e-mail cafe
delapaz@yahoo.com. MODERATE.

A welcome addition to Berkeley's growing culinary reputation is **Cesar**, a tapas bar next door to Chez Panisse. Opening at
4 p.m., the lively atmosphere invites you to have a drink and light
fare before dinner elsewhere, or sample the wide variety of tapas

Text continued on page 198.

Revolution
in the Kitchen

During the past several decades Berkeley has shed its image as a center of revolt and assumed the role of gourmet capital. Turbulence these days occurs not on the campus but in the Cuisinart. The shift in sensibility occurred during those dolorous days in the '70s when Berkeley's affluent graduates traded barricades for bouillabaisse.

Culinary consciousness is a cause célèbre. It means repudiating the fast food–frozen dinner mentality of the older generation and taking up the banner of fresh fruits and vegetables. Preservatives are out, natural foods are in. "Grow your own!" no longer refers to plants that are rolled and smoked.

Several exemplary restaurants were born of this movement. Developing a cooking style termed "California cuisine," they serve select dishes to small groups. All ingredients, from spice to shellfish, are fresh; the focus is on locally produced foods in season. Menus change daily and sometimes include dishes invented that afternoon to be tested on an adventurous clientele.

The vanguard of this culinary revolution is **Chez Panisse**. Set in a modest woodframe building, it hardly looks the part of a world-famous restaurant. But the owner, Alice Waters, has long been the guiding light in Berkeley kitchens. Her reputation is so imposing that the Dalai Lama stopped in for dinner during a Bay Area visit. Dinner is served downstairs in her two-tiered establishment and features a prix-fixe menu nightly. It's a multicourse extravaganza from appetizer to sorbet. A typical evening might include warm cabbage and spinach salad with goose confit and roasted apples, local fish and shellfish soup with garlic mayonnaise, grilled rack of lamb with green olive sauce, fried artichokes and celery root puree and passionfruit and kiwi sherbet Pavlova—all for an ultra-deluxe price. Reservations are *de rigueur* and must be made one month to the day in advance. Upstairs, however, the café offers more moderately priced meals in a lively setting, and reservations are also accepted up to a month in advance, but need only be made a week or two ahead of time. Open for lunch and dinner, it may serve calzone with goat cheese, oysters on the half shell, and sorrel soup, plus daily specials such as sautéed sole, fettuccine with sweetbreads, and grilled steak with rosemary butter. If time and budget permit, indulge yourself: this is where it all began. Closed Sunday. ~ 1517 Shattuck Avenue; dinner reservations 510-548-5525; café information 510-548-5049, fax 510-548-0140; www.chezpanisse.com. DELUXE TO ULTRA-DELUXE.

Alice Waters of Chez Panisse fame created her spinoff restaurant, **Café Fanny**, to accommodate those who wished to eat well without the hassle and expense of a "serious" restaurant. The bright little café is illuminated by a huge skylight and windows, and floored in handmade tiles. Most of the produce is purchased from local ranches that promote ecologically sound farming practices. The menu is simple and delicious: light sandwiches, and gourmet salads. Breakfast favorites include buck-wheat crêpes with fruit and organic yogurt. No dinner. ~ 1603 San Pablo Avenue, Berkeley; 510-526-7664; e-mail jhibbard@ix.netcom.com. BUDGET.

Rivoli Restaurant is run by a husband-and-wife team that set out to establish a neighborhood eatery featuring Chez Panisse–inspired California cuisine. They've maintained the mom-and-pop feel despite the popularity of the place. Service is flawless and unobtrusive, and the restaurant is elegantly lit. Tables, set close together, line a large dining room that looks out plate-glass windows onto a beautifully landscaped garden. The ever-changing menu consists of dishes made from fresh, local, organic produce. One delicacy that is a constant on the menu, luckily, is the portobello-mushroom fritters with lemon aïoli, parmesan, arugula, and caper vinaigrette. Dinner only. ~ 1539 Solano Avenue, Berkeley; 510-526-2542, fax 510-525-8412; www.rivolirestaurant.com, e-mail roscoe@rivolirestaurant.com. DELUXE.

Berkeley exported the revolution to Oakland's **Bay Wolf Restaurant**. Here, three partners founded a gourmet restaurant in a woodframe house. Its two dining rooms are decorated with modern art pieces. Run by a friendly staff, the place has the feel of home. Lunch and dinner menus vary weekly. If they're not serving sautéed duck breast or sword-fish with braised leeks, the chefs may be preparing roast leg of lamb, fresh pasta with scallops and mushrooms, or pork loin with artichoke purée. In any case, the food is outstanding, the service impeccable, and the ambience soft as candlelight. No lunch on weekends. ~ 3853 Piedmont Avenue, Oakland; 510-655-6004, fax 510-652-0429; www.baywolf.com. DELUXE TO ULTRA-DELUXE.

Bon appétit. Don't feel guilty. Former Communist leader Ho Chi Minh was once a pastry chef for Escoffier. *Vive la révolution!*

and stay until the midnight closing time. A communal table is available in the center of the room, with private tables along the wall. The eclectic menu includes items such as Spanish cheeses, salt cod and potato *cazuela*, and organic strawberries with rose for dessert. A fine selection of wines, cocktails, and beers complements the Spanish-inspired fare. ~ 1515 Shattuck Avenue, Berkeley; 510-883-0222. MODERATE TO DELUXE.

Berkeley may be known for California cuisine, but one of the great finds here is an Italian restaurant called **Caffe Venezia**. The walls in this eatery are decorated with murals portraying an Italian street scene. Adding three-dimensional reality is a clothesline hung with laundry stretched from one wall to another and a fountain. There are pasta dishes like cannelloni *al forno*, spaghetti puttanesca, and ravioli, plus fresh fish, chicken, and milk-braised pork. Rate this restaurant with a night sky worth of stars! No lunch on weekends and Monday. ~ 1799 University Avenue, Berkeley; 510-849-4681, fax 510-849-3104; www.caffe venezia.com. MODERATE TO DELUXE.

The gentrification of 4th Street in West Berkeley has produced a host of trendy restaurants. A popular eatery is the split-level **Café Rouge,** which serves a mix of southern French and northern Italian cuisine in a warm, modern setting. A cherry-wood zinc bar rounding the west wall adds a European flair. The menu changes weekly but may include a charcuterie plate and raw oysters for starters, and entrées such as spit-roasted chicken, steak *frite*, and seafood risotto. No dinner on Monday. ~ 1782 4th Street, Berkeley; 510-525-1440, fax 510-525-2776; www.caferouge.net. MODERATE TO DELUXE.

HIDDEN ▶ Definitely off the beaten path is **Meal Ticket**, a small restaurant hidden in the flatlands. Its red facade and yellow overlay provide a bright contrast to the dingy grays of the surrounding warehouses and garage shops. Inside are mouth-watering breakfast and lunch plates. Locals swear by the cornmeal pancakes and grilled salmon. No dinner. Closed Monday and Tuesday. ~ 125 San Pablo Avenue, Albany; 510-526-6385. BUDGET.

SHOPPING Situated on the Oakland waterfront, **Jack London Square** offers many opportunities for shopping. In addition to several national chains, there are interesting boutiques, specialty shops, and gift emporiums. Every Sunday, locals flock to the **farmers' market** for fresh fruit, produce, bread, and flowers. If you favor a literary respite, **Barnes & Noble**, one of the largest bookstores in northern California, will occupy you for hours. ~ 98 Broadway, Oakland; 510-272-0120.

College Avenue is one of the East Bay's major shopping sections. From its starting point at Broadway in north Oakland all the way to Russell Street in Berkeley, this thoroughfare hosts every type of store imaginable, from antique shops to clothing boutiques to children's secondhand stores.

Shattuck Avenue, a broad boulevard complete with landscaped median, is Berkeley's central district. The street divides into two entirely different sections, with University Avenue as a line of demarcation. To the south, from Durant Avenue to University, lies the city's old downtown section with traditional businesses.

North Berkeley, along Shattuck Avenue north of University Avenue, is far more interesting. This area, nicknamed "the gourmet ghetto" for its specialty food shops, is home to **The Cheese Board**. Run by an eclectic collective, this shop stocks a dizzying inventory of cheeses. With its baguettes, pizzas, and other breads, it's a perfect place to stock up for a picnic or pop down a few storefronts to their pizzeria that offers one or two types of pizza Tuesday through Saturday. Closed Sunday. ~ 1504 Shattuck Avenue, Berkeley; 510-549-3183, fax 510-549-9514; www.cheeseboardcollective.com.

> Moe's Books is a prime place to pick up secondhand books at reduced prices.

You can fill the rest of the basket with fresh flowers and goods from the wine shop, produce store, and pastry store, all of which are within whistling distance. And don't miss **Black Oak Books**, an exceptionally fine bookstore and an important literary gathering place. ~ 1491 Shattuck Avenue, Berkeley; 510-486-0698; www.blackoakbooks.com, e-mail blackoakbks@earthlink.net.

On the road again? Then stop by **Easy Going**. No matter where you're headed, this travel shop can help out with a wide array of guidebooks, maps, and accessories. ~ 1385 Shattuck Avenue, Berkeley; 510-843-3533, 800-675-5500; www.easygoing.com, e-mail info@easygoing.com.

A shopping district of another sort lies along Berkeley's **Telegraph Avenue** between Dwight Way and Bancroft Way. While this campus area is being steadily remodeled and made to conform to the chic standards of the new century, it still retains the native funk of Berkeley circa 1968. Street vendors line either side of the thoroughfare, selling clothes, metalwork, leather goods, and jewelry. Most of these artisans produce their own handiworks: there are painters, potters, weavers, and woodworkers here, dividing their days between studios at home and this open-air marketplace.

"Telegraph," as it's known locally, also supports enough bookstores to keep even a college town busy. Two of them, located practically next door to one another, are among the best in the country. **Moe's Books**, founded by a cigar-chomping bibliophile named Moe Moskowitz, contains four floors of new and used titles. ~ 2476 Telegraph Avenue, Berkeley; 510-849-2087; www.moesbooks.com, e-mail moe@moesbooks.com.

Cody's Books, with its beautiful design and smart layout, features new volumes. The selection here ranges from recondite titles to bestsellers. Cody's is also the best local bookstore for poetry. Don't forget to visit the bargain books section upstairs. ~ 2454 Telegraph Avenue, Berkeley; 510-845-7852.

West Berkeley has become a major center for design stores, art galleries, and discount outlets. Among the renovated warehouses and stores is **Smith and Hawken Outlet Store**, a trendy gardening supply store that also sells sportswear, books, and vases. ~ 1330 10th Street; 510-527-1076; www.smithandhawken.com. At **Earthworks Ceramics Coop** you'll find several potters creating functional dinnerware and decorative work. Fluctuating hours, call ahead. ~ 2547 8th Street; 510-841-9810. Many potters in the area offer open studios. One of the best is **Gary Holt**, whose award-winning work has an Asian influence. Open Saturday and by appointment. ~ 1449 5th Street; 510-527-4183; www.gary holt.com.

Fourth Street, a refurbished warehouse district in West Berkeley, has become ground zero for savvy shoppers. Outlet stores and stylish gift shops abound along this tree-lined street. **The Discovery Channel Store** has books, games, toys, and more, all focusing on the world of nature. ~ 740 Hearst Avenue at 4th Street; 510-841-1279. At **Hear Music** customers can don headphones and listen to a wide selection of classical and ethnic sounds. ~ 1809-B 4th Street; 510-204-9595; www.hearmusic.com. **The Gardener** has rustic home furnishings and upscale gardening supplies. ~ 1836 4th Street; 510-548-4545; www.thegardener.com.

NIGHTLIFE   Across the Bay from San Francisco, the evening activities revolve around places of high culture and those specializing in high spirits. From September to December, the **Oakland Ballet**, a nationally acclaimed company, presents dazzling premieres and performs classic ballets at the **Paramount Theatre**. This fully restored art-deco building is a showcase of flourishes and decorative details. A kind of architectural museum, the sumptuous theater alone is worth the price of admission. In addition to performing arts events

AUTHOR FAVORITE

In its latest incarnation, the historic **Parkway Theater**, which first opened in 1926, is a combination movie theater, pub, and pizzeria screening not-so-recent releases and experimental and foreign films at about half the price of a movie ticket anywhere else. Settle into a couch, cocktail lounge chair, or theater seat, put your pizza and beer on the table beside you, wait for the lights to dim, and enjoy the show. ~ 1834 Park Boulevard, Oakland; 510-814-2400; www.picturepubpizza.com, e-mail will@speakeasytheaters.com.

and concerts, the Paramount hosts a series of movie classics. ~ 2025 Broadway, Oakland; 510-465-6400; www.paramounttheatre.com, e-mail lstewart@paramounttheatre.com.

As for spirits, there's **Heinold's First and Last Chance**, a roisterous little bar once frequented by Jack London. ~ 56 Jack London Square, Oakland; 510-839-6761. While London aficionados crowd this rustic bar, blues enthusiasts head for **Eli's Mile High Club**, the Bay Area's finest blues club. Closed Sunday and Monday. Cover. ~ 3629 Martin Luther King Jr. Way, Oakland; 510-655-6161.

The **Bench & Bar** near the Oakland Museum is popular with gay men and women (particularly men). Get your groove on to latin dance music almost every night of the week. Drag shows Monday and Wednesday nights. The club is in the process of moving, call for details. ~ 120 11th Street, Oakland; 510-444-2266.

Yoshi's at Jack London Square, one of the Bay Area's premier jazz clubs, brings in locally and nationally known acts. It is also a full-service Japanese restaurant. Cover. ~ 510 Embarcadero West, Oakland; 510-238-9200; www.yoshis.com, e-mail yoshis@yoshis.com.

The brick-facaded **Berkeley Repertory Theater** offers an intimate alternative to the more commercial theaters in San Francisco, despite the 600-seat proscenium theater recently added to an existing 400-seat theater. This Tony award–winning group has a growing reputation in the performing-arts community, and is known for undertaking ambitious projects. ~ 2025 Addison Street, Berkeley; 510-845-4700, 800-427-8849, fax 510-647-2976; www.berkeleyrep.org, e-mail systems@berkeleyrep.org.

The **California Shakespeare Festival**, located near Orinda on Gateway Boulevard, is another highly visible example of the East Bay's rich dramatic tradition. Once devoted exclusively to Shakespeare, the Festival's recent change in management led to the inclusion of at least one non-Shakespeare production a season. Cal Shakes is perfect for a picnic dinner under the Orinda skies, accompanied by a bottle of wine and the Bard. ~ 510-548-9666; www.calshakes.org, e-mail letters@calshakes.org.

Also check with **Cal Performances** for a current listing of cultural events. They regularly present jazz concerts, chamber music, ballet and modern dance companies, ethnic performances, and countless other programs. ~ 101 Zellerbach Hall, UC Berkeley; 510-642-9988; www.calperfs.berkeley.edu, e-mail tickets@calperfs.berkeley.edu.

Pacific Film Archive, also connected with the University, is an extraordinary showcase for early and artistic movies. ~ Bancroft at Bowditch, Hearst Annex Field Building, Berkeley; 510-642-1412; www.bampfa.berkeley.edu.

On the Berkeley waterfront, **Skates on the Bay** provides other-worldly views of the Bay and San Francisco skyline. Just pull up to a plate-glass window, order a cocktail, and watch nature perform. ~ 100 Seawall Drive, Berkeley; 510-549-1900; www.r-u-i.com.

Being a college town, you'd expect Berkeley to have a healthy stash of bars. But here, espresso appears to be the addiction of choice, with cafés far outnumbering pubs. Still, there are a few good watering holes if you look for them. **Beckett's**, an authentic Irish pub, has a cozy and intimate atmosphere with stone walls, lots of woodwork, and a roaring fire. The charming set up and wonderful desserts make a visit definitely worthwhile. Occasional live entertainment. ~ 2271 Shattuck Avenue, Berkeley; 510-647-1790.

You can sample up to 40 of the best local brews at **Jupiter**. The setting is an early-20th-century building that originally housed a lumber merchant, with decor that the owner calls "beer gothic." This popular hangout also serves pizzas, focaccia sandwiches, and salads, and there's jazz several evenings a week in the beer garden out back. ~ 2181 Shattuck Avenue, Berkeley; 510-843-7625; www.jupiterbeer.com.

Another often-crowded brewery is **Triple Rock Brewery and Ale House**. Choose from a pale ale, an amber, or a porter and relax inside at one of the large wooden tables or outside on the upstairs back patio. ~ 1920 Shattuck Avenue, Berkeley; 510-843-2739; www.triplerock.com.

The **Freight and Salvage Coffee House** is a folk and acoustic music venue with national renown. Performers have included bluegrass legend Doc Watson, folksinger Tom Paxton, and country blues star Taj Mahal. Local musicians perform here as well, and on Tuesday night the famous (or infamous) open mike is, at $4.50, a great entertainment deal for the good-humored. Cover. ~ 1111 Addison Street, Berkeley; 510-548-1761; www.the freight.org.

Ashkenaz is a legend among Berkeleyites. This popular music and dance community center is a mecca for those who love the world's music, with groups playing world beat, salsa, folk, Cajun, or reggae most nights of the week. On many weekend nights the place is so packed you can't even get in the door. Cover. ~ 1317 San Pablo Avenue, Berkeley; 510-525-5054; www. ashkenaz.com, e-mail ashkenaz@ashkenaz.com.

Kimball's East is one of the Bay Area's leading jazz and R&B venues. Headliners have included Dizzy Gillespie and Wynton Marsalis. Modeled after a luxurious 1940s supper club, it has a full restaurant and bar, great acoustics, and an intimate ambience. Cover. ~ 5800 Shellmound, Emeryville; 510-658-2555; www.kim balls.com.

For online information on the East Bay's regional parks, go to www.ebparks.org.

ANTHONY CHABOT REGIONAL PARK AND REDWOOD REGIONAL PARK 🏃 🚲 🐎 ⛴ ⛴ ⛴ These contiguous facilities spread across nearly 7000 acres in the hills above Oakland. Foremost among their features are Lake Chabot, a haven for anglers and boaters, and the second-growth redwoods in Redwood Park. Chabot Park alternates between grass-covered hills and dense stands of eucalyptus, live oak, and madrone; the forests of Redwood Park are home to deer, raccoons, squirrels, and bobcats. Both parks have restrooms, picnic areas, and hiking trails. Chabot offers a golf course, an equestrian center, and a shooting range. Redwood has an archery range. There's a $4 parking fee at both parks. ~ The parks are located off Route 580 and can be entered from Skyline Boulevard or Redwood Road in Oakland or San Leandro; 510-635-0135, fax 510-569-4319.

> A wonderland for kids, Tilden Regional Park offers an antique merry-go-round with beautiful carved horses, a miniature steam train, pony rides, and a small farm.

▲ There are 75 sites (12 with RV hookups) near the lake in Chabot; $15 to $20 per night.

TEMESCAL REGIONAL RECREATIONAL AREA 🏃 🚲 🏊 ⛴ The highlight of this 48-acre park is Lake Temescal, created in 1868 when the Temescal Creek was dammed to supply water to Oakland. But soon larger reservoirs replaced Temescal and in 1936 it opened as one of the first recreational areas in the East Bay. Today this park, enhanced by lush growth of live oak, willow, and laurel, is a favorite spot among locals for swimming, sunbathing, fishing, picnicking, and hiking. In addition to a rose garden, fishing piers, and both paved and unpaved trails, facilities include picnic areas, restrooms, and showers. Swimming fee, $2 for kids and $3 for adults; fishing permit, $4; parking fee on weekends and holidays only, $4. ~ Located at the intersection of Routes 24 and 13 in Oakland. There are entrances from both highways; take the Broadway exit from Route 24, or the Broadway Terrace exit off Route 13; 510-652-1155, fax 510-652-0241.

TILDEN REGIONAL PARK AND WILDCAT CANYON REGIONAL PARK 🏃 🚲 🐎 🏊 ⛴ These two gems lie side by side in the hills above Berkeley. Tilden, by far the more diverse and popular, is a magnificent park. Stretching over 2000 acres, it features swimming in Lake Anza, a botanical garden that condenses California's 160,000 square miles of plant life into a six-acre preserve, a small environmental education center, and a rolling landscape that varies from volcanic rock to grassy meadows. Wildcat Canyon Park, with its meandering creek and forested arroyos, is a rustic counterpoint to Tilden's crowded acres. Both parks have restrooms, picnic areas, and hiking trails. Tilden also has a snack bar and a golf course. ~ Tilden Park is off Wildcat Canyon Road in the Berkeley hills; Wildcat Canyon Park is reached from McBryde Avenue in Richmond; 510-635-0135, fax 510-569-4319.

POINT PINOLE REGIONAL SHORELINE 🚶 🚲 ⛵ Located along San Pablo Bay, this 2400-acre park offers diverse possibilities. There are salt marshes to explore, as well as eucalyptus groves, open grasslands, and sea cliffs with sweeping vistas and pebble beaches. Anglers gravitate to the fishing pier, which extends several hundred yards into the Bay. Steelhead, salmon, sturgeon, striped bass, and leopard shark are a few of the game fish swimming these waters. Facilities include restrooms and picnic areas. Parking fee, $4. ~ Off Route 80 and can be reached by taking Hilltop Drive to San Pablo Avenue to Atlas Road in Richmond; 510-635-0135, fax 510-569-4319.

MOUNT DIABLO STATE PARK 🚶 🚲 🐎 Rising 3849 feet above sea level, Mount Diablo is the Bay Area's second loftiest peak (Mount Hamilton is the highest). From this surveyor's vantage point you can gaze east to the Sierra Nevada and west to the Pacific. Americans Indians considered it a place of power, the only point not submerged by the primordial flood. The mountain landscape ranges from shady cottonwood canyons to open woodlands to hillsides carpeted with wildflowers. Golden eagles, red-tailed hawks, and horned larks number among the many birds here. Rabbits, raccoons, coyotes, foxes, blacktail deer, bobcats, and an occasional mountain lion are also seen. In all, the park covers almost 20,000 acres. There are restrooms, picnic areas, and over 160 miles of hiking trails. A visitors center at the summit is closed Monday and Tuesday. Day-use fee, $4. ~ Located five miles east of Danville off Route 680, the park is reached via Mount Diablo Scenic Boulevard or North Gate Road out of Walnut Creek; 925-837-2525, fax 925-673-0160.

▲ There are 55 tent sites; $12 to $15 per night.

LAS TRAMPAS REGIONAL WILDERNESS 🚶 🚲 🐎 Within this 4000-acre expanse are sheer sandstone cliffs, chaparral-coated hillsides, and grassy meadows. It's a rugged region crossed by two ridges and containing a box canyon. Geologic forces have twisted and uplifted large sections of rock, which the wind has sculpted into exotic shapes. Golden eagles are often spotted here and wildlife is plentiful. The only facilities are picnic areas and restrooms. ~ Off Route 680 about seven miles northwest of San Ramon, the preserve lies along Bollinger Canyon Road; 510-635-0135, fax 510-569-4319.

COYOTE HILLS REGIONAL PARK 🚶 🚲 🐎 Adjacent to the Don Edwards San Francisco Bay National Wildlife Refuge, this

966-acre wildlife sanctuary provides both environmental education and recreation. Two shellmounds spanning more than 2000 years harken back to the days when American Indians settled this region of freshwater marshes, willow runs, fallow fields, and grassy hills. Trails traverse these habitats and a boardwalk extends through the marsh, allowing glimpses of native plants and wildlife, including thousands of migratory birds. The visitors center features exhibits and nature programs; closed Monday. There are picnic areas and restrooms. Parking fee, $4. ~ Paseo Padre Parkway and Route 84 off Route 880, north of the Dumbarton Bridge, Fremont; 510-795-9385, fax 510-795-8012.

Only 11 of Richardson Bay Audubon Center and Sanctuary's 900 acres are on land!

SUNOL/OHLONE REGIONAL WILDERNESS 🏃 🚲 🐎 An area of oak-covered hills, grasslands, and tumbling streams, this preserve stretches across more than 15,000 acres. Much of the land is cattle-grazing country, but more remote sections are covered with willows and inhabited by coyotes, mountain lions, and eagles. The foothills rise to almost 4000 feet, forming one of the wildest sections of the Diablo Range. An excellent trail system crosses the park. Facilities include a visitors center, restrooms, and picnic areas. Day-use fee, $4; trailer fee, $3; dog fee, $1. ~ Located about eight miles due east of Fremont, the park is at the end of Geary Road; 925-862-2244, fax 925-862-0810.

▲ There are four tent sites; $12 per night; there is also a backpack camp available for $5 per person. Reservations: 510-636-1684.

While the Pacific side of Marin County, described in Chapter Five, is known for its wave-lashed shoreline, the San Francisco Bay side of this wealthy region is renowned for posh homes and sleek shopping areas. Towns like Sausalito, Tiburon, and Mill Valley sit on dramatic hillsides and gaze out over the Bay toward the San Francisco skyline.

Marin County

Once across the Golden Gate Bridge in Sausalito, sightseeing begins on Bridgeway, a sinuous road paralleling the waterfront. I won't even begin to describe the views of Belvedere, Angel Island, and Alcatraz along this esplanade. Suffice it to say that the Sausalito waterfront offers the single element missing from every vista in San Francisco—a full-frame view of the city itself. It is also a perfect introduction to Marin County, a collection of luxurious bedroom communities that comprise one of the wealthiest counties in the nation.

Sausalito is a shopper's town: galleries, boutiques, and antique stores line Bridgeway, and in several cases have begun creeping

SIGHTS

uphill along side streets. **Plaza Vina del Mar** (Bridgeway and El Portal), with its elephant statues and dramatic fountain, is a grassy oasis in the midst of the commerce. Several strides seaward of this tree-thatched spot lies **Gabrielson Park**, where you can settle on a bench or plot of grass at water's edge.

Then continue along the piers past chic yachts, delicate sloops, and rows of millionaires' motorboats. To get an idea of the inland pond where the rich sail these toys, check out the U.S. Army Corps of Engineers **San Francisco Bay Model**. Built to scale and housed in a two-acre warehouse, this hydraulic model of San Francisco Bay is used to simulate currents and tidal flows. An audiotape guided tour leads you around the mini-Bay. When the model actually runs, you can watch the tide surge through the Golden Gate, swirl around Alcatraz, and rise steadily along the Berkeley shore. The tidal cycle of an entire day takes 14 minutes as you witness the natural process from a simulated height of 12,000 feet. Also part of the permanent exhibit is a display portraying Sausalito during World War II, when it was converted into a mammoth shipyard that produced almost 100 vessels in three years. Call ahead to make sure the model will be operating. Closed Monday in summer; closed Sunday and Monday the rest of the year. ~ 2100 Bridgeway, Sausalito; 415-332-3870, fax 415-332-0761; www.spn.usace.army.mil/bmvc.

Imagine a cluster of eight historic buildings and more than 100 hands-on activities all devoted to children ages one through ten. Throw in a multimedia center, a performing-arts theater, a science lab, and an indoor/outdoor "Tot Spot" for infants and toddlers and what you have is a place called the **Bay Area Discovery Museum**. Closed Monday. Admission. ~ 557 East Fort Baker, Sausalito; 415-487-4398, fax 415-332-9671; www.baykids museum.org, e-mail info@badm.org.

I heartily recommend the quarter-mile self-guided tour through the **Richardson Bay Audubon Center and Sanctuary**. It will provide an inkling of what Marin was like before the invention of cars and condominiums. During the winter months harbor seals can be seen in sanctuary waters. You can wander through dells and woodlands, past salt marshes and tidepools. Also contained on the property is **Lyford House**, a magnificent Victorian that commands a strategic spot on the shore of Richardson Bay. On Sunday afternoon from November through April, tours are given of the interior; on Sunday from September through May there are a variety of special programs. Admission. ~ 376 Greenwood Beach Road, Tiburon; 415-388-2524; e-mail rbac@earthlink.net.

Another field trip will lead you to a building, constructed of concrete and steel, which nevertheless evokes the rolling golden hills and blue-domed sky of Northern California. Perhaps that is because the **Marin County Civic Center** was designed by Frank

Lloyd Wright, an architect with a passion for blending a building to the surrounding landscape. Take Route 101 north to the North San Pedro Road exit in San Rafael; before even leaving the highway you'll see this long, low, graceful building that seems almost a landbridge between the three hills it spans. A self-guided tour will reveal interior corridors brilliantly illuminated by skylights and landscaped with trees and shrubs; there are docent-led tours Wednesday at 10:30 a.m. A singular structure, it represents the last commission of Frank Lloyd Wright, who died in 1959, several years before the Civic Center's dedication. Closed Saturday and

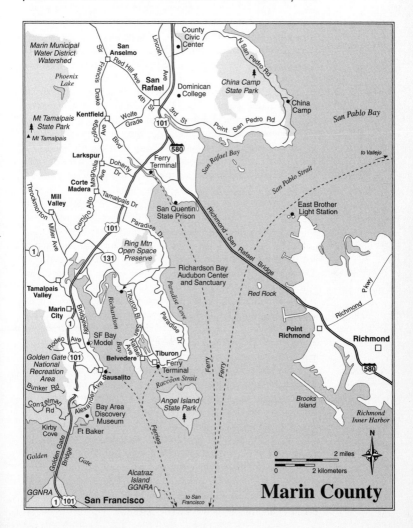

Marin County

Sunday. ~ 3501 Civic Center Drive, San Rafael; 415-499-6646; e-mail gholley@marin.org.

LODGING   **Casa Madrona Hotel & Spa** features a New England–style complex of rooms attached to a 19th-century landmark house and an expansive new Mediterranean wing. You'll find this tiered structure on a Sausalito hillside overlooking San Francisco Bay. The guest rooms in the B&B-style house have a personal feel and individual names. The "Artist's Loft" is decorated with antique artists' supplies and enjoys a bay view from its large deck, while the "La Posada" is styled after a grand Victorian. The contemporary wing features lavish accommodations with deep soaking tubs and fireplaces. There are also five private cottages available at this 63-room resort. ~ 801 Bridgeway, Sausalito; 415-332-0502, 800-567-9524, fax 415-332-2537; e-mail casa@casamadrona. com. ULTRA-DELUXE.

Staying at **The Waters Edge** in Tiburon is like a sleepover at Martha Stewart's house. The 23 elegant guest rooms all have fireplaces and are meticulously decorated in simple, modern design complete with vaulted wood ceilings. But you don't stay here for clever shelving or decorating tips. Wrap yourself in a hand-knitted blanket, curl up on the chaise lounge, and spend the day gazing at the view and pretending to turn a page every few hours. A continental breakfast is served in your room and there's complimentary wine and cheese every evening. ~ 25 Main Street, Tiburon; 415-789-5999, 877-789-5999, fax 415-789-5888; www.marinhotels.com, e-mail mgr@watersedgehotel.com. ULTRA-DELUXE.

If you're longing to get away to a quiet hideaway in a tropical setting reminiscent of Key West (but actually located in a residential Victorian neighborhood), book a room at the **Panama Hotel**. The 13 rooms and two garden cottages are decorated with a hodgepodge of antiques, some with clawfoot tubs and canopied beds. Most have ceiling fans and either a balcony or garden patio. Continental breakfast included. Gay-friendly. ~ 4 Bayview Street; San Rafael; 415-457-3993, 800-899-3993, fax 415-457-6240; www. panamahotel.com, e-mail innkeeper@panamahotel.com. DELUXE.

HIDDEN ▶   Calling the accommodations at **East Brother Light Station** unusual is a slight understatement. Where else can you find a bed-and-breakfast inn located within a lighthouse on an offshore island? The old beacon was built back in 1873 and has been operational for over a century. Today the two-story house and light station feature five bedrooms furnished with period pieces. Guests travel out to this one-acre hideaway by motorboat and enjoy wine and hors d'oeuvres followed by a multicourse dinner as well as breakfast the next morning. Of course, there's a premium on such seclusion: rates run in the ultra-deluxe range and reservations should be made. Shared and private bathrooms are available. Open Thursday through Sunday, this San Pablo Bay retreat is a unique opportunity to trade the trappings of civilization for your own private island. ~ 117 Park Place, Point Richmond; 510-233-2385; www.ebls.org, e-mail info@ebls.org. ULTRA-DELUXE.

DINING

You'll know the bill of fare by the name—**Hamburgers**; and you can tell the quality of the food by the line outside. Local folks and out-of-towners alike jam this postage stamp–sized eatery. They come not only for charcoal-broiled burgers, but for bratwurst, Italian sausage, and foot-long hot dogs as well. It's tough securing a table, but you can always pull up a bench in the park across the street. ~ 737 Bridgeway, Sausalito; 415-332-9471. BUDGET.

Sausalito sports many seafood restaurants, most of which are overpriced and few of which are good. So it's best to steer a course for **Seven Seas**. It lacks the view of the splashy establishments, but does feature an open-air patio in back. The menu includes scallops, bouillabaisse, and salmon. Landlubbers can choose from several meat platters; at lunch sandwiches are served; also open for breakfast. Closed January to mid-February. ~ 682 Bridgeway, Sausalito; 415-332-1304, fax 415-331-8015. MODERATE TO ULTRA-DELUXE.

If you long for a sea vista and an eyeful of San Francisco skyline, try **Horizons**. Housed in the early-20th-century San Francisco Yacht Club, this spiffy seafood restaurant has a wall of windows for those inside looking out, and a porch for those who want to be outside looking farther. Then, of course, there's the food: shellfish and other aquatic fare, with chicken, pasta, and steak dishes added for good measure. Some beautiful carpentry went into the design of this place. There's also a popular bar here, making it a choice spot to drink as well as eat. Open for brunch, lunch, and dinner. ~ 558 Bridgeway, Sausalito; 415-331-

AUTHOR FAVORITE

Sometimes I'll find a restaurant where the food is perfectly complemented by the surroundings. **Lark Creek Inn** is one such locale: A late-19th-century yellow house surrounded by redwoods, gardens, and a meandering creek, the Inn has garnered acclaim for its menu, farm-fresh ingredients, and country elegance. Dinner might feature cast-iron roasted striped bass with Yukon-gold potato gnocchi and chanterelle mushrooms. Lunch may find diners enjoying California quail stuffed with andouille sausage. In either case, finish your meal with the seasonal sorbet. No lunch on Saturday, but there is Sunday brunch. ~ 234 Magnolia Avenue, Larkspur; 415-924-7766, fax 415-924-7117; www.larkcreek.com.

3232, fax 415-332-0400; www.tavistockrestaurants.com MODERATE TO DELUXE.

If the tide doesn't carry you, current trends may very well deliver you to the door at **Guaymas** in Tiburon. This upscale Mexican restaurant bakes fresh tortillas and tamales daily. Pork, steak, and shrimp dishes are prepared on a mesquite grill; or try the duck with pumpkin seed sauce or the daily fresh fish catch. Located next door to the ferry dock, Guaymas rounds out the bill of fare with a bay view. ~ 5 Main Street, Tiburon; 415-435-6300, fax 415-435-6802; www.guaymas.com, e-mail guaymasrst@aol.com. MODERATE TO DELUXE.

Sit down to jalapeno cornbread, voodoo shrimp, and some Cajun loving at **Mudbugs Café**. Of course, you can always try the mudbugs (crawfish, that is). The menu also offers traditional dishes like tenderloin and filet mignon, but with a Creole kick. It's a vibrant and friendly place with a canvas-cloaked patio and decadent pecan pie. ~ 44 East Blithedale Avenue, Mill Valley; 415-381-2500; www.mudbugscafe.com. MODERATE TO DELUXE.

Another bayside spot that's accessible by ferry is **The Marin Brewing Company**. Famous for the beer (the Blueberry Ale has won a gold medal and Mt. Tam Pale Ale is a regional favorite), this spot also serves delicious pub grub. Clams, burgers, buffalo wings, and pizzas from the wood-fired oven are all tasty accompaniments to your brew of choice. The 50-foot-long wooden bar is claimed to be one of the longest in California. ~ 1809 Larkspur Landing Drive, Larkspur; 415-461-4677, fax 415-461-4688; www.marinbrewing.com. BUDGET TO MODERATE.

SHOPPING   The best shopping spot in all Marin is the town of Sausalito. Here you can stroll the waterfront along Bridgeway and its side streets, visiting gourmet shops, boutiques, and antique stores. One of the Bay Area's wealthiest towns, Sausalito sports few bargains, but it does host an assortment of elegant shops.

Several shops in the mini-mall at 660 Bridgeway are worth a browse. **Crescendo**, a one-of-a-kind boutique, features contemporary women's fashions and jewelry. ~ Sausalito; 415-332-0991, 800-266-0660.

A PASSAGE TO LITERARY LAND

Your next trip begins the minute you step in to **Book Passage**. Travel guides, maps, and accessories make this store a favorite among Bay Area travelers. After you've selected the books you need, sit down with an Italian soda in the café and begin plotting your itinerary. ~ 51 Tamal Vista Boulevard, Corte Madera; 415-927-0960, 800-999-7909; www.bookpassage.com, e-mail messages@bookpassage.com.

The **Northgate Mall** is an enclosed shopping center with about 100 stores, including the Gap, Macy's, Bath & Body Works, and other chains. There are several forgettable restaurants and a 15-screen movie theater. ~ 5800 Northgate Mall, San Rafael; 415-479-5955; www.themallatnorthgate.com.

Stretching for a half-mile and numbering two dozen stores is the antique-shop district of San Anselmo. You can bid on entire estates at spots like the **San Rafael Auction Gallery**. Open by appointment only. ~ 634 5th Avenue; 415-457-4488. Look for pewter and Early American furniture at **Oveda Maurer Antiques**. Open by appointment only. ~ 34 Greenfield Avenue; 415-454-6439. **Michael Good** specializes in a wide variety of antiquarian books including limited editions, fine art, and California history. Closed Sunday. ~ 35 San Anselmo Avenue; 415-459-6092.

NIGHTLIFE

The window simply reads "Bar"; the address is 757 Bridgeway in Sausalito; and the place is famous. Famous for its name, the **no name**, and because it's a favored hangout among young swingers and old salts alike. With an antique bar, piano, and open-air patio, it's a congenial spot to bend an elbow. You'll hear live jazz on Friday and Saturday, a variety of musical styles during the week including blues, folk, and Dixieland, and open-mike every Tuesday. ~ 757 Bridgeway, Sausalito; 415-332-1392.

One of the top repertory theater groups in the Bay Area is the **Marin Theater Company**, which performs classic and contemporary dramatic works in a state-of-the-art playhouse that many larger troupes would envy. ~ 397 Miller Avenue, Mill Valley; 415-388-5200; www.marintheater.org, e-mail info@marintheater.org.

Sweetwater jams every night. Featuring blues and rock sounds, the club often headlines big-name groups. Cover. ~ 153 Throckmorton Avenue, Mill Valley; 415-388-2820; www.sweetwatersaloon.com.

If you're in the mood for a mellow evening, several coffee-houses offer live acoustic music. **Mama's Royal Café** has jazz and cat house blues during the day on weekends. ~ 387 Miller Avenue, Mill Valley; 415-388-3261.

For a dose of outdoor drama, head to **Marin Shakespeare Company**'s amphitheater in San Rafael, where serious stage-strutting and fretting occur throughout the summer season, courtesy of the company's skilled, professional players. ~ Forest Meadows Amphitheater, Dominican College, Grand Avenue off Mission, San Rafael; 415-499-1108; www.marinshakespeare.org.

BEACHES & PARKS

CHINA CAMP STATE PARK This 1540-acre park, located shoreside along San Pablo Bay, is a perfect picnic spot. Heavily wooded and adorned with several midget islands just offshore, it has a particular lure. Part of the attraction is the old Chinese fishing village, dating to the 1860s. This ghost community of tumbledown houses was home to thousands of Chinese who were uprooted by the 1906 San Francisco earthquake and fire. Now it's a peaceful park inhabited by shore birds, anglers, and daytrippers. The park has picnic areas, restrooms, and 20 miles of hiking trails. ~ Located along North San Pedro Road about five miles east of San Rafael; 415-456-0766, fax 415-456-1743.

▲ There are 30 developed walk-in sites; $15 to $16 per night. Reservations: 800-444-7275.

The Delta Region

California's two major rivers, the Sacramento and San Joaquin, flow together around Sacramento, creating the state's fertile delta region. The heart of this bayou country lies about 70 miles northeast of San Francisco. From the city, the fastest way to go is by following Route 80 east to Fairfield, turning right on Route 12 and taking it to Route 160 in Rio Vista. Route 160 leads north through the heart of the Delta. An alternative course, taking Route 4 instead of Route 12, will also carry you near John Muir National Historic Site and the waterfront town of Port Costa.

SIGHTS

HIDDEN ▶

The **John Muir National Historic Site**, a grand 17-room Victorian on a nine-acre estate, was home to the renowned naturalist for almost a quarter-century until his death in 1914. It was here that Muir wrote voluminously on conservation and became a founder of the Sierra Club. Muir also helped create Yosemite National Park; he personally led Theodore Roosevelt through the Sierra, admonishing him for hunting big game and urging the president to preserve other wilderness areas.

The countryside that once surrounded the Scottish conservationist's house has given way to suburban plots. But nine acres of the orchards Muir once managed remain. Within the house, many rooms have been restored as they originally appeared. Muir's "scribble den," or study, remains littered with manuscripts and research materials, the family quarters are opulently furnished, and the parlor is filled with Victorian effects. While John Muir's primary love was the wild, a tour of his estate provides a singular glimpse into the life of the man. Closed Monday and Tuesday. Admission. ~ 4202 Alhambra Avenue, Martinez; 925-228-8860, fax 925-228-8192; www.nps.gov/jomu, e-mail jomu_interpretation@nps.gov.

Across the Carquinez Strait, the **Benicia Capitol** still stands, an imposing brick building marked by twin pillars. True to antiquity, every desk in the Senate chamber is set up to be illuminated by candle and has a spittoon by its side. Closed Monday and Tuesday. Admission. ~ West 1st and G streets, Benicia; 707-745-3385, fax 707-745-8912; www.parks.ca.gov, e-mail benicia@napanet.net.

Another relic of the past that didn't quite work out, the yellow sandstone **Benicia Camel Barn Museum** recalls the days in the 1850s when the U.S. Army imported a herd of dromedary camels from the Middle East in the belief that they might help open the desert West. Open Wednesday through Sunday. Admission. ~ 2060 Camel Road, Benicia; 707-745-5435.

◄ HIDDEN

There are walking tour booklets at the Capitol to lead you past the other historic sites that make Benicia the little town that couldn't. The **Benicia Chamber of Commerce** also has pamphlets and maps. ~ 601 1st Street, Benicia; 707-745-2120, 800-559-7377; www.beniciachamber.com, e-mail beniciachamber@aol.com.

THE DELTA   The Delta is an endless expanse of flatlands and orchards, levees and dikes. A thousand miles of waterways meander through this mazework. There are channels bearing names like Hog, Whiskey, Disappointment, and Montezuma Slough.

The gateway to this watery world is **Bethel Island**, one of the 55 islands that comprise the Delta. Featuring marinas, motels, restaurants, and boat rentals, it sits a few miles east of the intersection of Routes 4 and 160. Like the rest of the Delta, it is busiest during summer and on weekends. In the winter, many local businesses close for the season, so it's best to check in advance.

Two other points of interest border the southern fringes of the Delta. Listed on the National Register of Historic Places, the **Black Diamond Mines Regional Preserve**, a 5700-acre park at the foot of Mt. Diablo, features a 19th-century cemetery complete with

The Delta Region

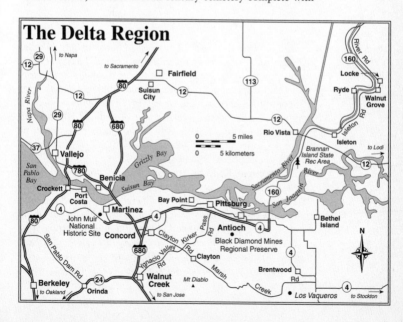

The Back Road to the Delta

Taking Route 4 instead of Route 12 will allow you to see a greater stretch of the Delta along Route 160. It will also carry you near two waterfront towns—Port Costa and Benicia—that should not be missed.

PORT COSTA   Port Costa enjoyed its heyday early in the century when the town served as a major grain-shipping port. Today it's a lazy community at the end of a country lane. A few sagging stores have been converted to artists' quarters and antique shops, and one of the warehouses has become a cavernous restaurant. Otherwise, the wrinkled hills all around seem like time warps in which this church-steeple village rests suspended. Farmland and forest enclose Port Costa, so finding your way becomes half the enjoyment of exploring the town: Well-marked side roads lead to it from Route 4. A few miles farther along this highway, past rounded hills tufted with grass, sits the **John Muir National Historic Site** (page 212).

MARTINEZ   From Port Costa, it's a short drive southeast on Route 4 to the bayside town of Martinez. Established as a trading post in the late 1840s, Martinez began to grow, enhancing its position by becoming a shipping port, county seat, and railroad center, not to mention the terminus for

cracked tombstones engraved in Welsh. Approximately 34 miles of hiking and biking trails traverse the park, which has picnic areas and campsites. In the lowest level of one of the mines is a visitors center that displays old photographs and mining artifacts. Two first-come, first-served underground tours of the mines begin at 12 p.m. and 3 p.m. on the weekend (arrive early to buy tickets). Weekend admission. ~ Somersville Road, three miles south of Route 4, Antioch; 925-757-2620, fax 925-757-0335; www.eb parks.org, e-mail bdvisit@ebparks.org.

The **Western Railway Museum** features dozens of vintage railroad cars, many of them in working order. Wander this 25-acre, open-air museum and you'll come across an Australian tram and a Gay Nineties streetcar. A nine-mile ride on one of the many historic cars is offered. Open on the weekends only September through May; open Wednesday through Sunday June through August. Admission. ~ 5848 Route 12, between Suisun City and Rio Vista; 707-374-2978, fax 707-374-6742; www. wrm.org.

the longest-running ferry service west of the Mississippi. Today the town is low-key, off the beaten track, relaxed, and friendly—more like a small town than a metropolitan suburb. Early-20th-century homes can be found scattered about town, and a historic downtown district boasts 23 antique stores.

BENICIA   Across the Carquinez Strait from Port Costa looms Benicia (from Route 4 in Martinez continue east a few miles, then take Route 680 north to Route 780), a community whose early dreams proved to be delusions of grandeur. The folks who founded the town foresaw it as the state capital. In 1853 it was actually named the seat of government, but by 1854 dissatisfied legislators had moved their operation to Sacramento. The founding mothers and fathers also pictured Benicia as a magnificent port. (For more information on Benicia, see page 212.)

BAYOU COUNTRY   On Route 160, you can travel north along the Sacramento River all the way to the current state capital. En route is a dreamy land of drawbridges, meandering waterways, and murky mists. This bayou country is as dateless as the Deep South. Back in the 1850s, steamboats sidewheeled upriver from San Francisco to the Gold Country outside Sacramento. Residents still tell of the pirates who stretched chains across the river to snag steamboats laden with gold. The area is renowned among anglers for its striped bass, blue gill, sturgeon, and black bass. Waterskiers and other aquatic enthusiasts favor it as well. (For more information on the Delta, see page 213.)

Chances are, you've marveled at the realistic gritty texture of the pear Jelly Belly, or the frothiness of the cappuccino-flavored bean. The Herman Goelitz company's **Jelly Belly Candyland Tour** will show you how it's done. During this 35-minute tour, you will receive samples and a color-coded Jelly Belly identification menu. In addition to the trademark beans, you will see the creation of Wiggle Worms, Tummy Bears, and Gummi Pet rats and tarantulas. Factory machinery does not operate on the weekends, though tours are still offered. ~ 2400 North Watney Way, Fairfield; 707-428-2838; www.jellybelly.com.

The high point of any Delta trip is a visit to **Locke** (population 75; elevation 13 feet), a creaky community of clapboard houses and falsefront stores. This intriguing town, located on Route 160, is the only rural community in the entire country built and occupied by Chinese. Many contemporary residents trace their ancestry back to the pig-tailed Asian immigrants who mined California gold fields and helped build the transcontinental railroad, then moved on to construct the Delta's intricate levee system.

◄ *HIDDEN*

During its heyday in the early 1900s, Locke was a wide-open river town. Chinese and non-Asians alike frequented its gambling parlors, speakeasies, and opium dens. These raffish denizens have long since disappeared, but little else has changed.

Today Locke is like an outdoor museum, an example of what America's small towns would be like if time were measured not in terms of human progress, but in the eternal effects of the elements. You can still stroll along wooden sidewalks, which now slope like the pathways in an amusement park funhouse. Elderly Asians sit in the doorways reading Chinese newspapers.

On either side of the town's block-long Main Street, there are tumble-down two-story buildings with balconies that lean toward the road. Rust streaks the tin roofs, and some structures have sagged so heavily that the doors are rectangular forms collapsing into parallelogram shapes. Some of the outer walls are covered with rose vines, others are buried in an avalanche of honeysuckle. Along the edge of town are the trim orchards and communal gardens that Chinese residents have tended for generations.

Every building has a story to relate. As you wander through town, glance up near the ridgetops of the falsefront buildings. On many you can still discern the outlines of hand-lettered signs proclaiming that once this place was a Chinese "Bakery and Lunch Parlor," the "Star Theatre," or "Waih & Co. Groceries & Dry Goods."

In the 1980s, the Department of Fish and Game purchased the land of a duck hunting club to create the **Tsenberg Crane Reserve**. Every Sunday and certain Saturdays and Thursdays from October through February, thousands of nature lovers embark on a two-hour tour to witness the gregarious nature and hear the trumpet-like gargling call of the sandhill crane. Marked by gray plumage and a bald red forehead, this threatened species

sights

AUTHOR FAVORITE

My Delta adventure lies along the filigree of waterways just behind Locke in a place known as **The Meadows**. The best way to explore this preserve is in a boat. By car, go south from Locke about 200 yards and turn left on the first paved road (just before the concrete bridge). Proceed about 100 feet and turn left on the gravel road; a mile in length, it leads into The Meadows. Generally considered the Delta's most picturesque region, The Meadows is like an everglades. Its narrow canals are shaded by oak and walnut trees that droop Spanish moss to the water's edge. Frogs croak in the lily pads. Pheasant, great horned owls, Canada geese, and a variety of ducks inhabit the place, and along the riverbanks you can pick blackberries and grapes.

stands at five feet tall with a seven-foot wingspan. Reservations required and mail-in registration needed, call for information. ~ In Woodbridge, ten miles southeast of Locke; 916-358-2869 or 916-358-2353.

Housed in a little yellow house circa 1854, surrounded by eucalyptus trees, and dotted with antiques and original art (most of which are for sale), the **Inn At Benicia Bay** is the epitome of quaint. All nine rooms are individually decorated and some feature pretty decks overlooking the garden. A continental breakfast is included, as is a wine and cheese "social hour" every evening. ~ 145 East D Street, Benicia; 707-746-1055, fax 707-745-8361; e-mail the innbb@aol.com. MODERATE TO ULTRA-DELUXE.

Good lodging places are rare around the Delta, but there's one that I recommend. **B & W Resort Marina**, set on the Mokelumne River, features a covey of wood-frame cottages scattered across spacious grounds. There's a marina as well as a picnic area and small beach. The units include one-bedroom cottages and two-bedroom duplexes. These are tidy efficiency units with knotty-pine walls, linoleum floors, and no decoration; they include kitchenettes but no utensils. During July and August, peak season, the minimum stay is one week. ~ 964 Brannan Island Road, Isleton; 916-777-6161, fax 916-777-5199; www.bandwresort.com, e-mail band wresor@aol.com. MODERATE.

A former speakeasy once owned by Lon Chaney, Jr., a star of early Hollywood horror flicks, **Ryde Hotel** retains its art-deco charm with 32 period-decorated guest rooms and a restaurant reminiscent of a 1930s supper club complete with arched windows, palms, and a grand piano. The restaurant is open Friday and Saturday, April through November, with Sunday brunch year-round. ~ Route 160 at Route 220, Ryde; 916-776-1318, 888-717-7933, fax 916-776-1195; www.rydehotel.com, e-mail ryde hotel@hotmail.com. MODERATE TO DELUXE.

The most adventurous lodging on the Delta is aboard a **houseboat**. These vessels are quite simple to operate with 45 minutes of instruction and require no captain's license. There's no finer way to experience California's bayou than by spending a few lazy days on the river. Among the many companies renting houseboats are **Herman & Helen's Marina**. ~ At the end of Eight Mile Road, Stockton; 209-951-4634, fax 209-951-6505; www.house boats.com, e-mail hth@inreach.com. DELUXE TO ULTRA-DELUXE.

In Benicia, en route to the Delta, **First Street Café** serves standard breakfast fare, soups, salads, and sandwiches for lunch, and seafood, meat, and pasta dishes for dinner. A contemporary café, this popular spot has an espresso machine and offers an assortment of fresh baked desserts. Head upstairs Thursday through

Sunday and munch on appetizers while gazing at the Carquinez Strait. Take out meals are also available. Weekend brunch. ~ 440 1st Street, Benicia; 707-745-1400, fax 707-745-1485; www.firstst cafe.com. MODERATE TO DELUXE.

For riverside dining, head for **The Point**, tucked into the Delta Marina Yacht Harbor in Rio Vista. A variety of seafood, pasta, steak, and chicken dishes are offered and you can dine in a cozy booth by the window and watch the Sacramento River scene in the River Room or on an enclosed patio known as the Garden Room. There's entertainment in the lounge on Saturday nights during the summer, and brunch on Sunday. Closed Monday. ~ 120 Marina Drive, Rio Vista; 707-374-5400, fax 707-374-2542; www.pointrestaurant.com, e-mail pointman@point restaurant.com. MODERATE TO DELUXE.

For local color, nothing compares to **Giusti's**, a reasonably priced seafood and prime rib restaurant. Dating to 1896, it's housed in a wooden building with a timeworn exterior. It's the kind of place where the walls are decorated with autographed photos inscribed to the owner and the ceiling is covered with 1250 baseball caps. At lunch they serve steaks, burgers, pasta, and daily specials; then for dinner, Giusti's features prawns, grilled halibut, veal cutlets, and fresh fish. Closed Monday. ~ 14743 Old Walnut Grove Road, Walnut Grove; 916-776-1808; www.giustis.com. MODERATE.

It seems almost too obvious to eat at a Chinese restaurant in Locke (founded and occupied by Chinese). But where better to find authentic Chinese cuisine? **Locke Garden Chinese Restaurant** occupies the town's first building, a 1912 structure that looks like a transplant from the Midwest. Formerly a beer parlor, the spacious dining room features basic but tasty Chinese staples such as cashew chicken, Szechuan beef, and chow mein. Closed Monday. ~ 13967 Eva Road, Locke; 916-776-2100. BUDGET.

SIX FLAGS AND A HAMMERHEAD SHARK

Six Flags Marine World, a 160-acre theme park, fuses education with an adrenaline rush. A 300,000-gallon shark tank, an aquarium of killer whales, and a 55-acre lake host a variety of stunt shows (both animal and human). On the thrill side, more than a dozen head-spinning rides with names like Zonga, Hammerhead Shark, and Boomerang defy gravity. Among other land-based attractions are the Elephant Encounter (where you'll have a chance to ride Asian and African species), Butterfly World, an animal nursery, and Looney Tunes Seaport (geared towards the under-48-inch set). Closed November through March. Steep admission. ~ 2001 Marine World Parkway, off Route 80, Vallejo; 707-643-6722; www. sixflags.com, e-mail marineworld@sftp.com.

The Delta's most bizarre restaurant is **Al's Place**, better known as "Al the Wop's." It may be the strangest joint you've ever entered. The bar out front is a saloon with hunting trophies protruding from the walls and a fading mural of a cowboy challenging a bucking bronco. The high ceiling is plastered with dollar bills (it'll cost you a buck to find out how they got there). Dinner consists primarily of steak and steak. A stack of sliced bread accompanies your slab of meat. At lunch, every table is set with big jars of peanut butter and jelly. The idea is to swab the peanut butter on the bread, add a dollop of jelly, and enjoy it with your steak. Sorry you asked? ~ Main Street, Locke; 916-776-1800. MODERATE.

◄ HIDDEN

Martinez is popular with antique collectors. Its plentiful stores offer a wild variety of items, with prices a bit lower than the city stores. Most are closed on Sunday, however, and some on other days, so call ahead. At **Asilee's Victorian Antiques** you'll discover a collection of colorful, elegant lamps, and other antiques. Closed Sunday. ~ 608 Ferry Street; 925-229-0653.

SHOPPING

Historic downtown Benicia is antique store heaven. **Hagen's House of Clocks** features a vast array of timepieces and music boxes. Closed Sunday and Monday. ~ 513 1st Street; 707-745-2643. To discover hidden treasures, head to the **Benicia Antique Shop**, where you'll find silver, glassware, furniture, and jewelry. Closed Monday. ~ 305 1st Street, Benicia; 707-745-0978.

In the Delta, try the antique community of Locke, where you can combine shopping with a search for the town's historic roots. **River Road Gallery** is housed in a building that has experienced several incarnations as a grocery, pool hall, and old-style ice cream parlor. Today it contains oil and pastel paintings, ceramics, and silver jewelry, all created by local artists. Closed Monday through Thursday, and January through February. ~ 13944 Main Street, Locke; 916-776-1132, fax 916-331-4398; www.locketown.com.

By car or boat you can cruise to several spots around the Delta, including the **Ryde Hotel**. This rambling, multistoried affair features a plush bar and an intimate dining room; the bar is open Sundays only during winter, but every day in summer. Back in Prohibition days, the hotel was a notorious speakeasy. Today it is one of the hottest nightspots in the Delta. ~ Route 160, Ryde; 916-776-1318; e-mail rydehotel@hotmail.com.

NIGHTLIFE

BRANNAN ISLAND STATE RECREATION AREA 🚶 🚴 ⚓ ⛵ 🚤 🛥 ⛴ 🎣 Located along the Sacramento River, this park sits in the midst of the Delta Country. With sloughs and levees all around, it's a region of willows and cottonwoods. There's a beach for swimmers, picnic tables for daytrippers, and a maze of waterways for anglers. Black bass, sturgeon, catfish, and perch number

BEACHES & PARKS

among the Delta's many gamefish. There are picnic areas, restrooms, and showers. ~ Route 160 about four miles south of Rio Vista; 916-777-6671, fax 916-777-7703.

▲ There are 102 sites; fees vary with season and day of week.

LOS VAQUEROS 🏃 🚴 🐎 ⛵ 🚤 🎣 This 18,500-acre watershed between Brentwood and Livermore is an ideal destination for a daytrip and picnic. The hiking is excellent, with a particularly pleasant eight-mile stroll along the side of the reservoir itself. The water and countryside are spectacular, but don't get so distracted that you forget to watch out for snakes. Because the reservoir stores drinking water, swimming and gas-powered boats are not allowed. Fishing's good here; the reservoir has been stocked with more than 200,000 gamefish such as rainbow trout and largemouth bass. In addition to picnic facilities, the recreation area has restrooms, a marina that rents electric boats, and 55 miles of hiking trails, including over 12 miles for biking and horseback riding. ~ 100 Walnut Boulevard, Brentwood; 925-513-2160, fax 925-513-2084; www.ccwater.com/losvaqueros.

> Sam Goldwyn once claimed that the California Delta "looks more like the Mississippi than the real thing," and chose it as the movie location for *Huckleberry Finn*.

Outdoor Adventures

Deep-sea and Bay expeditions for salmon, rock cod, halibut, and bass draw countless anglers to the Bay Area.

FISHING

THE EAST BAY For charters, contact **Berkeley Marina Sport Center**. Depending on the season, they fish the bay or the ocean. Bait is provided and tackle is for sale. ~ 225 University Avenue, Berkeley; 510-849-2727.

MARIN COUNTY **Caruso's Sportfishing Center** fishes the ocean exclusively for salmon (and sometimes tuna) aboard 40- to 60-foot cabin cruisers. Bait is included in the price; tackle can be rented. ~ At the foot of Harbor Drive, Sausalito; 415-332-1015. **Loch Lomond Live Bait House** handles charter reservations. ~ Loch Lomond Marina, San Rafael; 415-456-0321.

DELTA Fishing the Delta is a favored sport. **Crockett Sport Fishing** goes pot-luck fishing in a 42-foot boat. In the summer, they fish the bay around Angel Island. Bait and tackle are included in the price. ~ At the foot of Port Street, Crockett; 510-787-1047.

Go out on one of **The Fish Hookers Sportfishing**'s six-pack fishing boats and try your luck at catching striper, sturgeon, or catfish. ~ 1759 Circle Drive, Isleton; 916-777-6498; www.fish hookers.com.

SAILING

Nothing is more visually stunning than the sight of the sailboats on a clear, breezy San Francisco morning. Don't miss the experience of capturing the wind and drinking in endless vistas.

EAST BAY At the Berkeley Marina, **Cal Adventures** offers lessons and rentals on 15-foot Coronados. ~ U.C. Aquatic Center, foot of University Avenue, Berkeley; 510-642-4000; www.oski.org. For lessons and rentals on larger boats (24 to 43 feet), try **Olympic Circle Sailing**, also at the Berkeley Marina. ~ 1 Spinnaker Way, Berkeley; 510-843-4200.

MARIN COUNTY In the North Bay, try **Cass' Rental Marina**. In addition to running a sailing school, they rent keel sloops. ~ 1702 Bridgeway, Sausalito; 415-332-6789; www.cassmarina.com. For charters on San Francisco Bay call **Ocean Voyages**, which has luxury vessels. ~ 1709 Bridgeway, Sausalito; 415-332-4681, 800-299-4444; www.oceanvoyages.com.

KAYAKING

Your trip will take on a new dimension as you paddle among seals and seagulls, along the cityfronts and through the harbors of the world's largest landlocked bay. The popularity of kayaking has soared in the past few years, and the Bay Area certainly hasn't missed the boat; there are several small companies that cater to kayakers and would-be kayakers of all physical and financial abilities. While the most convenient place to paddle is on the Bay itself, there are also wonderful locations to the north in Marin County.

EAST BAY **California Canoe & Kayak**, at Oakland's Jack London Square, offers classes, sea and whitewater kayaking trips, retail sales, and rentals. ~ 409 Water Street; 510-893-7833, 800-366-9804; www.calkayak.com.

MARIN COUNTY To paddle across Richardson Bay under the bright silvery moon, contact **Sea Trek Ocean Kayaking Center**. They also do trips to Angel Island. ~ Schoonmaker Point Marina, Sausalito; 415-488-1000; www.seatrekkayak.com.

WIND-SURFING

The surf may not be up on San Francisco Bay, but the wind almost always is! The choice spot to windsurf in the East Bay is the Berkeley Marina. In Marin, everyone goes to Larkspur Landing. Candlestick Point in South San Francisco is also a very popular spot.

EAST BAY For sailboard rentals and lessons go to **Cal Adventures**. ~ U.C. Aquatic Center, foot of University Avenue, Berkeley; 510-642-4000; www.oski.org.

GOLF

It may not be the Monterey Peninsula, but the Bay Area offers many golfing opportunities at challenging, picturesque courses. Most places rent golf clubs and carts.

PENINSULA Duffers and professionals alike tee off at **Crystal Springs Golf Course**. This 18-hole course runs along the foothills with views of Crystal Springs Lake. ~ 6650 Golf Course Drive, Burlingame; 650-342-0603.

SOUTH BAY   San Jose Municipal Golf Course is an 18-hole tree-lined course. ~ 1560 Oakland Road, San Jose; 408-441-4653.

EAST BAY   With steep rolling hills, **Lake Chabot Golf Course** is quite challenging. Designed in the 1920s, the 18th hole is par 6. ~ Golf Links Road, Oakland; 510-351-5812. Traversed by a creek and dotted with redwood and pine trees, the 18-hole **Tilden Park Golf Course** is a choice spot. There's a driving range and putting green. ~ Grizzly Peak Boulevard and Shasta Road, Berkeley; 510-848-7373; www.tildenparkgolf.com. Located in a valley surrounded by rolling hills, **Sunol Valley Golf Club** encompasses two full golf courses. ~ 6900 Mission Road, Sunol; 925-862-2404; www.sunolvalley.com.

MARIN COUNTY   Situated in a valley surrounded by the China Camp Recreation Area, **Peacock Gap Golf and Country Club** is a relatively flat 18-hole course. ~ 333 Biscayne Drive, San Rafael; 415-453-4940.

TENNIS

The Bay Area is the third most active region in the nation for tennis. Cities all around the Bay have public courts, many lighted for night play.

PENINSULA   For tennis under the sun, try out the two courts at **Peers Park**. ~ 1899 Park Boulevard, Palo Alto. If you're looking to swing a racket, be sure to check out the seven lighted courts at **Mitchell Park**. ~ 600 East Meadow Park. For more information in Palo Alto, call 650-463-4900.

SOUTH BAY   In **Wallenberg Park** there are 12 lighted courts for your enjoyment. ~ Corner of Curtner and Cottle avenues, San Jose. Four lighted courts are open to the public at **Paul Moore Park**. ~ Corner of Hillsdale and Cherry avenues, San Jose.

EAST BAY   Perched high in the Berkeley hills, the four courts at the **Rose Garden** are the most picturesque courts in town. ~ 1201 Euclid Avenue. Also located in north Berkeley, the two courts in scenic **Live Oak Park** have night lighting. ~ Walnut and Berryman streets. The city of Berkeley has courts in six other locations. Call 510-644-6530 for information.

There are many public courts throughout Oakland. **Chabot** has three tennis courts. ~ Patton Avenue and Broadway. You can play in the evening on one of ten lighted courts at **Laney**. ~ 900 Fallon Street. **Davie Tennis Stadium** features five lighted courts. ~ 198 Oak Road. For more information, call 510-238-3494.

MARIN COUNTY   Sausalito has tennis courts in three locations. With a stunning view of the San Francisco Bay and skyline, **South View Park** has one court. ~ North Street. Three lighted courts are open to the public at **Marinship Park**. ~ North end of the San Francisco Bay Model. **M.L.K. Park** has five tennis courts. ~ Coloma and Olima streets.

With its Mediterranean climate and gentle terrain, the Bay Area is a perfect place to travel by bicycle. Thousands of local folks commute to work on two-wheelers. Bike paths are appearing everywhere and some public transportation systems accommodate passengers with bikes.

PENINSULA   Cycling is a great way to explore the sights of the Peninsula. There's a beautiful 15-mile loop through **Portola Valley** with an interesting side trip to the quaint town of Woodside. For a journey through a eucalyptus grove, try the four-mile loop in **Coyote Point Park**. To ride through academia, check out the numerous paths at **Stanford University** in Palo Alto.

SOUTH BAY   If you take your bicycle on a sightseeing tour of the South Bay, **Kelley Park** in San Jose is a great place to begin. There are 150 acres of rolling hills with numerous sights along the way. Another jaunt travels between two stunning garden parks—**Villa Montalvo** and **Hakone Gardens**. More challenging is the steep 24-mile climb up **Mount Hamilton Road** to the Lick Observatory.

EAST BAY   There are diverse routes for two-wheeling sightseers in the East Bay. The **Berkeley Marina** offers a gently rolling paved loop with sweeping views of the Bay Bridge, San Francisco, and the Golden Gate Bridge. In Oakland, there's a bike path around **Lake Merritt**, the city's saltwater lake. **Tunnel Road** and **Skyline Boulevard** climb the East Bay hills to several regional parks. The 3.5-mile paved Bayview Trail in **Coyote Hills Regional Park** treats bikers to views of marshes, hills, and the Bay. Out at **Point Pinole Regional Shoreline**, a path takes cyclists through grassy meadows to the shores of San Pablo Bay.

MARIN COUNTY   In Marin, the **Sausalito Bikeway** carries along the shoreline past marshes and houseboats. Another bikeway in Tiburon offers spectacular views of Sausalito and San Francisco.

AUTHOR FAVORITE

I've always found the **Berkeley Marina** a good spot to satisfy differing outdoor preferences. There's a harbor with boating facilities and the consistent sea breezes support great kite flying at 90-acre Cesar Chavez Park. You'll also find inline skaters, joggers, and dog owners (there's a dog park here) all sharing the same pavement. My advice: bike the fairly flat promenade around the park. You'll have a great ride and will enjoy the famous views of San Francisco as you go. ~ Located at the west end of University Avenue, Berkeley.

DELTA For a truly enjoyable bike ride past mud flats, ponds, sloughs, rickety towns, country lanes, and levees, take your bike to the **Delta**. The roads are flat, lightly traveled, and offer cyclists a chance to experience Huck Finn's Mississippi right here in Northern California.

Bike Rentals On the peninsula, try **The Bike Connection** for all your rental needs. ~ 211 El Camino Real, Stanford; 650-853-3000. For mountain bikes and trail information, the people at Summit Bicycles are friendly and eager to help. ~ 1111 Burlingame Avenue, Burlingame; 650-343-8483. **Bicycle Outfitter** sells road, mountain, hybrid, and tandem bicycles. On Sunday mornings, they lead a 20-plus-mile tour through Portola Valley. They also run several other local tours. Closed Monday. ~ 963 Fremont Avenue, Los Altos; 650-948-8092; www.bicycleoutfitter.com. **Stan's Cyclery** also has mountain bikes. Closed Monday. ~ 19685 Stevens Creek Boulevard, Cupertino; 408-996-1234; www.stans-bikes.com. In the East Bay, **Action Sports** rents mountain, racing, and children's bikes. ~ 27365 Industrial Boulevard #F, Hayward; 510-786-1025; www.sportsbay.com. **Karim Cycle** rents mountain, touring, and tandem bikes, as well as inline skates. Closed Sunday. ~ 2800 Telegraph Avenue, Berkeley; 510-841-2181; www.teamkarim.com.

HIKING

Though much of the landscape has been built up to serve growing urban needs, some of the surrounding wilderness regions have been preserved. So the Bay Area still offers diverse terrains for hikers—grassy hillsides, open meadows, stark mountainsides, and meandering creek beds. Where the pavement ends and the pathways begin, you can often find solitude and serenity. All distances listed for hiking trails are one way unless otherwise noted.

PENINSULA Several trails wind through **San Bruno Mountain County Park**, offering spectacular views of the Bay Area. **Summit Loop Trail** (3.1 miles) takes you past mountain springs to views of the bay and the ocean. **Old Guadalupe Trail** (.8 mile) is an easy walk through a "fog forest" of fern-bedecked Monterey cypress and eucalyptus. **Ridge Trail to East Peak Vista** (2.5 miles) offers a hawk's eye perspective on the Bay.

At the **San Francisco State Fish and Game Refuge**, the **Sawyer Camp Historic Trail** (6 miles) provides access to this beautiful preserve in the Santa Cruz Mountains. The road is paved, but open only to hikers, equestrians, and bicycle riders. The trail climbs past San Andreas and Crystal Springs lakes, providing excellent opportunities for birdwatchers and wildflower-gazers.

A fascinating journey through earthquake country is the high point of a trek through **Los Trancos Open Space Reserve**. The **San Andreas Fault Trail** (.6 mile) is a self-guided path along a portion of California's infamous earthquake fault. A brochure points out sag ponds, benches, and scarps near the fault. The **Franciscan–Lost Creek Loop Trail** (4.3 miles) crosses a high meadow, cuts through stands of bay and oak, and crosses Los Trancos Creek. Its final destination is open countryside dotted with wildflowers.

EAST BAY   **Anthony Chabot Regional Park** teems with wildlife and offers several good hikes. **Hidden Canyon Trail** (1.1 miles), near Anthony Chabot Campground, leads through stands of oak to an amphitheater set in a eucalyptus grove. **East Shore and West Shore Trails** (5.5 miles), bicycle paths with gentle slopes, also make for an enjoyable hike along Lake Chabot. If waterfalls, grass valleys, weeping willows, and wooded hillsides sound inviting, try the **Cascade** and **Columbine Trails** (2 miles). For a trek that covers the length of the park, there's **MacDonald–Brandon Trail** (8.7 miles). It's part of the 31-mile-long Skyline National Recreation Trail that connects Chabot with other regional parks. After the first uphill mile, the hike is fairly easy as it passes ridges and ravines, offering wonderful views to the south.

Tilden Regional Park, the most popular park in the East Bay, is a playground for naturalists. Its trails lead through nature areas, around lakes, and along mountain ridges. Be sure to visit the nature center. **Jewel Lake Trail** (.9 mile) is an easy walk through woods and fields to a marsh pond. Frogs, ducks, and bog vegetation are part of the setting. **Laurel Canyon** and **Wildcat Peak Trails** (3 miles) begin at the Little Farm and present striking views of the park as they carry you through groves of eucalyptus and Monterey pine. Another gentle hike nearby lies along **Sylvan Trail** (.7 mile).

The **Nimitz Way Trail** (3 miles) is also part of the 31-mile-long Skyline National Recreation Trail connecting six Bay Area parks. This section, a paved road, traverses San Pablo ridge.

The granddaddy of East Bay mountains, **Mount Diablo's State Park** is appealing both for its challenges and rewards. **Summit Trail** (7.2 miles) is an uphill climb across stark, rocky terrain, but

GET ROLLING

If you want to get downright serious about skating, roll over to the **Bladium**. Billed as "the biggest and the best," this popular sports center features an inline hockey rink, an indoor soccer field, a volleyball court, and a basketball court, as well as an equipment shop, changing rooms, and a snack shop. With open rink times and pick-up games every day, it's a great place to enjoy one of the nation's fastest growing sports. Admission. ~ 800 West Tower Avenue, Building 40, Alameda; 510-814-4999, fax 510-814-4990; www.bladium.com, e-mail alamedainfo@bladium.com.

the views are outstanding; bring water. **Devil's Slide and Oyster Point Trail** (3.8 miles) traverses rolling grasslands and oak forests en route to another stunning vista. **North Peak Trail** (1.4 miles) is a varied hike up steep slopes and down through shady woods. In the end it arrives atop Mount Diablo's second peak and offers marvelous views of the Bay Area.

Hiking through the wild and rugged chaparral country of **Las Trampas Regional Wilderness** evokes dreams of the early West. **Chamis Trail to Las Trampas Ridge Trail** (6 miles roundtrip) begins in a valley and climbs 1000 feet to an impressive view point. **Creek Trail** (1.5 miles) is an easy, shady trail through hardwood forests and grasslands past Bollinger Creek. **Devil's Hole Trail** (6.6 miles) requires a strenuous 2000-foot climb, both out and back. The rewards include a small creek, fern gorge, and magnificent views. Bring food and water.

> Finding sustenance to fuel your hike shouldn't be difficult in Berkeley. The city is corporate headquarters for both Clif and Powerbars, companies instrumental in the surge of energy bar consumption.

Sunol Regional Wilderness offers several pathways through hills and along tumbling creeks. **Flag Hill Trail** (1.3 miles) involves a 1000-foot climb to a grand view of the park. **McCorkle Trail via Cerro Este** (2.9 miles) follows Alameda Creek, then climbs a hill en route to a backpacking camp. To get away from other hikers, try the **Maguire Peaks Loop Trail** (3.9 miles). It carries past streams, oaks, and sage-scented grasslands to a pair of wind-sculpted peaks.

See Chapter Five for descriptions of hiking in Marin.

Transportation

CAR

The Bay Area is a sprawling region threaded with major highways. Along the Peninsula, **Routes 101, 280,** and **82** travel north and south. All three lead to the South Bay; from here, **Routes 880** and **80** travel up along the East Bay.

From San Francisco, **Route 101** streams north to Marin, and **Route 80** cuts through the East Bay and connects with other roads leading into the Delta.

AIR

Three major airports service the Bay Area: *San Francisco International Airport* (see Chapter Two), San Jose International Airport, and Oakland International Airport. To avoid the crowds and parking problems at San Francisco's mammoth airport, consider landing in Oakland, located just across the Bay. If you're interested in touring the South Bay or Central Coast, San Jose is very convenient.

Mineta San Jose International Airport: Airlines flying into San Jose include Alaska Airlines, American Airlines, America West Airlines, Continental Airlines, Delta Air Lines, Southwest Airlines, and United Airlines.

Several bus companies provide ground transportation from the San Jose airport. Check with the **Airport Connection** (408-730-5555) for schedules and destinations. **Santa Clara County Transit** (408-321-2300) provides frequent service to downtown San Jose. Taxi cabs are also available: **United Cab** (408-971-1111) or **Yellow Cab** (408-293-1234).

Oakland International Airport: Oakland's airport is serviced by Alaska Airlines, American Airlines, America West Airlines, Delta Air Lines, jetBlue, Southwest Airlines, and United Airlines.

Excellent ground transportation to and from the Oakland airport makes it one of the most convenient terminals in the area. **The Bayporter** (415-467-1800) serves both the Oakland and San Francisco airports. **Alameda–Contra Costa Transit**, or AC Transit, stops regularly at the terminal and transports passengers to downtown Oakland. ~ 510-817-1717; www.actransit.org. For a quick trip to various East Bay points, climb aboard the **Oakland Air-BART**, which connects the airport with the **Bay Area Rapid Transit**, or BART, system. ~ 510-465-2278; www.bart.gov.

Several cab and shuttle companies service the airport as well: try **Friendly Cab** (510-536-3000) or **Yellow Cab** (510-444-1234).

BUS

Greyhound Bus Lines offers extensive bus service to the Bay Area from around the country. There are stations in Oakland at 2103 San Pablo Avenue and San Jose at 70 Almaden Avenue. ~ 800-231-2222; www.greyhound.com.

TRAIN

Amtrak has several trains coming into the Bay Area daily. Two cover California routes: the "Coast Starlight" runs from San Diego to Seattle with stops in San Jose, Oakland, Emeryville, and Martinez. The "San Joaquin" covers the San Joaquin Valley, stopping in Oakland, Emeryville, Richmond, and Martinez. From Chicago, the "San Francisco Zephyr" traverses the western United States to Oakland, Emeryville, and Richmond. ~ 800-872-7245; www.amtrak.com.

CAR RENTALS

Most towns in the Bay Area have car rental agencies; check the Yellow Pages to find the best bargains. To pick up a car at the San Jose airport, call **Avis Rent A Car** (800-331-1212), **Budget Rent A Car** (800-527-0700), **Dollar Rent A Car** (800-800-4000), **Hertz Rent A Car** (800-654-3131), or **National Car Rental** (800-227-7368).

At the Oakland airport, check with **Avis Rent A Car** (800-331-1212), **Budget Rent A Car** (800-527-0700), **Dollar Rent A Car** (800-800-4000), **Hertz Rent A Car** (800-654-3131), or **National Car Rental** (800-227-7368). Several other companies, listed in the Yellow Pages, offer free pickup and delivery to both airports.

PUBLIC TRANSIT

Most sections of the Bay Area are accessible by some form of public transportation. It may be a bus, subway, or ferry boat, but it will get you to your destination.

On the Peninsula, **San Mateo County Transit**, or **Sam Trans**, carries passengers from San Francisco as far south as Palo Alto. ~ 800-660-4287; www.samtrans.org.

The South Bay is traversed by **Santa Clara County Transit** buses and the **Light-Rail System**, with service extending from Palo Alto through San Jose. ~ 408-321-2300; www.vta.org.

A network of bus routes crisscrosses the East Bay. Call **Alameda–Contra Costa County Transit**, or AC Transit, for schedules. ~ 510-839-2882; www.actransit.org.

Golden Gate Transit buses can take you from points in San Francisco to locations throughout Marin County (Sausalito, San Rafael, and beyond). ~ 415-923-2000; www.goldengatetransit.org.

Daily commuter trains run the length of the Peninsula from San Francisco to San Jose. Call **Caltrain** for information. ~ 4th and Townsend streets; 800-660-4287; www.caltrain.org.

Bay Area Rapid Transit, or BART, runs from Fremont north to Richmond, stopping in Oakland and Berkeley; from Colma through San Francisco to Pittsburg/Bay Point; and from Colma through San Francisco and Oakland to Dublin/Pleasanton. ~ 510-465-2278; www.bart.gov.

Public transportation from San Francisco to Marin can become a sightseeing adventure when you book passage on a **Golden Gate Transit** ferry boat. Cruises to Sausalito and Larkspur from the Ferry Building in San Francisco are crowded with commuters and vacationers alike. ~ 415-923-2000; www.goldengateferry.org. The **Red and White Fleet** also operates ferries from San Francisco to Sausalito, Vallejo, and Tiburon. ~ 415-447-0597. The **Alameda/Oakland Ferry** provides service from the East Bay to the Ferry Building and Pier 39 in San Francisco. ~ 510-522-3300.

FOUR

Wine Country

Just one hour from the streets of San Francisco lies an agricultural area that can match for beauty farmlands anywhere in the country. It's a region of tree-tufted mountains and luxurious valleys. Tilled fields create quiltlike patterns across the landscape and country roads wind into its hills.

Despite the grandeur of the place, its visual appeal is only a secondary feature. The lure of the land is its temptation to all the senses, particularly taste and smell. The plants stippling those picturesque fields are grapes and the product is wine, fine vintages that rival even those of France.

Winemaking in California dates back to the 18th century when Spanish padres planted vineyards at the missions. The Franciscans grew black grapes for sacramental wines, crushing them by foot in hide troughs, then fermenting the harvest in leather sacks.

Spanish vineyards spread north to Sonoma, where in 1823 church fathers established their last mission. In Napa Valley, across the mountains east of Sonoma, George Yount, the area's original settler, cultivated grapes in 1843. During the next decade numerous Europeans, drawn initially by the Gold Rush, forsook prospecting for planting. A Prussian immigrant named Charles Krug became a pioneer in commercializing Napa wines. He also taught other early vintners like Jacob Beringer and Carl Wente, whose names even today adorn wine bottles.

In 1857, Agoston Haraszthy, a Hungarian count, founded the Buena Vista Winery in Sonoma. Commissioned by the California governor, he traveled through France, Italy, and Germany a few years later, collecting cuttings from 300 grape varieties. Soon thereafter, the University of California perfected fermentation techniques and established a national center for viticulture and enology at its Davis campus.

California's wine business boomed. Four million gallons were produced in 1869, 28 million in 1900, and by 1911 the total rose to 58 million gallons. Then came Prohibition. From 1920 until 1933, an entire industry withered on the vine. Many wineries shut down; others converted their fields to orchards.

It took nearly 30 years for the industry to recover. Not until the 1960s, as wine became an increasingly popular national drink, did California's vineyards burgeon once more. This long-awaited renaissance proved extraordinary. Within a five-year period, vineyard acreage doubled. Wineries mushroomed in the Napa and Sonoma valleys, along the Russian River, and elsewhere throughout the state. Family-run wineries blossomed, national companies like Coca-Cola and Nestlé moved into the vineyards, and formerly aloof French winemakers, impressed with the quality of the wines, formed partnerships with local growers. Winemaking became a multibillion dollar business, with millions of people touring California's vineyards each year.

The natural elements for this success story have always been present, though only recently did the social factors begin to coalesce. Geography and climate play vital roles in winemaking and combine north of San Francisco to create ideal growing conditions. Here several valleys—Napa, Sonoma, and the Russian River—are protected by mountains from the cold winds and rain along the Pacific coast. They enjoy hot (very hot!) summers and cool, moist winters, ensuring good harvests.

In Napa Valley, sun, low hills, and fog drifting up from San Francisco Bay produce one of the world's finest winegrowing regions. Today, the area has become so well-known and fashionable that it is not only drawing fog from San Francisco. Celebrities and millionaires are moving here faster than new wineries. Gourmet restaurants and country inns have multiplied, and tourists are causing weekend traffic jams in this once-rustic realm. Even the health spa at Calistoga has gained such importance that France's Perrier took over the mineral water bottling. It's a far cry from a century ago when a penniless writer named Robert Louis Stevenson explored the isolated farming community.

Sonoma Valley's history traces back further than that of Napa, but lately the "valley of the moon" has been hard-pressed to keep pace with its starstruck neighbor. Resting between the volcanic Sonoma Mountains and the Mayacamas Mountains to the east, it was once inhabited by Coastal Miwok, Pomo, Wappo, and Patwin Indians. They gathered berries and acorns, fished the waters of nearby San Pablo Bay, and stalked the mountains for bear and deer. The advent of the Spanish mission changed their lifestyle unalterably and ushered in an era of international intrigue. During the early 1840s, Mexico's General Mariano Guadalupe Vallejo controlled Sonoma. Then in 1846 a band of roughhewn Americans arrested Vallejo and declared California the Bear Flag Republic. Within weeks the United States took control, eventually converting Sonoma to a military base.

Novelist Jack London settled in the nearby town of Glen Ellen in 1904, living there until his death in 1916. Interested in ranching as well as writing, London chose a region that today is an important dairy farming and sheep ranching area. The Sonoma Valley is also noted for its apple orchards, not to mention many excellent wineries.

Like the Russian River region to the north, it's planted with an extraordinary variety of grapes. Moving in a southerly course from Mendocino County, the Russian River passes Alexander Valley, Dry Creek Valley, and other regions that have greatly contributed to California's wine renaissance. Then, as it turns west toward the sea, it has given birth to a different sort of rebirth, a gay renaissance. Since the 1970s, the area around Guerneville, long popular for its excellent canoeing, and fishing, has become Northern California's top gay resort. Country inns, restaurants, and nightclubs catering to gays from San Francisco and around the country have mushroomed along the riverbanks and in the region's deep redwood forests.

Any of these areas—providing opportunities to taste fine wines, tour vineyards, visit historic sites, and explore the Russian River—can be visited in the course of a day trip from San Francisco. But you might want to take longer—a week, or lifetime perhaps, to wander California's luscious Wine Country. Then you can decide for yourself whether it's the beauty of the landscape or the flavor of the wine that creates the magical lure of the place.

A tour of the Wine Country will give you an opportunity to sample choice vintages, explore vineyards, and experience the art of winemaking. You'll find that most wineries, large or small, welcome visitors and provide tours and tasting.

To visit the area, pack a picnic lunch, wander through the growing region, and plan to stop at only three or four wineries during the day. Small wineries, where

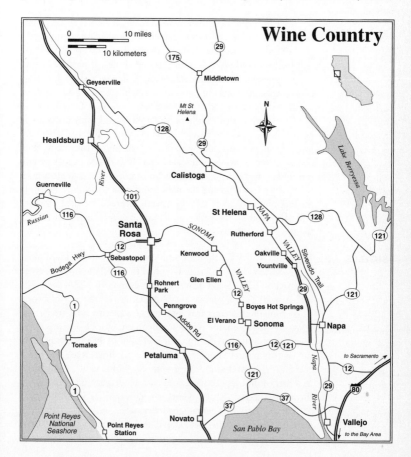

the operation is family run and tours are personalized, create the most memorable experiences. Usually the winemaker or a member of the family will show you around, providing a glimpse into their lives as well as their livelihoods. Since the winemakers will be leaving their normal duties to help you, small wineries usually require advance reservations. It's also a good idea to ask directions to these secluded vineyards.

Large wineries schedule tours and tasting all day and permit you to drop by unannounced. Though impersonal, they're convenient to visit and provide a wider variety of wines. Many are housed in beautiful buildings of historic interest.

Both family-run and multinational wineries are described here, though the vineyards listed are a small fraction of those you can visit. They also represent my favorites and are liable to the follies and foibles of my personal taste. So test for yourself; somewhere out there lies a hidden vineyard or unheralded vintage, waiting to be discovered.

▼▼▼▼▼▼▼▼▼▼
Napa Valley

California's premier winegrowing region is a long, narrow valley, laid out like a checkerboard and stretching 35 miles. Here grape arbors alternate with wild grasses and rich bottom land gives way to forested slopes. If natural beauty were a question for the palate, Napa Valley would be the rarest of vintages. It is a landscape of windmills and wooden barns, clapboard cottages and stone wineries.

The region is also a millionaire's preserve, a freshly fashionable place which draws the most affected people imaginable. There are pinch-faced connoisseurs who purse their lips as they taste, then comment on the wine in mangled French. It draws hordes of visitors and is fast becoming the state's most popular tourist attraction.

So try to visit during the week, and plan to explore not only the main highway, but also the Silverado Trail. An ideal itinerary will carry you up the valley on Route 29, then back down along the parallel roadway.

SIGHTS

The **Napa Valley Conference and Visitors Bureau** is a good place to get started. They will supply you with maps and brochures for the area. ~ 1310 Napa Town Center, Napa; 707-226-7459, fax 707-255-2066; www.napavalley.com, e-mail info@napavalley.org.

If someone in your traveling party wants to be a fireperson when she grows up, the whole family might like a brief stop at the **Napa Firefighters Museum,** just a couple of blocks away from the visitors bureau. Engines, ladder trucks, hose carts, and other equipment, as well as uniforms and old photos would look better in a real firehouse, but it's a nice enough display. Closed Sunday through Tuesday. ~ 1201 Main Street, Napa; 707-259-0609.

For anyone who's ever aligned themselves with Copia, the goddess of abundance, there's **Copia: The American Center for Wine, Food & the Arts,** an institution that uses multimedia exhibits to

A Day Trip to the Wine Country

- Leave San Francisco early. Cross the Golden Gate Bridge and head north to Petaluma on Route 101. From there, take the slower but more scenic Route 116 east over the Sonoma Mountains to the Sonoma Valley. Allow one hour for the trip.

- Visit the old mission and other historic buildings of **Sonoma State Historic Park** (page 254) around the town plaza. Allow one hour.

- Take the self-guided tour of **Buena Vista Historical Winery** (page 256) to see where California's wine industry got its start. Allow one hour.

- Back on the road, head north on Route 12 to **Jack London State Historic Park** (page 257) for a leisurely stroll around the author's estate. Allow one and a half hours.

- Stop off in Kenwood for lunch at **Cafe Citti** (page 260).

- Continue north on Route 12 to Santa Rosa. Soon after you enter the outskirts of town, turn north (right) onto Calistoga Road, which follows creeks among rolling hills and past the **Petrified Forest** (page 242) to Calistoga. Allow one hour for the trip.

- You are now deep in the heart of Wine Country, so you may wish to visit some of the wineries where they make the cabernets and chardonnays for which the area's steeply terraced vineyards are justly famous. Then again, you might want to spend the afternoon luxuriating at **Nance's Hot Springs** (page 242) or one of the other spas for which Calistoga is equally famous.

- Heading south along Route 29 on your way back to the Bay Area, countless more wineries will beckon to you, as will a number of fine restaurants. **Domaine Chandon** (page 248) in Yountville is both, and dinner here makes for a perfect end to your Wine Country excursion.

- At Yountville, Route 29 becomes a divided freeway and quickly zips you through Napa to Vallejo, where you can pick up Route 80 and return to San Francisco via the Bay Bridge in half an hour.

trace the connection between wine and food and the arts. The 12 acres of grounds include a 500-seat performance terrace, orchards, a vineyard, and an organic garden; products from the garden are used in food demonstrations (don't worry, you get to taste). I recommend one of the daily wine or food education classes, taught by knowledgeable vintners. Closed Tuesday. ~ 500 1st Street, Napa; 707-259-1600, 888-512-6742, fax 707-257-8601; www.copia. org, e-mail mail@copia.org.

An unusual option for touring the Wine Country is to climb aboard the **Napa Valley Wine Train**, which runs daily between the city of Napa and the vineyards slightly north of St. Helena. Travelers may choose the luncheon, brunch, or dinner trip, each of which takes three hours and smoothly chugs past some of the most scenic parts of the valley. The 1915–47 Pullman cars have been beautifully restored; the dining car is straight out of a romance novel. ~ 1275 McKinstry Street, Napa; 707-253-2111, 800-427-4124, fax 707-253-9264; www.winetrain.com.

If you choose to do tour the Wine Country on your own, you'll find one of the area's most interesting wineries right in Napa. Located on the site of the former Christian Brothers' Mont LaSalle winery, the **Hess Collection** is where fine wine meets fine art. The self-guided tour is unique: It is the only winery in the valley that includes two floors displaying some 130 museum-quality artworks by contemporary international artists. The Hess Collection also refers to the cabernets and chardonnays that are just being released and are available for sampling in the ground-floor tasting room. Tasting fee. ~ 4411 Redwood Road, Napa; 707-255-1144, fax 707-253-1682; www.hesscollection.com.

HIDDEN ▶   **Mayacamas Vineyards** provides a different setting entirely. Located deep in the mountains west of Napa Valley, it sits astride an extinct volcano. The blocks of vineyard appear hewn from surrounding rock walls. Indeed, the fields of chardonnay and cabernet sauvignon rest on terraces along the mountainside. Like the encircling hills, the winery is made of stone, built in 1889. Tours of this unique place are by appointment; it lies about ten miles off Route 29 along winding mountain roads. Closed weekends. ~ 1155 Lokoya Road, Napa; 707-224-4030, fax 707-224-3979; www.mayacamas.net, e-mail mayacama@napanet.net.

As you proceed north, the next group of major wineries lie clustered around **Yountville**. Residents of this rural town claim that their town is "where it all began." George Yount, the municipal namesake, was the first American to settle in Napa Valley. Arriving in 1836, he took control of an 11,000-acre land grant and built a Kentucky-style log house.

Domaine Chandon, owned by France's fabled champagne producer, Moët & Chandon, sits on a knoll west of town. Producing some of California's foremost sparkling wines, this win-

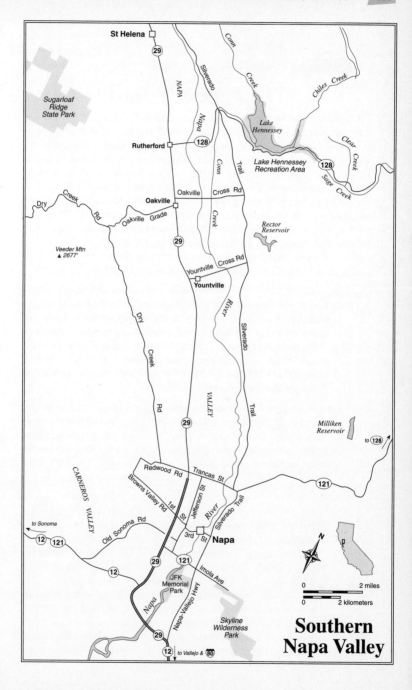

Southern Napa Valley

The Silverado Trail

The Silverado Trail, an old stagecoach road, parallels Route 29 on the east and links with it via a succession of cross-valley roads as it runs 29 miles from Napa to Calistoga. Fully paved, this route is a favorite among cyclists as well as leisurely drivers. In addition to glimpses of Napa Valley as it was in the 1960s, it's an excellent place to search out small wineries. All along this rural stretch are family-owned vineyards, set on the valley floor or tucked into nearby hills. To reach it, you can follow Trancas Street east from Route 29 through Napa and turn left onto the Silverado Trail. Or better yet, head north from Napa on Route 29 to Oak Knoll Avenue and turn right, which will take you past **Monticello Cellars** (call for tour and tasting; 4242 Big Ranch Road, Napa; 707-253-2802), a winery in a replica of Thomas Jefferson's mansion, before crossing the Napa River and intersecting the trail. Here's a sampling of the wineries you'll find along the route:

SHAFER VINEYARDS   About two miles north of the Oak Knoll intersection on the Silverado Trail, Shafer Vineyards lies at the base of a rocky outcropping surrounded by fields of chardonnay, merlot, and cabernet sauvignon grapes. Removed from the road, it's a placid spot with views of the fields and the valley. Tours of the winery and wine cave are by appointment only, as are tastings. Closed weekends. ~ 6154 Silverado Trail, Napa; 707-944-2877, fax 707-944-9454; www.shafervineyards.com, e-mail shafer@shafervineyards.com.

CAYMUS VINEYARDS   Nine miles north of Shafer Vineyards, after skirting the town of Yountville, the Silverado Trail brings you to this unpretentious winery run by Chuck Wagner. The winery was established by his parents, who were Napa winemakers in the early 1900s. Caymus focuses exclusively on its delicious cabernet sauvignon. ~ 8700 Conn

ery provides a close look into the production and bottling of the bubbly. It's housed in a modernistic building with barrel-vaulted ceilings and contains exhibits by local artists as well as a gourmet restaurant. The regularly scheduled tours are free. Tasting fee. ~ 1 California Drive, Yountville; 707-944-2280, fax 707-944-1123; www.chandon.com, e-mail info@chandon.com.

An airy, post-modern structure, the **Napa Valley Museum** houses displays on local history, culture, art, and the environment. You'll find an interactive wine exhibit, displays on the region's land and people, and rotating fine arts exhibitions; gardens and landscaped terraces enhance the series of indoor/outdoor

Creek Road, Rutherford; 707-967-3010, fax 707-963-5958. Open by appointment only; www.caymus. com.

STERLING VINEYARDS   In a few more miles you'll pass the turnoff to the village of St. Helena. Another seven miles will bring you to Sterling Vineyards near the outskirts of Calistoga. A tramway takes visitors up to this distinctive winery, built in the architectural style of the Greek island of Mykonos, perched 541 feet above the valley floor for wine tasting on a terrace with a magnificent view. ~ 1111 Dunaweal Lane, Calistoga; 800-726-6136; www.sterlingvineyards.com.

MOUNT ST. HELENA   If you continue north after arriving in Calistoga, the Silverado Trail trades the warm, level terrain of the valley for the cool, rugged landscape of the mountains. It climbs and winds through thick coniferous forests and past bald rockfaces. In touring Napa, you've undoubtedly noticed the stately mountain that stands sentinel at the north end of the valley. Mount St. Helena, named by 19th-century Russian explorers for their empress, rises 4343 feet, dominating the skyline.

ROBERT LOUIS STEVENSON STATE PARK   Perched on the side of Mount St. Helena is Robert Louis Stevenson State Park. The Scottish writer and his wife honeymooned in these parts, camping in the hills and enjoying the recuperative air. Here he wrote sections of *The Silverado Squatter* and studied settings later used in *Treasure Island*. Today the Memorial Trail leads through this undeveloped park one mile to an old mine and a monument commemorating the spot where Stevenson spent his honeymoon. Then a fire road continues four more miles to the top of Mount St. Helena. From this impressive aerie the entire Napa Valley lies before you, with views stretching from the Sierra Nevada to San Francisco. ~ Route 29, about eight miles north of Calistoga; 707-942-4575, fax 707-942-9560.

galleries. Closed Tuesday. Admission. ~ 55 Presidents Circle, Yountville; 707-944-0500, fax 707-945-0500; www.napavalley-museum.org.

Among the largest in the Napa Valley, **Robert Mondavi Winery** is a Spanish mission–style building offering a variety of seasonal informative tours by reservation. Popular picks include the basic production tour with tasting or a three-hour-long look at the entire process from vineyard to laboratory to winery (the latter is only offered a few days a week). The chardonnay and fumé blanc are excellent and you can also sample reserve wines by the glass. In addition to visiting the art gallery, you may want to attend summer jazz concerts held in the courtyard. Tasting fee. ~ 7801 St. Helena Highway, Oakville; 707-963-9611; www.robertmond avi.com, e-mail info@robertmondavi.com.

Continuing along Route 29 you'll drive through the tiny town of Rutherford, passing a patchwork of planted fields. In a valley virtually spilling over with wineries, how does a new one get noticed? In the case of **St. Supéry Winery**, it's by constructing a first-rate gallery with numerous exhibits on Napa Valley wine-making. Three-dimensional displays include a replica of an actual grapevine growing out of deep soil, smell-a-vision (a contraption that enables you to smell eight of the aromatic components of wine), and topographical maps that show why the valley is good for grapes. Daily guided tours available. An outdoor tasting area and a restored Victorian add spice to the winery tour. Tasting fee. ~ 8440 St. Helena Highway, Rutherford; 707-963-4507, 800-942-0809, fax 707-963-4526; www.stsupery.com, e-mail divine cab@stsupery.com.

One of the prettiest wineries in Rutherford is the **Niebaum–Coppola Estate Winery**, where movie great Francis Ford Coppola and his wife Eleanor have been making wine since 1975. In 1995 they purchased the adjacent Inglenook Château and vineyard, unifying the original 1879 estate of winemaker Gustave Niebaum. The ivy-draped château houses the Centennial Museum, where the history of winemaking at the estate is chronicled as is Coppola's career (five of his Oscars along with artifacts from several of his films are displayed). Specialties of the winery include rubicon, chardonnay, cabernet franc, merlot, and zinfandel. Tasting fee. ~ 1991 St. Helena Highway, Rutherford; 707-968-1100, fax 707-967-4178; www.niebaum-coppola.com, e-mail service@ niebaum-coppola.com.

A winery with an old French name, **Mumm Napa Valley** is a good place to see *methode champenoise* production via daily tours. Located on an oak-shaded hillside, the pitched-roof winery looks like a redwood barn. In the tasting room you can sample flutes of sparkling wine. Tasting fee. ~ 8445 Silverado Trail, Rutherford; 707-942-3434, 800-686-6272, fax 707-942-3470; www. mummcuveenapa.com, e-mail concierge@sparkling.com.

Capital of the Wine Country is the falsefront town of **St. Helena**. Surrounded by vineyards, this old farm town still retains much of its early charm. In the Victorian-style downtown area, the brick-and-stone IOOF **Building** looms several stories above the pavement, as it has for a century. ~ 1352 Main Street. The cynosure of St. Helena is the **Ritchie Block**, a stone structure with brick-and-wood facade. Featuring more frills and swirls than a wedding cake, it is a study in ornate architecture. ~ 1331 Main Street.

The town's **Robert Louis Stevenson Silverado Museum** houses a collection of artifacts from Robert Louis Stevenson's life and

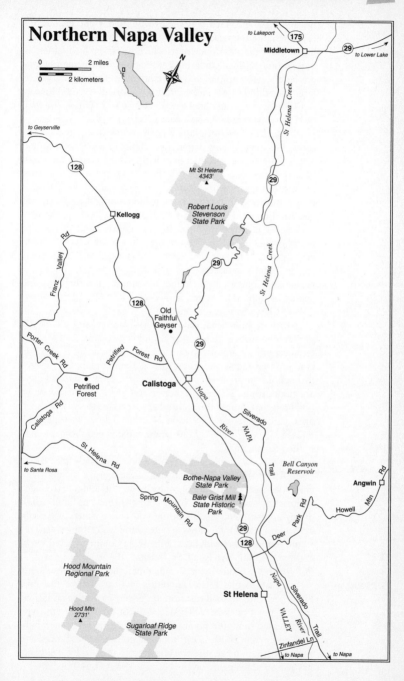

Northern Napa Valley

0   2 miles
0   2 kilometers

N

to Lakeport

175

Middletown

29

to Lower Lake

St Helena Creek

to Geyserville

128

Mt St Helena
4343'

Robert Louis
Stevenson
State Park

29

Kellogg

St Helena Creek

Franz Valley Rd

29

128

Old
Faithful
Geyser

29

Porter Creek Rd

Petrified Forest Rd

Petrified
Forest

Calistoga

Napa River

Calistoga Rd

St Helena Rd

Silverado

NAPA

to Santa Rosa

Bell Canyon
Reservoir

Angwin

Trail

Bothe-Napa Valley
State Park

Spring Mountain Rd

Bale Grist Mill
State Historic
Park

Deer Park Rd

Howell Mtn Rd

Howell

29
128

Hood Mountain
Regional Park

Hood Mtn
2731'

Sugarloaf Ridge
State Park

St Helena

Napa River

Silverado

VALLEY

Trail

Zinfandel Ln

to Napa

to Napa

his sojourn in the Napa Valley. Having visited Monterey and San Francisco, the Scottish author arrived in Calistoga in 1880, seeking a salubrious environment in which to escape his lifelong illnesses. Among the memorabilia at the museum are manuscripts, art, letters, photographs, and first editions, as well as personal effects left behind by the globe-girdling Victorian. Closed Monday. ~ 1490 Library Lane, St. Helena; 707-963-3757, fax 707-963-0917; www.silveradomuseum.com.

While the way to see Napa wineries is to visit the smaller concerns, big sometimes is better. Take **Beringer Vineyards**, for example. The vintage product here is the Rhine House, an 1880s Queen Anne–style mansion. With its mansard roof and stone inlay, it is a masterwork of spires, turrets, and gables. The interior, complete with tasting room, is illuminated through stained glass and paneled in hand-carved hardwoods. Among the winery's other features are 1000 feet of tunnels handcut into the neighboring hillside by 19th-century Chinese laborers. The adjacent historic bottling room has been converted into a gift shop/tasting room. You can take a tour, which covers several interesting parts of the operation, including the tunnels. Fee for tours and tasting. ~ 2000 Main Street, St. Helena; 707-963-7115, fax 707-259-4510; www.beringer.com.

North of St. Helena, **Bale Grist Mill State Historic Park** is a picturesque stop. Sitting beside a tumbling stream, an 1846 waterwheel mill creates a classic scene. It was built for a Mexican land grantee and served as an early gathering place for farmers throughout the area. The mill is now partially restored and there are guided tours. There's a visitors center plus a pair of raw wood buildings that housed the mill and granary. Due to staffing shortages, call for hours. Admission. ~ Route 29, St. Helena; 707-942-4575, fax 707-942-9560; www.napanet.net/~bothe, e-mail bothe@napanet.net.

Not far past the old mill stream, a side road leads from Route 29 to **Tudal Winery**. Touted as one of the world's smallest wineries, it consists of a cluster of contemporary buildings surrounded by luxurious grape arbors. Tours and tasting at this family affair are by appointment. A walk around the entire winery will probably take a grand total of ten minutes, after which the owner may regale you for hours with tales of the Wine Country. Closed weekends. ~ 1015 Big Tree Road, St. Helena; 707-963-3947, fax 707-968-9691; www.tudalwinery.com, e-mail tudalwinery@aol.com.

HIDDEN ►   It's easy to find **Litto Damonte's Hubcap Ranch**. Just take Howell Mountain Road east from the Silverado Trail in St. Helena to the hamlet of Pope Valley. Head north three miles until you see at least a thousand points of light. Those are Damonte's hubcaps, more than 2000 strong, adorning houses, barns, fences, and pastures. Just to make sure you know who's responsible, Damonte has plastered his name on the barn in—what else—hubcaps.

When Robert Louis Stevenson visited the **Schramsberg Vineyards**, he tasted 18 different wines. Today you'll have to settle for a tour (by appointment) of this historic facility. The road up to Schramsberg burrows through a dense forest before arriving at the original owner's home. The winery has added several buildings since Stevenson's day and now specializes in sparkling wine, but the old tunnels and cellars remain. Tasting fee. ~ Schramsberg Road, Calistoga; 707-942-4558, 800-877-3623, fax 707-942-5943; www.schramsberg.com, e-mail schram@schramsberg.com.

In the 19th century, roads were unpaved and no modern conveyances transported guests to hillside wineries. All that has changed at **Sterling Vineyards**. Set atop a knoll near the head of Napa Valley, this Greek monastery–style winery is reached via an aerial tramway (fee). The gondolas carry visitors to a multitiered building, painted a brilliant white, which commands sentinel views of the surrounding valley. Once atop this lofty retreat, a self-guided tour leads through various winemaking facilities to an elegant tasting room. It also takes in the spectacular stained-glass windows and 18th-century church bells that add an exotic element to this unusual winery. ~ 1111 Dunaweal Lane, Calistoga; 800-726-6136, fax 707-942-3467; www.sterlingvineyards.com, e-mail info@svclub.com.

Back on terra firma, you'll arrive in the town of **Calistoga**. Founded in 1859, this well-known health spa owes its origin and name to Sam Brannan. Brannan, of course, is the shrewd Mormon journalist and entrepreneur who first alerted San Francisco to the gold discovery. A decade later he saw liquid gold in Napa Valley's mineral springs and geysers. Determined to create a California version of New York's famous Saratoga spa, he named the region Calistoga. Indeed, its hot springs and underwater reservoirs were perfectly suited to a health resort.

Today Brannan's idea is carried on by numerous spas and health resorts. After imbibing at vineyards throughout the valley,

THAR SHE BLOWS

More evidence of Calistoga's infernal geology issues forth from **Old Faithful Geyser**, a subterranean stream heated to 350° that blows skyward approximately every 15 to 30 minutes, reaching 60 feet high. This geothermal gusher, a hokey but interesting tourist attraction, is caused when hot magma heats water deep within the earth and intense pressures force it violently to the surface. Admission. ~ 1299 Tubbs Lane, Calistoga; 707-942-6463, fax 707-942-6898; www.oldfaithfulgeyser.com, e-mail geyser@oldfaithfulgeyser.com.

visitors arrive in Calistoga to luxuriate in the region's mineral waters. I highly recommend that you sign up for "the works" at one of the local spas. You'll be submerged in a mud bath, led into a whirlpool bath, then a steam room, wrapped head to toe in a blanket, and finally given a massage. By the end of the treatment, your mind will reside somewhere in the ozone and your body will be completely loose. If you're game, contact **Nance's Hot Springs**, which opened in 1923 and is one of the oldest spas in Calistoga. ~ 1614 Lincoln Avenue, Calistoga; 707-942-6211, fax 707-965-0302. **Calistoga Village Inn and Spa** is another possibility. They offer the unique powdered mustard bath as well as the more standard steam baths, blanket wraps, and facials. ~ 1880 Lincoln Avenue, Calistoga; 707-942-0991, fax 707-942-5306; www.great spa.com, e-mail greatspa@napanet.net.

> Zinfandel wines are only made in California, not in Europe. The origin of this grape was a mystery until modern DNA testing traced it to an obscure vineyard in northern Italy.

About 3.5 million years ago, when nearby Mount St. Helena was an active volcano, the magma itself exploded. Evidently, eruptions from this firepit leveled an entire redwood grove, which transformed over the ages into a **Petrified Forest**. Located six miles from Calistoga, this eerie spot contains a succession of fallen giants. Redwoods measuring over 100 feet long and 8 feet in diameter lie along the forest floors, perfectly preserved in stone. Unfortunately, the place has the trappings of a tourist trap. Admission. ~ 4100 Petrified Forest Road, Calistoga; 707-942-6667, fax 707-942-0815; www.petrifiedforest.org, e-mail petrifiedforest@ap.net.

Other Calistoga points of interest are the **Sharpsteen Museum** and adjacent **Sam Brannan Cottage**. Dedicated to the town's original settlers, the museum displays tools from a blacksmith's shop and early California kitchen. Sam Brannan's cottage is furnished in period fashion with Victorian furniture and a glorious old piano. Highlight of the entire display, however, is an elaborate diorama portraying Brannan's health resort in miniature. Representing Calistoga circa 1865, it contains everything from railway station to racetrack, hotel to distillery. An annual spring lecture series is also held. ~ 1311 Washington Street, Calistoga; 707-942-5911, fax 707-942-6325; www.sharpsteen-museum.org, e-mail museum@napanet.net.

One of the Napa Valley's most intriguing wineries is 160-acre **Château Montelena**. Tours by appointment lead to a castle that overlooks a lake landscaped in classic Chinese manner. Oh, by the way, you'll also find a tasting room known for its chardonnays and cabernets. Closed the third Saturday in May. Tasting fee. ~ 1429 Tubbs Lane, Calistoga; 707-942-5105, fax 707-942-4221; www.montelena.com.

At **Clos Pegase** the tasting room is a post-modern affair designed by architect Michael Graves that features Honduran mahogany flourishes and antique glass decorations. There's a sculpture garden and fine works of art shown throughout the premises. A glass wall exposes the upright tank room where vintners make cabernet sauvignon, merlot, and chardonnay. Tasting fee. ~ 1060 Dunaweal Lane, Calistoga; 707-942-4981, fax 707-942-4993; www.clospegase.com, e-mail cp@clospegase.com.

LODGING

Reasonably priced bed and breakfasts are nearly nonexistent in the Wine Country, with one exception—**Churchill Manor**. Located on an acre of landscaped, flower-filled grounds just south of downtown Napa, the manor, built in 1889, is now a ten-room inn. The rooms are furnished with European antiques, and exquisite redwood columns front the main staircase. The innkeepers serve a full breakfast in the tile-floored sunroom, and on nice mornings you can take it out on the veranda, which surrounds three sides of the home. In the evenings, complimentary wine and cheese are offered. There are tandem bikes to ride and a sitting room with games and puzzles to enjoy. ~ 485 Brown Street, Napa; 707-253-7733, 800-799-7733, fax 707-253-8836; www.churchillmanor. com. DELUXE TO ULTRA-DELUXE.

Even in a town heavy on Victorians, **La Belle Epoque** is a standout. A colorful Queen Anne–style number built in 1893 by noted architect Luther M. Turton, it houses five spacious rooms and two suites named for wine varietals. Antiques such as an Eastlake queen bed, silk oriental carpets, and a Belgian armoire distinguish the accommodations, several of which have canopied beds and/ or stained-glass windows. The breakfasts are so elaborate that a menu for tomorrow's meal is displayed each afternoon. Tastings are held in the wine cellar each evening. The inn, which is near downtown shops and restaurants, also has two luxury suites in a Victorian across the street. ~ 1386 Calistoga Avenue, Napa; 707-257-2161, 800-238-8070; www.napabelle.com, e-mail lynnette@ napabelle.com. ULTRA-DELUXE.

The **Old World Inn** is at its most glorious in spring and summer, when wisteria and jasmine and then roses and other shrubs are at their peak of flowering. The unusual decor features a lot of stenciling, especially phrases sketched on the walls. Rooms are in bright colors such as mint green or blue and yellow; the 11th room is in a detached cottage on the far side of the outdoor hot tub. Two-night minimum April through November with a Saturday stay. ~ 1301 Jefferson Street, Napa; 707-257-0112, fax 707-257-0118; www.oldworldinn.com, e-mail innkeeper@oldworld inn.com. ULTRA-DELUXE.

For a dash of history with your evening glass of wine, consider the **Maison Fleurie**. A lodging place since 1873, this stone building is still a fashionable country inn. There are seven rooms in the old ivy-covered structure and six others in two adjacent buildings, each room crowded with antiques. Quilts and teddy bears adorn the beds, while chandeliers and brass lamps illuminate the historic setting; all have private baths and many have fireplaces and spa tubs. As a contemporary touch, there are a swimming pool, hot tub and bikes available for guest use. Breakfast is buffet style, and afternoon wine and tea are served daily. ~ 6529 Yount Street, Yountville; 707-944-2056, 800-788-0369, fax 707-944-9342; www.foursisters.com, e-mail msnflr@aol.com. DELUXE TO ULTRA-DELUXE.

The **Vintage Inn Napa Valley** is ideally located for exploring the Wine Country. Rose gardens and trickling fountains surround smart-looking, two-story villas with brick facades and wood shingles on the roof. Eighty rooms are like mini-suites, adorned with fireplaces and shuttered windows, marble wet bars and baths—all in all, some of the most desirable rooms in the valley. The complimentary breakfast buffet is quite extensive. An Olympic-sized pool and tennis courts are also found here, and Yountville's exclusive shops and eateries are but a short stroll. ~ 6541 Washington Street, Yountville; 707-944-1112, 800-351-1133, fax 707-944-1617; www.vintageinn.com. ULTRA-DELUXE.

Perched on a hillside studded with olive trees, **Auberge du Soleil** is a curious blend of French Mediterranean–style cottages named after French winegrowing regions and decorated in a breezy California/Southwest style. Bare Mexican tile floors, louvered doors, fireplaces, and private terraces are a refreshing change from the cluttered feel of older hotels in the valley. Thirteen low-rise cottages stagger down the hill, all but two of them containing four rooms. There's also a pool and spa to relax in. ~ 180 Rutherford Hill Road, Rutherford; 707-963-1211, 800-348-5406, fax 707-963-8764; www.aubergedusoleil.com, e-mail info@au bergedusoleil.com. ULTRA-DELUXE.

Crafted from white oak, the Spanish colonial **Rancho Caymus Inn** is a romantic retreat with stained-glass windows, a colonnade, a courtyard, and gardens. There is a total of 26 rooms; in the split-level rooms you'll find queen-size carved wooden beds, private balconies, and charming adobe beehive fireplaces. ~ 1140 Rutherford Road, Rutherford; 707-963-1777, 800-845-1777, fax 707-963-5387; www.ranchocaymus.com, e-mail ranchocaymus@ fcs.net. ULTRA-DELUXE.

In the center of town, the **Hotel St. Helena** is a traditional falsefront building dating to 1881. It features 18 guest rooms, all but four of which have private baths (the four share two European-style bathrooms down the hall). Many rooms include such decorative flourishes as caneback chairs, brass beds, antique armoires, marbletop vanities, and bent-willow headboards. Each is painted in warm pastel colors and plushly carpeted. Guests share an indoor reading room and sitting room with fireplace, plus other facilities like the hotel's wine bar. Continental breakfast is included. ~ 1309 Main Street, St. Helena; 707-963-4388, 888-478-4355, fax 707-963-5402; www.hotelst.helena.com. MODERATE TO ULTRA-DELUXE.

A gracious Victorian topped with a fanciful cupola affording 360° views of the Napa Valley, **Ink House Bed & Breakfast** offers a pleasant and serene place to stay. The 1884 house is encircled by a wide veranda with white wicker chairs and offers seven antique-filled guest rooms, five with private bath. In addition to a full gourmet breakfast, wine and appetizers are served in the afternoon. There's an antique pool table in the basement, and mountain bikes are available for guests. ~ 1575 St. Helena Highway, St. Helena; 707-963-3890, fax 707-968-0739; www.ink house.com, e-mail inkhousebb@aol.com. DELUXE TO ULTRA-DELUXE.

Set in the Mayacamas Mountains, just 12 minutes from Napa's wineries and restaurants, the contemporary-style **Hilltop House** is an excellent place to spot deer, raccoons, rabbits, hawks, and hummingbirds while enjoying the amenities of a 135-acre retreat. The four rooms are furnished with antiques, brass beds, and down comforters, and offer panoramic mountain views. There's a large deck, garden, a hot tub, and a network of hiking trails. Full breakfast is included. ~ 9550 St. Helena Road, St. Helena; 707-944-0880, fax 707-963-8743 (call first); www.cabbi.com. DELUXE TO ULTRA-DELUXE.

Spread across 45 acres and claiming to be the oldest hot-springs resort in California, **White Sulphur Springs Inn & Spa** dates to 1852. A deeply shaded creek and a walking trail run through

AUTHOR FAVORITE

When I need to balance my chakras (or just clear my head), I head for **Harbin Hot Springs**, the perfect place to hike in the hills, eat vegetarian, and bask naked (optional, of course) in a steaming pool full of New Agers. Although it may not be for everyone, it's a popular place, as witnessed by the crowds on weekends. Seven natural springs feed the warm, hot, and cold mineral-water pools of this New Age retreat center. You may stay in a dormitory, a retreat room, an ultra-deluxe cabin, or camp out, and enjoy quiet conversation with the other guests. There's a restaurant serving breakfast, lunch, and dinner (poolside café closed in winter), or you can bring your own vegetarian food to cook in a communal kitchen. Also on the vast property are a health food store, bookstore, and a small theater with nightly showings. ~ Harbin Springs Road, Middletown; 707-987-2477, fax 707-987-0616; www.harbin.org. BUDGET TO ULTRA-DELUXE.

the property, which also contains a redwood grove and a natural sulphur spring and pool. The cottages (five small, four large) and carriage house possess a rustic charm. The former have private baths, while the latter share a bathroom and hospitality room. There are also "inn rooms" with private baths available at moderate cost. In the health spa you can treat yourself to a massage, an herbal facial, a body wrap, or stone therapy. Or you can hop into the swimming pool, jacuzzi, or sulphur soaking pool. ~ 3100 White Sulphur Springs Road, St. Helena; 707-963-8588, 800-593-8873, fax 707-963-2890; www.whitesulphur springs.com, e-mail info@whitesulphersprings.com. MODERATE TO ULTRA-DELUXE.

Located at the end of a tree-shaded country road, **Meadowood Napa Valley** comprises 85 accommodations, a nine-hole golf course, two croquet lawns, two pools, tennis courts, and a fitness center and spa. Guests may choose to stay in cozy cottages or in the Croquet Lodge; either way, they'll have comfortable furnishings and serene views of the grounds. ~ 900 Meadowood Lane, St. Helena; 707-963-3646, 800-458-8080, fax 707-963-3532; www. meadowood.com, e-mail reservations@meadowood.com. ULTRA-DELUXE.

The **Calistoga Inn & Brewery** has reasonably priced rooms that include a continental breakfast. This 18-room hostelry sits atop a restaurant and pub that serve their own Napa Valley Brewing Company beer. The European-style accommodations are small but tidy, carpeted wall-to-wall, and plainly decorated. The furniture is simple and baths are shared, but each room does have its own sink. ~ 1250 Lincoln Avenue, Calistoga; 707-942-4101, fax 707-942-4914; www.napabeer.com, e-mail calistoga@napabeer.com. MODERATE.

CRUISIN' THROUGH THE COUNTRY

If you're in San Francisco and are planning to tour the Wine Country, the most unique—and likely the most luxurious—way to do so is by boat. Catch the **California Wine Country Cruises** at San Francisco's China Basin for three- or four-night excursions up the Sacramento River to Sonoma, Napa Valley, and Old Town Sacramento. In addition to soaking up views of the Bay and riverfront towns from the decks of these 100-passenger ships, you'll get to enjoy gourmet meals served in the dining room; and an on-board wine expert will impart knowledge about winemaking. So rest up in your comfortable stateroom before heading out to visit those wineries and historic sites. ~ 2401 4th Avenue, Seattle, WA 98121; 800-426-7702, fax 206-441-4757; www.cruisewest.com, e-mail info@cruisewest.com.

Several Calistoga spas also provide overnight accommodations. **Indian Springs Hotel Resort**, located on the same grounds as the town's original resort, offers bungalow-style cottages (actually duplexes) with kitchenettes. Guests are welcome to use the spa's olympic-sized swimming pool, mineral pool (heated between 90 and 102°), tennis courts, shuffleboard, croquet, hammocks, and bicycles. Indian Springs also features volcano ash mud baths, steam baths, massages, and facials, making it an excellent resting place for the health-minded. ~ 1712 Lincoln Avenue, Calistoga; 707-942-4913, fax 707-942-4919; www.indian springscalistoga.com. ULTRA-DELUXE.

Built in 1914, the renovated **Mount View Hotel** has the aura and feel of a classic small-town hotel. It's a 32-room affair with dining room and lounge downstairs and Victorian flourishes throughout. The lobby is spacious and elegant, featuring a fireplace and contemporary artwork. Guest rooms are nicely decorated with a mix of Victorian and modern touches. There are also three cottages, each with a private hot tub. Guests are free to use the hotel's pool and spa. Continental breakfast in your room in the morning. ~ 1457 Lincoln Avenue, Calistoga; 707-942-6877, 800-816-6877, fax 707-942-6904; www.mountview hotel.com, e-mail info@mountviewhotel.com. ULTRA-DELUXE.

Even in the over-touristed Napa Valley, there's a way to leave the crowds behind—head for the hills. Travel several miles upslope from Calistoga and you'll find **Mountain Home Ranch**, run by the same family since 1913. Once there, you may never make it back to the wineries. This is a fully equipped resort with a dining room, swimming pools, picnic areas, tennis court, and fishing lake. It rests on 300 acres threaded with hiking trails. Accommodations range from rustic cabins, to all-weather cabins to rooms in the main lodge. Rates include a full breakfast. ~ 3400 Mountain Home Ranch Road, Calistoga; 707-942-6616, fax 707-942-9091; www.mountainhomeranch.com, e-mail info@mountain homeranch.com. MODERATE TO DELUXE.

Meadowlark Country House is a beautiful 19th-century home with 20 acres of wooded grounds. Out beyond the mineral pool, hot tub, and sauna (enclosed, clothing optional) you can watch horses being trained for jumping events. Each of the seven rooms features contemporary or English country antique furniture, comforters, and a view of forest or meadow. A generous breakfast is served each morning and you will find the serene veranda a great place to catch up on your reading. ~ 601 Petrified Forest Road, Calistoga; 707-942-5651, 800-942-5651, fax 707-942-5023; www.meadowlarkinn.com. ULTRA-DELUXE.

If a room proves hard to reserve, or you need assistance with other bookings, several agencies offer reservation services. These can prove very convenient during peak tourist periods, or if you want to reduce long-distance calls. If interested, contact **Accommodations Referral**. Closed Saturday and Sunday. ~ P.O. Box 762, Angwin, CA 94508; 707-965-3400, 800-240-8466, fax 707-965-9595; www.apollotravel.net.

DINING

HIDDEN ►

If you wonder where the locals are, you can find a lot of them at the **Foothill Café**, a modest establishment off the tourist path on the unfashionable side of town. Hearty soups and salads, elegant entrées like lamb shank, duck breast and ahi tuna, and knockout desserts make this a delightful alternative to the fancier, pricier up-valley restaurants. Dinner only. Closed Monday and Tuesday. ~ 2766 Old Sonoma Road, Napa; 707-252-6178; e-mail foothill cafe@yahoo.com. MODERATE.

HIDDEN ►

Napa's culinary scene got a shot in the arm in 2000 with the opening of **Sake Tini Asian Diner and Lounge**, located in a shopping center on the north side of town. One long yellow wall and simple furnishings, including several counter seats, play second string to the food, a blend of things Chinese, Japanese, Thai and Hawaiian. Tiger shrimp satay, sushi, seared tuna, hibachi-style salmon with ponzu sauce and spicy baby-back pork ribs show off the talents of the chef. ~ 3900 Bel Air Plaza, Napa; 707-255-7423. BUDGET TO MODERATE.

The Restaurant at Domaine Chandon does more than bottle sparkling wine. This European concern also features a widely acclaimed restaurant at its winery. A multilevel structure with curved ceiling and colorful banners, it serves fine French cuisine with a California twist. Lunch includes such delicacies as mesquite-grilled asparagus salad, grilled quail, and tuna peppersteak with a mustard sauce. At dinner, the chef prepares special appetizers and entrées. These might include cream of tomato soup in puff pastry, home-smoked salmon carpaccio with onions and chives, and venison tournedos wrapped in pancetta. Little wonder Domaine Chandon has won national awards. No dinner Tuesday and Wednesday. Closed in January. Dress code. ~ 1 California Drive, Yountville; 707-944-2892, fax 707-944-1123; www.chandon.com. DELUXE.

Bouchon is a glamorous and glorified bistro, with lots of sparkle in the decor and on the menu. Entrées lean to *coq au vin*, *entrecote avec frites*, marinated leg of lamb, sole meuniere, onion soup, roast chicken, sautéed seasonal vegetables, fruit tarts and soufflés. Yet its most unusual feature may be its late-night dining—as late as 12:30 a.m. as a courtesy to night owls such as workers from area restaurants. ~ 6534 Washington Street, Yountville; 707-944-8037, fax 707-944-2769; www.bouchon bistro.com. MODERATE TO DELUXE.

Set in an old building, **The French Laundry** features contemporary American cuisine with a classic French influence. The food is excellent, the wine list extensive, and the prix-fixe menu changes nightly. It's very popular; reservations are a must. No lunch Monday through Thursday. Closed for remodeling until April 2004. ~ 6640 Washington Street, Yountville; 707-944-2380. ULTRA-DELUXE.

Mustards Grill is an ultramodern brass-rail restaurant complete with track lighting and contemporary wallhangings. There's an attractive wooden bar and paneled dining room, but the important features are the woodburning grill and oven. Here the chefs prepare rabbit, grilled pork chops, smoked duck, and hangar steak. This eatery specializes in fresh grilled fish like sea bass, ahi tuna, and salmon. ~ 7399 St. Helena Highway, Yountville; 707-944-2424, fax 707-944-0828; www.mustardsgrill.com. MODERATE TO DELUXE.

First and last word in Napa Valley elegance is **Auberge du Soleil**, a hillside dining room overlooking the vineyards. Modern in design, this gourmet hideaway is a curving stucco structure with a wood-shingle roof. The circular lounge is capped by a skylight-cum-cupola and the dining area is an exposed-beam affair with an open fireplace. Even architecture such as this pales in comparison with the menu, which changes seasonally. Lunch might begin with the Seven Sparkling Sins appetizer (which includes foie gras, caviar, and truffled quail eggs), then move on to a pan-seared foie gras and roasted duck sandwich. Dinner entrées include oak barrel–roasted sterling salmon, rack of lamb, and thyme-roasted pheasant. Vegetarian options include grilled asparagus and wild mushroom lasagna. Extensive wine list. ~ 180 Rutherford Hill Road, Rutherford; 707-963-1211, 800-348-5406, fax 707-963-8764; www.au bergedusoleil.com. ULTRA-DELUXE.

Tra Vigne can claim the most dramatic interior in the Wine Country. Soaring ceilings, unusual lighting, and festive displays of peppers and garlic make the setting as exciting as the menu. The

---

THE JOY OF WATCHING SOMEONE ELSE COOK

The Wine Spectator Greystone Restaurant at the Culinary Institute of America—just call it Greystone—is a cavernous restaurant in an 1889 National Historic Landmark in north St. Helena. The complex is a top-notch cooking school, but not to worry—the chefs are for real. The menu is devoted to California cuisine, focusing on fish, chicken, and lots of fresh vegetables. It's great fun to match dishes with different wines. Flanked by century-old stone walls, the restaurant is large enough to have cooking, baking, and grilling stations in full view, which provide a terrific distraction for fidgety kids. ~ 2555 St. Helena Highway, St. Helena; 707-967-1010, fax 707-967-2375; www.ciachef.edu, e-mail wsgr@culinary.edu. BUDGET TO DELUXE.

theme here is regional Italian: chewy breads, bold pizzas, hearty salads, rabbit, chicken, and grilled seafood dishes, and a first-rate wine list. ~ 1050 Charter Oak Avenue, St. Helena; 707-963-4444, fax 707-963-1233; www.travigne restaurant.com, e-mail travigne@napanet.net. MODERATE TO DELUXE.

During the summer months, several Napa Valley wineries sponsor concerts and other special events.

Within the Tra Vigne complex, **Cantinetta** is an upscale Italian deli with a wood-paneled bar serving espresso, campari, and wines by the glass. In addition to panini (Italian for sandwich), focaccia, and the like, you'll find a changing array of picnic and heat-at-home items. Lunch only. ~ 1050 Charter Oak Avenue, St. Helena; 707-963-8888, fax 707-963-1233. BUDGET.

HIDDEN ►

Pizzeria Vitte is a terrific place to bring the family. It's kid-friendly as well as budget-friendly, with thin-crust pizzas, pasta, salads, and other easy-to-eat fare in an upbeat setting. Inexpensive wines are sold by the glass. ~ 1016 Main Street, St. Helena; 707-967-9999, fax 707-967-0495. BUDGET TO MODERATE.

For southern French and northern Italian–style cooking with a Pacific Rim influence, head to **Terra Restaurant**. You might be treated to appetizers such as fried rock shrimp, crab cabbage egg rolls, and *tataki* of tuna on the seasonally changing menu. Entrées feature exotic preparations of seafood, beef, and squab. By way of ambience there are stone walls, terra-cotta features, and a wooden trim that lends an oriental overtone to this comfortable, Tuscan farmhouse–style dining room. Dinner only. Closed Tuesday. ~ 1345 Railroad Avenue, St. Helena; 707-963-8931; www.terra restaurant.com. DELUXE TO ULTRA-DELUXE.

The setting is informal and the menu Italian. Day or night at **Boskos,** you'll find fresh pasta dishes like bay scallops, mushrooms, and pesto cream over fettuccine, linguine with bay shrimp and asiago cream sauce, and spaghetti with meatballs. Or you can have a meatball, sausage, or Italian ham sandwich on their homemade focaccia. The wine list is extensive and the meals they offer are good and filling. ~ 1364 Lincoln Avenue, Calistoga; 707-942-9088, fax 707-942-9661; www.boskos.com. MODERATE.

Wappo Bar Bistro dishes up dazzling food that spans the globe with Asian noodles with shiitake mushrooms, Thai shrimp curry, Ecuadorean braised pork, osso bucco, chiles rellenos with walnut pomegranate sauce, and Turkish mezze (that hard-to-find treasure that in this case includes herb-and-cheese-stuffed eggplant sandwich, white bean salad, carrots, golden beets, shaved fennel, cracked green olives, hummus, yogurt sauce and, believe it or not, more). Closed Tuesday. ~ 1226 South Washington Street, Calistoga; 707-942-4712, fax 707-942-4741; www.wappobar. com, e-mail wappo@napanet.net. MODERATE TO DELUXE.

Triple S Ranch has been pleasing local palates for more than   ◄ HIDDEN
40 years. Head north of Calistoga into the Sonoma Mountains
to find this unique eatery in a century-old barn. It's one of those
timeless places that can't be categorized. Animal trophies, cookie
jars, tin trays, bottles, and old tools decorate the walls. Red-and-
white checked tablecloths adorn tables laden with huge portions
of fried chicken, barbecue ribs, steak, lobster, and other hearty fare.
The onion rings are legendary. Meals include a relish plate, soup
or salad, drink, and dessert. After dinner, you can play a game of
bocce ball or horseshoes. Closed January through March, and
Monday after Labor Days. ~ 4600 Mt. Home Ranch Road, four
miles north of Calistoga; 707-942-6730, fax 707-942-4250.
DELUXE.

Almost by definition, shopping malls are unattractive. **Vintage**   **SHOPPING**
1870 is a rare exception to a modern rule. Housed in the historic
Groezinger Winery, a massive brick building smothered in ivy, it
contains several dozen fashionable shops. Wooden corridors, designed with an eye to antiquity, lead along two shopping levels.
There are clothing stores galore, and several restaurants, as well
as specialty shops offering arts-and-crafts products. ~ 6525 Washington Street, Yountville; 707-944-2451, fax 707-944-2453; www.
vintage1870.com.

Across the street, the **Groezinger Wine Company** features
hard-to-find premium wines from California, Oregon, and Washington. Closed Sunday. ~ 6484 Washington Street, Suite E,
Yountville; 707-944-2331, 800-356-3970.

Oakville Grocery is a prime place to stock up for a picnic.
This falsefront country store sells wines and cheeses, fresh fruits,
specialty sandwiches, and baked goods, as well as a host of gourmet and artisanal items. ~ 7856 St. Helena Highway, Oakville;
707-944-8802, 800-973-6324; www.oakvillegrocery.com, e-mail
ogccorp@aol.com.

For people living in northern Napa Valley, going on a shopping spree means heading for either St. Helena or Calistoga. Both
towns combine local businesses with general merchandise stores.
Main Street, St. Helena, is a falsefront boulevard lined with a
hardware store, stationery shop, newspaper office, and grocery.
Of interest to visitors are the boutiques, bookstore, jewelers, and
wine shop.

The **Art on Main** features original works by Northern California artists as well as prints, posters, and ceramics. ~ 1359 Main
Street, St. Helena; 707-963-3350.

The **Napa Valley Olive Oil Manufacturing Co.** is more than a
gourmet shopping spot: it's a sightseeing adventure as well. Housed
in a former oil manufacturing plant, it contains the original press

and crusher. Railroad tracks run along the cement floor, and posters of old Italia cover the walls. Today this tiny factory sells its own olive oil, along with delicious cheeses, salami, pasta, and condiments. ~ 835 Charter Oak Avenue, St. Helena; phone/fax 707-963-4173.

Up the road at **St. Helena Premium Outlets** you will find a shopping mall with clothing stores and an assortment of other shops. ~ 3111 North St. Helena Highway, St. Helena.

Up in Calistoga, shops of general interest are mixed with those catering to local concerns. Along Lincoln Avenue, near the barber shop and town cobbler, are antique stores, clothing shops, and a bookstore. The historic **Calistoga Depot** has been converted to a mall. Within this former railway station are assorted stores, including the **Calistoga Wine Stop** (707-942-5556, 800-648-4521), housed in an antique railroad car. ~ 1458 Lincoln Avenue, Calistoga.

Hurd Beeswax Candles has, since 1954, elevated candle-making to the level of art. The waxworks resemble statues rather than tapers; fashioned by hand, they are formed into myriad intricate shapes (some are also handpainted). There's also a demonstration beehive on the premises. ~ 1255 Lincoln Avenue, Calistoga; 707-942-7410, 800-977-7211, fax 707-942-7415.

NIGHTLIFE   The Napa Valley has yet to learn the fine art of evening entertainment. Perhaps by nightfall visitors are already tipsy from tasting wine all day. In any case, there's not a lot to do; what scene there is centers around the wineries and the hotel and restaurant bars.

The **Ring's Lounge**, an upscale lounge at the Embassy Suites Napa Valley, is a pleasant spot for quiet conversation. ~ 1075 California Boulevard, Napa; 707-253-9540; www.embassynapa.com.

Downtown Joe's features rock, pop and blues bands nightly except Monday through Wednesday; open-mic on Wednesday. Cover on some Fridays and Saturdays. ~ 902 Main Street, Napa; 707-258-2337.

Silverado Brewing Co. and Restaurant has live entertainment on Friday and Saturday nights, usually cover bands playing blues and/or classic rock. Occasional cover. ~ 3020 North Route 29, St. Helena; 707-967-9876.

PARKS   **BOTHE–NAPA VALLEY STATE PARK** 🚶 🐎 🌲 Rising from the valley floor to about 2000 feet elevation, this outstanding park is fully developed along one side, wild and rugged on the other. For those seeking to escape the Wine Country crowds, there are ten miles of hiking trails leading along steep hillsides through redwood groves. More than 100 bird species inhabit the area, including hawks, quail, and six types of woodpecker. There are also coyotes, bobcats, deer, and fox here. For guided horseback riding, call 707-933-1600. The park's developed area features spacious picnic groves, campgrounds, a swimming pool open in the summer, restrooms, and showers (fee). Day-use fee, $4 per vehicle. ~ Route 29 about five miles north of St. Helena; 707-942-4575, fax 707-942-9560; www.napanet.net/~bothe, e-mail bothe@napa net.net.

▲ There are 40 tent/RV sites and 9 walk-in sites; $12 per night per site. Reservations recommended: 800-444-7275.

Sonoma Valley

Touring the wineries of Sonoma provides a perfect excuse not only for tasting California's fine varietals, but also for exploring the state's beautiful interior. Cutting a long, luxurious swath between the ocean and the distant Sierra, this piedmont country divides its terrain among vineyards, ranches, and dense forest.

SIGHTS

On the way to the Sonoma Valley via Route 101, you may want to make a slight detour to **Petaluma**. Once the state's largest egg producer, Petaluma has such a quintessential small-town flavor that it was chosen as the location for filming *American Graffiti* and several other movies about middle America. And the city's downtown district is listed on the National Register of Historic Places.

For information on Petaluma and other outlying areas, contact the **Sonoma County Tourism Program**. Closed weekends. ~ 520 Mendocino Avenue, Suite 210, Santa Rosa; 707-565-5383, 800-576-6662, fax 707-565-5385; www.sonomacounty.com, e-mail info@sonomacounty.com.

The logical place to begin a tour of the valley is in **Sonoma**, a Spanish-style town of 8200 people. And the spot to begin this tour-within-a-tour is the **Plaza**, bounded by 1st Street East, 1st Street West, Spain, and Napa streets. The center of Sonoma for more than 150 years, this shady park is an excellent picnic place. The largest plaza in the state, it contains a playground, an open-air theater, a duck pond, and a rose garden. At the **Sonoma**

sights

AUTHOR FAVORITE

If you're traveling with children, here's a trick that might make your trip a little easier: Kids who tire of all the dusty history can be bribed with a visit to **Train Town**. Miniature steam engines chug around a ten-acre park, passing over trestles, through three tunnels, and arriving at a scale-model Western town. Also visit the petting zoo, antique carousel, and cabooses. Closed Monday through Thursday during winter. Admission. ~ 20264 Broadway, Sonoma; 707-938-3912.

Valley Visitors Bureau there are maps and brochures of the area. ~ 453 1st Street East, Sonoma; 707-996-1090.

Spanish adobes, stone buildings, and falsefront stores surround the historic square. Mission San Francisco Solano, or **Sonoma Mission**, stands at the southeast corner. Founded in 1823, this was the last and most northerly of the 21 California missions. With its stark white facade, the low-slung adobe houses a small museum. There are dozens of paintings portraying other California missions; the chapel has also been painted brilliant colors and adorned with carved wood statues. ~ 1st Street East and East Spain Street, Sonoma.

The **Sonoma Barracks**, across the street, were built with Indian labor during the 1830s to house the troops of Mexico's General Mariano Guadalupe Vallejo. A two-story adobe with sweeping balconies, it also houses a museum devoted to early California history. ~ 1st Street East and East Spain Street, Sonoma.

Next door, the **Toscano Hotel** is furnished in 19th-century fashion with woodburning stoves, brocade armchairs, and two gambling tables with poker games in progress. Dating to 1852, this wood-frame structure was built as a general store but later was used to house Italian workers. ~ 20 East Spain Street, Sonoma.

The only remains of General Vallejo's 1840 house, **La Casa Grande**, is the servant's house with its sagging adobe facade. ~ West Spain Street between 1st Street East and 1st Street West. Together with the mission and other historic buildings encircling the plaza, it is part of **Sonoma State Historic Park**; all these noteworthy places can be toured for a single admission price. ~ Sonoma; 707-938-1519, fax 707-938-1406; www.napanet.net/~sshpa, e-mail sshpa@napanet.net.

Just north of the plaza stands the **Depot Park Museum**, where the displays commemorate railway history and the Bear Flag uprising when Americans revolted against General Vallejo in 1846. You can also see Sonoma as it was at the turn of the 20th century. Closed Monday and Tuesday. ~ 270 1st Street West, Sonoma; phone/fax 707-938-1762; www.vom.com/depot, e-mail depot@vom.com.

About one-half mile northeast of the town square, you'll find another antique structure. **Lachryma Montis** was the home General Vallejo built in 1852, after the United States had assumed control of California. Vallejo successfully made the change to American rule, becoming a vintner and writing a five-volume history of early California. Something was lost in the transition, however, and this yellow Victorian house with pretty green shutters fails to evoke images of a Mexican general.

Nevertheless, it's well worth touring. Every room is appointed in 19th-century style, as though Vallejo were expected to arrive

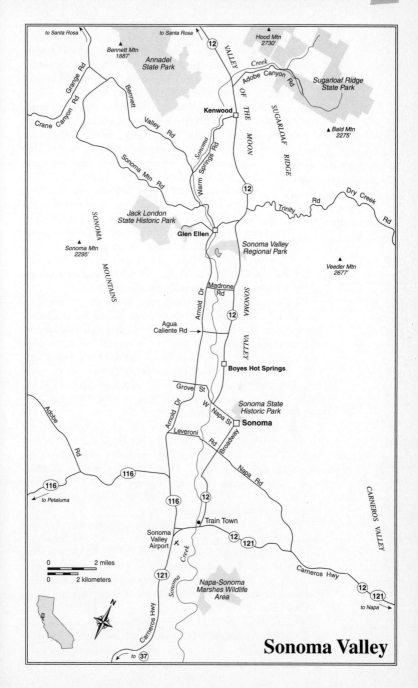

to Santa Rosa
to Santa Rosa
Bennett Mtn
1887'
Annadel
State Park
Hood Mtn
2730'
12
VALLEY OF THE MOON
Creek
Adobe Canyon Rd
Sugarloaf Ridge
State Park
Grange Rd
Crane Canyon Rd
Bennett
Valley Rd
Kenwood
Sonoma
SUGARLOAF
Bald Mtn
2275'
Sonoma Mtn Rd
Warm Springs Rd
RIDGE
SONOMA
MOUNTAINS
Jack London
State Historic Park
12
Trinity Rd
Dry Creek Rd
Sonoma Mtn
2295'
Glen Ellen
Sonoma Valley
Regional Park
Veeder Mtn
2677'
Arnold Dr
Madrone Rd
SONOMA VALLEY
12
Agua
Caliente Rd
Boyes Hot Springs
Grove St
Arnold Dr
W Napa St
Sonoma State
Historic Park
Sonoma
Adobe Rd
Leveroni Rd
Broadway
Napa Rd
116
116
to Petaluma
116
12
Train Town
CARNEROS VALLEY
Sonoma
Valley
Airport
12
121
0   2 miles
0   2 kilometers
121
Sonoma Creek
Napa-Sonoma
Marshes Wildlife
Area
Carneros Hwy
Carneros Hwy
12
121
to Napa
N
to 37

Sonoma Valley

any moment. The old pendulum clock still swings and the dinner table is set. Out back, the cookhouse contains personal effects of the Chinese cook and ducks flap around the pond. Part of Sonoma State Historic Park, it also features a cactus garden, mini-museum, and picnic area. Admission. ~ At the end of 3rd Street West, Sonoma; 707-938-1519, fax 707-938-1406.

While Vallejo was settling into his American-style home, Count Agoston Haraszthy, a Hungarian aristocrat, moved to Sonoma and founded **Buena Vista Historical Winery** in 1857. Popularly known as the "father of the California wine industry," he eventually imported 100,000 vines from Europe. Today the actual winemaking occurs at the vineyard estate in the Carneros area, but you can taste sample vintages in the old stone winery and take a self-guided tour around the grounds. Now a historical monument, the winery also has picnic tables for the crowds that visit. Tasting fee. ~ 18000 Old Winery Road, Sonoma; 707-938-1266, 800-926-1266, fax 707-939-0916; www.buena vistawinery.com, e-mail events@buenavistawinery.com.

After Jack London's untimely death, his wife built the House of Happy Walls and opened the property to wealthy vacationers as Jack London's Beauty Ranch.

One of Spain's premier winemaking families began winning awards with their very first vintages from **Gloria Ferrer Champagne Caves**. The Ferrers carved caves (typical in their native country) out of the hillside for storing premium sparkling wines. The wines are available for purchase or for tasting (at a nominal fee) either indoors or on a wide patio with lovely views of the surrounding countryside. Tasting fee. Closed weekends. ~ 23555 Route 121 (Carneros Highway), Sonoma; 707-996-7256, fax 707-601-0307; www.gloriaferrer.com.

Sam and Vicki Sebastiani, of the famous Sonoma family of vintners, opened their own winery, **Viansa Winery**, in the heart of the prolific Carneros region. A multilevel stucco compound mounted on a hill at the south end of the Sonoma Valley, this Tuscan-style winery offers self-guided tours and tastings. ~ 25200 Arnold Drive, Sonoma; 707-935-4700, 800-995-4740, fax 707-996-4632; www.viansa.com, e-mail tuscan@viansa.com.

If the Napa Valley is Stevenson country, Sonoma Valley belongs to Jack London. A world adventurer and self-described "sailor on horseback," London was not the type to settle down. Illegitimate son of an astrologer, he was in turn an oyster pirate, socialist, gold prospector, and internationally renowned author. But settle he did, a few miles northwest of Sonoma in the town of **Glen Ellen**.

Calling this area "the valley of the moon," London and his wife Charmian acquired a 1400-acre ranch and began construction of the Wolf House, an extraordinary mansion with 26 rooms and nine fireplaces. In 1913, when nearly completed, London's dream house mysteriously burned. Three years later, after producing 51 books and becoming America's first millionaire author, he committed suicide at age 40.

Today, at **Jack London State Historic Park**, you can wander the old estate. At the east end of the park, the House of Happy Walls, occupied by Charmian after her husband's death, is a museum containing first editions and original manuscripts. London's study is adorned with the original artwork for his stories, and many keepsakes from his world adventures are here. A half-mile path leads past the author's grave, simply marked by a stone boulder, to the west side of the park and the tragic ruins of the Wolf House, a monument to a lost dream. Nearby, the cottage where London lived and wrote from 1911 until his death in 1916 still stands. Admission. ~ 2400 London Ranch Road, Glen Ellen; 707-938-5216, fax 707-938-4827; e-mail jacklondonshp@aol.com.

Gray and almost brooding in the shadow of the Mayacamas Mountains, **Ledson Winery & Vineyards** was originally intended as a residence. Plans changed midway, however, and the sprawling Normandy-style château now houses the winery. Steve Ledson claims he used more than two million bricks in constructing what locals refer to as "the castle." The winery is best-known for its estate-grown merlot and zinfandel and its Russian River chardonnay. The well-stocked Marketplace sells old dishes, fresh sandwiches and some 100 cheeses, which may be enjoyed at oak-shaded picnic tables. Tasting fee. ~ 7335 Route 12, Kenwood; 707-833-2330; www.ledson.com, e-mail hospitality@ledson.com.

The strikingly beautiful **Château St. Jean Winery** sits beside a colonnaded mansion built during the 1920s. The winery has added several similar buildings, including one with an observation tower from which to view the surrounding countryside. Wine, not extraordinary vistas, is the business here, and the winery has won several awards for its chardonnays and cabernet sauvignons. You can taste these and other varietals and take a self-guided tour of the grounds. It's also a nice place to bring a picnic. ~ 8555 Sonoma Highway, Kenwood; 707-833-4134, 800-478-5326, fax 707-833-4200; www.chateaustjean.com.

LODGING

Immerse yourself in a bit of Petaluma history and stay in **Goltermann Gardens & Country Inn**, a 1930s chicken farm transformed into a bed-and-breakfast inn. Stay in the Egg House, which is decorated with chicken memorabilia, or one of the other two suites. All have feather beds with down comforters and private baths. The inn sits three miles outside of town in Leghorn Valley, where 100 farms once raised more than one million leghorns. Today only one chicken farm remains. Weekly or monthly rentals only. ~ 1000 Skillman Lane, Petaluma; 707-762-1761, fax 707-765-2145. ULTRA-DELUXE.

The **Fairmont Sonoma Mission Inn & Spa** lives up to its name, in all three senses of the word. The pale pink stucco facade on this gracious Mission Revival–style hotel harks back to the days when American Indians enjoyed the natural mineral waters of this area. The 228 accommodations are appointed in earthy tones, with wooden shutters and ceiling fans adding a touch of plantation to the place. Some rooms have fireplaces. A full-service spa, an 18-hole golf course, and two swimming pools add up to one of the best retreats in the Wine Country. ~ 18140 Route 12 at Boyes Boulevard, Boyes Hot Springs; 707-938-9000, 800-441-1414, fax 707-938-4250; www.fairmont.com/sonoma. ULTRA-DELUXE.

The **Swiss Hotel**, a State Historical Landmark, is an adobe building dating from 1840. This five-room hostelry features rooms with private baths and a refrigerator. One has a four-poster bed and pine furniture, others have a variety of antique and modern pieces. The hotel rests on the town's central plaza and contains a bar and restaurant downstairs. ~ 18 West Spain Street, Sonoma; 707-938-2884, fax 707-938-3298; www.swisshotel sonoma.com, e-mail swisshotel@rom.com. DELUXE TO ULTRA-DELUXE.

Sonoma's plaza features another historic hostelry, the **Sonoma Hotel**, which dates to around 1879 and is a 16-room facility decorated entirely with French Country furnishings. The lobby has a stone fireplace and the adjoining restaurant features a hand-carved bar. Combining history with comfort, this vintage hotel is worth a visit. Continental breakfast is included, as well as complimentary wine service. ~ 110 West Spain Street, Sonoma; 707-996-2996, 800-468-6016, fax 707-996-7014; www.sonomahotel. com, e-mail sonomahotel@aol.com. MODERATE TO ULTRA-DELUXE

The **El Dorado Hotel**, also located on the square, is a small gem. Originally an adobe built in 1843, this refurbished stucco establishment offers 27 small- to moderate-size rooms, as well as a full-service bar and restaurant. Appointed with four poster beds, down comforters, Mexican tile floors, and California/Spanish style

---

PACK-N-GO PICNIC

Sonoma Cheese Factory is the spot to stop on the way to the picnic grounds. In addition to a grand assortment of cheeses, it sells wines, sandwiches, and gourmet specialty foods. There's also a small, outdoor patio for diners. In back, where store gives way to factory, you can watch Jack cheese being made. ~ 2 West Spain Street, Sonoma; 707-996-1931, 800-535-2855; www.sonomajack.com, e-mail retailstore@sonomajack. com. BUDGET.

furniture, each has a private balcony. There's a heated swimming pool, and complimentary morning coffee. ~ 405 1st Street West, Sonoma; 707-996-3030, 800-289-3031, fax 707-996-3148; www.hoteleldorado.com, e-mail info@hoteleldorado.com. ULTRA-DELUXE.

DINING

Join the local crowd for a burger or some barbecued ribs and a brew at **McNears Saloon & Dining House**. Old pictures, mirrors, signs, and even tennis rackets decorate the brick walls of this popular hangout in a historic building that dates to 1886. ~ 23 Petaluma Boulevard, Petaluma; 707-765-2121. BUDGET TO MODERATE.

Santé, a handsome Southwestern-inspired dining room, is the best restaurant in the county. Startlingly innovative but not pretentious, the menu features a dozen entrées such as grilled fish and various chicken and lamb dishes, virtually all from local sources. No lunch. ~ Fairmont Sonoma Mission Inn & Spa, 18140 Route 12, Boyes Hot Springs; 707-938-9000, fax 707-938-4250; www.fairmont.com/sonoma. DELUXE TO ULTRA-DELUXE.

A less formal option is the **Big 3 Diner**. This bistro-style eatery also serves tasty, healthful fare with a northern Italian influence. You'll find pastas, pizzas, and salads on the lunch and dinner menu, while breakfast features freshly baked goods, pancakes, and egg dishes. ~ Fairmont Sonoma Mission Inn & Spa, 18140 Route 12, Boyes Hot Springs; 707-938-9000, 800-441-1414, fax 707-996-5358; www.fairmont.com/sonoma. MODERATE TO DELUXE.

Savor the flavors of Tuscany at **Cucina Viansa**, a classy Italian restaurant accented with a black-and-white tile floor and marble countertops. A wood-burning stove perfects seasonal dishes like ribeye with a potato torta or Sonoma chicken scented with thyme and orange. Oenophiles can visit the adjoining wine bar featuring vintages from Viansa Winery. ~ 400 1st Street East, Sonoma; 707-935-5656, fax 707-935-5651. MODERATE TO DELUXE.

Thin-crusted, New Haven–style pizzas were the raison d'être behind **The Red Grape** when it opened in early 2002, but the restaurant has become equally popular for generous portions of fresh pastas and salads. The high-ceilinged room features glass walls on three sides and an open kitchen; there's also patio seating. ~ 529 1st Street West, Sonoma; 707-996-4103. BUDGET TO MODERATE.

The General's Daughter is a gloriously restored yellow Victorian that once belonged to General Mariano Vallejo's daughter. High-ceilinged rooms, decorated with paintings of oversized farm animals and lots of greenery provide an appropriately residential atmosphere. The kitchen has faltered since it opened in the early 1990s but there is much to like on the wide-ranging California-cuisine menu, particularly among the appetizers. This is the place to bring an aunt or a group for a sedate Sunday brunch. Closed Monday. ~ 400 West Spain Street, Sonoma; 707-938-4004, fax 707-938-4099. MODERATE TO ULTRA-DELUXE.

If you prefer Mexican cuisine, try **La Casa**. Located just off the plaza, this colorful restaurant offers a full menu from south of the border. There are margaritas and other tequila drinks at the bar, plus a bill of fare ranging from snapper Veracruz to chile verde to chimichangas. Enjoy your meal on their outdoor patio. ~ 121 East Spain Street, Sonoma; 707-996-3406, fax 707-938-0285; www.la casarestaurant.com. BUDGET TO MODERATE.

Don't let the simplicity of the menu fool you. The half-dozen or so main courses at **Café La Haye** are the result of a sophisticated chef who manages to create delectable dishes in a postage stamp–size kitchen. Chicken, beef, pasta, and daily fish and risotto selections get the deluxe treatment in this split-level storefront restaurant just off the Sonoma plaza. Dinner only; Sunday brunch. No dinner on Sunday. Closed Monday. ~ 140 East Napa Street, Sonoma; 707-935-5994; www.cafelahaye.com, e-mail cafelahaye@vom.com. MODERATE TO DELUXE.

Family-owned and-operated, **Cafe Citti** is an Italian trattoria set amongst the vineyards of Kenwood and extremely popular with Sonoma Valley locals, who love its casualness and friendly atmosphere. Flowers and candles on the tables add a bit of romance, while summertime allows patio dining. The Italian chef serves up a variety of pastas; rotisserie chicken stuffed with fresh herbs, garlic, and rosemary; and weekend specials. He also makes his own mozzarella cheese and biscotti. ~ 9049 Sonoma Highway, Kenwood; 707-833-2690, fax 707-578-9499; www.cafe citti.com. MODERATE.

SHOPPING   Petaluma is a great place to shop, with some 25 antique stores and a factory outlet mall.

More than 25 dealers display their antiques, vintage clothing, furniture, and country collectibles at **Summer Cottage**. ~ 153 Kentucky Street, Petaluma; 707-776-2873.

Bargain seekers will discover lots of good deals at the **Petaluma Village Premium Outlets** mall. Ann Taylor, Brooks Brothers,

AUTHOR FAVORITE

On the way to Jack London State Historic Park, be sure to stop in at the **Jack London Bookstore**. An important resource center for London scholars and fans, it contains numerous first editions of the author's works. Closed Tuesday and Wednesday. ~ 14300 Arnold Drive, Glen Ellen; 707-996-2888; e-mail jlondon@vom.com.

Liz Claiborne, and Saks Fifth Avenue all have outlets here, as do Linen Barn, Corning Revere, Mikasa, and Harry and David. There are also several cafés to fortify hungry hunters. ~ 2200 Petaluma Boulevard North, Petaluma; 707-778-9300, fax 707-778-6963; www.premiumoutlets.com.

The old Spanish town of Sonoma contains a central plaza around which you'll find its best shops. Stroll the square (bounded by 1st Street East, 1st Street West, Spain, and Napa streets) and encounter gourmet stores, boutiques, a designer lingerie company, antique stores, poster galleries, and a brass shop. Many of these establishments are housed in historic Spanish adobes.

One place to consider is the **Arts Guild of Sonoma**, containing works by local artisans. Here are paintings, ceramics, and jewelry. Closed Tuesday. ~ 140 East Napa Street, Sonoma; 707-996-3115.

A nearby mall, **El Paseo de Sonoma**, contains more off-street shops. ~ 414 1st Street East, Sonoma.

The Sign of the Bear celebrates the pleasures of life in the Wine Country. The shop sells over 13,000 items from nutmeg to napkin rings, gadgets to glassware, cookware to make just about anything and cookbooks to teach you how to do it. ~ 435 1st Street West, Sonoma; 707-996-3722, fax 707-996-2046.

Robin's Nest specializes in discount kitchen accessories and gifts such as Italian bowls and platters. ~ 116 East Napa Street, Sonoma; 707-996-4169.

The glasses, goblets, ornaments, lamps, shades, wall sconces and art vessels created at **Bacchus Glass** are available for sale in the adjacent gallery, as are some works from other glass artists. Closed Sunday and Monday. ~ 21707 8th Street East, Sonoma; 707-939-9416.

Locally and nationally known bands, playing a variety of music to satisfy nearly every taste, pack in the crowds at **McNears Mystic Theater and Music Hall** on Friday and Saturday nights. Cover. ~ 21 Petaluma Boulevard, Petaluma; 707-765-2121, fax 707-765-4671; www.mcnears.com.

NIGHTLIFE

It's Oktoberfest all year at **Little Switzerland**, where you can dance the polka and waltz to live accompaniment and pretend you're in another time and place. Join your partner on the main dancefloor inside or outside in the beer garden. Dinners of steak, pasta, and chicken are also served. Reservations recommended. Open Friday, Saturday, and Sunday only. Cover. ~ Corner of Riverside and Grove, El Verano; 707-938-9990; e-mail lilswiss@vom.com.

As in the Napa area, Sonoma Valley nightlife revolves around summer events at the wineries. Check local calendars for concerts, theatrical performances, and other special programs. If that seems uninteresting, or it's not summertime, you'll have to rely on hotel and restaurant bars for entertainment.

With old photos adorning its walls, the bar of the historic **Swiss Hotel** is a favorite meetingplace of locals and travelers alike. You can also get a pretty filling meal here. ~ 18 West Spain Street, Sonoma; 707-938-2884, fax 707-938-3298.

Out in Jack London country, the **Jack London Saloon** is a pretty, brick-faced bar that draws a mixture of locals and visitors. Fashionably decorated with Tiffany-style lamps and old movie posters, it's a good drinking place. ~ Jack London Lodge, 13740 Arnold Drive, Glen Ellen; 707-996-3100, fax 707-939-9642.

PARKS

SUGARLOAF RIDGE STATE PARK 🚶🚴🐎⚓ Within this 2820-acre facility lie two different ecological systems, as well as 25 miles of hiking trails along which to explore them. There are chaparral-coated ridges (you can see San Francisco and the Sierra Nevada from the top of Bald Mountain), plus forests of maple, laurel, madrone, and alder. Sonoma Creek tumbles through the park; you can try for trout here. Spring brings a profusion of wild-flowers, and autumn is another popular season in the park. The Ferguson Observatory (707-833-6979) boasts a 40-inch telescope and offers public viewing nights. Horse rentals are available from Triple Creek Horse Outfit (707-933-1600). Facilities include picnic areas and restrooms. Day-use fee, $4. ~ Located east off Route 12 between Sonoma and Santa Rosa, the park is at 2605 Adobe Canyon Road in Kenwood; phone/fax 707-833-5712.

▲ There are 49 sites; $15 per car per night. Camping here offers a reasonably priced lodging option for a visit to the Wine Country and is popular with Bay Area families. Reservations: 800-444-7275.

▼▼▼▼▼▼▼▼▼▼▼▼▼▼▼▼

Northern Wine Country

Sonoma's vine-rich county continues north of Santa Rosa along Route 101 to Cloverdale, but the secret to touring this region resides along country lanes paralleling the highway. At the center of this area is Healdsburg, a country town centered on a plaza and dating back to 1852.

SIGHTS

Santa Rosa, the largest city in Sonoma County, is perhaps best known as the home of Luther Burbank, the great horticulturist who worked miracles on plantlife, creating the Santa Rosa plum, Shasta daisy, spineless cactus and hundreds of other hybrids. His legacy remains in full bloom at the **Luther Burbank Home & Gardens**, where visitors can stroll through gardens filled with the descendants of his plant "inventions" and tour the Victorian house where he lived for 20 years. The house is open Tuesday through Sunday from April through October. Admission to tour the house. ~ Santa Rosa and Sonoma avenues, Santa Rosa; 707-524-5445, fax 707-524-5827; www.lutherburbank.org, e-mail burbankhome@lutherburbank.org.

On the western edge of downtown, the **Historic Railroad Square** once was a busy commercial and transport center. Today its buildings, some of which survived the great 1906 earthquake that destroyed much of the city center, contain antique and specialty shops and restaurants. ~ Located west of Route 101 and east of the railroad tracks.

The old Santa Rosa Depot has been restored and turned into a visitors center and the **Northwest Pacific Rail Museum**. The museum in the former ticket office has a small display of memorabilia from the depot's past, including photographs and a model train the kids can operate. The **California Welcome Center** provides an overview of the region's wineries and attractions. ~ 9 4th Street, Santa Rosa; 707-577-8674, fax 707-571-5949; www.visit santarosa.com.

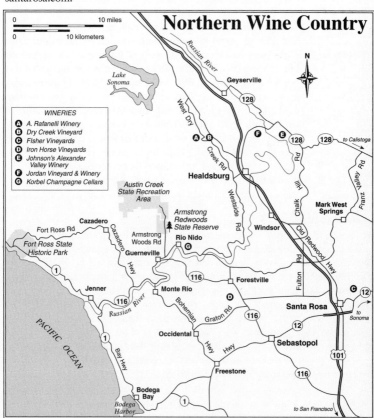

Northern Wine Country

WINERIES
- Ⓐ A. Rafanelli Winery
- Ⓑ Dry Creek Vineyard
- Ⓒ Fisher Vineyards
- Ⓓ Iron Horse Vineyards
- Ⓔ Johnson's Alexander Valley Winery
- Ⓕ Jordan Vineyard & Winery
- Ⓖ Korbel Champagne Cellars

Housed in a former 1909 post office, the **Sonoma County Museum** provides a historical and cultural perspective on the region with changing exhibits, some of them especially designed for kids. The museum includes the Christo Collection with over 80 works from the French avant garde artist. Closed Monday and Tuesday. Admission. ~ 425 7th Street, Santa Rosa; 707-579-1500, fax 707-579-4849; www.sonomacountymuseum.org.

Up in the mountains outside Santa Rosa, hidden along country lanes, lies **Fisher Vineyards**. Tucked into a fold in the hills and surrounded by redwood forest, this picturesque winery is a family-style operation. The main building, a lofty board-and-batten structure, was built with wood cut and milled on the site. It follows a contemporary California design and overlooks the surrounding vineyards. Planted primarily with cabernet sauvignon, chardonnay, and merlot vines, the winery produces a small but delicious quantity of wine each season. Visiting by appointment only. ~ 6200 St. Helena Road, Santa Rosa; 707-539-7511, fax 707-539-3601; www.fishervineyards.com.

Just north of Santa Rosa, around the tiny towns of **Forestville** and **Windsor**, are numerous family wineries. Without doubt, one

HIDDEN ►

of the prettiest vineyard settings in all California belongs to **Iron Horse Vineyards**. The driveway snaking into this hidden spot is bordered with flowers, olive trees, and palm trees. Hills roll away in every direction, revealing a line of distant mountains. The winery buildings, painted barn-red, follow the classic architecture of American farms. Laid out around them in graceful checkerboard patterns are fields of pinot noir and chardonnay grapes. At harvest time these will be handpicked and then barrel-aged, for the emphasis at this elegant little winery is on personal attention. The outdoor tasting area boasts a view of green valley and is open

"BOONTLING"

As Route 128 rolls down into Anderson Valley, it passes **Boonville**, a farming community of about 2000 folks. Back in the 1880s, this town invented a kind of local pig Latin, "boontling," known only to residents. With a vocabulary of over 1000 words, it neatly reflected Anderson Valley life. A photo became a "Charlie Walker" after the Mendocino fellow who took portraits. Because of his handlebar whiskers, "Tom Bacon" lent his name to the moustache. Rail fences were "relfs," heavy storms became "trashmovers," and pastors (those heavenly skypilots) were "skipes." Vestiges of the old lingo remain—restaurants, for instance, still boast of their "bahl gorms," or good food. They also produce good wine in these parts, and several award-winning wineries dot the Anderson Valley.

seven days a week by appointment. ~ 9786 Ross Station Road, Sebastopol; 707-887-1507, fax 707-887-1337; www.ironhorse vineyards.com, e-mail info@ironhorsevineyards.com.

In addition to wineries, there are countless orchards around **Sebastopol**, another town that has become gentrified in recent years. Known as the Gold Ridge region, it is California's premier apple-producing area. For details, contact the **Sebastopol Chamber of Commerce** and ask for a Sonoma County farm trails map. It will lead you to farms producing apples, pears, berries, cherries, peaches, and vegetables—some of which you can pick yourself. Closed weekends. ~ 265 South Main Street, Sebastopol; 707-823-3032, fax 707-823-8439; www.sebastopol.org, e-mail apples@sebastopol.org.

West of Sebastopol on Route 12 in the historic town of Free-stone is the five-acre **Osmosis Enzyme Bath & Massage**. While hot springs soaks and mud baths are possible at countless locations, Osmosis claims to be the only place in North America offering Japanese cedar enzyme baths, composed of cedar fiber, rice bran, and more than 600 active enzymes. ~ 209 Bohemian Highway, Freestone; 707-823-8231, fax 707-874-3788; www.osmosis.com.

At the **Healdsburg Chamber of Commerce & Visitors Bureau** you can pick up maps, brochures, and other information on the region. ~ 217 Healdsburg Avenue, Healdsburg; 707-433-6935, 800-648-9922, fax 707-433-7562; www.healdsburg.org, e-mail info@healdsburg.org.

Dry Creek Valley, a luxurious landscape of vineyards and forest, stretches to the west of Healdsburg. Two small family-owned wineries warrant special attention. **Dry Creek Vineyard** sits in an ivy-covered building surrounded by shade trees. There's tasting every day and the winery provides picnic tables for guests. Among the excellent wines produced are chenin blancs, fumés, cabernets, chardonnays, merlots, and zinfandels. ~ 3770 Lambert Bridge Road, Healdsburg; 707-433-1000, 800-864-9463, fax 707-433-5329; www.drycreekvineyard.com, e-mail dcv@drycreek vineyard.com.

Along the far rim of Dry Creek Valley rises **A. Rafanelli Winery**, a classic family-style enterprise. David A. Rafanelli, whose roots go far back in the wine industry, owns the place and does much of the work himself along with his wife, Patty. Now in their fourth generation, the winery specializes in producing high-qual-ity zinfandel, merlot and cabernet sauvignon, which are sold in limited quantities. The winery itself consists of an old barn be-hind the family home. Backdropped by forested hills, it over-looks the valley and surrounding countryside. Tours and tasting are by appointment. ~ 4685 West Dry Creek Road, Healdsburg; 707-433-1385, fax 707-433-3836; www.arafanelliwinery.com.

East of Healdsburg lies the **Alexander Valley**, a region whose wines are gaining an increasingly fine reputation. Because of its warm climate, the valley is sometimes compared with the Bordeaux area of France. Its vintages, however, have a quality all their own.

Jordan Vineyard & Winery is a lavish facility built along the lines of a Bordeaux château, and the winery is housed in a grand building that overlooks the Alexander Valley. Electronic gates protect the grounds, making it somewhat secluded. Tours are a real treat, providing a glimpse into a winery whose elegance matches its excellence; morning and afternoon tours are scheduled. Reservations required. Closed Sunday and for two weeks at Christmas. ~ 1474 Alexander Valley Road, Healdsburg; 707-431-5250, fax 707-431-5259; e-mail publicrelations@jordancos.com.

A long road leads to an unpainted redwood barn housing **Johnson's Alexander Valley Winery**. Within this nondescript tasting room sits a 1924 theater pipe organ used for the winery's occasional concerts and events. There is also a wealth of modern equipment around the place, which produces fine pinot noirs and cabernets. Family-owned, the little winery offers tasting anytime. Closed Tuesday through Thursday, December through February. ~ 8333 Route 128, Healdsburg; 707-433-2319, fax 707-433-5302.

Route 101 streams north past Ukiah and several more wineries. A more interesting course lies along **Route 128**, which leads northwest from Cloverdale through piedmont country. En route, the two-lane road meanders like an old river, bending back upon itself to reveal sloping meadows and tree-tufted glades. It's a beautiful country drive through rolling ranch land. Sheep graze the hills and an occasional farmhouse stands along the roadside, its windows blinking sunlight at solitary cars.

LODGING   You can stay in the heart of Santa Rosa's fascinating Historic Railroad Square at **Hotel La Rose**, built in 1907 by the same Italian stonemasons who were responsible for the depot across the street. It has been listed on the National Register of Historic Places and is a member of Historic Hotels of America. English country style describes the decor, with dark greens and rose-red colors. Some rooms sport four-poster beds. The fourth-floor attic rooms have sloping ceilings, and some are brightened by skylights. An outdoor spa is available to guests. ~ 308 Wilson Street, Santa Rosa; 707-579-3200, 800-527-6738, fax 707-579-3247; www.hotellarose.com, e-mail reservations@hotellarose.com. DELUXE TO ULTRA-DELUXE.

Now that the 90 acres of surrounding vineyards have matured, the **Vintners Inn** blends in with the landscape. Spacious accommodations are decorated in European country style, with antiques and comforters. Little piazzas and open landscaping between two-story townhouses create a luxurious ambience. Breakfast is included. ~ 4350 Barnes Road, Santa Rosa; 707-575-7350, 800-421-2584, fax 707-575-1426; www.vintnersinn.com, e-mail info @vintnersinn.com. ULTRA-DELUXE.

Healdsburg, located farther north along Route 101, is a perfect jumping-off point for visiting the many wineries in the area. Numerous country inns dot the area, including the **Haydon Street Inn**, a lovely eight-bedroom bed and breakfast set in a vintage 1912 house. Each room is beautifully appointed with antique furniture and artistic wallhangings. Both the private rooms and the common areas are quite spacious. The tree-shaded lawn, comfortable living room, and wraparound front porch are a perfect expression of Main Street, America. Serving a full breakfast and afternoon refreshments, the inn has eight rooms in the main building and the separate carriage house, all with private baths. (Several rooms feature jacuzzi tubs and/or fireplaces). ~ 321 Haydon Street, Healdsburg; 707-433-5228, 800-528-3703, fax 707-433-6637; www.haydon.com, e-mail innkeeper@haydon. com. DELUXE TO ULTRA-DELUXE.

In an area dotted with B&Bs and charming little hostelries, **Hotel Healdsburg** is a good option if you're looking for something a bit more modern. There's a spa, a pool, and pretty gardens for strolling. The guest rooms all have private balconies, wood floors, and huge bathrooms. With a good gourmet restaurant on the premises, you don't even need to bother venturing from the building. ~ 25 Matheson Street, Healdsburg; 707-431-2800, 800-889-7188, fax 707-431-0414; www.hotelhealds burg.com, e-mail concierge@hotelhealdsburg.com. ULTRA-DELUXE.

Built in 1881 as a private summer retreat, the **Madrona Manor Country Inn** is a charming example of Gothic Victorian architecture, complete with a balconied porch, turrets, and gables. The best rooms are in the main house; they are spacious (two upstairs sport a shared veranda) and furnished in serious antiques, including chaises longues and armoires. There are an additional 12 accommodations in several outbuildings on an eight-acre site, including a carriage house. Guests enjoy the pool and a breakfast buffet. The on-site restaurant whips up eclectic California

SKATING IN THE PEANUTS GALLERY

The Redwood Empire Ice Arena may be the only sports facility ever created by a cartoonist. Built by Charles Schulz of *Peanuts* fame for his children, the arena is open year-round from 6 a.m. until 10:30 p.m. Snoopy's Gallery and Gift Shop, also part of the facility, sells Snoopy memorabilia, books, clothing, and life-size comic strip characters. ~ 1667 West Steele Lane, Santa Rosa; 707-546-7147, fax 707-546-3764; www.snoopyshomeice.com.

cuisine. ~ 1001 Westside Road, Healdsburg; 707-433-4231, 800-258-4003, fax 707-433-0703; www.madronamanor.com, e-mail madronaman@aol.com. ULTRA-DELUXE.

HIDDEN ►   If you're yearning to retreat back into the '60s, check out **Isis Oasis**, a ten-acre hideaway that combines bed-and-breakfast facilities with massage, tarot readings, and past-life experiences. Set in the tiny town of Geyserville, you can wander the Egyptian-style grounds, which includes an obelisk, and luxuriate in the hot tub, sauna, and swimming pool. There is also a zoo with exotic animals and birds, an Egyptian meditation temple, and a "tomb room" for deep meditation. ~ 20889 Geyserville Avenue, Geyserville; 707-857-4747, 800-679-7387, fax 707-857-3544; www.isisoasis.org, e-mail isis@isisoasis.org. MODERATE.

Up in the Anderson Valley, Mendocino's winegrowing region, there's a two-story B&B called the **Philo Pottery Inn**. It sits in an 1888 redwood farmhouse (once an old stagecoach stop) built entirely of redwood. The five bedrooms are high-ceilinged, wood-paneled affairs with such decorative flourishes as oak dressers, patchwork quilts, and brass beds (some rooms share a bath). The garden cottage features a queen bed and a woodburning stove. Relax by the fire in the living room, lounge on the porches or stroll through the gardens. A great place for a few days of easy living. Full breakfast is included. ~ 8550 Route 128, Philo; 707-895-3069, fax 707-895-3352; www.philopotteryinn.com, e-mail info@philopotteryinn.com. MODERATE TO DELUXE.

The **Wine Country Inns of Sonoma County** is a referral service that can help you with local bed-and-breakfast reservations. ~ 707-433-4667, 800-946-2686; www.winecountryinns.com.

DINING   One of the most beloved restaurants in Sonoma County, **John Ash & Co.** resides in an elegant adobe-style building, decorated with local artwork that blends in with vineyards visible through

AUTHOR FAVORITE

I'm constantly amazed at the clever innovations provided by the chefs at **Zazu**, who have the nerve to pair seared tuna with bing cherries and make the combination work. In a ramshackle building west of Santa Rosa, Zazu peddles a seasonal mix of playful American food and northern Italian fare—with a twist—split between small and big plates. Typical of the former are squash blossoms fritti and poppyseed-crusted soft-shell crab; of the latter, star anise–rubbed duck and grilled rack of lamb with quinoa tabbouleh. Many housemade desserts feature fresh local fruit. No dinner on Sunday. Closed Monday and Tuesday. ~ 3535 Guerneville Road, Santa Rosa; 707-523-4814; www.zazurestaurant.com. MODERATE TO ULTRA-DELUXE.

enormous windows. Executive chef Jeffrey Madura upholds John Ash's style, and is known for a devotion to local fish, fowl, and produce prepared with a confident flair. The widely varied menu changes monthly and might include Dungeness crab cakes, venison, lamb, and filet mignon. No lunch on Saturday. ~ 4330 Barnes Road next door to the Vintners Inn, Santa Rosa; 707-527-7687, 800-421-2584; www.vintnersinn.com. MODERATE TO ULTRA-DELUXE.

Serving fresh Sonoma County cuisine, **Mixx Restaurant & Bar** makes good use of the region's agricultural bounty, including 25 wines that can be sampled by the glass. The contemporary dining room with Art Nouveau touches and an elegant mahogany bar imported from Europe is the place to sample liberty duck breast with Chinese five spice, black rice, and watercress, or zinfandel-poached hare with Sonoma greens. Closed Sunday. ~ 135 4th Street, Santa Rosa; 707-573-1344, fax 707-573-0631; www.mixx restaurant.com, e-mail mixx@ap.net. MODERATE TO ULTRA-DELUXE.

You cannot find fresher or tastier Thai food than what comes out of the kitchen at **Jhanthong Banbua**. Located in front of a motel near the Santa Rosa Junior College campus, this pretty place knocks itself out with service and a menu with something for everyone. Particularly fine are the *pad thai* and anything with shrimp. No lunch on Saturday. Closed Sunday. ~ 2400 Mendocino Avenue, Santa Rosa; 707-528-8048. MODERATE.

Sassafras, located in a westside office park, offers updated classics such as grilled chicken with butternut squash, sage, and cranberry coulis and seared tuna with pineapple salsa. No lunch on weekends. ~ 1229 North Dutton Avenue, Santa Rosa; 707-578-7600; www.sassafrasrestaurant.com. MODERATE TO DELUXE.

In the prime Mendocino County winegrowing region of Anderson Valley, there are a few cafés and family-style restaurants in the small towns along rural Route 128. When hunger strikes, Boonville presents the best possibilities. Particularly recommended for dinner is the **Boonville Hotel**, an outstanding California cuisine restaurant with a gourmet menu. Closed Tuesday, Wednesday, and the month of January. ~ Route 128, Boonville; 707-895-2210, fax 707-895-2243; www.boonville hotel.com. MODERATE TO ULTRA-DELUXE.

Winetasting is a much more popular sport in these parts than window-browsing. If intent on shopping, you'll have to skip from town to town searching out a few interesting stores. An exception to this is Santa Rosa, which has a busy downtown district and the Historic Railroad Square, with its many excellent shops.

SHOPPING

It's Halloween all year at **Disguise the Limit**, where you can find the paraphernalia to be a clown, a queen, or an alien creature. Also here are toys and a few magic tricks to put up your sleeve. ~ 100 4th Street, Santa Rosa; 707-575-1477, fax 707-579-4542.

Antique addicts beware: Sebastopol's **Antique Row** may be your undoing. Two hundred dealers in a dozen locations within eight miles? Lead on. ~ Gravenstein Highway (Route 116) between Route 101 and Route 12, Sebastopol; 707-823-3032.

Fifteen miles north of Cloverdale, **Real Goods Solar Living Center** showcases products utilizing renewable energy sources as well as items manufactured from natural fibers and alternative materials. Merchandise includes natural bed and bath products, cotton clothing, and gourmet kitchenware. More than just a retail store, the center also presents water-conservation and solar-panel demonstrations and offers guided tours of the facilities. ~ 13771 South Route 101, Hopland; 707-744-2100, fax 707-744-1342; www.realgoods.com.

NIGHTLIFE   Some of the area wineries feature programs during the summer. Otherwise, there are bars and hotel lounges scattered throughout the area in towns such as Healdsburg, Geyserville, Cloverdale, and Boonville.

PARKS   **ANNADEL STATE PARK** 🏃 ⛵ Possessing a wealth of possibilities, this 5000-acre facility has 40 miles of trails through meadow and forest. A volcanic mountain flanks one end of the park and a lake provides fishing for black bass and bluegill. There's also a marsh where many of the area's 160 bird species flock. Blacktailed deer and coyotes roam the region. The park has picnic areas and pit toilets. Day-use fee, $2. ~ Off Route 12 about five miles east of Santa Rosa; 707-539-3911, fax 707-538-0769.

▼▼▼▼▼▼▼▼▼▼▼
Russian River

With its headwaters in Mendocino County, the Russian River rambles south through north central California to Healdsburg. Here it turns west toward the sea, as the surrounding landscape changes from rolling ranch land to dense redwood forest. The area around Guerneville, where the river begins its headlong rush to the Pacific, has enjoyed a rebirth as a gay resort area. Earlier a family vacation spot, the Guerneville–Forestville–Monte Rio area became a raffish home to bikers and hippies during the '50s and '60s. Then in the '70s, gay vacationers from San Francisco began frequenting the region.

Today, the Russian River is San Francisco's answer to Fire Island. There are many gay resorts in and around Guerneville, and almost without exception every establishment in town welcomes gay visitors. The area is also a popular family resort area. This stretch of the river offers prime fishing and canoeing opportunities. As the river rumbles downslope, it provides miles of scenic runs past overhanging forests. Black bass, steelhead, bluegill, and silver salmon swim these waters, and there are numerous beaches for swimming and sunbathing. From Santa Rosa, the winding, two-lane River Road follows the northern edge of the Russian River taking you to the ocean, where it stops at Jenner.

The **Visitors Information Center** provides maps and brochures on facilities and water sports. ~ 16209 1st Street, Guerneville; 707-869-3533, 800-253-8800, fax 707-869-9009; www.russianriver. com, e-mail info@russianriver.com. The Center also operates the

SIGHTS

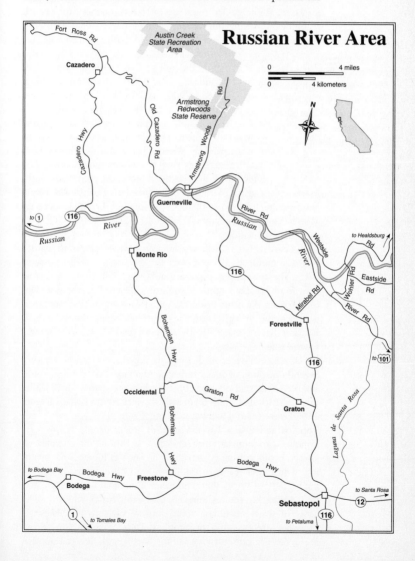

Visitors Bureau at Korbel Station. ~ 13250 River Road, Guerneville; 707-869-4096.

Founded in 1882 by three brothers, **Korbel Champagne Cellars** produces today's most popular sparkling wines. On any day of the week you may taste these award-winning bubblies and sample their still wines and brandies. The tasting room and attached gift shop offer nine different champagnes, some of which are available nowhere else; also on the premises is a gourmet delicatessen. While guided tours are offered throughout the year, I recommend visiting during spring and summer when the winery's century-old garden, which you can tour separately, is alive with roses, tulips, and daffodils. No garden tours on Monday. ~ 13250 River Road, Guerneville; 707-824-7000, fax 707-869-2981; www.korbel.com, e-mail info@korbel.com.

Russian River wines are distinctive because a 70-foot-deep stratum of gravel lies beneath the valley, forcing vine roots to reach deeper for water and adding trace minerals that give the grapes a complex flavor.

As you first arrive in downtown Guerneville you will come to a traffic signal at the intersection of Armstrong Woods Road. Turning north will take you to **Armstrong Redwoods State Reserve** (2.5 miles down the road), where you undoubtedly will marvel at the grove of ancient redwoods dating back 1400 years and reaching heights of 300 feet. Admission. ~ 17000 Armstrong Woods Road, Guerneville; 707-869-2015, fax 707-869-5629; e-mail armvs@mcn.org.

Of course, Guerneville would never have developed into a resort destination had it not been for the waters of the Russian River. The most popular spot around Guerneville to plunge in for a swim or launch a canoe is **Johnson's Beach**. Located just two blocks from the heart of downtown, this sunny waterfront strip is also home to many summer events, including the renowned Russian River Jazz Festival. ~ South end of Church Street, Guerneville.

Dozens of wineries distinguish the Russian River region. Several outstanding ones can be found along Westside Road and smaller roads that are sometimes little more than a lane, while others are located south on heavily traveled routes such as Route 116 (Gravenstein Highway). Along Route 116 you will find **Topolos at Russian River Vineyards** (most people simply say Topolos, pronounced taupe-uh-lohs). This rambling complex is known for its cutting-edge techniques such as biodynamic farming, which is believed to produce more vital crops by capitalizing on natural forces that tend to have minimal negative impact on the land. But the real fun is in the tasting room, where a wide array of wines, including some unusual varietals like Alicante Bouschet, are available for sampling. Don't miss the port. They also have a full restaurant open for breakfast, lunch and dinner.

Call for seasonal hours. ~ 5700 Route 116, Forestville; 707-887-1575, fax 707-887-1399; www.topolos.net, e-mail topolos@topolos.net.

Resting on 15 waterfront acres on the edge of downtown Guerneville, **Fifes Resort** is the Russian River's largest gay resort. In addition to a restaurant and a bar, Fifes offers such facilities as a beach, a pool, and volleyball courts, as well as a disco, gym, and massage services. Accommodations are as varied as the sports activities. There are 100 budget-priced campsites as well as moderate-to-deluxe-priced individual cabins that were built in the 1920s and haven't changed much since then. Each is simply furnished with a queen-sized bed and without TV or phone. Some two-room cabins have a woodburning stove and a sofa bed in one room. ~ 16467 River Road, Guerneville; 707-869-9500, 800-734-3371, fax 707-869-0658; www.fifes.com, e-mail info@fifes.com. budget to moderate.

Fondly called "Triple R," **Russian River Resort** offers 24 cheerfully decorated guest rooms situated around a clothing-optional hot tub area. Whereas most other resorts in the area can be described as rustic, this resort provides more modern, contemporary accommodations; each room is carpeted and has a private bath and cable TV (several have woodburning fireplaces as well). Throughout the year, the Russian River Resort organizes 15 to 20 events celebrating major holidays and festivities such as Women's Weekend. The guests are almost exclusively gay male but lesbians and gay-friendly straights are welcome. A restaurant and several bars are located on the premises, and there's a pool. ~ 16390 4th Street, Guerneville; 707-869-0691, 800-417-3767, fax 707-869-0698; www.russianriverresort.com, e-mail info@russianriverresort.com. DELUXE.

Catering primarily to gays and lesbians, **Highlands Resort** sits on three acres. Accommodations here come in many forms. Some are individual cabins with fireplaces, private baths, and kitchenettes; others are more standard motel-style rooms. The pool suite has both a queen- and king-sized bed, a TV, a refrigerator, and a view of the pool, where sunbathing is *au naturel*. A hot tub, a continental breakfast, and a guest lounge with a piano, TV, VCR, and books complete the amenities. There is also space for 20 tents. ~ 14000 Woodland Drive, Guerneville; 707-869-0333, fax 707-869-0370; www.highlandsresort.com, e-mail muffins@highlandsresort.com. BUDGET TO DELUXE.

Spread over five wooded acres along the Russian River, **The Willows** is a gay and lesbian guesthouse resort with spots for tent camping and barbecuing on the grounds. The main lodge has 13 bedrooms, most with private baths, and a spacious living room with a stone fireplace, library, and grand piano. The price tag includes breakfast, tea, and coffee served in the morning and afternoon, as well as use of the canoes. ~ 15905 River Road, Guerneville; 707-869-2824, 800-953-2828, fax 707-869-2764; www.willowsrussianriver.com. MODERATE TO DELUXE.

The **Fern Grove Cottages** sit at the foot of a mountain and are a five-minute walk from town. The 21 mustard-colored craftsmen cottages were built in 1926 and are furnished with antiques. Some have jacuzzi tubs, fireplaces, wood-burning stoves, or kitchens. Guests enjoy a buffet-style breakfast. ~ 16650 River Road, Guerneville; 707-869-8105, fax 707-869-1615; www.ferngrove.com, e-mail innkeepers@ferngrove.com. DELUXE TO ULTRA-DELUXE.

Monte Rio's historic **Village Inn**, a river resort dating back to 1908, was the location for Bing Crosby's 1942 film classic, Holiday Inn. Refurbished, this cozy country inn set amid redwood trees has a comfortable feel. You'll also find a good second-floor restaurant and bar with river views. All rooms come with private bath and begin in the moderate range; a deluxe price includes river views and a deck. They're trim little units: clean and carpeted. ~ 20822 River Boulevard, Monte Rio; 707-865-2304, 800-303-2303, fax 707-865-2332; www.villageinn-ca.com, e-mail village@sonic.net. MODERATE TO DELUXE.

Huckleberry Springs Country Inn sits on 56 acres in the hills above Monte Rio. The most unique of its four cottages, the round Cherry Barrel, formerly was a building for curing cherries. It's lined with cedar wood, and, like the others, has modern art on the walls, a CD player, a skylight over the bed, a refrigerator, and a wood stove. There's a separate massage cottage, and an outdoor jacuzzi and pool. Guests who stay four nights get 50 percent off on the fourth and fifth nights. Closed December through February. ~ P.O. Box 400, Monte Rio, CA 95462; 707-865-2683, 800-822-

AUTHOR FAVORITE

I love sleeping in one of the *casas* at the **Applewood Inn**, where I'm surrounded by giant redwoods that give the illusion of camping out in a treehouse. They're the prettiest accommodations in this neck of the redwoods, hidden on a hillside in tiny Pocket Canyon. Belden House, the original family home built in 1922, has the older, more staid rooms, while two two-story *casas* across the courtyard offer more space that in some cases includes a small balcony. With a pool, hot tub, and excellent restaurant (which uses produce from its own gardens), this estate, secluded among the redwoods, is the kind of place to which you can retreat and never leave the grounds until your visit is over. ~ 13555 Route 116, Guerneville; 707-869-9093, 800-555-8509, fax 707-869-9170; www.applewood inn.com, e-mail stay@applewoodinn.com. ULTRA-DELUXE.

2683; www.huckleberrysprings.com, e-mail mail@huckleberry springs.com. DELUXE TO ULTRA-DELUXE.

The **Farmhouse Inn** is a vision in yellow, with rose gardens and grapevines growing right out the front door. A stone's throw from the old farmhouse, eight attached cottages were totally overhauled in 2001 and decorated with distinction; one is done in peach-and-sage silk, another in whimsical prints, another in cream and green. All have personal saunas, fireplaces, jet tubs, and CDs and TV/VCRs. On-site amenities include a pool, restaurant, and spa. ~ 7871 River Road, Forestville; 707-887-3300, 800-464-6642, fax 707-887-3311; www.farmhouseinn.com, e-mail innkeep@farmhouseinn.com. DELUXE TO ULTRA-DELUXE.

DINING

While even remote Guerneville now offers more than a couple of places to get an espresso, none are better than the **Coffee Bazaar**. Located on Armstrong Woods Road a block off the main strip, this café's food and beverages are tasty and affordable. There is a wide range of coffee creations and a generous selection of pastries each morning. Lunch choices include soups, salads, sandwiches, quiches, and calzones; many vegetarian options are available. There is plenty of seating inside, but take a sidewalk table to people-watch. ~ 14045 Armstrong Woods Road, Guerneville; 707-869-9706; www.coffee-bazaar.com. BUDGET.

The restaurant at **Fifes** is an intimate dining room with a stone fireplace, pine walls, and an exposed-rafter ceiling. There's also a sundeck for warm-weather dining. Fifes has a sophisticated California-cuisine menu that changes seasonally. Dinner includes the likes of scampi, steak, chicken curry, and prosciutto tortellini. Dinner only. Weekend brunch. ~ 16467 River Road, Guerneville; 707-869-9500, 800-734-3371; www.fifes.com, e-mail info@fifes.com. MODERATE TO DELUXE.

The founder of **Cape Fear Café** hails from North Carolina, and the Southern influence cuts through the eclectic influences of Asian and Californian cuisine. Most notably, the place serves the unusual but tasty shrimp grits: a side of grits in a pool of broth and shrimp. Other entrées such as salmon crab cakes, and Carolina chicken are also delicious. The place is casual (as most restaurants around here are) and decorated with works by local artists. ~ 25191 Main Street, Duncans Mill; 707-865-9246.

The walls in the dining room at the **Farmhouse Inn** are the same yellow as the exterior, making a pretty backdrop for dining. (There's also patio seating.) The seasonal menu depends on what's growing in the chef's garden and other local sources, including a lamb farm down the road and a nearby dairy that makes goat cheese, and on the availability of fresh wild salmon. Desserts are housemade. No lunch. Closed Monday through Wednesday. ~ 7871 River Road, Forestville; 707-887-3300, 800-464-6642, fax 707-887-3311; www.farmhouseinn.com.

Just eight miles southeast of Guerneville in downtown Forestville, **Chez Marie** is a quaint lesbian-owned eatery. The cuisine (a mixture of country French and Cajun Creole) is always prepared and served by the owners themselves. Duck à l'orange, *poulet des nuits arabes* (chicken marinated in a ginger-honey-sage mixture, then baked in phyllo dough), and *ris de veau supreme* (veal sweetbreads in a nutmeg cream sauce) are among the recommended offerings. Closed Monday and Tuesday; call for winter hours. Dinner only. ~ 6675 Front Street, Forestville; 707-887-7503; www.chez marie.com, e-mail chezmarie@chezmarie.com. MODERATE TO DELUXE.

SHOPPING   An excellent bookstore and a true community resource, the **River Reader, Inc.** has a small but strong selection of books, magazines, cards, games, music, and gifts. Visitors will find plenty of choices for poolside reading in all categories including fiction, spirituality, and regional topics. There is also a good selection of gay reading material including books and magazines. ~ 16355 Main Street, Guerneville; 707-869-2240; e-mail rreader@sonic.net.

If you're traveling with your pets and they need a little attention, visit **River Wolf**, the "general store for pets." You can get gifts for Fluffy here, and there's self-service dog bathing. ~ 14016 Armstrong Woods Road, Guerneville; 707-869-3449.

On the main road to Forestville from Guerneville, you'll do your sweet tooth a favor by stopping at **Kozlowski Farms**. They make and sell all-fruit, sugar-free preserves, apple cider blends, and a variety of baked goods. Other condiments include mustards, salad dressings, salsas, and teriyaki sauces, among others. The farm also has a picnic area, a deli, a bakery, and an espresso bar. ~ 5566 Gravenstein Highway (Route 116), Forestville; 707-887-1587, 800-473-2767; www.kozlowskifarms.com, e-mail koz @kozlowskifarms.com.

NIGHTLIFE   **Fifes**, one of the area's first gay resorts, has a beautiful bar area that spreads through several pine-paneled rooms and extends out to a poolside deck. They offer deejays for dancing on Friday and Saturday night during the summer. ~ 16467 River Road, Guerneville; 707-869-9500; www.fifes.com, e-mail info@fifes.com.

Like Fifes, the **Russian River Resort** invites nonguests to enjoy the facilities and mingle with guests at the bar and around the pool. The bar isn't large but the crowd is friendly and if nothing is jumping in town, there will surely be some people hanging out at the "Triple R." ~ 16390 4th Street, Guerneville; 707-869-0691; www. russianriverresort.com, e-mail info@russianriverresort.com.

Russian River Eagle attracts a mixed crowd of gays and lesbians. A canoe and oars hang above the bar, and the rainbow flag adorns the walls, along with posters of nudes and old photos of

California Winetasting

The Greeks had it all wrong. They fervently believed that the gods drank nectar. Anyone who has explored the vineyards of California knows that wine, not sweet ambrosia, is the drink of the gods. It's also obvious that deciding on the finest wine is as simple as determining the true religion. This is not to say that a tour of the Wine Country is a pilgrimage, though it can have a lifetime effect on the drinking habits of mere mortals.

In order to find that ultimate wine, keep in mind a few principles. The best season to visit the vineyards is during the harvest in late September and early October. The scent of freshly fermenting wine fills the air and the vineyards are colored brilliant red and gold. Winter is the rainy season and a fallow period. It's also less crowded than the rest of the year and allows opportunities for more relaxed and personalized tours, particularly at small wineries. The growing season begins in March when buds appear on previously bare, gnarled vines. By early summer, the buds are miniature grape clusters that ripen during the torrid months of midsummer.

Once the grapes are picked in autumn, the activity shifts from the vineyard to the winery. The berries are crushed; white wines are then filtered or clarified and fermented in temperature-controlled tanks. Red wines are fermented, together with their skins and seeds, at higher temperatures (70° to 90°). Later the wines are racked, or stored, in wooden barrels to add flavor, and then bottled. Requiring two or three years to reach their potential, reds mature more slowly than whites.

There are two basic types of California wine: *varietals*, made primarily from a particular type of grape such as cabernet sauvignon or zinfandel, and lower-quality *generics*, wines generally blended from several different grapes and often named for a European wine region like Burgundy.

The true test, of course, is in the tasting. Unfortunately, winetasting also becomes a test of the taster's wine knowledge. Folks unversed in the liturgy and lexicon of wine sampling can feel mighty uncomfortable. Adding to their consternation are the region's self-styled wine connoisseurs.

Not to worry. It really only requires a sensitive nose, tongue, and eye to master the art of tasting. Just remember a few simple criteria. The look or appearance is important: wine should be clear and brilliant, not cloudy, in the glass. Consider the smell or *nose* of the vintage: this includes *aroma*, or scent of the grapes themselves, and *bouquet*, the smell from fermentation and aging. Of final importance is the taste. Let the wine wash around your mouth a moment and you'll be able to tell if it's sweet or dry, light-bodied (watery) or full-bodied, rough or mellow.

Guerneville. Tuesday is karaoke night, Wednesday country-and-western. A deejay spins tunes on weekends, and occasionally there's live entertainment. ~ 16225 Main Street, Guerneville; 707-869-4500; www.russianrivereagle.com, e-mail info@russianriver eagle.com.

Also in the middle of downtown is the **Rainbow Cattle Company**—a true gay bar. Offering nothing more than a couple of pool tables, three pinball machines, bar stools, and long benches, this nightspot doesn't provide much in the way of entertainment, but it's a congenial place for socializing and drinking. Happy hour is from 6 a.m. to 8 p.m. ~ 16220 Main Street, Guerneville; 707-869-0206.

Home of the Rat Bastard Pale Ale, **Stumptown Brewery** is a small seven-barrel brew pub. They have a deck overlooking the river and offers access to their two-acre beach complete with volleyball court. There's occasional live entertainment on weekend afternoons, and myriad meats from the smokehouse. ~ 15045 River Road, Guerneville; 707-869-0705; www.stumptown.com/brews, e-mail wwpints@stumptown.com.

PARKS

ARMSTRONG REDWOODS STATE RESERVE AND AUSTIN CREEK STATE RECREATION AREA These two parks, lying side by side, are a study in contrasts. Armstrong features a deep, cool forest of redwood trees measuring over 300 feet high and dating back 1400 years. Rare redwood orchids blossom here in spring and there is a 1200-seat amphitheater that was once used for summer concerts. Austin Creek offers sunny meadows and oak forests. Fox, bobcats, deer, wild pigs, and raccoons inhabit the region, and a nearby shallow bullfrog pond is stocked with sunfish and bass. A four-mile hike takes you to a few swimming holes that offer relief from the sun. There are 22 miles of trails threading the park. Facilities include picnic areas, restrooms, and a visitors center. Day-use fee, $4. ~ 17000 Armstrong Woods Road, Guerneville; 707-869-2015, fax 707-869-5629; e-mail armvs@mcn.com.

▲ Permitted in Austin Creek and Bullfrog Pond Campground, which has 24 campsites ($12 per night); there are also 3 hike-in campsites ($7 per night). For restrictions and permit information call 707-869-2015.

▼ ▼ ▼ ▼ ▼ ▼ ▼ ▼ ▼ ▼ ▼ ▼ ▼ ▼
Outdoor Adventures

WATER SPORTS

There are many opportunities for boating in the Wine Country, primarily along the Russian River. In addition, the lakes, rivers, and hot springs–fed swimming pools provide great places to swim during the sweltering Wine Country summers.

NAPA VALLEY **Lake Berryessa**, on the eastern edge of Napa County, attracts weekend crowds, who come to swim, boat, water-

ski, and fish. ~ Off Route 21, 25 miles northeast of Napa.
Getaway Adventures organizes day-long, weekend, and six-day
kayak trips. ~ 1117 Lincoln Avenue, Calistoga; 707-763-3040, 800-
499-2453; www.getawayadventures.com.

SONOMA VALLEY   The two swimming pools at **Morton's Warm
Springs** are kept at 85°F and are open year-round. There's a café
on the grounds. ~ 1651 Warm Springs Road, Kenwood; 707-833-
5511; www.sonoma springs.com. The historic Olympic-sized pool
at **Indian Springs Resort and Spa** is fed by the mineral water from
three natural geysers. Nuisance suits forced the resort to close the
pool to the general public in 1997, but guests can still swim in
what I consider one of the best swimming pools in Northern California, if not anywhere. ~ 1712 Lincoln Avenue; 707-942-4913,
fax 707-942-4919.

RUSSIAN RIVER   The Russian River is a Class I from April to
October, and during that time canoe and kayak rentals are plentiful. Several outfits offer everything from one-day excursions to
five-day expeditions. If you're ready for the adventure, contact
Burke's Canoe Trips. They offer a ten-mile day trip to Guerneville and outfit you with a canoe, lifejacket, and paddles before
sending you on a self-guided ride through the redwoods. Reservations required. ~ At the north end of Mirabel Road at River
Road, Forestville; 707-887-1222; www.burkescanoetrips.com.
W. C. "Bob" Trowbridge Canoe Trips has canoes and kayaks. ~
20 Healdsburg Avenue, Healdsburg; 707-433-7247.

The Russian River is also good for a swim. A popular spot is
Memorial Beach in the town of Healdsburg. Other favorites are
Monte Rio Beach in Monte Rio and **Johnson's Beach** in the town
of Guerneville.

All puns aside, no sport in the Wine Country has taken off like
hot-air ballooning. Every morning, colorful balloons dot the sky,
providing riders with a billowing crow's nest from which to view
the sweeping countryside.

**BALLOON
RIDES**

NAPA VALLEY   For a ride straight from the pages of *Around the
World in 80 Days*, call **Balloon Aviation of Napa Valley.** The

AUTHOR FAVORITE

The Russian River is *the* place to explore in a canoe or kayak. Most folks
rent for the day, canoe one way, and are picked up by the outfitter and
shuttled back. The scenery, ranging from rolling ranch land to dense redwood groves, is stunning. The experience of floating timelessly along
this magnificent river will long be remembered.

one-hour ride drifts over vineyards and wineries, and includes a continental breakfast before the ride and a full breakfast with sparkling wine afterwards. Run by the same people as Balloon Aviation, **Adventures Aloft** offers the same features but with a smaller group size. If you've ever considered renewing your wedding vows aloft, these are the folks for you. ~ 6525 Washington Street, Yountville; 707-944-4408, 800-944-4408; www.nvaloft.com, e-mail ballooning@nvaloft.com.

SONOMA VALLEY In business since 1974, **Air Flambuoyant Hot Air Balloon Excursions** take off from Healdsburg and soar above Sonoma Valley, offering views of Alexander and Dry Creek valleys, the Russian River, and more. Afterward, riders are treated to brunch. Capacity of four to eight people; they specialize in private flights. ~ P.O. Box 1416, Windsor, CA 95492; 707-838-8500, 800-456-4711; www.airflambuoyant.com, e-mail whmj@sonic.net.

GOLF

The Wine Country's excellent weather makes golf a popular pastime. This is one of the few places in the world where you can play golf amidst beautiful grape vines.

NAPA VALLEY Play a game on the oldest golf course west of the Mississippi. The **Aetna Springs Golf Course**, now public, opened in the 1890s as part of a hot-springs resort which had buildings designed by well-known architect Bernard Maybeck. ~ 1600 Aetna Springs Road, Aetna Springs; 707-965-2115, fax 707-965-1152.

HIDDEN ▶ The 18-hole **Napa City Municipal Golf Course** is surrounded by Kennedy Park and rents clubs and carts. ~ 2295 Streblow Drive, Napa; 707-255-4333. In Calistoga, the public nine-hole **Mount St. Helena Golf Course** has views of Mt. St. Helena. This mom-and-pop-style establishment has seven par 4s and two par 3s, and rents clubs and carts. Closed for five days over the Fourth of July weekend. ~ Napa County Fairgrounds, Calistoga; 707-942-9966, fax 707-942-5125.

SONOMA VALLEY Play a challenging game at the public 18-hole **Windsor Golf Course**. ~ 1340 19th Hole Drive, Windsor; 707-838-7888. **Oakmont Golf Club** features a par-72 championship course and a par-63 executive course. This tree-lined, semiprivate club rents clubs and carts. ~ 7025 Oakmont Drive; 707-539-0415, fax 707-539-0453.

RUSSIAN RIVER The Alister MacKenzie–designed **Northwood Golf Course** has nine holes. Clubs and carts are available for rent. ~ 19400 Route 116, Monte Rio; 707-865-1116. The **Sebastopol Golf Course** offers peaceful, countryside golfing. This public nine-hole course rents clubs. ~ 2881 Scott's Right of Way, Sebastopol; 707-823-9852.

RIDING STABLES

The hills and valleys of the Wine Country provide wonderful opportunities for equestrians. Slide into the saddle and saunter through the forest on a guided journey offered by **Sonoma Cattle Company & Napa Valley Trail Rides**. They operate horseback-riding trips out of Skyline Wilderness Park. These personally guided treks are intimate and offered only a few times a week. Closed in winter. ~ P.O. Box 5808, Napa, CA 94581; 707-255-2900; www.napasonomatrailrides.com.

One of the nicest ways to explore the region is to bike the back-roads, pedaling between wineries, historic sites, and health spas.

BIKING

NAPA VALLEY The **Silverado Trail** through Napa Valley is the best road to travel. It's less crowded than Route 29, the main thoroughfare, and is fairly level. Several steep mountain roads lead from Napa Valley across to Sonoma Valley through vineyards.

SONOMA VALLEY A bike path on the western edge of Sonoma passes numerous sightseeing spots.

At Sugarloaf Ridge, try the nine-mile **Bald Mountain Trail** to Gray Pine and then through the meadow loop. You'll pass open meadows sprinkled with oak trees.

RUSSIAN RIVER **River Road**, between Windsor and Guerneville, meanders past rolling hills and rural scenery, but carries a moderate amount of traffic.

Bike Rentals **Napa Valley Bike Tours** does rentals and outings. ~ 1988 Wise Drive, Napa; 800-707-2453; www.napavalleybike tours.com. For rentals (hybrids and tandems) and repairs, check out **St. Helena Cyclery**. Along with a sidebag, lock, and helmet, they'll throw in some suggested routes. Closed Monday in winter. ~ 1156 Main Street, St. Helena; 707-963-7736. **Getaway Adventures** rents bikes and operates day-long, weekend, and six-day cycling tours of the wineries. ~ 1117 Lincoln Avenue, Calistoga; 707-942-0332, 800-499-2453.

In the Sonoma area, head to **Norcal Bike Sport**. If you're in the mood to buy a bike, you can find a large selection of them here. They also do repairs. ~ 353 College Avenue, Santa Rosa; 707-528-3283. **Spoke Folk Cyclery** includes helmets, locks, and

THE VEHICLE LESS TRAVELED BY

To see the area by an organized bike tour, contact **Backroads**. They offer week-long trips throughout Northern California (and the rest of the world), giving you challenge options. The Wine Country excursion pedals through the towns of Healdsburg, Calistoga, Yountville, Sonoma, and Bodega Bay. Most meals and lodging are included, and bikes and helmets can be rented. ~ 801 Cedar Street, Berkeley; 510-527-1555, 800-462-2848; www.backroads.com, e-mail goactive@backroads.com.

backpacks with their rental bikes (hybrid, tandem, road). You can buy a bike and accessories, as well as have repairs done. ~ 201 Center Street, Healdsburg; 707-433-7171.

HIKING   For backpackers and daytrippers, state parks in the Wine Country offer a chance to escape the crowds while exploring forests, meadows, and mountain ridges. **Backroads** organizes five- to six-day hiking jaunts; most meals and lodging are included. ~ 801 Cedar Street, Berkeley; 510-527-1555, 800-462-2848; www.backroads.com, e-mail goactive@backroads.com. **Getaway Adventures** also operates weekend and six-day trips. ~ 1117 Lincoln Avenue, Calistoga; 707-942-0332, 800-499-2453; www.getawayadventures.com, e-mail info@getawayadventures.com.

All distances listed for hiking trails are one way unless otherwise noted.

NAPA VALLEY   For those interested in communing with nature amid splendid redwood groves, **Bothe–Napa Valley State Park** has ten miles of hiking trails.

History Trail (1.2 miles) is a fairly strenuous hike that begins at the picnic area and leads near an old pioneer cemetery, the site where an 1853 church once stood, and past Mill Creek en route to Old Bale Grist Mill.

The moderately difficult **Coyote Peak Trail** (1.5 miles) heads away from Ritchey Creek, then climbs up to 1170 feet elevation for scenic views of the Napa Valley.

Ritchey Canyon Trail (3.9 miles) starts off easy on an 1860 roadbed that wanders beside a stream and is shadowed by redwoods and firs. Farther along, the trail becomes moderate and leads past a small cascade that flows into a small canyon.

On a clear day, from the top of Bald Mountain Trail, you'll see as far as San Francisco, the Golden Gate Bridge and the Sierra Nevada.

A tranquil hike along Ritchey Creek can also be found on **Redwood Trail** (1 mile). In spring, redwood orchids and trilliums add to the beauty of this tree-shaded pathway.

The **South Fork Trail** (.9 mile) is a moderately strenuous hike that circles across the rim of Ritchey Creek and arrives at a vista point overlooking the canyon.

SONOMA VALLEY   The trails at **Sugarloaf Ridge State Park** (707-833-5712) provide opportunities to explore ridges and open fields. Every spring, wildflowers riot throughout the meadows. The park's most popular walk is along **Creekside Nature Trail** (.8 mile roundtrip). This self-guided stroll begins at the day-use picnic area and carries past stands of oak, alder, ash, maple, and Douglas fir. Watch for several species of lichen *and* poison oak! If you are up for a steep climb, try **Bald Mountain Trail** (2.7 miles), which leads to the top of the mountain. At an elevation of 2729 feet, the summit offers spectacular views of the Sonoma and Napa valleys. The climb begins at the day-use parking lot near the campground, which is already 1000 feet in elevation.

Once inhabited by Pomo and Wappo Indians, **Annadel State Park** is a mix of forest and meadow laced with 39 miles of hiking paths. ~ 707-539-3911. The **Warren B. Richardson Trail** (2.7 miles) wanders through a forest of Douglas fir en route to Lake Ilsanjo. Spring brings redwood orchid blossoms, adding a rare experience to an already splendid hike.

Marsh Trail (3.6 miles) climbs the side of Bennett Mountain and offers grand views of Lake Ilsanjo as well as nearby mountain ranges. For a trip to an old quarry site where cobblestones were once excavated, head down the aptly named **Cobblestone Trail** (2 miles).

Transportation

CAR

The quick, painless, and impersonal way to the Napa Valley is along **Route 80**. From San Francisco, the freeway buzzes northeast to Vallejo, where it connects with **Route 37** and then **Route 29**, the main road through Napa Valley.

An alternative course leads north from San Francisco along **Route 101**. From this freeway you can pick up Route 37, which skirts San Pablo Bay en route to its junction with Route 29.

For the most scenic drive, turn off Route 37 onto **Route 121**. This rural road, which also connects with Route 29, provides a preview of the Wine Country. The curving hills along the way are covered with vineyards, ranches, and sheep farms. Route 121 also connects with **Route 12**, which leads into the Sonoma Valley.

Route 101 runs like a spine through the Russian River region. Vineyards lie in clusters on either side of the highway. Another road, **Route 116**, leaves this freeway and heads to the gay resort area around Guerneville and on to the Pacific Ocean.

BUS

Greyhound Bus Lines has frequent service to the both Napa and Sonoma areas. It also stops in Healdsburg, Geyserville, and points farther north. ~ 800-231-2222; www.greyhound.com.

PUBLIC TRANSIT

There is no public transportation system in the Napa Valley. You'll have to take a Greyhound bus to Napa, then fend for yourself.

In Sonoma, **Sonoma County Transit** covers the area from Sonoma to Santa Rosa, stopping in Glen Ellen and Kenwood; it continues from Santa Rosa to Windsor, Healdsburg, and Geyserville. Sonoma County Transit also serves the area between Healdsburg and Guerneville. ~ 355 West Robles Avenue, Santa Rosa; 707-576-7433; www.sctransit.com.

FIVE

North Coast

When visitors to San Francisco seek a rural retreat, paradise is never far away. It sits just across the Golden Gate Bridge along a coastline stretching almost 400 miles to the Oregon border. Scenically, the North Coast compares in beauty with any spot on earth.

There are the folded hills and curving beaches of Point Reyes, Sonoma's craggy coast and old Russian fort, plus Mendocino with its vintage towns and spuming shoreline. To the far north lies Redwood Country, silent domain of the world's tallest living things.

Along the entire seaboard, civilization appears in the form of fishing villages and logging towns. Matter of fact, a lot of the prime real estate is saved forever from developers' heavy hands. California's Coastal Commission serves as a watchdog agency protecting the environment.

Much of the coast is also preserved in public playgrounds. Strung like pearls along the Pacific are a series of federal parks—Golden Gate National Recreation Area, Point Reyes National Seashore, and Redwood National Park.

The main highway through this idyllic domain is Route 1. A sinuous road, it snakes along the waterfront, providing the slowest, most scenic route. Paralleling this road and following an inland course is Route 101. This superhighway streaks from San Francisco to Oregon. It is fast, efficient, and at times boring. In the town of Leggett, Route 1 merges into Route 101, which continues north through Redwood Country.

Route 1 runs through San Francisco into Marin County, passing Sausalito before it branches from Route 101. While the eastern sector of Marin, along San Francisco Bay, is a suburban sprawl, the western region consists of rolling ranch land. Muir Woods is here, featuring 1000-year-old redwoods growing within commuting distance of the city. There is Mt. Tamalpais, a 2571-foot "sleeping maiden" whose recumbent figure has been the subject of numerous poems.

According to some historians, Sir Francis Drake, the Renaissance explorer, landed along the Marin shore in 1579, building a fort and claiming the wild region for dear old England. The Portuguese had first sighted the North Coast in 1543 when they espied Cape Mendocino. Back then Coastal Miwok Indians inhabited Marin, enjoying undisputed possession of the place until the Spanish settled the interior valleys during the early 1800s.

To the north, in Sonoma County, the Miwok shared their domain with the Pomo Indians. After 1812 they were also dividing it with the Russians. The Czar's forces arrived in California from their hunting grounds in Alaska and began taking large numbers of otters from local waters. The Russians built Fort Ross and soon proclaimed the region open only to their shipping. Of course, these imperial designs made the Spanish very nervous. The American response was to proclaim the Monroe Doctrine, warning foreign powers off the continent.

By the 1830s the Russians had decimated the otter population, reducing it from 150,000 to less than 100. They soon lost interest in the area and sold their fort and other holdings to John Sutter, whose name two decades hence would become synonymous with the Gold Rush.

Many of the early towns along the coast were born during the days of the '49ers. Established to serve as pack stations for the mines, the villages soon turned to lumbering and fishing. Today these are still important industries. About seven percent of California's land consists of commercial forest, much of it along the coastal redwood belt. Environmentalists continue to battle with the timber interests as they have since 1918 when the Save-the-Redwoods League was formed.

The natural heritage they protect includes trees that have been growing in California's forests since before the birth of Christ. Elk herds roam these groves, while trout and steelhead swim the nearby rivers. At one time the forest stretched in a 30-mile-wide swath for 450 miles along the coast. But in little more than a century the lumber industry has cut down over 90 percent of the original redwoods. Presently, 87,000 acres of ancient trees remain, over 90 percent of which are protected in parks. The fate of one unprotected grove, the Headwaters Forest in Humboldt County, which contains the world's largest privately owned stand of old-growth redwoods, has been an emotional issue, resulting in the arrest of scores of protesters during the past several years. The federal government is currently negotiating to purchase 7500 acres of old-growth and second-growth redwoods in the forest from the Pacific Lumber Company.

Another, much younger, cash crop is marijuana. During the '60s and early '70s, Mendocino and Humboldt counties became meccas for counterculturalists intent on getting "back to the land." They established communes, built original-design houses, and plunged into local politics. Some also became green-thumb outlaws, perfecting potent and exotic strains of sinsemilla for personal use and black-market sale. They made Northern California marijuana famous and helped boom the local economy. In 1996, California voters passed Proposition 215, an initiative legalizing the use of marijuana for medical purposes. Although 38 other states already had similar laws, and the herb had actually been available to cancer patients prior to the Reagan administration, marijuana was not currently available to patients anywhere because it was (and still is) prohibited by federal law. When bars where the recreational herb was actually dispensed for medical purposes began to open in San Francisco, the U.S. Drug Enforcement Administration was quick to close them down. The California statute reached the U.S. Supreme Court for a final determination of its legality and that of similar laws in other states across the country, in 2001, but the ruling, which deemed that state and federal laws need not conform with each other, only served to continue the dissonance.

The North Coast has become home to the country inn as well. All along the Pacific shoreline, bed and breakfasts serve travelers seeking informal and relaxing accommodations. Local artisans have also proliferated while small shops have opened to sell their crafts.

The great lure for travelers is still the environment. This coastal shelf, tucked between the Coast Ranges and the Pacific, has mountains and rivers, forests and ocean. Once the habitat of Yuki, Athabascan, Wiyot, Yurok, and Tolowa Indians, it remains an adventureland for imaginative travelers. Winters are damp, mornings and evenings sometimes foggy, but the weather overall is temperate. It's a place where you can fish for chinook and salmon, go crabbing, and scan the sea for migrating whales. Or simply ease back and enjoy scenery that never stops.

▼ ▼ ▼ ▼ ▼ ▼ ▼ ▼ ▼
Marin Coast

As frequently photographed as the Golden Gate Bridge, the coast of Marin County consists of rolling ranch lands and spectacular ocean bluffs. It extends from San Francisco Bay to Tomales Bay, offering groves of redwoods, meadows filled with wildflowers, and miles of winding country roads.

SIGHTS

An exploration of this vaunted region begins immediately upon crossing the **Golden Gate Bridge** on Route 101. There's a vista point at the far north end of the bridge affording marvelous views back toward San Francisco and out upon the Bay. (If some of your party want to start off with an exhilarating walk across the bridge, drop them at the vista point on the city side and pick them up here a little later.)

Once across the bridge, take the first exit, Alexander Avenue; then take an immediate left, following the sign back toward San Francisco. Next, bear right at the sign for Marin Headlands.

For what is literally a **bird's-eye view** of the Golden Gate Bridge, go three-tenths of a mile uphill and stop at the first turnout on the left. From here it's a short stroll out and up, past deserted battery fortifications, to a 360° view point sweeping the Pacific and Bay alike. You'll practically be standing on the bridge, with cars careening below and the tops of the twin towers vaulting above you.

Continue along Conzelman Road and you will pass a series of increasingly spectacular views of San Francisco. Ahead the road will fall away to reveal a tumbling peninsula, furrowed with hills and marked at its distant tip by a lighthouse. That is **Point Bonita**, a salient far outside the Golden Gate. After proceeding to the point, you can peer back through the interstices of the bridge to the city or turn away from civilization and gaze out on a wind-tousled sea.

Text continued on page 290.

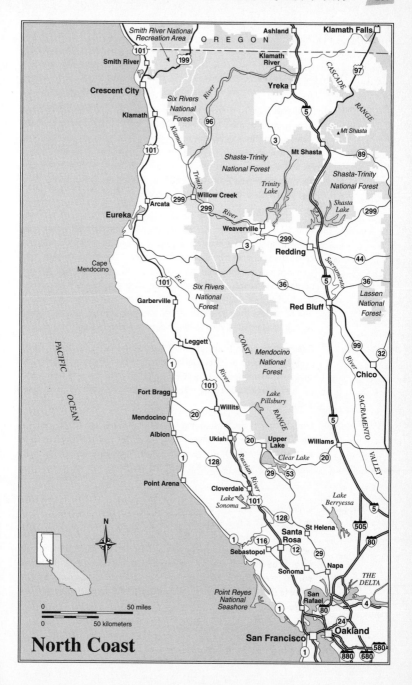

North Coast

Three-day Weekend

North Coast

DAY 1 From San Francisco, cross the Golden Gate Bridge. After the bridge, take Route 1 to the **Marin Headlands**, with increasingly spectacular views along the way. For an even more scenic and not much longer drive, turn north (left) at the crest of the Marin Peninsula onto Panoramic Highway, which takes you through deep forest in **Mount Tamalpais State Park** (page 303) before rejoining Route 1 at Stinson Beach on the peninsula's west coast.

It's a 150-mile drive along Route 1 to Mendocino, which may not sound like far (except on Saturdays, when heavy traffic can slow highway speeds to a crawl, giving passengers plenty of extra time to enjoy the scenery), but allow all day to get there. The two-lane highway is often winding and sometimes steep, and it passes through numerous 25-mph small towns. Most of these towns have restaurants where you can stop for lunch, or you may prefer to picnic in one of no less than 35 beautiful beaches and coastal parks along the way, all of them ideal for relaxing hours of hiking and enjoying nature.

Check into your hotel in the **Mendocino** area for two nights. Lodging tends to be pricey in Mendocino establishments such as the landmark **Stanford Inn by the Sea** (page 316) and less so in nearby Fort Bragg at places like the lovely little **Avalon House** (page 318).

Dine at one of the Mendocino coast's many fine restaurants, such as the **Café Beaujolais** (page 320) or the **MacCallum House Restaurant** (page 321), where you'll experience gourmet dining at its finest with a wide range of entrée prices.

DAY 2 Continue north on Route 1 for another 50 miles to join Route 101 at Leggett. This is Redwood Country, and although you could take Route 101 all the way to Redwood National Park, another 150 miles north, this would mean more driving than most people prefer to do on a three-day trip. Instead, why not take time to explore **Richardson Grove State Park** (page 328), drive the **Avenue of the Giants** (page 328), and hike in **Humboldt Redwoods State Park** (page 328)?

From Humboldt Redwoods State Park, loop west to Honeydew and south to Shelter Cove for a glimpse of California's **Lost Coast** (page 325). Protected from civilization by the towering sea cliffs and steep, treacherous slopes of the King Range, as well as by reclusive marijuana farmers, this is one of California's most thoroughly hidden corners.

Return to Route 101 at Garberville and retrace your route to your hotel in the Mendocino area for dinner and a well-earned night's rest.

DAY 3 Spend the morning exploring more of the beaches and headlands along the Mendocino coast. One good bet is **Russian Gulch State Park** (page 327) just north of Mendocino, where you'll find lofty vistas, a waterfall, and a sheltered beach. Another is **MacKerricher State Park** (page 327), one of the region's best, encompassing a cross-section of coastal environments that includes an ocean beach, sand dunes, high lookouts, a lush forest, and marshes that provide an edenlike habitat for an abundance of birds. South of Mendocino, the hiking trails of **Van Damme State Park** (page 326) take you from the beach through a pygmy pine forest to a verdant fern canyon and a pungent meadow of skunk cabbage.

In early or mid-afternoon, by taking Route 20 east from Noyo (between Mendocino and Fort Bragg) you can rejoin fast Route 101 at Willits and be back in San Francisco within four hours. This return route takes you through the heart of the Russian River wine country.

By the time you hit the freeway traffic waiting to cross the Golden Gate Bridge to the city, you may find that you've left your heart in Mendocino.

Nature writes in big letters around these parts. You're in the **Marin Headlands** section of **Golden Gate National Recreation Area**, an otherworldly realm of spuming surf, knife-edge cliffs, and chaparral-coated hillsides. From Point Bonita, follow Field Road, taking a left at the sign for the **Marin Headlands Visitors Center**, where you can pick up maps and information about the area, or make a camping reservation. ~ 415-331-1540, fax 415-331-6963; www.nps.gov/goga.

Walk along **Rodeo Beach**, a sandy corridor separating the Pacific from a tule-fringed lagoon alive with waterfowl. Miles of hiking trails lace up into the hills (see the "Hiking" section at the end of this chapter). At the far end of the beach you can trek along the cliffs and watch the sea batter the continent.

At the nearby **Marine Mammal Center** are seals, sea lions, and other marine mammals who have been found injured or orphaned in the ocean and brought here to recuperate. Center workers conduct rescue operations along 600 miles of coastline, returning the animals to the wild after they have gained sufficient strength. ~ From Alexander Avenue take Conzelman Road and follow the signs; 415-289-7325, fax 415-289-7333; www.marinemammal.org, e-mail members@tmmc.org.

Bunker Road leads through a long tunnel and out of the park. You've completed a lazy loop and will emerge near an entrance to Route 101. Follow this north a few miles, then pick up Route 1. You'll be on the northern leg of one of the most beautiful roads in America. With its wooded sanctuaries and ocean vistas, Route 1 is for many people synonymous with California.

> Over 45 percent of North America's bird species have been sighted at Point Reyes.

When Route 1 forks after several miles, turn right on Panoramic Highway toward Muir Woods and Mt. Tamalpais; the left fork leads to Stinson Beach, but that comes later. It's uphill and then down to **Muir Woods National Monument**, a 560-acre park inhabited by *Sequoia sempervirens*, the coast redwood. Though these forest giants have been known to live over two millennia, most enjoy a mere four-to-eight-century existence. In Muir Woods they reach 260 feet, while farther up the coast they top 360 feet (with roots that go no deeper than 10 feet!). ~ 415-388-2596, fax 415-389-6957; www.nps.gov/muwo.

Back up on Panoramic Highway, the road continues through Mt. Tamalpais State Park en route to **Mt. Tamalpais'** 2571-foot peak. Mt. Tam, as it is affectionately known, represents one of the Bay Area's most prominent landmarks. Rising dramatically between the Pacific and the Bay, the site was sacred to Indians. Even today some people see in the sloping silhouette of the mountain the sleeping figure of an Indian maiden. So tread lightly up the

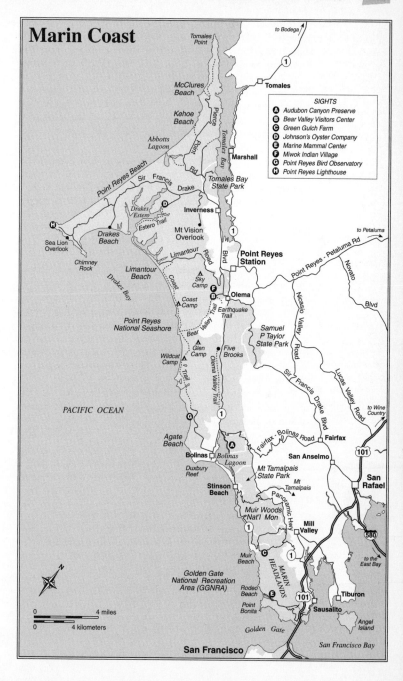

Marin Coast

SIGHTS

Ⓐ Audubon Canyon Preserve
Ⓑ Bear Valley Visitors Center
Ⓒ Green Gulch Farm
Ⓓ Johnson's Oyster Company
Ⓔ Marine Mammal Center
Ⓕ Miwok Indian Village
Ⓖ Point Reyes Bird Observatory
Ⓗ Point Reyes Lighthouse

to Bodega

Tomales Point

Tomales

McClures Beach

Kehoe Beach

Abbotts Lagoon

Pierce Point Rd

Tomales Bay

Marshall

Point Reyes Beach

Sir Francis Drake

Tomales Bay State Park

Drakes Estero

Estero Trail

Inverness

Sea Lion Overlook

Drakes Beach

Mt Vision Overlook

Point Reyes Station

Chimney Rock

Limantour Road

Blvd

to Petaluma

Point Reyes - Petaluma Rd

Novato

Blvd

Drakes Bay

Limantour Beach

Coast Trail

Sky Camp

Coast Camp

Point Reyes National Seashore

Olema

Earthquake Trail

Bear Valley Trail

Samuel P Taylor State Park

Nicasio Valley Road

Lucas Valley Road

to Wine Country

Bear Valley Trail

Glen Camp

Five Brooks

Olema Valley Trail

Sir Francis Drake Blvd

Wildcat Camp

Coast Trail

PACIFIC OCEAN

Agate Beach

Bolinas

Bolinas Lagoon

Duxbury Reef

Fairfax - Bolinas Road

Fairfax

San Anselmo

101

Stinson Beach

Mt Tamalpais State Park

Mt Tamalpais

San Rafael

Muir Woods Nat'l Mon

Panoramic Hwy

Mill Valley

580

Golden Gate National Recreation Area (GGNRA)

Muir Beach

MARIN HEADLANDS

to the East Bay

Rodeo Beach

Point Bonita

101

Tiburon

Sausalito

Angel Island

Golden Gate

San Francisco Bay

San Francisco

0   4 miles
0   4 kilometers

N

short trail that leads to the summit. You'll be rewarded with a full-circle view that sweeps across the Bay, along San Francisco's miniature skyline, and out across the Pacific. Contrary to rumor, on a clear day you cannot see forever, but you can see north toward Redwood Country and east to the Sierras.

Continue on Panoramic Highway as it corkscrews down to Stinson Beach. Better yet, take the longer but more spectacular route to Stinson: backtrack along Panoramic to where the fork originally separated from Route 1 (Shoreline Highway). Turn right and head north on Route 1.

Shortly, a turnoff will lead down to **Green Gulch Farm**, a 115-acre Zen retreat tucked serenely in a coastal valley. Residents here follow a rigorous program of work and meditation. There is a temple on the grounds and guests are welcome to tour the organic farm. Sunday is the best day to visit since a special meditation program and speaker is offered then. Closed January. ~ 1601 Shoreline Highway, near Muir Beach; 415-383-3134, fax 415-383-3128; www.sfzc.org, e-mail ggfzc@earthlink.net.

It's not far to **Muir Beach**, where you'll find a crescent-shaped cove with sandy beach. Though swimming is not advised, this is a good spot for picnicking. About a mile farther up the road, follow the "vista point" sign to **Muir Beach Overlook**. Here you can walk out along a narrow ridge for a view extending from Bolinas to the coastline south of San Francisco. It's an outstanding place for whale watching in winter. Matter of fact, this lookout is so well placed it became a site for World War II gun batteries, whose rusty skeletons remain.

You have entered a realm that might well be called the Land of a Thousand Views. Until the road descends to the flat expanse of Stinson Beach, it follows a tortuous route poised on the edge of oblivion. Below, precipitous cliffs dive to the sea, while above the road, rock walls edge upward toward Mt. Tamalpais. Around every curve another scene opens to view. Before you, Bolinas is

AUTHOR FAVORITE

Facts can't convey the feelings inspired by the towering coast redwoods at **Muir Woods National Monument**. You have to move among them, walk through Muir's Cathedral Grove where redwoods form a lofty arcade above the narrow trail. It's a forest primeval, casting the deepest, most restful shade imaginable. Muir Woods has the double-edged quality of being the redwood forest nearest to San Francisco. It can be horribly crowded. Since silence and solitude are vital to experiencing a redwood forest, plan to visit early or late in the day, and allow time to hike the more remote of the park's six miles of trails. For more information, see page 292.

a sweep of land, an arm extended seaward. Behind, the San Francisco skyline falls away into the past. If God built highways, they'd look like this.

Stinson Beach, that broad sandy hook at the bottom of the mountain, is one of Northern California's finest strands. Anglers haunt the rocks along one end in pursuit of blenny and lingcod, while birdwatchers are on the lookout for sandpipers, shearwaters, and swallows. Everyone else comes for sand, surf, and sun.

Birdwatchers also flock to **Audubon Canyon Preserve**, located astride Route 1 on Bolinas Lagoon. Open on weekends and holidays from mid-March to mid-July (or by appointment), the ranch includes four canyons, one of which is famed as a rookery for egrets and herons. From the hiking trails here you can see up to 90 bird species as well as gray fox, deer, and bobcats. ~ Route 1; 415-868-9244, fax 415-868-1699; www.egret.org, e-mail acr@egret.org.

Bolinas Lagoon is also a bird sanctuary. Great egrets, ducks, and great blue herons make this one of their migratory stops. A colony of harbor seals lives here permanently and is joined in summer by migrating seals from San Francisco.

To reach the next point of interest you'll have to pay close attention. That's because you're approaching **Bolinas**. To get there from Route 1, watch for the crossroad at the foot of the lagoon; go left, then quickly left again and follow the road along the other side of the lagoon; take another left at the end of the road.

There should be signs to direct you. But there probably won't be. Not because the state neglected them or highway workers forgot to put them up. It seems that local residents subscribe to the self-serving philosophy that since Bolinas is beautiful and they got there first, they should keep everyone else out. They tear down road signs and discourage visitors. The rest of Northern California is fair game, they seem to say, as long as Bolinas is left as some sort of human preserve.

The place they are attempting to hide is a delightful little town that rises from an S-shaped beach to form a lofty mesa. There are country roads along the bluff that overhangs the beach.

Whether you stroll the beach or hike the highlands, you'll discover in the houses here a wild architectural array. There are domes, glass boxes, curved-roof creations, huts, ranch houses, and stately brown-shingle designs.

Bolinas, abutting on the Point Reyes National Seashore, is also a gateway to the natural world. Follow Mesa Road for several miles outside town and you'll encounter the **Point Reyes Bird Observatory**, where scientists at a research station study a bird population of over 200 species.

The award-winning **Bolinas Museum** features exhibits on the history of the Marin coast, including displays of Miwok Indian artifacts as well as Living Artist Project shows presenting the work of Marin County painters and sculptors. The normally shy little community welcomes sightseers from mid-April to early June for the museum's biggest annual event, a series of guided tours of the public and private gardens of Bolinas. Open Friday through Sunday and by appointment. Admission. ~ 48 Wharf Road, Bolinas; 415-868-2006, fax 415-868-0607; www.bolinasmuseum.org, e-mail info@bolinasmuseum.org.

HIDDEN ►   On the way back to town take a right on Overlook Drive, then a right on Elm Road; follow it to the parking lot at road's end. Hiking trails lead down a sharp 160-foot cliff to **Duxbury Reef**, a mile-long shale reef. Tidepool-watching is great sport here at low tide: starfish, periwinkles, abalone, limpets, and a host of other clinging creatures inhabit the marine preserve. Back in 1971 a huge oil spill endangered this spectacular area, but volunteers from all around the state worked day and night to save the reef and its tenacious inhabitants. Just north of this rocky preserve is **Agate Beach**, an ideal spot to find agates, driftwood, and glass balls (however, no collecting is permitted).

Back on Route 1, continue north through Olema Valley, a peaceful region of horse ranches fringed by forest. Peaceful, that is, until you realize that the **San Andreas Fault**, the global suture that shook San Francisco back in 1906, cuts through the valley. As a matter of fact, the highway you are traveling parallels the fault line. During the great quake, houses collapsed, trees were uprooted, and fences decided to mark new boundaries.

As you turn off Route 1 onto Sir Francis Drake Boulevard headed for the Point Reyes Peninsula, you'll be passing from the North American Plate, one of the six tectonic plates on which the entire earth's surface rides, to the Pacific Plate, which extends across the ocean. It is the pressure formed by the collision of these two great land masses that causes earthquakes. No sign will notify you as you cross this troubled geologic border, no guide will direct you along the rift zone. If you're like the people who live hereabouts, within 15 minutes of crossing over you'll have forgotten the fault exists. Especially when you see what is served on the Pacific Plate.

POINT REYES NATIONAL SEASHORE   Point Reyes National Seashore, with 88 miles of shoreline, is without doubt one of the finest seaside parks on any of the world's six plates. It is a realm of sand dunes and endless beaches, Scottish moors and grassy hillsides, salt marshes and pine forests. Bobcats, mountain lions, fox, and elk inhabit its wrinkled terrain, while harbor seals and gray whales cruise its ragged shoreline. More than 45 percent of North American bird species have been spotted here. The seashore also supports dairies and cattle ranches. In 1995, fire ripped through Point Reyes, burning 12,000 acres. However, all areas have since been cleared and await your exploration. All trails listed here and in the "Hiking" section are open and additional trails lead through the charred area, giving you a close-up look at the awesome healing power of nature.

The first stage in exploring this multifeatured preserve involves a stop at the **Bear Valley Visitors Center**. Here you can obtain maps, information, and camping permits. ~ Bear Valley Road; 415-464-5100, fax 415-663-8132; www.nps.gov/pore. A short hike from the center will lead you to a **Miwok Indian Village**, where the round-domed shelters and other structures of the area's early inhabitants have been re-created. There is also an earthquake trail where you can see evidence of the San Andreas fault.

> A brass plate, purportedly left by Drake, was discovered near San Francisco Bay in 1936; later it was believed that the plate had been first located near Drakes Bay and then moved; finally the plate was deemed a counterfeit.

Most points of interest lie along Sir Francis Drake Boulevard, which rolls for miles through the park. It will carry you past the tiny town of **Inverness**, with its country inns and ridgetop houses, then out along **Tomales Bay**. Like the Golden Gate, this finger-shaped inlet is a drowned river valley.

Deeper in the park, a side road twists up to Mount Vision Overlook, where vista points sweep the peninsula. At **Johnson's Oyster Company**, along another side road, workers harvest the rich beds of an estuary. The farm is a conglomeration of slapdash buildings, house trailers, and rusty machines. The shoreline is heaped over with oyster shells and the air is filled with pungent odors. Raw oysters are for sale. Even if you don't care for them, you might want to visit anyway. After all, when was the last time you saw an oyster farm? ~ 17171 Sir Francis Drake Boulevard, Inverness; 415-669-1149, fax 415-669-1262.

The main road continues over folded hills that fall away to reveal sharp bluffs. Farm animals graze through fields smothered in wildflowers. There are ocean vistas stretching along miles of headland.

On **Drakes Beach** you can picnic and beachcomb. Or gaze at the surrounding cliffs and wonder whether they truly resemble the White Cliffs of Dover. In that question resides a story told by one school of historians and vehemently denied by others. It seems that in 1579 the English explorer Sir Francis Drake anchored somewhere along the Northern California coast. But where? Some claim he cast anchor right here in Drakes Bay, others say Bolinas Lagoon, even San Francisco Bay. Find out more at the **Ken Patrick Visitor Center**, which also features aquarium and interactive computer displays. Saturday and Sunday only.

Point Reyes Beach (also known as "North Beach" and "South Beach"), a windy ten-mile-long strip, is an ideal place for beachcombers and whale watchers. From there, it's not far to the end of Point Reyes' hammerhead peninsula. At one tip is **Chimney Rock**, a sea stack formed when the ocean eroded away the intervening land mass, leaving this islet just offshore. On the way to Chimney Rock you'll pass an **overlook** that's ideal for watching sea lions; then from Chimney Rock, if the day is clear, you'll see all the way to San Francisco.

At the other tip is **Point Reyes Lighthouse**, an 1870s beacon located at the foggiest point on the entire Pacific coast. The treacherous waters offshore have witnessed numerous shipwrecks, the first occurring way back in 1595. The original lighthouse, constructed to prevent these calamities, incorporated over a thousand pieces of crystal in its intricate lens. A modern beacon eventually replaced this multifaceted instrument, although the antique is still on view. The old lighthouse and an accompanying information center are still open to the public Thursday through Monday, weather permitting (lighthouse is inaccessible during winds exceeding 40 m.p.h.). ~ 415-669-1534.

Walking the steps between the Point Reyes Lighthouse and its observation platform is equivalent to ascending a 30-story building.

HIDDEN ►

From Olema you can continue north on Route 1 or follow a looping 25-mile detour through the region's **pastoral interior**. On the latter, Sir Francis Drake Boulevard leads east past bald-domed hills and isolated farms. Livestock graze at the roadside while overhead hawks work the range. Grassland gives way to dense forest as you enter the realms of **Samuel P. Taylor State Park**. Then the road opens again to reveal a succession of tiny, woodframe towns.

At San Geronimo, turn left on Nicasio Valley Road. This carries you farther into the pastoral region of west Marin, which varies so dramatically from the county's eastside suburban enclaves. Indeed, the inland valleys are reminiscent more of the Old West than the busy Bay Area. At the Nicasio Reservoir, turn left onto Point Reyes–Petaluma Road and follow it to Sir Francis Drake Boulevard, closing the circle of this rural tour.

From Olema, Route 1 continues north along Tomales Bay, the lovely fjord-shaped inlet. Salt marshes stretch along one side of the road; on the other are rumpled hills tufted with grass. The waterfront village of **Marshall** consists of fishing boats moored offshore and woodframe houses anchored firmly onshore. Then the road turns inland to **Tomales**, another falsefront town with clapboard church and country homes. It continues past paint-peeled barns and open pastureland before turning seaward at Bodega Bay.

LODGING

HIDDEN ►

Green Gulch Farm, a Zen meditation center and organic farm, offers a guest residence program. Located on a 115-acre spread in a lovely valley, it's a restful and enchanting stop. Enroll in the Guest Practice Retreat Program, available between Sunday and Thursday, stay three days or longer, and the price drops. The schedule involves meditation, chanting, and bowing as well as morning chores and includes all meals (vegetarian, of course). Or you can simply rent a room by the night (at deluxe prices including meals). With nearby hiking trails and beaches, it's a unique place. Closed three weeks in January; call ahead ~ 1601 Shoreline Highway near Muir Beach; 415-383-3134, fax 415-383-3128; www.sfzc. org, e-mail ggfdirector@sfzc.org. MODERATE TO DELUXE.

Most folks grumble when the fog sits heavy along the coast. At **The Pelican Inn**, guests consider fog part of the ambience. Damp air and chill winds add a final element to the Old English atmosphere at this seven-chamber bed and breakfast. Set in a Tudor-style building near Muir Beach, The Pelican Inn re-creates 16th-century England. There's a pub downstairs with a dart board on one wall and a fox-hunting scene facing on another. The dining room serves country fare like meat pies, prime rib, and bangers. Upstairs the period-print bedrooms contain time-honored antique furnishings including canopied beds. Highly recommended; reserve well in advance. ~ Route 1, Muir Beach; 415-383-6000, fax 415-383-3424; www.pelicaninn.com, e-mail innkeeper@pelicaninn.com. DELUXE.

Smiley's Schooner Saloon and Hotel, located in the rustic town of Bolinas, is a three-minute walk to the beach. Accommodations are clean and nicely refurbished. The rooms are done in a rose color with antiques and have no radio, TV, phones, or other new-fangled inventions. Six guest rooms are in the bungalows behind the saloon while two are above the bar. Light sleepers be fore-warned: The bar downstairs is a favorite haunt of late-night revelers. ~ 41 Wharf Road, Bolinas; 415-868-1311, fax 415-868-0502; www.coastalpost.com/smileys, e-mail editor@coastalpost. com. MODERATE.

There's also **Grand Hotel**, a tiny business where the two rooms share a bath and a kitchen. The proprietor also serves as a referral service for other places in town, so check with him about local accommodations. ~ 15 Brighton Avenue, Bolinas; 415-868-1757. BUDGET.

Within Point Reyes National Seashore, the **Hostelling International—Point Reyes Hostel** provides low-rent lodging. In addition to 44 dorm-style accommodations, the hostel has a patio, kitchen and a living room with a wood-burning stove. Perfect for explorers, it is situated two miles from the ocean near several hiking trails. The hostel is closed from 10 a.m. to 4:30 p.m. Reservations recommended. ~ Point Reyes National Seashore; Box 247, Point Reyes Station, CA 94956; phone/fax 415-663-8811, 800-909-4776 ext. 168; www.norcalhostels.org, e-mail marinhdl@ norcalhostels.org. MODERATE.

The **Blackthorne Inn** is an architectural extravaganza set in a forest of oak, bay trees, and Douglas fir. The four-level house is expressive of the flamboyant "woodbutcher's art" building style popular in the 1970s. Using recycled materials and heavy doses of imagination, the builders created a maze of skylights, bay windows, and French doors, capped by an octagonal tower. A spiral staircase corkscrews up through this multitiered affair to the top deck, where an outdoor hot tub overlooks the canyon. There are four bedrooms, all with private baths. Each room has been personalized; the most outstanding is the "Eagle's Nest," occupying the glass-encircled octagon at the very top of this Aquarian wedding cake. ~ 266 Vallejo Avenue, Inverness Park; 415-663-8621, fax 415-663-8635; www.blackthorneinn.com, e-mail susan@blackthorneinn.com. ULTRA-DELUXE.

Nearby in Inverness there's **Motel Inverness**, commanding a location along Tomales Bay that would be the envy of many well-heeled hostelries. Unfortunately, the architect who designed it faced the rooms toward the road, not the water. You can, how-ever, enjoy views of the bay in the motel's common room, which features a billiards table, stereo, and pinball machine. The guest rooms come equipped with color televisions and cable. The entire motel is a nonsmoking establishment. ~ 12718 Sir Francis Drake Boulevard, Inverness; 415-669-1081, 888-669-6909; www.motel inverness.com, e-mail reservations@motelinverness.com. DELUXE TO ULTRA-DELUXE.

Situated on 15 quiet country acres, the **Inverness Valley Inn and Tennis Ranch** offers an affordable retreat in the increasingly upscale Point Reyes area. Scattered over the well-groomed grounds are three contemporary A-frame buildings, each hous-ing large, light, and airy rooms complete with kitchenettes, bar-becues, and private patios. A pool, hot tub, and, of course, ten-nis courts round out the amenities. Perfect for families and active couples, the inn is a stone's throw away from secluded coves,

AUTHOR FAVORITE

Sometimes location is everything. That—plus a lively young clientele—is why I recommend the **Marin Headlands Hostel**. Also known as Golden Gate Hostel, the lodging is ideally located in the spectacular Marin Headlands section of the Golden Gate National Recreation Area. Housed in two his-toric woodframe buildings, this hostel's 104 dormitory-style accommo-dations go for low prices. There are kitchen and laundry facilities available, a game room, a living room, and a few private rooms. Like most hostels it is closed during the day; you're permitted access only after 3:30 p.m. and in the afternoon. Reservations are advised. ~ Fort Barry, Building 941; 415-331-2777, 800-909-4776 ext. 168, fax 415-331-3568; www.nor-calhostels.org. BUDGET.

spectacular hiking trails, and excellent kayaking. And if you forgot your tennis rackets, the friendly owners will be glad to provide them. ~ 13275 Sir Francis Drake Boulevard, Inverness; 415-669-7250, 800-416-0405; www.invernessvalleyinn.com, e-mail info@invernessvalleyinn.com. MODERATE TO DELUXE.

Another favorite bed and breakfast lies along the flagstone path at **Ten Inverness Way**. The place is filled with pleasant surprises, like fruit trees and flowers in the yard, a hot tub, a library, and a warm living room with stone fireplace. The five bedrooms are small but cozy, carpeted wall-to-wall, and imaginatively decorated with hand-fashioned quilts; all have private baths. It's a short stroll from the house to the shops and restaurants of Inverness. Another special treat: tea and fresh-baked cookies are served in the afternoon, and wine and cheese in the evening. ~ 10 Inverness Way, Inverness; 415-669-1648, fax 415-669-7403; www.teninvernessway.com, e-mail inn@teninvernessway.com. DELUXE TO ULTRA-DELUXE.

As country living goes, it's darn near impossible to find a place as pretty and restful as Point Reyes. People with wander in their hearts and wonder in their minds have been drawn here for years. Not surprisingly, country inns sprang up to cater to star-struck explorers and imaginative travelers. A good source for information on these local hostelries is **Point Reyes Lodging**, which offers 24-hour information on a dozen or so inns and cottages in coastal Marin. ~ 415-663-1872, 800-539-1872; www.ptreyes.com.

From the Marin Headlands region, the nearest restaurants are in the bayside town of Sausalito. Then, progressing north, you'll find dining spots scattered throughout the towns and villages along the coast.

DINING

Stinson Beach sports several restaurants; my favorite is the **Sand Dollar Restaurant**, with facilities for dining indoors or on the patio. At lunch this informal eatery serves hamburgers and sandwiches. At dinner there are fried prawns, scallops, fresh fish dishes, and pasta; they also serve meat dishes like chicken parmesan and steak. With a fireplace and random artwork on the wall, it is a cozy local gathering point. ~ 3458 Route 1, Stinson Beach; 415-868-0434, fax 415-868-8988. MODERATE.

The Station House Café comes highly recommended by several local residents. Maybe it's the artwork along the walls or the garden patio. Regardless, it's really the food that draws folks from the surrounding countryside. The dinner menu includes fresh oysters, plus chicken, steak, and fish dishes. There are also daily chef's specials, such as salmon with a dill-smoked salmon sauce. Dinners are served with soup or salad, and accompanied by a basket of cornbread and piping hot popovers. The Station House also features a complete breakfast menu; at lunch time there are

◀ HIDDEN

light crêpe, pasta, and seafood dishes, plus sandwiches and salads. Closed Wednesday. ~ 11180 Main Street, Point Reyes Station; 415-663-1515; www.stationhousecafe.com, e-mail stnhouse@svn.net. MODERATE.

Priscilla's Pizzeria & Cafe, a woodframe café in the center of tiny Inverness, serves delicious pizza and pasta as well as soups and salads. The place has a touch of city style in a country setting; there are overhead fans and an espresso machine. Closed Tuesday. ~ 12781 Sir Francis Drake Boulevard, Inverness; 415-669-1244. BUDGET TO MODERATE.

Manka's Inverness Lodge is set in a 1917 hunting lodge with an open fireplace and American arts and crafts. This white-tablecloth dining room prepares American regional cuisine. Diners can feast on a prix-fixe menu of poached salmon, grilled venison, boar, or duck, prepared on a wood fire. Dinner only. Closed weekdays from mid-February through March; closed January to mid-February. ~ 30 Callendar Way, Inverness; 415-669-1034, fax 415-669-1598; www.mankas.com, e-mail mankas@best.com. ULTRA-DELUXE.

Among the area's most unusual dining spots is **Vladimir's Czechoslovakian Restaurant**, operated at this location by a Czech refugee family for more than 40 years. Though, admittedly, sweet stewed red cabbage is an acquired taste, the menu also includes chicken paprikash, goulash, klobasa sausage, and roast duckling. The Old-World atmosphere—walls and ceiling painted deep red, accented with dark wood and decorated with hunting trophies and family heirlooms, with maudlin Czechoslovakian ballads emanating from the sound system—is at least as memorable as the food. Closed Monday. Hours vary so call before you go. ~ Inverness; 415-669-1021. DELUXE.

SHOPPING   Past Sausalito, the shopping scene along the North Coast is concentrated in a few towns. There are small shops scattered about in rural areas, but the best selection of arts and crafts is located around Point Reyes.

During the '60s and '70s many talented people, caught up in the "back to the land" movement, migrated to the state's northern counties. Here they developed their skills and further refined their art. As a result, crafts like pottery, woodworking, weaving, stained-glass manufacturing, jewelry, and fashion designing have flourished.

If the weather's nice take a stroll through the **Claudia Chapline Gallery and Sculpture Garden**. Featuring a variety of mixed media and three roomy skylight galleries, it's a great place to pick up an interesting work of art. Closed Tuesday through Thursday. ~ 3445 Shoreline Highway, Stinson Beach; 415-868-2308; www.cchapline.com.

There are small shops scattered about all along the coast, but the best selection of arts and crafts is located around Point Reyes.

Stinson Beach Books may be located in a small town, but it handles a large variety of books. Compressed within the confines of the place is an array of travel books, field guides, bestsellers, novels, how-to handbooks, etc. It's a great place to stop before that long, languorous day at the beach. Closed Tuesday from January through May. ~ 3455 Shoreline Highway, Stinson Beach; 415-868-0700.

For an idea of the local art scene, you should certainly stop by Bolinas Gallery. Judy Molyneux has stocked it with an impressive selection of her work, as well as other local, national, and international artists. Open weekends and by appointment. ~ 52 Wharf Road, Bolinas; 415-868-0782.

Gallery Route One spotlights sculptures, photographs, and paintings by contemporary regional artists. There's also mixed-media environmental art exhibits. Closed Tuesday. ~ 11101 Route 1, Point Reyes Station; 415-663-1347.

Shaker Shops West is a marvelous store specializing in reproductions of Shaker crafts, particularly furniture. In addition to rag rugs, candlesticks, and woven baskets, there are beautifully handcrafted boxes. The Early American household items range from cross-stitch needlepoint to tinware. Touring the store is like visiting a mini-museum dedicated to this rare American community. Open Friday and Saturday, and by appointment. ~ 5 Inverness Way, Inverness; 415-669-7256, 800-474-2537; www.shakershops.com, e-mail shaker@shakershops.com.

When the sun goes down in Bolinas, you are left with several options. Sleep, read, curl up with a loved one, fade into unrelieved boredom, or head for Smiley's Schooner Saloon. Since local folks often follow the latter course, you're liable to find them parka-to-parka along the bar. They come to shoot pool, listen to weekend live music, and admire the lavish wood-panel bar. Smiley's, after all, is the only show in town—and the longest continuously operating saloon in California (since 1851). Occasional cover. ~ 41 Wharf Road, Bolinas; 415-868-1311.

NIGHTLIFE

Local folks in Point Reyes Station ease up to a similar wooden bar at Old Western Saloon practically every night of the week. But on Friday and Saturday, when the place features live rock, blues, country—you name it—and dancing 'til the wee hours, the biggest crowds of all arrive. Occasional cover. ~ 11201 Route 1, Point Reyes Station; 415-663-1661.

KIRBY COVE 🚶 🚲 🐎 ⚓ 🦪 This pocket beach, located at the end of a one-mile trail, nestles in the shadow of the Golden Gate Bridge. The views from beachside are unreal: gaze up at the bridge's steel lacework or out across the gaping mouth of the Gate. When the fog's away, it's a sunbather's paradise; regardless of the

BEACHES & PARKS

weather, this cove is favored by those who like to fish. Facilities include a picnic area and toilets. ~ The beach is located in the Marin Headlands section of the Golden Gate National Recreation Area. Take the first exit, Alexander Avenue, after crossing the Golden Gate Bridge. Then take an immediate left, following the sign back toward San Francisco. Next, bear right at the sign for Marin Headlands. Follow Conzelman Road three-tenths of a mile to a turnout where a sign will mark the trailhead; 415-331-1540, fax 415-331-6963; www.nps.gov/goga.

▲ There are four campsites for tents only; $25 per night. Reservations are required: 800-365-2267. Closed November through March.

HIDDEN ▶

UPPER FISHERMAN'S BEACH 🚲 🐎 �-- This is a long, narrow corridor of sand tucked under the Marin Headlands. With steep hills behind and a grand view of the Golden Gate in front, it's a perfect place for naturists and nature lovers alike. It is a popular beach for nudists, although not officially recognized as such. It cannot be found on maps or atlases, but local folks and savvy travelers know it well (some call it "Black Sands"). There are no facilities here. ~ Located in the Marin Headlands section of the Golden Gate National Recreation Area. Follow the directions to Kirby Cove trailhead (see listing above). Continue on Conzelman Road for two and a third miles. Shortly after passing the steep downhill section of this road, you'll see a parking lot on the left with a trailhead. Follow the trail to the beach.

RODEO BEACH 🚶 🚲 🐎 🎿 💺 🛶 A broad sandy beach, this place is magnificent not only for the surrounding hillsides and nearby cliffs, but also for the quiescent lagoon at its back. It boasts a miniature island offshore, named appropriately for the creatures that turned its surface white—Bird Rock. Given its proximity to San Francisco, Rodeo Beach is a favorite among the natives. The beach has restrooms, cold-water showers, and a picnic area. Pets on leashes are allowed. Beware of the strong undercurrents and rip tides. ~ Located in the Marin Headlands section of the Golden Gate National Recreation Area. After crossing Golden Gate Bridge on Route 101, take the first exit, Alexander Avenue. Then take an immediate left, following the sign back toward San Francisco. Next, bear right at the sign for Marin Headlands. Follow this road to Rodeo Beach; 415-331-1540, fax 415-331-6963; www.nps.gov/goga.

▲ Though not permitted on the beach, camping is available at three campgrounds in the area. They are hike-in campgrounds, ranging from 100 yards to 3 miles. There are five sites at Haypress, three sites at Hawkcamp, and three sites at Bicentennial. No water, no fires, and no pets. These campgrounds are for tents only, all are free, but reservations and permits are required. Call the information number above for more details.

MUIR WOODS NATIONAL MONUMENT 🏃 If it weren't for the crowds, this redwood preserve would rank little short of majestic. Designated a national treasure by President Theodore Roosevelt in 1908, it features stately groves of tall timber. There are six miles of hiking trails, a snack bar, a gift shop, and restrooms. Day-use fee, $3. ~ Off Route 1 on Panoramic Highway, about 17 miles north of San Francisco; 415-388-2596, fax 415-389-6957; www.nps.gov/muwo.

> Salmon run the creeks at Muir Woods from November to April. The best viewing times are a few days after a heavy storm.

MT. TAMALPAIS STATE PARK 🏃 🚵 🐎 Spectacularly situated between Mt. Tamalpais and the ocean, this 6300-acre park offers everything from mountaintop views to a rocky coastline. More than 50 miles of hiking trails wind past stands of cypress, Douglas fir, Monterey pine, and California laurel. Wildlife abounds. The countryside draws nature lovers and sightseers alike. The park's facilities include picnic areas, restrooms, a refreshment stand, and a visitors center (open weekends only); ranger stations are located in various parts of the park. Every year since 1913 a mountain play has been staged in the amphitheater. Parking fee, $4. ~ Follow Route 1 north through Mill Valley; turn right on Panoramic Highway, which runs along the park border; 415-388-2070, fax 415-388-2968.

▲ There are 16 tent sites at Pontoll Park Headquarters (415-388-2070); facilities in this well-shaded spot include picnic areas, restrooms, and running water; $12 per night. There's also camping at Frank Valley Horsecamp (800-444-7275), located near Muir Beach in the southwest end of the park. You'll find picnic tables, pit toilets, and running water. Reservations are required and can be obtained at park headquarters. For information on Steep Ravine Environmental Camp see the listing below.

MUIR BEACH 🏃 🚵 🐎 🏊 🎣 Because of its proximity to San Francisco, this spot is a favorite among local people. Located at the foot of a coastal valley, Muir forms a semicircular cove. There's a sandy beach (with a rough surf) and ample opportunity for picnicking. Other than picnic tables the facilities are limited to toilets. ~ Route 1, about 16 miles north of San Francisco; 415-388-2596, fax 415-389-6957; www.nps.gov/muwo.

STEEP RAVINE ENVIRONMENTAL CAMP Set on a shelf above the ocean, this outstanding site is bounded on the other side by sharp slopes. Contained within Mt. Tamalpais State Park, it features a small beach and dramatic sea vista. This is a good place for nature study. ~ Located along a paved road off Route 1, about one mile south of Stinson Beach. Turn at the sign; 415-388-2070, fax 415-388-2968.

▲ There are six walk-in tent sites ($7 per night) and ten rustic cabins ($27 per night). Reservations are required seven months in advance for cabins; call 800-444-7275.

HIDDEN ▶ **RED ROCK BEACH** One of the area's most popular nude beaches, this pocket beach is wall-to-wall with local folks on sunny weekends. Well protected along its flank by steep hillsides, Red Rock is an ideal sunbathers' retreat. There are no facilities here. ~ Part of Mt. Tamalpais State Park, Red Rock is located off Route 1 about one mile south of Stinson Beach. Watch for a large (often crowded) parking area on the seaward side of the highway. Follow the steep trail down to the beach.

STINSON BEACH PARK One of Northern California's finest beaches, this broad, sandy corridor curves for three miles. Backdropped by rolling hills, Stinson also borders beautiful Bolinas Lagoon. Besides being a sunbather's haven, it's a great place for beachcombers and birdwatchers. To escape the crowds congregating here weekends, stroll up to the north end of the beach. You'll find a narrow sand spit looking out on Bolinas. You still won't have the beach entirely to yourself, but a place this beautiful is worth sharing. Because of currents from Bolinas Lagoon, the water at Stinson Beach Park is a little warmer than elsewhere along the Northern California Coast (but it's still brisk by Atlantic Coast standards). There are picnic areas, a snack bar, and restrooms; lifeguards in summer. If you dare swim anywhere along the North Coast, it might as well be here, where the waters are a tiny bit warmer. ~ Located along Route 1 in the town of Stinson Beach, 23 miles north of San Francisco.

BOLINAS BEACH Beginning near Bolinas Lagoon and curving around the town perimeter, this salt-and-pepper beach provides ample opportunity for walking. A steep bluff borders the beach. In the narrow mouth of the lagoon you can often see harbor seals and waterfowl. There are no facilities but the town of Bolinas is within walking distance. ~ Located at the end of Wharf Road in Bolinas.

AGATE BEACH AND DUXBURY REEF A prime area for beachcombers, Agate Beach is rich in found objects and objects waiting to be found—(however, collecting is not permitted). At low tide, Duxbury Reef to the south is also outstanding for tidepool gazing. Both are highly recommended for adventurers, daydreamers, and amateur biologists. There are no facilities. ~ From Olema–Bolinas Road in Bolinas, go up the hill on Mesa Road, left on Overlook Drive, and right on Elm Road. Follow Elm Road to the parking lot at the end; take the path down to the ocean; 415-499-6387, fax 415-499-3795.

HAGMAIER POND ➣ Favored by swimmers and nude sun- ◄HIDDEN
bathers, this miniature lake offers a variation from nearby ocean
beaches. It's fringed with grassland and bounded by forest, making it an idyllic spot within easy reach of the highway. There are
no facilities. ~ On Route 1 go three and a half miles north of the
Bolinas turnoff (at the foot of Bolinas Lagoon). You'll see a shallow parking lot on the right side of the highway. A dirt road leads
uphill several hundred yards to the lake; take the first left fork.

SAMUEL P. TAYLOR STATE PARK 🚶 🚴 🐎 ➣ Located several
miles inland, this redwood facility provides an opportunity to experience the coastal interior. The place is heavily wooded and offers 2900 acres to roam. In addition to the campgrounds, there
are hiking trails and a creek. Wildflowers adorn the park entrance
and gentle hiking trails. The park has picnic areas, restrooms,
and showers. Day-use fee, $4. ~ Located on Sir Francis Drake
Boulevard, east of Route 1 and six miles from Olema; 415-488-
9897, fax 415-488-4315.

▲ There are 60 sites, 25 for tents only (no hookups); $11
per night. Reservations are required from Memorial Day through
Labor Day; call 800-444-7275.

POINT REYES NATIONAL SEASHORE 🚶 🚴 🐎 ➣ 🏃 ⚓ 🚣
🚤 🎣 One of the great natural features of Northern California, this 72,000-acre park contains everything from wind-blown
beaches to dense pine forests. No traveler should miss it. The park's
facilities include three visitors centers, picnic areas, restrooms,
and 140 miles of hiking trails. ~ Off Route 1, about 40 miles
north of San Francisco; 415-464-5100, fax 415-663-8132; www.
nps.gov/pore.

▲ You may camp in any of four campgrounds, which are all
accessible only by hiking trails or bikes. Each campground charges
$12 per night. Sky Camp, with 12 primitive sites, sits on the side
of Mt. Wittenberg, commanding stunning views of Drakes Bay.
Wildcat Camp rests on a bluff above a pretty beach; there are 7
primitive sites. Glen Camp lies in a forested valley and has 12
primitive sites. Coast Camp nestles in a meadow near the beach;

TOMALES BAY'S GOURMET OYSTERS

Shacks and storefronts along Tomales Bay sell fresh local oysters, barbecued
or on the half-shell. Most oysters in the Point Reyes area are Pacific oysters, imported from Japan in the 1930s to replace local oysters that had
disappeared from San Francisco Bay because of pollution. Tomales Bay
is one of the few areas where the smaller, sweeter Olympia oyster
native to the Bay Area is still harvested. Gourmets consider Olympic
oysters a special delicacy.

there are 14 primitive sites. Each camp is equipped with toilets, non-potable water, and picnic areas. Wood fires are not allowed; plan to bring alternate campfire materials. Permits are required; camping fee is $12 per night. You are limited to four nights in the park. Reservations are strongly recommended. For reservations call 415-663-8054 between 9 a.m. and 2 p.m. Monday through Friday, or download a camping form from the website and fax to 415-464-5149. Permits can be obtained Monday through Friday until 2 p.m. at Bear Valley Visitors Center.

LIMANTOUR BEACH ⚓ This white-sand beach is actually a spit, a narrow peninsula pressed between Drakes Bay and an estuary. It's an exotic area of sand dunes and sea breezes. Ideal for exploring, the region shelters over 350 bird species. There's good (but cold) swimming and fishing seaside. The only facilities are toilets. ~ Once in Point Reyes National Seashore, follow Limantour Road to the end.

▲ None, but the Point Reyes Youth Hostel is located on the road to Limantour.

TOMALES BAY STATE PARK 🚶 ⚓ 🏖 🛶 This delightful park, which abuts on Point Reyes National Seashore, provides a warm, sunny alternative to Point Reyes' frequent fog. The water, too, is warmer here in Tomales Bay, making it a great place for swimming, as well as fishing and boating. Or check out the self-guided nature trail for a description of the relationship between American Indians and local plants. The virgin grove of Bishop pine is a special treat. Rimming the park are several sandy coves; most accessible of these is Heart's Desire Beach, flanked by bluffs and featuring nearby picnic areas. From Heart's Desire a self-guided nature trail goes northwest to Indian Beach, a long stretch of white sand fringed by trees. Hiking trails around the park lead

AUTHOR FAVORITE

sights

Of the many beautiful beaches in Point Reyes National Seashore, **McClures Beach** is by far my favorite. It is a white-sand beach protected by granite cliffs that stand like bookends on either flank. Tidepool watching is a great sport here; if you arrive during low tide it's possible to skirt the cliffs along the south end and explore a pocket beach next door. But don't let a waxing tide catch you sleeping! Swimming is dangerous here; surf fishing, birdwatching, and driftwood gathering more than make up for it. Quite simply, places like this are the reason folks visit Northern California. The only facilities are toilets (at the trailhead). ~ Located in Point Reyes National Seashore at the end of Pierce Point Road. A steep trail leads a half-mile down to the beach.

to other secluded beaches, excellent for picnics and day hikes. Dogs are restricted to the upper picnic area and must be kept on a leash. The park has picnic areas and restrooms. Day-use fee, $4. ~ From Route 1 in Olema take Sir Francis Drake Boulevard to Inverness. From Inverness it's another eight miles. When Sir Francis Drake forks, take the right fork, which becomes Pierce Point Road. Then follow Pierce Point Road to the park; 415-669-1140, fax 415-669-1701.

▲ There are six sites for tents only; $1 per night per person. Campsites are hike-in or bike-in only.

SHELL BEACH Actually part of Tomales Bay State Park, this pocket beach is several miles from the park entrance. As a result, it is often uncrowded. A patch of white sand bordered by steep hills, Shell Beach is ideal for swimming and picnicking. No dogs allowed. The only facilities are toilets. ~ Once in Point Reyes National Seashore, take Sir Francis Drake Boulevard one mile past Inverness, then turn right at Camino del Mar. The trailhead is located at the end of this street; follow the trail three-tenths of a mile down to the beach.

MARSHALL BEACH This secluded beach on Tomales Bay is a wonderful place to swim and sunbathe, often in complete privacy. The beach is a lengthy strip of white sand fringed by cypress trees. ~ Once in Point Reyes National Seashore, take Pierce Point Road. Immediately after passing the entrance to Tomales Bay State Park, turn right onto the paved road. This road travels uphill, turns to gravel and goes two and six tenths miles to a gate. From the gate you hike one and a half miles along the road/trail to the beach.

▲ Camping allowed on the beach; be sure to pack out everything you packed in. For information call 415-663-8054.

ABBOTTS LAGOON Because of its rich waterfowl population and beautiful surrounding dunes, this is a favorite place among hikers. From the lagoon it's an easy jaunt over the dunes to Point Reyes Beach. The only facilities are toilets. ~ Once in Point Reyes National Seashore, take Pierce Point Road. The trailhead is located along the roadside, two miles past the turnoff for Tomales Bay State Park; follow the trail one mile to the lagoon.

KEHOE BEACH Bounded by cliffs, this strand is actually the northern end of ten-mile-long Point Reyes Beach. It's a lovely place, covered with wildflowers in spring and boasting a seasonal lagoon. The isolation makes it a great spot for explorers. The only facilities are toilets (at the trailhead). ~ Once in Point Reyes National Seashore, take Pierce Point Road. The trailhead is along the roadside four miles past the turnoff for Tomales Bay State Park; follow the trail a half-mile to the beach.

POINT REYES BEACH ⚓ It will become wonderfully evident why this is nicknamed "Ten Mile Beach" when you cast eyes on this endless sand swath. A great place for whale watching, beachcombing, and fishing, this is not the spot for swimming. Sharks, riptides, and unusual wave patterns make even wading inadvisable. Also the heavy winds along this coastline would chill any swimmer's plans. But that does not detract from the wild beauty of the place, or the fact you can jog for miles along this strand (also referred to as North Beach and South Beach). Restrooms are the park's only facilities. ~ Located off Sir Francis Drake Boulevard, about 14 miles from park headquarters.

DRAKES BEACH ⚓ Edged by cliffs, this crescent beach looks out upon the tip of Point Reyes. Since it's well protected by Drakes Bay, this is a good swimming spot. It also provides interesting hikes along the base of the cliffs to the inlet at Drakes Estero. Facilities include picnic areas, restrooms, a visitors center, and a snack bar. ~ Located off Sir Francis Drake Boulevard, 15 miles from park headquarters.

OLEMA RANCH CAMPGROUND This roadside camping park has facilities for trailers and tent campers. The price, however, ain't cheap—$23 for a tent and two people ($32 for RV sites). That will buy a plot of ground in a grassy area. It's not exactly the great outdoors, but the place is strategically situated along Route 1 near the turnoff for Point Reyes National Seashore. There are picnic areas, restrooms, showers, a playground, and a laundromat. ~ 10155 Route 1, Olema; 415-663-8001, fax 415-663-8832; www.olemaranch.com, e-mail camping@olemaranch.com.

▲ There are 230 tent/RV sites (full hookups available); $23 to $32 per night.

Sonoma and Mendocino Coast

Just north of Marin County lie the coastlines of Sonoma and Mendocino, beautiful and still lightly developed areas. Placid rangeland extends inward while along the shoreline, surf boils against angular cliffs. Far below are pocket beaches and coves; offshore rise dozens of tiny rock islands, or sea stacks. The entire coast teems with fish—salmon and steelhead—as well as crabs, clams, and abalone. Rip currents, sneaker waves, and the coldest waters this side of the Arctic make swimming inadvisable. But the landscape is wide open for exploration, enchanting and exotic.

SIGHTS Jenner, Mendocino, and Fort Bragg are among the small towns along this endless coastline, but the first place you'll come to is a somewhat different type community. In fact the fishing village of **Bodega Bay** might look vaguely familiar, for it was the setting of Alfred Hitchcock's eerie film *The Birds*. It's questionable whether any cast members remain among the population of snowy egrets, but the Bay still supports a variety of winged creatures. Conservation efforts have encouraged a comeback among the endangered brown pelicans and blue herons. Serious Hitchcock fans in search of familiar structures from the movie can take a short side trip inland along the Bay Highway to the town of **Bodega**. Here they'll find the old Potter schoolhouse and the church from the film.

In Bodega Bay, at **Lucas Wharf**, and elsewhere along this working waterfront, you can watch fishermen setting off into the fog every morning and hauling in their catch later in the day. ~ Route 1 and Smith Brothers Lane, Bodega Bay.

For a rustic detour, follow Coleman Valley Road when it departs from Route 1 north of Bodega Bay. It weaves through farmland and offers great views of ocean and mountains, and leads to the forest-rimmed village of **Occidental**.

When Route 1 winds up to the woodframe town of **Jenner** (population 200, elevation 19), where the broad Russian River meets the ocean, you can take Route 116 up the river valley to the fabled Russian River resort area and the town of Guerneville.

The Russians for whom the river is named were explorers and trappers sailing down the Pacific coast from Russian outposts in Alaska. They came in search of sea otters and in hope of opening trade routes with the early Spanish settlers. In 1812 these bold outlanders went so far as to build **Fort Ross**, a wooden fortress overlooking the sea. The old Russian stronghold, 13 miles north of Jenner, is today a state historic park. Touring the reconstructed fort you'll encounter a museum, an old Russian Orthodox chapel, a stockade built of hand-tooled redwood, barracks and officers'

AUTHOR FAVORITE

Maybe it's just the name, but I have to rank the ride on the **Skunk train** through the redwoods as one of my favorite scenic rail trips. You can board the train near the center of Fort Bragg for a half- or full-day ride aboard a steam engine or a diesel-powered railcar. Dating from 1885, the Skunk was originally a logging train; today it also carries passengers along a 40-mile route through mountains and redwoods to the inland town of Willits and back. For information, contact California Western Railroad. Reservations recommended. ~ Fort Bragg; 707-964-6371, 800-777-5865, fax 707-964-6754; www.skunktrain.com, e-mail skunk@skunk train.com.

houses, and two blockhouses (one seven-sided and another eight-sided). Together they provide an insight into an unusual chapter in California history. Admission. ~ 707-847-3286, fax 707-847-3601; e-mail fria@mcn.com.

From Jenner north through Fort Ross and beyond, Route 1 winds high above the coast. Every curve exposes another awesome view of adze-like cliffs slicing into the sea. Driving this corkscrew route can jangle the nerves, but the vistas are soothing to the soul. With the exception of scattered villages, the coastline remains undeveloped. You'll pass sunbleached wooden buildings in the old town of Stewarts Point. Then the road courses through **Sea Ranch**, a development bitterly opposed by environmentalists, which nevertheless displays imaginative contemporary-design houses set against a stark sea.

Just north of Point Arena, a side road from Route 1 leads out to **Point Arena Lighthouse**. The original lighthouse, built in 1870, was destroyed in the 1906 San Francisco earthquake, which struck Point Arena even more fiercely than the bay city. The present beacon, rebuilt shortly afterwards, rises 115 feet from a narrow peninsula. The lighthouse is open for tours. The views, by definition, are outstanding. Open from 10 a.m. to 4:30 p.m. Memorial Day to Labor Day and from 11 a.m. to 3:30 p.m. the rest of the year. Admission. ~ 707-882-2777; www.mcn.org/1/palight, e-mail palight@mcn.org.

In Mendocino County, the highway passes through tiny seaside villages. **Elk, Albion**, and **Little River** gaze down on the ocean from rocky heights. The coastline is an intaglio of river valleys, pocket beaches, and narrow coves. Forested ridges, soft and green in appearance, fall away into dizzying cliffs.

The houses that stand amid this continental turmoil resemble Maine saltboxes and Cape Cod cottages. In the town of **Mendocino**, which sits on a headland above the sea, you'll discover New England incarnate. Settled in 1852, the town was built largely by Yankees who decorated their village with wooden towers, Victorian homes, and a Gothic Revival Presbyterian church. The town, originally a vital lumber port, has become an artists' colony. With a shoreline honeycombed by beaches and a villagescape capped with a white church steeple, Mendocino is a mighty pretty corner of the continent.

Mendocino Headlands State Park, located atop a sea cliff, offers unmatched views of the town's tumultuous shoreline. From the bluffs you can gaze down at placid tidepools and wave-carved grottoes.

In the park is the historic **Ford House**, an 1854 home with a small museum that also serves as a visitors center for the park. ~ 735 Main Street, Mendocino; 707-937-5397.

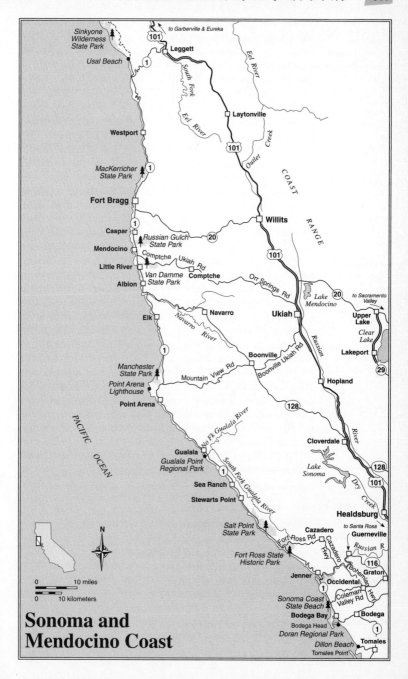

Sonoma and Mendocino Coast

The best way to experience this antique town is by stopping at the **Kelly House Museum**. Set in a vintage home dating from 1861, the museum serves as an historical research center (open Tuesday through Friday from 9 a.m. to 4 p.m.) and unofficial chamber of commerce. The museum is open daily from 1 to 4 p.m. from June through August, and Friday through Sunday from September through May. Admission. ~ 45007 Albion Street, Mendocino; 707-937-5791, fax 707-937-2156; e-mail kellyhs@mcn.org.

Among Mendocino's intriguing locales are the **Chinese Temple**, a 19th-century religious shrine located on Albion Street (open by appointment only); the **Presbyterian Church**, a national historic landmark on Main Street; and the **MacCallum House**, a Gingerbread Victorian on Albion Street, which has been reborn as an inn and restaurant. Another building of note is the **Masonic Hall**, an 1865 structure adorned with a hand-carved redwood statue on the roof. ~ Ukiah Street.

Then after meandering the side streets, stop at the **Mendocino Art Center**. Here exhibits by painters, potters, photographers, textile workers, and others will give an idea of the tremendous talent contained in tiny Mendocino. There's a pretty garden and a gift shop, and the complex also houses a local theater company. ~ 45200 Little Lake Street, Mendocino; 707-937-5818, 800-653-3328, fax 707-937-1764; www.mendocinoartcenter.org, e-mail mendoart@mcn.org.

North of town, on the way to Fort Bragg, stop at **Jug Handle State Reserve**. Here you can climb an ecological stairway which ascends a series of marine terraces. On the various levels you'll encounter the varied coast, dune, and ridge environments that form the area's diverse ecosystem. ~ Along Route 1 about one mile north of Caspar; 707-937-5804, fax 707-937-2953.

North of Fort Bragg, Route 1 runs past miles of sand dunes and traverses several small towns. Then, after having followed the

THE GARDEN BY THE SEA

For a thoroughly delightful stroll to the sea, meander through the **Mendocino Coast Botanical Gardens**. This coastal preserve, with three miles of luxuriant pathways, is "a garden for all seasons" with something always in bloom. The unique Northern California coastal climate is conducive to heathers, perennials, fuchsias, and rhododendrons, which grow in colorful profusion here. Trails lead past gardens of camellias, ferns, and dwarf conifers to a coastal bluff with vistas up and down the rugged shoreline. Admission. ~ 18220 North Route 1, Fort Bragg; 707-964-4352, fax 707-964-3114; www.gardenbythesea.org, e-mail mcbg@mcn.org.

coast all the way from Southern California, it abruptly turns inland. The reason is the mysterious Lost Coast of California. Due
north, where no highway could possibly run, the King Range vaults
out of the sea, rising over 4000 feet in less than three miles. It is
a wilderness inhabited by black bears and bald eagles, with an
abandoned lighthouse and a solitary beach piled with ancient
Indian shellmounds.

Though bed-and-breakfast prices are generally high, Northern
California's inns are unparalleled in intimacy and personal care.

LODGING

Located a few miles east of Bodega Bay, the **Inn at Occidental**
is a charming Victorian homestead encircled by a wide porch bedecked with potted plants and white wicker rockers. The 16
guest rooms feature fireplaces, spa tubs, antiques, and original
artwork. There is also a separate cottage with a full kitchen and
two master suites. A full breakfast is included, as are afternoon
wine and cheese. ~ 3657 Church Street, Occidental; 707-874-
1047, 800-522-6324, fax 707-874-1078; www.innatocciden-
tal.com, e-mail innkeeper@innatoccidental.com. ULTRA-DELUXE.

A prime Jenner resting spot is **Jenner Inn and Cottages**, a bed
and breakfast overlooking the river. Several buildings comprise
the spread: you can rent a room, a suite, even a house. One of the
less expensive accommodations, the personalized "Gull Room,"
features a quilted bed, old oak wardrobe, and a deck overlooking the river. The "Captain Will's Room," a higher-priced suite,
adds features like a hand-carved headboard, living room with a
wood stove and antique rocker, and a loft for extra guests. Some
of the rooms are outfitted with hot tubs or fireplaces ~ 10400
Route 1, Jenner; 707-865-2377, 800-732-2377, fax 707-865-
0829; www.jennerinn.com, e-mail innkeeper@jennerinn.com.
MODERATE TO ULTRA-DELUXE.

A fair bargain can be found along the coast at **Fort Ross Lodge**,
two miles north of the old Russian fort. Overlooking the ocean,
this 22-unit establishment consists of a cluster of woodframe
buildings. The rooms have ocean views; the ceilings are knotty
pine, and the varied decor includes everything from wicker to antique furniture. There are TVs, VCRs, and private baths in all rooms,
plus a community sauna and hot tub. ~ 20705 Route 1, Jenner;
707-847-3333, 800-968-4537, fax 707-847-3330; www.fortross
lodge.com. MODERATE TO ULTRA-DELUXE.

Several lodges along the California coast reflect in their architecture the raw energy of the surrounding sea. Such a one is
Timber Cove Inn. Elemental in style, it is a labyrinth of unfinished woods and bald rocks. The heavy timber lobby is dominated
by a walk-in stone fireplace and sits astride a Japanese pond. The
53 guest rooms are finished in redwood with beams and columns
exposed; they look a bit old and dated for my taste, but they do

afford marvelous views of the mountains and open sea. Many have decks, fireplaces, and hot tubs. All have TVs and phones. Timber Cove, fittingly, rests on a cliff directly above the ocean. Raccoons are a common sight; if you have critter issues you might want to steel yourself before wandering the grounds at night. Restaurant and lounge. ~ 21780 North Route 1, 15 miles north of Jenner; 707-847-3231, 800-987-8319, fax 707-847-3704; www.timbercoveinn.com. MODERATE TO ULTRA-DELUXE.

Set on a plateau above the ocean, **Stillwater Cove Ranch** is set on lovely grounds and populated with peacocks. Formerly a boys' school, this complex of buildings has been transformed into a restful retreat. Accommodations are varied and include single rooms, large kitchenettes, and a cottage with a fireplace. Even the dairy barn can house guests: it's been converted to a bunkhouse with kitchen. Stillwater Cove is certainly worth checking into. Closed for one week before Christmas. ~ 22555 Route 1, 16 miles north of Jenner; 707-847-3227. BUDGET TO MODERATE.

Mar Vista Cottages at Anchor Bay is a community of 12 separate cottages scattered around nine acres of oceanview property. Each is an old woodframe affair with a sitting room and kitchen as well as a bedroom and bathroom. Several are equipped with decks, fireplaces, or wood stoves. A soaking tub and barbecue facility on the property are surrounded by trees; a short path leads across Route 1 to the beach. Completely nonsmoking. Pets welcome. ~ 35101 South Route 1, Gualala; 707-884-3522, fax 707-884-4861; www.marvistamendocino.com, e-mail renata@marvistamendocino.com. DELUXE.

HIDDEN ► Built in 1903, the **Gualala Hotel** is a massive two-story structure. It's an old clapboard affair, fully refurbished, that includes a bar and dining room. The 19 rooms upstairs are small, but the wallpaper, decor, and old-time flourishes give the place a comfy traditional feel, making it a rare find on the North Coast. Because of the downstairs restaurant/bar, it can get noisy at times. ~ 39301 Route 1, Gualala; 707-884-3441. BUDGET.

Every one of the 16 rooms at **Seacliff Inn** stares straight at the Pacific Ocean, and some days you can see whales rubbing their bellies on the sandbar. Accommodations are simple but entirely comfortable, with everything you need for an atmospheric retreat: fireplaces, private decks, two-person whirlpool tubs with ocean views, downy king-size beds and plush comforters, coffee makers, and refrigerators stocked with complimentary champagne. The staff treats you like family. ~ 39140 South Route 1, Gualala; 707-884-1213, 800-400-5053, fax 707-884-1731; www.seacliffmotel.com, e-mail information@seacliffmotel.com. MODERATE TO DELUXE.

Country inns of this genre are quite abundant farther north. Near the town of Mendocino there are numerous bed and breakfasts, some outstanding. The seaside towns of Elk, Albion, Little River, Mendocino, and Fort Bragg each house several.

Among the more renowned is **Harbor House Inn**. Set on a rise overlooking the ocean, the house is built entirely of redwood. The living room alone, with its fireplace and exposed-beam ceiling, is an architectural feat. The house was modeled on a design exhibited at San Francisco's 1915 Panama–Pacific Exposition. Of the ten bedrooms and cottages, all are beautifully and individually decorated, many with ocean views, fireplaces, and antique appointments. The gardens are gorgeous, with paths leading down to the private beach. Rates include breakfast and dinner. The inn is closed the first two weeks in December. ~ 5600 South Route 1, Elk; 707-877-3203, 800-720-7474, fax 707-877-3452; www.theharborhouseinn.com, e-mail innkeepers@theharborhouseinn.com. ULTRA-DELUXE.

A message in a guest room diary at **Elk Cove Inn** reads: "A view, with a room." The view is of knobby coast and simmering surf of ice blue and shaggy dunes falling away. The room is perfect for watching it all: a comfortable cabin with dramatic beamed ceiling, gas fireplace at the foot of your featherbed, carafe of port waiting on the nightstand. In the morning the proprietor lays out an elaborate buffet—coffee cakes, corned beef hash—in the main 1883 Victorian house, a short walk from the four bluff-top cabins. There are seven guest rooms in the main house, some with dormer windows overlooking ocean, others with views of the riotous gardens. Four luxurious spa suites and an outdoor hot tub complete the picture. ~ 6300 South Route 1, Elk; 707-877-3321, 800-275-2967, fax 707-877-1808; www.elkcoveinn.com, e-mail innkeeper@elkcoveinn.com. DELUXE TO ULTRA-DELUXE.

Baby Face Nelson is reputed to have hidden in the old farmhouse that today serves as the Heritage House's reception and dining area.

Heritage House was constructed in 1877 and reflects the New England architecture popular then in Northern California. Most guests are housed in cottages that overlook the rocky coastline. Some of the 66 rooms have jacuzzis, fireplaces, and private decks. ~ 5200 North Route 1, Little River; 707-937-5885, 800-235-5885, fax 707-937-0318; www.heritagehouseinn.com, e-mail info@heritagehouseinn.com. ULTRA-DELUXE.

The New England–style farmhouse that has become **Glendeven** dates even further back, to 1867. The theme is country living, with a meadow out back and dramatic headlands nearby. The sitting room is an intimate affair with comfortable armchairs set before a brick fireplace. In the rooms you're apt to find a bed with wooden headboard, an antique wardrobe, and colorful orchids. Glendeven is as charming and intimate as a country inn can be. A full breakfast is brought to your room on a tray. There's also a two-bedroom rental house available, which is just as beautiful as the rest of the property. Closed first two weeks of January. ~ 8205 North Route 1, Little River; 707-937-0083, 800-822-4536, fax 707-937-6108; www.glendeven.com, e-mail innkeeper@glendeven.com. DELUXE TO ULTRA-DELUXE.

The **Little River Inn**, centered in a quaint 1850s-era house, has expanded into a mini-resort with 65 units, a restaurant, tennis courts, a day spa, a lounge, and a nine-hole golf course. Intimacy may be lacking, but the inn boasts a variety of rooms, from simple to super luxurious, and almost all afford grand ocean views. ~ 7751 North Route 1, Little River; 707-937-5942, 888-466-5683, fax 707-937-3944; www.littleriverinn.com, e-mail lri@mcn.org. MODERATE TO ULTRA-DELUXE.

Auberge Mendocino overlooks Van Damme State Park, with trails that deliver you instantly to rocky coast and the shiny bald heads of grey seals. Six rooms, three suites, and two cottages are extra spacious and decorated with pastel walls, folded linen draperies, antique dressers, and woodburning hearths. Bach streams through the living room. Breakfast, featuring savory items like baked apples and cranberry pancakes and herbed cheese omelettes with black beans, is served in the elegant dining room. ~ 8200 North Route 1, two miles south of Mendocino; 707-937-0088, 800-347-9252, fax 707-937-3620; www.aubergemendocino.com, e-mail innkeeper@aubergemendocino.com. DELUXE TO ULTRA-DELUXE.

A minute from downtown Mendocino, set right where Big River meets the ocean, **Stanford Inn by the Sea** is both woodsy and New Agey. The rambling lobby is paneled in Ponderosa pine and looks across to Pacific headlands; llamas and geese roam terraced lawns; and "biodynamic" nurseries provide fare for the inn's outstanding vegetarian menus. Families love it here, and pets are welcome. There's kayaking and redwood outrigger ca-

AUTHOR FAVORITE

Sea Ranch Lodge is the ultimate Sonoma coast retreat. Miles of secluded beaches and hiking trails, fields of wildflowers, and beautiful bluffs make this resort a perennial favorite. The lodge, which wears its weathered wood siding with dignity, offers 20 rooms with ocean or ridge views. The decor emphasizes earth tones that blend in with the natural surroundings. There is a bar with a solarium, a store, and nearby hiking and biking trails. ~ 60 Sea Walk Drive, Sea Ranch; 707-785-2371, 800-732-7262, fax 707-785-2917; www.searanchlodge.com. ULTRA-DELUXE.

noeing down Big River, and mountain biking along Pacific cliff trails. Couples go for the handsome, intimate rooms with Lexington furnishings, woodburning fireplaces, VCRs (the inn stocks 1400 videos), and DVD players. You'll also find a wonderful greenhouse pool with gardens of palms and bougainvillea, and water that's bathtub-warm year-round. Yoga classes are offered, as is massage. ~ Route 1 and Comptche Ukiah Road, Mendocino; 707-937-5615, 800-331-8884, fax 707-937-0305; www.stanford inn.com, e-mail stanford@stanfordinn.com. ULTRA-DELUXE.

Set in a falsefront building which dates to 1878, the 51-room **Mendocino Hotel** is a wonderful place, larger than other nearby country inns, with a wood-paneled lobby, full dining room, and living quarters adorned with antiques. There are rooms in the hotel with both private and shared baths as well as quarters in the garden cottages out back. ~ 45080 Main Street, Mendocino; 707-937-0511, 800-548-0513, fax 707-937-0513; www.mendocino hotel.com, e-mail reservations@mendocinohotel.com. MODERATE TO ULTRA-DELUXE.

The queen of Mendocino is the **MacCallum House Inn**, a Gingerbread Victorian built in 1882. The place is a treasure trove of antique furnishings, knickknacks, and other memorabilia. Many of the rooms are individually decorated with rocking chairs, quilts, and wood stoves. Positively everything—the carriage house, barn, greenhouse, gazebo, even the water tower—has been converted into a guest room. Full breakfast included. ~ 45020 Albion Street, Mendocino; 707-937-0289, 800-609-0492, fax 707-937-2243; www.maccallumhouse.com, e-mail info@maccallumhouse. com. MODERATE TO ULTRA-DELUXE.

Also consider **Mendocino Village Inn**, a vintage 1882 house that has two attic rooms, one with a sea view. A blue-and-white clapboard building with mansard roof, the place offers spacious accommodations with private baths, some with jacuzzis and fireplaces. The neighboring **Sweetwater Spa & Inn** offers a variety of accommodations, including cozy watertower rooms and private suites. Breakfast, afternoon wine and cheese, and evening wine and cheese are included. ~ 44860 Main Street, Mendocino; 707-937-0246, 800-882-7029, fax 707-937-0727; www.mendocinoinn.com, e-mail lodging@mendocinoinn.com. MODERATE TO ULTRA-DELUXE.

The nearby **Sea Gull Inn** has nine guest accommodations, some with ocean views. In a land of pricey hotels, this bed-and-breakfast establishment is a rarity. Choose to stay in the main house or in the cottage set in the garden. ~ 44960 Albion Street, Mendocino; 707-937-5204, 888-937-5204, fax 707-937-3550; www.seagullbnb.com, e-mail seagull1@mcn.org. BUDGET TO DELUXE.

Set on two landscaped acres overlooking Mendocino village and the coast, the **Joshua Grindle Inn** is a 19th-century New England–style farmhouse with ten spacious rooms, all with sitting areas, and some with woodburning fireplaces, whirlpool tubs, and ocean views. A separate two-bedroom cottage is also available. An inviting gathering spot during evening hours, the parlor offers a cheerful fire and an antique pump organ. Full breakfast included. ~ 44800 Little Lake Road, Mendocino; 707-937-4143, 800-474-6353; www.joshgrin.com, e-mail stay@joshgrin.com. DELUXE TO ULTRA-DELUXE.

For women guests only, **Sallie & Eileen's Place** offers a studio A-frame cottage and a spacious cabin three miles from Mendocino. The studio has a fireplace, a kitchen area, and a sunken tub, while the cabin, which can sleep up to six, has a loft bedroom, a woodstove, a deck, a full kitchen, and a private backyard. Hot tub available. ~ Box 409, Mendocino, CA 95460; 707-937-2028, fax 707-937-2918; www.seplace.com, e-mail innkeeper@seplace.com. MODERATE.

A white gate—what else?—marks the entrance to the **Whitegate Inn**, a Victorian-style inn surrounded by gardens and cypress trees. Within are six beautifully decorated rooms appointed with private baths, feather beds, fireplaces, and oceanviews; there's also a private cottage out back. Breakfast along with afternoon wine and hors d'oeuvres are included. ~ 499 Howard Street, Mendocino; 707-937-4892, 800-531-7282, fax 707-937-1131; www.whitegateinn.com. DELUXE TO ULTRA-DELUXE.

Tucked away in a quiet residential neighborhood, the **Avalon House**, a 1905 craftsman dwelling, has been lovingly converted into a B&B inn. Each room is individually appointed with handmade willow furniture and antiques. Gardens surround the house. A complimentary breakfast is served. A real gem. ~ 561 Stewart Street, Fort Bragg; phone/fax 707-964-5555, 800-964-5556; www.theavalonhouse.com, e-mail anne@theavalonhouse.com MODERATE TO DELUXE.

The **Lost Coast Inn** is an 1890-vintage bordello that has been converted into a country inn with four guest rooms. The place sits across the street from the ocean with a path that leads down to a sandy beach. There is an espresso bar, and a homemade continental breakfast is served. Closed January. ~ 38921 North Route 1, Westport; 707-964-5584; www.lostcoastinn.com. MODERATE.

DINING   For the best meal hereabouts (or for that matter, anywhere about), head for **River's End Restaurant**. Situated at that momentous crossroad of the Russian River and Pacific Ocean (and commanding a view of both), this outstanding little place is a restaurant with imagination. How else do you explain a dinner menu that ranges from *médallions* of venison to racklettes of elk to coconut-fried shrimp? Not to mention good service and a selection of over 150 local wines. River's End is a great place for ocean lovers and culinary adventurers. Closed Tuesday and Wednesday in summer, Monday through Thursday in winter. ~ 11048 Route 1, Jenner; 707-865-2484, fax 707-865-9621; www.rivers-end.com, e-mail bert@rivers-end.com. MODERATE TO DELUXE.

The **Salt Point Bar and Grill** features a small restaurant serving breakfast, lunch, and dinner. The menu relies heavily on seafood—halibut, oysters, prawns—but also includes chicken, steak, and other dishes. At lunch, enjoy a variety of salads, sandwiches, or seafood selections. Breakfast features a variety of omelettes. ~ 23255 North Route 1, 17 miles north of Jenner; 707-847-3234, fax 707-847-3002; www.saltpointlodgebarandgrill.com. MODERATE TO DELUXE.

The 1903 **Gualala Hotel** has an attractive dining room with a menu that varies from braised lamb shank to pan-seared duck breast. Stops along the way include linguini puttanesca, salmon, and New York steak. What makes dining here really special is the old hotel with its big front porch and antique decor. ~ 39301 Route 1, Gualala; 707-884-3441. MODERATE TO DELUXE.

Okay, so **St. Orres** is yet another California-cuisine restaurant. But it's the only one you'll see that looks as if it should be in Russia rather than along the California coast. With its dizzying spires, this elegant structure evokes images of Moscow and old St. Petersburg. The kitchen provides an everchanging menu of fresh game and fish dishes with an emphasis on organic, locally grown food. The fixed-price menu will include hot and chilled soups, poached salmon, rabbit, rack of lamb, stuffed wild boar, and several seasonal specialties. Even if you're not interested in dining, it might be worth a stop to view this architectural extravaganza. Dinner and Sunday brunch. Cash or check only. ~ 36601 Route 1, Gualala; 707-884-3303, fax 707-884-1840; www.saintorres.com, e-mail saintorres @yahoo.com. ULTRA-DELUXE.

Expert forager and St. Orres chef Rosemary Campiformio jokes that she can sniff out truffles that are still underground.

Arena Cove Bar & Grill looks out on a pier as well as a series of ocean bluffs. With a hand-carved bar and woodplank dining room, it's a local seafood restaurant serving fresh salmon, sautéed prawns, oysters, and broiled swordfish. If oysters and homemade clam chowder don't interest you, there are steaks and chops at this good-ol'-style eating place. There's "Mexican Fiesta" night on Wednesday, and sushi on Friday. ~ 790 Port Road, Point Arena; 707-882-2100, fax 707-882-2762. MODERATE TO DELUXE.

Although the dining room at **Harbor House Inn** mainly serves guests at this bed and breakfast, there are three extra tables for two people each evening. A fire in the fireplace will keep you warm and cozy on a cold coastal night, and in the summer you can watch the sunset over the ocean out of the huge windows. The chef prepares a set menu, served at 7 p.m., with entrées such as salmon, pork tenderloin, or halibut. A vegetarian meal can also be prepared with advance notice. Reservations are required. ~ 5600 South Route 1, Elk; 707-877-3203, 800-720-7474, fax 707-877-3452; www.theharborhouseinn.com, e-mail innkeeper@the harborhouseinn.com. ULTRA-DELUXE.

The **Albion River Inn**, set high on a cliff above the Albion Cove and the ocean, is a plate-glass dining spot serving California cuisine, and specializing in otherworldly ocean views. Entrées include grilled ginger-lime prawns, oven-roasted quail, and pasta tossed with roasted peppers, asparagus, and toasted pistachios, and can be perfectly paired with a selection from their award-winning wine list. Dinner only. ~ 3790 North Route 1, Albion; 707-937-4044, 800-479-7944, fax 707-937-2604; www.albionriver inn.com, e-mail ari@mcn.org. DELUXE TO ULTRA-DELUXE.

The Ravens provides a gourmet vegetarian alternative to the many seafood restaurants along the coast. Look for grilled polenta with sautéed peppers and portobello mushrooms, pistachio-encrusted tofu, and, for the adventurous, seapalm strudel. Pizzas and pastas are also available. Breakfasts include a variety of omelette and pancake dishes. No lunch. ~ In the Stanford Inn, Route 1 and Comptche Ukiah Road, Mendocino; 707-937-5615, 800-331-8884, fax 707-937-0305; www.ravensrestaurant.com, e-mail ravens@stanfordinn.com. MODERATE TO DELUXE.

A morning ritual for locals and visitors alike is to climb the rough-hewn stairs to the loft-like **Bay View Café** for coffee, French toast, or fluffy omelettes. On sunny afternoons, the deck over-

AUTHOR FAVORITE

Mendocino's best-known dining room is well deserving of its renown. **Café Beaujolais**, situated in a small antique house on the edge of town, serves designer dishes, which I try to sample on a regular basis. Dinner, served seven nights a week, is ever changing. Perhaps they'll be serving warm duck salad and Thai rock shrimp salad with entrées like *poulet verjus*, chicken braised with Navarro vineyards Verjus, leg of lamb stuffed with garlic, and steamed salmon with chervil *sabayon* sauce. Excellent cuisine. Closed from the day after Thanksgiving until early January. ~ 961 Ukiah Street, Mendocino; 707-937-5614; www.cafe beaujolais.com, e-mail cafebeau@mcn.org. MODERATE TO DELUXE.

looking Main Street and the coastal headlands makes an ideal lunch spot, especially for fish and chips or a jalapeño chile burger. ~ 45040 Main Street, Mendocino; 707-937-4197, fax 707-937-5300. BUDGET.

At the **Mendocino Hotel** you can enjoy California-style cuisine in the main dining room or out in the "garden room." The menu represents a mix of meat and seafood entrées such as prime rib, free-range chicken, and local salmon. The ambience in this 19th-century building evokes Mendocino's early days. ~ 45080 Main Street, Mendocino; 707-937-0511, 800-548-0513; www.mendocinohotel.com, e-mail reservations@mendocinohotel.com. DELUXE TO ULTRA-DELUXE.

Situated in a cozy little house, the **Moosse Café** offers imaginative seasonal dishes and organically grown comfort food. Try their seafood dishes, pot roast, or crispy chicken. For dessert, of course you have to sample the moosse puff. ~ 390 Kasten Street, Mendocino; 707-937-4323, fax 707-937-3611; www.theblue heron.com, e-mail moosse@mcn.org. MODERATE TO DELUXE.

For French and California cuisine, **955 Ukiah Street** is an address worth noting. Candles, fresh flowers, and impressionist prints set the tone here. Serving dinner only, it prepares brandied prawns, red snapper in phyllo pastry, roast duck, and calamari. For the diet-conscious, they also offer lighter dishes. Dinner only. Closed Monday and Tuesday. ~ 955 Ukiah Street, Mendocino; 707-937-1955, fax 707-937-5138; www.955restaurant.com. MODERATE TO DELUXE.

The dining rooms of the 1882 **MacCallum House Restaurant** are beautiful, the walls and ceilings covered with carved redwood and fir, the tables glittering with firelight and candlelight. Everything on the menu is excellent. Start with an Alexander's Antidote aperitif (champagne with puréed blackberries and schnapps) and an appetizer of Pacific Rim oysters with gazpacho relish. Then try the pan-seared ahi with tomatoes, capers, and mushrooms. Or the roasted chicken with a potato-chanterelle gratin, or the carmelized scallops with vanilla-saffron sauce. There's a lighter café menu served in the bar. Breakfast and dinner only. ~ 45020 Albion Street, Mendocino; 707-937-0289; www.maccallumdining.com, e-mail info@maccallumhouse.com. MODERATE TO ULTRA-DELUXE.

Fort Bragg's favorite dining spot is easy to remember—**The Restaurant**. Despite the name, this is no generic eating place but a creative kitchen serving excellent dinners. It's decorated with dozens of paintings by local contemporary artists, lending a sense of the avant garde to this informal establishment. The Restaurant's menu offers seasonal entrées like sautéed prawns, salmon, rockfish, and vegetarian selections. Choose from a selection of housemade desserts, including ice creams and sorbets. Dinner only except for Sunday brunch. Closed Tuesday and Wednesday. ~ 418

North Main Street, Fort Bragg; 707-964-9800; www.therestaurantfortbragg.com, e-mail info@therestaurantfortbragg.com. MODERATE TO DELUXE.

SHOPPING   In the New England–style town of Mendocino you'll discover a shopper's paradise. Prices are quite dear, but the window browsing is unparalleled. Housed in the town's old Victorians and Cape Cod cottages is a plethora of shops. There are stores specializing in soap, seashells, candles, and T-shirts; not to mention bookstores, potters, jewelers, art galleries, and antique shops galore.

Most shops are located along Mendocino's wood-frame Main Street, but also search out the side streets and passageways in this vintage town.

One particularly noteworthy gallery is the **William Zimmer Gallery**, which houses an eclectic collection of contemporary and traditional arts and crafts. ~ 10481 Lansing Street, Mendocino; 707-937-5121. Be sure to also check out **Highlight Gallery**, featuring, among other things, displays of handmade furniture, contemporary art, jewelry, ceramic, glass, and woodwork. ~ 45052 Main Street, Mendocino; 707-937-3132. The **Mendocino Art Center** houses numerous crafts studios as well as art galleries. ~ 45200 Little Lake Street, Mendocino; 707-937-5818.

Books are the order of the day at the **Gallery Bookshop and Bookwinkle's Children's Books**. ~ Main and Kasten streets, Mendocino; 707-937-2665.

Every Friday from mid-May to late October, Howard Street in central Mendocino is blocked off to vehicles as area growers assemble for the **Mendocino Farmers' Market**. Early in the season, the market showcases magnificent floral displays, while organic and specialty produce takes center stage later in the summer and fall. It only lasts from noon to 2 p.m. ~ 707-937-3632.

Many of the same growers also display their bounty at other open-air markets along the coast on other days of the week, including the **Gualala Farmers' Market** (Community Center, Saturdays, 10 a.m. to 12:30 p.m.; 707-882-2474) and the **Fort Bragg Farmer's Market** (Laurel and Franklin streets, Wednesdays, 3:30 to 6 p.m.; 707-937-4330).

NIGHTLIFE   There's music four nights a week at the **Caspar Inn**. This down-home bar room spotlights deejays, local bands as well as groups from outside the area. Hit it on the right night and the joint will be rocking. If you've overdone your partying by the end of the night, ask management about the rooms they have available. Cover. ~ 14961 Caspar Road, Caspar; 707-964-5565; www.casparinn.com.

For a night on the town, enjoy a quiet drink at the **Mendocino Hotel**. You can relax in a Victorian-style lounge or in an enclosed garden patio. ~ 45080 Main Street, Mendocino; 707-937-0511.

For a pint of Guinness, a game of backgammon, local characters and friendly chit chat, slip into **Patterson's Pub**. The pub is small, in keeping with its Irish persona, and furnished in dark wood and brass. There's occasional live entertainment. ~ 10485 Lansing Street, Mendocino; 707-937-4782.

DILLON BEACH 🕴 🚲 🐎 💰 ⚓ 🏃 ⚓ 🛶 🚤 ⛴ 🎣 Located at the mouth of Tomales Bay, this beach is popular with boaters and clammers. The surrounding hills are covered with resort cottages, but there are open areas and dunes to explore. There are picnic areas and restrooms, groceries, boat rentals, and fishing charters. Day-use fee, $5. ~ From Route 1 in Tomales take Dillon Beach Road west for four miles.

▲ Located nearby, Lawson's Landing (707-878-2443) has open-meadow tent/RV camping (no hookups); $17 per night. Take note: This campground hosts hundreds of trailers. Call in December and January for closures; they may lock the gates if it's too wet.

BEACHES & PARKS

DORAN REGIONAL PARK 🕴 🚲 🐎 ⚓ ⚓ 🐟 ⚓ 🚤 ⛴ 🎣 This peninsular park is situated on a sand spit between Bodega Harbor and Bodega Bay. With a broad sand beach and good facilities, it's an excellent spot for daytrippers and campers alike. You can explore the tidal flats or fish up on the jetty. There are picnic areas, restrooms, and showers. Day-use fee, $3 to $4. ~ Off Route 1 in Bodega Bay; 707-875-3540, fax 707-875-2171; e-mail groupwise@sonoma-county.org.

▲ There are 134 tent/RV sites (no hookups); $14 per night for Sonoma County residents and $16 for nonresidents.

BODEGA HEAD There are pocket beaches here dramatically backdropped by granite cliffs. A good place to picnic and explore, this is also a favored whale-watching site. There are restrooms and showers located in nearby Westside Park. ~ Off Route 1 in Bodega Bay along Bay Flat Road.

▲ Westside Park has 47 tent/RV sites (no hookups); $14 per night for Sonoma County residents and $16 for nonresidents. ~ 707-875-3540.

SONOMA COAST STATE BEACH 🕴 🚲 🐎 🏃 🎣 🎣 This magnificent park extends for 19 miles between Bodega Head and the Vista Trail. It consists of a number of beaches separated by steep headlands; all are within easy hiking distance of Route 1. The beaches range from sweeping strands to pocket coves and abound with waterfowl and shorebirds, clams, and abalone. The park headquarters and information center is at Salmon Creek Beach, where endless sand dunes backdrop a broad beach. Schoolhouse Beach is a particularly pretty pocket cove bounded by rocky cliffs; Portuguese Beach boasts a wide swath of sand; Blind Beach is rather secluded with a sea arch offshore; and Goat Rock Beach faces the town of Jenner and is decorated with offshore rocks. Pick your poison—hiking, tidepooling, birdwatching, whale watching, camping, picnicking, fishing—and you'll find it waiting along this rugged and hauntingly beautiful coastline. Bodega Dunes, Salmon Creek Beach, Schoolhouse Beach, Goat Rock, Portuguese Beach, and Wrights Beach have restrooms; Bodega Dunes and Wrights Beach also feature picnic areas. Day-use fee, $4. ~ Located along Route 1 between Bodega Bay and Jenner; 707-875-2603, fax 707-875-3876.

▲ At Bodega Dunes, there are 98 tent/RV sites (no hookups); $16 to $20 per night. At Wrights Beach, there are 30 tent/RV sites (no hookups); $18 to $20 per night. Reservations are required; call 800-444-7275. At Pomo Canyon and Willow Creek there are 33 walk-in primitive sites; $10 per night; closed December through March.

FORT ROSS REEF CAMPGROUND 🚶 🚵 🛶 🏊 ⚓ Set in a canyon surrounded by bluffs, this facility is beautifully located near the ocean and features a redwood grove. It is a state park with spectacular surroundings and gorgeous views. There are picnic areas and restrooms. Closed November through March. Day-use fee, $4. ~ 19005 Route 1, 12 miles north of Jenner; watch for a cluster of white barns on the west side of the highway; 707-847-3708, fax 707-847-3601.

▲ There are 20 tent/RV sites (no hookups); $12 per night. Closed November through March. Depending on the weather, fires may not be allowed.

STILLWATER COVE REGIONAL PARK 🚶 🛶 ⚓ Situated amid pine trees on a hillside above the ocean, this is a small park with access to a beach. The canyon trail leads up to the restored (but closed) Fort Ross Schoolhouse. There are picnic areas, restrooms, and showers. Day-use fee, $3. ~ Route 1, about 16 miles north of Jenner; 707-847-3245, fax 707-847-3325.

▲ There are 22 tent/RV sites (no hookups); $16 per night. Reservations must be made at least ten days in advance; 707-565-2267.

OCEAN COVE STORE AND CAMPGROUND 🚶 🚵 🎣 🚣 ⚓ This privately owned campground has sites on a bluff above a rocky shoreline. Anglers catch everything from salmon to rockfish. The scenery is mighty attractive, and the campsites are well removed from the road. There are hot showers and portable toilets. ~ Route 1, about 17 miles north of Jenner; 707-847-3422, fax 707-847-3624; www.ocean-cove.com, e-mail relax@oceancove.com.

▲ There are 150 tent/RV sites (no hookups); $15 per night; $2 extra for dogs. Closed December through March.

The Lost Coast

There are alternate routes to Eureka leading along the perimeter of California's Lost Coast region. One of the state's most remote wilderness areas, it is a tumbling region of extraordinary vistas. Here the King Range, with its sliding talus and impassable cliffs, shoots 4087 feet up from the ocean in less than three miles. No road could ever rest along its shoulder. The place has been left primitive, given over to mink, deer, river otter, and black bear; rare bald eagles and peregrine falcons work its slopes.

The range extends about 35 miles. Along the shore is a wilderness beach from which seals, sea lions, and porpoises, as well as gray and killer whales, can be seen. There's also an abandoned lighthouse and the skeletons of ships wrecked on the rocks.

To reach this remote area, from Route 101 near Redway take Briceland–Thorne Road, which turns into Shelter Cove Road as it winds through the King Range.

Shelter Cove is a tiny bay neatly folded between sea cliffs and head-lands. A point of embarkation for people exploring the Lost Coast, it has a few stores, restaurants, and hotels. Stock up here: The rest of this backcountry jaunt promises little more than a couple of stores.

Outside Shelter Cove you can pick up Kings Peak Road or Ettersburg–Honeydew Road, which connect with Wilder Ridge Road and lead to the general store town of **Honeydew**. This is a prime marijuana growing region and a colony of hippies is bound to be sitting on the stoop swapping tales.

Mattole Road heads northeast, meandering along the Mattole River, to another forest hamlet, **Petrolia**. Nestled in a river valley and marked by a white-steeple church, the town is a scene straight from a Norman Rockwell painting. Hawks glide overhead. Old men rock on their front porches.

Next, **Mattole Road** ascends a succession of plateaus to a ranch land of unpainted barns and broad shade trees, then noses down to the coast-line and parallels the waves for perhaps five miles. Here the setting is Scottish. Hillsides are grazed by herds of sheep and covered with tena-cious grasses that shake in the sea wind. The gray sand beach is covered with driftwood. Along the horizon peaks rise in jagged motions, seem-ingly thrust upward by the lash of the surf.

SALT POINT STATE PARK 🏃 🚵 ⛵ 🍴 Extending from the ocean to over 1000 feet elevation, this 6000-acre spread includes coastline, forests, and open range land. Along the shore are weird honeycomb formations called tafoni, caused by sea erosion on coastal sandstone. Up amid the stands of Douglas fir and Bishop pine there's a pygmy forest, where unfavorable soil conditions have caused fully mature redwoods to reach only about 20 feet in height. Blacktail deer, raccoons, mountain lions, and bobcats roam the area. Miles of hiking trails lace the park, including one through a rhododendron reserve. There are picnic areas and restrooms. Day-use fee, $6. ~ Route 1, about 20 miles north of Jenner; 707-847-3221, fax 707-847-3843.

> After the fall rains, chanterelles and other favored mushrooms abound at Salt Point. Pickers beware: carefully identify anything you plan to eat, since some mushrooms can be fatal.

▲ There are three campgrounds here with 108 tent/RV sites (no hookups); $20 per night. Reservations are required on weekends and from April to October; call 800-444-7275.

GUALALA POINT REGIONAL PARK 🏃 🚣 🎣 🍴 Located where the Gualala River meets the ocean, this charming place has everything from a sandy beach to redwood groves. Across the river, there are kayak and canoe rentals. There are picnic areas, restrooms, and an information center. Day-use fee, $3. ~ Located along Route 1 due south of Gualala; 707-785-2377, fax 707-785-3741.

▲ There are 19 tent/RV sites (no hookups), 1 hiker/biker site, 6 walk-in sites; $16 per night. Reservations: 707-565-2267.

MANCHESTER STATE PARK 🏃 🏊 🍴 This wild, windswept beach extends for miles along the Mendocino coast. Piled deep with driftwood, it's excellent for beachcombing and hiking. There are picnic areas, restrooms, and an information center. ~ Located along Route 1, about eight miles north of Point Arena; 707-937-5804, fax 707-937-2953.

▲ There are 43 tent/RV sites (no hookups) and 10 primitive, hike-in environmental sites; $15 per night; first-come, first-served.

VAN DAMME STATE PARK 🏃 🚵 🎣 🍴 Extending from the beach to an interior forest, this 2069-acre park has several interesting features: a "pygmy forest" where poor soil results in fully mature pine trees reaching heights of only six inches to eight feet; a "fern canyon" smothered in different species of ferns; and a "cabbage patch" filled with that fetid critter with elephant ear leaves—skunk cabbage. This park is also laced with hiking trails and offers excellent beachcombing opportunities. Facilities include a visitors center, picnic areas, restrooms, and showers. Day-use fee, $4 for the fern canyon. ~ Route 1, about 30 miles north of Point Arena, or three miles south of Mendocino; 707-937-5804, fax 707-937-2953.

▲ There are 74 tent/RV sites (no hookups); $13 per night. The upper campground is closed in winter. Reservations are essential during the summer: 800-444-7275.

MENDOCINO HEADLANDS AND BIG RIVER BEACH STATE PARKS 🏃 🏌 🚣 ⛴ These adjoining parks form the seaside border of the town of Mendocino. And quite a border it is. The white-sand beaches are only part of the natural splendor. There are also wave tunnels, tidepools, sea arches, lagoons, and 360-degree vistas that sweep from the surf-trimmed shore to the prim villagescape of Mendocino. The only facilities are restrooms; private canoe rental nearby. ~ Located in the town of Mendocino.

RUSSIAN GULCH STATE PARK 🏃 🚴 🐎 🚣 ⛴ Set in a narrow valley with a well-protected beach, this park has numerous features. There are marvelous views from the craggy headlands, a waterfall, and a blowhole that rarely blows. Rainbow and steelhead trout inhabit the creek while hawks and ravens circle the forest. There are picnic areas, restrooms, and showers. Day-use fee, $6. ~ Located along Route 1, two miles north of Mendocino; 707-937-5804, fax 707-937-2953.

▲ There are 30 tent/RV sites (no hookups); $20 per night. Reservations: 800-444-7275.

MACKERRICHER STATE PARK 🏃 🚴 🐎 🏌 🚣 ⛴ ⛵ Another of the region's outstanding parks, this facility features a crescent of sandy beach, dunes, headlands, a lake, a forest, and wetlands. Harbor seals inhabit the rocks offshore and over 90 bird species frequent the area. The park has picnic areas, restrooms, and showers. ~ Along Route 1, about three miles north of Fort Bragg; 707-937-5804, fax 707-937-2953.

▲ There are 140 tent/RV sites (no hookups), 10 walk-in and 3 hike-and-bike sites ($2 per night, per person); $16 per night. Reservations: 800-444-7275.

▼▼▼▼▼▼▼▼▼▼▼▼

Redwood Country

Near the nondescript town of Leggett, Route 1 joins Route 101. Logging trucks, those belching beasts that bear down upon you without mercy, become more frequent. You are entering Redwood Country.

This is the habitat of *Sequoia sempervirens*, the coastal redwood, a tree whose ancestors date to the age of dinosaurs and which happens to be the world's tallest living thing. These "ambassadors from another time," as John Steinbeck called them, inhabit a 30-mile-wide coastal fog belt stretching 450 miles from the Monterey area north to Oregon. Redwoods live five to eight centuries, though some have survived over two millennia, while reaching heights over 350 feet and diameters greater than 20 feet.

There is a sense of solitude here uncapturable anywhere else. The trees form a cathedral overhead, casting a deep shade across the forest floor. Solitary sun shafts, almost palpable, cut through the grove; along the roof of the forest, pieces of light jump across the treetops, poised to fall like rain. Ferns and a few small animals are all that survive here. The silence and stillness are either transcendent or terrifying. It's like being at sea in a small boat.

SIGHTS

The Redwood Highway, Route 101, leads north to the tallest, densest stands of *Sequoia sempervirens*. At **Richardson Grove State Park** the road barrels through the very center of a magnificent grove. A short nature trail leads through this virgin timber, though the proximity of the road makes communing with nature seem a bit ludicrous.

North of Garberville, follow the **Avenue of the Giants**, a 32-mile alternative route that parallels Route 101. This two-lane road winds along the Eel River south fork, tunneling through dense redwood groves. Much of the road is encompassed by **Humboldt Redwoods State Park**, a 52,000-acre preserve with some of the finest forest land found anywhere—17,000 acres are virgin-growth redwood. Park headquarters contains a nice visitors center. ~ 707-946-2409, fax 707-946-2326; www.humboldtredwoods.org, e-mail hrsp@humboldtredwoods.org.

Farther along is **Founder's Grove**, where a nature trail loops through a redwood stand. The forest is dedicated to early Save-the-Redwoods League leaders who were instrumental in preserving thousands of redwood acres, particularly in this park. Nearby **Rockefeller Forest** has another short loop trail that winds through a redwood grove. Avenue of the Giants continues through towns that are little more than way stations and then rejoins Route 101, which leads north to Eureka.

It's not far to **Cape Mendocino**, second-most westerly point in the contiguous United States. Here you'll have broad views of the ocean, including the menacing shoals where countless ships have been slapped to timber. Next, the road curves up through forest and sheep-grazing lands before rolling down to the gentle pastureland near the unique town of Ferndale.

A Victorian-style hamlet set in the Eel River valley, **Ferndale** is so perfectly refurbished it seems unreal. Main Street and nearby thoroughfares are lined with Gothic Revival, Queen Anne, Eastlake, and Italianate-style Victorians, brightly painted and blooming with pride. Tragedy struck this picturesque town in April 1992 when a 6.9-level earthquake and several powerful aftershocks rocked the entire area. Since then local residents have devotedly rebuilt the quaint Main Street district with its boutiques and gift shops and other affected neighborhoods. The film *Outbreak*, starring Dustin Hoffman, was shot in Ferndale.

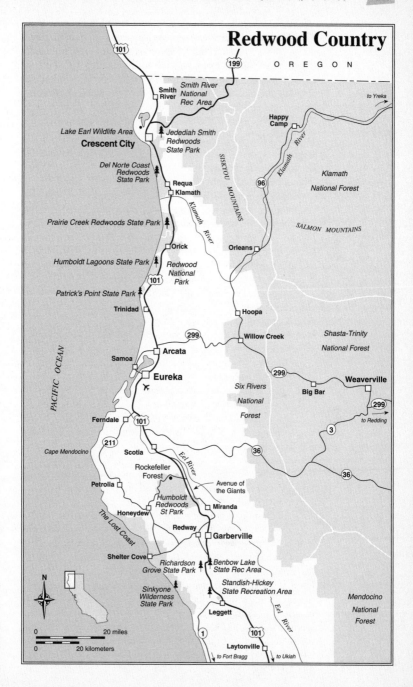

Redwood Country

OREGON

to Yreka

Smith River National Rec Area

Smith River

Lake Earl Wildlife Area
Crescent City

Jedediah Smith Redwoods State Park

Happy Camp

Klamath River

SISKIYOU MOUNTAINS

Klamath National Forest

Del Norte Coast Redwoods State Park

Requa
Klamath

Klamath River

SALMON MOUNTAINS

Prairie Creek Redwoods State Park

Orick

Orleans

Humboldt Lagoons State Park

Redwood National Park

Patrick's Point State Park

Hoopa

Trinidad

Willow Creek

Shasta-Trinity National Forest

Arcata

Samoa

Eureka

Weaverville

Big Bar

PACIFIC OCEAN

Ferndale

Six Rivers National Forest

to Redding

Cape Mendocino

Scotia

Eel River

Rockefeller Forest

Avenue of the Giants

Petrolia

Humboldt Redwoods St Park

Miranda

The Lost Coast

Honeydew

Redway

Garberville

Shelter Cove

Richardson Grove State Park

Benbow Lake State Rec Area

Sinkyone Wilderness State Park

Standish-Hickey State Recreation Area

Mendocino National Forest

Eel River

N

Leggett

0   20 miles
0   20 kilometers

Laytonville

to Fort Bragg   to Ukiah

The best way to see the town is by stopping first at the **Ferndale Museum**. Here is an ever-changing collection of antiques and memorabilia from the region, plus an old blacksmith shop. There are sometimes maps available for self-guided walking tours of this historic community. It's an architectural wonder that shouldn't be missed. Closed Monday during summer and Tuesday during winter; closed January. Admission. ~ 515 Shaw Avenue, Ferndale; phone/fax 707-786-4466; e-mail museum@quik.com.

EUREKA   Eureka's roughly 40,000 inhabitants make it the largest town on the Northern California coast. Founded in 1850, the town's first industry was mining; the name "Eureka!" came from an old gold mining exclamation meaning "I found it."

Today fishing and lumbering have replaced more romantic occupations, but much of the region's history is captured in points of interest. Stop at the **Greater Eureka Chamber of Commerce** on the way into town for maps, brochures, and information. Closed on the weekends in winter. ~ 2112 Broadway, Eureka; 707-442-3738, 800-356-6381, fax 707-442-0079; www.eurekachamber.com, e-mail chamber@eurekachamber.com.

Make certain to ask at the Chamber of Commerce for the **architectural tour** map. Eureka has over 100 glorious Victorian homes ranging from understated designs to the outlandish **Carson Mansion**, a multilayered confection that makes other Gothic architecture seem tame. It was built in the 1880s by William Carson, a wealthy lumber merchant with the same need for ostentation that afflicted the robber barons on San Francisco's Nob Hill. The Carson Mansion is a private club, but you can drive by and view its distinctive architecture. ~ 2nd and M streets, Eureka.

HIDDEN ►   Of a more subdued nature are the **covered bridges** on the southern outskirts of town. To reach them from Route 101, take Elk River Road two miles to Berta Road or three miles to Janes Road (there is a wooden span covering both). You'll enter a picture of red barns and green pasture framed by cool, lofty forest. The bridges, crossing a small river, evoke Vermont winters and New Hampshire sleigh rides.

Fort Humboldt is also stationed at this end of town. Built in the early 1850s to help resolve conflict between gold settlers and indigenous tribes of Yurok, Hoopa, Wiyot, and Mattole Indians; it has been partially restored. In addition to re-creating Army life (experienced here by a hard-drinking young officer named Ulysses S. Grant), the historic park displays early logging traditions. There's a drafty logger's cabin, a small lumber industry museum, a military museum displaying Army artifacts, a museum of American Indian artifacts, and a couple of remarkable old steam engines. In the winter, the museums are open only on weekdays. ~ 3431 Fort Avenue, Eureka; 707-445-6567, fax 707-445-5314.

Nearby **Sequoia Park** provides a nifty retreat from urban life. Tucked into its 52-acre preserve is a petting zoo (closed Monday), a picnic area, a playground, and a thick stand of redwoods. ~ W Street between Glatt and Madrone streets, Eureka.

Then head to **Old Town**, Eureka's answer to the nation's gentrification craze. This neighborhood was formerly the local bowery; the term "skid row" reputedly originated right here. It derived from the bums residing beside the nearby "skid roads," along which redwood logs were transported to the waterfront. Now the ghetto is gilded: old Victorians, woodframe warehouses, brick buildings, and clapboard houses have been rebuilt and painted striking colors. Stylish shops have sprung up and restaurants have opened.

At the foot of C Street in Old Town, where the bowery meets the bay, the vintage motor vessel **Madaket** departs. For several well-invested dollars, you'll sail past an egret rookery, oyster beds, pelican roosts, ugly pulp mills, and the town's flashy marina. The cruises are weather-dependent; always call ahead. Closed October through April. Admission. ~ Eureka; 707-445-7910, fax 707-445-3582; e-mail madaket1910@webtv.net.

Heading north from Eureka there are two towns worth noting. **Arcata**, home of Humboldt State University, is a student town with an outstanding collection of old Victorians. For a self-guided architectural tour, obtain a map at the **Arcata Chamber of Commerce**. ~ 1635 Heindon Road, Arcata; 707-822-3619, fax 707-822-3515; www.arcatachamber.com, e-mail arcata@arcata chamber.com.

Trinidad, one of the area's oldest towns, perches above a small port. Sea stacks and sailboats lie anchored offshore, watched over by a miniature lighthouse. For a tour of the pocket beaches and rocky shores lining this beautiful waterfront, take a three-mile trip south from town along Scenic Drive.

AUTHOR FAVORITE

sights Don't miss **Clarke Historical Museum**, with its outstanding collection of Northern California American Indian artifacts. Here are twined baskets, ceremonial regalia, and a dugout redwood canoe. It provides a unique insight into this splendid Humboldt Bay region before the age of gold pans and axe handles. There is also the museum's Victorian section, featuring items from the Gold Rush and the timber and maritime industries. Closed Sunday and Monday. ~ 240 E Street, Eureka; 707-443-1947, fax 707-443-0290.

Next is **Redwood National Park**, a fitting finale to this lengthy coastal journey. Park of parks, it's a necklace strung for over 33 miles along the coast. Among its gems are secluded beaches, elk herds, and some of the world's tallest trees.

First link in the chain is the **Redwood Information Center**. ~ 119441 Route 101, Orick; 707-464-6101 ext. 5265, fax 707-488-5335. In addition to information, the center issues permits for **Tall Trees Grove**. A one-and-one-third-mile hike leads to a redwood stand boasting some of the loftiest of all California's redwoods. **Lady Bird Johnson Grove**, located off Bald Hill Road on a one-mile trail, represents another magnificent cluster of ancient trees.

Another side road, Davison Road (day-use fee), leads along remote **Gold Bluffs Beach** eight miles to Fern Canyon. Here angular walls 50 feet high are covered with rioting vegetation.

Redwood National Park encompasses three state parks—Prairie Creek Redwoods, Del Norte Coast Redwoods, and Jedediah Smith Redwoods. Just after the main entrance to the first you'll pass **Elk Prairie**, where herds of Roosevelt elk graze across open meadows. Immediately past the entrance, Cal Barrel Road, another short detour, courses through dense redwood forest.

HIDDEN ►   Also plan to turn off onto **Coastal Drive**, a gravel road paralleling Route 101. Its numerous turnouts expose extraordinary ocean vistas. The road snakes high above the coast before emptying onto the main highway near the mouth of the Klamath River.

The Del Norte section of the park reveals more startling sea views en route to Crescent City, where the **main park headquarters** is located. ~ 1111 2nd Street, Crescent City; 707-464-6101, fax 707-464-1812. There is travel information aplenty at the headquarters and at the **Crescent City–Del Norte County Chamber of Commerce** building just across the street. Closed on weekends in winter. ~ 1001 Front Street, Crescent City; 707-464-3174, 800-343-8300, fax 707-464-9676; www.northerncalifornia.net, e-mail chamber@northerncalifornia.net.

◆◆

NORTH COAST BEACON

Perched on a rocky island off Route 101 in Crescent City is **Battery Point Lighthouse**, an 1856 stone and masonry structure that is one of the best preserved original lighthouses on the Pacific Coast, and the fifth-oldest on the West Coast. At low tide from April through September visitors can walk across a spit of sand and rock to the lighthouse for tours of the house, the lantern room, and a small museum. Closed Monday and Tuesday and from October through March. Admission. ~ Crescent City; 707-464-3089.

Woodlands, wetlands, grasslands—you'll find them all at **Lake Earl Wildlife Area**. This preserve also offers secluded sand dunes and a sufficient number of bird species, 260 at last count, to make it look like it was created by the Audubon Society. One of the finest birdwatching spots on the North Coast, this Pacific Flyway destination is the place to see hawks, falcons, bald eagles, Canada geese, and canvasback ducks. As many as 51,000 Aleutian Canadian geese stop here in the spring to fatten up before their 3000-mile non-stop flight back to the Aleutian Islands. Closed weekends. ~ Old Mill Road, three miles north of Crescent City; 707-464-2523, fax 707-464-2871; e-mail lakeearlwa@efg.ca.gov.

◄ HIDDEN

Route 101 north to Route 199 leads to the park's Jedediah Smith section with its mountain vistas and thick redwood groves. The Smith River, rich in salmon and steelhead, threads through the region. For further details on this remote area check with the **Hiouchi Information Center**. Closed Labor Day to Memorial Day. ~ Route 199, four miles east of Route 101; 707-464-6101 ext. 5067, fax 707-464-1812.

One of Northern California's finest old lodges is the imposing, Tudor-style **Benbow Inn**. Located astride the Eel River, this regal retreat is bounded by lawns, gardens, and umbrella-tabled patios. The structure itself is a bold three-story manor in the English country tradition. The lobby, paneled in carved wood and adorned by ornamental molding, is a sumptuous sitting area with a grand fireplace. Jigsaw puzzles lie scattered on the clawfoot tables and rocking horses decorate the room. The dining area and lounge are equally elegant. Guest quarters offer such flourishes as quilted beds with wooden headboards, hand-painted doors, period wall-prints, marble-topped nightstands, and complimentary sherry. Visitors also enjoy tea and scones in the afternoon and evening hors d'oeuvres. Closed January through March. ~ 445 Lake Benbow Drive, Garberville; 707-923-2124, 800-355-3301, fax 707-923-2122; www.benbowinn.com, e-mail benbow@benbowinn.com. DELUXE TO ULTRA-DELUXE.

LODGING

The cheapest lodging I've found in the southern redwoods area is **Johnston Motel**. Unlike the region's big-tag caravansaries, this 14-unit facility has rooms at budget prices. Don't expect a lot of shine. The plain rooms are small but comfortable. ~ 839 Redwood Drive, Garberville; 707-923-3327, fax 707-923-2108. BUDGET TO MODERATE.

Not that I have anything against Johnston's; it's just that Garberville is not my idea of paradise. For a few well-spent dollars more you can rent a room in any of several motels along redwood-lined Avenue of the Giants. **Miranda Gardens Resort** is a good choice. This 16-unit resort has rooms with kitchens and fully equipped cabins. The place features a heated swimming pool, playground, and market. The facilities are tucked into a redwood grove and the rooms are partially paneled in redwood. Closed January through March. ~ 6766 Avenue of the Giants, Miranda; 707-943-3011, fax 707-943-3584; www.mirandagardens.com, e-mail info@mirandagardens.com. MODERATE TO DELUXE.

The predominant business in Redwood Country is the lumber industry, which casts a lengthy shadow in surrounding towns like Scotia. Here the 1923 **Scotia Inn** lavishly displays the region's product in a redwood-paneled lobby. Antique furnishings decorate this sprawling hotel, which boasts a fashionable restaurant and lounge. The 22 guest rooms are appointed in oak and adorned with armoires, brass lamps, and silk wallpaper. The bathrooms, not to be upstaged, boast brass fixtures, clawfoot tubs, and medicine cabinets of carved wood. A gem. Continental breakfast is included. ~ Main and Mill streets, Scotia; 707-764-5683, fax 707-764-1707; www.scotiainn.com, e-mail stay@scotiainn.com. MODERATE TO DELUXE.

HIDDEN ►

Way out in Shelter Cove, at the southern end of California's remote Lost Coast, is the **Shelter Cove Beachcomber Inn**, which consists of three buildings with six units. Three rooms have kitchens and woodburning stoves; all seem to be lovingly cared for. All come with barbecue grills and patios, as well as ocean views. Considering that the price tag on this luxury is reasonable and that Shelter Cove is one of the coast's most secluded hideaways, the Beachcomber Inn is well worth the effort. ~ 412 Machi Road, Shelter Cove; phone/fax 707-986-7551, 800-718-4789; www.sojourner2000.com. BUDGET TO MODERATE.

HIDDEN ►

Mattole River Organic Farms Country Cabins offers full-facility cottages complete with kitchenettes. Each is plain but comfortably furnished and features a sitting room and a bedroom. This rustic colony sits amid shade trees and is backdropped by forested hills. ~ 42354 Mattole Road, Petrolia; phone/fax 707-629-3445, 800-845-4607; e-mail iansigman@hotmail.com. BUDGET TO MODERATE.

The cheapest lodging of all is in the neon motels along Route 101 on the outskirts of Eureka. Many advertise room rates on highway signs along the southern entrance to town. **Sunrise Inn and Suites** is perhaps the best of these. Because it is centrally located, guests can walk to Old Town and other points of interest. The rooms are simple but very clean, with carpeting and king or queen beds. Nearly half have jacuzzi tubs. ~ 129 4th Street, Eureka; phone/fax 707-443-9751, 800-404-9751. BUDGET.

For country-inn sensibility in an urban environment, **Old Town Bed & Breakfast Inn** comes highly recommended. Just a couple blocks from Eureka's fabled Carson Mansion, this four-bedroom house dates from 1871. It's a Greek Revival structure with a winding staircase and a wealth of antiques. Plushly carpeted and adorned with patterned wallpaper, the house has been beautifully redecorated; there's also a library/media room The cost includes a full country-style breakfast. ~ 1521 3rd Street, Eureka; 707-443-5235, 888-508-5235, fax 707-442-4390; www.oldtown bnb.com, e-mail info@oldtownbnb.com. MODERATE TO DELUXE.

Another of Eureka's spectacular bed and breakfasts is **Carter House**, one of the finest Victorians I've ever seen. This grand old four-story house is painted in light hues and decorated with contemporary artwork, lending an airy quality seldom found in vintage homes. The place is beautiful: light streams through bay windows; oriental rugs are scattered across hardwood floors; there are sumptuous sitting rooms, and oak banisters that seemingly climb forever. In the seven rooms are antique nightstands and armoires, beds with bold wooden headboards, ceramic pieces, and original local artwork. Two private cottages with fireplaces, spa tubs, and full kitchens are also available. The price includes a full breakfast, complimentary wine, and cookies before bedtime. ~ 301 L Street, Eureka; 707-445-1390, 800-404-1390, fax 707-444-8067; www.carterhouse.com, e-mail reserve@carterhouse.com. MODERATE TO ULTRA-DELUXE.

> How far back in time do redwoods go? Far enough to be present on earth at the same time as dinosaurs!

Mark and Christi Carter added the 23-room **Hotel Carter** to their lodging empire a number of years ago. Its pale pine furniture and peach-colored walls offer a refreshing counterpoint to the Carter House across the street. Accommodations are quite spacious; some have fireplaces and whirlpool baths. Complimentary breakfast is served in the ground-floor dining room, where colorful dhurrie rugs and silver candleholders add an elegant touch. ~ 301 L Street, Eureka; 707-444-8062, 800-404-1390, fax 707-444-8067; www.carterhouse.com, e-mail reserve@carter house.com. DELUXE TO ULTRA-DELUXE.

For traditional and stylish lodging, also consider **Eureka Inn**. Set in an imposing Tudor-gabled building near Eureka's Old Town section, it provides excellent accommodations. There's a wood-beamed lobby with large fireplace and comfortable sitting area, a pool, jacuzzi, and sauna, plus a café, gourmet restaurant, and piano bar. Built in 1922 and registered as a National Historic Landmark, this huge hotel has 104 guest rooms. These are well appointed and attractively decorated. ~ 7th and F streets, Eureka; 707-442-6441, 800-862-4906, fax 707-442-0637; www.eureka inn.com, e-mail innplacetobe@eurekainn.com. MODERATE TO DELUXE.

Built in 1905 by a local department store magnate, **The Daly Inn** is now an elegant bed and breakfast. Surrounded by colorful Victorian gardens, this picture-perfect inn has three comfortable rooms and two spacious suites, all furnished in early-20th-century antiques. A full breakfast and evening hors d'oeuvres are included in the rate. ~ 1125 H Street, Eureka; 707-445-3638, 800-321-9656, fax 707-444-3636; www.dalyinn.com, e-mail innkeeper@dalyinn.com. MODERATE TO ULTRA-DELUXE.

For an extra dash of history in your nightly brew, there's the **Shaw House Bed & Breakfast** in nearby Ferndale. It's only fitting to this bed and breakfast that Ferndale is an island in time where the Victorian era still obtains. The Shaw House, built in 1854, is the oldest home in town and is on the National Historic Register. A library, two parlors, a dining room, and balconies are available to guests, and the home is furnished throughout with precious antiques. All rooms have private baths. Tea and cookies are served in the afternoon. ~ 703 Main Street, Ferndale; mailing address: P.O. Box 1369, Ferndale, CA 95536; 707-786-9958, 800-557-7429, fax 707-786-9758; www.shawhouse.com, e-mail stay@shawhouse.com. MODERATE TO ULTRA-DELUXE.

> A Carpenter Gothic creation, the Shaw House Bed & Breakfast was modeled on Hawthorne's *House of the Seven Gables*.

In a town chockablock with precious Victorians, one of the most precious of all is **The Gingerbread Mansion**. Turrets and gables, an intimate garden, interesting antiques, and a delicious homemade breakfast are among the features; but what you'll find particularly special about this bed and breakfast are the bathrooms. One has mirrored ceilings and walls; another, his-and-hers clawfoot tubs set near a tiled gas fireplace. The 11 distinct accommodations (4 are top-floor suites), are comfortably cozy. Afternoon tea and handmade turn-down chocolates (port, too, for suite guests) are additional touches. ~ 400 Berding Street, Ferndale; 707-786-4000, 800-952-4136, fax 707-786-4381; www.gingerbread-mansion.com, e-mail innkeeper@gingerbread-mansion.com. DELUXE TO ULTRA-DELUXE.

Set in a quiet residential neighborhood within walking distance of downtown, the **Lady Anne** has five rooms and one suite in a 1888 Queen Anne–style home. Each is appointed with antiques. One has a woodburning stove. You can sit on the porch or in a chair in the front yard and watch the world go by, or play the grand piano and guitars in one of the inn's two parlors. ~ 902 14th Street, Arcata; 707-822-2797; e-mail ladyanne@humboldt1.com. MODERATE.

You will be hard pressed anywhere along the coast to find a view more alluring than that of **Trinidad Bay Bed & Breakfast**. This New England–style shingle house, set in a tiny coastal town, looks across Trinidad Bay, past fishing boats and sea rocks, seals and sandy beaches, to tree-covered headlands. The two country-style rooms are equipped with standard furnishings, private entrances, and come with a delivered breakfast. There is a fireplace and a living room for guests to share. Rates include breakfast. Closed December and January. ~ Edwards and Trinity streets, Trinidad; 707-677-0840, fax 707-677-9245; www.trinidadbaybnb.com. ULTRA-DELUXE.

Turtle Rocks Oceanfront Inn is located four and a half miles north of town on a rocky bluff overlooking seastacks that provide a refuge for barking seals. Decorated with seashells, driftwood, turtle figurines, and fresh flowers, the contemporary bed and breakfast has six spacious guest rooms, each with a sitting area with facing divans, a king-size bed, a private bath, and a private glass-paneled deck that's picture-perfect for whale-watching in spring or fall and enjoying sunsets any time of year. Trinidad State Beach and Trinidad Head Trail are close by, and Patrick's Point State Park, with its rock headlands and promontories, is less than a mile's walk. Rates include a full gourmet breakfast. ~ 3392 Patrick's Point Drive, Trinidad; 707-677-3707; www.turtle rocksinn.com, e-mail trocks@northcoast.com. DELUXE TO ULTRA-DELUXE.

Hostelling International—Redwood National Park, set in a 1908 settler's house, provides basic dormitory-style accommodations; there is one private room for couples. It's across the highway from a beach and features a laundry room, kitchen facilities, and a common room. ~ 14480 Route 101 at Wilson Creek Road, Klamath; 707-482-8265, 800-909-4776 ext. 74, fax 707-482-4665; www.norcalhostels.org, e-mail theredwoodhostel@earth link.net. BUDGET.

Farther north in Crescent City, along the scimitar strand that gave the town its name, is **Crescent Beach Motel**. This 27-unit motel has plate-glass views of the ocean. Rooms are small but decorated with oak furniture and a blue-green color scheme. They have TVs, and most rooms have those oh-so-priceless sea vistas. ~ 1455 Route 101 South, Crescent City; 707-464-5436, fax 707-464-9336; www.cresentbeachmotel.com. MODERATE.

DINING

Personally, my favorite dining place in these parts is the **Benbow Inn**. This Tudor lodge serves meals in a glorious dining room that will make you feel as though you're feasting at the estate of a British baron. The dinner menu relies on local produce and herbs grown in the inn's own garden. Though the menu changes seasonally, you are likely to find such items as lamb, salmon, duck, and filet of beef. Breakfast and dinner served year-round; lunch served June to mid-September. Closed January through March. ~ 445 Lake Benbow Drive, Garberville; 707-923-2124, 800-355-3301, fax 707-923-2122; www.benbowinn.com, e-mail benbow@benbow inn.com. MODERATE TO ULTRA-DELUXE.

Proceeding north along the Avenue of the Giants, you'll encounter cafés in tiny towns like Miranda, Myers Flat, Weott, and

Pepperwood. Most are tourist-oriented businesses, adequate as way stations, but undistinguished and slightly overpriced.

For a touch of good taste in the heart of Redwood Country try the **Scotia Inn**. The dining room of this revered old hotel is trimly paneled in polished redwood, furnished with captain's chairs, and illuminated by brass chandeliers. It features a menu with fresh fish dishes, tenderloin of elk, lobster, prime rib, steak, and lamb. Vegetarians will find an option or two, as well. **The Pub**, also within the Inn, serves a lighter version of the menu in a less dressy atmosphere. ~ Main and Mill streets, Scotia; 707-764-5683; www.scotiainn.com. MODERATE TO DELUXE.

The historic Old Town section of Eureka, a refurbished neighborhood of stately Victorians, supports several good restaurants. **Restaurant 301** in the Hotel Carter offers fresh, inventive gourmet food, with imaginative entrées such as teriyaki-bourbon portobello mushroom and coffee-dusted venison medallions. The menu changes seasonally but usually features fish, meat, and vegetarian dishes. Prix-fixe multicourse meals, complete with wine pairings for each course, are also available. Dinner only. ~ In the Hotel Carter, 301 L Street, Eureka; 707-444-8062, fax 707-444-8067; www.carterhouse.com. DELUXE TO ULTRA-DELUXE.

A meal at the **Sea Grill** is a chance to enjoy fine dining in a historic 1876 storefront. The place has an airy Victorian feel about it, with lots of peachy pastels, fabric drapes, and an antique mahogany bar. Oil paintings created by local artists add to the atmosphere. Chicken, steak, and seafood dishes are the specialties here. No lunch Saturday through Monday. Closed Sunday. ~ 316 E Street, Eureka; 707-443-7187, fax 707-825-9223; www.the seagrill.com, e-mail comments@theseagrill.com. MODERATE TO ULTRA-DELUXE.

For Asian fare there's **Samurai Restaurant**, a simple dining room appointed with Japanese antiques and folk art. It's dinner

AUTHOR FAVORITE

In the southern redwoods region you'll be hard pressed to find a better restaurant than **Woodrose Café**. T'aint much on looks—just a counter, a few tables and chairs, and a small patio out back. But the kitchen folk cook up some potent concoctions. That's why the place draws locals in droves. The breakfast menu offers buckwheat pancakes, lox and bagels, and spinach-and-feta-cheese omelettes. At lunch they make homemade soups, organic salads, sandwiches, and tofu burgers; no dinner served. The Woodrose Café is a good reason to visit otherwise drab Garberville. No lunch on Saturday and Sunday. ~ 911 Redwood Drive, Garberville; 707-923-3191. BUDGET.

only, folks, with a menu that includes seafood, standard suki-yaki, tempura, and teriyaki dishes. There's a large selection of imaginative sushi. You can also try the "Treasure Ship," a sampler of five different entrées. Dinner only. Closed Sunday and Monday. ~ 621 5th Street, Eureka; 707-442-6802; e-mail tengu@ humboldt1.com. MODERATE.

For a dining experience lumberjack-style, there's **Samoa Cook-**   ◄ HIDDEN
house just outside Eureka. A local lumber company has opened its chow house to the public, serving three meals daily. Just join the crowd piling into this unassuming eatery, sit down at a school cafeteria–style table and dig in. You'll be served redwood-size portions of soup, salad, meat, potatoes, vegetables, and dessert—you can even ask for seconds. Ask for water and they'll plunk down a pitcher, order coffee and someone will bring a pot. It's noisy, crowded, hectic, and great fun. Reduced rates for children and seniors. ~ Samoa Road, Samoa; 707-442-1659, fax 707-442-1699; www.humboldtdining.com/cookhouse. MODERATE.

The **Seascape Restaurant** is small and unassuming. There are only about three dozen tables and booths at this seafood dining room. But the walls of plate glass gaze out upon a rocky headland and expansive bay. Situated at the foot of Trinidad Pier, the local eating spot overlooks the town's tiny fishing fleet. The dishes, many drawn from surrounding waters, include halibut, rock cod, salmon, crab, and shrimp. Landlubbers dine on filet mignon. Lunch and breakfast menus are equally inviting. ~ Trinidad Pier, Trinidad; 707-677-3762, fax 707-677-3921. MODERATE TO DELUXE.

From Trinidad to the Oregon border the countryside is sparsely populated. Crescent City is the only town of real size, but you'll find nondescript cafés in such places as Orick, Klamath, and Smith River.

Crescent City—like the entire North Coast—is seafood country. Best place around is **Harbor View Grotto**, a family restaurant with an ocean view. This plate-glass eatery features a long inventory of ocean dishes—whole clams, fried prawns or oysters, scallops, red snapper, salmon, cod, halibut, and so on, not to mention the seafood salads and shrimp cocktails. There are also a few meat dishes plus an assortment of sandwiches, chicken, and pasta dishes. Worth a stop. ~ 150 Starfish Way, Crescent City; 707-464-3815, fax 707-464-3875. MODERATE.

In Ferndale, a picturesque Victorian town south of Eureka, there's   **SHOPPING**
a covey of intriguing shops. The community has attracted a number of artisans, many of whom display their wares in the 19th- and early-20th-century stores lining Main Street. There are shops selling needlework, stained glass, and kinetic sculptures; others deal in ironwork, used books, and handknits. There are even stores specializing in "paper treasures," boots and saddles, dolls, and

"nostalgic gifts." All are contained along a three-block section that more resembles a living museum than a downtown shopping district.

Eureka, too, has been gentrified. Most of the refurbishing has occurred in Old Town, where stately Victorians, falsefront stores, and tumbledown buildings have been transformed into sparkling shops and art galleries. Window browse down 2nd and 3rd streets from C Street to H Street and you're bound to find several inviting establishments. Of particular interest is the F Street corridor, which is becoming a nexus for the arts. The crown jewel is the Humboldt Arts Council's **Morris Graves Museum of Art**, featuring seven galleries of local fine arts. Closed Monday through Wednesday. ~ 636 F Street, Eureka; 707-442-0278, fax 707-442-2040; www.humboldtarts.org.

NIGHTLIFE   Now don't misunderstand—California's northern coast and redwood region are wild and provocative places. It's just that the word "wild" up here is taken in the literal sense, as in wilderness and wildlife. Somehow the urban meaning of crazy nights and endless parties was never fully translated.

The **Benbow Inn** features a fine old lounge with carved walls and an ornate fireplace. A pianist adds to the intimacy. ~ 445 Lake Benbow Drive, Garberville; 707-923-2124.

Entertaining for almost three decades, the **Ferndale Repertory Theater** puts on a variety of plays and musicals year-round in an old movie theater. ~ 447 Main Street, Ferndale; 707-786-5483; www.ferndale-rep.org.

BEACHES & PARKS   THE "LOST COAST" 🚶🚴🐎🎣🛶🚤⚓ California's coastal Route 1 is one of the greatest highways in America. Beginning in Southern California, it sweeps north through Big Sur, Carmel, San Francisco, and Mendocino, past ocean scenery indescribably beautiful. Then it disappears. At the foot of Redwood Country, Route 1 quits the coast and turns into Route 101.

The region it never reaches is California's fabled "Lost Coast." Most of the region is now protected as the King Range National Conservation Area. Three major trails traverse it: King Crest Trail, which climbs the main coastal ridge for 10.5 miles, with views of the ocean and Eel River Valley; the five-mile-long Chemise Mountain trail; and the 25-mile-long Lost Coast Trail along the wilderness beach.

One of the wettest areas along the Pacific Coast, King Range gets about 100 inches of rain a year. The precipitation is particularly heavy from October to April. Summer carries cool coastal fog and some rain. Weather permitting, it's a fascinating region to explore—wild and virgin, with the shellmounds of American

Indians who inhabited the area over a century ago still scattered on the beach.

Motels, restaurants, groceries, and boat rentals are available in Shelter Cove, at the south end of the Conservation Area. To get there from Garberville on Route 101, Shelter Cove Road leads to nearby Redway and then southwest to Shelter Cove. About 15 miles down this road, Kings Peak Road forks northwest, paralleling the Conservation Area, to Ettersberg and Honeydew. Just before Kings Peak Road, Chemise Mountain Road turns off into Nadelos and Wailaki campgrounds.

▲ There are numerous tent/RV campgrounds (no hookups): Wailaki is for RVs and tents, Nadelos for tents only. Fees range from free to $8 per night. For information contact the Arcata Field Office, U.S. Bureau of Land Management, 1695 Heindon Road, Arcata, CA 95521; 707-825-2300, fax 707-825-2301; www.ca.blm.gov/arcata, e-mail caweb 330@ca.blm.gov.

> Coast redwoods are one of just a few species that transpire, a process that allows them to create their own rain (one tree can produce 500 gallons a day).

SINKYONE WILDERNESS STATE PARK 🚶 🐎 ⛵ This 7500-acre park below the southern tip of the King Range is known for the narrow and steep winding dirt roads leading to its interior. For this reason trailers and RVs are discouraged from entering the park—especially since there are no RV facilities. Featuring old-growth redwood groves and clear-cut prairies, the park hugs the southern section of the Lost Coast. The ranch house and visitors center are a mere 200 yards from awe-inspiring bluffs. Other facilities include picnic tables and pit toilets. Keep an eye out for the majestic Roosevelt elk who inhabit Sinkyone Wilderness State Park. Day-use fee, $6. ~ Located 30 miles west of Redway on Briceland Road or 50 miles north of Fort Bragg on County Road 431; phone/fax 707-986-7711.

▲ There are 35 drive-in sites at Usal Beach and 17 hike-in sites at Needle Rock for tents only; $10 per night. All of the north end sites are hike-in only.

STANDISH-HICKEY STATE RECREATION AREA 🚶 🏊 🎣 ⛵ Near the southern edge of Redwood Country, this 1500-acre park primarily consists of second-growth trees. The single exception is a 1200-year-old giant named after the Mayflower pilgrim, Captain Miles Standish. The forest here also has Douglas fir, oak, and maple trees. The south fork of the Eel River courses through the area, providing swimming holes and fishing spots (catch-and-release only). There are picnic areas, restrooms, and showers. Day-use fee, $6. ~ Located along Route 101, two miles north of Leggett; 707-925-6482, fax 707-925-6402.

▲ There are 99 tent/RV sites (no hookups) and 63 tent sites; $15 to $20 per night. Reservations recommended during summer; call 800-444-7275.

RICHARDSON GROVE STATE PARK 🏃 🚴 🏊 🎣 The first of the virgin redwood parks, this 1500-acre facility features a grove of goliaths. For some bizarre reason the highway builders chose to put the main road through the heart of the forest. This means you won't miss the redwoods, but to really appreciate them you'll have to disappear down one of the three hiking trails that loop through the grove. The south fork of the Eel River flows through the park, providing swimming and trout fishing opportunities. In the summer there are nightly campfires and kids' programs. The park has an information center, picnic areas, restrooms, and showers. Day-use fee, $4. ~ Route 101, about 18 miles north of Leggett; 707-247-3318, fax 707-247-3300; e-mail rgspblsra@ humboldt.net.

▲ There are 176 tent/RV sites (no hookups); $12 per night. Reservations: 800-444-7275.

BENBOW LAKE STATE RECREATION AREA 🏃 🚴 🏊 🎣 🚣 🛶 🎣 One of the less desirable parks in the area, this facility fronts the Eel River near the dam that creates Benbow Lake. The lake is usually full and suitable for boating from July 1 to mid-September; it's a good idea to call first. Motorized boats are not allowed. Route 101 streams through the park's center, disrupting an otherwise idyllic scene. Nevertheless, there's good swimming and fishing in the river-lake. In summer there are nightly campfires and kids' programs here. There are picnic areas, restrooms, and showers. Day-use fee, $4. ~ Route 101, about 23 miles north of Leggett; 707-923-3238, fax 707-247-3300; e-mail rgsp-blsra@humboldt.net.

▲ There are 75 tent/RV sites (two have hookups) along the river; $12 to $16 per night. Closed in winter. Reservations: 800-444-7275.

HUMBOLDT REDWOODS STATE PARK 🏃 🚴 🏇 🏊 🎣 One of the state's great parks, it is set within a 20-million-year-old forest. The park is a tribute to early conservationists who battled lumber interests in an effort to save the area's extraordinary trees. Today 105 miles of hiking trails lead through redwood groves and along the south fork of the Eel River. Within the park's 35-mile length there are also opportunities for swimming, biking, horseback riding (you must provide your own horse), fishing, or tree gazing. Facilities include an information center, picnic areas, restrooms, and showers. Day-use fee, $6. ~ Located along the Avenue of the Giants between Miranda and Pepperwood; 707-

946-2409, fax 707-946-2326; www.humboldtredwoods.org, e-mail hrst@northcoast.com.

▲ There are four different campgrounds (only one in the winter) with a total of 256 tent/RV sites (no hookups); $19 per night. (The best, most private sites are, appropriately enough, at Hidden Springs Campground.) There are also five hike-in camps. Reservations: 800-444-7275.

CLAM BEACH COUNTY PARK 🏃🏇 🏊 ⛵ There's a broad expanse of beach here with good views of surrounding headlands. As its name suggests, this place was once known for its clams; unfortunately for mollusk-lovers, clamming has all but disappeared from these parts in the last few years. Still, it's a lovely local park. Horseback riders must provide their own horses. There's a picnic area and toilets. ~ Located along Route 101, about 15 miles north of Eureka; 707-445-7652, fax 707-445-7409.

▲ There is a number of open-ground tent/RV sites here (no hookups); $8 per night. No reservations accepted.

PATRICK'S POINT STATE PARK 🏃 🏊 ⛵ This 650-acre park is particularly known for Agate Beach, a long crescent backdropped by wooded headlands. It's one-third of a mile from the main parking area. Here it's possible to gather not only driftwood but semiprecious agate, jasper, and black jade. There are tidepools to explore, sea lions and seals offshore, and several miles of hiking trails. Leave Fido at home—dogs aren't allowed on the beach or trails. The facilities here include picnic areas, restrooms, and showers. Day-use fee, $2. ~ Off Route 101, about 25 miles north of Eureka; 707-677-3570, fax 707-677-9357; www.cal-parks.ca.gov, e-mail ncrdppsp@humboldt1.com.

> Drop by the reconstructed Yurok Indian village at Patrick's Point State Park, where rangers will tell you about life on the coast before the Europeans showed up.

▲ There are 124 tent/RV sites (no hookups); $12 per night. Reservations are recommended in the summer; call 800-444-7275.

HUMBOLDT LAGOONS STATE PARK 🏃🏊 🚣 ⛵🚤 ⛵ A 2000-acre facility, this beach park is full of surprises. The main entrance leads to a sandy beach tucked between rocky outcroppings and heaped with driftwood. Behind the beach an old lagoon has slowly transformed into a marsh of brackish water. Add the two areas together and you come up with a splendid park. Catch-and-release fishing at Stone Lagoon is good for cutthroat trout. Toilets and a visitors center are the only facilities. ~ Off Route 101, about 31 miles north of Eureka; 707-488-2041, fax 707-488-5555; e-mail ncrdt@humboldt1.com.

▲ There are 12 environmental hike-in and boat-in sites; $12 per night.

REDWOOD NATIONAL AND STATE PARKS 🚶 🚴 🐎 🛶 ⛵

Actually four parks in one, this 105,516-acre giant encompasses Prairie Creek Redwoods, Del Norte Coast Redwoods, Jedediah Smith Redwoods state parks and Redwood National Park. Together they stretch over 33 miles along the coast from Orick to the Crescent City region. Within that span, one of California's wettest areas (69 inches of rain yearly in Del Norte), are hidden beaches, ocean cliffs, deep redwood forests, and mile on mile of hiking trails.

Along the coast are wind-scoured bluffs and gently sloping hills. The beaches range from sandy to rocky; because of the rugged terrain in certain areas, some are inaccessible. In addition to beaches, many streams—including Prairie Creek, Redwood Creek, Klamath River, Mill Creek, and the Smith River—traverse this series of parks.

> The thick bark of a redwood—up to a foot wide in places—essentially makes the tree fire-proof.

Hikers and redwood lovers will find that several spectacular groves lie adjacent to Routes 101 and 199. Others can be reached along uncrowded trails. Tan oak and madrone grow around the redwoods, while farther inland there are Jeffrey pine and Douglas fir.

Birdwatchers will encounter mallards, hawks, owl, shorebirds, quail, and great blue herons. The mammal population ranges from shrews and moles to rabbit and beaver to black-tail deer, Roosevelt elk, and an occasional bear. Along the coast live river otters and harbor seals. These and other features make the parks a natural for swimming, fishing, canoeing, and kayaking.

Facilities include information centers, picnic areas, restrooms, and showers. Day-use fee, $4 at campgrounds. ~ Located along Route 101 between Orick and Crescent City; Jedediah Smith Redwoods State Park is along Route 199, nine miles east of Crescent City. The park headquarters is at 1111 2nd Street, Crescent City; 707-464-6101, fax 707-464-1812; www.nps.gov/redw.

▲ In the national park, there are four hike-in campgrounds: Nickel Creek, with five sites; Flint Ridge and Demartin, each with ten sites; and Little Bald Hills has four sites and one group site. All are free and completely primitive. The incorporated state parks offer more campgrounds: at **Prairie Creek Redwoods State Park** there are 75 tent/RV sites (no hookups); $12 per night. ~ 707-464-6101 ext. 5113. **Jedediah Smith Redwoods State Park** has 106 tent/RV sites (no hookups); $12 per night. ~ 707-464-6101 ext. 5112. **Del Norte Coast Redwoods State Park** has 145 tent/RV sites (no hookups); $12 per night. ~ 707-464-6101 ext. 5101. In winter, sites are on a first-come, first-served basis. In summer, call for reservations: 800-444-7275.

All along the coast, charter boats depart daily to fish for salmon, Pacific snapper, or whatever else is running. Most companies leave the dock at 6 a.m. and return by 3:30 p.m.

▼▼▼▼▼▼▼▼▼▼▼▼▼▼
Outdoor Adventures

SPORT-FISHING

MARIN COAST If you hanker to try your luck for salmon, contact **Caruso's Sportfishing**. ~ Harbor Drive, Sausalito; 415-332-1015. **Loch Lomond Live Bait House** sells bait and tackle. During the summer they cruise the bay for striper and halibut, winter yields sturgeon. ~ Loch Lomond Marina, San Rafael; 415-456-0321.

SONOMA AND MENDOCINO COAST Bodega Bay Sportfishing operates four boats. Besides salmon charters, they run charters for rock cod, ling cod, albacore, and crab. Whale-watching cruises run January through April, and in the summer there are sunset cruises. ~ 1410 Bay Flat Road, Bodega Bay; 707-875-3344; www.usafishing.com. Whatever your sportfishing tastes, **Anchor Charter Boats** aims to please. Besides the usual rockfish, tuna, salmon, and whale-watching excursions, they'll also take you on extended trips, or out for a funeral. ~ North Harbor Drive, Wharf Restaurant, Fort Bragg; 707-964-4550; www.anchorcharterboats.com.

REDWOOD COUNTRY For deep-sea fishing trips in search of salmon, halibut, or albacore, contact **King Salmon Sportfishing**. Bait and tackle are provided. ~ 3380 Utah Street, Eureka; 707-441-9075; www.kingsalmonsportfishing.com.

KAYAKING

Your trip will take on a new dimension as you paddle among seals and seagulls, along the cityfronts and through the harbors of the world's largest landlocked bay. There are several small companies that cater to kayakers and would-be kayakers of all physical and financial abilities. While the most convenient place to paddle is on the bay itself, there are also stellar locations to the north in Marin County.

MARIN COUNTY To paddle across Richardson Bay under the bright silvery moon, contact **Sea Trek Ocean Kayaking Center**. They also do trips to Angel Island and rent all the equipment you'll need. ~ Schoonmacher Point Marina, Sausalito; 415-488-1000; www.seatrekkayak.com.

RIVER RUNNING

With the Eel, Klamath, Smith, and Trinity rivers traversing many of the North Coast's parks, you're never far away from these mysterious fog-filled areas full of natural vegetation and wildlife.

All Outdoors Adventure Trips offers professionally guided rafting excursions ranging from Class III to Class V. Trips are half-day to three-day affairs, with all food and lodging included. ~ 1250 Pine Street, Suite 103, Walnut Creek; 925-932-8993, 800-247-2387; www.aorafting.com.

In addition to running trips on the Stanislaus, American, and Yuba rivers (Class I to Class V), **Beyond Limits** can arrange kayak and canoe trips. ~ P.O. Box 215, Riverbank, CA 95367; 209-869-6060; www.rivertrip.com.

The **Electric Rafting Company** has half-day to three-day trips on the Trinity, Smith, Klamath, and Eel rivers for all levels. ~ P.O. Box 4418, Arcata, CA 95518; 707-826-2861, 800-499-7238.

GOLF

From Marin to the Oregon border you'll find several clubs where it's relatively easy to get tee times.

SONOMA AND MENDOCINO COAST   On the Sonoma Coast, **Bodega Harbor Golf Links** is hilly and scenic. Part of the 18-hole course meanders around a freshwater marsh. ~ 21301 Heron Drive, Bodega Bay; 707-875-3538; www.bodegaharborgolf.com.

REDWOOD COUNTRY   In the home of that lofty tree, I recommend **Eureka Municipal Golf Course**, an 18-hole course nestled in redwoods. There's a pro shop, a driving range, a putting green, a restaurant, and carts. ~ 4750 Fairway Drive, Eureka; 707-443-4808; www.playeureka.com. In Crescent City, the challenging nine-hole **Del Norte Golf Course** is set amidst redwoods. ~ 130 Club Drive, Crescent City; 707-458-3214.

TENNIS

The best bet for finding a tennis court without staying at the most expensive hotels is to call the local parks and recreation department.

REDWOOD COUNTRY   In Eureka, you can play at **Highland Park**. ~ Highland and Glen streets. **Hammond Park** has two courts. ~ 14th and E streets, Eureka; 707-442-3738. In Crescent City there are three lighted courts available. ~ 301 West Washington Boulevard. For information on courts call 707-464-7237.

RIDING STABLES & PACK TRIPS

Riding along the hauntingly beautiful North Coast is not an experience easily forgotten. This area also offers opportunities for a more delightfully primitive mode of transport—llama riding.

MARIN COAST   There are few prettier places to ride than Point Reyes National Seashore, where you can canter through rolling ranch country and out along sharp sea cliffs. **Five Brooks Stables** conducts mounted tours of this extraordinary area. Reservations required. ~ 8001 Route 1, Olema; 415-663-1570.; www.five brooks.com.

BIKING

Two-wheeling north of San Francisco is an invigorating sport. Not only is the scenery magnificent, but the accommodations aren't bad either. Many state and national parks sponsor campgrounds where cyclists and hikers can stay for a nominal fee.

Route 1 offers a chance to pedal past a spectacular shoreline of hidden coves, broad beaches, and sheer headlands. Unfor-

Whale Watching

It is the world's longest mammal migration: 6000 miles along the Pacific coast from the Bering Sea to Baja California, then back again. The creatures making the journey measure 35 to 50 feet and weigh 40 tons. During the entire course of their incredible voyage they neither eat nor sleep.

Every year from mid-December to early February, the California gray whale cruises southward along the Northern California coast. Traveling in groups numbering three to five, these magnificent creatures hug the shoreline en route to their breeding grounds.

Since the whales use local coves and promontories to navigate, they are easy to spot from land. Just watch for the rolling hump, the slapping tail, or a lofty spout of spuming water. Sometimes these huge creatures will breach, leaping 30 feet above the surface, then crashing back with a thunderous splash.

The best crow's nests from which to catch this aquatic parade are Muir Beach Overlook, Chimney Rock at Point Reyes National Seashore, Bodega Head State Park, Sonoma Coast State Beach, Salt Point State Park, Mendocino Headlands State Park, Shelter Cove or Trinidad Head in Humboldt County, and Point St. George up near Crescent City. Visitors to California's Central Coast also enjoy this annual event.

Several outfits sponsor whale-watching cruises. During the winter and early spring, **Oceanic Society Expeditions** offers gray whale migration tours, which are led by qualified naturalists. June through November, full-day Farallon Islands trips to see humpback and blue whales are provided. ~ Fort Mason Center, Building E, San Francisco; 415-474-3385, fax 415-474-3395; www.oceanic-society.org. For a close look at our fellow mammals from December through May, contact **New Sea Angler & Jaws**. ~ 1445 Route 1, Bodega Bay; 707-875-3495, fax 707-875-9879.

California gray whales live to 40 or 50 years and have a world population numbering about 21,000. Their only enemies are killer whales and humans. They mate during the southern migration one year, then give birth at the end of the following year's migration. The calves, born in the warm, shallow waters of Baja, weigh a ton and measure about 16 feet. By the time they are weaned seven months later, the young are already 26 feet long.

Blue whales, humpback whales, dolphins, and porpoises also sometimes visit the coast. Gray whales can be seen again from March to mid-May, though farther from shore, during their return migration north. So keep an eye peeled: that rocky headland on which you are standing may be a crow's nest in disguise.

tunately, the highway is narrow and winding—for experienced cyclists only.

MARIN COAST   Point Reyes National Seashore features miles of bicycling, particularly along Bear Valley Trail.

SONOMA AND MENDOCINO COAST   Other popular areas farther north include the towns of Mendocino and where level terrain and beautiful landscape combine to create a cyclist's haven.
Bike Rentals   In Mendocino **Catch a Canoe and Bicycles Too!** rents and sells state-of-the-art equipment. ~ Coast Highway 1 at Comptche-Ukiah Road; 707-937-0273. Located on the bicycle migration route between Canada and Mexico, **Fort Bragg Cyclery** does full-service repairs. ~ 221-A North Main Street, Fort Bragg; 707-964-3509.

HIKING

To call California's North Coast a hiker's paradise is an understatement. After all, in San Francisco and north of the city is the Golden Gate National Recreation Area. Together with continuous county, state, and national parks it offers over 100,000 acres to be explored.

Within this ambit are trails ranging from trifling nature loops to tough mountain paths. The land varies from tidal areas and seacliffs to ranch country and scenic mountains. In the far north are the giant redwood forests, located within national parks and featuring networks of hiking trails.

All distances listed for hiking trails are one way unless otherwise noted.

MARIN COAST   The **Marin Headlands**, a region of bold bluffs and broad seascapes, contains many hiking paths in its unpredictable landscape.

The easy-to-moderate **Kirby Cove Trail** (1.5 miles) leads from Conzelman Road down to a narrow beach. The views of San Francisco en route provide a lot of adventure for a short hike.

The moderate **Wolf Ridge Loop** (4.5 miles) begins at Rodeo Beach, follows the Coastal Trail and Wolf Ridge Trail, then returns along Miwok Trail. It ascends from a shoreline environment to heights with sweeping views of both San Francisco and Mt. Tamalpais.

The easy **Tennessee Valley Trail** (2 miles) winds along the valley floor en route to a small beach and cove. The trailhead sits off Route 1 at the end of Tennessee Valley Road.

About 45 miles of trails loop through **Mt. Tamalpais State Park** (415-388-2070, fax 415-388-2968). These link to a 200-mile network of hiking paths through Muir Woods National Monument and Golden Gate National Recreation Area. Explorers are rewarded with a diverse terrain, startling views of the entire Bay Area, and a chance to hike within commuting distance of San Francisco. Most trails begin at Pan Toll Park Headquarters. Here you can pick up trail maps ($1) and descriptions from which to devise your own combination loop trails, or consult with the rangers in planning anything from an easy jaunt to a rugged trek.

Dipsea Trail (6.8 miles) is a favorite moderate path beginning in Mill Valley and heading along rolling hills, past sea vistas, then ending near Stinson Beach. The easiest way to pick up the trail is in Muir Woods, about a mile from the Mill Valley trailhead.

Matt Davis Trail (3.8 miles) descends 1200 feet from Pan Toll Park Headquarters to Stinson Beach; you'll encounter deep woods, windswept knolls, and views of San Francisco and Point Reyes.

Steep Ravine Trail (2.8 miles), true to its name, angles sharply downward from Pan Toll Park Headquarters through a redwood-studded canyon, then joins the Dipsea Trail.

Redwood Creek Trail (2.5 miles) loops through several remarkable redwood stands. A favorite with tourists, this easy trail begins near Muir Woods park headquarters and is often crowded. So it's best hiked either early or late in the day.

There are numerous other trails that combined form interesting loop hikes. For instance, from Bootjack picnic area in Mt. Tamalpais State Park, you can follow **Bootjack Trail** down a steep canyon of redwood and Douglas fir to Muir Woods, then take **Ben Johnson Trail** back up to Pan Toll Park Headquarters. From there it's a half-mile walk back to Bootjack. This 4.2-mile moderate circle tour carries through relatively isolated sections of Muir Woods.

For a more challenging (9.4 miles) circular trek to the top of Mt. Tamalpais, begin at Pan Toll Park Headquarters. You'll encounter Mountain Home, an inn located along Panoramic Highway. Follow **Old Railroad Grade**. This will lead to West Point Inn, a cozy lodging place for hikers. From here you climb to the road that goes to East Peak, one of Mt. Tamalpais' three summits. Heading down along **Fern Creek Trail**, you'll encounter Old Railroad Grade once more. En route are flowering meadows, madrone stands, chaparral-cloaked hillsides, and mountaintop views.

AUTHOR FAVORITE

A hike along the two-mile **Hiouchi Trail** in Del Norte Coast Redwoods State Park, with its huckleberries, trilliums, and rhododendrons, is one of the best ways I know to beat the big-city blues and get back in touch with nature. This nature trail goes right through a burned-out redwood; it also affords scenic vistas along the Smith River.

POINT REYES NATIONAL SEASHORE Within its spectacular 72,000-acre domain, this park contains over 140 miles of hiking trails plus four hike-in campsites. The trails form a latticework across forests, ranch lands, and secluded beaches and along sea cliffs, brackish inlets, and freshwater lakes. Over 350 bird species inhabit the preserve. Black-tailed deer, Eurasian fallow deer, and spotted axis deer abound. You might also encounter raccoons, weasels, rabbits, badgers, bobcats, even a skunk or two.

Most trailheads begin near **Bear Valley Visitors Center**, Palomarin, Five Brooks, or Estero. For maps and information check with the rangers at the visitors center. ~ 415-464-5100, fax 415-663-8132; www.nps.gov/pore.

Hikers can learn about the nearby San Andreas Fault on the short **Earthquake Trail** (.6 mile) that begins from the Bear Valley Visitors Center and leads along the epicenter of the 1906 earthquake. The ground here shifted over 16 feet during that terrible upheaval.

Woodpecker Trail (.7 mile) is an easy self-guiding trail with markers explaining the natural environment. The annotated path leads to a horse "museum" set in a barn.

Bear Valley Trail (4.1 miles), also beginning near the visitors center, courses through range land and wooded valley to cliffs overlooking the Pacific Ocean. The park's most popular trail, it is level and may unfortunately be crowded with hikers and bicyclists.

Coast Trail (16.3 miles) runs between Palomarin (near Bolinas) and Limantour Beach. Hugging the shoreline en route, this moderate, splendid trail leads past four freshwater lakes and two camping areas, then turns inland to Hostelling International's lodge.

Olema Valley Trail (5.2 miles) parallels Route 1 as it tracks a course along the infamous San Andreas Fault. Originating from Five Brooks, it alternates between glades and forest while beating a level path to Dogtown. The trail was damaged in the

BE PREPARED

Keep in mind that the "Lost Coast" is a wilderness area and not a heavily monitored state park. Hikers and campers need to bring water or water purifiers, sturdy hiking boots, and insect repellent. If you want to hike the beach, use a tide table; hikers often get trapped for hours by the tides. Mountain bikers should stick to the area east of King Range. Black Sands Beach is closed to motorized vehicles.

1998 winter storms; check with the visitors center before heading out. Moderate.

Estero Trail (4.4 miles) shadows the shoreline of Drakes Estero and provides opportunities to view local waterfowl as well as harbor seals, sea lions, and bat rays. This trail, also, was damaged in early 1998. Check with the visitors center before walking it.

REDWOOD COUNTRY There are more than 100 miles of hiking and riding paths within **Humboldt Redwoods State Park**. Many lead through dense redwood stands, others meander along the Eel River, and some lead to the park's hike-in camps.

Founder's Grove Nature Trail (.5 mile) tunnels through a virgin redwood forest that once boasted the national champion coastal redwood. Though a storm significantly shortened the 362-foot giant, it left standing a cluster of equally impressive neighbors.

Rockefeller Loop Trail (.5 mile) ducks into a magnificent grove of old-growth redwoods.

There are also longer trails leading deep into the forest and to the top of 3379-foot Grasshopper Peak.

Comprising three distinct state parks and extending for miles along California's northwestern corner, **Redwood National and State Parks'** diverse enclave offers adventure aplenty to daytrippers and mountaineers alike. There are over 150 miles of trails threading the parks, leading through dense redwood groves, along open beaches, and atop wind-buffeted bluffs. ~ 707-464-6101, fax 707-464-1812.

Yurok Loop Trail (1 mile), with its berry patches and wildflowers, begins near the terminus of Coastal Trail.

Enderts Beach Trail (.5 mile), south of Crescent City, features tidepools, seaside strolling, and primitive camping. It also offers access to the moderate **Coastal Trail** (8.2 miles), an old roadway that cuts through forests of redwood, alder, and spruce and features glorious ocean views.

Within **Prairie Creek Redwoods State Park** there are numerous trails to enjoy.

Redwood Creek Trail (9 miles) leads from a trailhead two miles north of Orick to Tall Trees Grove, home of the world's tallest trees. There is backcountry camping en route; permits available at the trailhead.

Tall Trees Trail (1.6 miles) provides a shorter route to the same destination.

Lady Bird Johnson Grove Nature Loop Trail (1 mile) winds through ancient redwood country.

The moderate **Rhododendron Trail** (7.8 miles) begins at park headquarters and continues along the eastern ridge of the park, which is filled with rhododendrons.

James Irvine Trail (4.3 miles) goes from the Prairie Creek visitors center along a redwood ridge to Fern Canyon. For a longer loop (10.3 miles), hike south on Gold Bluffs Beach, then pick up Miner's Ridge Trail. This last trail follows a corduroy mining road used early in the century.

The Fern Canyon Trail (.8 mile) courses along a gulch dripping with vegetation.

The easy Coastal Trail (5 miles) begins at Fern Canyon and parallels Gold Bluffs Beach.

The moderate West Ridge Trail (7.1 miles) traces a sharp ridgetop through lovely virgin forest, ending at the Butler Creek backpacking camp.

The Revelation Trail (.3 mile), a marvelous innovation, contains handrails and a tape-recorded description of the surroundings for the blind. For those of us gifted with sight, it provides a fuller understanding of the scents, sounds, and textures of a redwood forest.

Cathedral Trees Trail (1.4 miles) heads along streams and meadows to elk country.

Brown Creek Trail (1.2 miles), reputedly one of the park's prettiest hikes, leads along streams and through old redwood stands.

Del Norte Coast Redwoods State Park offers several areas ideal for short hikes. Coastal Trail (5.1 miles), located south of the state park, begins at Klamath River Overlook. In addition to ocean vistas, it offers a moderate walk through a spruce and alder forest, plus glimpses of sea lions, whales, and numerous birds.

Damnation Creek Trail (2.5 miles), a strenuous ancient Yurok Indian path, winds steeply down from Route 101 to a hidden cove and beach.

Hobbs Wall Trail (3.8 miles) leads through a former lumberjacking region.

Alder Basin Trail (1 mile) meanders along a stream through stands of willow, maple, and alder.

Farther north, Jedediah Smith Redwoods State Park has a number of trails to hike.

Stout Grove Trail (.5 mile) highlights several spots along its short easy course: a 340-foot redwood tree, swimming and fishing holes, plus rhododendron regions.

Hatton Trail (.3 mile) tours an ancient redwood grove.

Nickerson Ranch Trail (.8 mile) leads through a corridor of ferns and redwoods.

Howland Hill Road (8 miles), a moderate to difficult trail, now overgrown with salmonberries, was once a vital stagecoach route.

When traveling by car you can choose the ever-winding, spectacular coastal **Route 1**, which provides some of the prettiest scenery this side of Shangri-la. Or take **Route 101**, the faster, more direct freeway that follows an interior route.

Transportation

CAR

Eureka/Arcata Airport in McKinleyville is served by Alaska Air and Horizon Air. On a bluff above the Pacific, this is one of the most beautiful small fields in California. **Humboldt Transit Authority** provides roughly hourly service (Monday through Friday) from Eureka and Arcata to the airport. There's limited service on Saturday. ~ 133 V Street, Eureka; 707-443-0826; www.hta.org.

AIR

Greyhound Bus Lines (800-231-2222; www.greyhound .com) travels the entire stretch of Route 101 between San Francisco and Oregon, including the main route through Redwood Country. ~ 707-545-6495; www.greyhound.com.

BUS

It's advisable to rent an auto in San Francisco rather than along the North Coast. There are more rental agencies available and prices are lower. At the Eureka/Arcata Airport you can rent from **Avis Rent A Car** (800-331-1212), **Hertz Rent A Car** (800-654-3131), and **National Car Rental** (800-227-7368).

CAR RENTALS

Golden Gate Transit has bus service between San Francisco and Sausalito. It also covers Route 101 from San Francisco to Santa Rosa. ~ 415-923-2000; www.goldengate.org.

From Santa Rosa you can pick up coastal connections on **Mendocino Transit Authority**, which travels Route 1 from Bodega Bay to Point Arena. There's only one bus a day in either direction. ~ 800-696-4682; www.4mta.org.

Public transportation from San Francisco to Marin can become a sightseeing adventure when you book passage on a **Golden Gate Transit** ferryboat. ~ 415-455-2000.

PUBLIC TRANSIT

SIX

Central Coast

If the Central Coast were an oil painting, it would portray a surf-laced shoreline near the bottom of the frame. Pearly beaches and bold promontories would occupy the center, while forested peaks rose in the background. Actually, a mural would be more appropriate to the subject, since the coastline extends 150 miles from San Francisco to Big Sur. The artist would paint two mountain ranges parallel to the shore, then fill the area between with a patchwork of hills, headlands, and farmland.

Even after adding a swath of redwoods along the entire length of the mural, the painter's task would have only begun. The Central Coast will never be captured—on canvas, in print, or in the camera's eye. It is a region of unmatched beauty and extraordinary diversity.

Due south of San Francisco is Half Moon Bay, a timeless farming and fishing community founded by Italians and Portuguese during the 1860s. The oceanside farms are so bountiful that Half Moon Bay dubs itself the pumpkin capital of the world, and Castroville, farther south, claims to be the artichoke capital. While local farmers grow prize vegetables, commercial fishing boats comb the entire coast for salmon, herring, tuna, anchovies, and cod.

In the seaside town of Santa Cruz, on the other hand, you'll encounter a quiet retirement community that has been transformed into a dynamic campus town. When the University of California opened a school here in the 1960s, it created a new role for this ever-changing place. Originally founded as a Spanish mission in 1791, Santa Cruz became a lumber port and manufacturing center when the Americans moved in around 1849. Then in the late 19th century it developed into a tourist resort filled with elaborate Victorian houses.

Like every place on the Central Coast, Santa Cruz is reached from San Francisco along Route 1, the tortuous coast road that twists past sandy coves and granite cliffs. Paralleling it is Route 101, the inland freeway that leads through the warm, dry agricultural regions of the Salinas Valley. Between these two roadways rise the Santa Cruz Mountains, accessible along Routes 35 and 9. Unlike the low-lying coastal and inland farming areas, this range measures 3000 feet in elevation and is filled with redwood, Douglas fir, alder, and madrone.

Different still is the Monterey Peninsula, a fashionable residential area 125 miles south of San Francisco. Including the towns of Monterey, Pacific Grove, and Carmel, this wealthy enclave is a far cry from bohemian Santa Cruz. If Santa Cruz is an espresso coffeehouse, Monterey is a gourmet restaurant or designer boutique.

Farther south lies Big Sur, the most unique area of all. Extending from the Monterey Peninsula for 90 miles along the coast, and backdropped by the steep Santa Lucia Mountains, it is one of America's most magnificent natural areas. Only about 1000 residents live in this rugged region of bald crags and flower-choked canyons. None but the most adventurous occupy the nearby Ventana Wilderness, which represents the southernmost realm of the coastal redwoods. Once a nesting place for rare California condors, Ventana is still home to wild boar, black bear, and mountain lion.

The Esselen Indians, who inhabited Big Sur and its mountains, took Spanish names to avoid being slaughtered during the missionary period. In recent years, they have been organizing to make the state of California recognize their tribal status. Together with the Costanoans, who occupied the rest of the Central Coast, the Esselen may have been here for 5000 years. By the time the Europeans happened upon California, about 10,000 American Indians lived near the coast between San Francisco and Big Sur. Elk and antelope ranged the region. The American Indians also hunted sea lions, gathered seaweed, and fed on oysters, abalone, clams, and mussels.

Westerners did not settle Big Sur until after 1850, and Route 1 did not open completely until 1937. During the 1950s, novelist Henry Miller became the focus of an artists' colony here. Jack Kerouac trekked through the area, writing about it in several of his novels. Other Beat poets, lured by Big Sur's dizzying sea cliffs and otherworldly vistas, also cut a path through its hills.

Over 300 years before settlers arrived in Big Sur, Monterey was already making history. As early as 1542, Juan Rodríguez Cabrillo, a Portuguese explorer in Spanish employ, set anchor off nearby Pacific Grove. Then in 1602 Sebastian Vizcaíno came upon the peninsula again and told a whale of a fish story, grandly exaggerating the size and amenities of Monterey Bay.

His account proved so distorted that Gaspar de Portolá, leading an overland expedition in 1769, failed to recognize the harbor. When Father Junípero Serra joined him in a second journey the next year, they realized that this gentle curve was Vizcaíno's deep port. Serra established California's second mission in Monterey, then moved it a few miles in 1771 to create the Carmel Mission. Neither Serra nor Portolá explored the Big Sur coast, but the Spanish were soon building yet another mission in Santa Cruz.

In fact, they found Santa Cruz much easier to control than Monterey. By the 1820s, Yankee merchant ships were plying Monterey waters, trading for hides and tallow. This early American presence, brilliantly described in Richard Henry Dana's classic *Two Years Before the Mast*, climaxed in 1846 during the Mexican War. Commodore John Sloat seized the town for the United States. By 1849, while Big Sur was still the hunting ground of American Indians, the adobe town of Monterey had become the site of California's constitutional convention.

An added incentive for these early adventurers, and modern-day visitors as well, was the climate along the Central Coast. The temperature still hovers around 67° in summer and 57° during winter; Santa Cruz continues to boast 300 sunny days a year. Explorers once complained of foggy summers and rainy winters, but like today's travelers, they were rewarded with beautiful spring and fall weather.

Perhaps that's why Monterey became a tourist mecca during the 1880s. Of course the old Spanish capital also developed into a major fishing and canning region during the early 20th century. It was then that John Steinbeck, the Salinas-bred writer, added to the already rich history of Monterey with his novels and stories. Much of the landscape that became known as "Steinbeck Country" has changed drastically since the novelist's day, and the entire Central Coast is different from the days of Serra and Sloat. But the most important elements of Monterey and the Central Coast—the foaming ocean, open sky, and wooded heights—are still here, waiting for the traveler with a bold eye and robust imagination.

▼▼▼▼▼▼▼▼▼▼▼▼▼▼▼▼
South of San Francisco

An easy drive from the city, the coast south of San Francisco is full of surprises. You might see gray whales, watch the sea lions at Año Nuevo State Reserve, or visit one of the rural towns that dot this shoreline. The area along Route 1 between San Francisco and Santa Cruz also sports numerous beaches, bed-and-breakfast inns, and country roads that lead up into the Santa Cruz Mountains.

SIGHTS

Preceding the beauty, however, is the beast. The road south from San Francisco leads through one of America's ugliest towns. In fact, **Daly City** is the perfect counterpoint to the bay city: it is as hideous as San Francisco is splendid. If Tony Bennett left his heart in San Francisco, he must have discarded a gallbladder in Daly City. This town was memorialized in Malvina Reynolds' song, "Little Boxes," which describes its "ticky tacky" houses and over-developed hillsides.

No matter, this suburban blight soon gives way to Route 1, which cuts through Pacifica and curls into the hills. As the road rises above a swirling coastline you'll be entering a geologic hotspot. The **San Andreas Fault**, villain of the 1906 and 1998 earthquakes, heads back into shore near Pacifica. As the road cuts will reveal, the sedimentary rock along this area has been twisted and warped into bizarre shapes. At **Devil's Slide**, several miles south of Pacifica, unstable hillsides periodically collapse into the sea.

Now that I have totally terrified you, I should add that this is an area not to be missed. Drive carefully and you'll be safe to enjoy the outstanding ocean vistas revealed at every hairpin turn in this winding roadway. Rocky cliffs, pocket beaches, and erupting surf open to view. There are sea stacks offshore and, in winter, gray whales cruise the coast.

Text continued on page 360.

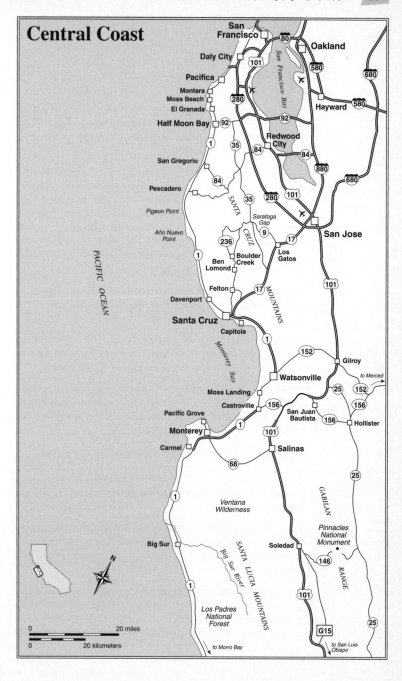

Central Coast

Three-day Weekend

Central Coast

DAY 1 • From San Francisco, follow the San Andreas earthquake fault south on Route 280 to the Routes 35/92 exit, and stay on Route 92 for seven miles to **Half Moon Bay**. Allow one-half to one hour depending on traffic conditions.

• Take coastal Route 1 south to Santa Cruz, a distance of 40 miles that takes about an hour to drive. Along the way you'll discover almost a dozen great beaches along with hidden fishing and farming villages, headlands, marshy estuaries, and sand dunes. Take your pick among such spots as **Pescadero State Beach** (page 368) and **Año Nuevo State Reserve** (page 369) for a mellow morning walk. In this world, it's hard to believe you're just over the hill from the big cities of San Francisco and San Jose.

• Arriving in Santa Cruz, if it's a summer day or weekend, be sure to visit the **Santa Cruz Beach Boardwalk** (page 376), one of the last old-fashioned amusement parks.

• Later in the afternoon, continue down Route 1, skirting **Monterey Bay**. This 30-mile stretch is four-lane divided highway all the way, but you're never far from an opportunity for a beach break.

• **Monterey** has accommodations in all price ranges. If money is no object, you'll find an array of ultra-deluxe resorts in nearby **Pacific Grove** and **Carmel**. Any of these towns makes a fine base for exploring the coast and the Sierra de Salinas.

• Take a **walking tour of Monterey** (page 398) before dinner.

DAY 2 • Visit the fabulous **Monterey Bay Aquarium** (page 397). Allow at least two hours.

• Follow Route 1 down the coast to **Big Sur** (page 420), one of the most spectacular scenic drives anywhere. Scattered restaurants offer lunch possibilities, while four scenic state parks provide perfect picnic spots.

• You could spend the rest of the day continuing to explore your way down Route 1, which winds between the sea and Los Padres National Forest for another 65 miles to San Simeon. Or you could choose to return to Carmel and head into the Santa Lucia Mountains to unwind in the hot springs at the **Tassajara Zen Center** (page 422).

- Return to your Monterey area lodging for the evening.

DAY 3 • Pack a picnic lunch.

- Drive inland from Carmel along pastoral Carmel Valley Road (Route G16) to Greenfield; take Route 101 north for 10 miles to Soledad. Turn east on Route 146 and go 13 miles to the west entrance of **Pinnacles National Monument** (page 415). Allow one and a half to two hours for the drive.

- Equipped with good hiking boots and plenty of water, explore the wild stone wonderland of Pinnacles.

- The return trip to San Francisco via Route 101 takes two hours (unless you encounter traffic snarls in Silicon Valley—a distinct possibility any day of the week).

At the village of **Montara**, you will pass an old lighthouse whose utility buildings have been converted to a youth hostel. As the road descends toward Moss Beach, precipitous rock faces give way to gentle slopes and placid tidepools. Then in Half Moon Bay a four-mile-long white-sand beach is backdropped by new homes built on farmlands.

Half Moon Bay is what happens when the farm meets the sea. It's a hybrid town, half landlubber and half old-salt. They are as likely to sell artichokes here as fresh fish. The town was named for its crescent beach, but thinks of itself as the pumpkin capital of the world. In October, this San Francisco suburb bedroom community hosts the **Pumpkin Festival**, which draws over 300,000 people. At times the furrowed fields seem a geometric continuation of ocean waves, as if the sea lapped across the land and became frozen there. It is Half Moon Bay's peculiar schizophrenia, a double identity that lends an undeniable flair to the community.

From Half Moon Bay, a connecting road leads to Route 35 and Route 9, providing an alternate course to Santa Cruz; this will be covered below, in the "Santa Cruz Mountains" sightseeing section of this chapter. For now, let's stay on Route 1, which continues south, poised between the mountains and the sea.

HIDDEN ► On the southern outskirts of Half Moon Bay, watch for the **Higgins–Purisima Road**, a country lane that curves for eight miles into the Santa Cruz Mountains, returning to Route 1. This scenic loop passes old farmhouses and sloping pastures, mountain meadows and redwood-forested hills. Immediately upon entering this bumpy road, you'll spy a stately old New England–style house set in a plowed field. That will be the **James Johnston House**, a saltbox structure with sloping roof and white clapboard facade. Dating back to 1853 and built by an original '49er, it is the oldest house along this section of coastline. The house is rarely open to the public; during the summer, it occasionally opens on the third Saturday of the month.

The farming plus fishing spirit of Half Moon Bay prevails as Route 1 continues south. A short distance from the highway, you'll encounter **San Gregorio**, a weather-beaten little town. Once a resort area, today it reveals a quaint collection of sagging roofs and unpainted barns. Be sure to drop by the **San Gregorio General Store**, a classic general store that's been around since the 1890s. You'll find live music here on weekend mornings. ~ Corner of Stage Road and Route 84, San Gregorio; 650-726-0565, fax 650-712-1845; www.sangregoriostore.com.

Pescadero represents another timeworn town hidden a short way from Route 1. It's a woodframe hamlet of front-porch rocking chairs and white-steeple churches. The name translates as "fisherman," but the Portuguese and Italian residents are farmers, planting artichokes, Brussels sprouts, beans, and lettuce in the patch-work fields surrounding the town.

A family-owned farm open to the public, **Phipps Ranch** offers a child-friendly barnyard and a market selling dried beans, herbs, and other products grown on the premises. During the summer visitors can pick several varieties of berries. ~ 2700 Pescadero Road, Pescadero; 650-879-0787, fax 650-879-1622; www.phipps country.com.

The beacon several miles south is **Pigeon Point Lighthouse**, a 110-foot sentinel that's one of the nation's tallest lighthouses. The point gained a nasty reputation during the 19th century when one ship after another smashed on the rocks. The lighthouse went up in 1872, and originally contained a 1000-piece lens. Doubling as a youth hostel, it now warns sailors while welcoming travelers.

The Ohlone Indians highly valued the region around **Año Nuevo State Reserve** for its abundant fish and shellfish population. It was here they experienced their first contact with whites in 1769 when Juan Gaspar de Portolá trekked through en route to his discovery of San Francisco Bay. Today, visitors come to Año Nuevo to observe the elephant seals who return to breed each year from December through March. (For further information, see "Beaches & Parks" below.) ~ 650-879-2025, fax 650-879-2031; www.anonuevo.org.

From here to Santa Cruz, the road streams past bold headlands and magnificent seascapes. There are excellent beaches to explore and marvelous vista points along the way. You'll also discover roll-ing farmlands where giant pumpkins grow at the edge of the sea.

About two miles north of Santa Cruz along Route 1 you'll discover **Wilder Ranch State Park**. This 6500-acre spread has 30 acres that have been designated a "cultural preserve" because of the historic houses found on the property. Hiking trails allowing horses and bikes wind throughout. In addition to an 1839 adobe, the complex features a Greek Revival farmhouse dating to 1859 and an 1897 Queen Anne Victorian. You can also tour the out-lying barns and workshops portraying life on a turn-of-the-20th-

AUTHOR FAVORITE

sights

Miles of sand dunes border **Año Nuevo State Reserve**, an en-chanting park that contains an offshore island where two-ton elephant seals breed in winter. With its tidepools, exotic bird population, sea lions, and harbor seals, the reserve is a natural playground. My favorite time to visit is during the mating season of the elephant seals from December to March. See above for more information.

century dairy farm, which this once was. Go on a weekend to see a living-history demonstration and the working Pelton water-wheel, used during the Gold Rush to operate mining equipment. Open Thursday through Sunday, and occasionally other weekdays; call for hours. Parking fee. ~ 831-426-0505, fax 831-423-3756.

LODGING If there were a hotel on the site of **Hostelling International—Point Montara Lighthouse**, it would easily charge $300 a night. Set on a bluff overlooking the ocean, on one of those dramatic points always reserved for lighthouses, the hostel charges down-to-earth prices (and requires a morning chore). The daily fee buys you a bunk in a cozy dorm-style room. Couple and family rooms are also available. There is a kitchen, a common room and an outdoor hot tub in this old lightkeeper's house. This is a good spot for whale watching (November through April). Reservations are strongly recommended. ~ Route 1 at 16th Street, Montara; 650-728-7177; www.norcalhostels.org, e-mail pmlh@slip.net. BUDGET.

The Seal Cove Inn, located 30 minutes south of San Francisco and six miles north of Half Moon Bay, is the perfect place to sojourn for one more night before heading farther afield. The decor is decidedly country inn, with flowers, grandfather clocks, antique furnishings, and a fireplace. But the setting is California-style, with seals, whales, long white beaches, and towering cypress trees sharing the surrounding acreage. ~ 221 Cypress Avenue, Moss Beach; 650-728-4114, 800-995-9987, fax 650-728-4116; www.sealcoveinn.com, e-mail innkeeper@sealcoveinn.com. ULTRA-DELUXE.

The Cape Cod look has become very popular with establishments in the Half Moon Bay area. One of the foremost, **Pillar Point Inn** is a fully modern bed and breakfast cloaked in 19th-century New England disguise. Overlooking the harbor, this 11-room inn combines VCRs, televisions, and refrigerators with traditional amenities like featherbeds, window seats, and fireplaces. Every guest room has a private bath, and there's a deck overlooking the waterfront. Breakfast is a full-course affair. ~ 380 Capistrano Road, Princeton-by-the-Sea; 650-728-7377, 800-400-8281, fax 650-728-8345; www.pillarpointinn.com, e-mail info@pillarpointinn.com. ULTRA-DELUXE.

Sitting right above the beach a few miles north of Half Moon Bay is the 54-room **Beach House**. This contemporary facility, designed in the style of a New England summer home, features "lofts" that include patios, fireplaces, and private balconies. One of the most comfortable hotels along this stretch of coastline, it creates a sense of easy elegance. There's a lobby with fireplace, a heated pool and a jacuzzi, not to mention a succession of beautiful sunsets

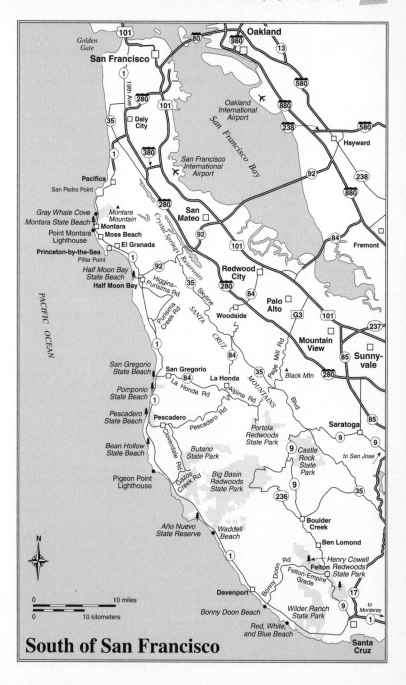

South of San Francisco

just beyond your patio door. ~ 4100 North Cabrillo Highway, P.O. Box 129, Half Moon Bay; 650-712-0220, 800-315-9366, fax 650-712-0693; www.beach-house.com, e-mail view@beach-house.com. ULTRA-DELUXE.

One of the finest country inns along the entire Central Coast is **Mill Rose Inn**. This inn, built in 1902, is adorned with hand-painted wallpapers, European antiques, and colorful tiles throughout. The grounds resemble an English garden and include an enclosed gazebo with a jacuzzi and flagstone patio. Each of the six guest rooms is brilliantly appointed; even the least expensive displays an antique armoire, European featherbed, and marble-top dresser covered with old-style combs and brushes. The sitting room and spacious dining room are equally elegant. ~ 615 Mill Street, Half Moon Bay; 650-726-8750, 800-900-7673, fax 650-726-3031; www.millroseinn.com, e-mail info@millroseinn.com. ULTRA-DELUXE.

Among lodgings on this stretch of coastline, **San Benito House** is a personal favorite. Set in a 1905 building, it's a 12-room bed-and-breakfast inn with adjoining bar and restaurant. The less expensive rooms are small but quite nice. One room I saw featured a brass light fixture, hanging plants, quilted beds, framed drawings, and wood furniture. There are both shared and private baths. Add a sauna plus a country-inn ambience and you have a bargain at the price. ~ 356 Main Street, Half Moon Bay; 650-726-3425; www.sanbenitohouse.com. MODERATE TO DELUXE.

The blue clapboard home of an early merchant in Half Moon Bay is now a bed-and-breakfast inn called the **Zaballa House**. Within the 1859 structure, the oldest in town, are 12 charming rooms, some with fireplaces and large whirlpool tubs. Eleven hotel-style rooms with queen beds, love seats, and fireplaces were recently added to another building on the property. A friendly, unpretentious atmosphere prevails throughout, with guests encouraged to put their feet up in the parlor and relax with a good book. All guests enjoy a full breakfast and afternoon wine and cheese. ~ 324 Main Street, Half Moon Bay; 650-726-9123, fax 650-726-3921; www.zaballahouse.net, e-mail zaballahouse@earthlink.net. DELUXE TO ULTRA-DELUXE.

Comparable to the low-cost lodging at Montara is **Hostelling International—Pigeon Point Lighthouse**. It has a similarly dramatic windswept setting above the ocean. The rooms are in several shared cottages with kitchens, living rooms, and accommodations for couples. Rates, as in other American Youth Hostels, are budget, and a chore is requested. Guests have access to a private, clifftop hot tub for a small fee. Set beneath California's second tallest lighthouse on a beautiful shoreline, the hostel is a charming place to stay. Four private rooms are available for an additional charge. Reservations strongly advised; couples should call four to six months in advance. ~ Route 1 at Pigeon Point Road, Pescadero; 650-879-0633, fax 650-879-9120; www.norcalhostels.org. BUDGET.

Davenport Bed & Breakfast Inn, located near the coast about ten miles north of Santa Cruz, has a singular appeal. A few rooms here are situated in a historic old house; most are upstairs from a gallery gift shop. The staff is congenial and the accommodations mighty comfortable. All rooms have private baths and are imaginatively decorated with watercolors. In fact, the owners are potters and have adorned some rooms with their handicrafts. You can also look for antique pieces, oak furniture, and wall-to-wall carpeting. Complimentary breakfast included. ~ 31 Davenport Avenue, Davenport; 831-425-1818, 800-870-1817, fax 831-423-1160; www.davenportinn.com. DELUXE.

DINING

Nick's Restaurant has been operated by the same Greek-Italian-American family for more than seven decades and is still pulling in the Pacifica crowds. Wood sculptures of sea life decorate the walls, but the main attraction is the million-dollar view of Rockaway Beach. Nick's is known for its grilled crab sandwiches, sautéed prawns, and fettuccine angelina. ~ 100 Rockaway Beach, Pacifica; 650-359-3900, fax 650-359-5624. DELUXE.

For dinner overlooking the ocean, there's nothing quite like **Moss Beach Distillery**. The place enjoys a colorful history, dating back to Prohibition days, when this area was notorious for supplying booze to thirsty San Francisco. Today it's a bustling plate-glass restaurant with adjoining bar and an indoor/outdoor patio with an incredible ocean view. The menu includes fresh seafood, gulf shrimp and Chicago steaks. The bootleggers are long gone, but those splendid sea views will be here forever. Brunch served on Sunday. Closed first three weeks of December ~ Beach Way and Ocean Boulevard, Moss Beach; 650-728-5595, fax 650-728-8135; www.mossbeachdistillery.com. DELUXE TO ULTRA-DELUXE.

AUTHOR FAVORITE

I find the countrified atmosphere at **New Davenport Cash Store Restaurant** a perfect match to the hearty, homestyle meals served here. It's decorated with colorful wall rugs, handwoven baskets, and fresh flowers. The cuisine at this eatery ranges from chorizo and eggs to tofu and vegetables to mushroom cheese-melt sandwiches to steamed clams. More ordinary fare—such as omelettes, hamburgers, steak, and seafood—is also on the agenda. They also feature dinner specials such as salmon, scallops, and chicken. Breakfast, lunch, and dinner daily. ~ 1 Davenport Avenue, Davenport; 831-426-4122; www.davenportinn.com. MODERATE TO DELUXE.

Speaking of seafood, **Barbara's Fishtrap** down on Half Moon Bay has some of the lowest prices around. Set in and around a small woodframe building smack on the bay, this unpretentious eatery features several fresh fish dishes daily. "The trap," as the locals call it, is liable to be serving fresh sea bass, local halibut, and salmon, as well as steak sandwiches and shellfish. Calamari rings are a specialty. Friendly, local, inexpensive—and highly recommended. ~ 281 Capistrano Road, Princeton-by-the-Sea; 650-728-7049, fax 650-728-2519. MODERATE.

For contemporary California cuisine in a country inn setting, there's **San Benito House**. This gourmet restaurant with moderate to deluxe prices incorporates fresh seafood and produce from the surrounding ocean and farm country. On a typical night you might choose salmon with mustard vinaigrette, homemade ravioli, or filet of beef with chanterelle mushrooms. The hotel also houses a budget-priced deli (open daily 11 a.m. to 3:30 p.m.) that serves homemade soup, salad, and bread. ~ 356 Main Street, Half Moon Bay; 650-726-3425; www.sanbenitohouse.com. MODERATE.

If you're in the mood for raw oysters, fresh produce and hearty Mediterranean dishes stop by **Cetrella** for dinner (or Sunday brunch). This bistro/café is a mix of the contemporary and the traditional, with its open, stainless-steel kitchen, roaring fireplace, and exposed-truss ceiling. Along with a tempting selection from the raw bar, they offer up intriguing appetizers from their cheese-and-charcuterie room. The menu changes daily: I started with shrimp ceviche and ended with a vanilla *panna cotta* and fresh cherries; my main course was milk-braised lamb shank with aromatic Moorish spices. ~ 845 Main Street, Half Moon Bay; 650-726-4090; www.cetrella.com. DELUXE TO ULTRA-DELUXE.

Once past Half Moon Bay, restaurants become mighty scarce. Practically anything will do along this lonesome stretch south; but rather than just anything, you can have **Duarte's Tavern**. Open since 1894, this restaurant and tavern has earned a reputation all down the coast for delicious food. There's a menu filled with meat and fish entrées, omelettes, and sandwiches. They also serve a variety of homemade desserts, and there's a full bar. Personally, I recommend trying the artichoke soup and olallieberry pie. Breakfast, lunch, and dinner daily. ~ 202 Stage Road, Pescadero; 650-879-0464, fax 650-879-9460; www.duartestavern.com. MODERATE TO DELUXE.

NIGHTLIFE   There's jazz and classical music most Sunday afternoons at the **Bach Dancing and Dynamite Society**. There's also occasional classical and jazz music on Saturday nights. Situated beachfront off Route 1 about two miles north of the Route 92 intersection, it's renowned for quality sounds. Call for dates. ~ Miramar Beach, off Medio Road, Half Moon Bay; 650-726-4143; www.bachddsoc. org, e-mail bachsociety@aol.com.

The **New Davenport Cash Store Bar** offers a mellow café-like setting. ~ 1 Davenport Avenue, Davenport; 831-426-4122; www. swanton.com.

BEACHES & PARKS

GRAY WHALE COVE This white-sand crescent is a well-known clothing-optional beach. Tucked discreetly beneath steep cliffs, it is also a beautiful spot. The undertow is strong, so swimming is not advised. The only facilities are toilets. Day-use fee. ~ Located along Route 1 three miles south of Pacifica. Watch for the parking lot on the east side of the highway. Cautiously cross the highway and proceed down the staircase to the beach.

MONTARA STATE BEACH Though this half-mile beach may be a haven to nude sunbathers, police controls occasionally pass out tickets. Volleyball players and frisbee throwers can be found everywhere. Backdropped by a rocky bluff, it's a very pretty place. Surfers ride the small swells. The only facilities here are primitive toilets and parking is limited. ~ The beach is located along Route 1 seven miles south of Pacifica. There is a trail leading to the beach from Route 1 and 2nd Street in Montara; 650-726-8820, fax 650-726-8816.

Spanish explorer Gaspar de Portolá dropped anchor at San Gregorio in October 1769.

JAMES V. FITZGERALD MARINE RESERVE Boasting the best facilities among the beaches in the area, this park also has a sandy beach and excellent tidepools. It's a great place to while away the hours watching crabs, sea urchins, and anemones. Since there are houses nearby, this is more of a family beach than the freewheeling areas to the immediate north and south. There are restrooms and a picnic area. ~ Off Route 1 in Moss Beach about eight miles south of Pacifica; 650-728-3584.

HALF MOON BAY STATE BEACH (OR FRANCIS BEACH) Despite a four-mile-long sand beach, this park receives only a guarded recommendation. Half Moon Bay is a working harbor, so the beach lacks the seclusion and natural qualities of other strands along the coast. Of course, with civilization so near at hand, the facilities here are more complete than elsewhere. Also, Francis Beach is part of a chain of beaches that you can choose from, including Venice Beach, Roosevelt Beach, and Dunes Beach. Personally, I pick the last. Surfers head to the sandy beach break at Francis Beach and below Half Moon Bay jetty. Restrooms or toilets are available at all four beaches; picnic areas at Francis Beach. Day-use fee, $2. ~ All four park segments are located along Route 1 in Half Moon Bay; 650-726-8820, fax 650-726-8816.

▲ There are 43 tent/RV sites (no hookups) and 4 additional tent sites at Francis Beach, available during the summer only; $12 per night. Hiker/biker camp available at Francis; $1 per night. First-come, first-served for all sites.

HIDDEN ► **SAN GREGORIO STATE BEACH** 🏃 🚣 🏄 🛶 There is a white-sand beach here framed by sedimentary cliffs and cut by a small creek. Star of the show, though, is the nearby private nude beach (admission) north of the state beach, reputedly the first beach of its type in California. Among the nicest of the state's nude beaches, it features a narrow sand corridor shielded by high bluffs. There are picnic areas and toilets at the state beach, no facilities at the nude beach. Day-use fee, $4. ~ Located along Route 1 about 15 miles south of Half Moon Bay. Entrance to the nude beach is several hundred yards north of the state beach entrance; 650-879-2170, fax 650-879-2172.

POMPONIO STATE BEACH 🏃 🏄 🛶 Less appealing than its neighbor to the north, this park has a white-sand beach that's traversed periodically by a creek. There are headlands on either side of the beach. Facilities include picnic areas and toilets. Day-use fee, $4. ~ Route 1, about 16 miles south of Half Moon Bay; 650-879-2170, fax 650-879-2172.

PESCADERO STATE BEACH 🏃 🏄 🛶 Backed by sand dunes and saltwater ponds, this lovely park also features a wide beach. There are tidepools to the south and a wildlife preserve across the highway. Steelhead run annually in the streams here, while deer, blue herons, and egrets inhabit the nearby marshland. Rangers lead guided tours. There are picnic areas and toilets. ~ Route 1, about 19 miles south of Half Moon Bay; 650-879-2170, fax 650-879-2172.

BEAN HOLLOW STATE BEACH 🏃 🏄 🛶 The small sandy beach here is bounded by rocks, so sunbathers go elsewhere while tidepool watchers drop by. Particularly interesting is nearby Pebble Beach, a coarse-grain strand studded with jasper, serpentine, agates, and carnelians. The stones originate from a quartz reef offshore and attract rockhounds by the pack. But don't take rocks away—it's illegal. Also not to be missed is the blufftop trail between Bean Hollow and Pebble Beach, from which you can espy whales and seals in season. Facilities include a picnic area and toilets. ~ Located along Route 1 about 21 miles south of Half Moon Bay; Pebble Beach is about a mile north of Bean Hollow; 650-879-2170, fax 650-879-2172.

BUTANO STATE PARK 🏃 🚴 🛶 This inland park, several miles from the coast, provides a welcome counterpoint to the beach parks. About 3600 acres, it features a deep redwood forest, including stands of virgin trees. Hiking trails traverse the territory. Not as well known as other nearby redwood parks, Butano suffers less human traffic. The park has picnic areas and restrooms. Day-use fee, $4. ~ Located 22 miles south of Half Moon Bay. Coming from the north on Route 1, go 20 miles south of Half Moon Bay; turn left (east) on Pescadero Road, and then right on Cloverdale Road about four miles to the park. Or, coming from the south, turn right (east) on Gazos Creek Road (two miles south of Pigeon Point Lighthouse) and then left on Cloverdale Road; phone/fax 650-879-2040.

> Pigeon Point is named for the *Carrier Pigeon*, a Yankee clipper that wrecked on the rocks here in 1854.

▲ There are 32 sites for tents, 7 for RVs (no hookups); $15 per night. Camping by reservation only from Memorial Day to Labor Day: 800-444-7275.

AÑO NUEVO STATE RESERVE 🏌 🏃 ⛵ 🚣 Awesome in its beauty, abundant in wildlife, this park is one of the most spectacular on the California coast. It consists of a peninsula heaped with sand dunes. A miniature island lies just offshore. There is a nature trail for exploring. Seals and sea lions inhabit the area; loons, hawks, pheasants, and albatrosses have been spied here. But most spectacular of all the denizens are the elephant seals, those lovably grotesque creatures who come here between December 15 and March 31 to breed. Elephant seals, reaching two tons and 16 feet, are adorned with bulbous, trunk-like snouts for which they are named. Back in 1800, elephant seals numbered in the hundreds of thousands; by the end of the century, they were practically extinct; it's only recently that they have achieved a comeback. When breeding, the bulls stage bloody battles and collect large harems, creating a spectacle that draws crowds every year. During breeding season, docents lead two-and-a-half-hour tours that must be booked eight weeks in advance by calling 800-444-4445. The tours cover seal-breeding areas, which otherwise are closed to the public throughout the breeding season; during the rest of the year the entire park and the seal rookery are open. Be forewarned that it's a three-mile roundtrip walk from the parking lot to the rookery. During the summer there are surf breaks off the end of beach, about ten minutes south of the rookery. Also be aware, the elephant seal population makes this beach attractive to sharks. Closed the first two weeks of December. The only facilities are toilets. Day-use fee, $4. ~ Off Route 1, about 26 miles south of Half Moon Bay; 650-879-2025, 650-879-0227 (recorded information), fax 650-879-2031; www.anonuevo.org.

GREYHOUND ROCK 🚣 One of the most secluded strands in the area, this beach is a beauty. There are startling cliffs in the back-   ◄ *HIDDEN* ground and a gigantic boulder—Greyhound Rock—in the foreground; the area is a favorite among those who love to fish. It is also, unfortunately, a favorite for thieves. Keep your valuables with you and lock your car. Although the beach has good conditions for swimming, it has been known to be "sharky." Restrooms and picnic areas are the only facilities. ~ Located along Route 1 about 30 miles south of Half Moon Bay. From the parking lot at the roadside follow the path down to the beach.

BONNY DOON BEACH ⚓ This spot ranks among the most popular nude beaches in California. Known up and down the coast, the compact beach is protected on either flank by rugged cliffs. There are dunes at the south end of the beach, caves to the north, plus bevies of barebottomed bathers in between. Currents are strong; be careful when swimming. Keep a close eye on your valuables. This beach has no security nor facilities. ~ Off Route 1, about eight miles north of Santa Cruz. Watch for the parking lot near the junction with Bonny Doon Road; follow the path across the railroad tracks and down to the beach.

RED, WHITE, AND BLUE BEACH 🏊 🎣 ⚓ 🚤 ⛵ There's a clothing-optional beach here surrounded by rocky headlands. There are also more RVs than at a Fourth of July picnic. The beach is monitored for safety and no cameras or dogs are allowed. Visitors have to pay upon entry. Of course, the beach does provide facilities and permit camping but somehow the management takes the nature out of bathing au natural. There are picnic areas, restrooms, and hot showers. Day-use fee, $10. ~ Off Route 1, five miles north of Santa Cruz. Watch for the red, white, and blue mailbox at Scaroni Road intersection; follow Scaroni Road a short distance west to the beach; phone/fax 831-423-6332.

▲ There are 35 sites; $15 per night, per person. Closed November through January.

Santa Cruz Mountains

▼▼▼▼▼▼▼▼▼▼▼▼▼▼

For a hawk's-eye view of the Santa Cruz Mountains and redwood country, leave the coast at Half Moon Bay and catch Route 35 (Skyline Boulevard) south. This rustic highway climbs along a ridgetop, revealing vistas of both the ocean and San Francisco Bay. From the tangled undergrowth on either side of the road, scattered trees, pine and deciduous, stand against open sky.

SIGHTS

The forest gathers around you as Route 35 tunnels through dense, tall timber. You are entering a land of giants. A gate and small sign, three miles north of the Route 84 turnoff, mark **Methuselah**, a stately 1800-year-old redwood.

For an interesting detour loop, take Route 84 (La Honda Road) south to **La Honda**, a knotty-pine town decorated with a bar, a restaurant, and a post office. This forest retreat is novelist Ken Kesey's old stomping ground. During the halcyon days of the '60s, his band of Merry Pranksters, like rebels in the hills, swept down from La Honda through Northern California and beyond. They were mind-guerrillas, set on overthrowing American consciousness with the "Trips Festival," a multimedia extravaganza of rock music, light shows, and street theater, raised to an electric pitch by massive doses of psychedelic drugs.

Today La Honda has lapsed back into rural consciousness. Rather than tripping out or experiencing heavy life changes, you'll

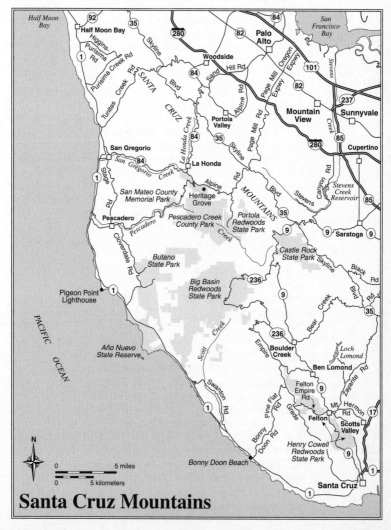

Santa Cruz Mountains

probably just pass through town and pick up Alpine Road, which returns to Route 35. En route you'll encounter **Heritage Grove**, a virgin redwood forest with a creek and hiking trails, and then emerge into rolling hill country marked by broad vistas.

Pick up Route 9 south, the redwood road that will eventually lead to Santa Cruz. Before this winding mountain road descends to the sea, it connects with an even narrower and more sinuous thoroughfare, Route 236, which goes to **Big Basin Redwoods State Park**. One of the area's prettiest parks, it offers nature trails galore, 2000-year-old redwood stands, and complete facilities for picnicking and camping.

Accommodations in the Santa Cruz Mountains cluster around the towns of Boulder Creek, Ben Lomond, and Felton. They are generally of two types: neon motels and piney lodges. The first are less expensive, the second more inviting.

Rejoining Route 9 in **Boulder Creek**, you'll find that this town, **Ben Lomond**, and **Felton** are central to the area's travel facilities. They house numerous antique stores and crafts shops. In addition to tourists, they also attract a lot of winter rain. In 1982 this became a disaster area: almost two feet of rain fell in just 36 hours, hillsides collapsed, mudslides buried homes, and 21 people died in Santa Cruz County. Outside Ben Lomond, a dozen people are buried in mudslides so deep their bodies have never been recovered.

Now that you're convinced never to go near the region, let me tell you some of its marvelous features—like the **Felton covered bridge** (at the edge of town on Covered Bridge Road). A wood-plank span with sagging shingle roof, the structure dates from 1892. Appropriately, it's set in a secluded spot along the San Lorenzo River.

At nearby **Henry Cowell Redwoods State Park** there are 2390 acres of redwood forest to explore; one trail here leads to the dean of the forest, an ambassadorial, 285-foot tree.

During the summer you can climb aboard the full-size Santa Cruz, Big Trees and Pacific Railway for a scenic eight-mile journey from the Santa Cruz boardwalk to the hillside town of Felton. In Felton you can catch the area's locomotive superstar, the **Roaring Camp & Big Trees Pacific Railroad**. This vintage steam engine whistles through redwood stands en route to Bear Mountain. Passengers are invited to picnic on the mountain, hike the area, then return on a later train. ~ Graham Hill Road, Felton; 831-335-4400; www.roaringcamp.com.

LODGING   **Merrybrook Lodge**, set in a redwood grove, has six pretty cottages right on a creek. They are one-bedroom structures, with living room, kitchen, and porch. The floors are hardwood, the walls knotty pine, and as a final touch, there's a woodstove. For rustic living high in the mountains, you'll be hard pressed to find a more inviting place. ~ 13420 Big Basin Highway, Boulder Creek; 831-338-6813. MODERATE TO DELUXE.

Innkeeper Hanna Peters greets all her guests at the **Felton Crest Inn Bed and Breakfast** with champagne and chocolate kisses. It's a pleasant arrival to an even more pleasing inn. All four rooms and suites are wonderfully furnished and have either a jacuzzi or add-on whirlpool. Outside the house is a peaceful redwood glade, which keeps the surroundings green and lush year-round; it's close to Henry Cowell Redwoods State Park. Continental breakfast included. ~ 780 El Solo Heights Drive, Felton; 831-335-4011; www.feltoncrest.com. ULTRA-DELUXE.

Tyrolean Inn, a rustic little restaurant, serves German and Bavarian dishes. During the dinner hour, they stoke the fires and prepare an array of German dishes. Sauerbraten, wiener-schnitzel, and smoked pork chops with sauerkraut are among the European dishes. Brunch and lunch on weekends only; dinner nightly. Closed Monday. ~ 9600 Route 9, Ben Lomond; 831-336-5188; www.tyroleaninn.com. BUDGET TO DELUXE.

DINING

Around since 1904, **Scopazzi's Inn** can still be trusted for a good meal. The place is perfectly fitted to its mountain environment, with wood-paneled walls, a lofty, exposed-beam ceiling and lots of windows for great views. Add a tile fireplace, a patio, and a lounge for a prize establishment in the heart of Santa Cruz redwood country. The menu is equal to all this: there are numerous dinners—roast beef, filet of sole, veal parmigiana—complete with soup, salad, antipasto, and dessert. At lunch they serve sandwiches, salads, pasta dishes, and several platters including veal cutlet and calamari. Closed Monday and Tuesday. ~ 13300 Big Basin Highway, Boulder Creek; 831-338-6441, fax 831-338-6442. MODERATE TO DELUXE.

Hailing from Italy, Chef Luca Rubino brings his culinary expertise to **La Bruschetta**, a house *cum* restaurant in a residential neighborhood. This unpretentious place cooks up traditional Sicilian dishes with organic and homegrown ingredients, from *gamberoni in unido* (prawns, sautéed garlic, capers, tomatoes, and white wine) to *agnolotti alla ragusana* (round ravioli stuffed with wild mushrooms and ciocavello cheese, and draped in a butter and sage sauce). If the weather's nice, dine on their outdoor patio. No lunch Monday through Thursday. ~ 5447 Route 9, Felton; 831-335-3337; www.labruschettasc.com. MODERATE.

SAN MATEO COUNTY MEMORIAL PARK 🚶 🚲 🏊 A 499-acre park, this redwood preserve is covered with hiking trails. There's a creekside swimming hole, a visitors center, and a redwood tree dating back 1500 years. In an area of extraordinary parks, this one's a sleeper, small but beautiful, and a good place to avoid the

PARKS

crowds found at more popular parks. It's also a gateway to 7400-acre **Pescadero Creek County Park**, with a network of trails and hike-in campsites. There's also the very special 38-acre Heritage Grove, an unusual stand of redwoods that are bigger and larger in diameter than others in the park. Facilities include picnic areas, restrooms, showers, a horse camp for those with horses, and a snack bar that also sells a few groceries. Day-use fee, $5. ~ 9500 Pescadero Creek Road, about six miles from La Honda; 650-879-0212, 650-879-0238, fax 650-879-1034.

▲ There are 158 sites; $18 per night; hike-in sites are free but you need a permit from the park.

PORTOLA REDWOODS STATE PARK 🏃 With dense stands of redwood, Douglas fir, and tan oak, this natural facility is a great place for exploration. There are 18 miles of hiking trails, including one leading to Tiptoe Falls, a five-foot waterfall. Add to the attributes of this lovely park several creeks filled with steelhead (no fishing, however) and an undergrowth thick with huckleberry. There are picnic areas, restrooms, and showers. Day-use fee, $5. ~ From Route 35, take Alpine Road west to Portola State Park Road; 650-948-9098.

▲ There are 53 sites plus a backpack camp; $16 per night. Closed in winter.

CASTLE ROCK STATE PARK 🏃🐎 A hiker's paradise, this 3800-acre semi-wilderness area has no entry roads. To experience the place you'll have to join the many hikers, backpackers, and rock climbers who number this among their favorite parks. The rewards are several: a network of trails, including one that descends 31 miles to the ocean; a waterfall; and the eponymous sandstone boulder which crowns this retreat at 3214 feet. Hike-in campsites feature picnic areas, toilets, and running water. Parking fee, $5. ~ The

SAVING THE GIANTS

Almost as fascinating as Big Basin Redwoods State Park's natural wonders is the history behind its founding. At the turn of the 20th century, most of these magnificent groves were marked for destruction by lumbermen. But Andrew P. Hill, a local photographer and conservationist, vowed to preserve the giants. Hill had been infuriated and inspired when an arrogant landowner refused him permission to photograph the redwoods because they were private property! Dedicated to "Save the Redwoods," Hill formed the Sempervirens Club, which lobbied for preservation of forests throughout the state. Today, you can hike to **Slippery Rock**, opposite a waterfall, where pioneer conservationists made a pact to protect the public's natural heritage.

parking lot and trailhead are on Skyline Boulevard, two and a half miles south of the intersection with Route 9; 408-867-2952.

▲ Permitted at 23 hike-in campsites; $10. For information, contact the park headquarters at 831-338-8861.

BIG BASIN REDWOODS STATE PARK 🚶 🚵 🐎 California's oldest state park, this 18,000-acre expanse reaches from the ocean to a 2300-foot elevation. Within that domain are 2000-year-old redwoods, a sandy beach, 88 miles of hiking trails, 20 to 30 miles of mountain-biking trails, and a host of facilities. You'll also find Homo sapiens in tents, black-tailed deer, coyotes, bobcats, raccoons, and salamanders inhabiting the area, as well as over 250 bird species that either live here or drop by. It's highly recommended that you do also. There are picnic areas, a mini-museum, a snack bar, a grocery, a gift shop, restrooms, and showers. Day-use fee, $5. ~ 21600 Big Basin Way (Route 236), nine miles north of Boulder Creek; Route 9 connects with Route 236, leading to the park; 831-338-8861.

▲ There are 183 designated sites plus several hike-in sites; $16 per night. Also, four-person tent cabins are available for $49 per night. Reservations: 800-874-8368. (Two especially recommended campsites near park headquarters are the Blooms Creek and Huckleberry campgrounds.)

HENRY COWELL REDWOODS STATE PARK 🚶 🚵 🐎 ⛵ An 1800-acre park on the San Lorenzo River, it features a short nature trail (three-quarter-mile loop) through a redwood forest. One of the sequoias here measures 285 feet; there are also stands of Douglas fir and madrone. With 18 miles of hiking trails, picnic areas, a mini-museum, a bookstore, restrooms, and showers, it's a favorite among locals. Fishing is prohibited during summer, and alcohol is not allowed. Day-use fee, $5. ~ Off Route 9, just south of Felton; 831-335-4598, fax 831-335-3156.

▲ There are 111 sites in a campground on Graham Hill Road three miles from the park center; $14 to $16 per night. Information: 831-438-2396.

▼▼▼▼▼▼▼▼▼▼

Santa Cruz

One of California's original missions, a University of California campus, a historic railroad, and some of the finest Victorian neighborhoods on the coast are just a few of the pluses in Santa Cruz. This town of 51,000 population is in many respects one big playground. It enjoys spectacular white sand beaches, entertaining nightlife, and an old-style boardwalk amusement park. The city faces south, providing the best weather along the Central Coast. Arts and crafts flourish here, and vintage houses adorn the area.

Route 1, California's magnificent coastal highway, veers slightly inland upon reaching Santa Cruz, which means it's time to find

SIGHTS

a different waterfront drive. Not to worry, the best way to begin exploring the place is at the north end of town around **Natural Bridges State Beach**. A pretty spot for a picnic, this is the place to pick up West Cliff Drive, which sweeps the Santa Cruz waterfront. The shoreline is a honeycomb of tiny coves, sea arches, and pocket beaches. From **Lighthouse Point** on a clear day, the entire 40-mile curve of Monterey Bay silhouettes the skyline. Even in foggy weather, sea lions cavort on the rocks offshore, while surfers ride the challenging "Steamer Lane" breaks.

Testament to the surfers' talent is the tiny **Santa Cruz Surfing Museum** situated in the lighthouse at Lighthouse Point. Here vintage photos and antique boards re-create the history of the Hawaiian sport that landed on the shores of Santa Cruz early in the 20th century. Closed Tuesday (and Wednesday in winter). ~ West Cliff Drive and Lighthouse Point, Santa Cruz; 831-420-6289; www. santacruzmuseums.org, e-mail carolyn@santacruzmuseums.org.

Beach Street continues this coast-hugging route to **Santa Cruz Municipal Pier**, a half-mile-long wharf lined with bait shops, restaurants, and fishing charters. Those early-morning folks with the sun-furrowed faces are either fishing or crabbing. They are here everyday with lawn chairs and tackle boxes. When reality overcomes optimism, they have been known to duck into nearby fresh fish stores for the day's catch. The pier is a perfect place to promenade, soak up sun, and seek out local color. It also provides a peaceful counterpoint to the next attraction.

Santa Cruz Beach Boardwalk is Northern California's answer to Coney Island. Pride of the city, it dates back to 1907 and sports several old-fashioned rides. The penny arcade features vintage machines as well as modernistic video games. You'll find shooting galleries and candy stalls, coin-operated fortune tellers and do-it-yourself photo machines. Shops sell everything from baubles to bikinis. Then there are the ultimate entertainments: a slow-circling Ferris wheel with chairs suspended high above the beach; the antique merry-go-round, a whirl of mirrors and flashing color; a funicular whose brightly painted cars reflect the sun; rides with names that instantaneously evoke childhood memories—bumper cars, tilt-a-whirl, haunted castle; and that soaring symbol of amusement parks everywhere, the roller coaster. Closed December and most non-summer weekdays. ~ 400 Beach Street; 831-423-5590, fax 831-460-3336; www.beachboardwalk.com.

The Boardwalk's 1911 Loof carousel and the 1924 Giant Dipper roller coaster are both listed as National Historic Landmarks.

The **Cocoanut Grove Ballroom**, located on the boardwalk, has hosted Big Band greats like Benny Goodman and the Dorsey brothers. It occasionally sponsors dancing, usually disco or salsa. ~ 400 Beach Street; 831-423-2053; e-mail jan@beachboard walk.com.

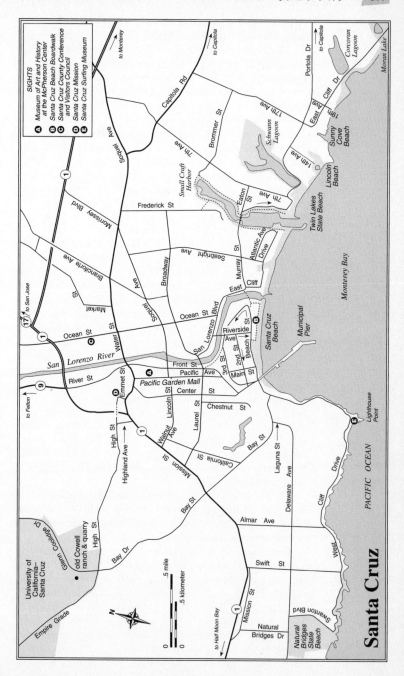

SIGHTS
- **A** Museum of Art and History at the McPherson Center
- **B** Santa Cruz Beach Boardwalk
- **C** Santa Cruz County Conference and Visitors Council
- **D** Santa Cruz Mission
- **E** Santa Cruz Surfing Museum

Santa Cruz

The playground for shoppers sits several blocks inland along Pacific Avenue. **Pacific Garden Mall** is a tree-lined promenade that stretches from Cathcart to Water streets. Beautifully executed, the entire mall is a study in urban landscaping and planning. On October 17, 1989, a 7.1 earthquake centered just a few miles from Santa Cruz sent most of the mall tumbling into the street, killing three people.

Within walking distance of the mall are several places that merit short visits. The **Museum of Art and History at the McPherson Center** features changing exhibits that focus primarily on California art. Exhibits relate to the social history of the Santa Cruz area, using photographs and artifacts. Also here is the **Museum Store**, which houses a gift shop for the museum within its century-old, eight-sided structure. Closed Monday. Admission. ~ 705 Front Street; 831-429-1964, fax 831-429-1954; www.santacruzmah.org, e-mail admin@santacruzmah.org.

And the **Santa Cruz Mission**, a half-scale replica of the 1791 structure, pales by comparison with the missions in Carmel and San Juan Bautista. Closed Monday. ~ 126 High Street; 831-426-5686.

A remarkable piece of restoration, **Santa Cruz Mission State Historic Park** provides a fascinating timeline on California's past. This 1822 adobe home was built for and by the Ohlone and Yocut Indians who sold the property to Californios (children of Spanish settlers). Later it was bought by Irish immigrants. Various rooms document each of these periods with artifacts excavated on the site. Reflecting the difficulties of early-19th-century interior design, the California Room is decorated with mismatched wallpaper that was sent at different times from the East Coast. Touring is self-guided, but guided tours are available by appointment. Special events including cooking demonstrations, candlemaking, and brick-making take place occasionally, as does American Indian storytelling (call for dates). Closed Monday through Wednesday. ~ 144 School Street near Mission Plaza; 831-425-5849, fax 831-429-6748.

The **Santa Cruz County Conference and Visitors Council** has information to help orient you with the area. ~ 1211 Ocean Street; 831-425-1234, 800-833-3494; www.santacruzca.org, e-mail comments@santacruzca.org.

Santa Cruz's rich history has left a legacy of elegant **Victorian houses**. Although there are no guided tours, if you set out on your own you won't be disappointed. In the Beach Hill area, not far from the Boardwalk, be sure to see the gem-like home at **1005 3rd Street**, counterpoint to the multilevel confection with Queen Anne turret at **311 Main Street**. Near Pacific Garden Mall is the Civil War–era **Calvary Episcopal Church**, with its clapboard siding and shingle roof. ~ 532 Center Street. The **200 block of Walnut Avenue** is practically wall-to-wall Victorians. Located near the Santa Cruz Mission is the white-painted brick **Holy Cross Roman Catholic Church**. The steeple of this 1889 Gothic Revival beauty is a landmark for miles around. ~ 126 High Street. Nearby **Francisco Alviza House**, vintage 1850s, is the oldest home in town. ~ 109 Sylvar Street. Around the corner, the **200 block of Mission Street** displays several houses built shortly afterwards. Nearby is **W. W. Reynolds House**, which was an Episcopal Church in 1850. ~ 123 Green Street.

From this last Victorian cluster, High Street leads to the **University of California–Santa Cruz** campus. Turn right at Glenn Coolidge Drive and you'll find an information booth dispensing maps, brochures, and words of wisdom. Those stone ruins and sun-bleached buildings nearby are the remains of the old Cowell ranch and limestone quarry from which 2000 of the campus acres were drawn. ~ 831-459-0111.

Due to the lack of lodging facilities in the early 20th century, visitors to Santa Cruz stayed in Tent City, where the accommodations consisted of striped tents on wooden frames, with wood floors, lights, and running water.

No ivory tower ever enjoyed the view that UC Santa Cruz commands of Monterey Bay. Set on a hillside, with redwood forest and range land all around, the campus possesses incredible beauty. The university itself is divided into eight colleges, insular and self-defined, each marked by a different architectural style. The best way to see this campus is simply to wander: Walk the fields, trek its redwood groves, and explore the different colleges that make it one of the West's most progressive institutions. Of particular interest at UC Santa Cruz are the organic farm as well as the arboretum, with its Mediterranean garden and outstanding collection of Australian and South African plants.

The **Seymour Marine Discovery Center** is located at the Joseph M. Long Marine Laboratory, a University of California research facility. Part museum, part working lab, the center is dedicated to teaching the public about the role of research in ocean conservation and features hands-on displays and working aquarium exhibits. The 87-foot blue whale skeleton (the largest on display in the world) is a highlight. Closed Monday. Admission. ~ End of Delaware Avenue; 831-459-3800, fax 831-459-1221; seymourcenter.ucsc.edu.

LODGING

When seeking overnight accommodations in Santa Cruz, the place to look is near the beach. That is where you'll want to be and, not surprisingly, where you'll find most hotels and motels. The problem during summer months is the cost. In winter you can have a room for a song, but come June the price tags climb.

An excellent facility is **Ocean Echo Motel and Cottages**, located near a quiet neighborhood beach. This 15-unit clapboard complex sits far from the madding Boardwalk crowd right on the beach. It represents a perfect choice for anyone seeking a studio or Cape Cod–style cottage. Some have kitchens and private patios. Weekly rentals are sometimes available. In summer there's a two-night minimum. ~ 401 Johans Beach Drive; 831-462-4192, fax 831-462-0658; www.oceanecho.com, e-mail beach@oceanecho.com. MODERATE TO ULTRA-DELUXE.

It's big, brash, and blocky, but the **Coast Santa Cruz Hotel** is also right on the beach. With pool, jacuzzi, oceanfront restaurants, and lounge, this multitiered establishment extends from a hilltop perch down to a sandy strand. Long on aesthetics it isn't, and it's sometimes noisy on weekends and in the summer, but for location it can't be topped. The boardwalk and fishing pier are a short stroll away. Each of the 163 guest rooms are trimly done with fabric walls and contemporary furnishings; each sports a private balcony and ocean view. The question is whether you'll endure the plastic atmosphere for the sake of proximity to the Pacific. It's your call. (Being lazy myself, I'd book reservations in a minute.) ~ 175 West Cliff Drive; 831-426-4330, 800-663-1144, fax 831-427-2025; www.coasthotels.com. DELUXE TO ULTRA-DELUXE.

Country inns are rare in Santa Cruz; this California custom is slowly catching on here. One exception is **Cliff Crest Bed & Breakfast Inn**, a five-bedroom establishment in a historic 1887 Victorian home. Among the features of the house are an outdoor belvedere, a yard landscaped by the designer of San Francisco's Golden Gate Park, and a solarium illuminated through stained-glass windows. Rooms vary in cost from a small room with private bath to the spacious "Rose Room," which has a fireplace. In any case, the decor you're apt to find includes patterned wallpaper and an antique bed. ~ 407 Cliff Street; 831-427-2609, fax 831-427-2710; www.cliffcrestinn.com, e-mail info@cliffcrestinn.com. MODERATE TO ULTRA-DELUXE.

There is also **Hostelling International—Santa Cruz**, located some distance from the beach. Set in restored Victorian cottages on well-located Beach Hill, it offers 40 dorm-style beds, two private family rooms and one private couple's room. The cottages are two blocks from the beach and boardwalk. There are also hot showers, a kitchen, a dining area, internet access, and a common room; all linen provided free of charge. There is an 11 p.m. curfew and in summer a three-night maximum stay. Non-members pay $3 more. ~ 321 Main Street; 831-423-8304, 800-909-4776 ext. 45, fax 831-429-8541; www.hi-santacruz.org, e-mail info@hi-santacruz.org. BUDGET.

Another member of this elite club, **Château Victorian** sits in a vintage home just one block from the Boardwalk. Guests here enjoy a sun deck and a sitting/dining room decorated with antique sideboard and wooden mantel. The entire house has been done by masterful decorators who placed plush carpeting throughout. The place is chockablock with antiques: a canopied bed, oak armoires, and so on. Less expensive rooms have carpets and are located in the cottage. Main house rooms are more costly. All rooms have fireplaces and feature tile bathrooms; expanded continental breakfast buffet included. ~ 118 1st Street; 831-458-9458; www.chateauvictorian.com. DELUXE TO ULTRA-DELUXE.

Less distinguished, but considerably cheaper, is **Harbor Inn** across town. The place sits in a two-story stucco house in a semi-residential neighborhood a couple blocks from the beach. It supports 19 bedrooms, all with refrigerators and microwaves. There are both private and shared baths. All are spacious, attractive, and inexpensively furnished. The staff is helpful and friendly, making this place a fortuitous addition to the local housing scene. ~ 645 7th Avenue; 831-479-9731, fax 831-479-1067; www.harborinn santacruz.com. MODERATE.

Santa Cruz also has a string of neon motels within blocks of the Boardwalk. Count on them to provide small rooms with color television, wall-to-wall carpeting, nicked wooden tables, naugahyde chairs, stall showers, etc.; if they have any decorations at all you'll wish they didn't. But what the hell, for a night or two you can call them home. Their rates fluctuate wildly depending on the season and tourist flow. (Generally they charge budget prices in winter; summer prices escalate to the moderate range.) The best of the lot is **St. Charles Court**, which has a pool and is spiffier and quieter than the others. ~ 902 3rd Street; 831-423-2091. BUDGET TO MODERATE.

Located within walking distance of the beach is **Big 6 Motel**. It sits in a two-story stucco building and contains 22 rooms with private baths. ~ 335 Riverside Avenue; 831-423-1651. BUDGET TO MODERATE.

Right next door is the **Super 8 Motel**, which has 23 rooms decorated in a white and burgundy color scheme. Guests here enjoy lounging at the pool or soaking in the spa. Continental break-

BEACH BARGAIN

The best bargain in town is **Surfside Apartments**. This seven-unit establishment contains several cottages and houses clustered around a flower garden and courtyard. They are truly efficiency units: no television, telephone, parking facilities, or housekeeping services. But they are comfortably furnished, possess a friendly "beach cottage" feel, and feature kitchens. Located two blocks from the Boardwalk, there are one- and two-bedroom apartments. They are only available from late June through Labor Day. ~ 311 Cliff Street; 831-423-5302. MODERATE.

fast is included. ~ 321 Riverside Avenue; 831-423-9449, 800-906-9066, fax 831-425-5100. DELUXE.

DINING   Most Santa Cruz restaurants can be found near the Boardwalk or in the downtown area, with a few others scattered around town. Of course, along the Boardwalk the favorite dining style is to eat while you stroll. Stop at **Hodgie's** for a corn dog, Italian sausage sandwich, or fried zucchini; sit down to a bowl of clam chowder or crab salad at the **Fisherman's Galley**; or pause at the **Barbary Coast** for cheeseburgers, baked potatoes, or "chicken nuggets." For dessert there are caramel apples, ice cream, cotton candy, popcorn, and saltwater taffy.

If all this proves a bit much, try one of the budget restaurants on Beach Street, across from the Boardwalk. Foremost is **Beach Street Café**, an attractive little cranny with white tablecloths and potted plants. This café houses the largest U.S. collection of Maxfield Parrish limited-edition prints. Breakfast begins with guacamole omelettes, bagels, croissants, or pancakes. Matter of fact, breakfast continues until late afternoon. Try the "Eggs Sardou" (artichoke bottoms with spinach, poached eggs, and hollandaise sauce) or the "Eggs Beach Street" (for which they replace the spinach with sautéed shrimp). The "mile-high" burgers are worth trying to get your teeth around. No dinner. ~ 399 Beach Street; 831-426-7621; www.beachstreetcafe.com. MODERATE.

Nearby **El Paisano Tamales** has the standard selection of tacos, tostadas, enchiladas, and burritos. Seasonal closures. ~ 605 Beach Street; 831-426-2382. BUDGET.

Ideal Bar and Grill is a tourist trap with tradition. It's been one since 1917. It also has decent food and a knockout view, especially from the outdoor deck right on the sand. The place is wedged in a corner between the beach and the pier, which means it looks out on everything, from boardwalk to bounding deep.

AUTHOR FAVORITE

I often join the locals at their favorite Mexican restaurant, **El Palomar**, named the best Mexican restaurant by the readers of *Good Times*, a local entertainment newspaper, for several years running. This leafy Mexican cantina is housed in a beautiful 1930s hotel and sports soaring ceilings and a giant mural of a Mexican woman cooking outdoors. El Palomar serves up such Mexican seafood dishes as prawn burritos and the Jose special—grilled skirt steak, snapper, and prawns. Homemade tortillas and specialty margaritas enhance the delicious fare. ~ 1336 Pacific Avenue; 831-425-7575, fax 831-423-3037. BUDGET TO DELUXE.

The specialty is seafood—calamari, oysters, lobster, and salmon. Several pastas, plus a few meat and fowl dishes, round out the menu. ~ 106 Beach Street; 831-423-5271, fax 831-423-3827. MODERATE TO DELUXE.

Cozy **Casa Blanca Restaurant**, with its overhead fans and Moroccan flair, is an excellent dinner choice. The place has a wraparound view of the ocean, not to mention a tony decor. The menu includes such gourmet selections as grilled duck, rack of lamb, seafood linguine, and filet mignon with brandy. Casa Blanca boasts one of the largest selections of wines in Santa Cruz County. Dinner only. ~ 101 Main Street; 831-426-9063, fax 831-423-0235; www.casablanca-santacruz.com, e-mail casabeach@aol.com. MODERATE TO ULTRA-DELUXE.

Among the many places in the Pacific Garden Mall area, my personal favorite is **The Catalyst**. I don't go there so much to eat as to watch. Not that the food is bad (nor particularly good, for that matter), but simply that The Catalyst is a scene. At night the place transmogrifies into a club with live music and unfathomable vibrations. By day, it's just itself, a cavernous structure with a glass roof and enough plants to make it an oversized greenhouse. Indeed, some of the clientele seem to have taken root. There are two bars if you're here to people watch. Otherwise meals are cafeteria-style and include a full breakfast menu, deli sandwiches, burgers, and a few dinner selections. ~ 1011 Pacific Avenue; 831-423-1338, fax 831-429-4135; www.catalystclub.com. BUDGET.

◀ HIDDEN

For Japanese food there's **Benten**, a comfortable restaurant complete with a sushi bar. They serve an array of traditional dishes including *yosenabe*, sashimi, tempura, teriyaki, and a special plate called *kaki* fry (deep-fried breaded oysters). Understated and reliable. Closed Tuesday. ~ 1541 Pacific Avenue, Suite B; 831-425-7079. BUDGET TO MODERATE.

Aldo's Harbor Restaurant, a café with patio deck overlooking Santa Cruz Harbor, whips up seafood dishes, pastas, soups, salads, and sandwiches. Conveniently located near Seabright Beach, this unassuming little place serves breakfast and lunch. ~ 616 Atlantic Avenue; 831-426-3736, fax 831-426-1362. BUDGET TO MODERATE.

Opa! For Greek food and fun hit up **Vasili's Greek Taverna**. It's a quirky place where the walls are chockablock with trinkets and the kebabs are great. Patrons like the flaming cheese appetizer, especially when the owner comes over and lights the dish up. Closed Monday. ~ 1501 Mission Street, Suite A; 831-458-9808. MODERATE.

The central shopping district in Santa Cruz is along Pacific Garden Mall, a six-block strip of Pacific Avenue converted to a promenade. The section is neatly landscaped with flowering shrubs

SHOPPING

and potted trees and its sidewalks, widened for window browsers, overflow with people.

You can stop by **Artisans Gallery**, which deals in fine handcrafts and gift items by local artists. They feature outstanding pottery, woodwork, glassware, and jewelry. ~ 1364 Pacific Avenue; 831-423-8183. The **Bookshop Santa Cruz** is the finest among this college town's many wonderful bookstores. ~ 1520 Pacific Avenue; 831-423-0900; www.bookshopsantacruz.com.

Strolling along **Pacific Avenue,** you will find galleries, gift stores, plus arts-and-crafts shops run by local artists. Also, many artisans' studios are located at the center, making it a gathering place for craftspeople as well as a clearinghouse for their wares.

NIGHTLIFE   In Santa Cruz, **The Catalyst** is the common denominator. A popular restaurant and hangout by day, it becomes an entertainment spot at night. There's live music most weekday evenings in the Atrium, where local groups perform. But on weekends the heavyweights swing into town and The Catalyst lines up big rock performers. Some all-ages shows. Cover charge for live bands. ~ 1011 Pacific Avenue; 831-423-1336, fax 831-423-7853; www. catalystclub.com.

The unassuming **Kuumbwa Jazz Center** headlines top-name musicians Monday and Thursday nights. Folks under 21 are welcome at this club. Cover. ~ 320 Cedar Street; 831-427-2227; www.jazzqwest.com/kuumbwa.

120 Union Street is a funky café in an old repair shop. Relax on a couch beneath the hanging plants and soak up the nightly music while sipping a soy espresso drink or a pint of beer. ~ 120 Union Street; 831-459-9876.

The Crow's Nest offers eclectic entertainment with an ocean view. On any given night they will be headlining jazz, reggae, salsa, rock, blues, or, on Sunday night, comedy. Cover. ~ 2218 East Cliff Drive; 831-476-4560; www.crowsnest-santacruz.com.

The crowd at **Blue Lagoon** dances to taped and deejay music during the week, and watches go-go dancers on Friday and Saturday night in summer. The club draws "gay boys and girls with a couple straight people thrown in for color." ~ 923 Pacific Avenue; 831-423-7117; www.thebluelagoon.com.

BEACHES & PARKS   **NATURAL BRIDGES STATE BEACH** 🏃 ⚓ 🎣 🚣 ⚓ 🛶 Northernmost of the Santa Cruz beaches, Natural Bridges is a small park with a halfmoon-shaped beach and tidepools. This is a popular windsurfing spot in the summer. It's quite pretty, though a row of houses flanks one side. In the winter, surfers gather on the reef break. This is also an excellent spot to watch monarch butterflies during their annual winter migration (from October to late February). During these months there are weekend guided

tours of the eucalyptus groves. Facilities include picnic areas, a
visitors center, a bookstore, and restrooms. No dogs are allowed.
Closed Monday and Tuesday in summer. Day-use fee, $5. ~
Located at the end of West Cliff Drive near the western edge of
Santa Cruz; 831-423-4609; e-mail naturalbridges@juno.com.

SANTA CRUZ BEACH Of the
three major beaches extending along the Santa Cruz waterfront,
this is the most popular, most crowded, and most
famous. All for a very simple reason: the Santa
Cruz Boardwalk, with its amusement park and
restaurants, runs the length of the sand, and the
Santa Cruz Municipal Pier anchors one end of the
beach. This, then, is the place to come for crowds and
excitement. "Steamer Lane" is the Santa Cruz surfing
hotspot. A series of reef breaks are located along West
Cliff Drive, extending west to Lighthouse Point. Facilities
include restrooms, showers, seasonal lifeguard, volleyball,
restaurants, and groceries. ~ Located along Beach Street; access
from the Municipal Wharf and along the Boardwalk.

> All but one of the sea
> arches at Natural Bridges
> State Beach have col-
> lapsed, leading local
> wags to dub the spot
> "Fallen Arches."

SEABRIGHT BEACH Also known as Castle
Beach, Seabright is second in Santa Cruz's string of beaches. This
beauty extends from the San Lorenzo River mouth to the jetty at
Santa Cruz Harbor. It's long, wide, and backdropped by bluffs.
The views are as magnificent as from other nearby beaches, and
the crowds will be lighter than along the Boardwalk. There are
restrooms, fire rings, and a lifeguard in summer. ~ Access to the
beach is along East Cliff Drive at Mott Avenue, or at the end of
3rd Avenue; 831-429-2850, fax 831-475-8350.

TWIN LAKES STATE BEACH Just the other
side of Santa Cruz Harbor is this odd-shaped beach. Smaller than
the two beaches to the north, it is also less crowded. The park is
94 acres, with a lagoon behind the beach and a jetty flanking one
side. A very pretty spot. Surfing is sometimes okay in winter or
after a storm. There are restrooms and lifeguards during the
summer. ~ At East Cliff Drive and 7th Avenue, south of Santa
Cruz Harbor; 831-429-2850, fax 831-475-8350.

LINCOLN BEACH, SUNNY COVE, MORAN LAKE BEACH Located
along the eastern end of Santa Cruz, these three sandy beaches
are in residential areas. As a result, they draw local people, not
tourists; they're also more difficult to get to, and, happily, are less
crowded. All are backdropped by bluffs. If you want to buck the
crowds, they're worth the trouble. There are restrooms and picnic
areas at Lincoln Beach and Moran Lake Beach; otherwise amenities are scarce. Parking is a problem throughout the area (though
Moran Lake Beach has a parking lot where you can park all day
for a fee during summer and weekends, otherwise free). ~ All three

beaches are near East Cliff Drive. Lincoln Beach (part of Twin Lakes State Beach) is at the end of 14th Avenue, Sunny Cove at the end of 17th Avenue, and Moran Lake Beach is near Lake Avenue.

▼▼▼▼▼▼▼▼▼▼▼▼▼▼▼▼▼▼▼▼

Santa Cruz to Monterey

From Santa Cruz, coastal Route 1 heads south through Capitola, known for its sparkling beach and September Begonia Festival, and through Aptos, another bedroom community with equally pretty beaches.

SIGHTS Aptos' most popular place these days is a foreboding forest located at latitude 37° 2' and longitude 121° 53'. That precise spot, at the end of a two-mile trail in the Forest of Nisene Marks State Park, is the **1989 earthquake epicenter.** A stake now marks ground zero of the 7.1 shaker that devastated Northern California. To reach the trailhead, follow Aptos Creek Road north from Aptos to the Nisene Marks parking lot. ~ 831-763-7063.

HIDDEN ▶ In nearby Rio del Mar, there's a **rural side trip** that carries you past miles of farmland before rejoining Route 1 near Watsonville. To take this side trip follow San Andreas Road, which tunnels through forest, then opens into rich agricultural acres. Intricately tilled fields roll down to the sea and edge up to the foot of the mountains. At the end of San Andreas Road, follow Beach Street to the ocean. The entire stretch of coastline is flanked by high sand dunes, a wild and exotic counterpoint to the furrowed fields nearby.

Beach Street leads back into **Watsonville**. Central to the surrounding farm community, Watsonville is the world's strawberry-growing capital. It's also rich in **Victorian houses**, which you can tour with a printed guide from the **Chamber of Commerce**. Closed weekends. ~ 444 Main Street, Watsonville; 831-724-3900, fax 831-728-5300; www.pvchamber.com, e-mail commerce@pv chamber.com.

Back on Route 1, you'll pass **Moss Landing**, a weather-beaten fishing harbor. With its antique stores, one-lane bridge, bright-painted boats, and unpainted fish market, the town has a warm personality. There is one eyesore, however, a huge power plant with twin smokestacks that stand out like two sentinels of an occupying army. Otherwise the place is enchanting.

HIDDEN ▶ Nearby, **Elkhorn Slough National Estuarine Research Reserve** is a 1400-acre world of salt marshes and tidal flats managed by a state and federal partnership between the California Department of Fish and Game and the National Oceanic and Atmospheric Administration. Within this delicate environment live some 400 species of invertebrates, 80 species of fish, and 300 species of birds (among them redshouldered hawks, peregrine falcons, and acorn woodpeckers), as well as harbor seals and sea otters. Guided tours on the weekend. To get to the visitors center from Route

1, follow Dolan Road for three miles, go left on Elkhorn Road, and then proceed two more miles. Closed Monday and Tuesday. Admission. ~ 1700 Elkhorn Road, Watsonville; 831-728-2822; www.elkhornslough.org, e-mail esf@elkhornslough.org.

Next in this parade of small towns is **Castroville**, "Artichoke Center of the World." Beyond it is a cluster of towns—Marina, Sand City, and Seaside—that probably represent the sand capitals of the world. The entire area rests on a sand dune that measures up to 300 feet in depth, and extends ten miles along the coast and as much as eight miles inland. From here you can trace a course into Monterey along wind-tilled rows of sand.

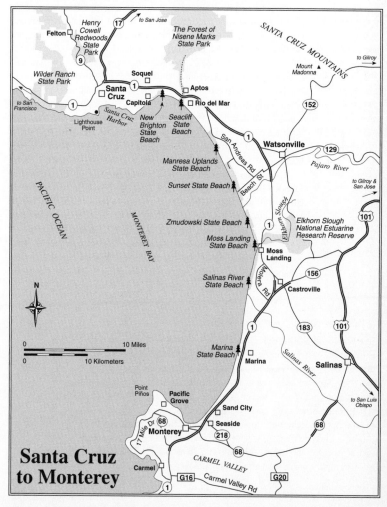

Santa Cruz
to Monterey

In Salinas, the **Steinbeck House** in which author John Steinbeck grew up is located a few blocks from the National Steinbeck Center. It now serves as a restaurant, open for lunch Monday through Saturday. Reservations are recommended. ~ 132 Central Avenue, Salinas; 831-424-2735. MODERATE.

John Steinbeck's grave is in the Garden of Memories cemetery. ~ 768 Abbot Street, Salinas.

LODGING

Capitola Venetian Hotel is a mock Italian complex next to Capitola Beach. With its stucco and red tile veneer, ornamental molding, and carved wooden doors, it's a poor cousin to the grand villas of Venice. The 20 guest rooms come equipped with kitchens. There are few wall decorations and the furnishings lack character, but the atmosphere is pleasant. Two-night minimum on weekend. ~ 1500 Wharf Road, Capitola; 831-476-6471, fax 831-475-3897, 800-332-2780; www.capitolavenetian.com, e-mail info rmation@capitolavenetian.com. MODERATE TO ULTRA-DELUXE.

Harbor Lights Motel, a few steps farther uphill from the beach, is similarly laid out but in a more modern fashion. This ten-unit stucco building has rooms with completely equipped kitchens and ocean views. The views of Monterey Bay are the real draw here. ~ 5000 Cliff Drive, Capitola; 831-476-0505, fax 831-476-0235. MODERATE TO ULTRA-DELUXE.

Does a trip around the world interest you? If so, the **Inn at Depot Hill** might save you time and money without sacrificing the feel of the trip. This 12-room bed and breakfast, fashioned from a former train station, features internationally decorated rooms with names like "Paris," "Côte d'Azur," and "Portofino." There is a fireplace in each room and most come with a patio and hot tub. Full breakfast, hors d'oeuvres with wine, and dessert are included with a night's stay. ~ 250 Monterey Avenue, Capitola;

FOR THE LOVE OF STEINBECK

The **National Steinbeck Center**, located in the heart of Oldtown Salinas (the historic district surrounding the town plaza), houses photographic, multimedia, and interactive exhibits about the life and work of Salinas-born author John Steinbeck, as well as a wing on the agricultural history of the region. It also contains a research library of more than 45,000 manuscripts, first editions, newspaper and magazine articles, reviews, letters, TV and radio scripts, theses, and historic photographs by and about Steinbeck and his works. Admission. ~ 1 Main Street, Salinas (eight miles southeast of Route 1 via Route 183); 831-796-3833, fax 831-796-3828; www.steinbeck.org, e-mail info@steinbeck.org.

831-462-3376, 800-572-2632, fax 831-462-3697; www.innsby thesea.com. ULTRA-DELUXE.

Attention to cozy detail is the forte of the **Blue Spruce Inn**. There are three rooms in the main house and three rooms in the garden area. Most have jacuzzis and fire places. One room has a hot tub in its private garden. Afternoon wine is served in the parlor (summer only). Full breakfast included. ~ 2815 South Main Street, Soquel; 831-464-1137, 800-559-1137, fax 831-475-0608; www.bluespruce.com, e-mail info@bluespruce.com. DELUXE TO ULTRA-DELUXE.

With two miles of beachfront, **Pajaro Dunes** is ideal for those who want to go down to the sea. Located midway between Santa Cruz and Monterey, this resort colony has 130 condominiums, townhouses, and beachhomes that range from one to five bedrooms. While decorating schemes vary from beach contemporary to brass and glass, all units offer kitchens, fireplaces, decks, and barbecues. There are 19 on-site tennis courts. The big units are a good bet for large family groups. A two-night minimum stay is required for houses. ~ 2661 Beach Road, Watsonville; 831-722-9201, 800-564-1771; www.pajarodunes.com, e-mail info@pajaro dunes.com. ULTRA-DELUXE.

DINING

The area's foremost dining room is actually outside Santa Cruz in a nearby suburb. True to its name, the multitiered **Shadow-brook Restaurant,** in operation since 1947, sits in a wooded spot through which a creek flows. Food is almost an afterthought at this elaborate affair; upon entering the grounds you descend either via a funicular or a sinuous, fern-draped path. Once inside, you'll encounter a labyrinth of dining levels and rooms, luxuriously decorated with potted plants, stone fireplaces, and candlelit tables. A mature tree grows through the floor and ceiling of one room here; in others, vines climb along the walls. When you finally chart the course to a table, you'll be offered a cuisine including prime rib, salmon, and other fresh seafood dishes. Definitely a dining experience. No lunch on Saturday. ~ 1750 Wharf Road, Capitola; 831-475-1511; www.shadowbrook-capitola.com, e-mail office@shadowbrook-capitola.com. MODERATE TO DELUXE.

Capitola Beach is wall-to-wall with seafood restaurants. They line the strand, each with a different decorative theme but all seeming to merge into a collection of pit stops for hungry beachgoers. If you're expecting me to recommend one you are asking more than mortal man can do. I say when in doubt, guess.

Touted as the best Mexican restaurant in Monterey County is **The Whole Enchilada**, specializing in seafood dishes. The chef uses locally grown produce like Castroville artichokes and chiles, fresh fish, prawns, and oysters. Try the "whole enchilada" entrée—fillet of red snapper wrapped in corn tortillas topped with

melted cheese and chile salsa. Save room for flan! ~ Route 1 at
Moss Landing Road, Moss Landing; 831-633-5398, fax 831-
633-5391. BUDGET TO MODERATE.

Right next door is the **Lighthouse Harbor and Grill**, offering
early breakfast (they open at 6:30 a.m.) and lunch. Mexican
dishes are available, but more standard fare such as omelettes
dominate the menu. There are even whole wheat hotcakes. Yum!
~ 7902 Route 1, Suite C, Moss Landing; 831-633-3858. BUDGET.

SHOPPING   Located along Route 1 south of Santa Cruz, the coastal village of
Moss Landing is a must for antique hounds. More than 20 shops
offer a wide array of treasures from the good old days. Clustered
around the intersection of Moss Landing Road and Sand Holt
Road are several shops that warrant a close look.

Stepping into **Yesterday's Books** is a bit like discovering a private library filled with antiquarian treasures. Closed Monday
through Wednesday. ~ 7902 Sand Holt Road, Building E, Moss
Landing; 831-633-8033.

NIGHTLIFE   For a relaxing evening, try **Shadowbrook Restaurant**. Its soft lighting and luxurious surroundings create a sense of well-being, like
brandy and a blazing fire. They present live music Thursday
through Monday nights in their Rockroom Lounge. ~ 1750
Wharf Road, Capitola; 831-475-1511, fax 831-475-7664; www.
shadowbrook-capitola.com.

Several of the restaurant lounges lining Capitola's waterfront
have nightly entertainment. Over at **Zelda's** you can enjoy a quick
drink on the patio, and occasional live music. ~ 203 Esplanade,
Capitola; 831-475-4900.

BEACHES   **CAPITOLA CITY BEACH** 🏊 🎣 🚶 🏖 ⛵ ⚓ Sedimentary
& PARKS   cliffs flank a corner of this sand carpet but the rest is heavily developed. Popular with visitors for decades, Capitola is a well-
known resort community. Seafood restaurants line its shore and
boutiques flourish within blocks of the beach. A great place for
families because of the adjacent facilities, it trades seclusion for
service. The ocean is well protected for water sports and in winter, surfers enjoy the breaks near the jetty, pier, and river mouth.
There are restrooms, showers, lifeguards, a fishing pier, and volleyball. ~ Located in the center of Capitola; 831-475-6522, fax
831-475-6530.

NEW BRIGHTON STATE BEACH 🏊 🎣 ⚓ This sandy crescent
adjoins Seacliff Beach and enjoys a wide vista of Monterey Bay.
Headlands protect the beach for swimmers and beginning
surfers. Clamming is also popular. Within its mere 94 acres, the
park contains a forested bluff. There are picnic areas, fire pits,
restrooms, and showers (for campers only). Note: Due to con-

struction, the park and campgrounds will be closed until mid-2004. Day-use fee, $5. ~ Off Route 1 in Capitola, four miles south of Santa Cruz; 831-464-6330, 831-464-6329, fax 831-685-6443.

▲ There are 112 tent/RV sites in a wooded area inland from the beach; $12 per night. There are no RV hookups. Reservations are required (people book up to seven months in advance): 800-444-7275.

SEACLIFF STATE BEACH 🏖 🏊 🎣 🛶 This two-mile strand is very popular. *Too* popular: During summer, RVs park along its entire length and crowds gather on the waterfront. That's because it provides the safest swimming along this section of coast. There are roving lifeguards on duty during the summer and a protective headland nearby. The visitors center offers guided walks year-round to look at fossils. The beach also sports a pier favored by anglers, but because of storm damage is closed. It's a pretty place, but oh so busy. There are picnic areas, restrooms, and showers. Day-use fee, $5. ~ Off Route 1 in Aptos, five miles south of Santa Cruz; 831-685-6500, fax 831-685-6443.

> Following a year of heavy storms, the beach at Capitola City Beach often disappears under the high tide.

▲ There are 26 sites for RVs and self-contained vehicles (full hookups); $26 per night. There are also 20 overflow sites for self-contained vehicles (no picnic tables, fireplaces, or hookups); $20 per night. Reservations are required: 800-444-7275.

THE FOREST OF NISENE MARKS STATE PARK 🚶 🚴 This semi-wilderness expanse, several miles inland, encompasses over 10,000 acres. Within its domain are redwood groves, meandering streams, rolling countryside, and dense forest. About 30 miles of hiking trails wind through the preserve. Along them you can explore fossil beds, deserted logger cabins, old trestles, and railroad beds; you can also hike to the epicenter of the 1989 earthquake. The park is a welcome complement to the natural features along the coast. There are picnic tables and barbecues. Day-use fee, $2. ~ From Route 1 southbound take the Seacliff Beach exit in Aptos, five miles south of Santa Cruz. Take an immediate left on State Park Drive, pass over the highway, and then go right on Soquel Drive. Follow this for a half-mile; then head left on Aptos Creek Road. This paved road turns to gravel as it leads into the forest; 831-763-7063, fax 831-763-7120.

MANRESA UPLANDS STATE BEACH 🏖 🏊 🛶 Here you'll find a strip of white sand bookended by blufftop homes. Popular with surfers, it provides a sweeping view of Monterey Bay. A bit more removed than other nearby beaches, Manresa nevertheless can be quite popular on summer afternoons. Facilities include restrooms, lifeguards (in summer), picnic tables, and, for campers, fire pits and showers. Day-use fee, $5. ~ Located 13 miles south of Santa Cruz; from Route 1, take the Larkin Valley Road and San Andreas Road exit, turn right onto San Andreas Road and follow it several miles to the park turnoff; 831-761-1795.

▲ There are 64 walk-in tent sites in Manresa Uplands Campground next to the beach; $12 per night. Reservations: 800-444-7275.

SUNSET STATE BEACH Over three miles of beach and sand dunes create one of the area's prettiest parks. There are bluffs and meadows behind the beach as well as Monterey pines and cypress trees. This 324-acre park is a popular spot for fishing. Surfers also come here. But remember, there's more fog here and farther south than in the Santa Cruz area. There are picnic areas, restrooms, and showers. Day-use fee, $5. ~ Located 16 miles south of Santa Cruz; from Route 1, take the Larkin Valley and San Andreas Road exit, turn right onto San Andreas Road and follow it several miles to the park turnoff; 831-763-7063, fax 831-763-7120.

▲ Permitted in 90 sites (no RV hookups), $16 per night; hiker/biker camp available, $2 per person. Reservations: 800-444-7275.

ZMUDOWSKI, MOSS LANDING, AND SALINAS RIVER STATE BEACHES These three state parks are part of a long stretch of sand dunes. They all contain broad beaches and vistas along Monterey Bay. Though relatively uncrowded, their proximity to Moss Landing's smoke-belching power plant is a severe drawback. Quite suitable anywhere else, they can't compete with their neighbors in this land of beautiful beaches. Surfing is good near the sandbar at Salinas River; great at Moss Landing, which draws locals from Santa Cruz. Each beach has toilet facilities. ~ All three are located off Route 1 within a few miles of Moss Landing; 831-384-7695; e-mail nbeaches@mbay.net.

MARINA STATE BEACH The tall, fluffy sand dunes at this 170-acre park are unreal. They're part of a giant dune covering 50 square miles throughout the area. A boardwalk takes you through the sand to the beach and gives you an up-close view of the unique vegetation. There are marvelous views of Monterey here, plus a chance to fish or sunbathe. It is also the perfect place to try out hang gliding with tandem rides for first-time gliders and hang-gliding rentals for the more experienced. Swimming is allowed, though rip tides do occur. Regarding surfing, there's a great beach break in summer but it's dangerous in winter. There are restrooms and a snack bar. ~ Located along Route 1, nine miles north of Monterey; 831-384-7695; www.mbay.net/~nbeaches, e-mail nbeaches@mbay.net.

Over two million visitors visit the Monterey area every
year. Little wonder. Its rocky coast fringed with cypress
forests, its hills dotted with palatial homes—the area is
unusually beautiful. The town of Monterey also serves as a gateway to the tumbling region of Big Sur.

For a tour of Monterey Peninsula, begin in Monterey itself.
Here are historic homes, an old Spanish presidio, Fisherman's
Wharf, and Cannery Row. Set in a natural amphitheater of forested hills, it is also home to one of the richest marine sanctuaries
along the entire California coast. Little wonder that this town, with
a population that numbers 32,000 people, has served as an inspiration for Robert Louis Stevenson and John Steinbeck. With a
downtown district that reflects small town America and a waterfront that once supported a rich fishing and canning industry, Monterey remains one of the most vital spots on the Central Coast.

Monterey

History in Monterey is a precious commodity that in most cases
has been carefully preserved. Ancient adobe houses and Spanish-
style buildings are so commonplace that some have been converted into shops and restaurants.

SIGHTS

For sightseeing tips and brochures, visit the **Monterey Peninsula Chamber of Commerce**. Closed Saturday and Sunday. ~ 380
Alvarado Street; 831-648-5360; www.mpcc.com, e-mail info@
mpcc.com. If you need a little touring advice on the weekend, the
Monterey County Convention & Visitors Bureau is open daily. ~
401 Camino El Estero; 831-649-1770, 800-221-1010, fax 831-
648-5373; www.montereyinfo.org, e-mail info@mccv.org.

In the **Maritime Museum of Monterey** you'll find model ships,
a World War II exhibit, and a two-story-tall rotating lighthouse
lens. Closed Monday. Admission. ~ 5 Custom House Plaza; 831-
375-2553, fax 831-655-3054.

Many of Monterey's historic buildings can be seen—and in
most cases toured—along the two-mile **Path of History** (see
"Walking Tour").

AUTHOR IN LOVE

Robert Louis Stevenson, the vivacious but sickly Scottish writer, sailed the
Atlantic and traveled overland across the continent to visit his wife-to-be
Fanny Osbourne in Monterey. Writing for local newspapers, depending in
part upon the kindness of strangers for sustenance, the fragile wanderer
fell in love with Fanny and Monterey both. From the surrounding
countryside he drew inspiration for some of his most famous books,
including *Treasure Island*.

Two other places of historical note are located in Monterey but a significant distance from the Path of History. The **Royal Presidio Chapel** is a graceful expression of the 18th-century town. Decorative molding adorns the facade of the old adobe church while the towering belfry, rising along one side, makes the structure asymmetrical. Heavy wooden doors lead to a long, narrow chapel hung with dusty oil paintings. This was the mission that Father Junípero Serra founded in 1770, just before moving his congregation a few miles south to Carmel. ~ 550 Church Street.

Argentine pirate Hipólito Bouchard sacked and burned the Monterey Presidio during his round-the-world rampage in 1818.

The **Presidio of Monterey** sits on a hill near the northwest corner of town. Established as a fort by the Spanish in 1770, it currently serves as a foreign language institute for the military. There are cannons banked in a hillside, marking the site of Fort Mervine, built by the Americans in 1846. There's some evidence that the Presidio may also be the site of an ancient Costanoan Indian village and burial ground. And a granite monument at the corner of Pacific and Artillery streets marks the spot where in 1602 the Spanish celebrated the first Catholic mass in California. In addition to historic points, the Presidio grounds enjoy marvelous views of Monterey. You can look down upon the town, then scan along the bay's curving horizon. Due to heightened security, the Presidio is not open to the public. ~ Pacific and Artillery streets; 831-242-5555, fax 831-242-5464; www.dli-army.mil.

Strangely, Monterey, which elsewhere demonstrates special care in preserving its heritage, has let its wharves and piers fall prey to tinsel-minded developers. **Municipal Wharf #2** is a welcome exception. It's actually all that remains from the heyday of Monterey's fishing fleet. Here broad-hulled boats still beat at their moorings, while landlubbing anglers cast from pierside. Gulls perch along the handrails, sea lions bark from beneath the pilings, and pelicans work the waterfront. On one side is the dilapidated warehouse of a long-defunct freezer company. At the end of the dock, fish companies still operate. It's a primal place of cranes and pulleys, forklifts and conveyor belts. There are ice boxes and old packing crates scattered hither-thither, exuding the romance and stench of the industry. ~ Located at the foot of Figueroa Street.

Then there is the parody, much better known than the original. **Fisherman's Wharf**, like its San Francisco namesake, has been transmogrified into what the travel industry thinks tourists think a fishing pier should look like. Something was lost in the translation. Few fishing boats operate from the wharf these days; several charter companies sponsor glass-bottom boat tours and whale-watching expeditions. Otherwise the waterfront haven is just one more mall, a macadam corridor lined on either side with

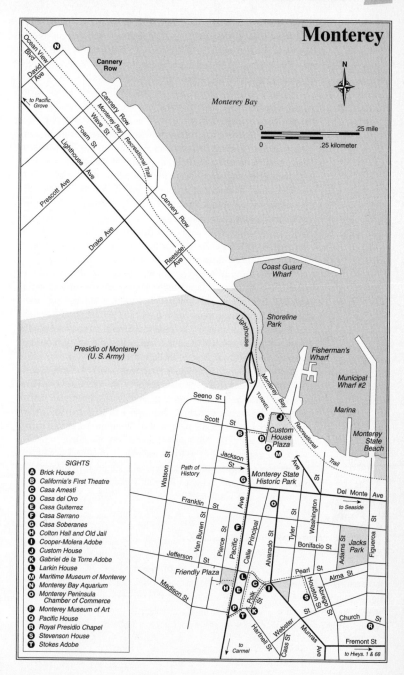

Monterey

Cannery Row

Monterey Bay

0 _____ .25 mile
0 _____ .25 kilometer

Ocean View Blvd
David Ave
to Pacific Grove
Cannery Row
Monterey Bay Recreational Trail
Wave St
Foam St
Lighthouse Ave
Prescott Ave
Drake Ave
Reeside Ave
Cannery Row

Coast Guard Wharf

Shoreline Park

Lighthouse

Presidio of Monterey
(U. S. Army)

Fisherman's Wharf

Municipal Wharf #2

Marina

Monterey State Beach

TUNNEL

Monterey Bay

Recreational Trail

Seeno St
Scott St
Watson St
Path of History
Jackson St
Monterey State Historic Park
Franklin St
Van Buren St
Jefferson St
Madison St
Friendly Plaza
Calle Principal
Pacific St
Pierce St
Polk St
Hartnell St
to Carmel
Alvarado St
Washington St
Tyler St
Bonifacio St
Pearl St
Webster St
Munras Ave
Cass St
Adams St
Houston St
Abrego St
Alma St
Church St
Jacks Park
Del Monte Ave
to Seaside
Figueroa St
Fremont St
to Hwys. 1 & 68

Custom House Plaza

SIGHTS

- **A** Brick House
- **B** California's First Theatre
- **C** Casa Amesti
- **D** Casa del Oro
- **E** Casa Guiterrez
- **F** Casa Serrano
- **G** Casa Soberanes
- **H** Colton Hall and Old Jail
- **I** Cooper-Molera Adobe
- **J** Custom House
- **K** Gabriel de la Torre Adobe
- **L** Larkin House
- **M** Maritime Museum of Monterey
- **N** Monterey Bay Aquarium
- **O** Monterey Peninsula Chamber of Commerce
- **P** Monterey Museum of Art
- **Q** Pacific House
- **R** Royal Presidio Chapel
- **S** Stevenson House
- **T** Stokes Adobe

shops. There are ersatz art galleries, shops vending candy apples and personalized mugs, plus a school of seafood restaurants. A few outdoor fish markets still sell live crabs, lobsters, and squid, but the symbol of the place is the hurdy-gurdy man with performing monkey who greets you at the entrance.

Actually this is only the most recent in the wharf's long series of role changes. The dock was built in 1846 to serve cargo schooners dealing in hides. Within a decade the whaling industry took it over, followed finally by Italian fishermen catching salmon, cod, and mackerel. During the Cannery Row era of the '30s, the sardine industry played a vital part in the life of the wharf. Today all that has given way to a bizarre form of public nostalgia.

The same visionary appears responsible for the resurrection of **Cannery Row**. Made famous by John Steinbeck's feisty novels *Cannery Row* and *Sweet Thursday*, this oceanfront strip has been transformed into a neighborhood of wax museums and dainty antique shops. As Steinbeck remarked upon returning to the old sardine canning center, "They fish for tourists now."

Cannery Row of yore was an unappealing collection of corrugated warehouses, dilapidated stores, seedy hotels, and gaudy whorehouses. There were about 30 canneries, 100 fishing boats, and 4000 workers populating the place. The odor was horrible, but for several decades the sardine industry breathed life into the Monterey economy. The business died when the fish ran out just before *Cannery Row* was published in 1945.

Before the entire oceanfront strip was developed in the early 1980s, you could still capture a sense of the old Cannery Row. A few weather-beaten factories remained. Rust stained their ribbed sides, windows were punched, and roofs had settled to an inward curve. In places, the stone pilings of old loading docks still stood, haunted by sea gulls. Now only tourists and memories remain.

At the other end of the Row, Steinbeck aficionados will find La Ida Café, now a fun restaurant and ice cream parlor called **Kalisa's La Ida Café**, which still retains its same tumbledown appearance. ~ 851 Cannery Row; 831-644-9316.

AUTHOR FAVORITE

sights

Monterey Bay features one of the world's biggest submarine canyons, deeper than the Grand Canyon. At the **Monterey Bay Aquarium** you'll encounter nearly 200 exhibits and display tanks representing the wealth of underwater life that inhabits this mineral-rich valley. Together the many displays and exhibitions make it one of the world's great aquariums. For more information, see page 397.

In the middle you'll encounter the scene of the malling of Cannery Row. Old warehouses were renovated into shopping centers, new buildings rose up, and the entire area experienced a face lift. Brightest tooth in the updated smile is the **Edgewater Packing Company**, a video arcade with miniature golf, bike rentals, and a hand-carved vintage-1905 carousel. ~ 640 Wave Street; 831-649-1899, phone/fax 831-648-2387.

The most impressive addition is the **Monterey Bay Aquarium**, a state-of-the-art museum that re-creates the natural habitat of local sea life. For instance, the Monterey Bay Habitat, a 90-foot-long acrylic enclosure, portrays the local submarine world complete with sharks, schooling fish, and wharf pilings. The Outer Bay Galleries contain, among other delights, a million-gallon tank filled with all kinds of ocean species, including black sea turtles, ocean sunfish, hammerhead sharks, barracuda, and the only tuna in an American aquarium; the vanishing wildlife exhibit allows a ground-floor view into the galleries. Another aquarium contains a mature kelp forest crowded with fish. Don't forget the hands-on exhibits where you can pet bat rays and touch crabs, starfish, and sea cucumbers. And don't miss the deep-sea video images beamed six to eight times a day live from research vessels in undersea Monterey Canyon, two miles beneath the surface of the bay. Definitely take the kids to the Splash Zone, where hands-on activities and animals like penguins, moray eels, and tropical sharks will keep them entertained for hours. Admission. ~ Cannery Row and David Avenue; 831-648-4888, 800-756-3737, fax 831-648-4810; www.montereybayaquarium.org, e-mail equarist@mo ntereybayaquarium.org.

LODGING

The problem with lodging on the Monterey Peninsula is the same dilemma plaguing much of the world—money. It takes a lot of it to stay here, especially when visiting one of the area's vaunted bed and breakfasts. These country inns are concentrated in Pacific Grove and Carmel, towns neighboring on Monterey. The town of Monterey features a few such inns as well as a string of moderately priced motels. Budget travelers will do well to check into the latter and also to consult several of the Carmel listings in the book. Monterey's motel row lies along Munras Avenue, a buzzing thoroughfare that leads from downtown to Route 1. Motels are also found along Fremont Street in the adjacent town of Seaside. These are cheaper, drabber, and not as conveniently situated as the Munras hostelries.

Since overnight facilities fill rapidly around Monterey, particularly on weekends and during summer, it's wise to reserve in advance. Contact **Resort II Me**, a free reservation agency for the Monterey Peninsula. ~ 831-642-6622, 800-757-5646, fax 831-642-6641; www.resort2me.com, e-mail info@resort2me.com.

Text continued on page 400.

Monterey's Path of History

The Path of History, carrying through the center of Monterey, measures over two miles if walked in its entirety.

CUSTOM HOUSE The best place to begin is the Custom House (c. 1827) across from Fisherman's Wharf. In 1846, Commodore Sloat raised the American flag here, claiming California for the United States. Today the stone and adobe building houses displays from an 1830s-era cargo ship. ~ 1 Custom House Plaza.

PACIFIC HOUSE Across the plaza rises Pacific House (c. 1847), a two-story balconied adobe with a luxurious courtyard. The exhibits inside trace California's history from American Indian days to the advent of Spanish settlers and American pioneers. ~ 10 Custom House Plaza; 831-649-7118; e-mail mshp1@mbay.net.

CASA DEL ORO Just behind Pacific House sits Casa del Oro, a tiny 1840s adobe that now houses the **Joseph Boston Store**, an old-fashioned mercantile shop selling Early American items. Closed Monday through Wednesday. ~ Olivier and Scott streets; 831-649-3364.

BRICK HOUSE Diagonally across the intersection on Olivier Street behind an office complex stands the oldest brick house, purportedly the first such house in California. Adjacent to this is the **Whaling Station**, an adobe with a balcony from which the early whalers spotted their migrating bounty.

CALIFORNIA'S FIRST THEATRE California's First Theatre, a block up the street, is still used to stage 19th-century melodramas that are performed by America's oldest continually operating theater troupe. The theater is partially closed for renovations. ~ Scott and Pacific streets; 831-649-7118; e-mail mshp1@mbay.net.

CASA SOBERANES A left on Pacific Street leads to Casa Soberanes, a Monterey-style house with red tile roof and second-story balcony. Completed in the 1840s, this impressive structure was built by a warden at the Custom House. ~ 6 Pacific Street; 831-649-7118; e-mail mshp1@mbay.net.

CASA SERRANO Casa Serrano (c. 1843) contains wrought-iron decorations over its narrow windows. Once home to a blind Spanish teacher, it is now open for touring only on weekends. For more information contact the Monterey History and Art Association. ~ 412 Pacific Street; 831-372-2608; www.mntmh.org.

FRIENDLY PLAZA   Nearby spreads Friendly Plaza, a tree-shaded park that serves as a focus for several important places. The **Monterey Museum of Art** exhibits works and artifacts by early and contemporary California artists. Closed Monday and Tuesday. Admission. ~ 559 Pacific Street; 831-372-5477; www.montereyart.org, e-mail mtry_art@ mbay.net. **La Mirada** is housed in an old adobe with period furnishings. Closed Monday and Tuesday. Admission. ~ 720 Via Mirada Avenue; 831-372-3689; www.montereyart.org, e-mail mtry_art@mbay.net.

COLTON HALL   Pierce Street, running along the upper edge of the plaza, contains a string of historic 19th-century homes. Colton Hall, site of California's 1849 constitutional convention, displays memorabilia from that critical event. ~ Pacific Street between Jefferson and Madison streets. The squat granite **Old Jail** next door, with wrought-iron bars across the windows, dates back to the same era. **Casa Gutierrez**, across the street, was built in 1846 by a cavalryman with 15 children.

LARKIN HOUSE   After exploring the plaza, turn left into Madison Street from Pacific Street, then left again along Calle Principal to one of the town's most famous homes, the Larkin House. Designed in 1834 by Thomas Larkin, the antique home is now a house museum filled with period pieces. The only United States Consul to California lived here. Admission. ~ 510 Calle Principal; 831-649-7118; e-mail mshp1@mbay.net.

HISTORIC HOMES   A right on Jefferson Street and another quick right on Polk takes you past a cluster of revered houses. **Casa Amesti** (c. 1824) is presently a private club. ~ 516 Polk Street. The **Cooper-Molera Adobe**, across the road, includes a 19th-century museum and a "historic garden" of herbs and vegetables of the Mexican era. Visit by guided tour (call for information). Admission. ~ 525 Polk Street; 831-649-7118; e-mail mshp1@mbay.net. Facing each other on either side of Polk and Hartnell streets are the **Gabriel de la Torre Adobe** (c. 1836) and the **Stokes Adobe**, erected in the 1840s.

STEVENSON HOUSE   Backtrack along Polk Street one block to the five-way intersection, take a soft right onto Pearl Street, walk a few short blocks, then turn right on Houston Street to the Stevenson House, Robert Louis Stevenson's residence for several months in 1879. The house features personal belongings, original manuscripts, and first editions, all of which can be viewed on a guided tour (call for tour information). Admission. Stevenson House is currently closed until late 2004 for renovations. ~ 530 Houston Street; 408-649-7118; e-mail mshp1@ mbay.net.

GUIDED TOURS   You can see Casa Soberanes, Larkin House, and Cooper-Molera Adobe (from the outside) on a daily guided 90-minute walking tour. For information, contact Monterey State Historic Park. Fee. ~ 831-649-7118; e-mail mshp1@mbay.net.

One standard located five blocks from downtown, the **Days Inn Monterey** features 35 rooms with private baths. ~ 1288 Munras Avenue; 831-375-2168, 800-329-7466, fax 831-375-0368. MODERATE.

For good cheer and homespun atmosphere, the **Old Monterey Inn** provides a final word. Before innkeepers Ann and Gene Swett decided to open their Tudor-style house to guests, they raised six children here. Now they raise rhododendrons and camellias in the garden while hosting visitors in their ten-room bed and breakfast. The house rests on a quiet street yet is located within a few blocks of downtown Monterey. The trimly appointed rooms feature feather beds, tile fireplaces, wicker furnishings, and delicate wallhangings; four have whirlpool tubs. There are spacious dining and drawing rooms downstairs and the landscaped grounds are studded with oak and redwood. An elaborate breakfast is included; they'll even serve you in bed. You'll find this friendly little inn a perfect spot for an evening fire and glass of port. ~ 500 Martin Street; 831-375-8284, 800-350-2344, fax 831-375-6730; www.oldmontereyinn.com, e-mail omi@oldmontereyinn.com. ULTRA-DELUXE.

Located in the downtown district, **Merritt House Inn** is not only an overnight resting place but also a stopping point along Monterey's "Path of History." Part of this lovely inn rests in a vintage 1830 adobe home. Accommodations in the old house (three lavish suites) and the adjoining modern quartersb (22 guest rooms) are furnished with hardwood period pieces and feature vaulted ceilings, fireplaces, and balconies. The garden abounds with magnolia, fig, pepper, and olive trees. Continental breakfast is served. ~ 386 Pacific Street; 831-646-9686, 800-541-5599, fax 831-646-5392; www.merritthouseinn.com, e-mail info@merritthouseinn.com. DELUXE TO ULTRA-DELUXE.

Oceanfront on Cannery Row stands the **Spindrift Inn**, an elegant 42-room hotel. The lobby is fashionably laid out with skylight and sculptures and there is a rooftop solarium overlooking the waterfront. Guest rooms carry out the award-winning architectural motif with bay windows, hardwood floors, woodburning fireplaces, and built-in armoires. ~ 652 Cannery Row; 831-646-8900, 800-232-4141, fax 831-646-5342; www.spindriftinn.com, e-mail reservations@innsofmonterey.com. ULTRA-DELUXE.

Catering to a mixed gay and straight clientele is the **Monterey Fireside Lodge,** a 24-room hostelry. In addition to comfortable accommodations, they have a jacuzzi and patio. Continental breakfast included. ~ 1131 10th Street; 831-373-4172, fax ; www.montereyfireside.com, e-mail tague68@attbi.com MODERATE TO ULTRA-DELUXE.

DINING

Few restaurants can compete with **Stokes Restaurant & Bar** for ambience. Housed in an 1833 California adobe with stucco walls, artwork by local artists, and European antiques, this restaurant serves California-Mediterranean cuisine including delicious pizzas and tapas. Featuring flavors from northern Italy, southern France, and Spain and an extensive wine list with French, Italian, Australian, and California vintages. No lunch on Sunday. ~ 500 Hartnell Street; 831-373-1110, fax 831-373-1202; www.stokes restaurant.com, e-mail stokes@mbay.net. MODERATE TO DELUXE.

Tasty *kalbi* and *bi bim bap* are among the traditional favorites at **Won Ju Korean Restaurant**. You'll find meat dishes as well as seafood and vegetarian options. Dinner comes with a Korean potato pancake, rice, and a wide variety of side dishes such as sesame-flavored spinach and spicy *kim chee* (pickled cabbage). ~ 570 Lighthouse Avenue; 831-656-0672. MODERATE TO DELUXE.

Eating at **Gianni's Pizza** is a guaranteed good time. You can feel it when you walk in the door of this casual restaurant. The tables sport red-and-white-checked tablecloths, there are bottles of wine and pictures of Italy on the walls, and on weekends banjo and accordion players serenade diners with lively tunes. You can order fresh pastas, hand-tossed, thick-crusted pizza, or oven-baked sandwiches from various stations, and they are prepared and delivered to your table. There's also a bar, an espresso counter, and wonderful gelato for dessert. No lunch Monday through Thursday. ~ 725 Lighthouse Avenue; 831-649-1500; www.restaurant eur.com/giannis. BUDGET TO MODERATE.

One of Monterey Bay's most abundant seafood products is squid, the inky creature that often turns up on local restaurant menus as the more palatable-sounding calamari. Under any name, the best place to enjoy it is **Abalonetti**, a casual wharfside restaurant overlooking the bay. The menu presents calamari in an array of guises, including deep-fried, sautéed with wine and garlic, and

AUTHOR FAVORITE

Small and personalized with an understated elegance is the most fitting way to describe **Fresh Cream**. Its light green and gray walls are decorated with French prints and leaded glass. One wall is floor-to-ceiling windows that provide a great view of the bay. Service is excellent and the menu, printed daily, numbers among the finest on the Central Coast. On a given night you might choose from beef tournedos in Madeira sauce, sautéed veal loin, blackened ahi tuna, duckling in black currant sauce, and rack of lamb. That's not even mentioning the appetizers, which are outstanding, or the desserts, which should be outlawed. Four stars. Dinner only. ~ Heritage Harbor, 99 Pacific Street; , fax 831-375-2283 www.freshcream.com, e-mail dining@freshcream.com. ULTRA-DELUXE.

baked with eggplant. Seven or more fresh fish specials round out the menu. ~ 57 Fisherman's Wharf; 831-373-1851, fax 831-373-2058; www.restauranteur.com/abalonetti. MODERATE TO ULTRA-DELUXE.

Enjoy a cuppa java in a coffee shop quite unlike any you've ever visited before. At **Plume's Coffee** they grind the beans for each cup and brew it individually. So that your own special cup of coffee is not mistakenly served to someone else, you pick up your order under a picture of, say, a waterfall or sunset. Plume's also serves cheesecake, fruit tarts, custard eclairs, and other sweet treats from the best bakeries in the area. ~ 400 Alvarado Street; 831-373-4526, fax 831-655-1621. BUDGET.

SHOPPING   In Monterey, there are stores throughout the downtown area and malls galore over on **Cannery Row**. Every year another shopping complex seems to rise along the Row. Already the area features cheese and wine stores, clothiers, a fudge factory, and a gourmet supply store. There's also a collector's comic book store, the inevitable T-shirt shop, knickknack stores, and galleries selling artworks that are like Muzak on canvas.

NIGHTLIFE   The classiest spot around is **Club Octane**. Entertainment changes nightly, with four different rooms featuring deejays spinning dance tunes. "Upscale" dress code enforced. Cover. ~ 321-D Alvarado Street; 831-646-9244.

Viva Monterey has been called the "Cheers of Monterey" and appeals to all ages (over 21, that is). A popular hangout with three blacklight pool tables, the club gets pumping with nightly music. Bands play a mix of cover and original tunes. ~ 414 Alvarado Street; 831-646-1415.

There are also several nightspots over by Cannery Row. **Kalisa's La Ida Café**, a funky restaurant and ice-cream parlor in a building that dates to the Steinbeck era, offers belly dancing on some weekends. This is also the home of John Steinbeck's birthday party every February 27, now a recognized town holiday. ~ 851 Cannery Row; 831-644-9316.

The only gay establishment in Monterey, the **Lighthouse Bar & Grill** serves American pub food. Patrons also shoot pool, play pinball, or relax with a drink on the patio. ~ 281 Lighthouse Avenue; 831-373-4488.

▼▼▼▼▼▼▼▼▼▼
Pacific Grove

Projecting out from the northern tip of Monterey Peninsula is the diminutive town of Pacific Grove. Covering just 1700 acres, it is reached from Monterey along Lighthouse Avenue. Better yet, pick up Ocean View Boulevard near Cannery Row and follow as it winds along Pacific Grove's surf-washed shores. A quiet town with a lightly developed waterfront, Pacific Grove offers paths that lead for miles along a rock-crusted shore.

Costanoan Indians once dove for abalone in these waters. By the 19th century, Pacific Grove had become a religious retreat. Methodist Episcopal ministers pitched a tent city and decreed that "bathing suits shall be provided with double crotches or with skirts of ample size to cover the buttocks." The town was dry until 1969. Given the fish canneries in Monterey and teetotalers in this nearby town, local folks called the area "Carmel-by-the-Sea, Monterey-by-the-Smell, and Pacific Grove-by-God."

SIGHTS

Today Pacific Grove is a sleepy residential area decorated with Victorians, brown-shingle houses, and clapboard ocean cottages. The waterfront drive goes past rocky beaches to **Point Pinos Lighthouse**. When this beacon first flashed in 1855, it burned sperm whale oil. Little has changed except the introduction of electricity; this is the only early lighthouse along the entire California coast to be preserved in its original condition. The U.S. Coast Guard still uses it to guide ships; it is the oldest continually operating lighthouse on the West Coast. Two rooms have been restored to look as they did in Victorian times, and there's a short history of Emily Fish, the woman who ran the lighthouse in the

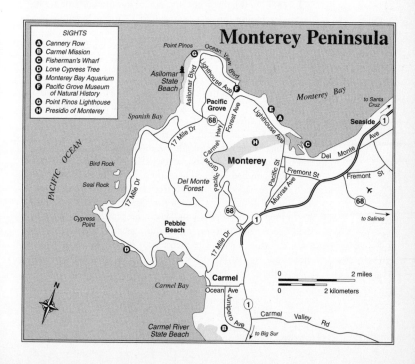

Monterey Peninsula

SIGHTS
Ⓐ Cannery Row
Ⓑ Carmel Mission
Ⓒ Fisherman's Wharf
Ⓓ Lone Cypress Tree
Ⓔ Monterey Bay Aquarium
Ⓕ Pacific Grove Museum of Natural History
Ⓖ Point Pinos Lighthouse
Ⓗ Presidio of Monterey

19th century. Open for self-guided tours. Closed Monday. ~ North of Lighthouse Avenue; 831-648-5716.

Sunset Drive continues along the sea to **Asilomar State Beach**. Here sand dunes mantled with ice plant front a wave-lashed shore. There are tidepools galore, plus beaches for picnics, and trails leading through the rolling dunes.

Pacific Grove's major claim to fame lies in an area several blocks inland: around George Washington Park on Melrose Street and in a grove at 1073 Lighthouse Avenue. This otherwise unassuming municipality is known as "Butterfly Town, U.S.A." Every mid-October, brilliant orange-and-black **monarch butterflies** migrate here, remaining until mid-March. Some arrive from several hundred miles away to breed amid the cypress and oak trees. At night they cling to one another, curtaining the branches in clusters that sometimes number over a thousand. Then, at first light, they come to life, fluttering around the groves in a frenzy of wings and color.

> The ivy-cloaked cottage at 147 11th Street is where John Steinbeck lived and wrote *In Dubious Battle* and *Of Mice and Men*. Unfortunately, it's not open to the public.

Also of interest are the **Pacific Grove Museum of Natural History**, an excellent small museum with exhibits on native animals and early peoples, and a touch gallery for children. Closed Monday. ~ Central and Forest avenues; 831-648-5716, fax 831-372-3256; www.pgmuseum.org, e-mail pgmuseum@mbay.net.

Gosby House Inn is a century-old Victorian mansion decorated in period antiques. ~ 643 Lighthouse Avenue. Next door, the **Hart Mansion** is another elaborate old Victorian house. It's currently closed to the public, but worth a look from the outside. ~ 649 Lighthouse Avenue.

17 MILE DRIVE From Pacific Grove, 17 Mile Drive leads to Pebble Beach, one of America's most lavish communities. This place is so exclusive that the rich charge a fee to anyone wishing to drive around admiring their homes. No wonder they're rich.

Galling as the gate fee might be, this is an extraordinary region that must not be missed. The road winds through pine groves down to a wind-combed beach. There are miles of rolling dunes tufted with sea vegetation. (The oceanfront can be as cool and damp as it is beautiful, so carry a sweater or jacket, or better yet, both.)

Among the first spots you'll encounter is **Spanish Bay**, where Juan Gaspar de Portolá camped during his 1769 expedition up the California coast. (The picnic area here is a choice place to spread a feast.) At **Point Joe**, converging ocean currents create a wild frothing sea that has drawn several ships to their doom.

Seal Rock and **Bird Rock**, true to their nomenclature, are carpeted with sea lions, harbor and leopard seals, cormorants, brown pelicans, and gulls. Throughout this thriving 17 Mile Drive area are black-tail deer, sooty shearwaters, sea otters, and, during migration periods, California gray whales.

There are crescent beaches and granite headlands as well as vista points for scanning the coast. You'll also pass the **Lone Cypress,** the solitary tree on a rocky point that has become as symbolic of Northern California as perhaps the Golden Gate Bridge.

The **private homes** en route are mansions, exquisite affairs fashioned from marble and fine hardwoods. Some appear like stone fortresses, others seem made solely of glass. They range from American Colonial to futuristic and were designed by noted architects like Bernard Maybeck, Julia Morgan, and Willis Polk.

This is also home to several of the world's most renowned **golf courses**—Pebble Beach, Spyglass Hill, and Cypress Point— where the AT&T National Pro-Am Championship takes place each year. More than the designer homes and their celebrity residents, these courses have made Pebble Beach a place fabled for wealth and beauty.

The best part of the drive lies along the coast between the Pacific Grove and Carmel gates. Along the backside of 17 Mile Drive, where it loops up into Del Monte Forest, there are marvelous views of Monterey Bay and the San Gabilan Mountains. Here also is **Huckleberry Hill,** a forest of Monterey and Bishop pine freckled with bushes.

LODGING

Asilomar Conference Center provides one of the area's best housing arrangements. Set in a state park, it's surrounded by 107 acres of sand dunes and pine forests. The beach is a stroll away from any of the center's 27 hotel lodges. There's a dining hall on the premises as well as meeting rooms and recreational facilities (pool and volleyball court). Breakfast is included in the price. Catering primarily to groups, Asilomar does provide accommodations (depending on availability) for independent travelers. Rooms in the "rustic buildings" are small and spartan but adequate (*and* designed by Julia Morgan). They lack carpeting on the hardwood floors and include little decoration. The "deluxe building" rooms are nicely appointed with wallhangings, study desks, and comfortable furnishings. Fireplaces are also available. Every lodge includes a spacious lounge area with stone fireplace. No doubt about it, Asilomar is a splendid place at a relaxing price. ~ 800 Asilomar Boulevard; 831-372-8016, fax 831-372-7227; www.asilomarcenter.com, e-mail asilomarsales@dncinc.com. MODERATE TO DELUXE.

One of Monterey Peninsula's less expensive bed and breakfasts is nearby. **Gosby House Inn,** a century-old Victorian mansion, includes 22 refurbished rooms. Each is different, and all have been decorated with special attention to detail. In any one you are liable to discover an antique armoire, brass lighting fixtures, stained glass, or a Tiffany lamp. The two rooms in the carriage house have jacuzzi tubs. They are all small after the Victorian fashion, which sacrifices space for coziness. The full breakfast, afternoon wine and hors d'oeuvres, and nightly turn-down service add to the homey feeling. ~ 643 Lighthouse Avenue; 831-375-1287, 800-527-8828, fax 831-655-9621; www.foursisters.com. DELUXE TO ULTRA-DELUXE.

Green Gables Inn represents one of the region's most impressive bed and breakfasts. The house, a Queen Anne–style Victorian, dates from 1888. Adorned with step-gables, stained glass, and bay windows, it rests in a storybook setting overlooking Monterey Bay. Five bedrooms upstairs and a suite below have been fastidiously decorated with lavish antiques. Four of these share two baths, but offer the best ocean views. Set in a town filled with old Victorian homes, this oceanside residence is an ideal representation of Pacific Grove. There are also five separate units in a building adjacent to the main house. These are suites with private bath and fireplace. All rooms have king or queen beds; full breakfast, afternoon wine and cheese, and access to the main house are included. ~ 301 Ocean View Boulevard; 831-375-2095, 800-722-1774, fax 831-375-5437; www.foursisters.com, e-mail info@four sisters.com. DELUXE TO ULTRA-DELUXE.

Commanding a front and center view of the spectacular waterfront is the **Martine Inn,** a pastel stucco Mediterranean-style villa with 24 individually decorated rooms, many with fireplaces. Among the accommodations is the Edith Head Room, which has 1920s furnishings from the Hollywood costume designer's estate. A full sit-down breakfast and afternoon wine and hors d'oeuvres are included. There is a two-night minimum stay on high-season weekends. ~ 255 Ocean View Boulevard; 831-373-3388, 800-852-5588, fax 831-373-3896; www.martineinn.com, e-mail info@mar tineinn.com. DELUXE TO ULTRA-DELUXE.

DINING

At **The Tinnery** you'll find an American-style seafood restaurant with a nautical theme and breakfast, lunch, and dinner. The restaurant overlooks the water and serves some of the best chowder around. ~ 631 Ocean View Boulevard; 831-646-1040, fax 831-646-5913. MODERATE TO DELUXE.

Or step up and over to the **Old Bath House Restaurant,** a luxurious building decorated in etched glass and sporting a Victorian-style bar. The Continental/California cuisine includes duckling, lamb, lobster, steak, and seafood dishes. Dinner only. ~ 620 Ocean View Boulevard; 831-375-5195, fax 831-375-5379; www.old bathhouse.com. DELUXE TO ULTRA-DELUXE.

The quaint, shingled **Red House Café** is a cozy place to join the locals for breakfast, lunch, or dinner. Morning brings Belgian waffles, frittatas, and croissant sandwiches, while the later meals feature oven-roasted chicken sandwiches and warm eggplant with fontina cheese. The freshly squeezed lemonade, which comes with free refills, is delicious. No dinner on Sunday. Closed Monday. ~

662 Lighthouse Avenue; 831-643-1060; www.redhousecafe.com, e-mail info@redhousecafe.com. BUDGET TO MODERATE.

Passionfish has a simple but charming ambience. Since the menu changes daily, gastronomic delights may include butternut-squash-and-marscapone ravioli, duck confit with Tasmanian honey sauce, and pepper-and-fennel-crusted mahimahi. The wine list is also impressive. Dinner only. Closed Tuesday. ~ 701 Lighthouse Avenue; 831-655-3311; www.passionfish.net, e-mail passion@passionfish.net. MODERATE TO DELUXE.

> For inexpensive snacks, try the hot dog stand at the bottom of the steps in Lover's Point Park. It's a local institution. ~ Ocean View Boulevard at the foot of 16th Street.

Peppers Mexicali Cafe pays homage to the red chile and has attracted an incredible number of devotees, as witnessed by the sometimes lengthy wait for a table. Chile posters and pepper prints by local artists decorate the walls, and the food is Mexican and Central American seafood. Among the offerings are grilled prawns with fresh lime and cilantro dressing, grilled seafood tacos, grilled halibut, snapper Veracruz, and more mundane dishes such as tacos, burritos, and enchiladas. No lunch on Sunday. Closed Tuesday. ~ 170 Forest Avenue; 831-373-6892, fax 831-373-5467. BUDGET TO MODERATE.

SHOPPING

The main area for window browsing in town can be found along Lighthouse Avenue. Just above this busy thoroughfare, on 17th Street, artisans have renovated a row of small beach cottages. In each is a creatively named shop. There's **Reincarnation Vintage Clothing**, which sells vintage and vintage-inspired contemporary clothing, jewelry, and accessories. Closed Sunday. ~ 214 17th Street; 831-649-0689. At **Mum's Place**, there's high-quality oak, maple, cherry, and pine furniture. ~ 246 Forest Avenue; 831-372-6250.

From designer fashions to gourmet cookware, the 35 shops at **American Tin Cannery Premium Outlets** are a shopper's paradise. A good place to look for luggage, books, shoes, housewares, and linens, this renovated two-story complex has a variety of outlet stores. If you're looking for bargains in the Monterey area, don't miss this gem. ~ 125 Ocean View Boulevard; 831-372-1442, fax 831-372-5707; www.premiumoutlets.com.

BEACHES & PARKS

ASILOMAR STATE BEACH 🏊 🏄 ♨ ⛱ This oceanfront facility features over 100 acres of pine forest, snowy white sand dunes, tidepools, and beach. It's a perfect place for daytripping and exploring. The best surfing here is just off the main sandy beach. Since northern and southern currents run together here, the waters are teeming with marine life. Swimming is not recommended. The conference grounds feature historic buildings and enchanting grounds (overnight accommodations are described in

"Lodging" above). ~ Located along Sunset Drive in Pacific Grove; 831-372-4076, fax 831-372-3759; www.visitasilomar.com.

Carmel

The first law of real estate should be this: The best land is always occupied by the military, bohemians, or the rich. Think about it. The principle holds for many of the world's prettiest spots. Generally the military arrives first, on an exploratory mission or as an occupying force. It takes strategic ground, which happens to be the beaches, headlands, and mountaintops. The bohemians select beautiful locales because they possess good taste. When the rich discover where the artists have settled, they start moving in, driving up the rents, and forcing the displaced bohemians to discover new homes, which will then be taken by another wave of the wealthy.

The Monterey Peninsula is no exception. In Carmel the military established an early beachhead when Spanish soldiers occupied a barracks in the old Catholic mission. Later the bohemians arrived in numbers. Poet George Sterling came in 1905, followed by Mary Austin, the novelist. Eventually such luminaries as Upton Sinclair, Lincoln Steffens, and Sinclair Lewis, writers all, settled for varying periods. Jack London and Ambrose Bierce visited. Later, photographers Ansel Adams and Edward Weston relocated here.

The figure most closely associated with this "seacoast of Bohemia" was Robinson Jeffers, a poet who came seeking solitude in 1914. Quarrying rock from the shoreline, he built the Tor House and Hawk Tower, where he lived and wrote haunting poems and epics about the coast.

Then like death and tax collectors, the rich inevitably moved in. As John Steinbeck noted when he later returned to this artists' colony, "If Carmel's founders should return, they could not afford to live there. . . . They would instantly be picked up as suspicious characters and deported over the city line."

It's doubtful many would want to remain anyway. Today Carmel is so cute it cloys. The tiny town is cluttered with over four dozen inns, about six dozen restaurants, and more than 300 shops. Ocean Avenue, the main street, is wall-to-wall with merchants. Shopping malls have replaced artists' garrets, and there are traffic jams where there was once solitude.

SIGHTS

Typifying the town is the **Tuck Box**, a gingerbread-style building on Dolores Street between Ocean and 7th avenues (there are no street numbers in Carmel), or the fairy tale–like **Hansel-and-Gretel cottages** on Torres Street between 5th and 6th avenues.

Still, reasons remain to visit Carmel, which is reached from Monterey via Route 1 or from the Carmel gate along 17 Mile Drive. The window shopping is good and several galleries are outstanding. Some of the town's quaint characteristics have appeal. There are no traffic lights or parking meters, and at night few street lights. Drive around the side streets and you will encounter an architectural mixture of log cabins, adobe structures, board-and-batten cottages, and Spanish villas.

A secret that local residents have long withheld from visitors is **Mission Trails Park.** No signs will direct you here, so watch ◀ HIDDEN for an entrance at the corner of Mountain View and Crespi avenues. Within this forest preserve are miles of hiking trails. They wind across footbridges, through redwood groves, and past meadows of wildflowers en route to Carmel Mission. There are ocean vistas, deer grazing the hillsides, and an arboretum seeded with native California plants.

Carmel's most alluring feature is the one that early drew the bohemians—the Pacific. At the foot of Ocean Avenue rests **Carmel Beach,** a snowy strand shadowed by cypress trees. From here, Scenic Road hugs the coast, winding above rocky outcroppings.

Just beyond stretches **Carmel River State Beach,** a sandy corridor at the foot of Carmel Bay. For additional information, see the "Beaches & Parks" section below.

Even for the non-religious, a visit to **Carmel Mission Basilica** becomes a pilgrimage. If the holiness holds no appeal, there's the aesthetic sense of the place. Dating back to 1770, its Old World

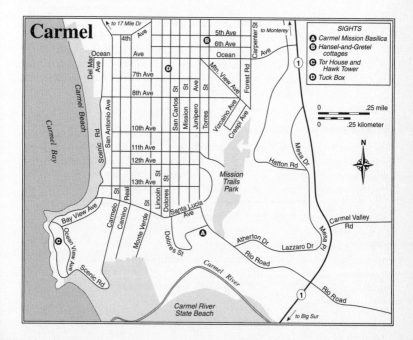

beauty captivates and confounds. The courtyards are alive with flowers and birds. The adobe buildings have been dusted with time—their eaves are hunchbacked, the tile roofs coated in moss. Admission. ~ Located on Rio Road just off Route 1; 831-624-3600, fax 831-624-0658.

Established by Father Junípero Serra, this mission is one of California's most remarkable. The basilica is a vaulted-ceiling affair adorned with old oil paintings and wooden statues of Christ; its walls are lime plaster made from burnt seashells. The exterior is topped with a Moorish tower and 11 bells.

Junípero Serra lies buried in the sanctuary, his grave marked with a stone plaque. There are also museum rooms demonstrating early California life—a kitchen with stone hearth and rudimentary tools, the state's first library (complete with waterstained bibles), and the cell where Father Serra died, its bed a slab of wood with a single blanket and no mattress. Close by, in the cemetery beside the basilica, several thousand American Indians are also buried.

Just two miles south of Carmel lies **Point Lobos State Reserve**, an incomparable natural area of rocky headlands and placid coves. The park features hillside crow's nests from which to gaze out along Carmel Bay. Before Westerners arrived, the American Indians gathered mussels and abalone here. Later Point Lobos was a whaling station and an abalone cannery. Today it's a park intended primarily for nature hikers. You can explore pine forests and cypress groves, a jagged shoreline of granite promontories, and wave-lapped coves. Every tidepool is a miniature aquarium pulsing with color and sea life. The water is clear as sky. Offshore rise sea stacks, their rocky bases ringed with mussels, their domes crowned by sea birds. This region, also rich in wildlife and underwater life, should not be bypassed; for complete information, see the "Beaches & Parks" section below.

STONE POEM

Just before the intersection with Stewart Way, gaze uphill toward those two stone edifices. Poet Robinson Jeffers' **Tor House and Hawk Tower** seem drawn from another place and time, perhaps a Scottish headland in the 19th century. In fact, the poet modeled the house after an English-style barn and built the 40-foot-high garret with walls six feet thick in the fashion of an Irish tower. Completed during the 1920s, the structures are granite and include porthole windows that Jeffers salvaged from a shipwreck. One-hour tours of the house and tower are conducted on Friday and Saturday by reservation. No children under 12 years allowed. Admission. ~ 26304 Ocean View Avenue; for information and reservations, call 831-624-1813, fax 831-624-3696; www.torhouse.org, e-mail thf@torhouse.org.

As if its shoreline was not enough, Carmel also boasts an extraordinary interior. Carmel Valley Road leads from Route 1 into the distant hills, paralleling the Carmel River in its circuitous course. The lower end of the **Carmel Valley** promises fruit orchards and fields of grazing horses before the road ascends into the wooded heights that separate Carmel from the farmlands of Salinas. Along the way you can stop by **Château Julien Winery** for a tasting and tour (reservations required for tour). ~ 8940 Carmel Valley Road, five miles from Route 1; 831-624-2600; www.chateau julien.com.

You may want to follow the trails that lead from the visitors center near the Carmel River through woodlands and meadows to Snively's Ridge, a 2000-foot peak in 3700-acre **Garland Ranch Regional Park**. Pick up a map at the visitors center for information about hiking and horseback riding. ~ 700 West Carmel Valley Road, nine miles from Route 1; 831-659-4488; www.mprpd. org, e-mail mprpd@mprpd.org.

LODGING

Carmel River Inn, located on the southern outskirts of town, is a 43-unit establishment with both a motel and woodframe cottages (the latter have greater appeal). The less expensive guest units are studio-size structures with wall-to-wall carpeting, televisions, refrigerators, and telephones; their interior designer was obviously a capable, if uninspired, individual. The pricier cottages vary in size and facilities, but all have DVD players, while some may contain extra rooms, a fireplace, or a kitchen. There's a heated pool and several patios. ~ Route 1 at Carmel River Bridge; 831-624-1575, 800-882-8142, fax 831-624-0290; www. carmelriverinn.com, e-mail carmelriverinn@hotmail.com. DELUXE TO ULTRA-DELUXE.

◀ **HIDDEN**

Carmel's most closely kept secret is a hideaway resort set on 22 acres and overlooking the ocean at a distance. Scattered about the tree-shaded grounds at the **Mission Ranch** are triplex cottages and a quadraplex unit, 31 rooms in all, in addition to the older white clapboard farmhouse. There are tennis courts, trim lawns, and ancient cypress trees. With mountains in the background, the views extend across a broad lagoon and out along sandy beachfront. The ranch dining room is favored by local people. A rare find indeed with continental breakfast included. On-site restaurant. ~ 26270 Dolores Street; 831-624-6436, 800-538-8221, fax 831-626-4163. MODERATE TO ULTRA-DELUXE.

The Pine Inn is not only Carmel's oldest hostelry, but also another of the town's more reasonably priced places. This 49-room hotel dates back to 1889 and still possesses the charm that has drawn visitors for decades. The lobby is a fashionable affair with black lacquered furniture, dark, warm woods, and a brick fireplace. The less expensive accommodations are smaller but do have canopied beds, private baths, TVs, and phones common to all the rooms. Each room has touches of both Europe and the Far East. Rather than a country inn, this is a full-service hotel with restaurant and bar downstairs as well as room service for the guests. ~ Ocean Avenue between Lincoln and Monte Verde streets; 831-624-3851, 800-228-3851, fax 831-624-3030; www.pine-inn.com, e-mail info@pine-inn.com. DELUXE TO ULTRA-DELUXE.

Highlands Inn, Park Hyatt Carmel is one of those raw-wood-and-polished-stone places that evoke the muted elegance of the California coast. Ultramodern in execution, it features a stone lodge surrounded by wood-shingle buildings. The lodge houses two restaurants and an oceanview lounge while the neighboring structures contain 142 guest rooms, each a warren of blond woods. Most have patios or balconies, and wood-burning fireplaces; several have double spa tub. Parked on a hillside overlooking an awesome sweep of ocean, the inn is the ultimate in Carmel chic. ~ Route 1 about four miles south of Carmel; 831-620-1234, 800-682-4811, fax 831-626-1574; www.highlands-inn.com. ULTRA-DELUXE.

DINING

In Carmel, the thing to do is drop by the **Tuck Box** for afternoon tea. The establishment sits in a dollhouselike creation with a swirl roof and curved chimney. The prim and tiny dining room also serves breakfast and lunch. During the noon meal there are omelettes, sandwiches, shrimp salad, and Welsh rarebit. Tea includes scones, muffins, or homemade pie. Jams and scone mix are available for purchase. ~ Dolores Street between Ocean and 7th avenues; 831-624-6365, fax 831-626-3939; www.tuckbox.com. BUDGET TO MODERATE.

Join the line in front of **Tuttomondo's Trattoria** for good times and a great meal. As you step through the door you might think you're in Italy: Wine bottles, cooking utensils, and strings of garlic adorn the walls, and the staff is very friendly, often breaking into song for impromptu celebrations. If that isn't enough, the

AUTHOR FAVORITE

The **Thunderbird Bookshop and Café** combines two of my favorite activities: eating and reading. You can browse the bookstore, then dine in the dining room or out on the patio. They serve lunch all day with entrées such as pot pies, soups, and salads. If you're just looking for a snack, they have a variety of desserts. ~ 3600 The Barnyard; 831-624-1803; www.thunderbirdbooks.com, e-mail info@thunderbirdbooks.com. BUDGET.

food is *molto deliziaso*. You can't go wrong with a fresh pasta dish such as the San Remo (sun-dried tomatoes and goat cheese in cream sauce) or *la mafiosa* (calamari, prawns, and scallops in a spicy tomato sauce). Dinner specials include veal, seafood, fish, and chicken entrées, and at lunch sandwiches are added to the menu. Save room for the desserts, especially the tiramisu! ~ Dolores Street between Ocean and 7th avenues; 831-624-8977, fax 831-624-4102; www.mondos.com. MODERATE TO DELUXE.

Reasonably priced, casual, and contemporary. Who could ask for more than what they're offering at critically acclaimed **Rio Grill**? The cuisine at this popular dining room is American grill with a Southwestern touch. Smoked chicken and artichokes and New York steak with a twice-baked potato are among the entrées. ~ Crossroads Shopping Center, Route 1 and Rio Road; 831-625-5436, fax 831-625-2950; www.riogrill.com. MODERATE TO DELUXE.

Patisserie Boissière belongs to that endangered species—the moderately priced French restaurant. The simple French country dining room adjoins a small bakery. In addition to outrageous pastries for breakfast, they offer brunch on the weekend. Entrées include coquilles St. Jacques, salmon in parchment paper, and braised lamb shank. Baked brie and French onion soup are also on the bill of fare. A bargain-hunter's delight in dear Carmel. No dinner on Monday and Tuesday. ~ Mission Street between Ocean and 7th avenues; 831-624-5008, fax 831-626-9155. MODERATE TO DELUXE.

Old-time Carmel residents will tell you about **The Restaurant at Mission Ranch**, how it dates back over a century to the days when it was a creamery. Today it's just a warm, homey old building with a stone fireplace plus a view of a sheep pasture and the neighboring ocean. The menu is a combo of fresh seafood and all-American fare: steak, prime rib, chicken, and pasta. Dinner served nightly, as well as Saturday lunch and Sunday brunch. ~ 26270 Dolores Street; 831-625-9040, fax 831-625-5502. MODERATE TO ULTRA-DELUXE.

Of course the ultimate dining place is **The Covey at Quail Lodge**, up in Carmel Valley. Set in one of the region's most prestigious hotels, The Covey is a contemporary European restaurant with a California influence, serving, for example, rack of lamb with tarragon mustard. Richly decorated, it overlooks the lodge's lake and grounds. Reservations, please. Breakfast and dinner. ~ 8205 Valley Greens Drive; 831-624-2888, 888-828-8787; www.quail lodge.com, e-mail qul@peninsula.com. DELUXE TO ULTRA-DELUXE.

SHOPPING

The major shopping strip is along Ocean Avenue between Mission and Monte Verde streets, but the best stores generally are situated on the side streets. The **Doud Arcade** is a mall featuring artisan shops. Here you'll find leather merchants, potters, and jewelers. ~ Ocean Avenue between San Carlos and Dolores streets.

Most of the artists who made Carmel famous have long since departed, but the city still maintains a wealth of art galleries. While many are not even worth browsing, others are outstanding. The **Carmel Bay Company** features posters by contemporary artists. ~ Lincoln Street and Ocean Avenue; 831-624-3868. The **Carmel Art Association Galleries**, owned and operated by artists, offers paintings and sculpture by local figures. ~ Dolores Street between 5th and 6th avenues; 831-624-6176; www.carmelart.org. Also of note is the **Chapman Gallery**, which features local artists as well. Closed Sunday and Monday, except by appointment. ~ 7th Avenue between Mission and San Carlos streets; 831-626-1766; www.chapmangallery.com.

> In Carmel, shopping seems to be the raison d'être. If ever an entire town was dressed to look like a boutique, this is the one. Its shops are stylish and expensive.

Carmel is recognized as an international center for photographers. Two of the nation's most famous—Ansel Adams and Edward Weston—lived here. **The Weston Gallery** displays photographs by both men, as well as works by other 19th- and 20th-century photographers. Closed Sunday and Monday, except by appointment. ~ 6th Avenue between Dolores and Lincoln streets; 831-624-4453; www.westongallery.com. At **Photography West Gallery** Weston and Adams are represented, as are Imogen Cunningham and Brett Weston. Closed Tuesday and Wednesday in January. ~ Dolores Street between Ocean and 7th avenues; 831-625-1587.

The **Barnyard Shopping Village** is an innovative mall housing about 50 shops and restaurants. Set amid flowering gardens is a series of raw wood structures reminiscent of old farm buildings. ~ Route 1 and Carmel Valley Road; 831-624-8886; www. thebarnyard.com. Browse the boutiques and gift shops, then follow those brick pathways to the **Thunderbird Bookshop and Café**. With a marvelous collection of hardbacks and paperbacks, it is one of the finest bookstores along the Central Coast. Better still, they have an adjoining café and there's a nearby book-and-toy store for children. ~ 3600 The Barnyard; 831-624-1803; www. thunderbirdbooks.com, e-mail info@thunderbirdbooks.com.

NIGHTLIFE The **Forge in the Forest** is a restaurant-cum-bar with its copper walls, hand-carved bar, and open fire. ~ Junipero Street and 5th Avenue; 831-624-2233.

Possibly the prettiest place you'll ever indulge the spirits in is the **Lobos Lounge** at Highlands Inn. An entire wall of this leather-armchair-and-marble-table establishment is plate glass. And the picture on the other side of those panes is classic Carmel—rocky shoreline fringed with cypress trees and lashed by passionate waves. If that's not entertainment enough, there's nightly piano music. ~ Route 1, about four miles south of Carmel; 831-620-1234, fax 831-626-1574; www.highlands-inn.com.

CARMEL RIVER STATE BEACH 🏃 This beach would be more attractive were it not upstaged by Point Lobos, its remarkable neighbor to the south. Nevertheless, there's a sandy beach here as well as a view of the surrounding hills. The chief feature is the bird refuge along the river. The marshes offer willets, sandpipers, pelicans, hawks, and kingfishers, plus an occasional Canadian snow goose. The beach has restrooms. ~ Located at the end of Carmelo Road in Carmel (take Rio Road exit off Route 1); 831-624-4909, fax 831-624-9265; pt-lobos.parks.state.ca.us, e-mail ptlobos@mbay.net.

POINT LOBOS STATE RESERVE 🏃 🚲 🛶 ⚓ In a region packed with uncommonly beautiful scenery, this park stands out as something special. A 1225-acre reserve, only 456 acres of which are above water, it contains over 300 species of plants and more than 250 species of animals and birds. This is a perfect place to study sea otters, harbor seals, and sea lions. During migrating season in mid-winter and mid-spring, gray whales cruise the coast. Along with Pebble Beach, Point Lobos is the only spot in the world where Monterey cypresses, those ghostly, wind-gnarled coastal trees, still survive in the wild. There are 80-foot-high kelp forests offshore, popular with scuba divers who know the reserve as one of the most fascinating places on the coast. Reservations to dive are necessary and can be made up to two months in advance by phone or e-mail. There are picnic areas and restrooms. Dogs aren't allowed. Parking fee, $6. ~ Route 1, about three miles south of Carmel; 831-624-4909; ptlobos.org, e-mail ptlobos@mbay.net.

PINNACLES NATIONAL MONUMENT 🏃 Set far inland amid the softly rolling Gabilan Mountains are the sharp, dramatic volcanic peaks that centerpiece this unusual park. Sheer spires and solitary minarets vault 1200 feet from the canyon floor. Comprising the weathered remains of a 23-million-year-old volcano, these towering peaks challenge day hikers and technical rock climbers alike. Rockclimbing is a major activity here in spring and fall (it's too hot in summer). There are caves to explore, and more than 30 miles of trails leading through the remnants of the volcano. Prairie falcons, coyote, gray fox, and bobcat roam the region, while golden eagles work the skies above. Since the cliffs are accessible only by trail, visitors should be prepared to hike. Bring water, durable shoes, loose clothing, and a flashlight for cave exploring. (Caves are subject to seasonal closures due to flooding and "bat protection.") The best time to visit is spring, when the wild-

Text continued on page 418.

The Old Spanish Mission Town

Time permitting, there's one overland excursion that must be added to your itinerary—a visit to the **Old Mission San Juan Bautista**. While this graceful mission town, located 90 miles south of San Francisco, is easily reached from Route 101, the most inspiring route is via Route 156 from the Monterey Peninsula.

Anyone who has read Frank Norris' muckraking novel about the railroads, *The Octopus*, will recognize this placid village and its thick, cool adobe church. And anyone who remembers the climax to Hitchcock's *Vertigo* will instantly picture the mission, even though the bell tower that Jimmy Stewart struggled to climb was a Hollywood addition that you won't see at the real San Juan Bautista. Founded in 1797, the mission was completed in 1812. Today it numbers among California's most enchanting locales. With its colonnade and sagging crossbeams, the mission has the musty scent of history. The old monastery and church consist of a low-slung building roofed in Spanish tile and topped with a belfry. ~ 831-623-4528; oldmission-sjb.org.

My favorite spot in this most favored town is **Mission Cemetery**, a small plot bounded by a stone fence and overlooking valley and mountains. It's difficult to believe that over 4300 American Indians are buried here in unmarked graves. The few recognizable resting places are memorialized with wooden crosses and circling enclosures of stone. Shade trees cool the yard. Just below the cemetery, symbolic perhaps of change and mortality, are the old Spanish Road (*El Camino Real*) and the San Andreas Fault.

The mission rests on a grassy square facing **Plaza Hall**. Originally a dormitory for unwed American Indian women, this structure was rebuilt in 1868 and used as a meeting place and private residence. Peek inside its shuttered windows or tour the building and encounter a child's room cluttered with old dolls, a sitting room dominated by a baby grand piano, and other rooms containing period furniture.

Behind the hall sits a **blacksmith shop**, filled now with wagon wheels, oxen yokes, and the "San Juan Eagle," a hook-and-ladder wagon drawn by a ten-man firefighting crew back in 1869. Nearby **Plaza Stable** houses an impressive collection of buggies and carriages.

The **Plaza Hotel** (admission) lines another side of the square. Consisting of several adobe structures, the earliest built in 1814, the place once served as a stagecoach stop. Today its myriad rooms contain historic exhibits and 1860s-era furnishings. Similarly, the **Castro-Breen Adobe** next door is decorated with Spanish-style pieces. Owned by a Mexican general and later by Donner Party survivors, it is a window into California frontier life. Nearby are **San Juan Jail**, an oversized outhouse constructed in 1870, and the

settler's cabin, a rough log cabin built by East Coast pioneers in the 1830s or 1840s.

All are part of the **state historic park** that comprises San Juan Bautista. Like the plaza, 3rd Street is lined with 19th-century stores and houses. Here, amid porticoed haciendas and crumbling adobe, are antique stores, a bakery, restaurants, and other shops. Admission. ~ 831-623-4881, fax 831-623-4612.

A block away is **El Teatro Campesino**, an excellent resident theater group. This Latino company originated *Zoot Suit*, an important and provocative play that was eventually filmed as a movie. With a penetrating sense of Mexican-American history and an unsettling awareness of contemporary Latino social roles, it is a modern expression of the vigor and spirit of this old Spanish town. From May to September summer productions are held in its theater; the Christmas show is staged in Mission San Juan Bautista. ~ 705 4th Street; 831-623-2444; www.elteatrocampesino.com, e-mail info@elteatrocampesino.com.

Accommodations are scarce in San Juan Bautista, but **Posada de San Juan** offers comfortable, unassuming rooms within walking distance of the mission and 3rd Street's shops and restaurants. The 34 rooms are equipped with wetbars, whirlpool bathtubs, and gas fireplaces. Decorated in a hacienda style, this inn reflects the distinctly Mexican flavor of San Juan Bautista. ~ 310 4th Street; 831-623-4030, fax 831-623-2378. MODERATE TO ULTRA-DELUXE.

Country Rose Inn Bed & Breakfast is a 20-minute drive away, but well worth the effort. At the end of a country lane and surrounded by fields of garlic and marigolds, this Dutch colonial manor has been on the cover of *Country Inns* magazine. Each of its five B&B rooms is done in a rose motif, with antique furnishings and a view of the mountains or foothills in the distance. You can relax on the front and back porches or in the parlor with its grand piano. A full breakfast is served. Reservations recommended. ~ 455 Fitzgerald Avenue, San Martin; 408-842-0441, fax 408-842-6646; www.countryrose-b-n-b.com. MODERATE TO DELUXE.

As for restaurants, **La Casa Rosa** sits in an 1858 house. Open for lunch only, this family-run eatery features an "old California casserole," a "new California casserole," a chicken soufflé, and a seafood soufflé. The first entrée is made with cheese, meat sauce, and a corn base; the second dish features green chiles. La Casa Rosa is charming and intimate. Closed Tuesday. ~ 107 3rd Street; 831-623-4563, fax 831-623-1031. MODERATE.

In the same block, **Jardines de San Juan** is recommended as much for its garden as its food. In addition to the usual tacos, burritos, and flautas, weekend specials get fancy: Veracruz-style red snapper served with *crema* on a bed of rice, or *pollos borrachos* cooked in sherry with ham and sausage. ~ 115 3rd Street; 831-623-4466; www.jardinesrestaurant.com, e-mail jardines@hollinet.com. BUDGET TO MODERATE.

flowers bloom, or autumn; summer brings stifling heat to the area and winter carries rain. The east side of the park has an information center, picnic areas, and restrooms. The west side offers a ranger station, picnic areas, and restrooms. There are no concession services in the park. Day-use fee, $5. ~ No road traverses the park. You must enter either on the east side by following Route 25 south from Hollister for 32 miles, then proceeding four miles west on Route 146; or on the west side along Route 146, about 13 miles east from Soledad (which is just off Route 101); 831-389-4485, fax 831-389-4489; www.nps.gov/pinn, e-mail pinn_visitor_information@nps.gov. The lengthy drive to the east entrance makes for a long day trip. If you plan to hike, start early in the day.

▲ **Pinnacles Campground Inc.**, a private facility with 139 sites (some with partial RV hookups), sits astride the park's east side. Hot shower, a pool, and campground activities are perks. Two-night stay may be required. Fees are $7 per person nightly or $28 for a group of up to six people. A small grocery store with limited hours is also on-site. ~ 2400 Route 146, Paicines; 831-389-4462; www.pinncamp.com.

▼▼▼▼▼▼▼▼▼▼
Big Sur

From Point Lobos, the highway hugs the coastline as it snakes south toward Big Sur. Like Route 1 north of San Francisco, this is one of America's great stretches of roadway. Situated between the Santa Lucia Mountains and the Pacific, Route 1 courses about 30 miles from Carmel to Big Sur, then spirals farther south along the coast toward San Luis Obispo and Los Angeles.

The Big Sur district is where the Santa Lucia Mountains encounter the Pacific. Backed by the challenging Ventana Wilderness, the region is marked by sharp coastal cliffs and unbelievable scenery. Though it's hard to conceive, Big Sur may be even more beautiful than the other sections of the Central Coast.

Along Route 1, each turnout provides another glimpse into a magic-lantern world. Here the glass pictures a beach crusted with rocks, there a wave-wracked cliff or pocket of tidepools. The canyons are narrow and precipitous, while the headlands are so close to the surf they seem like beached whales. Trees are broken and blasted before the wind. The houses, though millionaire affairs, appear inconsequential against the backdrop of ocean and stone.

SIGHTS

At **Soberanes Point**, eight miles south of Carmel, hiking trails lead out along the headlands. Here you can stand on a rock shelf directly above the ocean and gaze back at the encroaching hills.

HIDDEN ►

For an intriguing excursion into those hills, head about six miles up **Palo Colorado Road**, which intersects with Route 1 a couple of miles south of Garrapata Creek. Though paved, this country road is one lane. The corridor tunnels through an arcade of redwoods past log cabins and rustic homes. If you're feeling adventurous, follow the twisting eight-mile road to its terminus at Los Padres National Forest.

Back on Route 1 you'll traverse **Bixby Creek Bridge**, which stretches from one cliff to another across an infernal chasm. Local legend cites it incorrectly as the world's longest concrete arch span. With fluted hills in the background and a fluffy beach below, it may, however, be the world's prettiest.

For another incredible side trip, you can follow **Coast Road**   ◄ HIDDEN
for about 11 miles up into the Santa Lucia Mountains. Climbing along narrow ledges, then corkscrewing deep into overgrown canyons, the road carries you past exquisite views of forests and mountain ridges. There are hawk's-eye vistas of the Pacific, the rolling Big Sur countryside, and Pico Blanco, a 3709-foot lime-rich peak. This is the old coast road, the principal thoroughfare before Route 1 was completed in the 1930s. Take heed: It is so curvy it makes Route 1 seem a desert straightaway; it is also en-

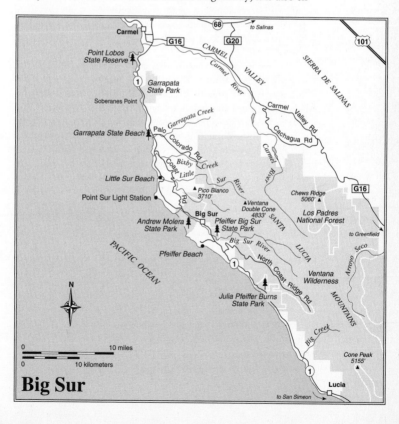

Big Sur

tirely unpaved, narrow, rutted, and impassable in wet weather. But oh those views!

Coast Road begins at Bixby Bridge and rejoins Route 1 at Andrew Molera State Park. If instead of detouring you stay on Route 1, it will climb along **Hurricane Point**, a promontory blessed with sweeping views and cursed by lashing winds, and descend toward **Little Sur Beach**. This sandy crescent is bounded by a shallow lagoon. There are dunes and lofty hills all around, as well as shore birds. Another lengthy beach leads to **Point Sur Light Station**, set on a volcanic headland. This solitary sentinel dates back to 1889. The only way to visit this lighthouse is by a three-hour guided tour. Tours run Saturday at 10 a.m. and 2 p.m., and Sunday at 10 a.m. There are additional tours added in summer, including a moonlight tour. Call for details. Admission. ~ 831-625-4419.

Then the road enters the six-mile-long Big Sur River Valley. **Big Sur**, a rural community of under 2000 people, stretches the length of the valley. Lacking a town center, it consists of houses and a few stores dotted along the Big Sur River. The place received its name from early Spanish settlers, who called the wilderness south of Carmel *El País Grande del Sur*, "the big country to the south."

Later it became a rural retreat and an artists' colony. Henry Miller lived here from 1947 until 1964, writing *Big Sur and the Oranges of Hieronymus Bosch*, *Plexus*, and *Nexus* during his residence. Today the artists are being displaced by soaring land values, while the region is gaining increased popularity among visitors. It's not difficult to understand why as you cruise along its knife-edge cliffs and timbered mountainsides. You can drive for miles past eye-boggling vistas, then turn back on Route 1 to the Monterey Peninsula, or continue on to a strange and exotic land called Southern California.

LODGING   For a variety of accommodations, consider **Big Sur Campground and Cabins**. Set in a redwood grove along the Big Sur River, this

---

HENRY MILLER LITE

There's not much to the **Henry Miller Library**, but somehow the unassuming nature of the place befits its candid subject. Occupying a small woodframe house donated by Miller's friend Emil White, the museum contains volumes from the novelist's library as well as his evocative artworks. Seasonal hours, call ahead. ~ Route 1 about a mile south of Ventana Inn; 831-667-2574; www.henrymiller.org, e-mail magnus@henrymiller.org.

13-acre facility has campsites, tent cabins, and A-frames. Camping out on the grounds includes access to hot showers, a laundry, a store, a basketball court, and a playground. The tent cabins consist of woodframe skeletons with canvas roofs. They come with beds, bedding, and towels, and share a bath house. The tent cabins are closed during the rainy season. The "cabins" along the river are actually mobile homes, neatly furnished but rather sterile. More intimate are the A-frame cabins with Franklin stoves and sleeping lofts. The newer modular units include pine floors with bedrooms as well as a kitchen and a private bath. ~ Route 1; 831-667-2322; www.bigsurcalifornia.org/camping.html. BUDGET TO DELUXE.

Ripplewood Resort has 16 cabins and a café. The least expensive cabin is a small, basic duplex unit with redwood walls, a gas heater, and carpeting. It has a bath but lacks a kitchen. The more expensive units are larger, with kitchens, sitting rooms, and decks, and are located above the river. My advice? Compromise with one of the riverfront cabins. They feature kitchens, decks, and spacious bedrooms. (No extra charge for the river tumbling past your doorstep.) ~ Route 1; 831-667-2242, fax 831-667-2108; www.ripplewoodresort.com. MODERATE.

Located within Pfeiffer Big Sur State Park is **Big Sur Lodge**, a complex containing 20 cottages with two to six units per cottage. The "lodge" represents a full-facility establishment complete with conference center, restaurant, gift shop, grocery, laundromat, and heated pool in the summer. It's very convenient, if undistinguished. The cottages are frame houses with wood-shingle roofs. They are simple in design, yet some have a kitchen and a fireplace. The interiors are pine and feature wall-to-wall carpeting and high beam ceilings; each cottage features a porch or a deck. ~ Route 1; 831-667-3100, 800-424-4787, fax 831-667-3110; www.bigsurlodge.com, e-mail info@bigsurlodge.com. DELUXE.

Big Sur has long been associated with bohemian values and an easy lifestyle. Today landed gentry and wealthy speculators have taken over many of the old haunts, but a few still remain. One such is **Deetjen's Big Sur Inn**, a 20-unit slapdash affair where formality is an inconvenience. The place consists of a hodgepodge collection of clapboard buildings. The outer walls are unpainted and the doors have no locks, lending the residence a tumbledown charm. Rooms are roughhewn, poorly insulated, and funky, but some have woodburning stoves. Throw rugs are scattered about, the furniture is traditional, and local art pieces along the wall serve as decoration. No in-room phones or TVs. If all this is beginning to discourage you, you're getting older than you think; after all, this offbeat hideaway does possess an enchanting quality. ~ 48665 South Route 1; 831-667-2377, fax 831-665-0466; www.deetjens.com. DELUXE TO ULTRA-DELUXE.

If, on the other hand, you spell Big Sur with a capital $, consider **The Post Ranch Inn**, located just across the highway from the Ventana Inn. Defying description, this cliff-edge hotel is a testimony to rustic perfection. Consisting of 30 separate units and designed to fit the surrounding landscape, some rooms are built into the hillside and covered by grass; others are perched on stilts high above the forest floor. Each room is decorated by wood and stone, has a king-size bed, and, best of all, offers an open view of the Pacific Ocean or tree-covered hillside. ~ Route 1; 831-667-2200, 800-527-2200, fax 831-667-2824; www.postranchinn.com, e-mail info@postranchinn.com. ULTRA-DELUXE.

HIDDEN ►

The ultimate resting place in this corner of the world is the **Tassajara Zen Center**. Set deep in the Santa Lucia Mountains along a meandering country road, Tassajara has been a hot springs resort since the 1860s. Before that its salubrious waters were known to American Indians and the Spanish. When the Zen Center purchased the place in 1966, they converted it into a meditation center. There are only a few telephones and electrical outlets in the entire complex, making it ideal for people seeking serenity. Every year from May until September, the Zen Center welcomes day-visitors and overnight guests to use the Japanese-style bath houses and natural steam showers. The hosts provide three vegetarian meals daily plus lodging in the private rooms and cabins dotted about the grounds. Day-visitors are also welcome; shuttle service into the resort is available from Jamesburg, south of the Carmel Valley. In summer, Tassajara hosts a number of special workshops and retreats, including tea ceremonies and calligraphy writing. For day and overnight visits be sure to make your reservations far in advance, since this unique place is very popular. Closed September through April. ~ For information, contact

AUTHOR FAVORITE

When I'm ready to spend *beaucoup* bucks, I book lodging at the **Ventana Inn and Spa**. Set along 243 mountainside acres overlooking the Pacific Ocean, this fabled resort is the *ne plus ultra* of refined rusticity. Buildings are fashioned from raw wood and most guest rooms are equipped with tile fireplaces. There are cedar walls and quilt beds. With Japanese hot baths, saunas, two pools, a spa, a fitness room, a library, and a clothing-optional sun deck, the place exudes an air of languor. Guests enjoy a continental breakfast and afternoon wine and cheese, hike nearby trails, and congratulate themselves for having discovered a secluded resort where doing nothing is a way of life. Leaving the kids at home is suggested. ~ Route 1; 831-667-2331, 800-628-6500, fax 831-667-2419; www.ventanainn.com. ULTRA-DELUXE.

the Zen Center, 300 Page Street, San Francisco, CA 94102; 415-863-3136; for reservations, call 415-865-1899; www.sfzc.com. DELUXE.

The Big Sur Roadhouse Restaurant has a prime location along Big Sur. The menu highlights fresh local seafoods; it also features teriyaki steak, chicken pot pie, and a variety of pasta dishes. The wine list features central California vintages. This small restaurant is a local favorite; reservations are recommended. Dinner only. Closed Tuesday. ~ Route 1; 831-667-2264, fax 831-667-2865. MODERATE TO DELUXE.

DINING

Fernwood, a combination restaurant-bar-store, has a changing menu that usually includes hamburgers, salads, and the like. This local gathering spot is your best bet for an inexpensive lunch or dinner. Closed Wednesdays. ~ Route 1; 831-667-2422, fax 831-667-2663. BUDGET TO MODERATE.

Cielo, part of the extraordinary complex that includes a prestigious inn, is one of the region's most elegant dining places. Resting on a hillside overlooking the mountains and sea, it's a perfect spot for a special meal. At lunch you'll be served salad, steak sandwiches, or fresh pasta, either inside the wood-paneled dining room, or alfresco on a sweeping veranda. For dinner you can start with oysters on the half shell or steamed artichoke, then proceed to such entrées as quail, rack of lamb, salmon, filet mignon, or fresh fish grilled over oak. ~ Route 1; 831-667-2331, 800-628-6500, fax 831-667-2419; www.ventanainn.com. DELUXE TO ULTRA-DELUXE.

Whether or not you're staying at the Post Ranch Inn, you will hardly want to miss dinner at the resort's signature restaurant, **Sierra Mar**. The magnificent views of the ocean and surf 1100 feet below become tenfold more dramatic at dinnertime when the sun drops behind the Pacific. The menu features health-conscious California cuisine and changes daily. Among the flexible prix-fixe menu selections are lean beef, seafood, poultry and vegetarian dishes. The bar serves a light luncheon all afternoon. Reservations required.~ Route 1; 831-667-2800, fax 831-667-2824; www.postranchinn.com. ULTRA-DELUXE.

Another bird's-eye view is offered at **Nepenthe**. Perched on a cliff 800 feet above the Pacific, this fabled dining spot has plenty of personality. People come across the continent to line its curving bar or dine along the open-air patio. It's a gathering place for locals, tourists, and everyone in between. There are sandwiches, quiches, and salads for lunch. At dinner the menu includes fresh fish, broiled chicken, and steak. If you're not hungry, stop in for a drink—the scene is a must. ~ Route 1; 831-667-2345, fax 831-667-2394; www.nepenthebigsur.com. MODERATE TO ULTRA-DELUXE.

For breakfast or lunch, try the outdoor **Café Kevah**, downstairs. Personally, I think it's a much better deal than Nepenthe.

They serve standard breakfast fare—waffles, omelettes—and lunch dishes with a Mexican twist. Their homemade pastries are the perfect companions for an afternoon gazing out at the ocean. Closed in January and February and when it rains. ~ 831-667-2344, fax 831-667-2394; www.nepenthebigsur.com. BUDGET TO MODERATE.

SHOPPING   Set in a circular wooden structure resembling an oversized wine cask (and made from old water tanks) is one of Big Sur's best-known art centers. The **Coast Gallery** is justifiably famous for its displays of arts and crafts by local artists. There are lithographs by novelist Henry Miller as well as paintings, sculptures, ceramics, woodwork, handmade candles, and blown glass by Northern California craftspeople. An adjoining shop features a wide selection of Miller's books. ~ 49901 Route 1, 33 miles south of Carmel; 831-667-2301, fax 831-667-2303; www.coastgalleries.com.

NIGHTLIFE   Down in Big Sur the lights go out early. There is one place, **Big Sur River Inn**, that has a wood-paneled bar overlooking the Big Sur River and keeps a candle burning. Live-music on Sunday in the summer. ~ Route 1; 831-667-2700, 800-548-3610; www.bigsur riverinn.com.

BEACHES & PARKS   **GARRAPATA STATE PARK** 🏃 🏊 🎣 🛶 This broad swath of white sand is particularly favored by local people, some of whom use it as a nude beach (which remains illegal). Easily accessible, it's nevertheless off the beaten tourist path, making an ideal hideaway for picnicking and skinny dipping. There are no facilities. A rough current and lack of lifeguards make swimming inadvisable. ~ It's along Route 1 about 7 miles south of Carmel. Watch for the curving beach from the highway; stop at the parking lot just north of the Garrapata Creek bridge. From here a path leads down to the beach; 831-667-2315, fax 831-667-2886.

ANDREW MOLERA STATE PARK 🏃 🚴 🐎 🏊 🎣 🛶 An adventurer's hideaway, this 4800-acre park rises from the sea to a 3455-foot elevation. It features three miles of beach and over 15 miles of hiking trails. The forests range from cottonwood to oak to redwood, while the wildlife includes mule deer, bobcat, harbor seals, and gray whales. Big Sur River rumbles through the landscape and surfers try the breaks on the beach. The only thing missing is a road: this is a hiker's oasis, its natural areas accessible only by heel and toe. The wilderness rewards are well worth the shoe leather. This is the only place in Big Sur where you can ride a horse; you can hire a horse from a concessionaire and check out Captain Cooper's Cabin, a late-19th-century pioneer log cabin. Toilets are the only facilities. Day-use fee, $5. ~ Located along Route 1 about three miles north of Big Sur; 831-667-2315, fax 831-667-2886.

▲ There are 24 hike-in sites (tents only); $7 per night. Primitive facilities, but water and flush toilets are available.

PFEIFFER BIG SUR STATE PARK 🏃 🏊 🎣 One of California's southernmost redwood parks, this 1000-acre facility is very popular, particularly in summer. With cottages, a restaurant, a grocery, a gift shop, picnic areas, restrooms, showers, and a laundromat on the premises, it's quite developed. However, nature still retains a toehold in these parts: the Big Sur River overflows with trout and salmon (fishing is prohibited, however), Pfeiffer Falls tumbles through a fern-banked canyon. Day-use fee, $5. ~ Located along Route 1 in Big Sur; 831-667-2315, fax 831-667-2886.

> The beach scenes from *Basic Instinct*, starring Sharon Stone and Michael Douglas, were filmed at Garrapata State Beach.

▲ There are 218 sites for both tents and RVs (no hookups); $16 to $20 per night. Reservations: 800-444-7275.

PFEIFFER BEACH 🏃 🏊 🐟 🎣 ⛵ Of Big Sur's many wonders, this may be the most exotic. It's a sandy beach littered with boulders and bisected by a meandering stream. Behind the strand rise high bluffs that mark the terminus of a narrow gorge. Just offshore loom rock formations into which the sea has carved tunnels and arches. Little wonder poet Robinson Jeffers chose this haunting spot for his primal poem "Give Your Heart to the Hawks." The only facilities are toilets. Day-use fee, $5. ~ Follow Route 1 for about a mile south past the entrance to Pfeiffer Big Sur State Park. Turn right onto Sycamore Canyon Road (unmarked), which leads downhill two miles to the beach; 831-667-2315, fax 831-667-2886.

JULIA PFEIFFER BURNS STATE PARK 🏃 This 3700-acre extravaganza extends from the ocean to about 1500 feet elevation and is bisected by Route 1. The central park area sits in a redwood canyon with a stream that feeds through a steep defile into the ocean. Backdropped by sharp hills in a kind of natural amphitheater, it's an enchanting glade. A path leads beneath the highway to a spectacular vista point where 80-foot-high McWay Waterfall plunges into the ocean. Another path, one-and-eight-tenths miles north of the park entrance, descends from the highway to an isolated beach near Partington Cove that has been declared an underwater park (permit required). There are picnic areas and restrooms. ~ Route 1, about 11 miles south of Pfeiffer Big Sur State Park; 831-667-2315, fax 831-667-2886.

▲ There are two hike-in environmental campsites for tents only; $14 per night with an eight-person maximum. Reservations are required; call 800-444-7275.

VENTANA WILDERNESS 🏃🐎 ⚓ 🛶 Part of Los Padres National Forest, this magnificent 216,500-acre preserve parallels Route 1 a few miles inland. It covers a broad swath of the Santa Lucia Mountains with elevations ranging from 600 feet to 5800 feet. Within its rugged confines are 237 miles of hiking trails. Wild boars and turkeys, mountain lions, and deer roam its slopes. Bald eagles soar the skies. The only facilities are ranger stations. Parking fee, $4. ~ From Route 1 in the Big Sur area, there are two entry points. The ranger station, where maps and fire permits can be acquired, is just south of Pfeiffer Big Sur State Park. For information and permits, contact the U.S. Forest Service (Monterey District, 406 South Mildred Avenue, King City, CA 93930; 831-385-5434), or 831-667-2315, fax 831-667-2886.

▲ There are more than 100 sites, some for self-contained RVs, others for walk-in tent camping. RV sites range from $12 to $18; hike-in is free.

Outdoor Adventures

The Central Coast is renowned for its open-sea fishing. Charter boats comb the waters for rock cod, salmon, and albacore. Most trips leave the dock by 6 a.m. and return by 3 p.m.

SPORT-FISHING

SOUTH OF SAN FRANCISCO If you want to test your skill, or luck, contact **Captain John's Fishing Trips**. They operate two boats, ranging from 55 to 65 feet. You can go deep-sea fishing for rock cod or ling cod any day of the week. April through November there's salmon fishing and December through March there's whale watching. Bait and tackle available. ~ 111 Johnson Pier, Princeton-by-the-Sea; 650-726-2913.

SANTA CRUZ To take a charter from Santa Cruz in search of tuna, salmon, or rock cod, call **Shamrock Charters**. Bait and tackle available. They run two boats, a 55-footer and a 64-footer. ~ 2210 East Cliff Drive at the Santa Cruz Yacht Harbor; 831-476-2648; www.scurfslanding.com, e-mail steve@scurfslanding.com. For do-it-yourself adventures, **Santa Cruz Boat Rentals** has 20 boats to rent and a 16-foot wood skiff that seats up to four adults. Fishing gear is provided. There is also bait, tackle, and a gift shop. ~ Santa Cruz Municipal Pier; 831-423-1739; www.santacruzboatrentals.net.

MONTEREY Spend the day on one of two boats with **Randy's Fishing Trips**. Advance reservations recommended. ~ 66 Old Fisherman's Wharf; 831-372-7440. **Sam's Fishing Fleet** also offers charters and day-long fishing trips for albacore, salmon, and deep-sea catches. ~ 84 Old Fisherman's Wharf; 831-372-0577.

WHALE WATCHING

To see the whales during their annual migration, head for whale-watching lookouts at Pillar Point in Half Moon Bay, the coast around Davenport, Point Pinos in Pacific Grove, or Cypress Point in Point Lobos State Reserve. (See the "Whale Watching" section in Chapter Five.)

SOUTH OF SAN FRANCISCO Captain John's Fishing Trips offers two whale-watching excursions daily. The party boat plies the coast in search of cetaceans, pinnipeds, and other marine life. ~ 21 Johnson Pier, Princeton-by-the-Sea; 650-726-2913.

> The summer whale-watching season typically runs from mid-June through September while the winter migration is viewable from mid-December to mid-March.

MONTEREY If you'd prefer a close look at these migrating mammals and other marine life—sea lions, seals, otters, sea birds—catch a cruise with **Randy's Fishing Trips.** They can accommodate up to 48 people, and the two-hour trip is fully narrated by a marine biologist. ~ 66 Old Fisherman's Wharf; 831-372-7440. To catch glimpses of blue whales, humpbacks, and dolphins, hop on board a 65-foot vessel with **Monterey Whalewatching.** Trips last about three hours and sonar equipment is used to help locate whales. ~ 96 Old Fisherman's Wharf #1; 831-372-2203. **Sam's Fishing Fleet** offers cruises that last anywhere from two to six hours. Their three boats are fully equipped with fish finders and radar. ~ 84 Old Fisherman's Wharf; 831-372-0577.

SEA KAYAKING

Whether you are young or old, experienced or a novice, the Central Coast awaits discovery by sea kayak.

MONTEREY Explore Monterey Bay and Elkhorn Slough, or paddle your way along the coastal waters with **Monterey Bay Kayaks.** They also offer naturalist-led trips around the Monterey National Marine Sanctuary, where you'll see a wide variety of marine life. The tour to Elkhorn Slough goes through an inland saltwater marsh to view seals, otters, and birds. Reservations recommended. ~ 693 Del Monte Avenue, Monterey; 831-373-5357, 800-649-5357; www.montereybaykayaks.com. **Adventures by the Sea** has 150 double and single kayaks for rent. A two-to-three-hour tour is led by a marine biologist who describes the history of Cannery Row, local geology, natural history, and native lore. ~ 299 Cannery Row; 831-372-1807; www.adventuresbythesea.com, e-mail sales@adventuresbythesea.com.

DIVING

The Central Coast offers premiere diving in Northern California. Although coastal waters are quite frigid, the unique kelp forests, wide array of fish, spotted harbor seals, and other fascinating marine life make for unforgettable diving.

SANTA CRUZ Adventure Sports offers everything from one- or two-week-long dive trips taking you to hotspots to brunch dives leaving from Monastery Beach. They rent and sell all the gear, and give classes ranging from beginning to assistant instructor. ~ 303 Potrero Court #15, Santa Cruz; 831-458-3648, 888-839-4286; www.asudoit.com, e-mail dennis@asudoit.com.

MONTEREY   Aquarius Dive Shop offers beach dives unless otherwise requested. One- and two-tank dives are available, as are night dives. They rent and sell all the gear. Classes are offered for open water, advanced rescue, dive master, and nitrox. ~ 2040 Del Monte Avenue, Monterey; 831-375-1933; www.aquariusdivers. com. For morning or afternoon dives, contact **Monterey Bay Dive Center**. All equipment is available to rent. ~ 225 Cannery Row; 831-656-0454.

CARMEL   Point Lobos State Reserve has some of the finest shore diving opportunities on the Pacific Coast. You'll spot sea otters, sea lions, and schools of fish. The numbers of divers per day is limited so reservations are a must. ~ Route 1; 831-624-8413; www.ptlobos.org, e-mail ptlobos@mbay.net.

SURFING & WIND- SURFING

Catching a wave when the surf's up near Lighthouse Point north of Santa Cruz is a surfer's dream. Known as "Steamer Lane," this stretch of coastline hosts many international surfing competitions. On the east side, Pleasure Point is a popular surf spot with several reef breaks. Mavericks Break, located north of Half Moon Bay, is world-renowned among surfers for its huge—sometimes deadly—waves. Even experienced wave riders need to be careful here. Avoid surfing too far north near Año Nuevo—the waters are popular with great white sharks. On the east side, long and short fiberglass boards, boogieboards, and wet suits can be rented or purchased from **Freeline Design**. ~ 821 41st Avenue, Santa Cruz; 831-476-2950. **O'Neill's Surf Shop**, a one-stop surf mecca, rents surfboards, boogieboards, and wetsuits, and sells all the accessories. ~ 1115 41st Avenue, Capitola; 831-475-4151.

Or catch the wind on a windsurfing board. Rentals and lessons are available at **Club Ed**, as are regular surfing lessons and equipment. Besides surfboards they also rent body boards and wetsuits. ~ Look for the trailer on Cowell Beach next to the Santa Cruz wharf; 831-464-0177; www.club-ed.com.

RIDING STABLES

Exploring the coast and inland trails astride a galloping horse is one way to enjoy a visit to the Central Coast.

SOUTH OF SAN FRANCISCO   With its four-mile white-sand beach and surrounding farm country, Half Moon Bay is a choice region for riding. **Seahorse Ranch and Friendly Acres Ranch**, located on the coast, rents more than 150 horses. They also have pony rides for kids. No reservations are necessary, and you can ride without a guide if you like (with adequate riding experience). ~ 2150 Route 1, Half Moon Bay; 650-726-9903; www. horserentals.com.

PACIFIC GROVE   There are escorted tours at the **Pebble Beach Equestrian Center**. A one-and-a-half-hour ride takes you through the forest and down to the beach. Call ahead to reserve a horse. ~ Portola Road and Alva Lane, Pebble Beach; 831-624-2756; www.ridepebblebeach.com, e-mail info@ridepebblebeach.com.

GOLF

For golfers, visiting the Monterey Peninsula is tantamount to arriving in heaven. Pebble Beach is home to the annual AT&T National Pro-Am Golf Championship. Several courses rank among the top in the nation.

With stunning views of the rugged coastline, **Pebble Beach Golf Course** is the most noted. Three U.S. Open Tournaments have been held here. The 7th, 8th, 17th, and 18th holes are world-renowned as highly difficult ocean holes. Reservations are required a day in advance for non-hotel guests. ~ 17 Mile Drive, Pebble Beach; 831-625-8518, 800-654-9300. **Spyglass Hill Golf Course,** known as one of the toughest courses in the nation, has six of the holes with ocean views while the rest are set in the forest. Reservations are required. ~ Stevenson Drive, Pebble Beach; 831-625-8563, 800-654-9300. Set on a century-old property, **Old Del Monte Golf Course** is a relatively flat course studded with ancient trees. ~ 1300 Sylvan Road, Monterey; 831-373-2700. **Pacific Grove Golf Course** overlooks Monterey Bay and the Pacific Ocean. It has a pro shop and driving range. ~ 77 Asilomar Avenue, Pacific Grove; 831-648-5777.

BIKING

The **Pacific Coast Bikecentennial Route** follows Route 1 through the entire Central Coast area to Big Sur and beyond. There are camping sites along the way. The ocean views and rolling pastures make this an ideal course to peddle, if you are experienced and careful.

Both Santa Cruz and Monterey have bike paths for beginners and skilled riders alike. Especially good for touring are **17 Mile Drive,** the bike trail along the bayshore from **Seaside to Marina,** the trail from **Seaside to Lover's Point** (via Cannery Row), and the roads in **Point Lobos State Reserve.**

AUTHOR FAVORITE

Of all the adventures in nature that await along the Central Coast, the one I remember most vividly is kayaking among the playful sea otters and boisterous sea lions on Monterey Bay. Guided excursions of the bay or Elkhorn Slough afford an up-close and personal look at the region's greatest treasures. See page 427 for kayaking tour outfitters.

Bike Rentals In Monterey, **Bay Bike Rentals** carries hybrids, mountain bikes, tandems, and sunreys (four-wheeled, pedal-powered vehicles). ~ 640 Wave Street, Monterey; 831-646-9090. They also have a store in Carmel. ~ 255 Heritage Harbor, Carmel; 831-655-8687.

HIKING To fully capture the beauty and serenity of the region's woodlands, chaparral country, and beaches, explore its hiking trails. The Santa Cruz and Santa Lucia mountains offer several hundred miles of trails through fir, madrone, and redwood forests. Getting lost, so to speak, among these stands of ancient trees is a splendid way to vacation. Or hike the inland hills with their caves and rock spires. Down at the sea's edge you'll discover more caves, as well as tidepools, sand dunes, and a world of marine life.

All distances listed for hiking trails are one way unless otherwise noted.

SOUTH OF SAN FRANCISCO If you've an urge to see elephant seals breeding, take the three-mile guided walk led by docents at **Año Nuevo State Reserve**. To protect these mammoth mammals, the preserve is open during breeding season only to those on the guided tours. Tours are scheduled from December through March. The tours are popular and space is limited so make reservations well in advance; call 800-444-4445. To explore this area after mating season, you can hike on your own past sand dunes, tidepools, and sea caves. Follow **Año Nuevo Trail** (2.5 miles), beginning at the west end of the parking lot, to Año Nuevo Point.

SANTA CRUZ MOUNTAINS For hikers and beginning rock climbers, **Castle Rock State Park** offers a chance to try out skills and enjoy magnificent views. **Castle Rock Trail** (3 miles) is a moderate hike through oak and madrone woodlands. The trail starts at the south side of the Skyline Boulevard parking lot. Castle Rock is about a half-mile from the trailhead. Continue along the

SKYLINE TO THE SEA

For a backpacking trip over the Santa Cruz Mountains, take the magnificent **Skyline-to-the-Sea Trail** (28.4 miles). The trail begins at Saratoga Gap (Skyline Boulevard and Route 9) or Castle Rock State Park (adding three miles to the trek) and climaxes on the Pacific shore. Campgrounds at Waterman Gap, Big Basin, and along Waddell Creek provide resting places for hikers traveling this heavily forested path. Be sure to make reservations for campsites; information, 831-338-8860 or 831-338-8861; www.bigbasin.org, e-mail info@bigbasin.org.

Castle Rock Trail, then pick up the **Saratoga Gap Trail** (2.8 miles), which leads to Castle Rock Trail Camp.

There are hikes for everyone along the 60 miles of trails in **Big Basin Redwoods State Park**, the oldest of California's state parks. Covering 18,000 acres, Big Basin has spectacular trails leading to waterfalls and redwood groves. **Redwood Trail** (.6 mile) is a self-guiding nature trail easy enough for the entire family. Take the trail that begins west of the parking lot and stroll past a grove of giants.

Berry Creek–Sunset Loop Trail (10 miles) is an arduous trek through the most beautiful scenery in the park. Follow Redwood Trail, then pick up Skyline-to-the-Sea Trail, which will run into Berry Creek Trail. The trek climaxes at Lower and Upper Berry Creek Falls, which tumble more than 50 feet over sandstone cliffs. A return on the Sunset Trail completes the journey; allow about six hours.

The **Howard King Trail** (3 miles) begins at the Middle Range Fire Road and ascends gradually to Mt. McAbee overlook. En route you'll encounter meadows, old-growth redwoods, and views of the Pacific.

MONTEREY AREA   One of California's most beautiful spots is the six-mile shoreline at **Point Lobos State Reserve**. The park is laced with trails leading to tidepools, sandy coves, and whale-watching vistas.

Cypress Grove Trail (.8 mile), one of the most popular (and populated) in the park, leads through a stand of Monterey cypress trees and offers cliff-top views of the ocean.

Bird Island Trail (.8 mile) takes you through coastal shrubbery to two exquisite white-sand beaches—China Cove and Gibson Beach. The path also overlooks Bird Island, a refuge for cormorants and brown pelicans.

Pine Ridge Trail (.7 mile), beginning near Piney Woods, goes inland through forests of Monterey pines and Coast live oak. Deer, squirrel, and such birds as pygmy nuthatches and chestnut-backed chickadees make this a tranquil nature hike.

South Shore Trail (1 mile), an oceanside walk between Sea Lion Point and the Bird Rock parking area, allows close looks at tidepool life and shore birds. You can also play amateur geologist, examining multicolored patterns in sedimentary rocks.

For rock climbers and hikers alike, **Pinnacles National Monument** offers great sport. Because of the summer heat and winter weather, it's recommended that you come in spring or fall to explore the park's rock spires, talus caves, and covered canyons. At any time of year, bring plenty of water and a flashlight.

Hiking along the narrow ledges of **High Peaks Trail** (5.4 miles), you'll find splendid views of the entire park. The steep trail begins across from the Chalone Creek picnic area, travels up through the High Peaks and ends up at the Moses Spring parking lot. Allow at least three to four hours.

Old Pinnacles Trail (2.3 miles) begins at Chalone Creek picnic area and goes along relatively level terrain near the west fork of the creek to Balconies Caves.

Juniper Canyon Trail (1.8 miles) starts near the west end of the park at the Chaparral ranger station and climbs 760 feet to connect with the park's east side High Peaks Trail. It's the steepest trail in the monument.

BIG SUR   Over 216,500 acres of rugged mountain terrain comprise the **Ventana Wilderness** of Los Padres National Forest. About 200 miles of hiking trails make it easy to explore the Santa Lucia Mountains while escaping the trappings of civilization. Several roads off Route 1 will take you onto the preserve. Big Sur Station and Bottchers Gap Station are the only staffed coastal entrances.

Be careful when driving along the coast in the summer—thick fogs occasionally creep in, making for dangerous driving conditions.

Bottchers Gap–Devils Peak Trail (4 miles) is a steep hike through coniferous forests to spectacular vistas overlooking the northern section of the Ventana Wilderness.

Kirk Creek–Vicente Flat Trail (5.1 miles) winds along ridgelines that afford mountain views.

Pine Ridge Trail (40.7 miles) begins at Big Sur Station and carries two miles to the park boundary before heading into the Ventana Wilderness. First stop is Ventana Camp, near the Big Sur River. Then the trail leads past several campgrounds and ends at China Camp.

Transportation

CAR

From San Francisco, coastal highway **Route 1** is the most scenic way to explore the Central Coast. In the Santa Cruz Mountains, **Routes 35** and **9** lead through redwood forests and rural towns. **Route 101**, which runs inland parallel to the coast is the fastest route. Numerous side roads lead from this highway to points along the Central Coast.

AIR

Several airlines fly regular schedules to the **Monterey Peninsula Airport**. America West, American Eagle Airlines, United and United Express service this area from San Francisco and other departure points. ~ Route 68 and Olmstead Road; 831-648-7000; www.montereyairport.com.

BUS

Greyhound Bus Lines has continual service to Santa Cruz (425 Front Street; 831-423-1800) and Monterey (1042 Del Monte Avenue at the Exxon station; 831-373-4735) from San Francisco and Los Angeles. ~ 800-231-2222; www.greyhound.com.

For railroad buffs, **Amtrak** offers daily service on the "Coast Star-light." The train runs from Seattle to Los Angeles with stops in Oakland, San Jose, and Salinas (11 Station Place). Once in Salinas, passengers can transfer to a Greyhound or Monterey–Salinas Transit bus. ~ 800-872-7245.

If flying directly into Monterey, you can rent a car at the airport from **Avis Rent A Car** (800-331-1212), **Budget Rent A Car** (800-527-0700), **Hertz Rent A Car** (800-654-3131), or **National Car Rental** (800-227-7368). Additional rental agencies are located in town. Try **American International Rent A Car** (800-392-8724).

San Mateo County Transit, or **SamTrans**, departing from the Daly City and Colma BART stations, has local bus service to Pacifica, Moss Beach, and Half Moon Bay. Bus service is also available between Año Nuevo and San Mateo and Half Moon Bay during seal season (January through March). Reservations are required (through SamTrans). ~ 800-660-4287; www.transitinfo.org.

From Waddell Creek in northern Santa Cruz County, the **Santa Cruz County Transit System** covers Route 1 as far south as Watsonville. ~ 831-425-8600.

From Watsonville, connections can be made to Monterey and Big Sur via the **Monterey–Salinas Transit Company**. These buses carry passengers to many points of interest including Cannery Row, Point Lobos, and Andrew Molera and Pfeiffer Big Sur State Parks. Buses from Monterey to Big Sur run twice daily from May to early September. ~ 831-899-2555; www.mst.org, e-mail cus tomerservice@mst.org.

SEVEN

Gold Country & High Sierra

Setting out from a flat, warm, agricultural region several hundred feet above sea level, this chapter ends far past timberline amid snow-domed peaks 13,000 feet high. The rivers that irrigate the farmland begin high in the Sierra Nevada. These whitewater currents slice through the mountains, carving canyons and dumping rich minerals along the riverbanks. Among the precious metals is one that altered the course of California history. It also gave its name to the foothill region that lies between the heights and the lowlands—the Gold Country.

Sacramento rests at the heart of California's Central Valley, the richest farming area in the world. Sacramento's other business is politics; this city of nearly 410,000 is the state capital. Originally, however, its business was gold. No yellow metal was ever found along Sacramento streets. Sacramento made its fortune supplying the gold fields, providing men and materials for the nearby strikes.

The man who founded the town was also directly responsible for the original discovery of gold. John Sutter created Sacramento in 1839 when he built a fort to protect the huge land grant that the Spanish government bestowed upon him. Using American Indians as serfs, he set out to create an inland empire, New Helvetia. With Sacramento as headquarters, his domain spread to the nearby Sierra foothills.

Then occurred an event of historic import, which should have secured his power and fortune. Instead, it destroyed him. Gold was discovered on John Sutter's land. That was January 1848. By the next year, machinists and farm hands, scoundrels and preachers, filled with hope and a hunger for gold, began descending in mobs. Over 40,000 miners arrived in 1849; three years later there were 100,000. They came to John Sutter's land. His workers quit to join the miners, farmland fell fallow, projects went unfinished, buildings were stripped for firewood. By 1852, Sutter was bankrupt.

His town, however, boomed. In 1854, Sacramento became the capital. By 1856 it boasted California's first railroad, and in 1860 the city was a center for the Pony Express. The transcontinental railroad was conceived in Sacramento, and by the turn of the century, this river town was adorned with the beautiful Victorian homes it still displays.

The precious metal that built Sacramento was found throughout the Gold Country east of the capital. There a rich vein of quartz and gold, the Mother Lode, parallels the Sierra Nevada range for several hundred miles.

The Gold Country became a land of dreams, but its gold fields were often a nightmare. Eventually two *billion* dollars worth of yellow metal was mined, yet for many argonauts, prospecting meant coming up empty-handed and then facing inflated prices for provisions. Little wonder that most of the towns that mushroomed in the wilderness have long since vanished. The towns remaining go by names such as Mariposa, Sonora, Coloma, and Nevada City. Still maintaining antique buildings and old mining scars, they are located along a 300-mile stretch of Route 49.

If time and territory can possibly be compared, perhaps the historic importance of the Gold Rush is equal to the grandeur of the mountains that forged the gold. The Sierra Nevada is the largest single mountain range in the country. It's a solitary block of earth, tilted and uplifted, 430 miles long and 80 miles wide. A mere child in the long count of geologic history, it rose from the earth's surface a few million years back and did not reach its present form until 750,000 years ago. During the Pleistocene epoch, glaciers spread across the land, grinding and cutting at the mountains. They carved river valleys and deep canyons, and sculpted bald domes, fluted cliffs, and stone towers.

The glaciers left a landscape dominated by ragged peaks where lakes number in the hundreds and canyons plunge 5000 feet. There are cliffs sheer as glass that compete with the sky for dominance. It is, as an early pioneer described it, a "land of fire and ice."

To the pioneers, however, the beauty of the place was of little consequence compared to its magnitude. The Sierra Nevada was a hellish gateway to the promised land, the final obstacle before entering California. The first to cross it was Jedediah Smith, a mountain man who followed the Stanislaus River in 1827. Then, in 1841, the Bidwell-Bartleson party became the first emigrant wagon train to trek the Sierra. By 1845, the mountain migration route was opening as 250 settlers crossed; twice that number traveled the "California Trail" the next year. Present-day hikers can explore a network of old emigrant trails throughout the mountains. Trees still living near timberline bear blazes left by pioneers back in the 1850s.

Before the settlers, Maidu and Miwok peoples hunted the western slopes, while Washoes and Paiutes stalked the eastern heights of Nevada. Today much of the land is preserved in a series of state parks and national forests. There's Calaveras Big Trees with its solitary trails through dense sequoia stands; Mono Lake, a prehistoric sea adorned with rock statues; and the High Sierra wilderness, domain of backpackers and golden eagles.

The hot spot of the Sierras is Lake Tahoe, an alpine resort that goes year-round. Tahoe enjoys 300 sunny days annually, but also manages to receive 18 feet of snow. Skiers challenge its slopes at Squaw Valley, Alpine Meadows, Sugar Bowl, and a dozen other runs. Spring and fall carry crisp weather to Tahoe; since summers are warm, anglers, boaters, and waterskiers replace snow lovers.

In the Gold Country, winter usually brings rain, spring covers the hillsides with wildflowers, and summers are hot. Not so hot, however, as Sacramento. There the weather can be torrid, though spring and fall are cool and winter is foggy and overcast.

That means Yosemite enjoys the finest weather of all: summers are mild, and in winter Yosemite Valley itself receives little snow while the high country is wide open to skiers. Climate is only one of the elements that makes Yosemite a special place. The Park is our national heritage etched in stone; a land where glaciers, sequoias, and alpine meadows are ringed by stately mountains. If Sacramento is the state capital, then Yosemite is the capital of the Sierra, representing in its angled cliffs and tumbling rivers a unique land of gold and granite. Since businesses in the area may be seasonal, travelers should call ahead.

Sacramento

Remember those quizzes in grammar school? What's the capital of Illinois?
—*Chicago.*
No, Springfield. How about New York?
—*Brooklyn.*
Wrong, dodo, it's Albany. And Florida?
—*Orlando.*
No, not Miami either, but Tallahassee.

I flunked every one of those tests simply because the state capital is never where it should be. It's rarely obvious, and almost never the state's big, famous city. They always put the capital in some backwater no one ever heard of, hoping that because it's the capital the place will become great. It never does. It only means kids have to spend four times as long doing their homework.

California is no different. The seat of government should be San Francisco or Los Angeles. But instead it's Sacramento, which is north of both those cities. Sacramento is actually closer to a town called Vacaville, which translates as "cow town."

Sacramento is not my favorite city. (Neither is Harrisburg, Pennsylvania, nor Jefferson City, Missouri.) Not that it's a bad place. In fact, Sacramento is more than the capital city: It's also a gateway to the Gold Country and the center of the richest agricultural area in the world. If you decide to tour the town, you'll discover it has several faces. Who knows? Sacramento might even become your favorite capital.

SIGHTS

One entertaining way to reach Sacramento is by **Amtrak**. Daily rail service from the San Francisco Bay Area is very convenient. The ride is especially fun for children. Best of all, the train stops just a couple of blocks from the most interesting part of town. ~ 800-872-7245.

Old Sacramento, a National Historic Landmark, provides a perfect introduction to the Gold Country. Lined with wooden sidewalks and heavy-masonry storefronts, its streets date to Sacramento's gilded era. Once considered the city's skid-row section, Old Sacramento today is a 28-acre historic park comprising more than 100 restored and re-created buildings. The neighborhood, situated between the Sacramento River and roaring interstate Route 5, can easily be seen in the course of a short walking tour.

Start at the **B. F. Hastings Building** at 2nd and J streets. Behind the iron doors of this 1852 structure is a museum commemorating the western headquarters of the Pony Express.

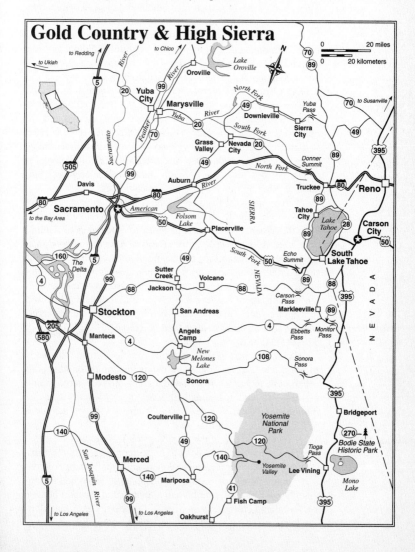

Gold Country & High Sierra

A walking tour will also carry you past the **Eagle Theatre**, an 1849 playhouse where Gold Rush–era plays and dramas are occasionally presented. Free guided tours are available, complete with a video about Old Sacramento. ~ 925 Front Street; 916-323-6343.

You'll also pass the **Globe**, a replica of a brig that sailed around Cape Horn in 1849. ~ Foot of K Street. At Front and L streets, the **Old Sacramento Schoolhouse**, with its bolted desks and wood stoves, evokes the days when stern taskmasters wielded cane rods. Then continue past the balconied buildings and brick warehouses that create a sense of nostalgia throughout this antique enclave.

From Old Sacramento, walk south to Capitol Mall, a tree-lined boulevard, and follow it to the **State Capitol Building**. Set in a gracefully landscaped park, adorned with statuary and lofty pillars, it's an impressive sight. Looking like capitols everywhere, the Roman Corinthian structure is capped with a golden dome and dominated by a grand rotunda. What makes this building different from others is that many rooms have been restored and are open to the public. The old governor's office has been furnished with period pieces, equipped with a coal-burning pot-bellied stove, and returned to its 1906 glory. The state treasurer's office has been converted to a historical condominium—half re-creating 1906 and the other half portraying the Depression era.

Wander up to the third floor when the legislature is in session and you can sit in the gallery watching the solons battle it out. Both the **Assembly** and **Senate galleries** are often open to visitors, even when the Legislature is not in session. Like the rooms downstairs, they feature antique furnishings and traditional decor, but the chambers also incorporate such newfangled devices as automatic vote counters and electronic sound systems. A museum offers exhibits about California history and government; a film and free guided tours are available. The Capitol is wheelchair accessible. ~ 10th Street between L and N streets; 916-324-0333, fax 916-445-3628; www.capitolmuseum.ca.gov.

Having listened to the legislators ramble on, you'll be ready to adjourn to **Capitol Park**. Surrounding the Capitol Building, this urban oasis includes a trout pond, cactus and rose gardens, and a grove of trees transplanted from Southern battlefields to memorialize the Civil War dead. There's also a Vietnam memorial to Californians lost in that war.

From the east end of the park, Capitol Avenue leads to **Sutter's Fort**. It was back in 1839 when John Sutter founded Sacramento, building an adobe fort near the American River. Having received a 76-square-mile land grant from the Spanish, he named the domain "New Helvetia" after his native Switzerland. The fort became a cultural and strategic center for all Northern California. Donner Party survivors sought refuge here, Captain John Fremont and Kit Carson visited, and in 1846, during the Mexican War, a key Spanish leader was imprisoned and the American flag raised over the fort.

The original fortress has long since dissolved to dust and a re-created version raised in its stead. Lacking the feel of authenticity, it nevertheless possesses some interesting displays. There are weaving rooms with large but primitive looms, plus living quarters complete with rusty utensils and the most uncomfortable beds imaginable. You'll see a cooper shop where buckets and barrels were fashioned, museum cases portraying early California life, and a room hung with traps and animal skins. Admission. ~ 2701 L Street; 916-445-4422; www.parks.ca.gov.

Then from the adjacent **California State Indian Museum**, you will gather an idea of California before the advent of Sutter and his Mexican benefactors. On permanent display are tools, baskets, dance regalia, and other items from California's first peoples. Admission. ~ 2618 K Street; 916-324-0971, fax 916-322-5231.

The capital city features several other points of interest. Contact the **Sacramento Convention & Visitors Bureau** for information. Closed weekends. ~ 1300 J Street; 916-264-4740, 800-292-2334, fax 916-264-7788; www.discovergold.com, e-mail scvb@cityofsacramento.org.

The **Crocker Art Museum** provides a grand example of Californian art and sculpture as well as decorative arts from

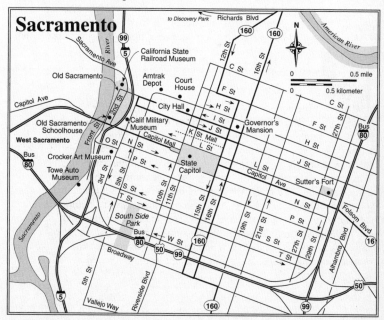

Europe and Asia. But the entire collection is dominated by the building it is housed in. With its parquet floors and repoussé ceilings, the E. B. Crocker mansion represents the ultimate artwork. Browsing the museum means wandering through a grand ballroom, along sweeping staircases, and past walls carved by hand. If you can overcome the impact of the interior, there are many interesting artworks to study. Or you can adjourn to the glass-walled pavilion, which houses part of the museum's contemporary California art collection. Children will enjoy the museum's student artwork and craft activities. Closed Monday. Admission. ~ 216 O Street; 916-264-5423, fax 916-264-7372; www.crocker artmuseum.org, e-mail cam@cityofsacramento.org.

Then there's the **Governor's Mansion** that houses no governors. Not any longer, that is. It did serve as home to 13 state leaders from 1903, when it was built, until 1966, when Ronald Reagan and wife Nancy refused to live there. The rest of the story is typical of California's wacky history. Reagan decided to build a new mansion, which wasn't ready until he left the governorship and went on to other things. The place was completed in time for Jerry Brown to occupy. But it looked more like an architectural testimonial to Reagan than a house. Brown refused to take up residence, preferring to slap a mattress on an apartment house floor and call it home. Which he did—for eight years. The next governor finally decided he'd like to move in, but the legislature, controlled by the opposition party, refused to let him have the place.

Anyway, that's the tale of the "new" governor's mansion. The 30-room old mansion became a museum open to tours. It's a

---

sights

AUTHOR FAVORITE

The highpoint of any visit to Old Sacramento is the **California State Railroad Museum**. The sights, sounds, and smells of the railroads are evocatively displayed here. Trains hoot, station-yard dogs bark, and steam engines hiss as you wander past antique locomotives and narrow-gauge passenger trains. Docents are always on hand to explain the history of railroading. There's a full-scale diorama showing the construction of the transcontinental railroad in the High Sierra during the 1860s. If the re-creation is not enough for you, take a six-mile train ride on a historic locomotive from the nearby Central Pacific Freight Depot (every weekend from April through September). Admission. ~ 2nd and I streets; 916-323-9280, 916-445-6645, fax 916-327-5655; www.californiastaterailroad museum.org, e-mail foundation@californiastaterailroadmuseum.org.

Victorian-Empire structure that looks like a woodframe wedding cake. Within its 15 rooms are antiques and artifacts from the early 20th century. Admission. ~ 16th and H streets; 916-323-3047, fax 916-322-4775.

At **Towe Auto Museum,** you can relive the development of the automobile and the visionary who brought us this modern convenience. Approximately 160 cars are on display at any one time, featured in rotating exhibits with themes such as the Dream of Mobility, the Dream of Luxury and the Dream of Cool. In addition to unusual cars—a 1906 Model N, a 1966 Cobra—the museum also houses automotive costumes, tools, and equipment. Be sure to check out the library, which has an extensive collection of automotive manuals and brochures. Admission. ~ 2200 Front Street; 916-442-6802, fax 916-442-2646; www.toweautomuseum. org, e-mail info@toweautomuseum.org.

A tribute to the men and women of California who have served in the U.S. Armed Forces since the Spanish-Mission period, the **California Military Museum** exhibits non-activated weapons, uniforms, and artifacts. In addition to profiling the California National Guard's role in the country's major wars, the museum looks at peacetime relief work such as the rescue efforts following the 1906 earthquake. Closed Monday. Admission. ~ 1119 2nd Street; 916-442-2883, fax 916-442-7532; www.militarymuseum.org, e-mail info@militarymuseum.org.

For a taste of country life right here in the city, you can pick your own fruits and vegetables at one of Sacramento's **farms.** ◄ HIDDEN Many of the region's farmers allow visitors to wander the fields, plucking produce right from the tree. The seasons are summer and autumn, but it's best to call ahead to find out what's ripe; costs for picking are minimal. For a list of farms in the Sacramento area and elsewhere, check the website of the Small Farm Center at University of California–Davis: www.calagtour.org.

Every city has its motel row, a single street illuminated in neon and **LODGING** offering dozens of overnight possibilities. In Sacramento it's West Capitol Avenue, a busy highway extending out from the city's freeway nexus. As you buzz along this boulevard, the motels fly past in furious fashion, becoming a blur along the periphery of vision.

For inexpensive accommodations near the downtown area, it's hard to compete with the **Econo Lodge.** Nothing special—just your basic 41-room motel—but at a budget price you were hoping maybe for the Ritz? There is wall-to-wall carpeting, a television, and a phone in every unit. So if you aren't expecting to spend a lot of time in the room anyway, give it a try. ~ 711 16th Street; 916-443-6631, 800-553-2666, fax 916-442-7251; www.econo lodge.com, e-mail mineshp@pacbell.net. BUDGET.

Once a stately mansion built in 1936, **Inn at Parkside** now serves as an extravagant boutique hotel. Decorated in Old World elegance with an Asian twist, most of the seven rooms feature jacuzzi tubs. Soothing easy-listening music fills the inn nightly, and evening wine-and-cheese service, in-room breakfast, and heavenly spa facilities make this one of Sacramento's most romantic places to stay. ~ 211 6th Street; 916-658-1818, 800-995-7275, fax 916-658-1809; www.innatparkside.com, e-mail info@innatparkside.com. ULTRA-DELUXE.

Amber House features a 1905 Craftsman's-style main house, an adjacent Mediterranean-style house built in 1913, and a century-old Colonial Revival. Each of the 14 guest rooms is named for a painter, poet, or composer; all feature private baths. Among the amenities are marble bathrooms with jacuzzis, canopy beds, and antique washstands. A lovely patio/garden area can serve as the setting for the full breakfast. ~ 1315 22nd Street; 916-444-8085, 800-755-6526, fax 916-552-6529; www.amberhouse.com, e-mail info@amberhouse.com. DELUXE TO ULTRA-DELUXE.

B&B inns, many of which are in the fine old mansions that were built in Sacramento during the early part of the 20th century, now provide a welcome alternative to motels and faceless business hotels.

The **Sterling Hotel** doesn't have to be as pretty as it is to succeed. A typical guest room has a four-poster bed, armoire, Henredon furniture, fine art, an elegant chandelier, and a jacuzzi in the marble-tiled bathroom. When this 1894 mansion was remodeled, 12 accommodations were arranged on the three upper floors and the cellar was converted into a restaurant. ~ 1300 H Street; 916-448-1300, 800-365-7660, fax 916-448-8066; www.sterlinghotel.com, e-mail rick@sterlinghotel.com. ULTRA-DELUXE.

They aren't kidding about the breakfast at the **Capitol Park Bed and Breakfast**. Omelettes, pancakes, french toast, and eggs—it almost makes you forget the beautifully appointed guest rooms and elegant parlor. Each of the four suites are named after a famous 19th-century railroad baron and feature a private bath and antique furnishings (except for the queen- or king-sized beds, which are comfortable contemporary); several have jacuzzis and one unit has a fireplace. Cookies and port are served every evening. ~ 1300 T Street; 916-414-1300, 877-753-9982, fax 916-414-1304; www.capitolparkbnb.com, e-mail info@capitolparkbnb.com. DELUXE TO ULTRA-DELUXE.

DINING

Situated in Old Sacramento, the city's antique neighborhood, **West End Bar & Grill** conveys a sense of the 19th century. The setting is an 1860s building with brick-and-wood paneled interior. True to the name, the menu specializes in beef dishes, but also includes such seafood selections as shrimp, salmon and ahi tuna. Lunch offers a typical selection of burgers, sandwiches, and salads. No lunch on Monday. ~ 900 2nd Street; 916-444-9641, fax 916-444-9292; MODERATE TO ULTRA-DELUXE.

Sacramento's capital restaurant is **The Firehouse**, a plush Victorian-style dining room set in an 1850s-era fire station. The cuisine at this jacket-and-tie establishment is California cuisine, as in lavender salmon, sesame-seared ahi, scallops, and rack of lamb. During summer months you can dine outdoors in a brick courtyard. No lunch on Saturday. Closed Sunday. ~ 1112 2nd Street; 916-442-4772, fax 916-442-6617; www.firehouseoldsac. com, e-mail comments@firehouseoldsac.com. DELUXE TO ULTRA-DELUXE.

For inexpensive Asian food, there's only one **New Lu-Shan**. The all-you-can-eat Chinese buffet is perfect for wallet-conscious diners. There's also a menu with over 130 dishes. Since the restaurant is located in the Chinese Cultural Center, you can tour the Asian enclave after dining. ~ 403 J Street; 916-444-2543. BUDGET.

Within the hustle and bustle of downtown stands **Kyoto Restaurant**, which dishes out tasty Japanese food. The place gets busy and noisy during lunch with businessfolk, but it's worth a stop. Favorites include the salmon teriyaki and the spicy chicken *yakiniku*. No lunch on weekends. ~ 1001 6th Street; 916-448-3570. BUDGET.

At **Biba**, Italian specialties include lasagna, osso buco *alla Milanese*, homemade stuffed pasta, and braised rabbit with prosciutto. Among the featured pasta dishes you might find a fresh seafood linguine and angelhair pasta with sun-dried and fresh tomatoes. The mirrored, off-white dining room features both modern and neon art. No lunch on Saturday. Closed Sunday. ~ 2801 Capitol Avenue; 916-455-2422; www.biba-restaurant.com, e-mail biba@biba-restaurant.com. DELUXE TO ULTRA-DELUXE.

A favorite neighborhood haunt for locals with a discerning sweet tooth, **Rick's Dessert Diner** is a tiny little retro-style joint that turns out a parade of decadent goodies. The on-site bakery has a repertoire of some 200 cakes and pies—Key lime pie and carrot, German chocolate, midnight torte, and poppyseed cakes are just a fraction of the 30 or so daily offerings. ~ 2322 K Street; 916-444-0969. BUDGET.

Another option is to climb aboard the **Delta King**, a five-decked riverboat that serves as a floating restaurant, hotel, and cultural curiosity. Seafood, of course, is the specialty, but you'll also find steaks and other meats on the menu. ~ Foot of K Street; 916-444-5464, 800-825-5464; www.deltaking.com, e-mail dking@deltaking.com. MODERATE TO DELUXE.

There are two prime sections for shoppers in the capital city. First is **Old Sacramento**, a warren of 19th-century buildings that have

SHOPPING

been renovated and converted into shops and malls. Within the course of a few short blocks are knickknack stores, antique shops, and clothiers. The **California State Railroad Museum Shop** has books, hats, T-shirts, and children's toys. ~ 111 I Street; 916-324-4950; www.csrmf.org.

Artists' Collaborative Gallery is an excellent place to pick up locally wrought items. The crafts here include woodwork, glass, jewelry, metal sculpture, ceramics, and watercolors. ~ 1007 2nd Street; 916-444-3764; www.artcollab.com.

The other shopping district lies along **K Street**, a 14-block pedestrian walkway. Extending from Old Sacramento past the Capitol Building to 14th Street, this street-cum-shopping mall is lined with stores. There are major department stores, small shops, and fashionable restaurants along the strip. Also, the mall has been attractively landscaped with fountains and flowering trees, lending a natural feel to this consumer park.

NIGHTLIFE   After sundown in the state capital, there are two places to look for entertainment. Old Sacramento, the city's historic sector, has several saloons and dancehalls. Better yet, head for the downtown area, where you'll find an array of nightclubs and watering holes.

Without doubt the weirdest spot in Old Sacramento is **Fanny Ann's Saloon**, a multitiered bar and restaurant. The staircase rises past an endless series of rooms, each decorated in high tack fashion with old boots, wagon wheels, dangling bicycles, and striped barber poles. The main action occurs along the ground-floor bar where drinkers line up elbow to elbow. ~ 1023 2nd Street; 916-441-0505, fax 916-441-7189.

Music that ranges from alternative to progressive to retro brings a lot of diversity to **The Rage**. A state-of-the-art laser and light system, a two-level dancefloor, mirrored walls, and bars are just a few of the added attractions. Cover. ~ 1890 Arden Way; 916-929-0232, fax 916-929-5905; www.ragenightclub.com.

AUTHOR FAVORITE

I'm all for enjoying gourmet California cuisine in a garden setting and contributing to a good cause at the same time. **Casa Garden Restaurant** serves up such specialties as Chinese dumpling and roasted vegetable salad, chicken with artichoke crowns, turkey enchiladas, and salad nicoise. The menu changes weekly. The staff are all volunteers, and the proceeds go to the Sacramento Children's Home. The restaurant only serves lunch from Monday through Friday. Reservations recommended. ~ 2760 Sutterville Road; 916-452-2809. BUDGET TO MODERATE.

With room for 556 guests, **Faces** is Sacramento's largest gay nightclub. There's dancing to a mix of house, R&B, Latin, country, and disco music in the dance annex and a chance to relax on the patio. Six bars offer ample opportunity to quench that thirst. Occasional cover. ~ 2000 K Street; 916-448-7798, fax 916-448-2000; www.faces.net.

For a laid back atmosphere, the **Fox & Goose** delivers. There's 15 beers on tap, darts, and live music on the weekend. Occasional cover. ~ 1001 R Street; 916-443-8823; www.foxandgoose.com.

AMERICAN RIVER PARKWAY 🚶 🚴 🐎 ⛵ 🚤 🛥 ⚓ This chain of parks stretches for 23 miles along the American River, providing access for anglers, bikers, hikers, and picnickers. The parkway leads from Discovery Park in Sacramento to Nimbus Dam near Lake Folsom. Unfortunately, access roads do not follow the river too closely, so to reach the water you must use a series of side roads. The parkway provides opportunities to explore the riverbanks and engage in the area's numerous watersports. There are also miles of equestrian and bike trails. Within the park are picnic areas and restrooms. Day-use fee, $4. ~ The three major parks lie along this strip—Discovery Park, C. M. Goethe Park, and Ancil Hoffman Park (916-875-6672, fax 916-875-6632; www. sacparks.net, e-mail parkway@sna.com). To reach C. M. Goethe Park (916-875-6961, fax 916-875-6050), follow Route 50 east from Sacramento for several miles to the Watt Avenue exit. Take Watt Avenue to La Riviera Drive. La Riviera Drive and Folsom Boulevard parallel the river parkway for most of its length. From Folsom Boulevard, Rod Beaudry Road leads to C. M. Goethe Park. To reach Ancil Hoffman Park from Route 50 east take the Watt Avenue exit. Turn right on Fair Oaks Boulevard, then right on Van Alstine Avenue. Turn left on California Avenue, then right on Tarshes Drive. This will take you through the main gate of the park.

PARKS

Extending from Mariposa to the restored Gold Rush town of Columbia, the southern Mother Lode consists of gentle, rolling foothill country laced by rivers that pour down from the Sierra Nevada. Sparsely populated, it is dotted with small towns, covered bridges, a steam railroad, and numerous monuments to the region's 19th-century heyday. Sonora is the region's hub, a good base for excursions into the Gold Country's emerald forests.

Southern Gold Country

A likely place to start is the town of **Mariposa**. The mine here was discovered in 1849 by the famous scout Kit Carson and became part of the 45,000-acre tract owned by his colleague, Colonel John

SIGHTS

C. Fremont. The **Mariposa Museum** displays a collection of artifacts from that era ranging from children's boots to Indian baskets to mining tools. Closed weekdays in January. Admission. ~ 5119 Jessie Street, Mariposa; 209-966-2924; e-mail mmhc@sti.net.

Along Bullion Street, on a hill overlooking town, the **old jail** and **St. Joseph's Catholic Church** still stand. A study in contrast, the jail is a squat granite building with formidable iron door, while the church is tall and slender with a lofty steeple. Most impressive of these period structures is the **Mariposa County Courthouse**. The state's oldest court of law, it was built back in 1854 with wooden pegs and square-cut nails. Still in use, the courtroom contains a wood stove, kerosene lanterns, and original wooden benches.

Gold—the mineral that shaped this area's history—is the focus at the **California State Mining and Mineral Museum**. Also on display are California diamonds and benitoite (the state gem), as well as gems and minerals from around the world. Among the historic mining artifacts is a scale model of a quartz mill. Closed Tuesday in winter. Admission. ~ Mariposa County Fairgrounds, south of Mariposa on Route 49; 209-742-7625, fax 209-966-3597; e-mail mineralmuseum@sierratel.com.

HIDDEN ► North of Mariposa, there's a memorable side trip to the ghost town of **Hornitos**. Just pick up Old Toll Road in Mt. Bullion, then catch Hornitos Road; on the way back take Bear Valley Road. All are paved country roads leading through tree-studded hills on this 25-mile roundtrip detour.

A Mexican-style village centered around a plaza, Hornitos was a hideout for the notorious bandito Joaquin Murieta. According to legend, this Robin Hood figure, a semi-mythical hero to the Spanish miners, used a secret tunnel in the fandango hall to escape the law.

The Anglos in this rowdy mining town also claimed a famous citizen. Domingo Ghirardelli, the San Francisco chocolate manufacturer, built one of his earliest stores here in 1859. Several walls still remain, as do many of the town's old buildings. There's also an old jail, measuring little more than the size of a cell but possessing granite walls two feet thick.

The community contains something more than ruins of brick and stone. Because of its removal in time and space, Hornitos reflects the old days more fully than surrounding towns. There are windmills and range fences, grazing cows and crowing roosters. The tiny population goes about its business with an intensity not unlike that of the 15,000 who once lived here. And up on a hill, at a point closer to heaven than the rest of town, the old stone-and-wood church gazes down on the scene.

The region between Mariposa and Jamestown represents the least developed section of the Gold Country. It's a perfect place to capture a pure sense of the past. Particularly picturesque is the stretch from Mariposa to Coulterville, where Route 49 weaves wildly through the Merced River valley. The sharp slopes and hairpin turns provide grand vistas of the surrounding mountains.

Nestling beneath forested slopes, **Coulterville** is an architectural hodgepodge that includes several historic buildings. The **Northern Mariposa County History Center** sits astride a sturdy stone-and-iron structure, the former home of McCarthy Pharmacy and Coulter Hotel. Closed Monday and Tuesday (though tours can be arranged by appointment); closed January. ~ Coulterville; 209-878-3015, fax 209-878-0744; www.northernmariposacoun ty.museum.com, e-mail nmchc@inreach.com.

In **Chinese Camp**, another falsefront town with a gilded past, are ruins of the Wells Fargo building, a 19th-century store, plus an old church and cemetery. Once home to 5000 Chinese miners, this placid area was the scene of a violent tong war. About 2000

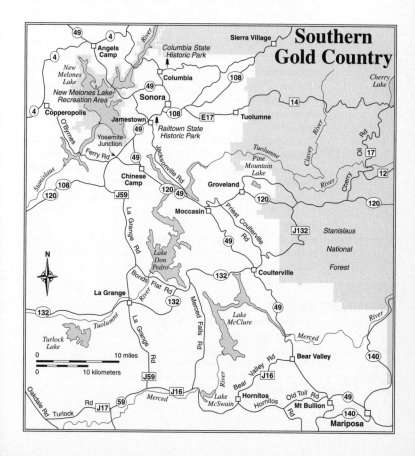

members of the Yan Wo and Sam Yap fraternities settled a mining dispute in 1856 with pikes, tridents, and axes.

North of Chinese Camp, Route 49 leads to **Jamestown**. More commercially developed than mining centers to the south, this town has been ambitiously gentrified. Its restored hotels, attractive restaurants, and antique shops are a prelude to the new, improved Gold Country awaiting you. *High Noon* and *Butch Cassidy and the Sundance Kid* were filmed here.

The **Railtown State Historic Park** hosts a roundhouse museum with blacksmith shop, a turntable, and historic locomotives. On weekends in April through October, you can also ride several miles through the Mother Lode country aboard a steam-powered train. ~ 5th Avenue and Reservoir Road, Jamestown; 209-984-3953, fax 209-984-4936; www.railtown1897.org, e-mail foundation@csrmf.org.

Sonora marks the center of the southern Gold Rush region. The seat of Tuolumne County and one of the largest towns in the Mother Lode, it has been preeminent almost since its founding in 1848. Settled by Mexicans, Sonora gained an early reputation both for its lawlessness and commercial potential. When rich strikes were discovered here, racist Americans pushed the Mexicans out of the action. They levied a $20-a-month residence tax on "foreigners," which they soon repealed when local merchants complained that the emigration of Mexican miners was hurting business!

Much of the history is written in the town's architecture. The best way to explore is with a walking-tour brochure available from the **Tuolumne County Museum and Historical Society**. With about 20 points of interest, the tour will carry you through the historic and geographic heart of the old "Queen of the Southern Mines." ~ 158 West Bradford Avenue, Sonora; 209-532-1317; www. tchistory.org.

Of the countless gold towns strung along Route 49, Columbia is not to be missed. Much of the old mining center has been preserved as **Columbia State Historic Park**. Here is a window on

THE BRIDGE OF STANISLAUS COUNTY

The gold town of **Knight's Ferry**, located on the Stanislaus River, features a rare California sight—a covered bridge. Built on a stone foundation, the wood-plank span adds an air of New England to the old mining center. The local general store has been operating over a century. Among the many Gold Rush–era buildings still standing is the unmarked **Dent House**, owned by relatives of former President Ulysses S. Grant, and visited by Grant himself in 1854. ~ Route 120.

19th-century life in the Sierra foothills. The refurbished buildings and rare artifacts create a picture that will help make sense of the random ruins found elsewhere in the Mother Lode.

Wandering the several streets that comprise this time-capsule town, you'll pass the old newspaper office, miners' boarding house, livery stable, and schoolhouse. There are hook-and-ladders so ancient they resemble Roman chariots, and a dentist's office containing fiendish-looking tools. Former Chinese residents are represented by a temple and herb shop, while the nearby apothecary remains stocked with Western-style potions and nostrums.

The old justice court serves the legal system no longer. It does, however, serve the public as it is open for touring. Over at the blacksmith shop are tools that bear an unsettling resemblance to those in the dentist's office. Like the four dozen buildings in this outdoor museum, it presents a perfect reconstruction of an imperfect era. ~ Route 49, Columbia; 209-532-0150, fax 209-532-5064.

Jamestown features several historic hotels that have been refurbished. Least expensive is the **Royal Carriage Inn**, a 19-room hostelry with a small lobby. Neither so grand nor so old as the town's other lodges, it attracts visitors with reasonable prices. Accommodations are small but freshly decorated. You'll find wall-to-wall carpeting, patterned wallpaper, and furnishings that range from pockmarked dressers to appealing brass beds. Ask for a room facing north, since the other side abuts another building, or rent one of the prim cottages out back. Continental breakfast is served daily, with an expanded version on weekends and holidays. ~ 18239 Main Street, Jamestown; 209-984-5271, fax 209-984-1675; www.royalcarriageinn.com. DELUXE TO ULTRA-DELUXE.

LODGING

The **Jamestown Hotel** is one of the best-restored hostelries in the Gold Country. An attractive two-story brick building with a balconied falsefront, it blends modern comforts such as whirlpool tubs with old-fashioned Victorian decor, including floral wallpaper, brass beds, patchwork quilts, and wicker settees. There's also a restaurant that serves lunch and dinner, Thursday through Monday. A full breakfast is served. ~ 18153 Main Street, Jamestown; 209-984-3902, 800-205-4901, fax 209-984-4149; www.jamestownhotel.com, e-mail info@jamestownhotel.com. MODERATE TO DELUXE.

Set in a sprawling Spanish-style structure, the **Sonora Days Inn** has 65 rooms. This is a full-service hotel complete with restaurant, lounge, and seasonal, rooftop swimming pool. The inn is made up of two buildings—a motel near the parking lot and the historic hotel. You'll encounter simulated-wood desks and naugahyde chairs, as well as telephones and televisions. The rooms are tidy and equipped with lovely tile showers. ~ 160 South Washington

Street, Sonora; 209-532-2400, 800-580-4667, fax 209-532-4542; www.sonoradaysinn.com, e-mail info@sonoradaysinn.com. MODERATE.

Staying at the **City Hotel** is almost a civic responsibility. Situated in Columbia State Historic Park, this charming establishment is a nonprofit organization and a training ground for hospitality management students from nearby Columbia Junior College. The ten-room hotel, dating from 1856, has been nicely restored and furnished with period pieces. There's a dining room and saloon downstairs. The guest rooms feature rugs across refinished pine floors, patterned wallpaper, and wall sconces. All include half-baths, with shared showers down the hall. "Balcony rooms" include patios overlooking the town's quiet Main Street. ~ Main Street, Columbia; 209-532-1479, 800-532-1479, fax 209-532-7027; www.cityhotel.com, e-mail info@cityhotel.com. MODERATE TO DELUXE.

The **Harlan House**, one of Columbia's finest homes at the turn of the 20th century, sits on a hill across from the old schoolhouse. You'll sleep among Victorian and other American antiques, lounge in front of your own fireplace, and relax on a shady front porch. ~ 22890 School House Street, Columbia; 209-533-4862, fax 209-533-9080; www.harlan-house.com. MODERATE TO DELUXE.

DINING

Some evening when Mexican food sounds appealing, consider the **Café Smoke**. It's a friendly, upbeat place decorated with local artwork, Mexican tile floors, and potted cacti. The menu features the full gamut of Mexican-style dishes and the adjoining saloon cooks up some mean margaritas. ~ Main Street, Jamestown; 209-984-3733, fax 209-984-4306. MODERATE.

This being Gold Country, you might expect to find mostly meat and potatoes, but **Banny's Café** offers a more sophisticated menu. At lunch, opt for a grilled chicken sandwich with prosciutto, provolone, and a fig balsamic vinaigrette on foccacia. For dinner, try

AUTHOR FAVORITE

In some hotels, if you've slept in one room you've slept in them all. Not so at the **Blue Nile Inn**, where each of the four guest rooms is decorated in a unique theme. If you choose the Gold Rush Room, you'll sleep in a four-poster bed, relax in a rocking chair, and read by the light of a miner's lamp. In the Angel Room, a satin spread covers the brass bed, crystal lamps provide light, and angels are ever present. Closed Monday through Wednesday, except with reservations. ~ 11250 Pacific Street, Columbia; 209-532-8041; www.blue-nile-inn.com, e-mail innkeeper@blue-nile-inn. com. MODERATE TO DELUXE.

the salmon filet prepared with wasabi ginger soy aioli and served over scallion rice, or pan-roasted duckling with apricot mustard port wine sauce. Daily quiches and a plentiful salad menu are always available. No lunch on Sunday. ~ 83 South Stewart Street, Suite 1, Sonora; 209-533-4709, fax 209-533-0747; www.bannys cafe.com, e-mail linlog@mlode.com. MODERATE.

For gourmet dining in a Gold Rush–era atmosphere, try **The City Hotel**. Built in 1856, the hotel is part of Columbia State Historic Park. The dining room is appointed in period with brass chandeliers, high-back chairs, and gold-framed oil paintings. Dinner is an extravaganza featuring roasted rack of lamb, pan-seared salmon and roast breast of pheasant. Sunday champagne brunch is also served. The food is delicious here and highly recommended. Closed Monday and the first two weeks in January. ~ Main Street, Columbia; 209-532-1479, 800-532-1479; www.cityhotel.com, e-mail info@cityhotel.com. MODERATE TO ULTRA-DELUXE.

SHOPPING

Jamestown has almost as many antique stores as saloons. Dotted along falsefront Main Street are shops selling pieces that date back almost as far as the stores themselves. Matter of fact, other than an occasional pharmacy, hardware store, and knickknack shop, that's pretty much all you'll find here.

Up in **Sonora**, you'll encounter a full-blown shopping scene. This is the commercial center for Southern Gold Country. Washington Street is lined with stores along its entire length. Since the shops cater to local residents, many are service outlets of little interest to travelers. But you will find clothiers, camera stores, jewelers, art galleries, bookshops, and antique stores.

Columbia has its own collection of shops—mostly antique, some touristy. Satisfy your sweet tooth at the **Columbia Candy Kitchen**, where much of the appetizing assortment of hard candy, taffy, fudge, and chocolate is dipped, pulled, and made on-site. ~ Main Street, Columbia; 209-532-7886.

NIGHTLIFE

Jamestown is one place that remembers its past. Main Street in this 19th-century community is still decorated with a string of drinking spots. For casual drinking in an easy setting, the hotel bars, such as the one in the **National Hotel**, are best. ~ 18183 Main Street, Jamestown; 209-984-3446; www.national-hotel.com, e-mail info@national-hotel.com.

The Rawhide Saloon is another get-down country bar complete with pool tables, jukebox, dancefloor, and wide-screen TV. On Friday and Saturday night, country-and-western bands crank up and wail into the wee hours. Cover. ~ Route 108, Jamestown; 209-984-5113.

In Columbia, the **Sierra Repertory Theatre** performs dramas, musicals, and comedies year-round at the Fallon House Theatre.

~ Columbia State Historic Park; 209-532-4644; www.sierrarep.org, e-mail srt@mlode.com.

PARKS

COLUMBIA STATE HISTORIC PARK 🚶🏇 A fully reconstructed Gold Rush town, this park represents an extraordinary outdoor museum. It stretches across many acres and provides a graphic representation of life in mid-19th-century California. Facilities include restrooms, picnic areas, restaurants, groceries, hotels, a museum, and much more. ~ Located off Route 49 about three miles north of Sonora; 209-532-0150; e-mail calavera@goldrush.com.

> Children of all ages will enjoy a ride in the old stagecoach that tours the perimeter of Columbia's historic town center (making one unannounced stop along the way to be held up by "bandits" on horseback).

▲ There is no camping in the park, but two private campgrounds for tents and RVs lie adjacent to the park. **'49er RV Ranch** (fax 209-532-9898) charges $29.50 double nightly for tent camping; full hookups and cable available. **Marble Quarry RV Park** (209-532-9539; www.marblequarry.com, e-mail info@marblequarry.com) collects $31.50 for partial hookups, $25 for full hookups and cable. Both feature picnic areas, hot showers, and other facilities. My vote goes to Marble Quarry RV Resort, where the folks are particularly friendly.

NEW MELONES LAKE TUTTLETOWN RECREATION AREA AND NEW MELONES LAKE GLORYHOLE RECREATION AREA 🚶🚴 🎣⛵🚤 Set on the shores of spacious New Melones Lake, these areas are popular with boaters and anglers. The entire lake is surrounded by oak trees and rolling hills, making it a pretty place to picnic. It was even more beautiful, conservationists claim, before the reservoir was created by the controversial Melones Dam, which flooded the historic Stanislaus River Valley. The Visitor Center/Museum addresses this controversy, and also features exhibits on Miwok culture, local ecology, and gold rush and mining history. Both recreation areas have toilets and showers. ~ Tuttletown and Acorn are off Route 49 about ten miles north of Sonora; Gloryhole is about 16 miles north of Sonora; 209-536-9094, fax 209-536-9652; www.usbr.gov, e-mail pguida@mp.usbr.gov.

▲ There are 144 sites (including hike-ins) at Gloryhole Campground; $12 to $16 per night; two-week limit. Reservations required. Tuttletown Campground features 175 sites with a few spaces big enough for larger RVs; there are also 65 sites at Acorn Campground; $12 to $16 per night. Reservations recommended. ~ 877-444-6777.

STANISLAUS NATIONAL FOREST 🚶🚴🏇🥾🚵🏠🎣⛵🚤 Rising along the western slope of the Sierra Nevada, this rugged region extends from the Gold Country to

Yosemite National Park. Elevations range from 1100 to over 11,000 feet, and there are hiking trails through much of the forest's 1700 square miles. Since it parallels Route 49 and represents the nearest high country to San Francisco, Stanislaus is quite popular. Among its attractions are the Merced, Tuolumne, Clavey, Stanislaus, and Mokelumne rivers, which have cut deep canyons through the forest. There are also ponderosa pine, incense cedar, cottonwood, and willows. Grouse, quail, black bear, and blacktail deer inhabit the mountains and wildflowers grow in brilliant profusion throughout the spring. Within the forest are picnic areas and restrooms; ranger stations are dotted around the area. ~ From Route 49 you can take Route 120, Route 108, or Route 4 east through the forest; 209-532-3671, fax 209-533-1890; www.fs.fed.us/r5/stanislaus.

▲ There are 49 campgrounds, including Pinecrest Campground, which has 200 sites; $19 per night; and Fraser Flat Campground, which has 38 sites; $13 per night. Some campgrounds are on a first-come, first-served basis; others by reservation only.

Central Gold Country

Mark Twain and Bret Harte helped immortalize it. Birthplace of the California Gold Rush and a good place to visit American Indian landmarks, the central Mother Lode is also home to giant sequoias and wineries, a famous frog jumping contest, white-water rafting, and some favorite hiking trails. Spread out along Route 49 between Angels Camp and Placerville, this area is a great escape.

SIGHTS

About nine miles north of Sonora, a side road leads from Route 49 to the reconstructed **Mark Twain Cabin**, where the fledgling writer lived for five months during the 1860s. It was Twain's Gold Country story, "The Celebrated Jumping Frog of Calaveras County," that first propelled him to fame.

The annual jumping-frog contest takes place every May up in **Angels Camp**, an old mining town which Twain visited during his California sojourn. The community boasts several antique buildings and a museum, but its chief notoriety is literary; it hosted not only the creator of Huckleberry Finn, but also Bret Harte, who probably used the mining center as a model in his story, "The Luck of Roaring Camp."

From Angels Camp, Route 4 leaves Route 49 and heads east toward the High Sierra. On the way it passes several points of interest including limestone caverns, the town of Murphys, and Calaveras Big Trees State Park.

Murphys is an attractive little town, established by two enterprising Irishmen in 1848. Among the historic buildings fronting its tree-lined streets is **Murphys Historic Hotel**. Built in 1856, it has housed an impressive assemblage of guests, among them Bret

Harte, Jacob Astor, Jr., Count Von Rothschild, and Ulysses S. Grant. ~ 457 Main Street, Murphys; 209-728-3444, 800-532-7684; www.murphyshotel.com, e-mail mhotel@caltel.com.

Many of the 19th-century luminaries signing the Murphys Hotel guest book were en route to the "Big Trees," which had been recently discovered and were fast becoming a world-famous tourist destination. Today **Calaveras Big Trees State Park** preserves these "Monarchs of the Forest." Located along Route 4 about 25 miles east of Angels Camp, the park rests at 4000 to 5000 feet elevation. Admission. ~ 209-795-2334, fax 209-795-7306; www.parks.ca.gov, e-mail cbt@goldrush.com.

Within it are two groves of giant sequoias, the largest living things on earth. Closely related to coastal redwoods, these trees trace their ancestry back to the age of dinosaurs. One tree in the park stands 320 feet high, another measures 27 feet in diameter. Like their coastal cousins, they create a hushed sense of awe that cannot be described, but must be experienced as you stand amidst these mountain goliaths.

The spirit of '49 remains alive and well on Route 49 as it continues north from Angels Camp. There are buildings of note in **San Andreas**. The argonaut community of **Mokelumne Hill** contains a Main Street lined with old-time buildings, including an IOOF **hall** that represents the Gold Country's first three-story structure.

HIDDEN ▶

Two **country tours** in this region will carry you past ancient mining claims tucked in the mountains. Little evidence remains of the '49ers, but the routes lead through pretty places away from civilization. First is an alternative 25-mile route from Angels Camp to San Andreas via Dogtown, Calvaritas, and Mountain Ranch roads. These country lanes wind past rolling ranchlands and mountain streams. Second is a westward course 11 miles each way to Campo Seco. From Mokelumne Hill take Route 26 to Paloma Road to Campo Seco Road. Settled by Mexicans in 1849, **Campo Seco** reveals its gilded past in a series of stone ruins lining the road.

If you haven't tired of walking tours, pick up a map of **Jackson** at the **Amador County Chamber of Commerce**. Closed weekends. ~ 125 Peek Street, Suite B, Jackson; 209-223-0350, fax 209-223-4425; www.amadorcountychamber.com, e-mail info@amadorcountychamber.com.

In addition to a balconied Main Street, this county seat features the **Amador County Museum**. One of the region's best museums, it honors the Chinese with displays of abacuses, Chinese drums, and coolie hats. Also here are a Kennedy Mine Model, geologic showcases, and a photograph collection featuring the dourest-looking people imaginable. Closed Monday, Tuesday, and December. ~ 225 Church Street, Jackson; 209-223-6386.

The next town along Route 49 is named for the man on whose land gold was first discovered, John Sutter. **Sutter Creek** warrants

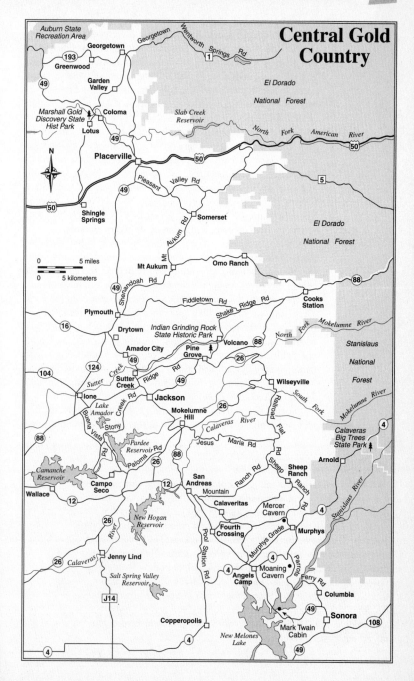

Central Gold Country

a walking tour, too. Within a few blocks along Main and Spanish streets are dozens of buildings and homes rich with history.

Volcano is another well-preserved mining center. Located on Sutter Creek Road about 12 miles east of the town of Sutter Creek, Volcano was a booming town of 5000 back in the days of the argonauts. In addition to a Masonic hall, express office, and three-story hotel, the community sports another relic—"Old Abe." According to local folks, this cannon was used during the Civil War to warn off Confederate sympathizers who sought to divert the town's gold to the Rebel cause. There are other motives for visiting this mountainside retreat. **Limestone caves**, where secret orders of Masons once held meetings, are open for exploration; they lie just outside Volcano along Pine Grove–Volcano Road. **Black Chasm** conducts guided tours daily. ~ 15701 Pioneer–Volcano Road, Volcano; 209-736-2708, 866-762-2837, fax 209-736-0330; www.caverntours.com, e-mail caverns@caverntours.com.

On the same road two miles from Volcano is **Indian Grinding Rock State Historic Park**. Here along a limestone outcropping the Miwok Indians gathered to collect acorns and grind seeds, berries, and nuts. Using the limestone bedrock as a natural mortar, they eventually ground over a thousand cavities in the rock. These unusual mortar holes, together with several hundred petroglyphs, can be toured along a self-guided trail. You'll also pass facsimile displays of bark houses, granaries, and a Miwok playing field. An on-site museum covers Sierra American Indian tribes. Nearby is an authentic roundhouse, still used by local Miwok. Admission. ~ Pine Grove–Volcano Road; 209-296-7488, fax 209-296-7528.

North from Sutter Creek, Route 49 bisects **Amador City**. The focus of a quartz mining operation, this pretty community still

sights

AUTHOR FAVORITE

Despite the tourist trappings, I still enjoy a visit to **Moaning Cavern** and **Mercer Caverns**. These extraordinary limestone formations descend hundreds of feet underground; guided tours lead into these subterranean cathedrals where rock formations are twisted into bizarre figures. Entering them is like descending into an ice palace filled with sparkling creations. Above ground, you can mine for gemstones in a flume system or walk the interpretive nature trail. Admission at both. ~ Moaning Cavern: 209-736-2708, 866-762-2837, fax 209-736-0330; www.caverntours.com, e-mail caverns@caverntours.com. Mercer Caverns: phone/fax 209-728-2101; www.mercercaverns.com. If you prefer a fullbore spelunking tour at Moaning Cavern or in another nearby cavern, you can schedule that as well.

contains many of its original brick and woodframe buildings. It was the creek, not the miners, that was dry in neighboring **Drytown**. Matter of fact, the place contained about 25 saloons during its golden youth.

From Plymouth, just north of Drytown, take a side trip up Shenandoah Road (County Road E16) to the **Shenandoah Valley wine-growing region**. Vineyards have prospered here since Gold Rush days and at present almost two dozen wineries dot the area. Many are clustered along a ten-mile stretch of Shenandoah Road.

◄ HIDDEN

Foremost is **Sobon Estate**, which dates from 1856. Enjoy the tasting room or take a self-guided tour through the original cellar. This rock-walled enclosure still contains the old handmade oak casks and hewn wooden beams. Specializing in zinfandel, Sobon also produces French syrah and viognier. While this winery is open daily, others have limited schedules and often require reservations. ~ 14430 Shenandoah Road, Plymouth; 209-245-6554, fax 209-245-5156; www.sobonwine.com, e-mail info@sobonwine.com.

It's wise to pick up a free winetasting brochure from the **El Dorado County Chamber of Commerce**. Closed Saturday and Sunday. ~ 542 Main Street, Placerville; 530-621-5885, fax 530-642-1624; www.visit-eldorado.com, e-mail chamber@eldoradocounty.org.

If visiting between September and December during the apple harvest, ask at the Chamber of Commerce for information about **Apple Hill**. Located on a mountain ridge east of Placerville, this area is crowded with orchards where for a modest fee you can pick your own apples. Many of the orchards lie just off Route 50 on Carson Road.

◄ HIDDEN

Placerville, one of the largest towns in the Mother Lode, has been heavily developed and lacks the charm of neighboring villages. There are a few historic places remaining, however, such as the **Gold Bug Mine**, where you can step between the timbers and explore a narrow stone tunnel that leads deep into the earth. One of the few mines open to the public, Gold Bug also features a weatherbeaten stamp press mill used to grind gold from bedrock. ~ Gold Bug Lane, off Bedford Avenue, one mile from downtown Placerville.

Placerville also served as a supply center for other mining towns, including several that can be visited via a **side trip** along Route 193. Just north of town you can pick up this mountain road and follow it in a 28-mile semicircle, rejoining Route 49 a few miles south of Auburn. In the course of its arc, the road curls along the sides of the mountains as it curves up from the American River Valley. There are open views of pine-fringed peaks and dark green canyons. Among the old mining communities are **Chili Bar**, perched astride the American River, **Georgetown** with its antique buildings lining a boulevard-wide Main Street, and the one-street town of **Greenwood**.

This country detour is recommended only if you plan to cover the Placerville to Auburn span along Route 49 as well. Otherwise you'll miss **Marshall Gold Discovery State Historic Park**. Like Columbia, this park features the remains of the Gold Rush town of Coloma. It also happens to be the place where it all began. Here on January 24, 1848, James Marshall found shining metal in a sawmill owned by John Sutter. "Boys," Marshall exclaimed, "I believe I have found a gold mine." The history of California and the West was changed forever. Within the park, a self-guiding trail leads past a reconstruction of Sutter's mill and to the discovery site on the banks of the American River. With the skeletal-looking mill on one hand and a foaming river on the other, it's an eerie sensation standing on the spot that once lured tens of thousands across a continent. Admission. ~ Route 49, Coloma; 530-622-3470, fax 530-622-3472.

There's also a museum with display cases portraying the days of '49 and a miner's cabin complete with long johns and animal pelts hanging from the rafters. In all, this 285-acre park features two dozen points of interest and is second only to Columbia in its ability to evoke California's glittery past.

LODGING
Step back into the days of yore at the **Ione Hotel**, a restored inn dating from the 1850s. Today, 14 guestrooms, each located on the second floor with easy balcony access, are all decorated with antiques. A number of rooms have clawfoot tubs, while all are fully carpeted and air-conditioned. For an added thrill, request the more rustic Room 13. It's supposedly haunted by a ghost named George. ~ 25 West Main Street, Ione; 209-274-6082; www.ione hotel.com, e-mail info@ionehotel.com. MODERATE.

One of the better bargains in all the Gold Country is found at the **National Hotel**. This hulking 25-room hotel claims every California governor since 1862 (until 1960) as a guest, not to mention Presidents Garfield and Hoover. Standard rooms are small, furnished with antiques, and eschew TVs. There's a Western-style saloon downstairs. ~ 2 Water Street, Jackson; 209-223-0500, fax 209-223-4845; e-mail nationalhotel@volcano.net. MODERATE TO DELUXE.

Sutter Creek Inn provides the most commodious lodging in town. Innkeeper Jane Way has been running this 18-room facility since 1966 and doing so with special flair. Among her trademarks are four rooms with swinging beds, a complete country-style breakfast, and a spacious lawn with secret gardens, shade trees and hammocks for lounging guests. Some of the guest rooms are located in the main house, a New England–style home built of redwood in 1859; others are located in the cottages that dot the grounds. Each room is individual in size, decor, and furnishings, but all feature private baths and many have fireplaces and private patios. There's also a library where guests can cozy up with a good book. ~ 75 Main Street, Sutter Creek; 209-267-5606, fax 209-267-9287; www.suttercreekinn.com, e-mail info@suttercreek inn.com. MODERATE TO ULTRA-DELUXE

The **Mine House Inn** represents the region's most intriguing hostelry. It's located in the former office building of the Old Keystone Consolidated Mining Company. Millions of dollars worth of gold was assayed and smelted in this century-old building. As a result, the place is built of brick with walls 13 inches thick. Each of the eight guest rooms was once an individual office, so if you check into the "Vault Room" be prepared to share the space with a ceiling-high iron vault. The "Keystone Room" was fashioned from the dumbwaiter shaft used to transport bullion, and the "Retort Room" features a keystone arch built to support the vault. Three luxury suites occupy the former superintendent's quarters, and feature canopy beds, jacuzzis, and fireplaces. There's also a separate building, the "Victorian House," that contains two other luxurious suites, one of which boasts an original Louis XV bedroom set. An inn since 1957, the Mine House is creatively furnished with period pieces and has a swimming pool and spa on the premises. A full breakfast is served. ~ 14125 Route 49, Amador City; 209-267-5900, 800-646-3473; www.minehouseinn.com, e-mail minehse@cdepot.net. MODERATE TO ULTRA-DELUXE.

 ◄ HIDDEN

A gay resort located along the Cosumnes River, **Rancho Cicada Retreat** offers rustic accommodations in two comfortably furnished cabins (year-round) and 24 cabins/tents set on platforms

AUTHOR FAVORITE

I get a kick out of spending the night in the same room where Mark Twain once slept at **Murphys Historic Hotel**. I wonder if I'd feel richer or just less funny if I stayed in William Randolph Hearst's room there, but so far I haven't tried. The place dates to 1856 and also numbers among its previous guests Ulysses S. Grant and Black Bart. The nine rooms are still maintained much as they were back when, with oak wardrobes, antique dressers, and patterned wallpaper. Each room has the name of a famous guest painted on the door. All the rooms share baths. For a historic splurge, book the presidential suite, containing the same bed on which Grant slept. (There's also an adjoining motel, but staying there contradicts the reason for coming to Murphys.) ~ 457 Main Street, Murphys; 209-728-3444, 800-532-7684, fax 209-728-1590; www.murphyshotel.com, e-mail mhotel@caltel.com. MODERATE TO ULTRA-DELUXE.

and equipped with mattresses (May through October, weather permitting). Although catering primarily to private groups, the resort also welcomes individuals. The grounds include rock gardens, lawns, hiking trails, a large hot tub, and places for sunbathing, volleyball, croquet, and swimming. Reservations required. ~ P.O. Box 225, Plymouth, CA 95669; 209-245-4841, 877-553-9481, fax 209-245-3357; www.ranchocicadaretreat. com. ULTRA-DELUXE.

When it was built in 1857, the three-story **Historic Cary House Hotel** was reputed to be the finest hotel in the Gold Country. Its name was changed twice, and in 1915 it was demolished and rebuilt using the same bricks. In 1997, after a complete renovation, the original name was restored. The lobby is richly appointed with deep teal carpeting, dark wood trim, and leather couches. The 37 guest accommodations are Victorian in style, decorated in hues of peach and blue. All have private baths and air conditioning, and most have kitchenettes and king- or queen-size beds. ~ 300 Main Street, Placerville; 530-622-4271, 866-245-9439, fax 530-622-0696; www.caryhouse.com, e-mail hchh@caryhouse.com. DELUXE.

DINING

A 19th-century hostelry, **Murphys Historic Hotel** features an informal dining room. Though there are antiques dotted about, the restaurant lacks the charm of the hotel. The Continental menu features a full breakfast, lunch, and an array of dinnertime spreads. ~ 457 Main Street, Murphys; 209-728-3444; www.murphyshotel. com, e-mail mhotel@caltel.com. MODERATE TO DELUXE.

The Upstairs Restaurant and Streetside Bistro is a small affair decorated with plenty of greenery and attractive prints on the walls. It's popular among residents and visitors alike. The menu features California-cuisine dishes such as New Zealand lamb in a zinfandel and gorgonzola sauce and grilled salmon with a citrus-dill sauce. Midday offerings include a variety of gourmet sandwiches and salads. Closed Monday and Tuesday. ~ 164 Main Street, Jackson; 209-223-3342. MODERATE TO ULTRA-DELUXE.

A restored 19th-century bar stands as the centerpiece of the **Golden Star Saloon.** Fashioned into a Chicago-style pub, this restaurant features chandeliers, shiny wooden floors, and the feel of the Old West. Dine on pasta, steaks, or other hearty cowboy fare. Local wines complement any meal. Breakfast and lunch served daily; dinner served Thursday through Sunday. ~ 25 West Main Street, Ione Hotel, Ione; 209-274-6982; www.ionehotel. com, e-mail info@ionehotel.com. MODERATE.

Zachary Jacque, a provincial French restaurant, is trimly appointed with paintings and decorative china plates. Wood paneling and a cozy fireplace add to its warm appeal. Though the menu is seasonal, you can always choose from staples like rack of lamb, duck with ginger and lavender, and fresh fish. Closed Monday and Tuesday. ~ 1821 Pleasant Valley Road, Placerville; 530-626-8045. DELUXE TO ULTRA-DELUXE.

There are several arts-and-crafts shops in Angels Camp, Murphys, Jackson, and Volcano. Then, proceeding north, you'll encounter a pair of towns with antique buildings that have been remodeled into charming shops. Foremost is **Sutter Creek**. Along the 19th-century Main Street are shops like **Old Hotel Antiques**. It boasts Depression glass, old Coca-Cola advertisements, and antique jewelry. ~ 68 Main Street, Sutter Creek; 209-267-5901. **SHOPPING**

Within a couple of blocks are no fewer than a dozen antique shops. Of course in this historic town, the stores as well as their contents are antiques: even the local plumbing company is situated in an 1869 building.

Amador City has been renovated in like fashion. Route 49 barrels through the center of this aged town, past handicrafts shops, art galleries, and those places that seem more plentiful than restaurants—antique stores.

Placerville serves as a regional shopping area for the Central Gold Country, with stores of all sizes.

There are nondescript bars in Angels Camp, San Andreas, and Mokelumne Hill. Up at the old **Murphys Historic Hotel** there's an old-time miners' saloon. The crowd here is drawn not only by the nightlife, but also because of the fame of this hostelry. There's occasional live music. ~ 457 Main Street, Murphys; 209-728-3444, 800-532-7684; www.murphyshotel.com, e-mail mhotel@caltel.com. **NIGHTLIFE**

There's a Western-style saloon in the historic old **National Hotel**. The place is complete with bright red wallpaper, gilded mirrors, and glittery chandeliers. On weekends karaoke and live bands are offered. ~ 2 Water Street, Jackson; 209-223-0500; e-mail nationalhotel@volcano.net.

PJ's Roadhouse, just outside Placerville, hosts bands every Friday and Saturday night. Other evenings you can play shuffleboard, shoot pool, or watch sports on big-screen televisions. ~

GEARING UP

For unique Gold Country mementos, check out the **Two Feathers Trading Post**, where you'll find buckskinning and craft supplies, trade goods, gold-panning kits, and gold samples found near the Sutter's Mill discovery site on the American River. Limited winter hours, call ahead. ~ 381 Route 49, Coloma; 530-621-0793.

5641 Mother Lode Drive, Placerville; 530-626-0336, fax 530-626-5463.

The **Coloma Club,** just north of historic Coloma, features rock-and-roll or country bands every weekend. It's a down-home bar complete with pool table and dancefloor as well as karaoke nights. ~ 7171 Route 49, Coloma; 530-626-6390, fax 530-333-4118; www.colomaclub.com.

High culture is also part of the Gold Country tradition. If visiting during a weekend in summer, you might take in a show by one of the region's many repertory groups. Several feature traditional drama, though most present light melodramas.

Out in Volcano, the **Volcano Theatre Company** headlines at the Cobblestone Theatre. ~ Volcano; 209-223-4663. The **Coloma Crescent Players** are featured at the Coloma Theatre. ~ Coloma; 530-626-5282.

PARKS

CALAVERAS BIG TREES STATE PARK 🚶 🚴 🛶 Straddling the north fork of the Stanislaus River, this magnificent park covers almost 6300 acres of mountainous terrain. Its 18 miles of hiking trails lead along deep canyons and riverside beaches. The chief attractions, however, are the two groves of giant sequoias. Of particular interest is the South Grove, explored along a five-mile trail, which still possesses a sense of the primeval. Facilities in the park include an information center, museum, picnic areas, and restrooms. Day-use fee, $6. ~ Route 4, about 25 miles east of Angels Camp; 209-795-2334; e-mail cbt@goldrush.com.

▲ There are 74 sites at Northgrove Campground and 55 sites at Oak Hollow Campground; both campgrounds have showers; $15 to $19 per night.

> The meadows at Indian Grinding Rock State Historic Park are brilliant with wildflowers in spring.

INDIAN GRINDING ROCK STATE HISTORIC PARK 🚶 Set at about 2400-feet elevation, this facility features interesting American Indian displays in the Regional Indian Museum. There are bedrock mortars, petroglyphs, and a reconstructed Miwok village complete with dwellings. The forest is filled with manzanita and ponderosa pine, as well as black oak trees from which the Miwok gathered acorns. Facilities include picnic areas, restrooms, and showers. Day-use fee, $3. ~ About 12 miles east of Jackson; from Route 49 in Jackson take Route 88 east to Pine Grove, then follow Pine Grove–Volcano Road to the park. Or from Volcano take Pine Grove–Volcano Road one mile to the park; 209-296-7488, fax 209-296-7528.

▲ There are 23 sites; $12 per night.

MARSHALL GOLD DISCOVERY STATE HISTORIC PARK 🚶 🚴 🏊 🛶 This re-created Gold Rush town was the site of the original strike. The primary interest is historic and the park is fully described in the "Central Gold County" section above. Canoeing and kayaking are at North Beach only. Facilities include an information center and museum, historical buildings and displays, picnic areas, and restrooms. Day-use fee, $4. ~ Located along Route 49 in Coloma; 530-622-3470; www.isgnet.com/coloma, e-mail coloma@jps.net.

▲ Camping is not permitted within the park, but there are campgrounds located nearby. The closest is **Coloma Resort**, with close to 100 campsites; $34 per night (showers and general store are available). ~ Route 49, Coloma; 530-621-2267, fax 530-621-4960.

Adjacent to the park is **American River Resort**, with riverside sites for $15 to $25 per night (showers, restaurant, grocery, and swimming pool on the premises). ~ Route 49, Coloma; 530-622-6700.

Camp Lotus, a few miles from Coloma, also has riverbank camping and is very popular with river rafters (fees are $7 per person during the week or $9 on Friday and Saturday; $18 minimum per party during the week and $25 minimum on weekends). There's a deli here with sandwiches and espresso drinks, and a store selling camping and rafting supplies. Closed November through February. ~ Bassi Road, Lotus; 530-622-8672, fax 530-622-0103; www.coloma.com/camplotus.

This forested region features colorful pinnacles, covered bridges, mining museums, and some of the state's more notable Victorians. The fastest growing part of the Gold Country, it also offers cross-country skiing, inviting river swimming holes, ghost towns, and 19th-century hotels that are a journey back in time. Extending from Auburn to Sierra City, the northern section of the Mother Lode is traversed by the historic transcontinental railroad.

Northern Gold Country

SIGHTS

Auburn, like Placerville, has grown too large to enjoy the rural charm of other Mother Lode communities. The only section of note is "Old Town," built near the American River in the 19th century. There's an interesting walking tour through this brick-and-woodframe neighborhood, which you should take after obtaining an Old Town map from the **Auburn Area Chamber of Commerce**. Closed weekends. ~ 601 Lincoln Way, Auburn; 530-885-5616, fax 530-885-5854; www.auburnchamber.net, e-mail info@auburnarea.com. Among the sights are a trim three-story firehouse capped with a bell tower, an old town antique shopping center, and a maze of falsefront streets.

The mines to the north along Route 49 were a far cry from the simple mining claims that started the Gold Rush. Prominent

during the latter half of the 19th century, these big buck operations were heavily industrialized. **Grass Valley**, for instance, has
367 miles of tunnels running beneath its streets. The town's **North
Star Mining and Pelton Waterwheel Museum** displays the sophisticated machinery that replaced the gold pan and rocker.
Closed October to mid-May. ~ End of Mill Street on Allison Ranch
Road, Grass Valley; 530-273-4255.

At nearby **Empire Mine State Historic Park** you can view the
engineering office and machine shops of the richest hardrock gold
mine in California. Walk about 50 feet into the black entranceway of a shaft that leads nearly a mile down and wander through
the many buildings comprising this multimillion dollar venture.
With its eroded hillsides, the surrounding area presents a graphic
illustration of how mining destroyed the landscape. It's ironic that
the rich mine owners, whose opulent homes you can view here,
chose to build their estates in neighborhoods they were turning
to rubble heaps. Admission. ~ 10791 East Empire Street, Grass
Valley; 530-273-8522, fax 530-273-0602; www.cal-parks.ca.gov.

Despite the scars, Grass Valley still reveals several pretty sections. Along Mill and Main streets, the gas lamps, awnings, balconies, and brick facades remain from the gold era. A replica of
the Lola Montez House contains the **Nevada County Chamber
of Commerce**, where you can obtain brochures and walking maps.
Together with Lotta Crabtree, Lola represents Grass Valley's
early days of glory. After rising in Europe as a dancer and the
mistress of King Ludwig of Bavaria, Lola settled in Grass Valley
in 1852. Her seven-year-old protégée, Lotta Crabtree, eventually
became a nationally renowned theatrical entertainer. Closed Sunday. ~ 248 Mill Street, Grass Valley; 530-273-4667, fax 530-
272-5440; www.grassvalleychamber.com, e-mail info@grassvalley
chamber.com.

Nevada City was once the third largest city in California. Still
grand by local standards, it nevertheless has a country village
charm. There are gaslights, turreted houses, and balconied stores
along Broad Street. Much of the Victorian elegance remains amid
the widow's walks, church steeples, and gingerbread facades, and
the downtown is listed on the National Register of Historic Places.
A walking map of the town, available from the **Nevada City
Chamber of Commerce**, will guide you through the historic heart
of town. Closed Sunday. ~ 132 Main Street, Nevada City; 530-
265-2692, fax 530-265-3892; www.nevadacitychamber.com, e-
mail info@nevadacitychamber.com.

For an adventurous side trip from town, head to **Malakoff
Diggins State Historic Park**. While it is a fully developed park,
this area is so remote it represents a good example of "hidden
California." You reach it from Nevada City on North Bloomfield–Graniteville Road, a 17-mile journey that will carry you

over the Yuba River, where the scenery is startling and the seclusion splendid.

The park includes the rustic town of North Bloomfield, built during the 1850s as one of the nation's largest hydraulic gold-mining centers. There's a livery stable filled with wagons, plus a whitewashed church, a saloon, an 1890s furnished home, and an old general store, all neatly preserved. The immediate area has been heavily eroded by hydraulic mining, which involves washing away hillsides with hoses, then sifting gold from the mud. Bald

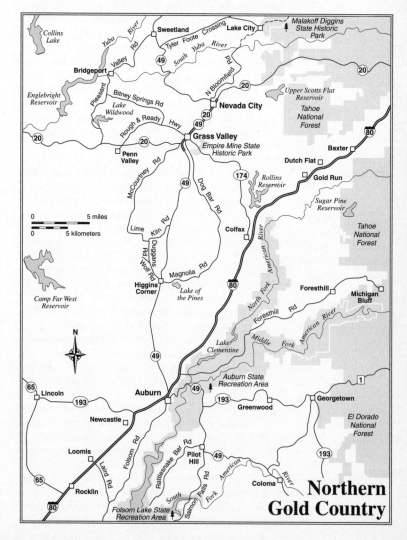

Northern Gold Country

cliffs and a miniature lake remain as evidence of these destructive techniques. But the rest of the region is wild and untouched, wide open for exploration. Tours are available daily during the summer and on weekends in winter. Admission. ~ North Bloomfield–Graniteville Road; phone/fax 530-265-2740.

To delve deeper into the mountains, continue north from Nevada City on Route 49. Towns are few and far in this region of tall pines and deep river valleys. About 13 miles from town you can take a 14-mile (roundtrip) detour along Pleasant Valley Road **HIDDEN ►** to the **Bridgeport covered bridge**. Stretching 230 feet, it is reputedly the West's longest single-span covered bridge.

Route 49 follows a serpentine course along the Yuba River as it climbs to **Downieville**, an enchanting town cradled in a canyon. The crooked streets and tin-roof houses of this 1849 settlement are completely encircled by mountains. The town gallows and many picturesque buildings still stand in this natural amphitheater.

Higher still is **Sierra City**, built in the shadow of the Sierra Buttes. The highway streams past fruit orchards and alpine meadows en route to this avalanche-plagued town, then climbs 6700-foot Yuba Pass and heads for the High Sierra.

LODGING The **Travelodge** is a 1970s time warp with 77 units spread across three buildings. Rooms offer king- and queen-sized beds, vanities, and small tables convenient for workaholics and families that

Be sure to see Nevada City's art-deco Courthouse (on Church Street) and City Hall. They're welcome anomalies amid the Gold Country's masonry-and-iron-door architecture. ~ 317 Broad Street, Nevada City.

like to dine in. There's a seasonal swimming pool and whirlpool on the premises. ~ 13490 Lincoln Way, Auburn; 530-885-7025, 877-885-7025, fax 530-885-9503; www.auburntravellodge.com. MODERATE.

Anchoring the center of Nevada City, the **National Hotel** claims to be the oldest continuously operating hotel west of the Rockies. With its bar, dining room, and Victorian decor, the place has served travelers since the 1850s. Accommodations vary from rooms that are plain but comfortable to suites that feature love-seats, canopy beds, and 19th-century frills. ~ 211 Broad Street, Nevada City; 530-265-4551, fax 530-265-2445. MODERATE TO DELUXE.

HIDDEN ► For a true living-history experience, delve into the secret treasures of **The Parsonage Bed & Breakfast**. Each of the six guest bedrooms honors a Dane family pioneer who settled in the Gold Country in the 1850s. The house is decorated with authentic period pieces and attention to detail is a way of life. You'll sleep on line-dried and hand-pressed linens. The full breakfast includes fresh baked muffins and croissants, and homemade jams and fresh fruit, all served on Haviland china. Closed first two weeks of January. ~ 427 Broad Street, Nevada City; 530-265-9478, 877-265-9499,

fax 530-265-8147; www.gv.net/~histinns.pars. MODERATE TO
DELUXE.

Several good restaurants cluster around the "Old Town" section   **DINING**
of Auburn. Among them is **Shanghai Bar & Restaurant**, a Chinese eatery that has been around since 1896, making it the oldest
family-owned bar and restaurant in the state. This high-ceilinged
establishment features a standard array of Cantonese dishes, patio
dining, and live music Thursday through Sunday. *Phenomenon*,
with John Travolta and Robert Duvall, was filmed here. Closed
Tuesday. ~ 289 Washington Street, Auburn; phone/fax 530-885-
1705; www.auburnshanghai.com. MODERATE.

At **Friar Tuck's** you can dine in a cozy back room, in a live-
lier dining area next to the bar, or in the Pine Street Room overlooking the historic district. With its brick walls, exposed beams,
and heavy posts, the restaurant is reminiscent of an old gold mine.
But potted plants, private booths, and a guitarist performing
through dinner add warmth to one of the region's most popular
restaurants. Fondue is the specialty here, with steak, chicken, meatball, shrimp, and cheese fondue available; and you can also order
teriyaki steak or fresh fish. Dinner only. ~ 111 North Pine Street,
Nevada City; 530-265-9093; www.friartucks.com, e-mail friars
@oro.net. DELUXE TO ULTRA-DELUXE.

The Country Rose Cafe is the latest incarnation of an 1861
brick building originally built as a grocery store. Huge trees shade
the patio; inside, flowered table cloths adorn the tables, while
copper pots and pans and bouquets of dried flowers decorate the
walls. Seafood is the specialty here: salmon with spinach and brie
and halibut with almond crust number among the favorites. Steak,
pasta, and lamb are also served. The blackboard menu changes
weekly. Lunches tend toward soups, sandwiches, and an array of
specials. Closed Monday. ~ 300 Commercial Street, Nevada City;
530-265-6248. MODERATE TO ULTRA-DELUXE.

Auburn contains expansive shopping sections and serves as a re-   **SHOPPING**
gional center for folks throughout the central Mother Lode.
Window browsing Auburn's "Old Town" section is tantamount
to a historic adventure. Most of the 19th-century buildings have
been converted to shops. The Empire Livery Stable is now a
minimall, the old Hop Sing Laundry and Chinese Joss Houses are
antique stores. Located along Sacramento, Washington, and Commercial streets are other new shops in old clothing.

Grass Valley and **Nevada City** are the chief shopping destinations in the northern Mother Lode area. The better of the two
is Nevada City, where early stores have received a face-lift. And
if you're looking for books about Gold Country history, you've
definitely come to the right place. Independent bookstores seem

to thrive here. Within a few blocks of the historic district, you'll find **Harmony Books** (231 Broad Street, Nevada City; 530-265-9564), **Brigadoon Books** (108 North Pine, Nevada City; 530-265-3450), and **Broad Street Books & Espresso Café** (426 Broad Street, Nevada City; 530-265-4204). You'll also find a jewelry shop beside the family barber, a T-shirt store near an old saloon, and an oriental rug shop next door to a historic hotel. The best places to browse are along Broad, Commercial, and North Pine streets. Happy hunting!

NIGHTLIFE Nevada City has two varied nightspots within a few doors of one another. **McGee's** is a posh brick-walled drinking emporium with overhead fans and stained-glass decoration that's good for a quiet cocktail. There's live music on weekends. Cover. ~ 315 Broad Street, Nevada City; 530-265-3205; www.mcgheesannex.com. **Cirino's** is neither so formal nor as neatly decorated. ~ 309 Broad Street, Nevada City; 530-265-2246, fax 530-265-1954.

PARKS **AUBURN STATE RECREATION AREA** This sprawling facility covers over 30,000 acres and includes Lake Clementine, a small reservoir. Long and narrow in its configuration, the park follows the American River basin for about 30 miles. There are opportunities to hike, swim, and fish in this former placer mining region. No facilities. ~ The ranger station is located along Route 49 about one mile south of Auburn; 530-885-4527; e-mail asra@cyber.com.

▲ Permitted in 50 primitive sites; $15 to $24 per night.

FOLSOM LAKE STATE RECREATION AREA One of California's most popular parks, this mammoth facility completely encircles Folsom Lake's 75-mile shoreline. Visitors come to boat, waterski, ride horseback, picnic, swim, and camp. Anglers try for trout, bass, perch, and sturgeon. There are also 65 miles of hiking trails around the lake. Quite

THE KING'S LADY

Grass Valley's most famous resident was Lola Montez, a dancer notorious for her love affairs with European notables such as Alexander Dumas, Czar Nicolas I of Russia, and "Mad" King Ludwig of Bavaria. After a performance tour of Gold Country opera houses, Montez retired to a house in Grass Valley, but scandal pursued her. Though prostitutes worked the streets of this mining town openly, the aging mistress of a foreign king aroused moral indignation. Montez was ultimately forced to flee California after horsewhipping a local newspaper editor who had attacked her in print.

crowded in summer, the park is best visited during the week. Facilities include a water education center at Folsom Dam, an information center, marinas, picnic areas, restrooms, and showers. Day-use fee, $5. ~ Located along Folsom–Auburn Road between Auburn and Folsom; 916-988-0205; e-mail folsom@sna.com.

▲ There are 150 sites in two campgrounds; $15 per night.

MALAKOFF DIGGINS STATE HISTORIC PARK 🏃 🚲 🛶 🎣
🚣 Remote and beautiful, this 3000-acre facility includes a well preserved Gold Rush town. The park rests near the Yuba River, where anglers catch rainbow and brook trout; there are also black bass and bluegill in nearby Blair Reservoir. The park's slopes, climbing from 2200 to 4200 feet, are open to hikers. Swimming is good in the reservoir. The park has an information center and museum, picnic areas, and restrooms. Day-use fee, $4. ~ From Nevada City, take Highway 49 north for 11 miles and make a right onto Tyler Foote Crossing Road. Follow the paved road 17 miles to Derbec Road, which leads to the park. 530-265-2740.

▲ Permitted in 30 sites, $10 per night; four primitive sites, $10 per night. There are also three rustic cabins for rent; $18 per night.

PLUMAS-EUREKA STATE PARK 🏃 🚲 🎿 🏊 🛶 🚣 Set deep
in the Sierra, this 4500-acre spread contains waterfalls, creeks, and two small lakes. The park rises from 4600 feet to 7447-foot Eureka Peak and is home to the pileated woodpecker, the largest woodpecker in North America, and the caliope hummingbird, the smallest of its kind on the continent. The park is also home to golden eagles, great blue herons, deer, and beaver. This area is also a pioneer ski region, which hosts winter sports events. Displays in the museum (admission) focus on the hard-rock mining of the area. During the summer, gold panning is offered. Get some basic instructions and tips, then try your hand at the sport. Call ahead to sign up. Other facilities include an information center, picnic areas, restrooms, and showers. ~ From Route 49 north of Sierra City take Gold Lake Road to Graegle, then go five miles west on County Road A14, which begins near the intersections of Routes 89 and 70; 530-836-2380.

▲ There are 67 sites (including 14 walk-in) from approximately May 15 to October 15; $15 per night; first-come, first-served.

Lake Tahoe Area

There aren't many places in America where you can waterski from one state to another. Nor can I think of many spots perfect for wilderness hiking during the day and shooting craps at night. And how many lakes can you name that are so clear you can see objects 75 feet below the surface? One of the West's most unique areas, the Lake Tahoe region is a remarkable blend of nature and kitsch.

In addition to its raw beauty and Nevada gambling, Lake Tahoe is also very popular simply because it is so easily accessible. From Route 49 in the Gold Country, numerous highways lead east into the Sierra and on toward Tahoe. The main road from San Francisco is Route 80, a fast, efficient freeway that bisects Sacramento and traverses the Sierra about 12 miles north of Lake Tahoe.

SIGHTS

It was not always so simple. During the terrible winter of 1846–47, a party of stalwart pioneers, unable to cross the Sierra because of drifting snow, camped for the winter. Many perished from exposure and hunger, others went insane, and some resorted to cannibalism. Today the **Emigrant Trail Museum** at **Donner Memorial State Park** commemorates their passing. There is also a monument on the grounds. Its base stands 22 feet high—the depth of the snow that winter. Today Route 80, the transcontinental interstate, passes within yards of the Donner Party's tragic resting place. Admission. ~ Donner Pass Road, Truckee; 530-582-7892, fax 530-582-7893.

For a more hospitable sense of the Old West, truck on over to **Truckee**, two miles east on Route 80. This 19th-century town sits astride a mountain pass high in the Sierra. Framed by forested slopes, Truckee is a woodframe town overlooking an old railroad yard and depot. The main street, Commercial Row, is lined with falsefront buildings. Clapboard warehouses and meeting halls with second-story balconies remain from the town's old lumbering and railroad days. Then as now, Truckee was a gateway. Today it leads to the gambling palaces and ski resorts of Tahoe.

To tour one of the most famous of the ski resorts, head south from Truckee toward Lake Tahoe on Route 89, and follow the signs to **Squaw Valley**. The 1960 Winter Olympics put this vale on the map, and ski bums have been making the pilgrimage ever since. Ringed by 8200-foot-high mountains, and sprinkled with lodges and condos, it's a favored jet-set landing ground.

As soon as the highway from Squaw Valley rises to meet **Lake Tahoe**, it becomes evident why the region's rivers run fast and pure. This lake, situated 6225 feet above sea level, contains water so clear that objects 75 feet below the surface are visible. With depths reaching an incredible 1645 feet, it is the biggest alpine lake of such purity in all North America. Tahoe is 22 miles long and measures 72 miles around. The entire lake is framed by 10,000-foot mountain peaks, a translucent gem set in a granite ring.

Unlike nearby lakes of glacial origin, Tahoe was formed by faulting. About 150 million years ago the basin was created when the Carson Range rose to the east while the Sierra Nevada grew to the west, leaving a giant trough between. When volcanoes dammed the end of the basin, rain and snow filled the natural bowl to brimming. Washoe Indians eventually inhabited the lakeshore regions, and enjoyed uninterrupted predominance until 1844 when Captain John Fremont and Kit Carson, searching a mountain pass into California, "discovered" the lake. By the 1870s, with the advent of the railroad, Tahoe emerged as a popular resort area.

Today the tourist scene along this alpine jewel centers around the "North Shore" and the "South Shore." The former includes a series of small towns, each featuring resort facilities, restaurants, and various attractions. The latter highlights South Lake Tahoe, the region's most populous town.

On either shore, crossing the border between California and Nevada is like passing from one country to another. The reason is simple—gambling. It's legal in Nevada, but not in California. Within a few steps of the border rise the casinos of Incline Village and Stateline, with their brilliant lights and promise of quick and easy wealth.

Mark Twain visited the lake over a century ago, long before the gaming palaces, and was overwhelmed. "As it lay there with the

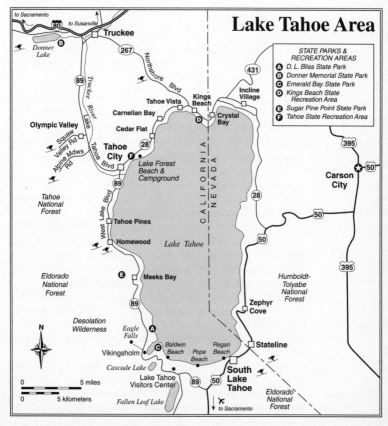

Lake Tahoe Area

to Sacramento
80
to Susanville
to Susanville
Truckee
Donner Lake
B
267
Northshore Blvd
89
Truckee River
431
Incline Village
Tahoe Vista
Kings Beach
Carnelian Bay
D
Crystal Bay
Olympic Valley
Cedar Flat
Squaw Valley Rd
Alpine Mdws Rd
Tahoe City
F
28
Tahoe Blvd
395
Lake Forest Beach & Campground
89
CALIFORNIA
NEVADA
Carson City
50
Tahoe National Forest
West Lake Blvd
28
Tahoe Pines
50
Homewood
Lake Tahoe
50
Eldorado National Forest
E
Meeks Bay
Humboldt-Toiyabe National Forest
89
395
Zephyr Cove
Desolation Wilderness
Eagle Falls
A
N
Baldwin Beach
Regan Beach
Stateline
Vikingsholm
C
Pope Beach
0   5 miles
Cascade Lake
Lake Tahoe Visitors Center
89
50
South Lake Tahoe
0   5 kilometers
Fallen Leaf Lake
to Sacramento
Eldorado National Forest

STATE PARKS & RECREATION AREAS
Ⓐ D. L. Bliss State Park
Ⓑ Donner Memorial State Park
Ⓒ Emerald Bay State Park
Ⓓ Kings Beach State Recreation Area
Ⓔ Sugar Pine Point State Park
Ⓕ Tahoe State Recreation Area

Around Lake Tahoe

To see Lake Tahoe fully, you should circle the entire lake, a loop of about 70 miles. The loop cuts through dense conifer forests, then passes dramatic outcroppings of granite. Intermittently the highway opens onto broad lake vistas, swept by westerly winds and adorned with the sails of careening sloops. Along the way are private residences worthy of a prince, magnificent stone edifices with lawns rolling down to the lip of the lake, leaded-glass mansions that appear drawn from *The Great Gatsby*.

VIKINGSHOLM   Starting from Tahoe City, head south along Route 89, past **Homewood Mountain Resort** (page 504). As you approach the south end of the lake, you'll come to the best known of all the great Lake Tahoe estates, Vikingsholm, a 38-room castle. Open for tours in the summer, this unusual structure was designed along the lines of a 9th-century Norse fortress. It's built of granite and hand-hewn timbers and marked by a series of towers. Admission. ~ 530-525-7277. Anchored offshore, near Vikingsholm, is tiny **Fanette Island**, where a stone teahouse built to similar specifications still sits.

EMERALD BAY   As if all this extraordinary stonework were not enough, the Vikingsholm castle rests beside two-mile-long Emerald Bay. From the vista point located along Route 89, this spectacular cove, guarded by lofty conifers, presents the most picturesque site along the entire lake. At the

shadows of the mountains brilliantly photographed upon its still surface," he remarked in *Roughing It*, "I thought it must surely be the fairest picture the whole earth affords."

Tahoe. The word still carries power. But in recent decades it has become a riddle, an oxymoron. To some it conjures images of dark casinos and fateful gaming tables. To others it evokes thoughts of pristine trackless wilderness and oceanic depths. Never the twain shall meet: Tahoe is an environmental battleground. Developers, wedded to tomorrow's dollar, struggle against environmentalists committed to yesterday's beauty. Every fight the conservationists lose results in more structures along the lake, greater erosion, and another cloud across that glassy water. The resource they seek to protect is a magical place.

For a driving tour of Lake Tahoe, see the Scenic Drive above.

LODGING   In a chic and flashy area like Lake Tahoe, where everything was constructed tomorrow, it's a pleasure to discover a place such as far end, poised between two peninsulas, is a slender opening into the lake; at the near edge, cascading along granite steps, is **Eagle Falls**. A short path leads from the vista point to a wooden footbridge below the falls, or you can hike one mile down from the vista point to Vikingsholm.

TALLAC HISTORIC SITE ESTATES   Continuing around the south end of the lake, you'll pass the **Lake Tahoe Visitors Center** (775-588-4591, fax 775-588-4598) and the turnoffs to two of the best beaches on the lake—**Baldwin Beach** and **Pope Beach** (page 483). Along the western outskirts of South Lake Tahoe, between the two beaches, are the Tallac Historic Site Estates, representing more of Tahoe's fabulous old mansions. Here you can stroll through the woods on a path strewn with pine needles. You'll pass a cluster of old brown-shingle buildings, a log cabin, and the fabled estates. These include the Pope House, built in 1884; Valhalla, a brown-shingle beauty; and the McGonagle estate, a prestigious house designed ironically in the fashion of a log cabin. Closed in winter. The Estate Trail lies between the Lake Tahoe Visitors Center and Camp Richardson Resort.

SOUTH LAKE TAHOE   Turning east onto Route 50, continue to the town of South Lake Tahoe, where you'll find **Regan Beach** and **Eldorado Beach**. Soon after, at the gambling village of **Stateline**, you'll cross into the state of Nevada. Continue north along the east side of the lake. Soon after passing through the village of Glenbrook, turn north (left) onto Route 28, which passes pretty **Spooner Lake**, curves around the lake's northern perimeter, crosses back into California at **Crystal Bay**, and brings you back eventually to the point where you began.

the **Truckee Hotel**. Built in 1873, and nicely renovated, this four-story falsefront building sprawls across an entire block. The guest rooms, with either shared or private bath, possess an Old West charm. They are cluttered with antiques and crowded with character. Even if you don't plan on staying there, the hotel is well worth the visit. ~ Corner of Bridge Street and Commercial Row, Truckee; 530-587-4444, 800-659-6921, fax 530-587-1599; www.thetruckeehotel.com, e-mail thetruckeehotel@sierra.net. MODERATE TO DELUXE.

For lakefront lodgings on the North Shore, try **Sun and Sand Lodge**. This knotty-pine motel has 26 units near the water. There's a sandy beach along one edge of the property and a sunny smile at the front desk. ~ 8308 North Lake Boulevard, Kings Beach; 530-546-2515, 800-547-2515, fax 530-546-0112; www.tahoeguide.com. MODERATE TO DELUXE.

How can anyone go wrong at a place named **Rustic Cottages**?   ◄ HIDDEN
With 18 cottages clustered across the street from the lake, this

charming complex offers a clapboard alternative to the chic lodges hereabouts. The houses are neatly furnished and feature knotty-pine interiors; all are tucked under an awning of pine trees. Some units have kitchens, some have fireplaces, many have both. It's a cute and cozy place. Many of the units are pet-friendly. ~ 7449 North Lake Boulevard, Tahoe Vista; 530-546-3523, 888-778-7842, fax 530-546-0146; www.rusticcottages.com, e-mail rustic@rusticcottages.com. MODERATE TO ULTRA-DELUXE.

Another great lakefront facility is **Beesley's Cottages Resort**, a collection of pine-frame houses fronting a private sand beach. Set in a grove of lodgepole pines, this homey establishment has cottage rooms and individual cottages. The latter are cozy affairs with full kitchen and living room. They are small and rustic but neatly furnished, paneled in that ever-present knotty pine and carpeted wall-to-wall. Closed in winter. ~ 6674 North Lake Boulevard, Tahoe Vista; 530-546-2448. MODERATE TO ULTRA-DELUXE.

You could get lost in the enormous suites at beachfront **Tahoe Vista Inn & Marina**. Five of the six accommodations in this multilevel, wood-shingled inn offer sweeping lake views. They each have bedrooms, as well as a living room, stone fireplace, full kitchen, and private porch. A few of the suites have jacuzzis. Sun pours through windows into rooms lightened even more by soft grays and off-white modern decor. Worth the price. ~ 7220 North Lake Boulevard, Tahoe Vista; 530-546-8222, 800-521-6656, fax 530-546-0667; www.sierravacations.com, e-mail info@sierravacations.com. ULTRA-DELUXE.

Mountain lodge meets high-class resort at the redwood, multi-gabled **Sunnyside Restaurant and Lodge**. Nestled in pine woods and sitting before its own marina, the lodge features a cozy country lobby with river rock fireplace adorned with hunting trophies. Ducks and decoys are everywhere in the 23 lakefront or lakeview accommodations, simply furnished in wicker and wood and featuring individual touches like an old sea chest or armoire. Many have fireplaces and wet bars. ~ 1850 West Lake Boulevard, Tahoe City; 530-583-7200, 800-822-2754, fax 530-583-2551; www.sunnysideresort.com. DELUXE TO ULTRA-DELUXE.

Mayfield House, a six-room bed and breakfast set in a 1930s-era house, is one block from the lake and within walking distance of shopping areas. In addition to cozy guest accommodations there is a living room with stone fireplace. All rooms have private baths. Occasionally closed in May and November; call ahead. ~ 236 Grove Street, Tahoe City; 530-583-1001, 888-518-8898, fax 530-581-4107; www.mayfieldhouse.com, e-mail innkeeper@mayfieldhouse.com. DELUXE TO ULTRA-DELUXE.

The **Resort at Squaw Creek** lures guests with an extravagant 405-room hotel that is showcased by a stream and waterfall which plunge 250 feet through the property. Situated a half-mile from

Squaw Valley's vaunted ski slopes, the resort is a summer destination as well as winter hideaway. For warm-weather enthusiasts
there are two tennis courts, an 18-hole golf course, bike paths,
miles of equestrian and hiking trails in the surrounding mountains,
and an aquatic center with three pools and a water slide, and a full-
service spa. In winter it provides ice skating facilities and easy access to the ski slopes with an on-site property. ~ 400 Squaw
Creek Road, Olympic Valley; 530-583-6300, 800-327-3353, fax
530-581-6632; www.squawcreek.com, e-mail info@squawcreek.
com. ULTRA-DELUXE.

Historic Camp Richardson Resort & Marina, a multifaceted
facility, sits along a pretty beach on the western outskirts of South
Lake Tahoe. In addition to a spacious lodge with traditional guest
rooms, this switch-hitting establishment has cabins for rent as well
as a multitude of campsites. The lodge is a classic mountain retreat.
It offers a cozy lobby with knotty-pine walls, log beams, and a
stone fireplace. The rooms are neatly if unimaginatively decorated.
The cabins are rustic in appearance, but furnished in comfortable
fashion. Woodframe in construction, they are set around the resort's wooded acres not far from the lake, with some located right
on the water's edge. The cabins include complete kitchen facilities. A gazebo with a hot tub is on the grounds, too. In summer
the resort only rents cabins by the week. ~ 1900 Jameson Beach
Road, South Lake Tahoe; 530-541-1801, 800-544-1801, fax 530-
541-1802; www.camprichardson.com, e-mail info@camprichard
son.com. MODERATE TO ULTRA-DELUXE.

Sky Lake Lodge is a 23-unit motel located on the South Shore's
main drag. The guest rooms here are nicely furnished and decorated with flair. Some have been shingled along the interior; all
have phones, carpets, color televisions, and stall showers. Ask for
a room away from the highway. ~ 2644 Lake Tahoe Boulevard,
South Lake Tahoe; 530-544-0770. BUDGET.

Tahoe travelers who just have to be where the action is will
find refined charm amid the chaos along Route 50 at the stone-

BEACH BLANKET MOTEL

Positively the best lodging bargain in hectic South Lake Tahoe is **Sail In
Motel Apartments**. Not only is the place away from the busy section of
town, it's also located right on a beach. The rooms are few, which might
be why the owners have taken such care in furnishing them. The interior
decoration shows imagination. And the exterior? Step outside and you'll
find a knockout view of Lake Tahoe. ~ 861 Lakeview Avenue, South
Lake Tahoe; 530-544-8615, 800-303-8246, fax 530-544-3098; e-mail
sailinmotel@aol.com. MODERATE.

and-shingle **Inn by the Lake**. The 100 accommodations, set back from the highway on landscaped grounds, feature blond woods and lush pastel bedspreads and wallhangings. Many view the lake across the street; suites have full kitchens. There's also a pool, sauna, and bi-level hot tub. ~ 3300 Lake Tahoe Boulevard, South Lake Tahoe; 530-542-0330, 800-877-1466, fax 530-541-6596; www.innbythelake.com, e-mail info@innbythelake.com. MODERATE TO ULTRA-DELUXE.

HIDDEN ►   Another recommended spot is **Hansen's Resort**, on the road to Heavenly Valley ski area. A collection of cabins tucked beneath arching pines, this facility is splendidly situated. It's a short stroll to the center of South Lake Tahoe or to the ski region. For a quiet but convenient retreat, the place is ideal. There's an individual cabin (with bedroom, living room, and kitchen) as well as two single-room motel units. All facilities are pine-paneled, very well-furnished, and immaculately clean. Cool and spiffy. ~ 1360 Ski Run Boulevard, South Lake Tahoe; 530-544-3361, fax 530-541-3824; www.hansensresort.com, e-mail hansens@etahoe.com. MODERATE TO DELUXE.

Holly's Place provides a serene getaway in the pines just two blocks from the lake. Each of its ten cabins are architecturally different. One is a converted barn and another a former greenhouse. They all have natural knotty-pine walls, carpeting, a couch, and a kitchen. There's a hot tub, a library, and free use of bicycles. ~ P.O. Box 13197, South Lake Tahoe, CA 96151; 530-544-7040, 800-745-7041, fax 530-541-6543; www.hollys place.com, e-mail reservations@hollysplace.com. DELUXE TO ULTRA-DELUXE.

Lake Tahoe is named for a Washoe word meaning "lake" or "water in high place."

At the very edge of South Lake Tahoe, near the gambling casinos and Nevada border, are countless motels. These are all within walking distance of the gaming tables and cater mainly to gamblers. Because of competitive rates, they can also be attractive to travelers. The problem is they're often crowded and their rates fluctuate wildly. Count on paying more during the summer and on weekends. Even the rates quoted below constitute little more than an estimate. I'll list two of the area's motels; it's advisable to shop among others nearby for the best deal.

Just two blocks from a private beach, **7 Seas Inn at Tahoe** is a 17-unit establishment with a hot tub. Some rooms have gas fireplaces. ~ 4145 Manzanita Avenue, South Lake Tahoe; 530-544-7031, 800-800-7327, fax 530-544-1208; www.sevenseastahoe.com, e-mail info@sevenseastahoe.com. BUDGET TO MODERATE.

The nearby **Blue Jay Lodge** is a sprawling 65-unit hostelry. ~ 4133 Cedar Avenue, South Lake Tahoe; 530-544-5232, 800-258-3529, fax 530-544-0453; e-mail jc@bluejaylodge.com. BUDGET TO MODERATE.

French-country dining to the max, **Le Petit Pier** greets guests with blue awnings outside and a partially glass-enclosed, candlelit dining room highlighted by white linens, and walls covered with culinary awards. A horde of black-tie waiters serve entrées such as pheasant *souvaroff* and *filet sauté au poivre vert*. Closed Tuesday and the first three weeks in November. ~ 7238 North Lake Boulevard, Tahoe Vista; 530-546-4464, fax 530-546-7508; www. lepetitpier.com. DELUXE TO ULTRA-DELUXE.

The folks at the **Old Post Office Coffee Shop** only serve breakfast and lunch, but they do it with country flair. Popular with local people, the restaurant offers pancakes, waffles, and omelettes from the early hours. By lunchtime, the griddle is blazing with a variety of chicken breast sandwiches and the cook is ladling out homemade soup and chili. ~ 5245 North Lake Boulevard, Carnelian Bay; 530-546-3205. BUDGET.

During the summer, dine on the **River Ranch Restaurant and Lodge**'s sprawling outdoor patio and watch river rafters roll down the Truckee River. When winter rolls around, head indoors and cozy up near a roaring fire. Both casual and formal, River Ranch's menu is as varied as its seating options. Try hamburgers and hotdogs on the deck, or portobello mushroom napoleon and roasted elk loin in the lavish dining room. The food is as enjoyable as the view. ~ 2285 River Road, Tahoe City; 530-583-4264; www.riverranchlodge.com. BUDGET TO DELUXE.

Bacchi's Inn has been owned and operated by the same family for three generations. Famed for its minestrone soup, this Italian eatery serves family-style meals. The dining room, open for dinner only, is decorated with traditional red-checkered tablecloths and lantern candles. ~ 2905 Lake Forest Road, Tahoe City; 530-583-3324, fax 530-583-4924. MODERATE TO ULTRA-DELUXE.

Tahoe House is owned by a Swiss family. Mainly a bakery, gourmet shop, and deli, their delicious sandwiches can be ordered to go, or enjoyed at a comfy little nook in front of the fireplace. Definitely give their fresh bread a try, and don't get me started on their desserts. ~ 625 West Lake Boulevard, Route 89, Tahoe City; 530-583-1377, 877-367-8246, fax 530-583-4909; www.tahoe-house.com, e-mail tahoehouse@ltol.com. BUDGET.

Rosie's Café is one of those laidback eating spots California is famous for harboring. Just across the street from the lake, the place is bizarrely decorated with old sleds, bicycles, skis, and wall mirrors. It's open all day and into the night, featuring imaginative cuisine. At breakfast there are lots and lots of egg specialties. Lunch carries salads, sandwiches, tostadas, and more. Come dinner, the menu expands to include pasta, vegetarian and stir-fry dishes, roast duckling, steak, and seafood. Tasty and popular. ~ 571 North Lake Boulevard, Tahoe City; 530-583-8504; www. rosiescafe.com, e-mail rosiescafe@aol.com. MODERATE TO DELUXE.

With a wraparound glass dining room, the chalet-style **Christy Hill** commands great lake views that complement its modern, minimalist decor. This California-cuisine eating spot is highly regarded by guests and locals. Fresh food in light sauces are Christy Hill's hallmark, with entrées such as Hawaiian *ono* in mango, ginger, and lime sauce. Dinner only. Closed Monday. ~ 115 Grove Street, Tahoe City; 530-583-8551, fax 530-583-6158; www.christy hill.com. DELUXE TO ULTRA-DELUXE.

A lovely little Tahoe cottage houses **Evan's American Gourmet Café**, where the menu ranges from Continental to Asian to American regional. Soft lighting and cream and burgundy tones with gold accents set off an appealing room of only 11 tables. The far-ranging menu might include entrées such as grilled garlic tenderloin of beef with gorgonzola cheese. Killer homemade desserts. Dinner only. ~ 536 Emerald Bay Road, South Lake Tahoe; 530-542-1990; www.evanstahoe.com, e-mail tahoewino@aol.com. MODERATE TO DELUXE.

The European-style **Christiania Inn** is a shingled restaurant with lots of lace and antiques, a large fireplace, and three wine cellars. Dinner choices include rack of lamb, fresh seafood platters, and a variety of Continental dishes that change seasonally. Desserts range from tableside flambées to baked Alaska. There's live jazz and blues on winter weekends. Closed Monday in spring, summer, and fall. ~ 3819 Saddle Road, South Lake Tahoe; 530-544-7337, fax 530-549-5342; www.christianiainn.com, e-mail the chris@sierra.net. MODERATE TO ULTRA-DELUXE.

The Dory's Oar Restaurant is a unique and fashionable establishment. The place sits in a Tudor-style cottage surrounded by green lawns and a white picket fence. Continental cuisine and an eclectic selection of seafood are featured in the downstairs restaurant, while Friday evenings are host to live harp music. This is a choice place for a special occasion. A more casual pub on the second floor serves traditional fare such as fish and chips,

AUTHOR FAVORITE

Living in the Bay Area, I guess I'm spoiled when it comes to great dining experiences. That's why, when visiting Lake Tahoe, dinner at **Wolfdale's** is one of the few I'll settle for. Located on Tahoe's north shore, the eatery touts itself as a "cuisine unique restaurant." It's well known and critically acclaimed. The menu changes frequently but always offers fresh seafood, quality meats, and unusual game. It's well worth a taste test. Dinner only. Closed Tuesday, except in July and August. ~ 640 North Lake Boulevard, Tahoe City; 530-583-5700, fax 530-583-1583; www.wolfdales.com. MODERATE TO DELUXE.

bangers and mash, and shepherd's pie. ~ 1041 Fremont Avenue, South Lake Tahoe; 530-541-6603; www.dorysoar.com, e-mail dorysoar@aol.com. MODERATE TO DELUXE.

Traditional diner fare is at its best when served up at the **Red Hut Cafe**. Only offering breakfast (opening at 6 a.m.!) and lunch, it's a great way to start your day. Choose from egg dishes or pancakes and waffles (even coconut ones), or all-American classics like grilled cheese and hamburgers for lunch. Prepare for some tasty grub in a homey and relaxed joint. ~ 749 Lake Tahoe Boulevard, South Lake Tahoe; 530-541-9024. BUDGET.

Among the cheapest places to eat on the South Shore are the casino hotels just across the border in Stateline, Nevada. All of them feature "gambler's specials" of one sort or another: breakfast for a buck or perhaps a full-course meal in a good restaurant at budget prices.

At the **Horizon Casino Resort**, LeGrande Buffet provides an incredible spread that on a typical night will include Mexican and Chinese selections, including international favorites such as prime rib. A salad and gourmet dessert bar caps off the feast. ~ 50 Route 50, Stateline, Nevada; 775-588-6211, fax 775-588-3110, 800-648-3322; www.horizoncasino.com. MODERATE.

Over at **Harvey's Lake Tahoe**, there's a huge, 12-station seafood buffet. Dinner only. ~ Route 50, Stateline, Nevada; 775-588-2411, 800-427-8397; www.harveys.com, e-mail info@harveys.com. ULTRA-DELUXE.

Harrah's Lake Tahoe Resort has a Forest Buffet up on the 18th floor where you can enjoy an array of dishes as well as a panoramic view. Typical specialties include pizza, a pasta and Asian bar, and baked turkey. The prices are quite affordable and children under the age of four dine for free. The catch, of course, is that you must escape from the casino before gambling away the money you just saved on breakfast, lunch, or dinner. ~ Route 50, Stateline, Nevada; 775-588-6611, fax 775-586-6607; www.harrahstahoe.com. MODERATE.

NIGHTLIFE

For a get-down, stomping good time, the place to head is Truckee. This Old West town, 12 miles north of Lake Tahoe, has as many saloons as any self-respectin' frontier outpost. Lining the false-front main drag are places like **O. B.'s Pub & Restaurant**. ~ 10046 Donner Pass Road, Truckee; 530-587-4164. At **Bar of America** there's live music every Friday and Saturday. Cover on weekends in summer. ~ Donner Pass Road at Bridge Street, Truckee; 530-587-3110.

There are other saloons that wail through the weekend with live music. All of them are hat brim to hat brim with ten-gallon locals. This is a Wild West town that knows how to party.

There are waterfront lounges and other nightspots around Lake Tahoe, particularly along the North Shore and in South Lake Tahoe. The real action, though, lies across the line in Nevada. Here legalized gambling has resulted in miles of neon casinos.

These garish, enticing establishments offer slot machines, roulette wheels, keno, and sports betting as well as gaming tables for poker, twenty-one, and other pastimes. The clubs also have plush lounges featuring top-name entertainers. As a result, the shows are extravaganzas complete with dance troupes and orchestras.

On the North Shore, the scene centers around Incline Village. Down along the South Shore everyone gravitates over to Stateline, Nevada. Here a string of casinos lines a Vegas-like strip. One top club is the **Aspen Lounge**, which offers live music dancing on weekends. ~ Route 50, Stateline, Nevada; 775-588-6211; www. horizoncasino.com. Be sure to check out the scene at **Harvey's Resort Hotel**. ~ Route 50, Stateline, Nevada; 775-588-2411; www.harveys.com. At **Caesar's Tahoe** there are 76 table games and 1060 slot machines. ~ Route 50, Stateline, Nevada; 775-588-3515, 888-829-7630; www.caesars.com. Good luck!

PARKS

DONNER MEMORIAL STATE PARK 🚶 🚴 🏠 ⛵ 🏊 🚣 🚤
Set in a pine-and-fir forest astride three-mile-long Donner Lake, this facility lies north of Lake Tahoe. It was here in the winter of 1846–47 that the ill-starred Donner party, trapped in heavy snow, was confronted with cannibalism or death. Today the accommodations are more commodious. There are campgrounds, a museum, and a resident population of porcupines, beaver, raccoons, and bears (plus perhaps the ghosts of several hungry pioneers). In addition to an information center and museum (open year-round), the park features picnic areas, restrooms, and showers. Closed August to Memorial Day. Day-use fee, $4. ~ Located just off Route 80, two miles west of Truckee; 530-582-7892, fax 530-582-7893.

▲ Permitted during the summer in 150 sites; $15 per night.

TAHOE NATIONAL FOREST 🚶 🚴 🐎 🎿 🏠 ⛵ 🚣 🚤
🚤 Rising from the Gold Country to the Sierra crest, this mammoth forest covers over 800,000 acres. Its scenic beauty and recreation facilities make it very popular year-round. Swimming and horseback riding opportunities are available during warm months, with skiers taking over in winter. Hunters, anglers, and gold panners also frequent the area. Within the forest are picnic areas and restrooms. ~ Located northwest of Lake Tahoe, the region is traversed by Routes 49, 80, and 89. The Tahoe National Forest Headquarters is located at **Route 49 and Coyote Street**, Nevada City; 530-265-4531, fax 530-478-6109; www.fs.fed. us/r5/tahoe.

▲ There are 68 campgrounds throughout the forest; $8 to $36 per night. Located at Sugar Pine Reservoir, Giant Gap Campground has 30 sites; $12 to $24 per night. At Jackson Meadow Reservoir, you'll find Pass Creek Campground, which has 30 sites; $10 to $16 per night. Reservations required: 877-444-6777.

KINGS BEACH STATE RECREATION AREA 🚣 ⛴ 🏖 🚤 ⛵ 🛶 A tiny eight-acre plot, this facility is important because it's one of the few public beaches near Nevada on the North Shore. Anticipate a small sandy beach plus a picnic area, playground, and restrooms. ~ Located in Kings Beach along Route 28, about 12 miles east of Tahoe City; 530-546-4212; www.northlaketahoe. net, e-mail ntpud@jps.net.

LAKE FOREST BEACH AND CAMPGROUND 🚴 🚣 🏖 🛶 ⛴ ⛵ 🛶 These are two discrete units situated within walking distance of one another (about a mile apart). The beach consists of a stretch of sand bordered by aspen trees. There are picnic areas and toilets. The campground, which is inland from the lake, features sites near a grove of trees. It's equipped with picnic areas, a playground, and restrooms. Parking fee for boat launch only, $10. ~ Off Route 28 along Lake Forest Road about two miles east of Tahoe City; 530-583-3796 ext. 29, fax 530-583-8452; www.tahoecity-pud.com, e-mail lvannoy@tcpud.org.

> If Lake Tahoe was drained onto the Golden State, Californians would be wading in more than a foot of water.

▲ There are 20 sites, first-come, first-served; $15 per night. Campground closed November to mid-April.

TAHOE STATE RECREATION AREA 🚶 🚴 🚣 🛶 Little more than a pocket park, this 62-acre facility possesses a small patch of lakefront property. The beach is unattractive, but the area behind it is studded with shady conifer trees. Facilities here include picnic area and restrooms. Closed Labor Day to Memorial Day. Day-use fee, $4. ~ Route 28 just east of Tahoe City; 530-525-7232 or 530-583-3074, fax 530-525-3380; e-mail sierrahq@jps.net.

▲ There are 20 sites; $25 per night.

SUGAR PINE POINT STATE PARK 🚶 🚴 🚣 🛶 One of the Tahoe region's most precious jewels, this magnificent park extends along almost two miles of lakefront. Inland it runs nearly four miles. Within that expanse is a forest of Jeffrey and sugar pines. The lakefront is dotted with sandy beaches, and the park possesses several historic structures, among them a pioneer log cabin and an old mansion that's been converted to a museum. There are also hiking trails, a tennis court, picnic areas, restrooms, and showers. Day-use fee, $4. ~ Route 89 about ten miles south of Tahoe City; 530-525-7232, fax 530-525-3383; www.ceres.ca. gov/sierradsp, e-mail sierrahq@jps.net.

▲ There are 175 forested sites; $15 per night.

D. L. BLISS AND EMERALD BAY STATE PARKS

These contiguous beauties curve along six miles of lakefront. Within their borders lie some of the area's most picturesque sites. Emerald Bay, a narrow cove bounded all around by dense forest, is a shimmering body of water. A spectacular waterfall feeds the cove. The forest that dominates both parks includes Jeffrey and ponderosa pines, incense cedar, quaking aspen, mountain dogwood, and willows. Wildflowers and berries flourish throughout the area. Tours of Vikingsholm Mansion (530-525-7277) are held daily. There are picnic areas, restrooms, and showers in both parks. Day-use fee, $4. ~ Both parks are along Route 89; D. L. Bliss is 17 miles south of Tahoe City, Emerald Bay is 22 miles south; 530-525-7232; e-mail sierra hq@jps.net.

> The amount of water that evaporates from Lake Tahoe in one day could provide Los Angeles with water for five years.

▲ There are 168 sites at D. L. Bliss and 100 sites plus 20 boat-in sites at Emerald Bay; $12 per night. Camping is allowed from late spring to early fall, depending on weather conditions.

DESOLATION WILDERNESS

This preserve, extending across 63,475 acres of alpine terrain, is a favorite among outdoor adventurers. With elevations ranging from 6500 to 10,000 feet, the domain encompasses about 130 lakes. Juniper, fir, and pine grow along the streams that tumble through the mountains, but large stretches, stripped by glacial action, are devoid of trees and appear like a moonscape. Because of heavy snowfall, the best time to explore is summer. Other than miles of hiking trails, there are no facilities here. A wilderness permit is necessary to enter. Contact the Taylor Creek Wilderness for more information, 530-543-2736. ~ Located a few miles southwest of Lake Tahoe; accessible from Route 89 or Route 50.

▲ Camping is hike-in only. Because of heavy summer use, a reservation fee and quota system has been instituted. Some wilderness permits can be reserved up to 90 days in advance; others are available on a first-come, first-served basis. Reservations: 530-644-6048.

LAKE TAHOE BASIN MANAGEMENT UNIT

This extremely beautiful region is concentrated around the south shore of Lake Tahoe. Its 148,800 acres include some of Tahoe's prettiest beaches (see listing below), several campgrounds, picnic areas, plus ski and horseback riding opportunities; restrooms throughout. Day-use fee at several locations. ~ Located along Route 50 around the lake's south shore. For more information contact the Taylor Creek Visitors Center on Route 89 along the western outskirts of South Lake Tahoe, near Fallen Leaf Lake; 530-573-2674 (summer and fall only); 530-543-2400 (year-round).

▲ There are several campgrounds surrounding Lake Tahoe. My favorite is Meeks Bay, located on a pretty white-sand beach; there are 40 sites; $14 per night. There are also campsites in another part of Tahoe National Forest north of Lake Tahoe; these are located along Route 89 between Truckee and Tahoe City. Information: 530-587-3558, fax 530-587-6914.

SOUTH SHORE BEACHES

Located within a few miles of South Lake Tahoe are several of the region's loveliest beaches. Matter of fact, the stretch from Baldwin Beach, near Emerald Bay, to the edge of South Lake Tahoe, is a golden swath of sandy beach dotted by a few businesses and private homes. Edged by trees and vegetation, backdropped by mountains, it's an idyllic site overlooking the entire lake. The sandy skein includes **Baldwin Beach** and **Pope Beach**. There are picnic areas, restrooms, and information centers at the Tallac Historic Site and Taylor Creek Center. ~ Located along Route 89 west of South Lake Tahoe; 530-573-2674 (summer only), 530-573-2600 (year-round).

HISTORIC CAMP RICHARDSON RESORT & MARINA

This lakefront facility includes a campground among its many features. Situated in piney woods within strolling distance of the beach, this private campground is part of a full-facility complex that includes access to a marina, lawn sports, riding stable, and bike rentals. There are also picnic areas, restrooms, and showers. ~ Located on Route 89 near the western outskirts of South Lake Tahoe; 530-541-1801, 800-544-1801; www.camprichardson.com, e-mail info@camprichardson.com.

▲ There are more than 250 sites, some with RV hookups. Fees are $18 for tent sites; $23 for water and electric hookups; $26 for water, electric, and sewage hookups.

REGAN BEACH

Not really a beach, this is an open picnic area along the waterfront. Nevertheless, it's nicely landscaped with a lawn and shade trees. Central to South Lake Tahoe, the park is still off the main thoroughfare. Facilities include picnic tables, barbecue grills, sand volleyball courts, and restrooms. ~ Located five blocks from Route 50 on Lakeview Avenue at Sacramento Street in South Lake Tahoe.

ELDORADO BEACH

This pocket park, with its patch of sand, commands a sweeping view of the lake. Unfortunately, it's located right on a busy highway. Things can become rather schizophrenic with pristine nature extending out before you and civilization rumbling along behind. But its location in the center of South Lake Tahoe makes it popular nonetheless. The only facilities are picnic tables. ~ Located in South Lake Tahoe along Route 50 near the intersection with Lakeview Avenue.

ELDORADO NATIONAL FOREST 🚶 🚵 🐎 🎿 🛶 ⛷ 🎣 🚣

🚤 🚤 ⚓ Rising from 1620 to 10,380 feet, this 668,000-acre national forest extends from the Gold Country to the High Sierra. Within its domain are numerous lakes, plus over 600 miles of fishing streams. Anglers try for brown, rainbow, and eastern brook trout; birdwatchers search out golden and bald eagles, quail, and several owl species; hunters stalk deer and bear. There are also 350 miles of hiking trails. There are picnic areas and restrooms within the forest. ~ Located southwest of Lake Tahoe, the region is traversed by Routes 50 and 88; 530-647-5400, fax 530-647-5405.

▲ There are 60 campgrounds, including the beautiful Silver Lake and Caples Lake campgrounds, along Route 88; $8 to $18 per night.

▼ ▼ ▼ ▼ ▼ ▼ ▼ ▼ ▼ ▼ ▼ ▼ ▼ ▼ ▼

Lake Tahoe to Yosemite

There are few better ways to experience High Sierra country than by following the mountain roads leading from Lake Tahoe to Yosemite. Route 89 heads from South Lake Tahoe and intersects with Route 395, which in turn links with Route 120, the back road into Yosemite.

Along the way are views of bald-domed mountains, lofty and elegant, backdropped by even taller ranges. The road courses just below the ridge of the world, where jagged peaks dominate the sky, with valleys spread below, flat and broad. There are alpine meadows wild with flowers and aspen trees palsied in the wind.

SIGHTS

The route cuts through **Monitor Pass**, an 8300-foot plateau across which early pioneers and gold seekers once trekked. Today it is unchanged, tufted with grass, like an elevated prairie. Then the highway dives into boulder-strewn defiles, along rumbling rivers with white water like lace. There are tiny towns along the way—Topaz, Coleville, and Bridgeport—plus an occasional rest area.

In the mountains high above Yosemite, Route 395 arrives at **Mono Lake**, one of California's strangest and most controversial spots. Located along the western edge of the Great Basin, it's a saline-alkaline body of water, the remnant of a prehistoric inland sea. At first glance it seems eerie and forbidding, an alien place with weird stalagmite-like formations that resemble a moonscape.

Actually, those spire-shaped figures are "tufa" towers, composed of calcite and formed by the confluence of fresh-water springs and salt water. Many have taken the form of delicate statuary, rising like minarets and rock candy mountains from the surface. They create a provocative landscape of bone-white rock against turquoise water.

The reason these underwater fossils are presently above the lake surface is the key to a bitter environmental controversy. For over five decades the distant city of Los Angeles drained water from streams feeding the lake. Together with natural evaporation, that action dropped the lake level about 40 feet and doubled salinity.

Since Mono Lake breeds brine shrimp and brine flies, favored food for gulls, it is home to the world's second-largest California Gull population. Grebes and phalaropes also gather in great numbers. Their habitat has been threatened because water diversions drastically lowered the lake. In 1994, the State Water Board intervened, declaring that water diversion must decrease. Now the lake is at half its ordered level. Thirsty Los Angeles will continue to divert a small amount of water but Mono Lake has been mandated to reach a stabilization level in 15 to 20 years. However, the future of this surreal and beautiful lake still hangs in the balance since the Water Board's decision could be appealed. ~ Route 395; 760-647-3044, fax 760-647-3046; www.monolake.org, e-mail info@monolake.org.

Just beyond Mono Lake, Route 395 meets Route 120, along the backside of Yosemite. Before entering the Park, the road cuts through **Inyo National Forest**, where jagged peaks angle upwards so sharply they seem like fortress walls. Below the road, other cliffs dive into gorges of granite and swirling water. The waterfalls cutting into these rockfaces have worked at the granite for thousands of years, barely chiseling a bed.

The road spirals up through **Tioga Pass** (9941 feet) and streams past **Ellery Lake,** an alpine crystal set at 9523 feet. Then it begins a steady descent into one of the country's prettiest parks—Yosemite.

sights

AUTHOR FAVORITE

Whenever I see a Western ghost town that has crumbled into ruins, suffered massive looting, or been commercialized beyond recognition, I gain more respect for the preservation of the 19th-century wood-frame storefronts at **Bodie State Historic Park**. Seven miles south of Bridgeport and 13 miles east (three of which are along a dirt road), the park rests like a kind of woodframe time capsule in a high-desert setting. One of the West's finest ghost towns, this 1880 boom center, once home to 10,000 people, is now an outdoor museum complete with the houses, taverns, stores, and churches of a bygone era. Mill and ridge tours are available in summer. Because of unmaintained roads, the park is usually accessible only to skiers and snowmobilers during winter. Admission. ~ 760-647-6445, fax 760-647-6486; e-mail bodie@qnet.com.

LODGING   Set high in the Sierras, just off a highway, there is a perfect mountain facility called **Sorensen's**. The 30 cabins (including ten log cabins) are scattered among a grove of aspen trees and look out upon rugged granite heights. Most are efficiency units, complete with kitchen facilities and everything you need for a few secluded days in the hills. Nicely remodeled and decorated with wallhangings, they have a rustic charm. Eight cabins feature fireplaces and private decks, and one has a hot tub. Sorensen's also operates the **Hope Valley Resort** down the road, which offers fly-fishing instruction, walking tours, llama treks, and kayaking lessons; they also rent mountain bikes, rafts, and kayaks. Skiing is excellent here, and the resort incorporates the Hope Valley Cross Country Ski Center. ~ 14255 Route 88, Hope Valley; 530-694-2203, 800-423-9949; www.sorensensresort.com, e-mail sorensensresort@yahoo.com. MODERATE TO ULTRA-DELUXE.

Caples Lake Resort** is another alpine jewel. Set on a sparkling lake at 7800 feet, it features a lodge with a restaurant and seven individual cabins. There are fishing and boating facilities available, and the resort is also favored by skiers. The six bed-and-breakfast rooms in the lodge have private baths. And views of lake and mountains are extraordinary. The cabins have complete kitchen units (plus those oh-so-outrageous views). There's a marina with fishing boat and kayak rentals and a convenience store. Closed November, December, April, and May ~ Route 88, Kirkwood; 209-258-8888, fax 209-258-8898; www.capleslakeresort.com, e-mail caples@volcano.net. MODERATE TO ULTRA-DELUXE.

Deep in the mountains seems hardly the place to find a historic hotel. But there it is, **Bridgeport Inn**, contained in an 1877 white-shingle building. Add a valley setting surrounded by snowy peaks and it becomes an even more remarkable establishment. Downstairs there is a white-linen dining room and an Irish bar, as well as a parlor with chandelier and granddaddy wood stove. The restored Victorian rooms are appointed with Monterey furniture. The decor is period, simple and elegant. Be sure to ask for a room in the inn proper. Open March 1 to the day before Thanksgiving. ~ 205 Main Street, Bridgeport; 760-932-7380, fax 760-932-1160; www.thebridgeportinn.com, e-mail reservation@thebridgeportinn.com. MODERATE.

Situated at 9600 feet, directly above Yosemite National Park, is **Tioga Pass Resort**. With ten log cabins, four motel rooms, a restaurant, and other facilities, this is a perfect jumping-off place for the adventure-minded. The resort is surrounded by Inyo National Forest, providing ample opportunity for trout fishing, hiking, and boating during the summer, and cross-country skiing during the winter. The cabins come complete with kitchens and are rented on a weekly basis. There are also motel units that are rented nightly. This resort's proximity to Yosemite makes it extremely popular, so book your reservations early. Summer season runs from mid-May to mid-October; winter season runs from the week before Christmas through April. ~ Route 120, Lee Vining; 209-372-4471; www.tiogapassresort.com. MODERATE TO DELUXE.

DINING

High in the Sierras, out in the no man's land between Lake Tahoe and Yosemite, there's a waterfront restaurant at **Caples Lakes Resort**. This eatery is a favorite among mountain-bound adventurers. The menu ranges from steak to seafood to daily specials. ~ Route 88, Kirkwood; 209-258-8888; www.capleslakeresort.com, e-mail caples@volcano.net. MODERATE TO DELUXE.

◀ **HIDDEN**

Restaurants are rare and far between along Route 395. There is a homey café en route, **Meadowcliff**. The folks hereabouts serve hamburgers and chili at lunch. Dinner features an array of Mexican dishes, and breakfast is available too. The food's good, which is mighty fortunate, since this is the only game around. Grab a table out back for spectacular views of the bordering cliffs. Dinner Thursday through Tuesday in summer and Friday through Sunday in winter. ~ Route 395, Coleville; 530-495-2180; www.meadowcliff.com, e-mail stay@meadowcliff.com. BUDGET TO MODERATE.

The Mono Craters, south of the lake, represent the youngest mountain range in North America.

The 1877 **Bridgeport Inn** contains a very attractive dining room. With its ceiling fans and antique wall fixtures, the place radiates a congenial atmosphere. The dinner menu, offering prime rib, veal chops, lobster, and catch-of-the-day, is deluxe in price, but breakfasts and lunches here are fairly inexpensive. Open March 1 to the day before Thanksgiving. ~ 205 Main Street, Bridgeport; 760-932-7380; www.thebridgeportinn.com, e-mail reservation@thebridgeportinn.com. MODERATE.

Way up behind Yosemite, more than 5000 feet above the valley, there's a friendly restaurant at **Tioga Pass Resort**. Serving three meals daily, this mountain retreat features a menu ranging from sandwiches to homemade chili to hearty full-course dinners with delicious homemade desserts. It's particularly welcome for travelers heading from the High Sierra down to Yosemite. ~ Route 120, Lee Vining; 209-372-4471; www.tiogapassresort.com. MODERATE.

NIGHTLIFE

For after-dinner drinks in an old-time bar, head over to **Wolfcreek Restaurant and Cutthroat Saloon**. Once the Alpine Hotel back in the boom days when the town of nearly 3000 was the gateway to the mines of Silver Mountains, it's now a low-key watering hole. ~ 14830 Route 89, Markleeville; 530-694-2150.

PARKS

HUMBOLDT-TOIYABE NATIONAL FOREST 🚶 🚴 🐎 🏕 ⛵ 🚤 This is the biggest national forest in the lower 48 states. Its 600,000 High Sierra acres reach from Lake Tahoe to Mono Lake and extend across the California border into Nevada. Routes 89 and 395, the main High Sierra roads between Lake Tahoe and Yosemite, traverse the heart of Toiyabe. In addition to alpine meadows and rugged mountain peaks, it contains coniferous forests inhabited by deer, black bear, porcupine, and mountain lion. There are numerous hiking trails and trout streams. Skiing, canoeing, and rafting are also popular here. Permits are required for wilderness backpacking. Facilities include picnic areas and restrooms. ~ The easiest access is along Routes 89 and 395, south of Lake Tahoe. For information, contact the Bridgeport Ranger District at Route 395, Bridgeport; 760-932-7070; www.fs.fed.us/htnf.

▲ There are 38 campgrounds; $11 to $13 per night.

GROVER HOT SPRINGS STATE PARK 🚶 🚲 ♨ 〰 Set in a mountain meadow and backdropped by 8000-foot peaks, this 650-acre park is a lovely sight. The Toiyabe National Forest and Mokelumne Wilderness Area completely surround it; hiking trails lead from the park to lakes and other points throughout the forest. There is fishing for rainbow and cutthroat trout. The central attractions, however, are the springs. Water from underground springs bubbles up at 148° and is cooled to an inviting 102° to 104° for the park's hot bath (fee). This, together with a swimming pool, is situated in the meadow and open to the public. If you long for an outdoor hot pool in an alpine setting, this is the ticket. Other facilities include picnic areas, restrooms, and showers. Closed for two weeks in September. Day-use fee, $6. ~ Off Route 89, about four miles from Markleeville; 530-694-2248, fax 530-694-2502; e-mail grover@gbif.com.

▲ There are 76 sites (20 winter sites) in two campgrounds within walking distance of the pools. Campgrounds require reservations from about May 15 to Labor Day; during the rest of the year sites are on a first-come, first-served basis; $20 per night. Reservations: 800-444-7275.

INYO NATIONAL FOREST 🚶 🚲 🏇 🎣 〰 ⛵ 〰 Part of this sprawling facility lies along both Route 395, near Mono Lake, and Route 120, directly above Yosemite. Within

LAND OF THE FLY PEOPLE

Mono Lake was inhabited for five thousand years by the Kuzedika, a Northern Paiute Indian tribe, who thrived on a high-protein diet of fly pupae and brine shrimp mixed with ground piñon nuts. The name "Mono," which comes from the language of the neighboring Yokut Indians, means "fly eaters."

this section of Inyo are several excellent campgrounds that have picnic areas access is along Routes 395 and 120. For information, contact the Lee Vining Ranger District at Route 120, Lee Vining; 760-873-2408; e-mail inyovis/r5_inyo@fs.fed.us.

▲ There are 90 campgrounds. Particularly recommended are Tioga Lake Campground and Ellery Lake Campground, both located along Route 120 directly above Yosemite. They're situated on lovely alpine lakes; $15 per night.

Yosemite National Park

It is a national institution, one of America's foremost playgrounds, a spectacular park climbing across the Sierra Nevada from 2000 feet elevation to a dizzying 13,000 feet—Yosemite. Within its domain is a valley whose sheer granite cliffs have been carved by the cold blade of a glacier. It's a region of bald domes, sunshot waterfalls, and stately sequoias. At the lower elevations are broad mountain meadows browsed by deer. During summer the place riots with wildflowers; in winter it's cloaked in snow. For general information on the goings-on in Yosemite, contact 209-372-0200; www.nps.gov/yose.

SIGHTS

Center of this natural wonderland is **Yosemite Valley**. Formed about two million years ago, this Sierra canyon has a flat meadow floor surrounded by vertical precipices. It seems that glacial action tore away softer sections of granite, leaving the more durable rocks like El Capitan and Half Dome.

For thousands of years, the Ahwahneechee and other Indians inhabited the valley. After its "discovery" by whites in the 19th century, the region became a curiosity point for tourists. To protect the place, President Lincoln in 1864 declared Yosemite Valley and the Mariposa Grove to be public parks. Several years later, John Muir, a Scottish naturalist, moved to Yosemite and began a campaign to further protect the natural environment by having it declared a national park. In 1890 his efforts succeeded.

The valley which Muir saved must be experienced; it cannot adequately be described. It was once a massive lake fed by the glaciers that created the surrounding cliffs. Erosion and stream sediment eventually filled it, creating fields rich in vegetation.

Above the valley bed, vertical cliffs extend on either side to the limit of sight. In the far distance rises **Clouds Rest**, at 9926 feet the highest mountain visible from the valley. In front of that stands **Half Dome**, a monstrous rock which appears to have been cleft in two by the hand of God, leaving a sheer wall 2000 feet straight up. There is **Mirror Lake**, a mountain jewel named for the peaks reflected in its gleaming waters, and **Royal Arches**, granite shells that have been formed into great arcs by time and glaciation.

Before them looms **Sentinel Rock,** last remnant of a mammoth block of granite, the rest of which has been cracked and dumped into the valley. It's named for its resemblance to a watchtower, while **Leaning Tower** gains its name from the rock's disconcerting tilt.

There are the **Cathedral Spires,** granite shafts rising about 2000 feet above the floor; **Three Brothers,** imposing forms honoring the three sons of Tenaya, Yosemite's greatest Indian chief; and **Yosemite Falls,** among the world's tallest waterfalls, tumbling 2425 feet in three dramatic cascades.

King of Kings among these grand geologic formations is **El Capitan.** It might well be the largest exposed monolith on earth, for this hard granite giant measures twice the size of the Rock of Gibraltar. Composed of several types of granite, its sheer cliff rises over 3000 feet from the valley floor. Solitary and unshakable, it seems to peer down upon the human antics occurring far below.

For Yosemite Valley is generally a beehive of activity. The busiest spot of all is **Yosemite Village,** a cluster of buildings and shops along the northern wall of the valley. The visitor center keystones the complex. In addition to an information desk, the center hosts a photographic display of the valley and a regionally oriented bookstore. ~ 209-372-0200; www.yosemitepark.com.

Next door is the building housing the **Yosemite Museum** with exhibits illustrating the cultures of the Miwok and Paiute peoples who once inhabited the area. The museum gallery has rotating exhibits on Yosemite Valley. Directly behind the museum spreads a mock village complete with bark dwellings called *umachas* and earth-covered houses.

Also within Yosemite Village is a shop selling prints by the great photographer Ansel Adams, whose shots of the valley are renowned for their beauty and mystery. There's an art center nearby, as well as a post office, gift shop, grocery, and restaurants.

Summer, holidays, and weekends are particularly crowded in Yosemite Valley. In recent years the place has sometimes assumed the quality of a human zoo, with traffic jams and long lines. If possible, it's best to visit during the week or in the off-season, and to arrive before 10 a.m. A particularly nice time to visit is in May (before Memorial Day), when the waterfalls are at their peak due to snow melt and the wildflowers and dogwood are in bloom. Best of all, the summer crowds have not yet descended upon the valley. Also consider walking, bicycling, or using the free shuttle service around the valley; it will save you a headache and help cut down on the traffic flow.

Something else to remember: Yosemite Valley covers seven square miles, and everyone seems intent on crowding into its confines. For good reason—the valley is an extraordinary sight and must not be missed. But there are 1200 square miles of Yosemite

National Park, many of them hardly touched by visitors. These outer reaches also possess singular beauty and should be part of your itinerary.

Plan to visit the High Sierra country above the valley by following Route 120, Tioga Road, in its eastward climb toward the top of the mountain range. This road is closed during snowy months, but in periods of warm weather it leads past splendid alpine regions with meadows, lakes, and stark peaks.

At about 7000 feet, it passes a virgin stand of red fir, then continues up to **White Wolf**. The lodge here provides cabins, a campground, and a restaurant. Past this enclave a spectacular view of the **Clark Range** is revealed; then the road passes a grove of quaking aspen.

Olmsted Point has a short trail leading to a granite dome that looks down toward the north side of Half Dome and up to **Tenaya**

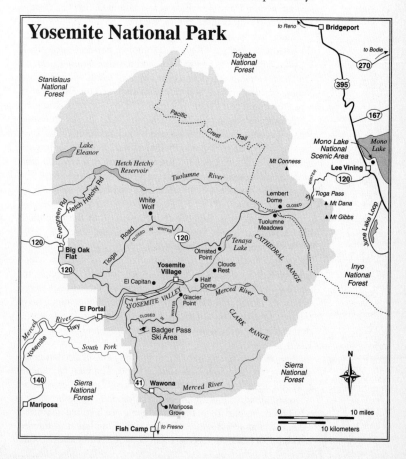

Lake. This long, slender body of water, set at 8149 feet, is shadowed on either side by bald rockfaces.

Soon **Mt. Conness**, 12,590 feet in elevation, comes into view. Then the highlight of the journey, **Tuolumne Meadows**, with its information center, campground, lodge, store, and restaurant. Statistically speaking, this wonderland constitutes the Sierra's largest subalpine meadow. Located at 8600 feet, its sunglinted fields are populated with smooth granite boulders and cut by a meandering stream. Conifers border the meadow and are in turn backdropped by bald domes and sharp faces. In summer, mountain wildflowers carpet the hillsides with brilliant shades of red, blue, and yellow, counterpointing the hard gray rocks with gentle forms and soft colors.

Beyond is **Lembert Dome**, a lopsided peak carved by glaciers. Glittering patches of glacial polish can still be seen along the dome surface. **Mount Dana** (13,053 feet) and **Mount Gibbs** (12,764 feet) are also part of this incredible landscape.

Then the road rises into **Tioga Pass**. Constructed at 9941 feet, this roadway marks the highest automobile pass in California. It is also the gateway to Mono Lake, and to other mountain roads. On these you can travel north to Oregon, south toward Death Valley, or turn around and return to that extraordinary valley now over 5000 feet below.

Another interesting trip from Yosemite Valley carries you along Route 41 to the park's southwestern boundary. Shortly after leaving the valley, the road passes **Bridalveil Fall**, where a short path leads to a 620-foot cascade. Tumbling along a sharp rockface, buffeted by breezes, the waterfall twists into intaglio designs. The edges of the cascade are blown to mist and fall like soft rain on the people below.

Soon afterwards, just before burrowing into the mountain, the highway arrives at **Tunnel View**. From here, Yosemite Valley looks like God's playpen, bounded by sharp walls and domed in azure sky. On the right, you'll see the hanging valley from which Bridalveil Falls descends. Behind it are Cathedral Rocks, appearing like hunchbacks bent to meet the valley. Sentinel Dome is a stone rapier, and Half Dome, from this unique angle, takes the form of a dolphin's bottlenose. To the left, a single figure predominates, its vertical profile at once alluring and frightening—El Capitan.

For an even finer view, follow the long side road that corkscrews up to 7214-foot-high **Glacier Point**. The vital fact here is that you are *above* Yosemite Valley, looking into the chasm and outward along its granite profile. You're also on the brink of a 3200-foot precipice (there but for the grace of a handrail go we all). Gaze out and you'll see that Half Dome now has transformed into a bird's head. Across the valley a two-tiered cascade, Upper and Lower Yosemite Falls, tumbles thousands of feet. This is the most spectacular of all Yosemite viewpoints, with the High Sierra stretching along a limitless series of snowcapped peaks. Below, the Merced River meanders past camps and hotels deep in Yosemite Valley. Glacier Point is open only during the summer.

The main road continues through miles of tall, cool forest to Wawona, a small settlement in the park's southwest corner. Here, just past an old covered bridge, is the **Pioneer Yosemite History Center**. There are log cabins and houses dating back well into the 19th century, plus a blacksmith shop and Yosemite transportation company office. This intriguing outdoor museum also features a collection of wagons and buckboards.

Beyond, near the park's south entrance, rises **Mariposa Grove**. Most impressive of Yosemite's three giant sequoia groves, it can be reached by tram or along a two-and-a-half-mile trail. Within the grove stands Grizzly Giant, a 2700-year-old forest denizen. Giant sequoias, the world's largest living things, can weigh more than two million pounds. Within this grove are about 200 trees measuring over ten feet in diameter. Unlike redwoods, which hug the cool, moist coastal areas, sequoias flourish between 5000 and 8000 feet in sunny climates. Here in the cathedral silence of the grove, these forest giants number not only among the earth's biggest life forms, but its most regal as well.

LODGING

Accommodations in Yosemite are varied, plentiful, and, paradoxically, difficult to reserve. Four million people a year pour through the Park's granite arches, many in search of a place to rest their wonder-struck heads. As a result, the park provides several locations with facilities ranging from canvas tents to cabins to cottages to hotel rooms to deluxe suites.

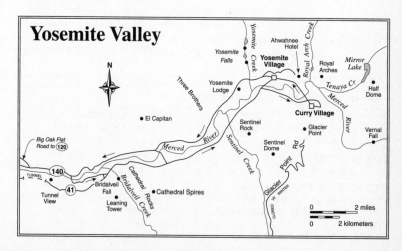

Yosemite Valley

Still it is not enough. Particularly during the summer months, facilities are booked far in advance. Matter of fact, it's not a bad idea to make reservations the year before your arrival. During the colder months the situation eases: even then, however, weekends, holidays, or good skiing snow can draw summer-size crowds back to the park. To make your reservations, contact **Yosemite Reservations, Yosemite Concession Services**. ~ 6771 North Palm Avenue, Fresno, CA 93704; 559-252-4848, fax 559-456-0542; www.yosemitepark.com.

Most facilities are located right in the valley—at the Yosemite Lodge, Curry Village, and The Ahwahnee Hotel. Others—White Wolf, Tuolumne Meadows, and Wawona—are situated in distant parts of the park and offer retreats from the crowds in the valley. Prices quoted below are summer rates; during the week in winter, rates are sometimes significantly lower.

Yosemite Lodge hosts several styles of accommodations. Foremost are the lodge rooms; these are motel-type affairs in a series of low-slung buildings near the central lodge facility. One I stayed in was nicely furnished in oak, modern in design, spacious, and quite comfortable. It had a telephone but no television, and enjoyed a private patio looking out upon a pine grove. Deer browsed 20 feet from the window. There are also cabins available, small but cozy duplex units with private bath. These lack wall decorations, but are adequately furnished and carpeted wall-to-wall. The "cottage rooms," contained in multi-unit buildings nearby, are more spacious and slightly upscale. ~ MODERATE TO DELUXE.

Over at **Curry Village**, in a nearby section of the valley, cabins are available at the same prices. Hotel rooms here have natural wood furnishings and stall showers. The wall decorations are tastefully selected and some rooms have lofts providing extra sleeping areas. The village also contains "canvas tent cabins," which provide an excellent means to visit Yosemite at an inexpensive price. They're wall tents on raised wooden platforms, with mosquito nets, windows, and canvas flaps for privacy. Furnishings

---

A SHOT OF SOUTHERN COMFORT

In Yosemite National Park's southwest corner is the **Wawona Hotel**. Its rolling lawn and white-pillared building make this century-old establishment a vision of the Old South. Indeed, the pace here is much slower, and the living easier, than in Yosemite Valley. There's a nine-hole golf course, tennis court, inviting swimming pool, and a covey of ivy-clad cottages. Rooms in this glorious old place often contain brass beds. Several share a bath (clawfoot tubs, as a matter of fact). Closed January through April. ~ 209-375-6556, fax 209-375-6601. MODERATE TO DELUXE.

include beds with complete bedding, plus time-battered shelves; basic but sufficient. Most of the tents are not heated, so prepare accordingly for winter stays. People staying in any Curry facility have access to the sitting room, swimming pool, shops, and restaurants on the premises. Closed weekdays from January through March. ~ 209-372-8333, reservations 209-252-4848, fax 209-372-4816; www.yosemitepark.com. MODERATE.

Yosemite provides the opportunity to bivouac in a flowering meadow, sleep in a pine forest, or rest yards away from the world's greatest geologic wonders. Nowhere, though, are the accommodations as grand and dramatic as at **The Ahwahnee Hotel**. Built in 1927, the place is an architectural marvel, a multitiered building of wood and stone backdropped by rain-fluted cliffs. Its manicured lawns and natural arbors place it among world-class hotels. The high-ceilinged interior is decorated after American Indian designs with intricate rugs and patterned glass. There are grand fireplaces large enough to stand inside and chandeliers that belong in a castle. Befitting the rest of the hotel, the bedrooms are spacious affairs decorated in the same motif. Even if you decide not to stay here at least plan to tour the hotel. It's a singular feature in an extraordinary park. ~ 559-252-4848, fax 559-456-0542; www.yosemitepark.com. ULTRA-DELUXE.

Tuolumne Meadows Lodge, nestled along Route 120 at 8775 feet, has tent cabins available. These are similar to the facilities in the valley, consisting of a bed, complete bedding, sparse furnishings, and, to warm those chilly mountain nights, a wood stove. There is no electricity; candles are provided. The experience here is somewhere between hotel living and camping; bathrooms and showers are shared. The nearby lodge contains a dining room and lobby available to tent sleepers. The entire complex sits in a beautiful meadow bounded by thick forest. Idyllic and easy. Open Memorial Day to early September.. ~ BUDGET.

White Wolf Lodge, located midway between Yosemite Valley and Tuolumne Meadows at 7700 feet, also has tent cabins as well as wood cabins with private baths. With its dining room, stables, and nearby hiking trails, it makes a great escape hatch. Closed in winter and early spring. ~ MODERATE.

Or try the nearby **The Redwoods in Yosemite**, a privately owned facility within the park. Here are cabins set in the woods just off a side road. Accommodations range from one- to six-bedroom vacation homes and feature living rooms, fireplaces, decks, and barbecues. ~ Box 2085, Wawona Station; 209-375-6666, fax 209-375-6400; www.redwoodsinyosemite.com, e-mail info@redwoodsinyosemite.com. MODERATE TO ULTRA-DELUXE.

One of the great frustrations of visiting Yosemite National Park is landing a reservation at the often sold-out Ahwahnee Hotel. Now **Tenaya Lodge at Yosemite** offers 244 rooms near the park's southern entrance. The hotel has a spacious lobby decorated with American Indian art, nicely landscaped grounds, indoor and outdoor pools with jacuzzis, and a variety of recreational programs centered around the park. The resort-style lodge also offers a bar and lounge and an exercise room. The only drawback is the 45-minute trip down to the Yosemite Valley floor. ~ 1122 Route 41, Fish Camp; 559-683-6555, 800-635-5807, fax 559-683-6834; www.tenayalodge.com, e-mail jfarrington@destination travel.com. ULTRA-DELUXE.

DINING

Yosemite Village, at the northern edge of the valley, provides three dining possibilities. In addition to **Degnen's Delicatessen** (by definition, budget-priced), there's an informal dining room called **Denigan's Loft.** Dominated by a mammoth fireplace, this restaurant boasts a daily assortment of appetizers and decent pizza. The **Village Grill** serves basic dinner fare, with a menu featuring hamburgers, chicken strips, and ice cream. Lunch only. Closed in winter. ~ BUDGET TO MODERATE.

Over at Yosemite Lodge there are three more restaurants, providing a fuller array of dining possibilities. It doesn't take much imagination to picture the **Food Court,** serving steam-tray food at low, low prices. Though the meals sometimes sit too long above the steam, and the dining hall is cavernous and impersonal, this is a place for anyone who believes that a full stomach shouldn't mean an empty wallet. ~ BUDGET.

The **Mountain Room Restaurant** provides an upscale step to a large but comfortable dining room. An exposed-beam ceiling adds a touch of class to the surroundings, where dinner is served. The interior is dominated by a striking photo of a rock climber dangling upside down from a granite cliff. At the tables outside, the scene is highlighted by the actual rockfaces that draw such climbers from around the world. All of which is enough to make you forget the menu. To refresh your memory, they serve steak, steak, and steak—as in sirloin, prime rib, filet mignon, and New York cut. Though they do have tasty seafood and pasta dishes—broiled salmon, rainbow trout almondine, pepper-vodka penne or breast of chicken. Sorry, dinner only. ~ DELUXE.

Curry Village features five dining locations with offerings such as burgers, pizza, Mexican fast food, meat and potatoes, and all-you-can-eat buffets. Closed in winter. ~ BUDGET.

For special occasions, or just a personal indulgence, there's the **Ahwahnee Dining Room.** An entire wing of this grand old hotel is dedicated to the fine art of dining. Part of the experience simply involves sitting in the dining room, a high-ceilinged affair with exposed-log beams. The interior is fashioned of stone and glass, with wood-paneled sections painted in American Indian designs. Service is impeccable. The breakfast menu is standard; lunch includes salads and sandwiches. Dinner is the hotel's premier meal. Appetizers range from charred, peppered buffalo carpaccio and salmon rillette to Dungeness crab. Entrées include pan-seared filet mignon, pistachio-crusted venison loin, and pasta primavera *aglio eolio*, to name a few. Dining here is an experience unto itself. Reservations required; dress code. ~ 209-372-1489, fax 209-372-1463; www.yosemitepark.com. DELUXE TO ULTRA-DELUXE.

Scattered around the various corners of this expansive park are several other restaurants. Outside the valley, up on Route 120, there's a dining facility at **White Wolf Lodge.** Farther up the highway, you'll encounter **Tuolumne Meadows Lodge,** a mountain hideaway with surprisingly sophisticated cuisine. The dining tent beside the Tuolumne River features a variety of beef, chicken, and vegetarian offerings, as well as soups, salads, and desserts. They also serve hearty breakfasts, but no lunch. Reservations required for dinner. ~ MODERATE.

Keep a keen eye open for rock climbers on the face of El Capitan—ant-like in proportion, they inch along its unyielding walls.

Then over at Wawona, located in the park's southwest corner, is the **Wawona Hotel.** An old establishment in the style of the Deep South, this splendid place contains a white-linen dining room that overlooks manicured lawns. Decorated with antique photos of Yosemite and illuminated by hooded lamps, it's a regal affair. In addition to a breakfast buffet, they feature a hearty lunch. Dinner presents angus beef, trout, prime rib, lasagna, or lamb chops. Such good food and elegant surroundings are hard to match out here deep in the forest. A special barbecue dinner is available on Saturday during the summer, and Sunday brunch is served from Easter through Thanksgiving and during the Christmas holidays. Closed the first two weeks of December; open Friday through Sunday only from mid-January to mid-March. ~ 209-375-6556, fax 209-375-6601. MODERATE TO DELUXE.

NIGHTLIFE

In Yosemite National Park, the **Mountain Room Bar** at Yosemite Lodge is a spacious, oak-paneled lounge complete with fireplace. The perfect spot for a late-night brandy, the room is walled-in glass and looks out toward Yosemite Falls. If you need a taste of the "real world," there's a large-screened TV that shows major sporting events. Over at the beautiful Ahwahnee Hotel, you'll encounter the intimate **Ahwahnee Bar,** a plushly appointed drinking place.

PARKS

YOSEMITE NATIONAL PARK 🏃 🚲 🐎 🏠 ⛵ 🛶 ⛴ One of the country's most extraordinary and renowned parks, this 761,000-acre giant offers every activity from sightseeing a spectacular glacial valley to skiing alpine meadows. About 95 percent of the park has been targeted for wilderness status. Its domain spreads from 2900 to 13,000 feet, climbing from the foothills to the roof of the Sierra. Since its features are so extensive, Yosemite is discussed at length in most other sections of this chapter, so consult them for details. Among the many facilities here are hotels, restaurants, stores, museums, shuttle service, organized nature programs, information centers, picnic areas, restrooms, showers, a ski area, almost 800 miles of hiking trails, stables, and more than 600 miles of riding trails. Day-use fee, $20 (good for one week). ~ Located along Routes 120, 140, and 41 about 200 miles southeast of San Francisco; 209-372-0200; www.nps.gov/yose. For information on weather, road conditions, and campground status, call 209-372-0200.

▲ Camping is permitted in campgrounds in Yosemite Valley and throughout the park ($15 fee in Yosemite Valley). There is a seven-day limit in the valley during the summer, fourteen days in other areas. Since the park's 1500 sites are in great demand, arrive early; some campsites are on a first-come, first-served basis. Call the reservation center at 800-436-7275 to secure a site. Wilderness permits are required for backcountry camping; these are available at the Yosemite Valley visitors center, and in Big Oak Flat, Yosemite Valley Wilderness Center, Tuolumne Meadows, and Wawona. ~ 209-372-0740; www.yosemitepark.com.

There are also five High Sierra camps with dormitory tents and dining facilities. Spaced about seven miles apart and open during the summer, these are ideal for hikers exploring the high country. Contact High Sierra Reservations, Yosemite Concession Services, 6771 North Palm Avenue, Fresno, CA 93704; 559-252-4848, fax 559-456-0542; www.yosemitepark.com.

TRAFFIC-FREE YOSEMITE

If possible, it's best to visit Yosemite during the week or in the off-season. Remember, though, that Tioga Pass Road and other scenic routes over the mountains are closed in winter. A particularly nice time to visit is in May (before Memorial Day), when the waterfalls are at their peak due to snow melt and the wildflowers and dogwood are in bloom. Best of all, the summer crowds have not yet descended upon the valley. Also consider walking, bicycling, or using the free shuttle service around the valley; it will save you a headache and help cut down on the traffic flow.

Pick almost any lake or river in the Gold
Country and High Sierra, bait a hook, and
you're bound to come up with trout for dinner.

FISHING

SACRAMENTO   Sacramento Sport Fishing Guides can arrange
trips on the Sacramento River for salmon from July through
October. Steelhead trips are available in September and October.
~ 1531 Wyant Way, Sacramento; 916-487-3392, 800-344-4871;
www.fishingtrips.com, e-mail captjack@fishingtrips.com.

SOUTHERN GOLD COUNTRY   Moccasin Point Marina rents
fishing boats on Lake Don Pedro where anglers try for bass,
crappie, trout, and salmon. ~ 11405 Jacksonville Road, Jamestown; 209-989-2206.

LAKE TAHOE AREA   One of the area's best bets is **Tahoe Sport
Fishing**. A morning or afternoon charter includes a light meal,
drinks, bait and tackle, and fish cleaning. Common catches are
mackinaw, rainbow and brown trout, and kokanee salmon. ~
900 Ski Run Boulevard, South Lake Tahoe; 530-541-5448, 800-
696-7797; www.tahoesportfishing.com, e-mail info@tahoesport
fishing.com.

**WATER
SPORTS**

From rafting and waterskiing on the American and Sacramento
rivers to sailing and windsurfing on Lake Tahoe, the Gold Country
and High Sierra are prime places for water sports.

SACRAMENTO   American River Rafting will shuttle you back
to your car after the three-and-a-half-hour lazy kayak or raft
ride. Open May through August. ~ 11257 South Bridge Street,
Rancho Cordova; 916-635-6400; www.raftrentals.com.

LAKE TAHOE AREA   *The* place for recreational boating—including sailing, canoeing, ski boating, and board sailing—is Lake
Tahoe. **Richardson's Resort Marina** rents 18-foot Bow Riders,
20-foot patio boats, and personal water crafts. Open May through
September. ~ 1900 Jameson Beach Road, Camp Richardson; 530-
542-6570; www.camprichardson.com.

**RIVER
RUNNING**

Whitewater rafting in the Gold Country and High Sierra combines spectacular scenery with high adventure.

SACRAMENTO   American River Recreation offers runs on the
American, Klamath, and Merced rivers. Trips range from Class
III to V, and last up to five days. Closed October through March.
~ P.O. Box 465, Lotus, CA 95651; 800-333-7238; www.arraft
ing.com.

SOUTHERN GOLD COUNTRY   Beyond Limits Adventure Tours
provides trips on various rivers. They also rent rafts, and any camping gear you might need. ~ P.O. Box 215, Riverbank, CA 95367;
209-869-6060; www.rivertrip.com. **Zephyr River Expeditions**

leads tours of the Tuolumne, Kings, Merced, and American rivers. Trips are on a six-person raft and last from a half day to five days. ~ P.O. Box 510, Columbia, CA 95310; 209-532-6249; www.zrafting.com.

CENTRAL GOLD COUNTRY Chili Bar Outdoor Center runs Class III and IV rapids on the American River. ~ P.O. Box 554, Coloma, CA 95613; 530-621-1236; www.cbocwhitewater.com.

NORTHERN GOLD COUNTRY In business for more than two decades, **Tributary Whitewater Tours** leads expeditions on the American, Yuba, and Truckee rivers; difficulty ranges from Class II to Class V. Closed in winter. ~ 20480 Woodbury Drive, Grass Valley; 530-346-6812, 800-672-3846; www.whitewatertours.com, e-mail rafting@whitewatertours.com.

LAKE TAHOE AREA Call **Mountain Air Sports** for a family ride on the gentle Class I Truckee River. Open in summer only. Don't forget your sunscreen! ~ 205 River Road, Tahoe City; 530-583-5606; www.truckeeriverrafting.com.

ROCK CLIMBING Ready to scale a sheer granite cliff? Then Yosemite National Park is your playground. Lessons and guides are available at **Yosemite Mountaineering and Cross-Country Ski School.** ~ Badger Pass, Yosemite National Park; 209-372-8444; www.yosemitemountaineering.com.

BALLOON RIDES A hot-air balloon may not get you there sooner, but it will carry you higher while offering spectacular views of Sacramento's rich farm country.

LAKE TAHOE AREA For a flight above the Sierras, call **Mountain High Balloons**. There are several special surprises in store for you, and kids between ten and fifteen fly free with an adult. ~ Truckee; 530-587-6922, 888-462-2683.

GOLD PANNING If sifting dirt along cold mountain streams sounds like fun, try your luck panning for gold. You may not strike it rich, but then again, who knows?

AUTHOR FAVORITE

The chances of striking it rich might be greater if I bought a state Lotto ticket, but I'd rather pan for gold, which transports me back to the days of the '49ers. Even if sluicing for riches in the Gold Country's streams won't fund my dream house, it will connect me to that bygone era that shaped California's history. See above for gold-panning outfitters.

SOUTHERN GOLD COUNTRY   Gold Prospecting Adventures will take you to their own private 1849 gold-mining camp. You'll find Mark Twain's cabin and Sutter's Mill as well as original pistols, lanterns, and flumes used during that serendipitous era. ~ 18170 Main Street, Jamestown; 209-984-4653, 800-596-0009; www.goldprospecting.com, e-mail info@goldprospecting.com. **California Gold** offers a five-hour mining trip where you'll dig and pan for gold just like the '49ers did. ~ P.O. Box 1132, Jamestown, CA 95327; 209-984-4914; www.goldfun.com.

CENTRAL GOLD COUNTRY   Roaring Camp Mining Co. is the place to contact for daily guided tours along the Mokelumne River. They also have cabins where you can vacation while seeking out your fortune. Closed October through April. ~ P.O. Box 278, Pine Grove, CA 95665; 209-296-4100; e-mail parrc@vol cano.net.

You don't have to be an Olympic medal winner to ski the Sierra, but you might run into one on the slopes.

SKIING

LAKE TAHOE AREA   Sugar Bowl has 1500 acres of skiable terrain accessed by 13 chairlifts. Seventeen percent of the 83 runs are beginner slopes, 45 percent are for intermediate, and 38 percent are for experts. There are two terrain runs for snowboarders designed by Noah Salasnek, plus a 17-foot super pipe. They rent downhill skis and snowboards. ~ Norden; 530-426-3651, 866-843-2695; www.sugarbowl.com, e-mail info@sugarbowl.com.

With 15 lifts and 70 runs, there is plenty to keep you busy at **Northstar**. Fifty percent of the slopes are intermediate level, with the other half split evenly between beginner and advanced runs. The summit reaches 8610 feet and the vertical drop is 2280 feet. A snowboard terrain has two half pipes and several jumps. There are also extensive cross-country and snowshoe trails, and a snow-tube run. The rental shop has downhill, telemark, and Nordic skis, cross-country skates, and snowboards. ~ Six miles east of Truckee on Route 267; 530-562-1010; www.northstarattahoe.com, e-mail northstar@boothcreek.com.

Nestled in the High Sierra amidst 8000 acres of wilderness preserve with 4000 skiable acres, **Squaw Valley** boasts 33 chairlifts, 6 mountain peaks, and a 2850-foot vertical drop. Twenty-five percent of the runs are beginner slopes, 45 percent are intermediate, and 30 percent are expert. The snowboard park includes two half pipes and three terrain parks; it is one of several runs open until 9 p.m. Lessons for skiing, telemarking, and snowboarding are available, and they rent all necessary equipment. ~ Olympic Valley; 530-583-6985, 800-545-4350; www. squaw.com, e-mail squaw@squaw.com.

Text continued on page 504.

Trekking Yosemite

alled the "Incomparable Valley," Yosemite is *the* place for hikers to seek the solitude, excitement, and grandeur of the wilderness. More than 100 hiking trails, both within and outside Yosemite Valley, lace the park. Remember, multiday hikes require a wilderness permit. Oftentimes, some trails are closed due to storm or fire damage. Call ahead before planning your hike. All distances listed are one way unless otherwise noted.

Happy Isles Trail (.5 mile), the easiest trail in the park, is wheelchair-accessible and crosses bridges to two islands in the Merced River. The Mist Trail and John Muir Trail start here.

Mist Trail (3.5 miles) starts about a mile away from Vernal Fall. This moderate to strenuous hike continues up to Nevada Fall.

John Muir Trail (8.5 miles) is a strenuous path that parallels the Mist Trail, but extends past Nevada Fall up to Half Dome.

Valley Floor–West Loop Trail (6.9 miles) carries past Bridalveil Fall, Cathedral Rocks, and El Capitan.

Valley Floor–Yosemite Village Loop Trail (2 miles) offers views of Yosemite Falls, Half Dome, and Royal Arches.

Valley Floor–Mirror Lake–Meadow Loop Trail (3 miles) wends past Mirror Lake Meadow and Half Dome along a tree-shaded route. The lake is naturally evolving into a meadow and dries by the end of summer. The trail also features views of treacherous Tenaya Canyon.

Yosemite Falls Loop Trail (7.2 miles roundtrip), a strenuous half-day hike, climbs to the top of Upper Yosemite Fall.

Sentinel Dome Trail (1.2 miles), one of the most-traveled paths in the park, carries across bedrock to the summit of Sentinel Dome. At the top are views of El Capitan, Yosemite Falls, Half Dome, and the lone Jeffrey pine that crowns this peak.

Vernal–Nevada Falls Loop Trail (7.8 miles) is one of the most scenic hikes in the valley. Initially it follows Mist Trail, where you'll be sprayed with rain from Vernal Fall (bring rain gear, or in summer, a bathing suit). After enjoying the views from Clark Point, pick up John Muir Trail for the climb to Nevada Fall.

Little Yosemite Valley Trail (7.9 miles) is a semi-loop trail that is best hiked in two days. This trail is a major starting point for backpackers heading deep into Yosemite. Watch out for bears!

Half Dome Trail (8.2 miles) is a strenuous mountain climb that ends at the most spectacular summit in the park. Not a hike for acrophobes.

Lembert Dome–Dog Lake Loop Trail (4.2 miles) begins in the Tuolumne Meadows parking lot and leads to the top of Lembert Dome. It continues to Dog Lake with views of Mt. Dana, Mt. Gibbs, and Mt. Lewis.

Elizabeth Lake Trail (4.5 miles), one of the most popular trails in the park, offers impressive views of the usually snowcapped Cathedral Range on its way from Tuolumne Meadows to a beautiful alpine lake.

Harden Lake Trail (3 miles) is an easy hike from White Wolf Campground to one of the area's warmest lakes.

Alder Creek Trail to Bishop Creek (3.5 miles) is a moderate half-day trek in the Wawona area. Hard to find but very beautiful, this trail is best hiked in springtime when the creeks flow and the temperature is moderate. One of the most outstanding features is the flowering plant life, including mountain misery, a lightly scented shrub.

Panorama Trail from Glacier Point to Nevada Falls (5.5 miles) is one of the more scenic routes into the valley. It begins at the Glacier Point parking lot and gives startling views of Tenaya Canyon, Half Dome, Illilouette Fall, Clouds Rest, Nevada, and Vernal falls—to name just a few!

Pohono Trail (13 miles) also starts from Glacier Point. Following the south rim of Yosemite Valley, it offers spectacular views as it descends 1800 feet to the Wawona Tunnel. This trail is known for its abundance of wildflowers in spring and early summer.

May Lake Trail (3 miles) makes its way through cool forest and across granite slabs to reach May Lake High Sierra Camp. Although it's hard to get reservations for the camp, fishing for rainbow and brook trout is permitted in the lake.

Mono Pass Trail (8.5 miles), one of the park's most ambitious hikes, takes all day. The scenery and the 10,600-foot altitude will leave you breathless.

Alpine Meadows is a skier's paradise with 12 chairlifts and more than 100 runs (25 percent beginner, 40 percent intermediate, and 35 percent expert). A terrain park for snowboarders has a half pipe and natural jumps. The base elevation is 6835 feet, and the steepest vertical drop is 60°. Lessons are available, and they rent downhill and telemark skis, big feet, and snowboards. ~ 2600 Alpine Meadows Road, Tahoe City; 530-583-4232, 800-441-4423; www.skialpine.com, e-mail info@skialpine.com.

Located six miles south of Tahoe City, **Homewood Mountain Resort** features a base elevation of 6230 feet and a 1650-foot vertical drop. Eight chairlifts cover the 56 runs (15 percent beginner, 50 percent intermediate, and 35 percent advanced). Shredwood Forest is a run made for boarders and skiers who like quarter and half pipes. Ski and snowboard lessons and rentals are available. ~ 5145 West Lake Boulevard, Homewood; 530-525-2992, 877-525-7669; www.skihomewood.com, e-mail smile@skihomewood.com.

For 4800 acres of pure white powder, head over to **Heavenly Ski Resort**. Catering to downhill skiers and snowboarders, the resort has a base elevation of 6540 feet. There are 31 lifts and 86 runs (20 percent beginner, 45 percent intermediate, and 35 percent expert). A snowboard park includes a super-pipe and jumps. Lessons are available for skiing and snowboarding. Hotels, restaurants, infant day care, and day lodges round out the amenities. ~ Wildwood and Saddle roads, South Lake Tahoe; 775-586-7000; www.skiheavenly.com, e-mail info@skiheavenly.com.

Located in a lovely alpine valley, **Kirkwood Ski Resort** sports 2300 acres of skiable terrain along with a 2000-foot vertical drop. The base elevation is at 7800 feet. There are 12 lifts and 65 runs (15 percent beginner, 50 percent intermediate, and 35 percent expert). Four terrain parks have jumps, spines, and a half pipe; there's also a super pipe. There are also 80 kilometers of groomed cross-country trails. They offer lessons for downhill and cross-country skiing, telemarking, and snowboarding. All equipment is available to rent. ~ 1501 Kirkwood Meadows Drive, Kirkwood;

LLAMA TREKS

For expeditions of another kind, call **Highland Llama Trekkers,** which offers multiday trips through Tahoe National Forest (July through October), Trinity Alps Wilderness Area (July and August) and Mokelumne Wilderness (August). Year-round daytrips traverse privately owned wilderness areas in Auburn and Grass Valley. ~ 14223 Highland Drive, Grass Valley; phone/fax 530-273-8105; e-mail llamahi@nccn.net.

209-258-6000; www.kirkwood.com, e-mail kwd-info@kirk wood.com.

Cross-country skiers can contact **Royal Gorge**, which encompasses 9172 acres of skiable terrain. You can rent Nordic skis and travel over 330 kilometers of groomed trails. ~ 9411 Hillside Drive, Soda Springs; 530-426-3871; www.royalgorge.com, e-mail info@ royalgorge.com.

YOSEMITE NATIONAL PARK Located 29 miles from Yosemite Valley, **Badger Pass Ski Area** features five chairlifts, nine runs, and an 800-foot vertical drop. ~ Glacier Point Road, Yosemite National Park; 209-372-8430; www.yosemitepark.com. Forty-five kilometers of trails are groomed at **Yosemite Cross-Country Ski School**. Countless miles of ungroomed trails are also open for exploration. Cross-country ski, telemark, and snowshoe rentals are available at the Badger Pass Ski Area. ~ Badger Pass, Yosemite National Park; 209-372-8344; www.yosemitemountaineer ing.com.

For further information on both downhill and cross-country skiing, see the "Ski California" section in this chapter.

Ski Rentals **Porter's Ski & Sport** in Tahoe City rents snowboards and skis. ~ 501 North Lake Boulevard, Tahoe City; 530-583-2314; www.porterstahoe.com.

You'll feel like you're in a Currier & Ives print when you climb aboard a sleigh for a romantic winter ride. **Camp Richardson Corral** offers 50- to 55-minutes rides daily, usually every hour, weather permitting. Closed mid-October through April. You must make reservations a day or two in advance. ~ Camp Richardson; 530-541-3113.

SLEIGH RIDES

Cantering through the parks of Sacramento or packing in to the Sierra wilderness . . . nothing brings you closer to the Old West than horseback riding.

RIDING STABLES

SACRAMENTO For one- and two-hour trail rides through an oak-filled meadow near the American River, contact **Shadow Glen Riding Stables**. Lessons are given year-round; trails are open April through September. ~ 4854 Main Avenue, Fair Oaks; 916-989-1826.

LAKE TAHOE AREA Around Lake Tahoe, call **Camp Richardson's Corral**. Their guided one- and two-hour trips pass aspen, pine, and fir trees en route to Fallen Leaf Lake. ~ Emerald Bay Road, Camp Richardson; 530-541-3113; www.camprich.com. In the spring, **Alpine Meadows Stable** will take you on a ride through wildflower-filled meadows and forests. It is not uncommon to see deer or black bears. Open Memorial Day to October. ~ Alpine Meadows, Tahoe City; 530-583-3905.

Text continued on page 508.

Ski California

As a travel destination, California offers everything. Even during winter, when rain spatters the coast and fog invades the valleys, the Golden State has one more treat in its bottomless bag—snow.

No sooner has the white powder settled than skiers from around the world beeline to the region's high-altitude resort areas. They come to schuss through fir forests in the Cascades, challenge the runs above Lake Tahoe, and breathe the beauty of Yosemite at Christmas.

The season begins in late fall and sometimes lasts until May. During those frosty months dozens of ski areas offer both downhill and cross-country skiing. In the Far North, the **Shasta Cascade Wonderland Association** provides information on facilities. Here, 14,162-foot Mt. Shasta features downhill skiing as well as miles of trackless wilderness. ~ 1699 Route 273, Anderson, CA 96007; 800-474-2782, fax 530-365-1258; e-mail scwa@shastacascade.org.

The center of California skiing lies in the Sierra, where large resorts surround Lake Tahoe and extend south toward Yosemite National Park and beyond. Squaw Valley played host to the 1960 Winter Olympics and numerous other resorts have won plaudits from world-class skiers. With temperatures hovering between 20 and 40 and snowfall measuring 200 to 400 inches, the region is ideal for winter sports. The **California Ski Industry Association** has full information. ~ 74 New Montgomery Street, Suite 750, San Francisco, CA 94105; 415-543-7036, fax 415-543-0112; www.californiasnow.com, e-mail info@californiasnow.com.

Many resorts focus on downhill and alpine-style skiing and provide complete facilities for their athletic guests. Some, like **Squaw Valley**, are self-contained villages offering every facility imaginable. Such "G-rated" resorts often feature boutiques, pools, tennis courts, groceries, restaurants, and après-ski spots. Squaw Valley also has ice skating, snow tubing, and an indoor climbing wall. There are instructors for every level of skier or snowboarder, snow school for children, and enough diversions to keep even a non-skier content. ~ Olympic Valley, CA 96146; 530-583-6985, 800-545-4350, fax 530-581-7106; www.squaw.com, e-mail squaw@squaw.com.

The more demanding Nordic style of cross-country skiing is gaining increased popularity around the state. This is the adventurer's way to explore the slopes—fill a daypack, strap on skis, and take off across the mountains. In the pack are extra clothes, food, water, flashlight, knife, map, compass, blanket, matches, equipment repair tools, and a first-aid kit.

Unrestricted by ski lifts and marked runs, cross-country skiers venture everywhere that geography and gravity permit. Their sport is tantamount to hiking on skis, with the entire expanse of the Sierra Nevada their domain. Some skiers disappear into the wilderness for days on end, emerging only when supplies run low. Particularly favored by these explorers is Desolation Wilderness, a stark, glaciated region just west of Lake Tahoe.

If you prefer a base of operations from which to experience the wild, more than a dozen Nordic ski centers operate extensive trail systems in the Tahoe region. **Royal Gorge Wilderness Lodge**, for instance, houses guests in a 60-year-old building formerly used by hunters. The 30 private rooms share baths and offer modern conveniences like heat, electricity, a sauna, and an outdoor hot tub. The lodge's chef specializes in French country cuisine.

Royal Gorge Lodge sits amid the largest network of cross-country trails in the nation. About 200 miles of groomed track and 90 trails extend in every direction, leading through forests of fir and lodgepole pine. There are frozen lakes to explore, extraordinary mountain vistas, and secluded warming huts where you can enjoy afternoon tea. ~ 9411 Hillside Drive, Soda Springs, CA 95728; 530-426-3871, 800-500-3871, fax 530-426-9221; www.royalgorge.com, e-mail info@royalgorge.com.

Other Nordic lodges offer moonlight tours through alpine meadows, overnight trips to backwoods cabins, cross-country races, and guided tours of the High Sierra. There are workshops in snow survival and winter photography. Or maybe you're ready for the Tahoe-version triathlon—six miles cross-country skiing, followed by twelve miles bicycling, six miles running, and finished off with a mere five miles kayaking along the Truckee River. What better time than winter to work up a sweat.

YOSEMITE NATIONAL PARK   Yosemite National Park has stables in the Valley, at Wawona, and at Tuolumne Meadows. Most of the Yosemite stables are closed in winter. ~ 209-372-1000; www.yosemitepark.com.

BIKING

Exploring the Gold Country and High Sierra by bicycle can be an exhilarating experience. It's an area best toured by physically fit folks on mountain bikes. Almost all roads are open for bikes, but heavy traffic, steep grades, and the high altitude make for an arduous journey. To enjoy touring this area, cyclists should plan their trips carefully, if possible scouting out the routes in advance.

SACRAMENTO   The Jedediah Smith Memorial Bicycle Trail runs along the American River Parkway for 30 miles and is ideal for a family outing.

NORTHERN GOLD COUNTRY   Auburn State Recreation Area offers more than 100 miles of mountain bike trails. The two-mile **Stagecoach Trail** runs from Russell Road in Auburn to the old Foresthill Bridge on the north fork of the American River. The **Old Lake Clementine Road** meanders for nine miles along the American River. To ride past a creek through oak-and-pine-filled meadows, try the ten-mile **Olmsted Loop Trail.**

Roads came slowly to the northern Gold Country. Decades after the Gold Rush, many people lived in areas that could only be reached by single-track mountain trails impassable in wagons. Many such trails still exist around **Downieville**, making the little town a mountain bike mecca.

LAKE TAHOE AREA   When it comes to mountain biking, few places can beat the Sierra Nevada. Some of the best off-road trails are found in **Tahoe National Forest**. At the forest office you can pick up information on mountain biking trails throughout the region. ~ 631 Coyote Street, Nevada City; 530-265-4531, fax 530-478-6109; www.fs.fed.us/r5/tahoe, e-mail psexton@fs.fed.us.

Other trails in the area that are not in the national forest include the **Flume Trail** off Spooner Summit at the junction of Routes 50 and 28. It offers challenging rides of 10 to 30 miles. **Angora Lakes Trail** (12 miles) in the Fallen Leaf Lake area is another possibility.

Another good bet is **Kirkwood Ski Area** 30 miles south of Lake Tahoe. This resort offers a mountain biking program in the summer months. There are 50 miles of trails within the Kirkwood property. Spring wildflower and fall foliage trips are highly recommended. ~ Route 88, Kirkwood; 209-258-6000, 800-967-7500; www.kirkwood.com, e-mail info@skikirkwood.com. In addition, the resort provides easy access to hundreds of miles of trails in the **Eldorado National Forest**. The easy **Kirkwood Meadow Loop** (6 miles) is a good way to get acclimated. If you're in great shape and feeling ambitious take the grueling **Mr. Toad's**

Wild Ride off Luther Pass. This 35-mile trip runs from Hope Valley to the Tahoe basin. Alternatively, ride from Kirkwood to Hope Valley up Old Luther Pass Road to the Grass Lake area (40 miles). **Schneider Camp** (7 miles) is another enjoyable ride offering great views of Caples Lake. Remember, it takes a few days to adjust to the high altitude; also plan on drinking plenty of fluids.

YOSEMITE NATIONAL PARK There is a paved **loop trail** (8 miles), which circles the valley floor and takes you as far as Mirror Lake-Meadow.

Bike Rentals For bike rentals and information in Sacramento, contact **American River Bicycle Shop**. They rent hybrids and sell accessories. ~ 9203 Folsom Boulevard, Sacramento; 916-363-6271; www.americanriverbike.com.

For bike rentals, trailhead shuttles, and guided tours, contact **Yuba Expeditions**. ~ Route 49, Downieville; 530-289-3010; www. yubaexpeditions.com. Another local enterprise that offers rentals, shuttles, and organized group trips is **Downieville Outfitters**. ~ 208 Main Street, Downieville; 530-289-0155; www.downieville outfitters.com.

Mountain bikes are the speciality at **Cycle Path Mountain Bikes**. If you are interested in a tour ask about the custom-designed trips of the area. ~ 1785 West Lake Boulevard, Tahoe City; 530-581-1171. The **Tahoe Bike Shop** rents mountain bikes and cruisers. ~ 2277 Lake Tahoe Boulevard, Tahoe; 530-544-8060; www. tahoebikeandski.com.

At Yosemite National Park you can rent single-speed cruisers and Schwinns with trailers at **Curry Village**. ~ 209-372-8319; www.yosemitepark.com. There are similar rentals available at the **Yosemite Lodge Bike Stand**. ~ 209-372-1208.

HIKING

The Gold Country and High Sierra represent two of nature's most magnificent contributions to Northern California. In the old mining territory you'll find groves of giant sequoias to explore. Then in the High Sierra, Lake Tahoe and Yosemite National Park offer networks of trails and Desolation Wilderness provides

CUTTING THROUGH THE HEART

The **Pacific Crest Trail**, a 2600-mile path from Canada to Mexico, passes through the heart of the Gold Country and High Sierra. Traversing the Desolation Wilderness, it continues south to Yosemite, then follows the mountains past Mount Whitney into Southern California. While it's doubtful you'll be making the entire international trek, you might want to hike a short distance along this amazing trail.

the closest wilderness area to San Francisco. All distances listed are one way unless otherwise noted.

CENTRAL GOLD COUNTRY   Two trails wind through **Calaveras Big Trees State Park**'s ancient forest of giant sequoias. **North Grove Trail** (1 mile) is a gentle loop through a stand of sequoia, ponderosa, and sugar pine. Included along the way is **Three Senses Trail** (600 feet) where you can touch, smell, and hear the forest around you. **South Grove Trail** (3 miles), more remote and primitive, winds up Big Trees Creek past nearly 1000 giant sequoias.

NORTHERN GOLD COUNTRY   Though formerly the site of one of the world's largest hydraulic mining operations, **Malakoff Diggins State Historic Park** has been partially healed by nature. About 15 miles of trails lead past mining-era ruins, colorful pinnacles, minarets, and lakes created by the miners. **Blair Trail** (1.5 miles) is an easy hike on a tree-shaded path that ends at an old-time swimming hole. **Rim Trail** (3 miles), beginning at Shoot Hill Campground, leads to a vista point above the pond at the site of the diggings.

LAKE TAHOE AREA   Donner Summit offers **Summit Lake Trail** (2 miles), located off Route 80 near the Donner Summit rest stop. It is an easy hike to Summit Lake through a conifer forest and flowering meadows.

Sandridge Lake Trail (6 miles) begins on the Pacific Crest Trail near Donner Summit and carries through pine and fir forests. It passes two alpine meadows en route to a small lake.

Because of its easy accessibility, **Desolation Wilderness** is extremely popular with daytrippers and campers alike. The number of backpackers is therefore held to a quota from June 15 to Labor Day, and a wilderness permit is required year-round of all who enter (for further information, consult Chapter One).

Mt. Tallac via Gilmore Lake Trail (5.7 miles) starts near Glen Alpine Creek and ends at Mt. Tallac Summit. From the summit, you'll have one of the region's most dramatic views of Lake Tahoe.

Pacific Crest Trail to Lake Aloha (3 miles) begins with a ride in a water taxi operated by Echo Lake Resort (information, 530-659-7207). Closed Labor Day to Memorial Day. The trail, one of the most heavily traveled in Desolation Wilderness, leads to sparkling mountain lakes. (It's another three miles to the lake if you opt to bypass the water taxi.)

Meeks Bay Trail (7 miles) starts near Meeks Bay Resort and follows the northern part of lengthy Tahoe–Yosemite Trail to glimmering Rubicon Lake.

Bay View Trail to Velma Lake (5 miles) offers some stunning views of Lake Tahoe.

Glen Alpine to Lake Aloha Trail (5.8 miles) starts near Glen Alpine Spring, and winds up at Lake Aloha, the most popular lake in Desolation Valley.

Eagle Falls–Eagle Lake Trail (1 mile) begins at the Eagle Falls picnic area and traverses the cascade along a wooden footbridge. Then it crosses a blocky talus slope that offers beautiful views of the Tahoe Basin, and finally arrives at Eagle Lake.

Lake Tahoe has numerous hiking adventures. One of the most popular—and most trafficked—hike is the Five Lakes Trail (3 miles), which begins on Alpine Meadows Road off Route 89. This fairly steep trail goes past beautiful alpine scenery to a group of small, cold mountain lakes.

Shirley Lake Trail (2.5 miles) traverses spectacular Squaw Valley and passes stunning waterfalls. If you're so inclined, take the tram up and then hike down.

Rubicon–Emerald Point Trail (4.7 miles) passes Lake Tahoe's only lighthouse and offers wonderful views of Emerald Bay.

Loon Lake Trail (4.5 miles), beginning at Loon Lake Campground, is an easy hike through a wild area. The trail crosses seasonal creeks as well as fir and pine groves en route to Spider Lake.

YOSEMITE NATIONAL PARK   For information on hiking in Yosemite National Park, see "Trekking Yosemite" on page 502.

Transportation

CAR

The large section of the state covered in this chapter is serviced by numerous highways. From San Francisco, Route 80 travels northeast directly to Sacramento, then bisects the Gold Country, and continues into the High Sierra, passing within ten miles of Lake Tahoe's North Shore. The quickest way to the South Shore is via Route 50 from Sacramento. To reach Yosemite, follow the freeways leading east from San Francisco, then pick up either Route 120 or Route 140 into the park. The Gold Country can be toured along Route 49.

AIR

Several major airlines fly into Sacramento International Airport. These include Alaska Airlines, America West, American Airlines, Continental, Delta Air Lines, Horizon Air, Northwest Airlines, Southwest Airlines, and United Airlines. ~ www.sacairports.org.

Airlines with flights into Reno–Cannon International Airport include Alaska Airlines, America West, American Airlines, Continental, Delta Air Lines, Reno Air, Southwest Airlines, and United Airlines. ~ www.renoairport.com.

BUS

Greyhound Bus Lines provides service to Sacramento and Lake Tahoe. ~ 800-231-2222. ~ www.greyhound.com.

TRAIN

Train aficionados can climb aboard Amtrak for an excursion to Sacramento, Lake Tahoe, or Yosemite. From Oakland, the "Coast Starlight" provides service to Sacramento, while the "Zephyr" carries passengers to Truckee in the Tahoe area. ~ 800-872-7245; www.amtrak.com.

Those traveling to Yosemite from Oakland or Los Angeles can take Amtrak's "San Joaquin" to Merced, where **Yosemite Area Regional Transportation System (YARTS)** provides connecting bus service into Yosemite Valley. ~ 877-989-2787; www.yarts.com.

CAR RENTALS

The following agencies are at Sacramento International Airport: **Alamo Rent A Car** (800-462-5266), **Avis Rent A Car** (800-331-1212), **Budget Rent A Car** (800-527-0700), **Enterprise Rent A Car** (800-736-8222), **Hertz Rent A Car** (800-654-3131) and **National Rent A Car** ()800-227-7368). Other agencies offer airport pick-up service. Check the Yellow Pages for agencies in town.

PUBLIC TRANSIT

To get around Sacramento by bus, call **Sacramento Regional Transit**. ~ 916-321-2877; www.sacrt.com. **Tahoe Area Regional Transit,** or **TART**, services North Lake Tahoe and offers a shuttle service between Tahoe City and Truckee. ~ 530-550-1212; www.laketahoetransit.com. In South Lake Tahoe, **South Tahoe Area Ground Express**, or **STAGE**, provides transportation around the South Shore and from one end of Tahoe City to the other. ~ 530-542-6077. In Yosemite Valley, a free **shuttle bus** ferries folks between various points of interest. ~ 209-372-1240, fax 209-372-8443; www.yosemitepark.com.

TOURS

To travel between the south and north shores of Lake Tahoe in winter, try **Lake Tahoe Cruises.** ~ 530-541-3364. **North Tahoe Cruises** explores the west shore of the lake and Emerald Bay from mid-April through October. ~ 850 North Lake Boulevard, Tahoe City; , 800-218-2464; www.tahoegal.com.

EIGHT

Far North

California's best-kept secret is a sprawling, thinly populated area full of history and incredible natural beauty. Much of the sector's lush terrain is virtually untouched. Reaching from Redding to Oregon and from the Coast Range to Nevada, the Far North encompasses a huge swath of California. Siskiyou, Modoc, Shasta, and Lassen counties are part of this tumbling block of territory.

A wilderness of alpine lakes and granite heights, its mountains include the Klamath, Marble, Salmon, Trinity, and Warner ranges. Foremost is the Cascade Range, extending south from Washington and Oregon. Mt. Shasta, rising over 14,000 feet, is lord of the land, a white-domed figure brooding above a forested realm. Lassen Peak, its infernal cousin, is an active volcano that last erupted in 1921.

Sprinkled along the region's panoramic byways are tiny hamlets where traffic lights are nonexistent. Virtually every town with more than a gas station has a museum showcasing its early history, but the most revealing glimpses are in the countryside, where small farms keep in step with an ancient drummer.

The Far North represents "hidden California" in its truly pristine state. Thousands of lakes and rivers make it a paradise for whitewater rafting. Chinook run 50 pounds and the fishing is excellent for trout and bass as well. Most of the region is preserved in a series of national forests, making it a retreat for hikers and campers.

The wilderness here has given birth to all sorts of things—rare species, trophy fish, and big game animals. The most prized find of all may not even exist. For over a century, people have been sighting an elusive creature, kin perhaps to the abominable snowman, named Bigfoot. Said to range in height up to 14 feet, he weighs as much as 800 pounds. His skin is dark and tough as leather; hair covers his entire body. Bigfoot has a flat nose, short ears, human-like features, and walks with a ten-foot stride. He inhabits deep river valleys and thick forests, leaving huge footprints in the untrammeled wilderness.

In addition to a rich mythology, the countryside boasts a history that dates back millions of years when volcanic activity created the Cascade Range and other geologic forces formed neighboring mountains. Modoc, Paiute, Pit River, and Shoshone peoples originally inhabited the Far North, fishing its endless waterways and hunting the surrounding forests. The region was not opened to Europeans until 1817 when Captain Luis Arguello, a Spanish adventurer, probed the wilds. By the 1840s, American wagon trains were rolling through the territory. When gold was discovered around the end of the decade, prospectors began panning the rivers.

The original inhabitants, pushed from their lands by settlers and gold-seekers, struck back in the "Modoc War." During the tragic climax in 1873, the U.S. Army fought a pitched battle in the Lava Beds area against a group of Modocs led by Chief Kientpoos, also known as Captain Jack. "Nobody will ever want these rocks," the American Indian leader pleaded. "Give me a home here."

Except for a handful of descendants, the American Indians have disappeared, but cowboys continue to ride the range, thanks in part to a thriving cattle business. With ranches everywhere, particularly around Alturas, the Far North ranks as the largest beef-producing region in the state. Since practically any place that's not a granite mountain or alpine lake is covered with forest, the lumber industry is also an important factor in the economy.

Tourism reigns as the biggest source of local revenue. Despite a major chemical spill along the Sacramento River in 1991, the Far North remains a year-round vacation zone. The spill, which resulted from a train derailment north of Dunsmuir, was contained, though fishing is limited to catch and release between Lake Siskiyou and Scarlett Way and between Soda and Campbell creeks.

Everywhere else in the Far North aquatic enthusiasts arrive in ever-increasing numbers during the warm summer months and skiers pile in during the winter. Many facilities shut down during the cold season, and many roads are closed, so sightseers are advised to visit between late spring and early fall. Mid-summer brings large crowds, so if touring then, plan ahead, make reservations well in advance.

Regardless of the season, the Far North rarely disappoints the adventurous traveler. A land of giant dams and endless waterways, it is a wonderland for outdoor sports and a place of exquisite beauty.

Redding

▼▼▼▼▼▼▼▼▼▼▼▼

Route 5 runs like a spine through this rural region, moving north and south from Sacramento to Oregon. Redding, capital of the "Inland Empire," is the closest facsimile around to a buzzing metropolis. This town of 80,000 folks is also the major jumping-off point for sightseers.

From here, it's less than an hour along Route 299 to Whiskeytown, Shasta, and Trinity lakes, as well as the history-book towns of Shasta and French Gulch. Farther north on Route 5 are the ski slopes of Mt. Shasta and the antique town of Yreka. Route 44 leads from Redding to Lassen Volcanic National Park, and Route 395 winds into the far northeast corner of California.

SIGHTS

No matter where you plan to visit, you should contact the **Shasta-Cascade Wonderland Association**, which also serves as a California Welcome Center. The friendly staff here is knowledgeable and can provide you with a comprehensive visitors guide. Furthermore, a series of scenic byways surround Redding. Most range from one to four hours in length, making for pretty and interesting side-trips. Stop off at the association and pick up a free 48-page guide. ~ 1699 Route 273, Anderson; 530-365-7500, 800-474-2782, fax 530-365-1258; www.shastacascade.org, e-mail scwa@shastacascade.org.

All of Redding's major sightseeing attractions are clustered together at the **Turtle Bay Exploration Park** complex, an ongoing $47-million project set on both banks of the Sacramento River, linked by a footbridge. A general admission fee gives you access to all the sites on the grounds. At the heart of the complex is the **Turtle Bay Museum**, which features a multitude of interactive exhibits including computers, microscopes, and puzzles. Its art gallery has fascinating historical displays re-creating local pioneer and American Indian life as well as selected contemporary items. The museum also houses a natural science display. At the hourly animal discovery time, two or three injured animals

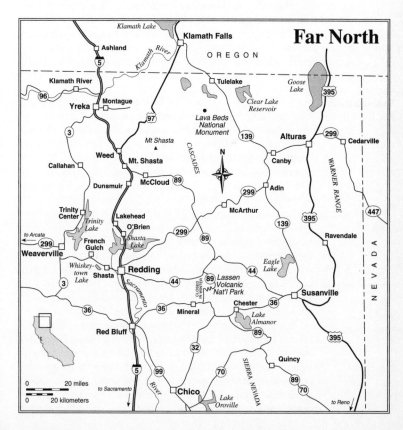

Far North

are brought out from their indoor cages for a show-and-tell session. Also check out the river aquarium with underwater fish viewing and the large ever-changing Exploration Hall.

A short jaunt north of the main complex is the **McConnell Arboretum.** Located along the Sacramento River, it provides acres of wildflowers and grass gardens. Visitors can walk or bike the nature trails where turtle ponds allow you to see the indigenous western pond turtles up close. The seasonal wetlands, streams, and oak woodland landscape this 200-acre preserve.

Paul Bunyan's Forest Camp, located just outside the museum, has a woodsy, pseudo-rustic play area for kids along the bank of the Sacramento River, as well as a life-size replica of a logging camp. Exhibits show how to identify trees and make forest crafts. A nature trail presents a cross-section of Northern California forests. Close by is the **Butterfly House,** which features about 1000 live butterflies inside a greenhouse filled with flowering plants.

The rest of the Turtle Bay Exploration Park is slated for completion in summer 2004. The new additions will include a sundial foot bridge, a wildlife center, and a nursery. Closed Monday in winter. ~ 840 Auditorium Drive, adjacent to the freeway entrance where routes 299 west and 44 east meet Route 5; 530-243-8850; www.turtlebay.org, e-mail info@turtlebay.org.

LODGING

For a last, luxurious taste of civilization before heading into the hills, try **La Quinta Inn.** This stylish establishment features positively huge rooms with plush wall-to-wall carpeting. The furnishings have a cherrywood finish with pastel upholstery and the decor is quite inviting. Despite the proximity to Route 5, this is an extremely quiet inn. ~ 2180 Hilltop Drive; 530-221-8200, 800-531-5900, fax 530-223-4727; www.laquinta.com, e-mail lq0192@laquinta.com. MODERATE.

On a bluff overlooking the Sacramento River, **Palisades Paradise Bed & Breakfast** is a contemporary inn. The spacious Sunset Suite, with its mix of contemporary and antique furnishings, features an outdoor spa and 50-foot long patio. The inn's other guest room, the "Cozy Retreat," offers queen-size beds and a muted color scheme. A continental breakfast is served daily. ~ 1200 Palisades Avenue; 530-223-5305, fax 530-223-1200; www.palisades paradise.com, e-mail bnbo1@jett.net. MODERATE TO DELUXE.

In a town where the lodging scene is dominated by chain motels and motor inns, a delightful exception is the **Tiffany House Bed & Breakfast Inn.** This late Victorian home in a residential area with a great view of distant Lassen Peak has three upstairs guest rooms, each with private bath, queen-size bed, and sitting area plus special touches like hand-crocheted bedspreads and embroidered pillowcases. There is also a separate cottage with a seven-foot spa tub and an antique laurel wreath iron bed. The parlor is furnished in Victorian-era antiques. There is also a music room with an upright piano and old-time sheet music; afterwards, you can plunge into the backyard pool. A full gourmet breakfast is served in the dining room or outdoors in the gazebo. ~ 1510 Barbara Road; 530-244-3225; www.sylvia.com/tiffany.htm, e-mail tiffanyhse@aol.com. MODERATE TO DELUXE.

Less lavish yet still quite comfortable, the **Best Western Hospitality House** is located in the heart of Redding's neon motel strip. Biggest and best of the bunch, it boasts 62 clean but sterile rooms. Amenities include color cable television in your room, and a swimming pool and spa on the grounds. ~ 532 North Market Street; 530-241-6464, 800-700-3019, fax 530-244-1998; www.reddinghh.com. MODERATE.

Bargain hunters take note: You'll find many inexpensive motels along this strip, each proudly displaying its nightly rates as part of a local price war. The local **Travelodge** features rooms with kitchenettes. ~ 540 North Market Street; 530-243-5291, 800-525-9055. BUDGET.

Just as economical is the **Economy Inn,** which features standard amenities. ~ 525 North Market Street; 530-246-9803, fax 530-244-5011. BUDGET.

DINING

It's tough to bust your budget while dining in Redding. With surroundings as pleasant as those at **Casa Ramos**, there's no reason to even stretch it. This restaurant is decorated with colorful posters, stained glass, and murals. And then there's the food—an extensive menu includes everything from a chile relleno, taco, and enchilada combination to huevos rancheros. ~ 460 North Market Street; 530-243-2493, fax 530-243-1065. BUDGET TO MODERATE.

It looks like a typical roadside restaurant, complete with flashing neon sign and naugahyde booths, but **Lim's Cafe** offers a large

- -

A REDDING REPAST

A special Redding restaurant is the **C. R. Gibbs American Grille**. Its bright, modern, wood-trimmed blue-and-white interior features an open exhibition kitchen that lets you watch as your meal is prepared and a central bar that offers a carefully selected assortment of California wines and microbrews as well as "the biggest selection of martinis around." The menu includes full dinner entrées such as Boston-style halibut filet and grilled ribeye steak, along with salads, sandwiches, pasta dishes, and a creative array of brick oven–baked pizzas. ~ 2300 Hilltop Drive; 530-221-2335, fax 530-221-2867; www.crgibbs.com, e-mail info@crgibbs.com. MODERATE TO DELUXE.

selection of Chinese and American dishes. The Asian dinners include a combo plate that consists of chicken noodle soup, pork chow mein, sweet and sour pork, and fried shrimp. For those with an American palate there are chicken dishes, sandwiches, and steaks. ~ 592 North Market Street; 530-241-9747. BUDGET TO MODERATE.

SHOPPING If you're in the market for locally produced arts and crafts, the **Turtle Bay Museum Store** has jewelry, handcrafted pottery, baskets, and wood crafts. Postcards and booklets describing the area's history are also available. ~ 840 Auditorium Drive; 530-243-8850; www.turtlebay.org, e-mail info@turtlebay.org.

Just south of Redding in Anderson lies **Prime Outlets**, with close to 50 stores offering a smorgasbord of clothing, accessories, housing items, and shoes. Retailers include Mikasa, Van Heusen, and The Gap. ~ 1699 Route 273, Anderson; 530-378-1000; www.primeoutlets.com.

▼▼▼▼▼▼▼▼▼▼▼▼▼▼▼

Redding to Weaverville

Rising up from the Central Valley the road from Redding to Weaverville leads west toward the gateway to one of Northern California's premier recreational destinations. While best known for water sports, this area is also the place to find old mining towns, historic commercial districts, and American Indian landmarks.

SIGHTS From Redding, Route 299 leads west for a few miles to the late, great gold mining outpost of **Shasta**. This brickfront ghost town was the region's "Queen City" back in the 1850s, producing over $100,000 in gold dust every week. A trail leads along a row of old ruins.

At **Shasta State Historic Park**, you'll find a restored county courthouse, American Indian artifacts, antique photos, Wanted posters, and paintings by early California artists. The old jail features holograms, and an 1880s mercantile store stands nearby. Admission. ~ Route 299W, Shasta; 530-243-8194, fax 530-225-2038.

Five miles farther west along Route 299 lies **Whiskeytown Lake**, one of California's best boating, fishing, camping, and swimming spots. With 36 miles of shoreline, green rolling hills, tiny wooded islands, and dense stands of ponderosa pine, it's a paradise for backcountry explorers.

HIDDEN ► The historic mining town of **French Gulch**, settled in 1849, is situated off Route 299 along Trinity Mountain Road. Once an important way station on the Old Oregon Pacific Trail, it's a place where time has refused to budge for the last 100 years. The townsfolk still take family walks down Main Street, paint their picket fences white, and rarely lock their bikes. Among the municipal heirlooms there is **St. Rose's Church**, a picturesque wood-frame structure.

From here, Route 299 winds past beautiful mountain vistas en route to **Weaverville**, a country-style Victorian town shaded by honey locusts. In addition to its small-town charm, Weaverville has a colorful past worth exploring.

At the **Jake Jackson Memorial Museum**, displays re-create the tragedy and romance of the Gold Rush days. There's a complete blacksmith's shop, as well as early mining tools (including a stamp mill used for obtaining gold from ore), archaic medical supplies, and a fascinating display of Chinese weapons, gowns, and money. From January through March, only open on Tuesday and Saturday afternoon; call for hours. ~ 508 Main Street, Weaverville; 530-623-5211.

LODGING

To complete the sense of old-time California, stay at the **Best Western Weaverville Victorian Inn**. The guest rooms of this 65-unit hotel are huge; 17 of them have hot tubs. There's a pool on the premises and you'll be within walking distance of the town's sights and outdoor activities. In addition, the place has an interesting old drugstore to poke around in, and an active Taoist temple. ~ 1709 Main Street West 299 West, Weaverville; 530-623-4432, fax 530-623-4264. MODERATE.

Tucked away in a woodsy corner, the **Red Hill Motel** delivers comfortable rooms and cabins. Most of the quaint accommodations feature knotty-pine walls and include color cable television, but the best deals are the individual cabins. Some of these include

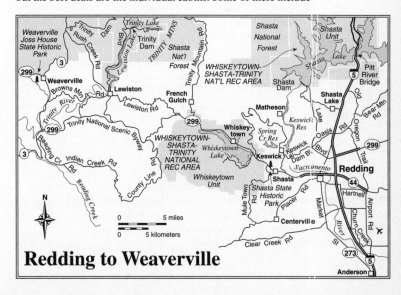

Redding to Weaverville

full kitchenettes, afford ample privacy, and cost a few dollars more. They also offer knockout views of the Trinity Alps through the pines. ~ Red Hill Road, Weaverville; 530-623-4331, fax 530-623-4341; www.redhillresorts.com, e-mail redhill@snow crest.net. BUDGET TO MODERATE.

DINING

Noelle's Garden Café sits on the upper part of a two-story flat and provides an excellent vantage point for studying the town's street life. Mornings, sample homefries, the breakfast burrito, or an omelette. At lunch, you'll find vegetarian sandwiches, quiche, gourmet salads, and cool fruit smoothies. On warm days, you can eat outdoors on the deck. Dinner served Wednesday through Saturday only. Call for winter hours. ~ Corner of Routes 299 and 3, Weaverville; 530-623-2058, fax 530-623-1123. BUDGET.

If there's a vegetarian in your midst, **Allan's Oak Pit Bar-B-Q** is probably not the place for you. The menu reads like a meat-lover's dictionary: sandwich options are barbecued steak, pork, beef, or chicken. Hamburgers are available with cheese, bacon, both, or, if you're watching your weight, just with fries. Closed Sunday. ~ 1324 Nugget Lane, Weaverville; 530-623-2182. BUDGET TO MODERATE.

SHOPPING

On Saturday evenings, locals head to the **Highland Art Center** for their monthly reception. The center, a non-profit established in the 1960s, sells locally made works of all types. Closed Sunday from January through April. ~ 503 Main Street, Weaverville; 530-623-5551. Behind the art center is the **Steve Hubble Studio**, a working art gallery where you can see the artist in action, painting mainly landscapes, with a few bronze sculptures for sale as well. His hours fit his fancy, so call ahead. ~ 410 Center Street, Weaverville; 530-623-3900.

A nice little shop, **Hays Bookstore** has a section devoted to local authors. They also have occasional book signings. ~ 106 Main Street, Weaverville; 530-623-2516, fax 530-623-2507.

AUTHOR FAVORITE

Weaverville Joss House State Historic Park, known as the "Temple Amongst the Forest Beneath the Clouds," has always appealed to me as one of the region's most unique places since it is here that Chinese Taoists have worshipped since 1874. Nestled in a grove of trees near a wooden footbridge, this temple is a tribute to the Chinese miners whose hard labor brought them neither riches nor acceptance in the Old West. Closed Monday and Tuesday. Admission. ~ Main and Oregon streets, Weaverville; phone/fax 530-623-5284.

Weaverville nightlife is scarce at best, but there's some entertain-   **NIGHTLIFE**
ment to be enjoyed at the **New York Saloon**. You don't visit the
1859 bar for dancing or karaoke—you go just to enjoy the sense
of a time gone by (and to play a little Ping-Pong). ~ 225 Main
Street, Weaverville; 530-623-3496.

The town's local theater troupe, the **Trinity Players**, quaintly
performs out of the Veteran's Memorial Hall. The season tends
towards the comedic and musical, although their Independence
Day production is usually a melodrama from the gold-digging
era. ~ 503 Main Street North, Weaverville; 530-623-8695, 800-
623-8695.

The best path between Weaverville and Yreka
is Route 3, a sinuous track plagued with fast-   # Weaverville to Yreka
moving lumberjacks on wheels, but offering
extraordinary mountain vistas. The old California-Oregon Wagon
Road, it parallels Trinity (Clair Engle) Lake and the Trinity Alps
on its 105-mile journey back to civilization at Yreka.

If you're feeling even more adventurous, you can travel west
from Weaverville on Route 299 into Humboldt County, connect
with Route 96, and head north into Salmon River country. This
winding roadway passes Six Rivers National Forest and ap-
proaches whitewater stretches of the mighty Klamath River. Slow
but scenic, it's the long way home to Yreka, doubling the distance
to 213 miles, and leading along poorly maintained roads.

If you opt for Route 3, watch for the Buckeye Creek Road turn-   **SIGHTS**
off about seven miles from Weaverville. Turn right and you'll discover some striking panoramas of **Trinity (Clair Engle) Lake**, a
16,500-acre expanse.

At **Scott Museum** you'll see displays representing the pioneer
days, everything from Indian baskets to snowshoes for horses. It
also boasts one of the country's largest collections of barbed wire—
nearly 500 different samples. Closed Sunday and Monday from
September through May. ~ Airport Road, Trinity Center.

To explore the **Trinity Alps Wilderness Area**, or for a closer
look at the mountains, go eight miles past Trinity Center and turn
left on Coffee Creek Road. It carries past waterfalls and rushing
rivers, through deep forest and dark canyons. Just past the North
Fork Coffee Creek Bridge lies the wilderness area, with its granite peaks and glacial lakes.

Back on Route 3, continue north into the placid Scott Valley
region. **Callahan**, once an important trade center, still sports boardwalks and 19th-century buildings along its one-block commercial
strip. Other small towns along the way—Etna, Greenview, and
Fort Jones—also feature antique buildings.

In **Yreka**, you'll find a reconstructed mining town, as well as hiking trails and a fishing lake in **Greenhorn Park**, located on Greenhorn Road.

At the **Siskiyou County Museum** are displays of American Indian artifacts, as well as exhibits on mining, the military, and Chinese pioneers. There are also vintage photographs, hand-colored panoramic images of Yreka and vicinity in the 1920s, and pioneer, logging, and Chinese exhibits. The Davis Cabin, part of this excellent facility, was built in 1856. Closed Sunday and Monday. Admission. ~ 910 South Main Street, Yreka; 530-842-3836, fax 530-842-3166; e-mail hismus@inreach.com.

Be sure to visit **Miner Street**, a timeworn commercial row where most of the buildings have been standing since the late 19th century, and explore the town's **Victorian home district** (bounded by 3rd, Oregon, Gold, and Lane streets). Some of the wealth that built these grand homes is displayed at the **Siskiyou County Court House**. Here, behind a glass case, rests a king's ransom in gold nuggets from neighboring mines. ~ 311 4th Street, Yreka.

Railroad fans won't want to miss diesel train rides from the 1910 **Yreka Depot**. The eight-mile trip heads up the Shasta Valley to Montague, where you'll have plenty of time for a picnic before returning south. Trains run Memorial Day through September. (Their steam locomotive, *The Blue Goose*, is undergoing extensive rebuilding and is scheduled for completion in late 2004.) Admission. ~ 300 East Miner Street, Yreka; 530-842-4146, 800-973-5277, fax 530-842-4148; www.yrekawesternrr.com.

LODGING
"A complete 90-acre vacation village on Trinity (Clair Engle) Lake" is the way **Wyntoon Resort** bills itself. This multifaceted enclave consists of 20 fully equipped cottages, a trailer park, 80 campsites, a marina with rental boats, supermarket, gas station, and more. Although the cabins don't have TV or phones, they have fully equipped kitchens and provide a good location for exploring the nearby Trinity Alps. The cottages house up to four people; there are two- and three-day minimums on weekends and holidays, respectively. ~ Route 3, Trinity Center; 530-266-3337, 800-715-3337, fax 530-266-3820; www.wyntoonresort.com, e-mail wyntoon@tds.net. MODERATE.

The **Historic Carrville Inn** is a gracious abode imbued with the glory of pure laziness: the swinging hammock beckons, the pool invites contemplative laps, and the veranda evokes images of napping with that book you've always meant to read. You can also wander out to the barn to visit the potbelly pig, llamas, and peacocks. Enjoy appetizers in the evening, then retire to the saloon to pound away on the dancehall piano or play a quiet game of checkers. The rooms are decorated in Victorian flare with ceiling fans and fresh flowers. ~ Carrville Loop Road, Trinity Center; 530-

Great Lakes of the Far North

Whiskeytown-Shasta-Trinity National Recreation Area, established by Congress in 1965, offers numerous recreational activities. With environments that vary from coniferous forest to mountain lake, hiking, horseback riding, swimming, and boating are just a few of the sports available here. Bear, mountain lion, raccoon, and deer are plentiful throughout the area and bald eagles and osprey are often spotted soaring in the sky. The recreation area, jointly administered by the National Park Service and the National Forest Service, consists of three large lakes north of Redding. ~ www.nps.gov/whis.

The main event at Whiskeytown Unit is **Whiskeytown Lake**, a 3220-acre body of water that's ideal for swimming, canoeing, and sailing. There are beaches at Brandy Creek and Oak Bottom; the fishing for bass, kokanee salmon, and brown and rainbow trout is good. There are picnic areas, restrooms, a summer hamburger stand at both beaches, an information center, and canoe rentals at Oak Bottom. Rangers often lead free educational programs; call for information. For campers, there are 37 free RV sites (no hookups) at Brandy Creek. Reservations are available at Oak Bottom (800-365-2267) which offers 42 RV sites and 100 tent sites; $14 to $18 per night. You'll also find seven primitive campgrounds (permit required). Day-use fee, $5. ~ Located along Route 299 around eight miles west of Redding; 530-246-1225, fax 530-246-5154; www.nps.gov/whis.

California's largest artificial lake, **Shasta Lake** boasts more than 372 miles of shoreline in Whiskeytown's Shasta Unit. The lake's water temperature in the summer months averages 76°, making it ideal for houseboating, swimming, windsurfing (although winds are tame), and waterskiing. Fishing is excellent year-round, with bass, trout, bluegill, and sturgeon among the most frequent catches. There are restrooms, picnic areas, and boat ramps; restaurants, groceries, boat rentals, and hotel facilities are located near the lake. Camping is permitted in several forest service campgrounds, including several reached only by boat; free to $26 per night depending on the campsite. ~ The lake is off Route 5 about ten miles north of Redding; 530-275-1587, fax 530-275-1512; www.r5.fs.fed.us/shastatrinity.

The Trinity (Clair Engle) Unit's centerpiece, **Trinity (Clair Engle) Lake** has 145 miles of shoreline and sits in the shadow of the Trinity Alps. Popular for swimming, waterskiing, and houseboating, it's also recommended for trout and smallmouth bass fishing. There are picnic areas and restrooms; restaurants, groceries, boat rentals, and hotel facilities are located near the lake. Some of the ten forest service campgrounds are located on a sandy beach at Clark Springs; $6 to $15 per night depending on the site. ~ The lake parallels Route 3 just a few miles north of Weaverville; 530-623-2121, fax 530-623-6010.

266-3511, fax 530-266-3778; www.carrvilleinn.com, e-mail info @carrvilleinn.com. DELUXE.

You won't find much in the way of exotic rentals up in Siskiyou County, but the 44-unit **Economy Inn** does have a few extras to make it stand out from the rest. Like exceptionally spotless rooms, color televisions, and a pool. The accommodations at this neon motel are comfortably but unimaginatively furnished. ~ 526 South Main Street, Yreka; 530-842-4404, fax 530-841-0439; e-mail previa@snowcrest.net. BUDGET.

If the Thunderbird is already booked, try the **Best Western Miner's Inn**. With 134 rooms (some are two-bedroom apartments with kitchenettes), it has two swimming pools and a free continental breakfast; a coffee shop is nearby. ~ 122 East Miner Street, Yreka; 530-842-4355, fax 530-842-4480. MODERATE.

DINING

Chinese dishes, teriyaki steak and seafood are the main attractions at **Ming's Restaurant and Lounge**. The menu offers crab legs, roast duck, and several different combination plates. ~ 210 West Miner Street, Yreka; 530-842-3888, fax 530-842-3889. BUDGET TO MODERATE.

SHOPPING

Antique stores are one of Yreka's strongest attractions. **James Place** is reputedly the largest single-owner shop of its type in the Pacific Northwest, and has been doing business since 1971. Here you'll find vintage clothing, quilts, miniatures, and folk art. There's also a large variety of antique toys, including dolls, stuffed bears, and carousel animals. Closed Sunday. ~ 216 3rd Street, Yreka; 530-842-5454.

PARKS

SHASTA-TRINITY NATIONAL FOREST Shasta and Trinity (Clair Engle) lakes are just two of the 131 lakes found in this seemingly unending paradise. It's visited by more than five million people each year, but there's still plenty of room to spare within the forest's 2,159,001 acres. About 3100 miles of hiking trails, including part of the Pacific Crest Trail, wind through the forest. Towering Mt. Shasta, the region's most

VEGGIE DELIGHTS

Nature's Kitchen will be a welcome sight for vegetarians. Breakfast means an assortment of baked goods and coffee. Lunch brings a menu of salads, cold and hot sandwiches, and a delicious veggie chiliburger. Desserts are made with local honey and organic wheat flour. No dinner. Closed Sunday. ~ 412 South Main Street, Yreka; 530-842-1136; www.yreka-natural-foods. com, e-mail hotek@snownet.net. BUDGET.

prominent peak, overlooks nearly 2000 miles of tributaries and streams. Wildlife includes bald eagles, ospreys, great blue herons, black bears, mule deer, striped skunks, gray fox, and golden-mantled squirrels. There are numerous visitors centers, restrooms, and picnic areas throughout the forest. ~ The forest is northeast, south, and west of Redding. Principal access is from Routes 3, 5, 89, and 299. For Whiskeytown, Shasta, and Trinity (Clair Engle) lakes, and for Trinity Alps Wilderness Area and Mt. Shasta, see listings below. Forest headquarters is located at 2400 Washington Avenue, Redding; 530-244-2978, fax 530-242-2233; www. r5.fs.fed.us/shastatrinity.

▲ There are more than 100 campgrounds; $6 to $14 per night. Some free campsites (without facilities) are scattered throughout the forest, and with a wilderness permit and a campfire permit you can camp anywhere in the forest.

TRINITY ALPS WILDERNESS AREA A high, sharp mountain range, the Trinity Alps vault from glacial canyons to 9000-foot heights. In addition to startling granite peaks, the region contains alpine lakes, pristine streams, and giant talus boulders. There are no facilities here. A wilderness permit is required, as is a free campfire permit. ~ Located 48 miles west of Redding, the area is accessible from Routes 299 and 3; 530-623-2121, 530-623-6106, fax 530-623-6010.

▲ Permitted for backpacking campers; no fee. Motorized vehicles are not allowed within the wilderness area.

SIX RIVERS NATIONAL FOREST Stretching from the Oregon border almost into Mendocino County, this 980,285-acre playground is the home of six major waterways—the Smith, Klamath, Trinity, Mad, Van Duzen, and Eel rivers. Although there are 251 miles of hiking trails, fishing is the most popular sport, followed by river rafting. There are picnic areas and restrooms. ~ Extending 140 miles along the western perimeter of the Far North, this facility is accessible from Routes 101 (via Routes 36, 299, and 199); 707-442-1721, fax 707-442-9242; www.r5.fs.fed.us/sixrivers.

▲ Permitted in 13 specified campgrounds and in other areas throughout the forest; $8 to $15 per night; group sites are extra. A cabin is available from June to October at Smith River; $75 for up to 8 people. Fire permits are required for fires outside of developed areas. For more information call any of the national forest's ranger districts: Smith River National Recreation Area (Gasquet; 707-457-3131), Orleans Ranger District (Orleans; 530-627-3291), Lower Trinity Ranger District (Willow Creek; 530-629-2118), or Mad River Ranger District (Mad River; 707-574-6233). Reservations are available at Snake River; all other campgrounds are first-come, first-served. ~ 877-444-6777.

▼ ▼ ▼ ▼ ▼ ▼ ▼ ▼ ▼ ▼ ▼ ▼ ▼ ▼

Redding to Mt. Shasta

A cross between Valhalla and Shangri-la, Mt. Shasta is the quintessential Cascade mountain backdrop. Driving north from Redding toward this volcanic peak, you'll pass manmade and natural attractions alike before ascending this magic mountain.

SIGHTS

Due north along Route 5, you'll encounter **Shasta Lake**, an extremely popular recreation area that is a paradise for naturalists and statisticians alike. Why the strange combination of interests? Because Shasta Lake, with its 365-mile shoreline and 30,000-acre expanse, is the largest manmade lake in the state. Its four arms stretch into the Sacramento, McCloud, and Pit rivers, as well as Squaw Creek. It boasts 17 types of game fish, a colony of houseboats, hiking trails, and every other possible outdoor diversion imaginable.

Then there's **Shasta Dam**, located along Shasta Dam Boulevard five miles west of Route 5. Three times taller than Niagara Falls, it measures 602 feet, making it the second highest dam in the United States. Nearly seven years labor and six and a half million cubic yards of concrete went into its completion. If those superlatives are insufficient, continue north on Route 5 a few miles and you'll cross **Pit River Bridge**, the world's highest double-deck bridge.

From the nearby town of **O'Brien** (population 2), you can visit **Lake Shasta Caverns**. Guides will take you on a 15-minute ride across the lake by boat, then along a picturesque road by bus, to this mazework of limestone caves. Within are strangely shaped stalactites and awesome stalagmites, dating back perhaps 250 million years. This natural statuary comes in the form of spires and minarets, stone curtains and Disneyesque figures. Within these tunnels, the temperature is always 58° with 95 percent humidity. Admission. ~ 20359 Shasta Caverns Road, O'Brien; 530-238-2341, 800-795-2283, fax 530-238-2386; www.lakeshastacaverns. com, e-mail shascav@aol.com.

Castle Crags State Park, farther north along Route 5 in Castella, is a land of granite domes and startling landscapes. From vista points, you can gaze out upon the Cascade Range. ~ Off of Castle Creek Road, Castella; 530-235-2684.

Foremost among these majestic peaks is awesome **Mount Shasta**, a 14,162-foot giant that carries five glaciers along its flanks. Dominating the skyline, it consists of two volcanic cones and features alpine lakes, flower-choked meadows, and deep forests. For a closer look at this sacred mountain, follow Route A10 through Mt. Shasta Recreation Area. The road winds to an elevation of 6800 feet and offers a different view at every hairpin turn.

In the shadow of Mount Shasta along Route 89 sits **McCloud**, one of California's most picturesque villages. A lumber center established in 1897, McCloud was a company town until the mid-

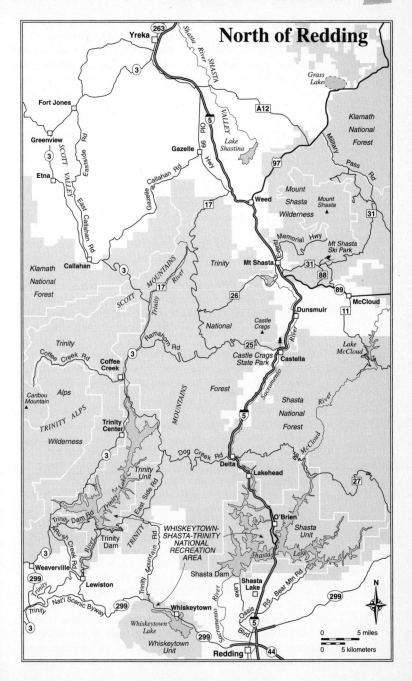

North of Redding

1960s. It still maintains much of its original architecture as well as its economic base of logging and tourism. In the winter, it's a mecca for skiers, while in the summer Dance Country calls square dancers from around the nation who do-si-do most evenings in McCloud's historic dance hall. The **McCloud Chamber of Commerce** doesn't have an office, but you can write them and request information. ~ P.O. Box 372, McCloud, CA 96057; 530-964-3113.

LODGING Idyllically situated in the Sacramento Arm of Shasta Lake, **Tsasdi Resort** is the perfect place to get away from it all without leaving all the conveniences behind. It offers 20 cabins that come complete with kitchens, patio decks, picnic tables, and barbecues. Fairly plush by rustic standards, they have knotty-pine interiors and sit in a black-oak forest overlooking Shasta Lake. The facilities also include a heated swimming pool, private dock, recreation room, and small convenience store. During the summer, cabins rent by the week only. ~ 19990 Lakeshore Drive, Lakehead; 530-238-2575, 800-995-0291, fax 530-238-8660; www.tsasdiresort.com, e-mail tsasdi@snowcrest.net. DELUXE TO ULTRA-DELUXE.

Neighboring **Antlers Resort** rents both houseboats and cabins. Many folks claim the only way to experience Shasta Lake is by houseboat, but the thrill doesn't come cheap. Prices for the smallest seagoing accommodations *start* in the ultra-deluxe range, with a three-day minimum. You can make the costs quite reasonable by bringing along a few friends. The comforts of home include a complete kitchen, bathroom, and TV with VCR or DVD. Landlubbers may find the housekeeping cabins more to their liking, with rates starting lower than the houseboats. Rustic but well appointed, half have wood stoves and all include open porches. These are among the most comfortable cabins on the lake (seven-night minimum during the summer). ~ Antlers Road at Shasta Lake, Lakehead; 530-238-2553, 800-238-3924, fax 530-238-2340; www.shastalakevacations.com, e-mail antlers@shastalake vacations.com. DELUXE TO ULTRA-DELUXE.

Farther south is **Holiday Flotels**, a houseboat haven. The houseboats are well maintained and come complete with kitchen, barbecue, and stereo system. All you need to add is food, linens, pillows, and gasoline. Each of the four available houseboats sleeps 10 to 14 people. There's a four-day minimum off-season and a one-week minimum from early June until early September. Closed October through April. ~ Packers Bay Marina at Shasta Lake; phone/fax 530-275-5570, 800-331-3137; www.packersbay.com, e-mail info@packersbay.com. ULTRA-DELUXE.

Town living is combined with a touch of rusticity at **Bavaria Lodge**. Here eight log cabins sit along the edge of town. Nothing fancy, mind you; each is decorated with a few paintings along raw-wood walls and all but two are equipped with a fully stocked kitchenette. The entire complex is nestled in the trees. ~ 4601 Dunsmuir Road, Dunsmuir; phone/fax 530-235-4707; www. bavarialodge.bizonthe.net, e-mail bavarialodge@snowcrest.net. BUDGET TO MODERATE.

Since the town of Mount Shasta doesn't offer much in the way of nightlife, it's important to pick a hotel that features more than just a bed and hot shower. **Mountain Air Lodge** covers more than the basics and does so with flair. There is one jacuzzi, a community kitchen, and a recreation room. The suites themselves are spacious, carpeted, and decorated with attractive wood furnishings. Family units with kitchens are available. ~ 1121 South Mount Shasta Boulevard, Mount Shasta; 530-926-3411, 800-727-3704, fax 530-926-0842. MODERATE.

A two-story Bavarian-style lodge, the **Alpenrose Cottage Guest House** is an ideal retreat. Panoramic views of Mount Shasta and proximity to skiing, hiking, rafting, and cycling make this retreat a great vacation base. A lovely deck makes for great lounging. There's a complete kitchen, a charming garden and TV room. Reservations are recommended—there's only two rooms offered. Free laundry facilities. No credit cards. ~ 204 East Hinckley Street, Mount Shasta; 530-926-6724, fax 530-926-6343. MODERATE.

A registered National Historic Landmark dating to 1916, the **McCloud Hotel** was, in its former incarnation, a 93-room rooming house for single lodgers and the town's teachers. Condemned in 1982, it emerged in 1995 as a 16-room B&B, after a total renovation. Each room is unique and individually designed; some have four-poster beds. In many rooms, the upholstery of the couches and chairs matches the wallpaper and curtains. Breakfast is served in the lobby sitting room or, if you're staying in a suite, brought to the guests' room. ~ 408 Main Street, McCloud; 530-964-2822, 800-964-2823, fax 530-964-2844; www.mccloudhotel.com, e-mail mchotel@snowcrest.net. MODERATE TO ULTRA-DELUXE.

AUTHOR FAVORITE

I've slept in all kinds of places, from tents to palaces, but I've rarely spent the night in accommodations as unique as one of the converted cabooses at the **Railroad Park Caboose Motel**. Part of the Railroad Park Resort, this historic hostelry features 23 cabooses, each transformed into a sleeping unit. The facility also offers four cabins, two with kitchens. The adjacent restaurant is housed in old railroad cars. Amenities at the resort include a swimming pool and jacuzzi. ~ 100 Railroad Park Road, Dunsmuir; 530-235-4440, fax 530-235-4470; www.rrpark.com. MODERATE.

DINING   For an incredible view of 4000-foot granite spires and a nostalgic trip back to the time when the railroad was king, climb aboard the **Railroad Park Restaurant and Lounge**. You'll discover two restored dining cars—decorated with antique hand tools, steam gauges, and plush pile carpeting—which brilliantly re-create the romance of the rails. The dinners include chicken dishes, seafood entrées, or prime rib dinners. Dinner only. Closed January to mid-March. ~ 100 Railroad Park Road, Dunsmuir; 530-235-4611, 800-974-7245, fax 530-235-4470; www.rrpark.com. MODERATE.

"Welcome back to homemade food—eat and enjoy" is the rule at **Michael's**. This downtown restaurant offers seafood, pasta, sandwiches, and a long list of wine and beers. At lunchtime, try the Rancho-burger, while pasta alfredo, linguine with white clam sauce, Russian ravioli, and prime rib top the dinner listings. A large window provides a breathtaking view of Mt. Shasta from the dining room. Closed Sunday and Monday. ~ 313 North Mount Shasta Boulevard, Mount Shasta; 530-926-5288, fax 530-926-5288; e-mail michaelsinc@snowcrest.net. MODERATE TO ULTRA-DELUXE.

You can shoot some pool or try your hand at pinball while waiting for your order at **Say Cheese Pizza**. At this sports-theme pizza parlor, pictures of sports stars decorate the walls. Pizza and sandwiches dominate the menu, and there's a great salad bar. ~ 304 Maple Street, Mount Shasta; 530-926-2821. BUDGET TO MODERATE.

The **Black Bear Diner** has taken the diner one step further with a themed restaurant specializing in bears. Pictures of black bears and old-time shots of Mt. Shasta decorate the walls, and you can chow down on sandwiches and burgers with names like Papa Bear. Just in case you're interested, the Papa Bear is a half-pound of ground beef on a grilled French roll with Swiss cheese, bacon, tomato, and lettuce, with a mountain of fries on the side. ~ 401

WHERE THE CONDUCTOR RINGS A DINNER BELL

For a different sort of dining experience, hop aboard the **Shasta Sunset Dinner Train**, which operates three-hour-long dinner runs. The mahogany-paneled dining cars with their antique brass lamps and luxurious upholstery harken back to the glory days of travel. The four-course dinner is pricey but an experience you'll never forget. During the summer months, theme nights like winetasting to murder mysteries are featured. If you can't afford it, there are open-air excursions through September that cover the same route. Trains run Saturday. They also operate Friday, May through October, and Thursday, June through September. ~ 328 Main Street, McCloud; 530-964-2142, 800-733-2141; www.shastasunset.com, e-mail info@shastasunset.com. ULTRA-DELUXE.

West Lake Street, Mount Shasta; 530-926-4669; www.blackbear diner.com, e-mail bbeardiner@yahoo.com. BUDGET TO MODERATE.

Past the picket fence, flower trellis, and leaded-glass doors of **Lily's Restaurant**, you'll discover a huge, filling breakfast (try the salmon omelette). For lunch and dinner, they have lots of vegetarian options, from an eggplant hoagie to veggie burgers. They also serve charbroiled hamburgers and a delicious shrimp and crab sandwich. Thai dishes, Mexican staples, even Italian influences are represented here. ~ 1013 South Mount Shasta Boulevard, Mount Shasta; 530-926-3372; www.lilysrestaurant.com, e-mail lilys@lilys restaurant.com. MODERATE.

The elegant dining room at **Serge's Restaurant** belies the reasonable prices. The menu is a blend of influences, with choices such as pork chop Normandy in an apple brandy sauce and Thai curry chicken. There's a cozy fire on weekends when the weather gets chilly; in warmer seasons, you can dine on the pretty patio. Dinner only. Closed Monday and Tuesday. ~ 531 Chestnut Street, Mount Shasta; 530-926-1276. MODERATE TO DELUXE.

Part of a 50-chalet exclusive resort, **The Mount Shasta Resort Restaurant** offers stunning vistas of Mt. Shasta and the golf course amidst a wine-colored atmosphere of teal green carpets and burgundy tabletops. The chef creates an array of pasta, chicken, beef, pork, lamb, seafood, and vegetarian entrées that include shrimp and scallop sauté pasta, chicken marsala, shrimp scampi, and châteaubriand. ~ 1000 Siskiyou Lake Boulevard, Mount Shasta; 530-926-3030, 800-958-3363; www.mountshastaresort.com, e-mail info@mountshastaresort.com. MODERATE TO ULTRA-DELUXE.

Raymond's Italian Ristorante can be found in a historic building at the upper end of McCloud's Main Street. The decor is simple—polished wooden walls and tables with Italian print table cloths—but the food is considered the best in town. Fettuccini alfredo, scampi, gnocchi, homemade beef and chicken ravioli, and other Italian favorites are the specialties here. There's a full bar. Dinner only. Closed Monday and Tuesday. ~ 424 Main Street, McCloud; 530-964-2099; www.raymondsitalian.com, e-mail info@raymondsitalian.com. BUDGET TO DELUXE.

Enchanted Forest Porcelain Doll Factory sells beautiful dolls in a beautiful shop in the same building where they are made. The workshop ships its porcelain dolls to collectors all over the world. Even if you have no intention to buy, this place is worth a look. Closed Sunday and Monday. ~ 4100 Pine Street, Dunsmuir; 530-235-0441; www.snowcrest.net/enchantedforest, e-mail enchanted forest@snowcrest.net.

SHOPPING

Village Books specializes in books on the Mount Shasta region and works by local authors. ~ 320 North Mount Shasta Boulevard, Mount Shasta; 530-926-1678.

Even if you're not planning to take a run down the nearby slopes, **The Fifth Season** warrants a walk-through. This sports trading post provides ski equipment, mountaineering and bicycling gear, and a complete line of all-weather clothing. ~ 300 North Mount Shasta Boulevard, Mount Shasta; 530-926-3606, fax 530-926-1337; www.thefifthseason.com.

HIDDEN ►

The **Golden Bough Bookstore** caters to the many spiritual seekers who look to nearby Mt. Shasta for magical power. For books about local folklore, or for a dash of friendly conversation, drop by. ~ 219 North Mount Shasta Boulevard, Mount Shasta; 530-926-3228, 877-674-7282; www.goldenboughbooks.com, e-mail goldenbough@jps.net.

The Gallery is a large gallery space full of prints and paintings, jewelry, and wall hangings by local artists and American Indians. ~ 201 North Mount Shasta Boulevard, Mount Shasta; 530-926-2334.

NIGHTLIFE

HIDDEN ►

Evenings tend to be quiet in the Mount Shasta region, but there is nightlife if you look for it, at least on some nights. At the **McCloud River Lodge**, the atmosphere is rustic. Deer trophies and carved wooden plaques decorate the walls. Old-fashioned tools hang from the ceiling beams and cattle brands are burned into the posts. In the winter, customers are warmed by a wood-burning stove in the center, and in the summer there's a grassy lawn with picnic tables in the back. There's live music—bluegrass, blues, rock and country—on Saturday evenings and line dancing on Wednesday. If that's not to your liking, play a game of pool or darts instead. ~ 140 Squaw Valley Road, McCloud; 530-964-2700; www.mccloud lodge.com, e-mail thelodge@snowcrest.net.

PARKS

CASTLE CRAGS STATE PARK 🏃 🛶 🛶 They might look like the work of an avant-garde sculptor, but the granite spires highlighting this 4000-acre facility were created more than 200 million years ago. In addition to the hiking on these 4000-foot statues, the park features rafting along the Sacramento River. The park has picnic areas, restrooms, and showers. Day-use fee, $6 per ve-

NATURAL BOUNTY

Outside Susanville, a 28-mile (roundtrip) detour on County Road A1 leads to **Eagle Lake**, one of the state's biggest natural lakes. The high alkaline content of this 22,000-acre body of water has created an environment that supports an incredible variety of animal life. In addition to the native Eagle Lake trout, there are antelope, porcupine, deer, white pelicans, and a rare species of osprey along its shores.

hicle. ~ Located six miles south of Dunsmuir, just west of Route 5 in Castella; 530-235-2684.

▲ There are 76 tent sites and 10 RV sites (no hookups); $17 per night.

MT. SHASTA RECREATIONAL AREA Dominated by 14,162-foot Mt. Shasta, this facility is favored by sightseers and climbers alike. Here you can explore living glaciers, whitewater canyons, and pristine lakes. A county road rises to 7800-feet elevation and hiking trails crisscross the mountain. Facilities include picnic areas and restrooms. ~ Located about 55 miles north of Redding off Route 5; turn east on Everitt Memorial Highway (Route A10); 530-926-4511, fax 530-926-5120; www.r5.fs.fed.us/shastatrinity.

▲ There are six campgrounds, including two on the south side of the mountain; $8 to $12 per night.

KLAMATH NATIONAL FOREST Fishing and river rafting are popular sports in this remote park. Covering parts of five different mountain ranges, it extends from Oregon across most of Siskiyou County. The Klamath, Scott, and Salmon rivers are explored here by many commercial outfitters, while fishing lodges have sprouted up near Happy Camp. Motorized boats are prohibited. Also within the forest is **Marble Mountain Wilderness Area**, a 213,363-acre preserve crowded with wildlife and sport fish. There are picnic areas and restrooms at the trailheads. ~ Accessible along Routes 96 and 97; 530-842-6131, fax 530-841-4571; www.r5.fs.fed.us/klamath.

▲ There are 34 campgrounds with 377 sites; free to $15 per night. For more information contact any of the four ranger districts: Happy Camp (Happy Camp; 530-493-2243), Scott River (Fort Jones; 530-468-5351), Salmon River (Fort Jones; 530-468-5351), or Goosenest (Macdoel; 530-398-4391).

▼▼▼▼▼▼▼▼▼▼▼▼

Northeast Loop

The best way to explore California's hidden northeastern corner is along a 400-plus mile odyssey from Redding. Heading east to Lassen Peak and beyond, it will carry you past mountain lakes and one-street towns. Then turning north, you'll skirt the Warner Mountains, detour to Lava Beds National Monument, and return to Redding via lonely Route 299.

SIGHTS

First stop on this wilderness expedition is **Lassen Volcanic National Park**, located about 50 miles from Redding off Route 44. Lassen Peak, a 10,457-foot volcano, is the highlight and highpoint of this extraordinary region. This is part of the same mountain chain that brought you the Mt. St. Helens catastrophe. Lassen's last eruptions were between 1914 and 1921. Spewing fumes and ash 20,000 feet in the air, one explosion tore away an entire side of the mountain and flicked 20-ton boulders down the hillside. Today it's still a semi-active volcano, and the surrounding area is filled with steam vents, mud pots, and moonscape features.

The Lassen Peak Park Road curves along three sides of the volcano, reaching an elevation of 8512 feet. Along this magnificent roadway are startling views of Lassen Peak, which still reveals scars from its furious eruptions. Also be sure to see **Bumpass Hell**, near the southern park boundary; it's a roaring region of boiling springs, mud pots, and pools colored gold and turquoise. (Although this 106,000-acre park is open year-round, the Lassen Peak Park Road is closed from the end of October until mid-June. If you're traveling during the ski season, consider taking Route 36 east from Red Bluff to the park's southwest entrance.) ~ 530-595-4444, fax 530-595-3262; www.nps.gov/lavo, e-mail lavo_information@nps.gov.

From Lassen, Route 36 heads east to **Lake Almanor**, a crystal blue expanse which mirrors the surrounding mountains. Measuring 52 square miles and bounded by evergreen forests, it's a prime place for swimming, boating, and waterskiing. Among the sport fish here are brown and rainbow trout as well as bass. Over 50 other lakes dot this pristine region and 500 miles of streams tumble through the area.

There are restaurants and lodgings in Chester, Susanville, and other small towns along the way. The **Lassen County Chamber of Commerce** can help you get your bearings in this sparsely populated region. Closed Saturday and Sunday. ~ 84 North Lassen Street, Susanville; 530-257-4323, fax 530-251-2561; www.lassencountychamber.org, e-mail info@lassencountychamber.org.

Leading into the state's vast, empty northeastern corner, Route 395 proceeds north through high desert country. Sage brush hills and whistling winds are your sole companions. You'll pass **Standish** (population 100), **Litchfield** (population 65), **Termo** (population 50), and **Madeline** (population 100) en route to the grand metropolis of **Alturas** (population 2600).

If you're interested in American folklore, be sure to take a detour to the tiny historic logging town of **Westwood**, where Paul Bunyan became a folk hero. Although the legend of Paul Bunyan had been told for generations in the lumber camps of the northeastern U.S., he was unknown outside the logging community. In 1913, the Walker family moved their mill from Minnesota to the northern Sierras, where they created the town of Westwood.

The Walkers hired W. B. Laughead to promote the new town and their company's Paul Bunyan Pine products by writing a series of small books on the exploits of Paul Bunyan and his blue ox Babe between the years of 1914 to 1944. Today, the mill is gone, but

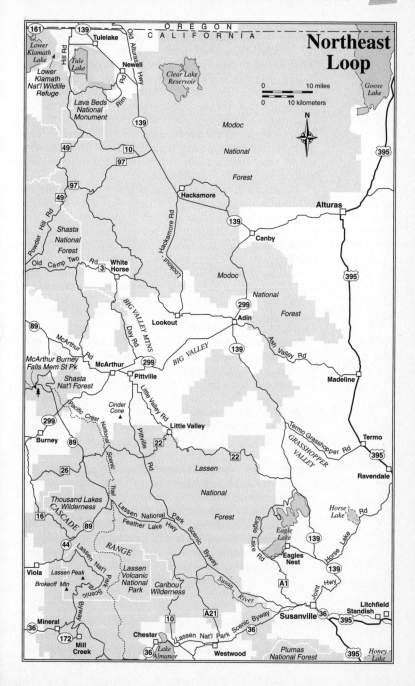

Northeast Loop

OREGON
CALIFORNIA

Lower Klamath Lake

Lower Klamath Nat'l Wildlife Refuge

Tulelake

Newell

Tule Lake

Clear Lake Reservoir

Goose Lake

0   10 miles
0   10 kilometers

N

Lava Beds National Monument

Modoc

National

Forest

Hackamore

Alturas

Shasta National Forest

White Horse

Canby

Modoc

National

Forest

Big Valley Mtns

Lookout

Adin

Madeline

McArthur Burney Falls Mem St Pk

Shasta Nat'l Forest

McArthur

Pittville

Cinder Cone

Little Valley

Termo Grasshopper Rd

Termo

Burney

Grasshopper Valley

Ravendale

Thousand Lakes Wilderness

Lassen

National

Forest

Horse Lake

Eagle Lake

CASCADE

Lassen National Park Scenic Byway

Feather Lake

RANGE

Lassen Nat'l Park Scenic Byway

Viola

Lassen Peak

Brokeoff Mtn

Lassen Volcanic National Park

Caribou Wilderness

Susan River

Eagles Nest

Litchfield

Standish

Mineral

Mill Creek

Chester

Lake Almanor

Westwood

Susanville

Plumas National Forest

Honey Lake

Paul Bunyan lives on in the annals of American folklore, and a giant statue of Paul and Babe stands guard at the edge of town.

The **Modoc County Museum** has an extensive collection of Paiute and Pit artifacts and the counter from a turn-of-the-20th-century general store with its inventory of corsets, high button shoes, and other period pieces. There's also an entire wall of weaponry, a rock and gem collection, and an intriguing exhibit on the region's bird life. Another display tells the story of Fort Bidwell, the pioneer military headquarters for this region. Here you'll learn about California's last Indian battle. Closed Sunday and Monday, and from November through May. ~ 600 South Main Street, Alturas; 530-233-6328.

The **Alturas Chamber of Commerce** can provide information and direct you to local attractions. Closed weekends. ~ 522 South Main Street, Alturas; phone/fax 530-233-4434; www.alturascham ber.homestead.com. One recommended stop is **Lava Beds National Monument**. This amazing park is a land of cinder cones, craters, and 30,000-year-old lava flows. It also features one of the world's finest series of lava tube caves, many open to exploration (the total number is over 500 caves). Once occupied by the Modoc people, this volcanic area contains numerous petroglyphs and pictographs. ~ Along Routes 299 and 139; 530-667-2282, fax 530-667-2737; www.nps.gov/labe.

HIDDEN ►   Nearby **Klamath Basin National Wildlife Refuge** is a migration point for one of the greatest concentrations of waterfowl on the continent. Together with neighboring areas, it draws two million birds during the spring and fall, including mallards, pintails, and snow geese. Vehicle fee for certain areas, $3. ~ Tulelake, off Route 139; head five miles west on East-West Road, then a half-mile south on Hill Road; 530-667-2231, fax 530-667-3299; www. klamathnwr.org.

From this remote preserve you can return to civilization, following Route 139 and then Route 299 as it cuts an alpine path back to Redding. Before leaving the wilderness entirely, stop at **McArthur–Burney Falls Memorial State Park**. Located midway between Mount Shasta and Lassen Park, it features a spectacular waterfall, fed by springs, which cascades over a 129-foot cliff. Ornamented with rainbows and an emerald pool, this fall was reputedly deemed the eighth wonder of the world by President Theodore Roosevelt. It's a fitting climax to this long, lonely loop into California's most secluded realm. ~ 530-335-2777, fax 530-335-5483.

LODGING   Modern amenities can be found at the **Lassen Mineral Lodge**, although it was established in 1896. Here the rooms are conventionally styled with wall-to-wall carpeting, some with wood paneling. Rooms with kitchenettes are available, as are RV and tent sites. A restaurant, general store, and ski shop are also on the grounds. ~ Route 36 East, Mineral; 530-595-4422, fax 530-595-4452; www.lassenminerallodge.com. MODERATE TO DELUXE.

Tucked between Mount Lassen and Lake Almanor you'll find **Cedar Lodge**. More of a motel than rural lodge, its cedar walls surround rather bland furnishings—second-hand-store bedroom sets—but in such technicolor territory, your eyes probably need a rest. The rooms that come equipped with kitchenettes offer a lot of space. ~ Junction of Routes 36 and 89, Chester; 530-258-2904. BUDGET.

For a true sense of life on the plains, you can rent a 19th-century homestead at Spanish Springs in Ravendale.

Farther east, set among towering pines, is the **Timber House Lodge**. Rooms here are plain but comfortable, with large beds, shower-tub combinations, color televisions, and wood furnishings. There's also a restaurant. ~ Route 36 and 1st Street, Chester; 530-258-2989. BUDGET.

Drakesbad Guest Ranch looks like it hasn't changed for generations. This resort, with its rustic wood-paneled rooms and hardwood floors adorned by braided rugs, sits at the end of a gravel road within Lassen National Park. The cabins are lit by kerosene lanterns and the pool warmed by thermal hot springs. Guests enjoy simple pleasures like horseback rides, horseshoes, hiking, fishing, volleyball, and badminton. The place is so popular, reservations often must be made a year in advance for the June to mid-October season. Three meals are included in the room rate. ~ End of Warner Valley Road, Chester; 530-529-1512 ext. 120, fax 530-529-4511; www.drakesbad.com, e-mail calquest@internetmci.com. ULTRA-DELUXE.

Since many of its 34 rooms are filled by permanent residents, the **St. Francis Hotel** provides a glimpse into small town hotel living. Little has changed since the hotel opened its doors back in 1914. The modestly decorated rooms feature furniture from early in the 20th century and the entire place has the aura of a bygone era. The hotel offers three reasonably priced suites and, despite its location in Historic Uptown Susanville, remains exceptionally quiet. In the summer, there's entertainment in the hotel courtyard. No phones in rooms; some baths shared. A steakhouse and bar are also on-site. ~ 830 Main Street, Susanville; 530-257-4820, fax 530-257-4195. BUDGET TO MODERATE.

The **Niles Hotel** is a museumlike hotel with an incredible array of antiques, including several vintage Wurlitzers and hundreds of sepia-toned photographs. It was established by J. Eugene Niles, a local entrepreneur who parlayed the county's only flour mill into ownership of an insurance company, an electric company, and the first (and only) movie theater in the valley, as well as the hotel and saloon. A major restoration was done in the 1980s, returning the frosted-glass doors, brass lighting fixtures, and hardwood floors to their original elegance. Note: At presstime, the hotel was for sale; it's future remains uncertain so call ahead. ~ 304 South Main Street, Alturas; 530-233-3261, fax 530-233-3440; www.nileshotel.com, e-mail info@nileshotel.com. MODERATE.

Located within half a mile of the Modoc County Museum, the **Super 8** has 49 rooms. It's a typical generic motel with the usual dresser-desk combination and dime-store paintings; the staff is friendly, though, and it happens to be the nicest place in town. ~ 511 North Main Street, Alturas; 530-233-3545, fax 530-233-3305. BUDGET TO MODERATE.

For breathtaking views of snow-capped mountains and lush fields, spend the night (or week) at **Cockrell's High Desert Lodging**. This three-bedroom house has two bathrooms, a fully equipped kitchen, and a backyard jacuzzi. Located on a working ranch, it's a great getaway and affords a truly Western experience. ~ Star Route 11-A, County Road 31, Cedarville; 888-279-2209, fax 530-279-6348; www.highdesertlodging.com. BUDGET TO MODERATE.

DINING

HIDDEN ►

The **Kopper Kettle Cafe** has the formica-counter-and-metal-chair appearance of a typical coffee shop, but the food is great. Just ask any of the local residents who crowd into this gathering spot. For a hearty breakfast, try the pork chops and eggs, which come with hash browns, toast, and applesauce. Then for lunch there are giant hamburgers and fries. Dinner is a selection of excellent fried chicken, liver and onions, and roast beef. If you're on a budget, it's a good place to chow down. ~ Route 36 and Myrtle Street, Chester; 530-258-2698, fax 530-258-3182. MODERATE.

HIDDEN ►

"Time paid a visit to the Grand Cafe around 1935," a roving reporter once noted, "and it hasn't been back since." Open since 1909, the **Grand Cafe** has been operated by the same family since 1921. This humble eatery is an uncrowded place where old-timers congregate to sip coffee and swap tales. Probably the most striking features in the Grand Cafe are the 30-foot-long formica counter and the wooden swivel chairs with hat clips. You'll also find art-

AUTHOR FAVORITE

The St. Bernard Lodge is one of those rare roadside inns that serves gourmet quality food. With its wood-paneled walls, lace tablecloths, and snowshoes on the wall, you might think you were in the Alps. Specialties include steaks, scampi, seafood, and fried chicken. Breakfast is also served Thursday through Monday (summer) and weekends (winter). ~ 44801 Route 36 East, ten miles west of Chester; 530-258-3382; www.stbernardlodge.com. MODERATE TO DELUXE.

deco wooden booths, a wooden refrigerator, and seven deer heads mounted on the walls. Even the prices seem like something out of the past. In addition to standard breakfast and lunch coffee shop offerings, there are also homemade soups and breads. Closed Sunday and the last two weeks in December. ~ 730 Main Street, Susanville; 530-257-4713. BUDGET.

Mi Casa Restaurant at the Niles Hotel is a dining place "where the West still lives." An incredible array of antiques, including several vintage Wurlitzers, accompany your meal, which is authentic Mexican. ~ 304 South Main Street, Alturas; 530-233-3261, 877-233-5510; www.nileshotel.com, e-mail info@niles hotel.com. MODERATE TO DELUXE.

The **Brass Rail Restaurant,** located just outside of the Alturas city limits, dishes up hefty portions of traditional Basque cuisine. It's a family-style restaurant, so when you and your compadres sit down, be prepared for lots of food, fun, and conversation. A prix-fixe menu gets you wine, homemade bread, salad, soup, an entrée, and coffee (doggy bags are often served with the food). Favorites include top sirloin, lamb steak, and scallops. Chow down. No lunch on Saturday. Closed Monday. ~ 395 Lakeview Highway, Alturas; 530-233-2906. MODERATE.

SHOPPING

Morrison's Warehouse is not the kind of store you'd expect to find in a small town. Hundreds of items, most costing $1 or less, crowd the shelves of this discount store. There are toys, personal care products, jewelry, cookware, cutlery, and fishing supplies. Closed Sunday and Monday from January through May; closed Sunday from June through December. ~ 317 Birch Street, Westwood; 530-256-3272, fax 530-241-7389.

You'll find some unusual gifts at **Country Victorian Charm**, an elegant boutique that sells handmade Victorian dolls, handcrafted furniture, pewter picture frames, Victorian angels, and everlasting floral arrangements. Closed occasionally on Sunday; call ahead. ~ 718 Main Street, Susanville; 530-257-8392.

NIGHTLIFE

You will find restaurant bars and local saloons in small towns throughout the Far North. Many are short on entertainment, but provide a glimpse into this roughhewn, backwoods region.

The **Brass Rail Restaurant** is a great place to stop for a drink. Their lounge is a low-light affair with a late-night bar and occasional musical entertainment. ~ 395 Lakeview Highway, Alturas; 530-233-2906.

PARKS

LASSEN NATIONAL FOREST Sprawling across 1,100,000 acres, this giant facility fronts numerous lakes, including the popular Lake Almanor and Eagle Lake. It also contains Thousand Lake Wilderness, with its glacier-carved valley and 9000-foot peaks; **Caribou Wilderness**, a pine-forested plateau area featuring numerous lakes; and **Ishi Wilderness**, a 41,000-acre oak brushland with pine-covered plateaus. Facilities include picnic areas and restrooms. ~ Accessible from Routes 44, 32, 36, and 89; 530-257-2151, fax 530-252-6428; www.r5.fs.fed.us/lassen.

▲ There are sites in 39 campgrounds; $10 to $15 per night for standard sites. Reservations: 872-444-6777.

LASSEN VOLCANIC NATIONAL PARK 🏃 🎣 🏕 🚶 🚣 ⛵
🛶 Lassen Peak, a 10,457-foot plug dome volcano, tops the horizon in this 106,000-acre coniferous forest. Manzanita Lake provides limited catch-and-release fishing. This area is popular with sightseers, cross-country skiers, and hikers (there are 150 miles of hiking trails). Motorized boats are prohibited. The park has picnic areas, restrooms, and a snack bar. ~ The Lassen Peak Park Road (which is closed during the snow season) bisects the park, which is located about 50 miles east of Redding; 530-595-4444, fax 530-595-3262; www.nps.gov/lavo, e-mail lavo_information@nps.gov.

▲ There are sites in eight campgrounds; $10 to $16 per night. The Manzanita Lake and Summit Lake campgrounds are the most popular, right off the Lassen Park Road.

MCARTHUR–BURNEY FALLS MEMORIAL STATE PARK 🏃 🚲
🚶 🎣 🚣 ⛵ 🚤 🛶 The chief attraction at this 910-acre facility is it's 129-foot waterfall, but the park also features a ponderosa pine forest, lake and stream fishing, and a bird population that includes bald eagles, black swifts, owls, and ospreys. The beach and swim area of the lake prove popular. Picnic areas and restrooms are within the park. Day-use fee, $4. ~ Off Route 89 about 11 miles northeast of Burney; 530-335-2777, fax 530-335-5483.

A bicycle helmet is acceptable as headgear when visiting the caves at Lava Beds National Monument.

▲ There are 128 campsites; $15 per night. Reservations are required Memorial Day through Labor Day: 800-444-7275.

LAVA BEDS NATIONAL MONUMENT 🏃 🚲 Known primarily for its extensive network of lava tube caves (over 500 of them), this amazing place features an active volcano, high desert plateaus, and large wilderness area. There are 25 miles of hiking trails. The visitors center provides free flashlights, which are essential for exploring, and sells headgear ($3.25), which is highly recommended for entering the caves. A visitors center and restrooms are the only facilities. Day-use fee, $10 ~ Off Route 139, 26 miles northwest of Canby; 530-667-2282, fax 530-667-2737; www.nps.gov/labe.

▲ There are 44 designated campsites; $10 per night.

MODOC NATIONAL FOREST 🏃 🚴 🐎 🚣 ⛷ 🚤 🛶 🚢 ⛴ ⚓ Nestled in the remote northeastern corner of California, this 1,654,392-acre facility is infrequently visited. Nevertheless, its features include obsidian cliffs, lava tubes, volcanic craters, open rangeland, basalt-domed plateaus, and mountain meadows. There are 118 miles of trails, plus numerous lakes and streams with fishing for trout and bass. The Warner Mountains and South Warner Wilderness are part of the forest. Toilets are the only facilities. ~ Located both east and west of Alturas, this noncontiguous facility is accessible from Route 395 or Route 299; 530-233-5811; www. r5.fs.fed.us/modoc, e-mail mailroom/r5_modoc@modoc.fs.fed.us.

▲ There are 26 campgrounds; $6 to $7 per night for sites with tested water and garbage facilities; free for campsites without these amenities.

Outdoor Adventures

Some of the best year-round fishing in the American West is found right here in the Far North. Steelhead, salmon, trout, and sturgeon run the region's countless rivers and trout and bass inhabit the mountain lakes. For an unforgettable adventure, check with one of the many outfitters offering fishing expeditions.

FISHING

REDDING The Fly Shop offers professional guides who will tailor a trip to suit your abilities and interests year-round. ~ 4140 Churn Creek Road, Redding; 800-669-3474; www.thefly shop.com.

WEAVERVILLE TO YREKA Klamath River Outfitters can lead you to the region's great fishing holes. They also provide rafting trips. ~ 3 Sandy Bar Road, Somes Bar; 530-469-3349. Trinity Fly Shop arranges fishing charters on the Sacramento River and Trinity Lake. They offer both half- and full-day trips on rafts and furnish flies and all gear. ~ Bottom of Ohio Hill, on Old Lewiston Road, Lewiston; phone/fax 530-623-6757.

REDDING TO MT. SHASTA Dunsmuir Fly Fishing Company has hand-tied flies and offers fishing in private waters known for their rainbow trout. Its tours are led by local licensed guides. Closed January to mid-April. ~ 5844 Dunsmuir Avenue, Dunsmuir; 530-235-0705; www.dunsmuirflyfishing.com. Jack Trout International Fly Fishing and Guide Service will take you on hiking excursions to local rivers or their own private ranch for a fruitful day of fishing. They rent all the equipment you may need. ~ P.O. Box 94, Mt. Shasta, CA 96067; 530-926-4540; www. jacktrout.com.

BOATING

Whether you prefer gliding across a crystal-blue lake in a rowboat, on waterskis, or paddling a canoe, the Far North resorts will cater to every desire.

REDDING To spend your days idling away on the water, contact **Bridge Bay Resort**. They rent houseboats, ski boats, patio boats, Sea Doos, and fishing boats for use on Shasta Lake. ~ 10300 Bridge Bay Road, Redding; 530-275-3021, 800-752-9669; www.seven crown.com.

REDDING TO WEAVERVILLE Nestled in a valley surrounded by trees and water, **Oak Bottom Marina** rents waterskis, innertubes, and several kinds of recreational boats for use on Whiskeytown Lake. For those who like to sail, there are small sailboats. Closed October through March. ~ Oak Bottom Marina Northwest, Whiskeytown; 530-359-2269, phone/fax 530-359-2027.

REDDING TO MT. SHASTA Shasta Lake provides ample opportunities for fishing, waterskiing, and houseboating. **Antlers Resort & Marina** rents houseboats, patio boats and Sea Doos. ~ 20679 Antlers Road, Lakehead; 530-238-2553, 800-238-3924; www. shastalakevacations.com, e-mail antlers@shastalakevacations. com. Located on the Sacramento arm of Shasta Lake, **Shasta Marina Resort** offers houseboats. They also rent wakeboards and skis. ~ 18390 O'Brien Inlet Road, Lakehead; 530-238-2284, 800-959-3359; www.shastalake.net, e-mail request@shastalake.net.

WEAVERVILLE TO YREKA Situated in the lovely Trinity Alps, **Cedar Stock Marina** is the perfect spot to rent a houseboat. They also rent speed boats, patio boats, and fishing boats. Waterski equipment and innertubes are available here. ~ Trinity Lake, 45810 Route 3, Trinity Center; 530-286-2225, 800-982-2279; www. cedarstock.com, e-mail info@cedarstock.com.

BALLOON RIDES & GLIDING

For a hawk's-eye view of Shasta Valley (and southern Oregon) consider taking a sailplane ride with **North Valley Aviation**. Basic rides average 15 to 20 minutes. You can also ride in a motor-powered airplane to see Mt. Ashland, Lassen Peak, Mt. Shasta, and the Klamath National Forest. ~ Montague Airport; 530-459-3456; e-mail flymontague@snowcrest.net.

There are few more peaceful ways to explore the Shasta area than in a hot-air balloon. **Shasta Valley Balloons** operates daily one-hour flights, which include brunch and a champagne toast. It also offers meditation flights. In the winter you can participate in a ski-and-fly package with a balloon flight in the late morning and an afternoon on the slopes. ~ Mount Shasta; phone/fax 530-926-3612; www.hot-airballoons.com, e-mail balloons@inreach.com.

SKIING

Ski enthusiasts can explore the Far North's winter wonderland on both downhill runs and cross-country treks. The skiing is particularly popular around Mt. Shasta. The **Shasta–Cascade Wonderland Association** can provide general information. ~ 1699 Route 273, Anderson; 530-365-7500, 800-474-2782; www.shastacascades.org.

Roller Coaster
River Rides

If your favorite carnival ride is the roller coaster, you're ready for the adrenaline-pumping, spine-chilling thrill of whitewater river rafting. At one time it was strictly a sport for daredevils, but more and more vacationing adventurers are taking to the rapids. As a result, over 60 professional guide services in Northern California now combine expertise and equipment in a variety of tour packages.

Whether you're looking for a true test of nerve or prefer excitement in smaller doses, these knowledgeable river pilots can provide an enjoyable whitewater experience. You're liable to wind up in the drink at least once, especially if you choose one of the more challenging runs. But getting wet is part of the intoxicating rush created by a fast-moving stretch of river. There's also the serenity of paddling past untracked forests and bald mountains. In spite of river rafting's increasing popularity, the Far North's endless river system makes it a solitary wilderness activity.

Tours vary in length from one to seven days, and generally include food and all the equipment necessary except sleeping bags. Camping is usually the rule, but lodge trips are also available.

River rafting is primarily a summertime sport, centered in the Klamath, Shasta, Trinity, and Six Rivers National Forests. The most frequently explored routes include Hell's Corner Gorge in the Upper Klamath River, the Salmon River, and Upper Sacramento River. For whitewater pioneers, Burnt Ranch Gorge in the south fork of the Trinity River, the Scott River, and Lower McCloud River Canyon offer unmatched challenges.

William McGinnis' Whitewater Voyages offers an array of river trips including one- and two-day trips as well as extended expeditions. ~ 5225 San Pablo Dam Road, El Sobrante, CA 94803; 510-222-5994; www.whitewatervoyages.com. To experience the thrill of a river run, contact **Wilderness Adventures**. Besides that, they'll point out plenty of wildlife—eagles, deer, hawks, beavers, and otters. ~ 108 Ski Village Drive, Mount Shasta, CA 96067; 530-926-6282.

REDDING TO MT. SHASTA   Located at the foot of beautiful Mt. Shasta, **Mt. Shasta Board & Ski Park** features three chairlifts that accommodate both skiers and snowboarders, and a 1390-foot vertical drop. You can also cross-country ski on the 30 kilometers of groomed Nordic trails. Most of the runs are beginning or intermediate level. ~ Ski Park Highway and Route 89, Mount Shasta; 530-926-8686, 800-754-7427; www.skipark.com, e-mail skipark @snowcrest.net.

NORTHEAST LOOP   Lassen's most popular Nordic trails begin at the Lassen Chalet (near Mineral on the park's south side) and lead to such enticing spots as Forest Lake. On the north side of Lassen, there's a nice beginner trail around Manzanita Lake (1.6 miles) and a popular medium-difficulty trail up the drainage of Manzanita Creek (10 miles). No rentals are available in the park. ~ Mineral; 530-595-4444; www.nps.gov/lavo, e-mail lavo_infor mation@nps.gov.

GOLD MINING

Seek your fortune in gold in the Klamath River and its tributary creeks. For a very minimal fee, you can spend a weekend, or maybe a week, mining with **The New 49'ers**, a private club that has 60 river miles of placer claims on National Forest Service land near Happy Camp. The club operates hands-on training in high banking every summer. Bring your tent or an RV. You may strike it rich, or just have a good time picking up some new skills. ~ Happy Camp; 530-493-2012, fax 530-493-2095; www.gold gold.com.

RIDING STABLES & PACK TRIPS

For the ultimate Western-style vacation, consider a horseback expedition through the Far North's mountainous wilderness. Experienced guides offer pack trips deep into this region of lost mountains and alpine rivers.

WEAVERVILLE TO YREKA   To explore new frontiers, call **Six Pak Packers** for an exciting trip through the wilderness. They offer seasonal trips on horses and mules through the Trinity Alps' pine forests. ~ 903 Mill Street, Weaverville; 530-623-6314.

NORTHEAST LOOP   South of Lake Almanor you can explore the Plumas National Forest by horseback. Ride through the Lakes Basin (Gold Lake Highway) or Bucks Lake (off Route 70, north of Quincy) recreation areas. **Reid Horse & Cattle Company, Inc.** operates guided trail rides out of Bucks Lake Stables ranging from one-hour to day-long trips. They also operate Gold Lake Stables, which offers overnight trips. ~ 1540 Chandler Road, Quincy; 530-283-1147; www.reidhorse.com, e-mail info@reidhorse.com.

BIKING

Biking in the Far North is a challenge rewarded with spectacular mountain scenery. It's a region for cyclists with experience: The climbs are often steep and the narrow-shouldered roadways are traveled by lumber trucks and RVs. But there are several highways well worth exploring. Beginner to moderate trails can be found.

WEAVERVILLE TO YREKA   Route 3 passes Trinity (Clair Engle) Lake and the historic town of Callahan on a lengthy journey from Weaverville to Yreka.

REDDING TO WEAVERVILLE   For a ride through Shasta State Historic Park and along Whiskeytown Lake, try **Route 299** outside Redding. Be careful; it's a popular road with moderate traffic.

NORTHEAST LOOP   Route 89 from Mt. Shasta to McArthur–Burney Falls State Park rolls from 2000 to 4500 feet elevation while passing pristine countryside and tiny towns. **Route 44** between Lassen Volcanic National Park and Susanville traverses unspoiled timber country.

Bike Rentals   Bikes Etcetera rents and repairs bikes; they also offer literature on area trails. ~ 2400 Athens Avenue, Redding; 530-244-1954.

More than any other part of the state, the Far North earns the description "Hidden California." Inhabited by black bears, coyotes, black-tailed deer, and an occasional bald eagle, the land offers hikers a glimpse of nature in its unspoiled state. The Trinity Alps feature more than 500 miles of trails for exploring glacial lakes, cool forests, and silent meadows. Mt. Shasta's snow-domed summit rewards mountaineers with other-worldly views, and Lassen Peak reveals the explosive side of this highly volcanic countryside.

HIKING

REDDING TO WEAVERVILLE   For a scenic, moderate, two-hour hike, turn off to the right from Route 299 on Crystal Creek Road, about a mile west of the French Gulch turnoff. After a couple of miles the road deteriorates into a washed-out former logging road that is no longer maintained. Follow this road on foot for about two miles to reach **Crystal Creek Falls**, a string of cascades that fall a total of 200 feet, set in a pocket of primeval forest.

WEAVERVILLE TO YREKA   **Trinity Alps Wilderness Area** is an extraordinary haven for backpackers. Less crowded than other

AUTHOR FAVORITE

Even if I can't bring home a bouquet of blooms, I enjoy trekking the **Paradise Meadows Trail** (1.5 miles), the best spot for summer wildflowers. Beginning at the Hat Lake parking area, the moderate trail climbs for a mile before reaching the meadows. Bring a lunch—this is a lovely place to picnic.

California wilderness areas, it possesses knife-edge peaks, deep pine forests, and lakes crowded with trout. You can camp anywhere in the forest with a wilderness permit (and a campfire permit, if you plan to build a fire).

Tangle Blue Lake Trail (4 miles) begins off Route 3 and leads through a flowering meadow to a lake rimmed by jagged peaks. It is an easy-to-moderate trail.

The Trinity Alps section of the **Pacific Crest Trail** (17 miles) starts at Scott Mountain Campground. It's one of the most scenic trails in the wilderness area, carrying past alpine lakes, meadows, and forests.

There's a choice to make when hiking the **Caribou Basin and Sawtooth Ridge Trail** (9.6 miles). You can follow an age-old trail across Caribou Mountain, or take a newer trail that's easier to trek, more crowded, and is two miles longer. Both hikes lead past mountain lakes and afford singular views from Sawtooth Ridge.

Stuart Fork to Emerald, Sapphire, and Mirror Lakes Trail (14.5 miles) is one of the most popular hikes in the Trinity Alps. It's one of Northern California's most picturesque hikes, resembling the Alps. It traverses an area teeming with wildlife en route to three subalpine lakes and is easy to moderate.

Beginning at Coffee Creek Road, the **Adams Lake Trail** (2.5 miles) leads to a tiny lake shadowed by a 7500-foot granite mountain and can be difficult to hike because of the steep path.

For a journey to three excellent fishing lakes, take **Big Bear Lake Trail** (4.7 miles) located off Route 3. This steep path climbs through fir and cedar forests and past thickets of willow and alder. An added treat is the 200-foot Bear Creek waterfall. En route, beware of rattlesnakes basking in the sun.

Mavis Lake–Fox Creek Lake Trail (4.7 miles) leads to another group of lakes. Beginning seven miles from Callahan, it climbs through heavy timber country to four trout lakes.

A lake covered with lilypads and a desolate canyon populated by coyotes, deer, and black bears are the destinations along **Boulder Lake to Poison Canyon and Lilypad Lake Trail** (4 miles). A steep ridge makes this a hike for the hearty.

REDDING TO MT. SHASTA Unparalleled adventure awaits skilled mountaineers in **Mt. Shasta Recreation Area**. The 14,162-foot Mt. Shasta is accessed via three routes: **Horse Camp to Avalanche Gulch Trail**, **Mt. Shasta Ski Bowl Lodge Trail**, and **Horse Camp to Shastina Trail**; however, only expert climbers can accomplish this feat.

At Bunny Flat, hikers will find the trail to Horse Camp and the beginning of the Avalanche Gulch climbing route. Hikers entering the Mt. Shasta Wilderness can self-issue a wilderness permit at the trail head. Climbers going above 10,000 feet need to self-issue an additional summit pass (fee, $15).

NORTHEAST LOOP   Lassen Volcanic National Park offers 150 miles of hiking trails leading past lava flows, volcanic craters, and boiling mud pots. Most of these trails are moderate to strenuous.

Starting from the park's southwest entrance station, the **Brokeoff Mountain Trail** (3.7 miles) carries past open meadows and thick forest. Offering scenic views of Mt. Shasta, it's also an excellent route for flower-gazing and birdwatching.

For a hike to a 75-foot waterfall, follow **Mill Creek Falls Trail** (2.3 miles) along its scenic course.

The **Ridge Lakes Trail** (1.1 miles) cuts through fir and pine forests and arrives at two jewel-like lakes (which become a single lake when the water level rises). This strenuous hike has a 1000-foot elevation change.

During wet years a small lake forms in a "recently" (300-year-old) collapsed dome at the top of Chaos Crags and Crags Lake Trail.

The largest hydrothermal area in Lassen lies along **Bumpass Hell Trail** (1.5 miles). One of the region's most dramatic hikes, the trail passes hot springs, steam vents, and mud pots.

Still, the finest hike in the park is **Lassen Peak Trail** (2.5 miles). Leading to the summit, it provides 360° degree views of the surrounding countryside and reveals evidence of recent volcanic activity. Hikers should be in good physical condition, bring water and jackets, and turn back in case of thunderstorms.

Devastated Area Trail (.3 mile) is an easy way to see a variety of rock formations and park panoramas. Highlights of this walk are volcanic formations from the May 1915 eruption and lava flow. Wheelchair accessible.

Chaos Crags and Crags Lake Trail (1.8 miles) begins near the Loomis Museum parking lot. Along this relatively easy walk are half a dozen immense crags, as well as wildflowers and a variety of geologic formations.

Terrace, Shadow, and Cliff Lakes Trail (1.5 miles) begins at a high elevation and follows a flower-banked path to three lakes.

Crystal Lake Trail (.4 mile) begins on the east side of Juniper Lake and goes through forests and meadows to one of the park's most beautiful lakes. For views of Lassen and other nearby peaks, climb **Inspiration Point Trail** (.8 mile). It tracks through western white pine and red fir forests and offers unforgettable vistas.

Cinder Cone Nature Trail (2 miles) travels up one of the nation's most perfectly formed cinder cones. The trail begins at Butte Lake Campground. High-top boots are recommended.

Beginning at Badger Flat, the Lassen Park section of the **Pacific Crest Trail** (17 miles) carries past Soap Lake, Fairfield Peak, Lower Twin Lake, Swan Lake, Pilot Mountain, Boiling Springs Lake, and Red Mountain to Little Willow Lake. In this area, the trail (which in its entirety extends from Canada to Mexico) is fairly level and can be hiked in two days at a comfortable pace.

▼▼▼▼▼▼▼▼▼▼▼▼
Transportation

CAR

From San Francisco, **Route 80** connects with **Route 5**, which leads through the heart of the Far North. It passes through Redding, Dunsmuir, Mount Shasta, and Yreka en route to Oregon.

AIR

For those traveling by air, Horizon Air, SunAir Express, and United Express fly into **Redding Municipal Airport**. ~ 6751 Woodrum Circle; 530-224-4321.

BUS

Greyhound Bus Lines travels Route 5, stopping in Redding, Dunsmuir, Mount Shasta, and Yreka. ~ 800-231-2222; www.greyhound.com.

TRAIN

Amtrak provides daily service on their "Coast Starlight" to Redding and Dunsmuir. ~ 800-229-9424; www.amtrak.com.

CAR RENTALS

Avis Rent A Car (800-331-1212) and **Hertz Rent A Car** (800-654-3131) have facilities at Redding Municipal Airport.

Index

Lodging Index

Dining Index

HIDDEN GUIDES

Adventure travel or a relaxing vacation?—"Hidden" guidebooks are the only travel books in the business to provide detailed information on both. Aimed at environmentally aware travelers, our motto is "Where Vacations Meet Adventures." These books combine details on unique hotels, restaurants and sightseeing with information on camping, sports and hiking for the outdoor enthusiast.

THE NEW KEY GUIDES

Based on the concept of ecotourism, The New Key Guides are dedicated to the preservation of Central America's rare and endangered species, architecture and archaeology. Filled with helpful tips, they give travelers everything they need to know about these exotic destinations.

PARADISE FAMILY GUIDES

Ideal for families traveling with kids of any age—toddlers to teenagers—Paradise Family Guides offer a blend of travel information unlike any other guides to the Hawaiian islands. With vacation ideas and tropical adventures that are sure to satisfy both action-hungry youngsters and relaxation-seeking parents, these guides meet the specific needs of each and every family member.

Ulysses Press books are available at bookstores everywhere. If any of the following titles are unavailable at your local bookstore, ask the bookseller to order them.

You can also order books directly from Ulysses Press
P.O. Box 3440, Berkeley, CA 94703
800-377-2542 or 510-601-8301
fax: 510-601-8307
www.ulyssespress.com
e-mail: ulysses@ulyssespress.com

HIDDEN GUIDEBOOKS

____ Hidden Arizona, $16.95
____ Hidden Bahamas, $14.95
____ Hidden Baja, $14.95
____ Hidden Belize, $15.95
____ Hidden Big Island of Hawaii, $13.95
____ Hidden Boston & Cape Cod, $14.95
____ Hidden British Columbia, $18.95
____ Hidden Cancún & the Yucatán, $16.95
____ Hidden Carolinas, $17.95
____ Hidden Coast of California, $18.95
____ Hidden Colorado, $15.95
____ Hidden Disneyland, $13.95
____ Hidden Florida, $18.95
____ Hidden Florida Keys & Everglades, $13.95
____ Hidden Georgia, $16.95
____ Hidden Guatemala, $16.95
____ Hidden Hawaii, $18.95
____ Hidden Idaho, $14.95

____ Hidden Kauai, $13.95
____ Hidden Maui, $13.95
____ Hidden Montana, $15.95
____ Hidden New England, $18.95
____ Hidden New Mexico, $15.95
____ Hidden Oahu, $13.95
____ Hidden Oregon, $15.95
____ Hidden Pacific Northwest, $18.95
____ Hidden Salt Lake City, $14.95
____ Hidden San Francisco & Northern California, $18.95
____ Hidden Southern California, $18.95
____ Hidden Southwest, $19.95
____ Hidden Tahiti, $17.95
____ Hidden Tennessee, $16.95
____ Hidden Utah, $16.95
____ Hidden Walt Disney World, $13.95
____ Hidden Washington, $15.95
____ Hidden Wine Country, $13.95
____ Hidden Wyoming, $15.95

THE NEW KEY GUIDEBOOKS

____ The New Key to Costa Rica, $18.95

____ The New Key to Ecuador and the Galápagos, $17.95

PARADISE FAMILY GUIDES

____ Paradise Family Guides: Kaua'i, $16.95
____ Paradise Family Guides: Maui, $16.95

____ Paradise Family Guides: Big Island of Hawai'i, $16.95

Mark the book(s) you're ordering and enter the total cost here ⟹ [   ]

California residents add 8.25% sales tax here ⟹ [   ]

Shipping, check box for your preferred method and enter cost here ⟹ [   ]

❑ BOOK RATE   **FREE! FREE! FREE!**

❑ PRIORITY MAIL/UPS GROUND   cost of postage

❑ UPS OVERNIGHT OR 2-DAY AIR   cost of postage

[   ]

Billing, enter total amount due here and check method of payment ⟹

❑ CHECK   ❑ MONEY ORDER

❑ VISA/MASTERCARD _____EXP. DATE_____

NAME _____PHONE_____

ADDRESS _____

CITY_____ STATE _____ ZIP _____

ABOUT THE AUTHOR

RAY RIEGERT is the author of nine travel books, including *Hidden Southern California* and *Hidden Coast of California*. His most popular work, *Hidden Hawaii*, won the coveted Lowell Thomas Travel Journalism Award for Best Guidebook as well as a similar award from the Hawaii Visitors Bureau. In addition to his role as publisher of Ulysses Press, he has written for the *Chicago Tribune*, *San Francisco Chronicle* and *Travel & Leisure*. A member of the Society of American Travel Writers, he lives in the San Francisco Bay area with his wife, co-publisher Leslie Henriques, and their son Keith and daughter Alice.